Author and journalist Peter Irvine, is also Scotland's leading-edge event organizer. His company, Unique Events, created Edinburgh's annual Hogmanay Programme ten years ago in the year that he started this book; it has become the world's biggest New Year's celebration. He's also the director of Scotland's newest festival, Burns and a' That, and Scotland's annual contemporary art gathering – the Glasgow Art Fair.

In 2000 he received the Silver Thistle Award for his 'outstanding contribution to the development of tourism in Scotland' and the MBE for services to Edinburgh.

'Makes all other guides to Scotland redundant'
Sunday Times

'Infallible and quite brilliant'
Daily Telegraph

'The only guide to Scotland the Scots use'
Glasgow Evening Times

'The only guide worth a damn'
The Scotsman

Comments from readers of previous editions of *Scotland the Best* include:

'We never go out without it'

'Your book gave us the trip of a lifetime'

'Having this book is like having you in the car'

'Please do England'

Pete Irvine is happy to receive comments about this edition and recommendations for entries for the next by post (sent c/o HarperCollins Publishers in Glasgow). He is however, unable to reply to submissions personally.

Scot land the best

PETER IRVINE

HarperCollins Publishers
Westerhill Rd, Bishopbriggs Glasgow G64 2QT

www.collins.co.uk

First published in Great Britain in 1993
by Mainstream Publishing Company (Edinburgh) Ltd

First published by HarperCollins Publishers in 1997

This edition published in 2003

© Peter Irvine 2003 (text)
© HarperCollins Publishers 2003 (maps on pp. 326-329)
© Collins Bartholomew Ltd 2003 (maps on pp. 324-325, 331-339)

ISBN 0 00 716530 7

Peter Irvine asserts his moral right to be identified as the author of this work.

A catalogue record for this book is available from the British Library

Printed in Italy by Legoprint

CONTENTS

INTRODUCTION

Welcome to the 10th year and the 7th edition of *Scotland the Best*. Sometimes we take the opportunity to make some changes in the reprints of the intervening years, but this edition for 2004/5 is the fully updated edition where every place has been revisited. I hope that once again you can rely on *Scotland the Best* to give you the current and definitive picture of what's good about Scotland. Because of other commitments, I've used a few 'researchers' this time just to make sure that we can cover the country. My fellow contributors, like our regular readers, all understand that some places are better than others; we have been diligent in seeking them out. My thanks to them and all who write and email. We do check out all suggestions and these contributions all help to make *Scotland the Best* the inside track guide that it purports to be. Please keep them coming (see p. 14).

In 10 years that *Scotland the Best* has been reporting Scotland, there have been huge changes. Even between this edition and the last, hundreds of places have been dropped or have closed and hundreds have been added. While we continue to hear about poor service and lack of progress in the offering restaurants and hotels make to visitors, it's my belief that things have hugely improved from what I found 10 years ago. It's true that if somewhere is very good, it is more likely to survive – and there are many places in this edition that have been there since the start – but the general standard of food and service, of décor and PR, particularly in Edinburgh and Glasgow and in the Highlands, has seen a remarkable transformation. Overall, we're as good as anywhere in the UK or Europe. In this edition, I've tried as always to register and reflect the changes.

When I started 10 years ago, there were hardly any other guides to Scotland – now there are loads. I know that many people buy every edition of this book and that Scottish people particularly seem to refer to it above others. This is a great source of both inspiration and responsibility. Nevertheless, as I've set off every other spring around the country again, the fact that it means so much to so many people, both the people who are in the book (and many are mentioned) and you people who use it, helps to keep me going. What I've found this time is that Scotland is better than ever – I hope you agree.

Peter Irvine
Edinburgh, October 2003

A DECLARATION

Scotland the Best is a handbook of information about all the 'best' places in Scotland. 'Best', you will understand, is a subjective term; it means 'best' according to what I think, but it's intended to be obvious that I am conveying opinions and impressions. We believe in what we are saying. We take no bribes and have no vested interest in any of the places recommended, other than that we do talk things up and shamelessly proclaim the places we like or admire.

Along with observations, every 'item' conveys factual information; I hope it is plain where the facts end and the opinions begin. In guide books, this is not always the case. However, it's with the 'facts' that inconsistencies may appear. We try to give accurate and clear directions explaining how to find a place and basic details that might be useful. This information is gleaned from a variety of sources and may be supplied by the establishment concerned. We do try to verify everything, usually by visiting, but the process of acquiring and transcribing information is tricky when there's so much of it. Things change and because nowhere we mention has solicited their inclusion (or if they have, it has made little difference), nor been invited to check what we say – well, mistakes can be made. With this density of information, it's impossible to run it past proprietors, and they might well not like what we say because it's our opinion, not theirs. So I'm sorry if we get something wrong. Please let us know if there are any mistakes, so we can fix them.

This admission is therefore made in advance. My cringing excuse is that we are merely human. This guide is made by fallible humans, of which I hope you are one. However, be clear of one thing; this book is more than about trying to get it right. As with many of the people we celebrate in these pages, we do strive for perfection.

HOW TO USE THIS BOOK

There are three ways to find things in this book:

1. There's an index at the back.

2. The book can be used by category, e.g. you can look up the best restaurants in the Borders or the best scenic routes in the whole of Scotland. Each entry has an item number in the outside margin. These are in numerical order and allow easy cross-referencing.

3. You can start with the maps and see how individual items are located, how they are grouped together and how much there is that's worth seeing or doing in any particular area. Then just look up the item numbers. If you are travelling round Scotland, I would urge you to use the maps and this method of finding the best of what an area or town has to offer.

   The maps correspond to the recognisable regions of Scotland. There's also an overall map to show how the regions fit together. The list of maps is on p.323 and the map section is at the back of the book.

   All items have a code which gives (1) the specific item number; (2) the map on which it can be found; and (3) the map co-ordinates. For space reasons, items in Glasgow and Edinburgh are not marked on Maps A and B, although they do have co-ordinates in the margin to give you a rough idea of the location. City maps are readily available from any tourist office or newsagent.

A typical entry is shown below, identifying the various elements that make it up.

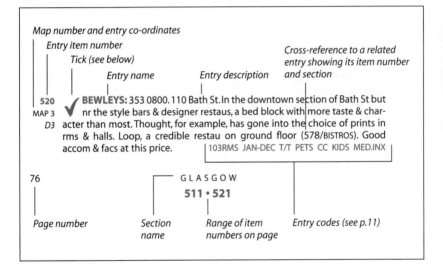

TICKS FOR THE BEST THERE IS

Although everything listed in the book is notable and remarkable in some way, there are places that are outstanding even in this superlative company. Instead of marking them with a rosette or a star, they have been 'awarded' a tick.

✓ Amongst the very best in Scotland

✓ ✓ Amongst the best (of its type) in the UK

✓ ✓ ✓ Amongst the best (of its type) in the world, or simply unique

Listings generally are not in an order of merit although if there is one outstanding item it will always be at the top of the page and this obviously includes anything which has been given a tick. Hotels and restaurants are also grouped according to price and this is why a cross-marked place may appear further down the page (ticks also indicate exceptional value for money).

A NOTE ON CATEGORIES

Edinburgh and Glasgow, the destinations of most visitors and the nearest cities to more than half of the population, are covered in the substantial Sections 2 and 3. You will probably need a city map to get around, although Maps A and B should give you the rough layout.

For the purposes of maps, and particularly in Section 4 (Regional Hotels and Restaurants), I have used a combination of the subdivision of Scotland based on the current standard political regions along with the historical ones, e.g. Argyll, Clyde Valley. From Sections 5 to 12, categories are based on activities, interests and geography and refer to the whole of Scotland. Section 13 covers the islands, with a page-by-page guide to the larger ones.

Section 14 is intended to give a comprehensive and concise guide to the best of the major Scottish towns in each area. Some of the recommended hotels and restaurants will be amongst the best in the region and will have been referred to in Section 4, or even amongst the best in Scotland and referred to in Sections 5 to 13, but otherwise they have been selected because they are the best there is in the town or the immediate area.

There are some categories like Bed and Breakfasts, Fishing Beats, Antique Shops that haven't been included because they are impracticable to assess (there are too many of them, are too small, or they change hands too often).

If there are other categories that you would like to see in future editions, please let us know (see p. 14).

THE CODES

1. The Item Code

At the outside margin of every item is a code which will enable you to find it on a map. Thus **1269** MAP 1 *C2* should be read as follows: **1269** is the item number, listed in simple consecutive order; MAP 1 refers to the Argyll/Ayrshire/Clyde Valley – the map section is at the back of the book; *C2* is the map co-ordinate, to help pinpoint the item's location on the map grid. A co-ordinate such as *xC1* indicates that the item can be reached by leaving the map at grid reference *C1*.

2. The Hotel Code

Below each hotel recommended is a band of codes as follows:

20RMS JAN-DEC T/T PETS CC KIDS TOS LOTS

20RMS means the hotel has 20 bedrooms in total. No differentiation is made as to the type of room. Most hotels will offer twin rooms as singles or put extra beds in doubles if required. This code merely gives an impression of size.

JAN-DEC means the hotel is open all year round. **APR-OCT** means approximately from the beginning of April to the end of October.

T/T refers to the facilities: **T/** means there are direct-dial phones in the bedrooms while **/T** means there are TVs in the bedrooms.

PETS means the hotel accepts dogs and other pets, probably under certain conditions (e.g. pets should be kept in the bedroom). It's usually best to check first.

XPETS indicates that the hotel does not generally accept pets.

CC means the hotel accepts major credit cards (e.g. Access and Visa).

XCC means the hotel does not accept credit cards.

KIDS indicates children are welcome and special provisions/rates may be available.

XKIDS does not necessarily mean that children are not able to accompany their parents, only that special provisions/rates are not usually made. Check by phone.

TOS means the hotel is part of the Taste of Scotland scheme and has been selected for having a menu which features imaginative cooking using Scottish ingredients. The Taste of Scotland produces an annual guide of members.

TR Top Rooms – the best rooms in the house!

GF means the establishment is gay-friendly.

LOTS Rooms which cost more than £75 per night per person. The theory is that if you can afford over £150 a room, it doesn't matter too much if it's £150 or £175.

Other price bands are:

EXP Expensive: £55-75 per person.

MED.EX Medium (expensive): £40-55.

MED.INX Medium (inexpensive): £32-40.

INX Inexpensive: £25-32.

CHP Cheap: less than £25.

Rates are per person per night. They are worked out by halving the published average rate for a twin room in high season and should be used only to give an impression of cost. They are based on 1999 prices. Add between £2 to £5 per year, though the band should stay the same unless the hotel undergoes improvements.

3. The Restaurant Code

Found at the bottom right of all restaurant entries. It refers to the price of an average dinner per person with a starter, a main course and dessert. It doesn't include wine, coffee or extras.

EXP Expensive: more than £30.

MED Medium: £20-30.

INX Inexpensive: £12-20.

CHP Cheap: under £12.

These are based on 2001 rates. With inflation, the relative price bands should stay about the same. Where a hotel is notable also for its restaurant, there is a restaurant line below the hotel entry and a separate code in the corner.

SD indicates the signature dish of the chef.

4.   The Walk Code

A great number of walks are described in the book, especially in section 9. Found at bottom-right corner of item:

2-10km   CIRC   BIKE   1-A-1

2-10km means the walk(s) described may vary in length from 2km to 10km.

CIRC means the walk can be circular, while **xCIRC** shows the walk is not circular and you must return more or less the way you came.

BIKE indicates the walk has a path which is suitable for ordinary bikes.
xBIKE means the walk is not suitable for, or does not permit, cycling.
mtBIKE means the track is suitable for mountain or all-terrain bikes.

The **1-A-1** Code

First number (**1, 2 or 3**) indicates how easy the walk is.
1 the walk is easy.
2 medium difficulty, e.g. standard hillwalking, not dangerous nor requiring special knowledge or equipment.
3 difficult: care and preparation and a map are needed.

The letters (**A, B or C**) indicate how easy it is to find the path.
A the route is easy to find. The way is either marked or otherwise obvious.
B the route is not very obvious, but you'll get there.
C you will need a map and preparation or a guide.

The last number (**1, 2 or 3**) indicates what to wear on your feet.
1 ordinary outdoor shoes, including trainers, are probably okay unless the ground is very wet.
2 you will need walking boots.
3 you will need serious walking or hiking boots.

Apart from designated walks, the **1-A-1** code is employed wherever there is more than a short stroll required to get to somewhere, e.g. a waterfall or a monument.

LIST OF ABBREVIATIONS

As well as codes and because of obvious space limitations, a personal shorthand and ad hoc abbreviation system has had to be created. I'm the first to admit some may be annoying, especially 'restau' for restaurant, but it's a long word and it comes up often. The others which are used are …

Aber	Aberdeen	N	north
accom	accommodation	NTS	National Trust for Scotland
adj	adjacent		
admn	admission	no smk	no smoking
app	approach	nr	near
approx	approximately		
atmos	atmosphere	o/look	overlook(s)/ing
av	average	opp	opposite
AYR	all year round	o/side	outside
bedrms	bedrooms	pl	place
betw	between	poss	possible
br	bridge	pt	point/port
BYOB	bring your own bottle		
		R	river
cl	closes/closed	rep	reputation
contemp	contemporary	r/bout	roundabout
cotts	cottages	road	rd
		refurb	refurbished/ment
def	definite/definitely	restau	restaurant
dining-rm	dining room	ret	return
		rm(s)	room(s)
E	east	RSPB	Royal Society for the Protection of Birds
Edin	Edinburgh		
esp	especially	rt	right
excl	excluding or excellent		
exhib(s)	exhibition(s)	S	south
exp	expensive	SD	signature dish
		self/c	self-catering
facs	facilities	sq	square
ft	fort	st	street
		stn	station
gdn(s)	garden(s)	SYHA	Scottish Youth Hostel Association
GF	gay-friendly		
Gillian G	Gillian Glover, notable Scottish food critic	🍵	Worth going to for the tearoom alone
Glas	Glasgow	TDH	Table d'hôte
gr	great	TGP	Time of going to print
HS	Historic Scotland	TIC	Tourist Information Centre
hr(s)	hour(s)		
		TO	tourist office
incl	including	TR	top rooms
inexp	inexpensive	t/away	take-away food
info	information	t/off	turn off
		trad	traditional
j/tie	jacket and tie	tratt	trattoria
jnct	junction		
Joanna B	Joanna Blythman, notable Scottish food critic	univ	university
		v	very
L	loch	VC	visitor centre
LO	last orders	vegn	vegetarian
LO10pm/11pm	usually, last orders at 10pm during week, 11pm weekends	W	west
		w/end(s)	weekend(s)
min(s)	minute(s)	yr(s)	years
mt(s)	mountain(s)		

YOUR HELP NEEDED
(AND WIN GOOD WHISKY)

Scotland the Best wouldn't be the best if I didn't receive feedback and helpful suggestions from so many people. It really has become an interactive book because so many of you seem to know what sort of places are likely to fit. With each new edition I believe I get closer to the definitive best guide including everywhere in Scotland that's any good. It bothers me if I miss something – a new restaurant might be forgiveable, but there may be an established one that I've omitted from this edition. There are pubs for example that have been doing great food for years and as each edition passes I get closer to knowing all of them. This completeness is because people write to tell me. And I hope very much that they will continue to do so. *Scotland the Best* is supposed to follow the inside track to Scotland and you who live here, or are experiencing it as a visitor, are on it. Send me the word!

Write and let me know whether you have found the information helpful and accurate and whether you agree or disagree with my selections. Have places lived up to your expectations and, in particular, are there any superlative places that ought to have been mentioned? Even if it's your own place and you think it deserves wider attention, let me know. Everywhere you recommend will be checked out for the next edition in 2004/2005. Please send your comments or suggestions to:

Peter Irvine/*Scotland the Best*
Reference Department
HarperCollins Publishers
Westerhill Rd
Bishopbriggs
Glasgow
G64 2QT

For sharing this information, HarperCollins will be happy to share out some good whisky and cheese. A bottle of malt (any from the list of my suggestions on p. 194) together with a drum of Tobermory cheddar will be presented at the launch of the next edition, to the best three suggestions received by 30 September 2005. Recommendations can be for any category or for any number of categories, and anywhere that you recommend will be included next time, if it checks out. Please give reasons for your recommendation and specific directions if it is difficult to find.

SECTION 1

The Likes of You and Me

THE BIG ATTRACTIONS

✓ ✓ ✓ *Amongst the 'top 10' (paid admn) and the 'top 10' (free) visitor attractions, these are the ones really worth seeing. Find them under their item nos.*

EDINBURGH CASTLE; HOLYROOD PALACE; EDINBURGH ZOO; THE NATIONAL GALLERY; OUR DYNAMIC EARTH: 390/392/398/397/396/MAIN ATTRACTIONS.

THE PEOPLE'S PALACE, GLASGOW; THE BURRELL COLLECTION; SCIENCE CENTRE: 760/758/761/MAIN ATTRACTIONS.

THE MUSEUM OF TRANSPORT; THE GLASGOW BOTANICS; THE GALLERY OF MODERN ART: 764/765/766/OTHER ATTRACTIONS.

THE EDINBURGH BOTANICS: 402/OTHER ATTRACTIONS.

CULZEAN CASTLE; STIRLING CASTLE: 1825/1822/CASTLES.

OTHER UNMISSABLES ARE:

1
MAP 2
E4
✓ ✓ ✓ **LOCH LOMOND:** App via Stirling and A811 to Drymen or from Glas, the A82 Dumbarton rd to Balloch. Britain's largest inland waterway and a trad playground, especially for Glaswegians; jet-skis, show-off boats. **LOMOND SHORES** at Balloch is the new, heavily retail gateway to the loch & the **LOCH LOMOND NATIONAL PARK** which covers a vast area. Orientate & shop here.

W bank Balloch-Tarbert is most developed: marinas, cruises, ferry to Inchmurrin Island. Luss is tweeville, like a movie set (it is used in the Scottish TV soap High Road) but has ok tearm (1495/TEAROOMS). Rd more picturesque beyond Tarbert to Ardlui (1232/HOSTELS); see 1374/BLOODY GOOD PUBS for the non-tourist/real Scots experience of the Drover's Inn at Inverarnan.

E bank more natural, wooded; good lochside and hill walks (2016/MUNROS). Rd winding but picturesque beyond Balmaha towards Ben Lomond.

2
MAP 5
A2
✓ ✓ ✓ **THE CUILLINS, SKYE:** This hugely impressive mt range in the S of Skye, often shrouded in cloud or rain, is the romantic heart-land of the Islands & was 'sold' in 2003 to a combination of public agencies so... it's ours now! The Red Cuillins are smoother and nearer the Portree-Broadford rd; the Black Cuillins gather behind and are best approached from Glen Brittle (2031/SERIOUS WALKS; 1681/WATERFALLS). This classic, untameable mt scenery has attracted walkers, climbers and artists for centuries. It still claims lives regularly. For best views apart from Glen Brittle, see 1711/SCENIC ROUTES; 1727/VIEWS. Vast range of walks and scrambles (see also 1742/PICNICS).

3
MAP 5
D2
✓ ✓ ✓ **LOCH NESS:** Most visits start from Inverness at the N end via the R Ness. Ft Augustus is at the other end, 56km. S. L Ness is part of the still-navigable Caledonian Canal linking the E and W coast at Ft William. Many small boats line the shores of the R Ness, and one of the best ways to see the loch is on a cruise from Inverness (Jacobite Cruises 01463 233999), Drumnadrochit or Fort Augustus. Most tourist traffic uses the main A82 N bank rd converging on Drumnadrochit where the L Ness Monster industry gobbles up your money. If you must, the 'official' L Ness Monster Exhibition is the one to choose. On the A82 you can't miss Urquhart Castle (1860/RUINS). But the two best things about L Ness are: the S rd (B862) from Ft Augustus back to Inverness (1716/SCENIC ROUTES; 1690/WATERFALLS); and the detour from Drumnadrochit to Cannich to Glen Affric (20-30km) (1665/GLENS; 2037/GLEN AND RIVER WALKS; 1667/WATERFALLS).

4
MAP 3
B4
✓ ✓ **FALKIRK WHEEL, FALKIRK:** 08700 500 208. Tamfourhill, halfway betw Edin & Glas, signed from M9 & M80 & locally. The splendid & deliberately dramatic massive boat-lift at the convergence of the (Millennium-funded) reinstated Union and Forth & Clyde canals – the world's first coast-to-coast ship canal (to wonder or plooter along). The 35-m lift is impressive to watch & gr to go on. Boats leave Vis Centre every 30 mins for 45-min journey. There are now 3 reasons to visit Falkirk (22/EVENTS, 1632/PARKS).

5 WEMYSS BAY-ROTHESAY FERRY: Calmac 01475 650100. The glass-roofed
MAP 2 stn at Wemyss Bay, the railhead from Glas (60km by rd on the A78), is redolent
E4 of an age-old terminus. The frequent ferry (Calmac) has all the Scottish traits
and sausage rolls you can handle, and Rothesay (with its period seaside mansions) appears out of blood-smeared sunsets and rain-sodden mornings alike,
a gentle watercolour from summer holidays past. Visit the (Victorian) toilet
when you get there and Mt Stuart (1886/HOUSES). Both are superb.

6 LOCH ETIVE CRUISES: 01866 822430, though booking not essential. From
MAP 2 Taynuilt (Oban 20km) through the long narrow waters of one of Scotland's
D2 most atmospheric lochs, a 3hr journey in a small cruiser with indoor and out-
door seating. Pier is 2km from main Taynuilt crossroads on A85. Easter-mid
Oct. Leaves 2pm (and 10am & 12 noon in summer not Sat/Sun). Also **LOCH
SHIEL CRUISES**: 01687 470322. From nr Glenfinnan House Hotel (1321/SCOT-
TISH HOTELS) on Rd to the Isles, A830. A 1-2-stop cruise on glorious L Shiel.
Various trips avail.

7 GLENELG-KYLERHEA: The shorter of the 2 remaining ferry journeys to Skye,
MAP 5 and definitely the best way to get there if you're not pushed for time. The drive
B2 to Glenelg from the A87 is spectacular (1705/SCENIC ROUTES) and so is this 5min
crossing of the deep Narrows of Kylerhea. Apr-Oct (frequent) 9am-5.45pm and
Sun in summer (from 10am). 01599 511302. Otter watch hide at Kylerhea.

8 CORRAN FERRY: From Ardgour on A861-Nether Lochaber on the A82 across
MAP 2 the narrows of L Linnhe. A convenient 5min crossing which can save time to
D1 pts S of Mallaig and takes you to the wildernesses of Moidart and
Ardnamurchan and which is a charming and fondly regarded journey in its
own rt. Runs continuously until 8.50pm summer, 7.50pm winter.

9 THE MAID OF THE FORTH CRUISE TO INCHCOLM ISLAND: 0131 331 4857.
MAP 3 The wee boat (though they say it holds 225 people) which leaves every day at
C4 different times (phone for details) from Hawes Pier in S Queensferry (15km
Central Edin via A90) opp the Hawes Inn, just under the famous railway br
(391/MAIN ATTRACTIONS). 45min trips under the br and on to Inchcolm, an
attractive island with walks and an impressive ruined abbey. Much birdlife
and also many seals. 1hr 30mins ashore. Tickets at pier.

10 THE WAVERLEY: 0845 130 4647. See the Clyde, see the world! Report:
MAP B 774/GLASGOW ATTRACTIONS.

11 THE WEST HIGHLAND LINE: Rail info: 08457 484950. One of the most pic-
MAP 5 turesque railway journeys in Europe and quite the best way to get to Skye
C2 from the S. Travel to Ft William from Glas, then relax and watch the stunning
scenery, the Bonnie Prince Charlie country (MARY, CHARLIE AND BOB, p. 242) and
much that is close to a railwayman's heart go past the window. Viaducts (incl
the Harry Potter one) and tunnels over loch and down dale. Also possible to
make the same journey (from Ft William to Mallaig and/or return) by steam
train on certain days. Journey time just under 2hrs. Check on 01463 239026.
There's a museum in the restored stn at Glenfinnan. Trains for Mallaig leave
from Glas Queen St, 3 times a day and take about 5hrs.

12 FROM INVERNESS: Info on 08457 484950. Two less-celebrated but mes-
MAP 5 merising rail journeys start from Inverness. The journey to Kyle of Lochalsh no
D2 longer has an observation car in the summer months, so get a window seat
and take an atlas; the last section through Glen Carron and around the coast
at Loch Carron is especially fine. There are 3 trains a day and it takes 2hrs
30mins. Inverness to Wick is a 3hr 50min journey. The section skirting the E
coast from Lairg-Helmsdale is full of drama, followed by the transfixing
monotony of the Flow Country. 3 trains a day in summer.

13 THE PLANE TO BARRA: Most of the island plane journeys pass over many
MAP 7 smaller islands (e.g. Glas-Tiree, Glas-Stornoway, Wick-Orkney) and are fasci-
A5 nating on a clear day, but BA's daily flight from Glas to Barra is doubly special
because the island doesn't have an airport and you land on Cockleshell Beach
in the N of the island (11 km from Castlebay) after a splendid app. The 12-
seater Otter leaves and lands according to the tide. 08457 733377.

THE ESSENTIAL SCOTTISH BOOKS

FICTION

Iain Banks, *The Wasp Factory*; *The Crow Road*; *Excession*

Christopher Brookmyre, *One Fine Day In The Middle Of The Night*

George Douglas Brown, *The House with the Green Shutters*

George Mackay Brown, *Greenvoe*; *The Masked Fisherman*

John Buchan, *The 39 Steps/Short Stories*

Lewis Grassic Gibbon, *Sunset Song*

Neil Gunn, *Highland River*; *The Silver Darlings*

Alasdair Gray, *Lanark*

Archie Hind, *The Dear Green Place*

James Hogg, *Confessions of a Justified Sinner*

Robin Jenkins, *The Cone Gatherers*

James Kelman, *How Late It Was, How Late*

A L Kennedy, *Night Geometry and the Garscadden Trains*

William McIlvanney, *Docherty*

Nancy Brysson Morrison, *The Gowk Storm*

Ian Rankin, *The Rebus Collection*

Bess Ross, *A Bit of Crack and Car Culture*

J K Rowling, The Harry Potter series

Sir Walter Scott, *The Heart of Midlothian*; *The Two Drovers and Other Stories*; *Old Mortality*

Ian Crichton Smith, *Consider The Lilies*

Alexander McCall Smith, *The No.1 Ladies' Detective Agency*

Alan Spence, *Its Colours They Are Fine*

Robert Louis Stevenson, *Kidnapped*; *Master of Ballantrae*; *Catriona*; *Dr Jekyll and Mr Hyde*; *Weir of Hermiston*

Muriel Spark, *The Prime of Miss Jean Brodie*

Alexander Trocchi, *Cain's Book*; *Young Adam*

Alan Warner, *Morvern Callar*; *The Sopranos*

Irvine Welsh, *Trainspotting*; *Maribou Stork Nightmares*

NON-FICTION

Boswell and Johnson, *Journey to the Western Islands*

Derek Cooper, *Skye*

Jim Crumley, *A High And Lonely Place*

Tom Devine, *The Scottish Nation: 1700–2000*

Raymond Eagle, *Seton Gordon: A Highland Gentleman*

Antonia Fraser, *Mary Queen of Scots*

George MacDonald Fraser, *The Steel Bonnets*

Douglas Gifford (ed), *Scottish Literature*

Elizabeth Grant of Rothiemurchus, *Memoirs of a Highland Lady*

Phillip Hills, *Appreciating Whisky*

Michael Lynch (ed), *Oxford Companion to Scottish History*

Osgood Mackenzie, *100 Years in the Highlands* (out of print but still available at Inverewe Gdns)

Charles Maclean, *The Story of St Kilda*

Cameron McNeish, *The Munros*

Gavin Maxwell, *Ring of Bright Water*

Edwin Muir, *Scottish Journey*

William Poucher, *The Magic of Skye*

John Prebble, *1000 Years of Scotland's History*; *The Lion in the North*; *The Highland Clearances*; *Culloden*; *Glencoe*

TC Smout, *A History of the Scottish People*

Nigel Tranter, *The Story of Scotland*

George Way and Romilly Squire, *The Collins Scottish Clan & Family Encyclopedia*

Christopher Whyte (ed), *Gendering The Nation: Studies In Modern Scottish Literature*

The West Highland Way: Official Guide

POETRY

Robert Burns, *Collected Songs and Poems*

Robert Fergusson, *Selected Poems*

Sorley Maclean, *Collected Poems*

Norman McCaig, *Collected Poems*

Edwin Morgan, *New Selected Poems*

A FEW THINGS THE SCOTS GAVE THE WORLD

The population of Scotland has never been much over 5 million and yet we discovered, invented or manufactured for the first time the following quite important things.

The decimal point

Logarithms

The Bank of England

The overdraft

Cannabis (the active principle)

Documentary films

Colour photographs

Encyclopaedia Britannica

Postcards

The gas mask

Theory of Combustion

The advertising film

The bus

The steam engine

The locomotive

The fax machine

The photocopier

Video

The telephone

Television

Radar

Helium

Neon

The telegraph

Street lighting

The lawnmower

Kinetic energy

Electric light

The alpha chip

The Thermos flask

The hypodermic syringe

Finger-printing

The kaleidoscope

Anaesthesia

Antiseptics

Golf clubs

The 18-hole golf course

Tennis courts

The bowling green

Writing paper

The thermometer

The gravitating compass

The threshing machine

Insulin

Penicillin

Interferon

The pneumatic tyre

The pedal bicycle

The modern road surface

Geology

Artificial ice

Morphine

Ante-natal clinics

Bovril

Marmalade

The fountain pen

The Mackintosh

Gardenias

Dolly, the cloned sheep

Auld Lang Syne

14 UP HELLY AA: Info: 01595 693434. Traditionally on the 24th day after Christmas, but now always the last Tues in Jan. A mid-winter fire festival based on Viking lore where 'the Guizers' haul a galley thro the streets of Lerwick and burn it in the park; and the night goes on. JAN

15 CELTIC CONNECTIONS, GLASGOW: Tickets and info: 0141 353 8000. A huge
MAP B festival of Celtic music from round the world held in the Royal Concert Hall
D3 and other city venues over 3 weeks. Concerts, ceilidhs, workshops. JAN

16 BURNS NIGHT: The National Bard celebrated with supper. No single major event (but see below). JAN 25TH

17 GLASGOW ART FAIR, GLASGOW: Info: 0141 552 6027. Britain's most signifi-
MAP B cant commercial art fair o/side London held in mid-April in tented pavilions
D3 in George Sq with selected galleries from Scotland and UK. APRIL

18 MELROSE SEVENS: Info TIC 01896 822555. Border town of Melrose com-
MAP 3 pletely taken over by tournament in their small is beautiful rugby ground. 7-
D6 a-side teams from all over incl international. It's just a good place to go, fanat-
ical or not. See p. 122 for accom and eats. APRIL

19 FIFE POINT TO POINT, LEVEN, FIFE: 01333 360229. Major 'society' i.e. county
MAP 3 set, get-together at Balcormo Mains Farm. Sort of Scottish equivalent of
C3 Henley with horses organised by Fife Fox and Hounds. Range Rovers, ham-
pers, Hermès and what's left of the Tories in Scotland. APRIL

20 PAPS OF JURA HILL RACE, ISLE OF JURA: Details from the hotel 01496
MAP 2 820243. The amazing hill race up and down the 3 Paps or distinctive peaks
B4 (total of 7 hills altogether) on this large remote island (2295/MAGICAL ISLANDS).
About 150 runners take part on the 16-mile challenge from the distillery in
Craighouse, the village. MAY

21 BURNS AND A'THAT, AYR & AYRSHIRE: Info 01292 678100. Fledgling festival
MAP 2 (the first outing in 2002 was a big critical success and now set to be annual)
E6 mainly in Ayr and Alloway with flagship open-air classical concert at Culzean
Castle. Celebrates the bard but programme focuses on contemporary music
and theatre. MAY

22 BIG IN FALKIRK, FALKIRK: Info 0141 552 6027. Held mainly in Callander Park
MAP 3 outside town centre so a delightful, almost rural setting for 'Scotland's
B4 International Street Arts Festival'. Street theatre usually incl one big finale
show with fireworks. Gala-day feel to daytime family programme. MAY

23 MOUNTAIN BIKE WORLD CUP, FT WILLIAM: 01397 703781. Actually held at
MAP 2 Nevis Range 5K run, around the ski gondola. Awesome course with truly inter-
D1 national competitors over 2 days with evening events in town. May move to
Sept.

24 FLOWER SHOWS, INGLISTON & AYR: Many Scottish towns hold flower
MAP 2 shows, mainly in the autumn, but the big spring show at the Royal Highland
E6 Centre by Edinburgh Airport (Ingliston) is well worth a look. Call 0131 333
0969 for info. Meanwhile the annual show in Ayr in early August is huge!
Check local TIC for details. SPRING & AUG

25 COMMON RIDINGS, BORDER TOWNS: Info Jedburgh TIC 01835 863435. The
MAP 3 Border town festivals. Similar formats over different weeks with 'ride-outs' (on
C5, D6, horseback to outlying villages etc) ,'shows', dances and games, culminating on
E6 the Fri/Sat. Total local involvement. Hawick is first, then Selkirk, Peebles/
Melrose, Gala, Jedburgh, Kelso and Lauder end of July. MAY-JULY

26 ROYAL HIGHLAND SHOW, INGLISTON SHOWGROUND, EDINBURGH: 0131
MAP A 335 6200. The premiere agricultural show (over 4 days) in Scotland and for the
xA3 farming world, the event of the year. Animals, machinery, food, crafts and
shopping. A big day out for 150,000 in 2003. JUNE

27 SCOTTISH TRADITIONAL BOAT FESTIVAL, PORTSOY: Perfect little festival in
MAP 4 perfect little Moray coast town nr Banff over a w/end in late June/early July.
C1 Old boats in old and new harbours, open-air ceilidhs, great atmos. 01261
842951. LATE JUNE

28 **MENDELSSOHN ON MULL:** Classical music festival in various halls & venues
MAP 2   around the island that celebrates the connection betw the composer & this
B2   rocky far-flung part of the world. Nice Idea, gr time to be here (see Mull, p.
299). Info 0131 225 8282.   END JUNE

29 **SCOTTISH GAME CONSERVANCY FAIR, PERTH:** Held in the rural and histor-
MAP 3   ical setting of Scone Palace, a major Perthshire day out and gathering for the
C3   hunting, shooting, fishing and of course, shopping brigade. Details: 01620
850577.   JULY

30 **T IN THE PARK, BALADO AIRFIELD nr KINROSS:** Scotland's highly successful
MAP 3   pop festival with all that is current in Britpop and beyond. The T stands for
C3   Tennents, the sponsors who are much in evidence. Not as lifestyle-affirming as
Glastonbury, but among the best fests in the UK.   JULY

31 **ART WEEK, PITTENWEEM:** 01333 312168. Remarkable local event where the
MAP 3   whole vill of Pittenweem in Fife becomes a gallery. Over 70 venues showing
D4   work incl public building & people's houses. Other events incl fireworks. AUG

32 **EDINBURGH INTERNATIONAL FESTIVAL, EDINBURGH:** 0131 473 2000. The
MAP A   3 week 'biggest arts festival in the world' with the Military **TATTOO** and major
opera/music/drama. The **BANK OF SCOTLAND FIREWORKS** are on the final
Saturday. Incorporates **THE FRINGE** Festival with hundreds of events every
night; **FRINGE SUNDAY** on the second w/end. Also the **INTERNATIONAL
FILM FESTIVAL, JAZZ FESTIVAL** and (mainly for delegates on a bit of a jolly)
the TV festival. Edin in Aug is the best place to be in the world. (471/ESS. EDIN
CULTURE)   AUG

33 **EDINBURGH INTERNATIONAL BOOK FESTIVAL:** 0131 228 5444. A tented
MAP B   village in Charlotte Sq Gardens. Same time as the above but deserving of a
E5   separate entry because it is so uniquely good. (471/ESS. EDIN CULTURE)   AUG

34 **THE WORLD PIPE BAND CHAMPIONSHIPS, GLASGOW:** 0141 221 5414.
MAP B   Unbelievable numbers (3-4000) of pipers from all over the world competing
E5   and seriously doing their thing on Glasgow Green.   AUG

35 **LEUCHARS AIR SHOW, LEUCHARS nr ST ANDREWS:** Info: 01334 839000.
MAP 3   Major air-show held over one day in RAF airfield with flying displays, exhibi-
D3   tions, classic cars etc.   SEPT

36 **THE PEDAL FOR SCOTLAND GLASGOW-TO-EDINBURGH BIKE RIDE:** Fun,
MAP 3   charity fund-raiser annual bike event. From George Sq to Meadowbank with
a pasta party at the halfway point.   SEPT

37 **TOUR OF MULL RALLY, ISLE OF MULL:** Info Tobermory TIC 01688 302182.
MAP 2   The highlight of the national rally calendar is this raging around Mull w/end.
B2   Though drivers enter from all over the world, the overall winner has often
been a local man (well plenty time for practice). There's usually a waiting list
for accom, but camping ok and locals put you up.   OCTOBER

38 **ST ANDREWS NIGHT:** Not such a big deal, but dinners etc and cultural ID.
NOV 30TH

39 **EDINBURGH'S HOGMANAY, EDINBURGH:** Everywhere gets booked up, but
MAP A   call TIC for accom, 0131 557 3990 for info. One of the world's major winter
events. Launched with a Torchlight Procession through the city centre and
with a full, largely populist programme. Main event is the Street Party on 31st;
you need a wrist-band. Huge, good-natured crowd. If you come from elsewhere, you'll be amazed. It's the Scots at their best! (471/ESS EDIN CULTURE)
DEC/JAN

40 **LOCHNAGAR ON THE LONGEST DAY:** Nr Ballater via L Muick. Leave evening
MAP 3 before and camp/keep your vigil kind of thing. 4hrs to get up. Take map, good
C1 boots, food, dram etc. From first light across the Cairngorm Plateau, the Dee
Valley, Morvern, Bennachie appear; and God, if you're lucky. Later, in Aug the
Royal Family are beneath you (2021/MUNROS).

41 **SANDWOOD BAY, KINLOCHBERVIE:** Another place to go in the long light of
MAP 6 summer days. It's a fair trek from the N (Cape Wrath) or even (more usually) the
B1 southern app via Balchrick and Kinlochbervie (1648/BEACHES). Take a tent,
some beers and wine; a few friends. Sit in the long sunset and/or the dawn.
The summer will pass; and the winter.

42 **A WEEKEND AWAY WITH GOOD FRIENDS OR SOMEONE YOU LOVE:** As
long as it's sympatico, does it really matter where? There are plenty suggestions in the following pages (*see esp pp. 160–162,* GET-AWAY-FROM-IT-ALL). But
for that special pampering **GLENEAGLES, KINNAIRD, CROMLIX, ISLE OF
ERISKA RAEMOIR** are among the v best country hotels in Britain. The food,
the service, the grounds are yours (1211/1209/1206/1210/COUNTRY-HOUSE
HOTELS). **THE HOUSE OVER-BY** in faraway Skye (1252/INNS) – the treat retreat
and **THE FARAWAY INNS: APPLECROSS** (1258/INNS), **GLENELG** (1255/INNS),
STEIN INN, SKYE (1260/INNS).

43 **THE TRESHNISH ISLANDS:** Go especially when the puffins are there too. The
MAP 2 trip to the Treshnish (from Ulva Ferry on Mull) on a summer's day is a voyage of
B2 discovery (incl Staffa). Go in July, walk amongst these enchanting creatures
before they disappear back into the cold Atlantic. Purify the soul. **HANDA
ISLAND** is a much shorter crossing, but you have the island & the birds to your-
self. (1792/BIRDS)

44 **ST KILDA:** The most westerly islands in the UK, 110 miles into the Atlantic.
MAP 7 Remote, symbolic, superlative in every way, ingrained deep in the spiritual
xA3 heart of the Scots. The community evacuated in 1930 represented the last in
an age of innocence and freedom now gone forever; life was hard but perfectly attuned to this dramatically beautiful place. Highest sea cliffs in UK, premier sea bird breeding stn. Village of Hirta conserved. NTS (01463 732622)
arrange 'working parties' (May-Aug, 14-day trips from Oban) or boat charter:
from Oban 01967 421654, Mull 01680 814260, Lewis 01851 672381.

45 **THE AONACH EAGACH or THE FIVE SISTERS OF KINTAIL:** Two awe-inspiring
MAP 2 high-level walks; in good weather among the most exhilarating in the world.
E2 The first is definitely not for the faint-hearted. The sisters are more forgiving,
MAP 5 but the walk, tho not perilous, is arduous; most of us should do them once in
C2 a lifetime, so do them before you're too doddery. And go with someone who's
done them before or knows hillwalking. Just go with somebody good as I did
on a rainy day in 2002 & a perfect day in autumn 2003 (thanks Neil & Sarah)
(2032/2034/SERIOUS WALKS).

46 **SUMMER PICNICS:** It's a warm, dry summer's day (think 2003): you stock up
from one of the great delis on pp. 188–189 like Valvona in Edinburgh
(1546/DELIS) or the wonderful Ndebele (288/CAFÉS) or Heart & Buchanan
(698/T/AWAY) or Delizique (1553/DELIS) in Glasgow – or Clare Ramsay in Bridge
of Allan which is nr some gt spots – and head for the river. There's a lot of good
river picnic sites listed on p. 213. Most are places that the locals know and
have gone for generations (when those summer's days were longer and
somehow, better). But you find your spot with your family or your mates,
maybe light a fire, and cool off in the pool. It's best to take old sandals or trainers and of course take care. Afterwards, a game of rounders. There may be
midgies, there may be showers, but to my mind this is the most blissful way to
spend a summer's day in Scotland.

SECTION 2

Edinburgh

The telephone code for Edinburgh is 0131
Refer to MAP A, unless otherwise stated

47
D2 ✓✓ **THE BALMORAL:** 556 2414. Princes St at E end above Waverley Stn. Capital landmark with its clock always 2 min fast (except at Hogmanay) so you don't miss your train. The old pile especially dear to Sir Rocco Forte's heart. Exp for a mere tourist but if you can't afford to stay there's always afternoon tea in the refurbished Palm Court. Few hotels anywhere are so much in the heart of things. Good business centre, fine sports facs; luxurious and distinctive rms have ethereal views of the city, tho' some don't and are simply not worth the money. Main restau, Number One Princes Street (110/BEST RESTAUS), is tops and less formal brasserie, Hadrian's (good power b/fast venue). Even the non-pretentious bar, NB, works (occ has music). **TR:** the 3 'Royal' suites – Presidential, Balmoral & Glamis. 188RMS JAN-DEC T/T PETS CC KIDS LOTS

48
C3 ✓✓ **THE CALEDONIAN HILTON:** 222 8888. Princes St, W End. Edin institution – former stn hotel built in 1903. Now in Hilton hands & upgrading continues to reinforce 5-star status. Good business hotel with all facs you'd expect (tho not in all rms). 'Living Well' spa with not large pool. Endearing lack of uniformity about the rms. Executive rms on fifth floor (and deluxe rms elsewhere) have gr views. Capital kind of place in every respect. Main restau, The Pompadour, for fine and très formal dining, being refurbed at TGP. Brasserie on ground floor. Cally Bar (or Chisholms) a famous rendezvous. **TR:** the Caledonian Suite. 249RMS JAN-DEC T/T XPETS CC KIDS LOTS

49
C3 ✓✓ **THE SHERATON GRAND:** 229 9131. Festival Sq on Lothian Rd and Conference Centre, this city-centre business hotel won no prizes for architecture when it opened late 1980s, but now both Festival Sq & the newly emerged Conference Sq behind one part of the shiny new financial district & Edin looks like a real city at last. This is a reliable stopover with excellent service. Larger rms and castle views carry premiums, but make big difference. Terrace restau adequate, but 'The Grill' menu prepared under the supervision of Nicolas Laurent is elegant, with innovative Auld Alliance menu (112/BEST RESTAUS) and Santini behind the hotel also excl (162/BEST ITALIAN). The health club 'One' is routinely identified as one of the best spas in the UK, with gr pool. **TR:** the 2 'Diplomatic Suites'. 260RMS JAN-DEC T/T PETS CC KIDS LOTS

50
xE4 ✓✓ **PRESTONFIELD HOUSE:** 668 3346. Off Priestfield Rd, 3km S of city centre. The Heilan' cattle in the 14-acre grounds tell you this isn't your average urban bed for the night. A romantic, almost other-worldly 17th-century building with period features still intact. The big news of 2003 is that James Thomson of The Tower (106/BEST RESTAUS) and The Witchery (107/BEST RESTAUS) has taken over this bastion of Edinburgh sensibilities and soon it will arrive in the 21st C. The architecture and the detail is exceptional; one expects the dining & maybe even the DVDs to follow. Prestonfield is the one to watch! **TR:** 5/6/16/17. 28RMS JAN-DEC T/T PETS CC XKIDS LOTS

51
B2 ✓ **CHANNINGS:** 315 2226. S Learmonth Gdns, parallel to Queensferry Rd after Dean Br. tasteful alternative to hotel chain hospitality. 5 period town houses joined to form a quietly elegant West End hotel. Efficient and individual service incl 24-hr rm service. Gr views from top-floor rms, incl the Prime Minister's alma mater – Fettes College. **TR:** 12/14/16 & 20 good enough for Sean/Elton/David Coulthard so prob good enough for the rest of us. Restau superb under chef Hubert Lamort & Mediterranean-style Ochre Vita make a surprising duo of destination eating spots in this quiet corner of the W End.
46RMS JAN-DEC T/T XPETS CC KIDS TOS LOTS

52
E2 **LE MERIDIEN EDINBURGH:** 557 3222. 18 Royal Terr. Romanesque plunge pool, other sports facs, multi-level terraced gdn out back, deceptively large number of rms and town house décor a tad on the Baroque side make this fabulous for some & a good business bet for others. Bar/restau not so notable among the natives but we do love the terrace in summer. **TR:** Aberlour Suite.
108RMS JAN-DEC T/T XPETS CC KIDS LOTS

53
D3 **CROWNE PLAZA:** 557 9797. 80 High St. Modern but sympathetic building on the Royal Mile, handy for everything. Good facs but some say service lacking. Thin walls, not gr views. Another of the **HOLIDAY INN** family out west nr the Zoo (08704 009026) with acres of rms, leisure facs & 2 restaus is a superior bed box. **TR:** 429. 238/303RMS JAN-DEC T/T PETS CC KIDS TOS LOTS

54 **THE GEORGE:** 225 1251. George St (betw Hanover St and St Andrew Sq). An
C2 Inter-Continental Hotel but Robert Adam-designed and dating back to late
18th century. Good views to Fife from the top 2 floors. Pricey, but you pay for
the location and the Georgian niceties (and extra for the views). Carvery plus
good restau, the Chambertin (216/SCOTTISH RESTAUS). Good Festival &
Hogmanay Hotel close to the heart of things (taken over by luvvies during TV
fest). **TR:** Stewart or Melville (quieter) suites.

195RMS JAN-DEC T/T PETS CC KIDS LOTS

INDIVIDUAL & BOUTIQUE HOTELS

55 ✓✓✓ **THE SCOTSMAN:** 556 5565. North Bridge. De-luxe boutique hotel in
D3 landmark building (the old offices of *The Scotsman* newspaper group)
converted into chic, highly individual accom with every modern fac: internet,
flat-screen TV, privacy locker in all rms. Labyrinthine lay-out (stairs & firedoors
everywhere) & slow lifts apart, this is the convenient cool hotel in town. Nice art,
intimate dining in Vermillion (114/BEST RESTAUS) & buzzy brasserie (119/BISTROS).
Excl leisure facs – Escape – with low-lit, steel pool gr for grown-ups. **TR:**
Penthouse & Director's suites. 68RMS JAN-DEC T/T XPETS CC KIDS LOTS

56 ✓✓ **THE HOWARD:** 315 2220. 34 Gr King St in the heart of the Georgian
C1 New Town. 3 townhouses in splendid st imbued with quiet elegance
tho only 5 mins Princes St. No bar or restau but restful drawing rm & 15 spacious
individual rms, sympatico with architecture but not old-fashioned. 3 new suites
(TR) downstairs have own entrances for discreet liaisons or just convenience &
own drawing rm for entertaining. A very Edinburgh accommodation.

15RMS+3SUITES JAN-DEC T/T XPETS CC XKIDS LOTS

57 ✓✓ **THE MALMAISON:** 468 5000. Tower Pl, Leith, at the dock gates.
xE1 Award-winning, praise-laden designer chain hotel with lavish yet
homely rms. All facs we smart, young, modern people expect eg CD players in
each chambre (borrow CDs from reception). **TR** have harbour views & 4-
poster beds. Brasserie and café-bar have stylish ambience too (132/BEST
BISTROS) and there are many other caffs nearby in this waterfront quarter. Pity
about the new flats outfront, but Leith still onwards & upwards.

101RMS JAN-DEC T/T PETS CC KIDS EXP

58 ✓✓ **THE POINT:** 221 5555. 34 Bread St. You'd never guess this used to be
C3 a Co-operative department store. Space and colour combinations
manage to look simultaneously rich and minimal, some castle views. **TR,** the
suites (LOTS), come with side-lit Jacuzzis. Once mentioned as one of the gr
designery hotels in the world and on the cover of *Hotel Design.* Café-bar
Monboddo and restau have modern and spacious, mid-Euro feel. Good places
to meet Edinburgers tho food & service can be off the point. Conference
Centre adj with gr penthouse often used for cool Edin launches & parties.
140RMS JAN-DEC T/T PETS CC KIDS EXP

59 ✓✓ **THE BONHAM:** 226 6050. 35 Drumsheugh Gdns. Discreet town-
B3 house in quiet W End cres. Cosmo service and ambience a stroll
from Princes St. Much favoured by visiting celebs. Owned by same people as
the Howard and Channings (51/BEST HOTELS). Rms stylish but not minimalist.
Elegant dining in calm, spacious restau (esp end table by back window). Chef
Michel Bouyer forges a foody Auld Alliance of top Scottish ingredients &
French flair. Nice wine-list. No bar. 48RMS JAN-DEC T/T XPETS CC XKIDS GF LOTS

60 ✓ **THE GLASSHOUSE:** 525 8203. 2 Greenside Pl betw Playhouse Theatre &
D2 the Warner Omni multiplex cinema. First of new urban chain, this 'boutique' hotel is in many ways more like a v upmarket travel lodge or motel. It's
built above the multiplex (rms on 2 floors) & the restaus in the mall below.
Main feature is extensive lawned garden on roof around which about half the
rms look out – with patios incl their standard 'de-luxe doubles'. No restau
(b/fast in rm or 'the Observatory'), honesty bar (how long will that last?). The
Omniplex itself is a big disappointment & the restaus within are all high st staples, but guests can use Holmes Place health facs & spa (incl 25m pool –
(438/EDIN SPORTS). Interesting concept not least because of the upmarket &
the downmarket juxtapositions. 65RMS JAN-DEC T/T XPETS CC XKIDS LOTS

61 ✔ **EDINBURGH RESIDENCE:** 226 3380. 7 Rothesay Terr. Another town
B3 house affair but on extravagant scale. Several Georgian town houses
have been joined into an elegant apartment hotel by the Townhouse Group
who own the Howard & the Bonham (above). No restau, but the Bonham do
b/fasts & 24-hr room service, so a discreet & distinctive stopover in 3 diff levels of suite. Big bathrms, views of Dean Village. Drawing rm if you're feeling
lonely in this quiet W End retreat but nightlife & shops a stroll away.

29RMS JAN-DEC T/T XPETS CC KIDS LOTS

62 ✔ **APEX CITY HOTEL:** 243 3456. 61 Grassmarket, the picturesque but rowdy
C3 Sat night city centre. Modern, soi-disant – been here before but close to
castle, club life & other bits of essential Edin. Cool to roam from. Restau called
Aqua. Another Apex adj has another 175 rms & there's a more lodgy lodging
beyond the W End (79/TRAVEL LODGES). 119RMS JAN-DEC T/T XPETS CC KIDS LOTS

63 ✔ **ROYAL GARDEN APARTMENTS:** 625 1234. York Buildings, Queen St opp
D2 Nat Portrait Gallery (389/ATTRACTIONS) nr Playhouse Theatre and funky
Broughton St. Self-cat v well turned-out apts with coffee-shop on grd floor &
access to private gdns. Access to the superior leisure facs at the Scotsman
Hotel (above) tho you wouldn't want to walk there in your dressing gown. Gr
views esp top floor. Nightly let avail (3 days' min at peak periods).

31APTMS JAN-DEC T/T XPETS CC XKIDS MED.EX

64 **RICK'S:** 622 7800. 55 Frederick St. Very city centre hotel and bar/restau in
C2 downtown location a stone's throw from George St. By same people who
have indigo yard (141/GASTROPUBS) and nearby Opal Lounge (378/STYLE BARS)
so the bar is full-on esp late. Restau (143/BISTROS) has (loud) contemporary
dining. Rms upstairs surprisingly quiet. Modern, urban feel eg DVD players as
standard. Same rate single or twin. Don't let the rms above the bar thing put
you off. Go as high as you can – these rms among the best in the centre at this
price. 10RMS JAN-DEC T/T XPETS CC XKIDS MED.EX

65 **BOROUGH:** 668 2255. 72 Causewayside. V urban & self-consciously hip hotel
xD4 in conversion of former snooker hall/warehouse on s side. Notable designer
Ben Kelly (of the legendary Hacienda) somehow failed to warm this place up
or excite. Stark look & cold lighting. Rms small & furnishings not gr, but this is
still a fairly cool place to stay. Bar & restau are southside hang-outs – food
improved of late. 9RMS JAN-DEC T/T XPETS CC XKIDS MED.EX

66 **HANOVER HOTEL:** 226 7576. 37 Rose St slap in the middle of town (betw
C2 Hanover & Frederick St) opp Yo Sushi & Easyeverything. Central & serviceable
hotel one-up from a travel-lodge tho no b/fast (tray in rm). Does have ground
floor wine-bar. 40RMS JAN-DEC T/T XPETS CC XKIDS MED.EX

67 **PARLIAMENT HOUSE:** 478 4000. 15 Calton Hill. Good central location, only
E2 200m from E end of Princes St and adj to Calton Hill (430/BEST VIEWS), although
tucked away. Small bar in residents lounge and restau for b/fast, even meals –
but OK town house-style décor. About half the rms have views – so you know
where to go. 54RMS JAN-DEC T/T XPETS CC KIDS EXP

68 **WEST END HOTEL:** 225 3656. 35 Palmerston Pl. Capital haunt for Highlanders
B3 and Islanders who feel like a blether in Gaelic or a good folk music session in
the bar (decent measures). Popular with folkie non-guests too. Spacious rms –
no sae cheap anymore, but real. And real Scottish b/fast.

8RMS JAN-DEC T/T XPETS CC KIDS MED.INX

69 **CANON COURT APARTMENTS:** 474 7000. Canonmills at foot of New Town
C1 and nr Botanics (402/ATTRACTIONS). Self-cat 1 & 2 bedrm aptms often avail for
short lets, even 1 night. No café, but an inx stopover. Cable TV. Some rms
o/look water of Leith. The gas station over the rd is a social hub esp middle of
the night. 42APTMS JAN-DEC T/T PETS CC KIDS MED.INX

70 ✓✓ **INNER SANCTUM** and the **OLD RECTORY** at the **WITCHERY:** 225
C3 5613. Castlehill. 2 highly individual rms and an apartment above the Witchery restau (107/BEST RESTAUS) at the top of the Royal Mile were supplemented 2003 with 5 sumptuous aptms across the st that put a whole new look into the Old Town. A stone's throw from the castle, few accoms anywhere are as emphatically it as this. Prob the most exceptional and atmospheric in town – designed by owner James Thomson and Mark Rowley – fairly camp/theatrical, OTT and v sexy. B/fast & everything else you need en suite. Go with somebody good.   2+6 APT JAN-DEC T/T XPETS CC XKIDS GF LOTS

71 ✓✓ **19 ST BERNARDS CRES:** 332 6162. In leafy and elegant New Town
B1 crescent (the one that's often used in period movies), an exemplary Georgian townhouse stuffed with antiques and the impeccable good taste of its owner, one William Balfour. All niceties are here incl lovely bathrms (tho not en suite) and b/fast in the dining rm. A not-so-wee gem.
    4RMS JAN-DEC X/X XPETS XCC XKIDS GF MED.INX

72 ✓ **SOUTHSIDE:** 668 4422. 8 Newington Rd. On main st in s side with many
xE4 hotels/GH stretching halfway to Dalkeith, a surprisingly civilised haven. Careful attention to decor & detail & excl b/fast. 'Café South' operates in on-street dining rm in summer. Some traffic noise, but upstairs rms double-glazed. Nice prints. Parking nearby.
    8RMS JAN-DEC T/T XPETS CC KIDS GF MED.INX

73 ✓ **ARDMOR HOUSE:** 554 4944. 74 Pilrig St which is off Leith Walk & with lots
xE1 of other B&Bs – this the top spot. Individual, contemporary and relaxed – & that's just the proprietors Colin and Robin & their gorgeous wee dog, Lola. Love that garden, chaps.   5RMS JAN-DEC X/T PETS CC KIDS GF MED.INX

74 **24 NORTHUMBERLAND ST:** 556 8140. A definitive New town B&B. Georgian
C2 townhouse in mid-New Town full of antiques (owner a notable dealer). Only 3 rms so often booked.   3RMS JAN-DEC T/T XPETS CC XKIDS MED.EXP

75 **17 ABERCROMBY PLACE:** 557 8036. Another plush and private Georgian
C2 town house; discreet lack of signage. Once abode of the New Town's architect, Playfair, now belongs to advocate Eirlys Lloyd. No smk. Lovely st with gdns opp. A Wolsey Lodge.   10RMS JAN-DEC T/T XPETS CC KIDS MED.EXP

76 **SIX ST MARY'S PLACE:** 332 8965. Vegn-friendly GH on main st of Stockbridge
B1 (St Mary's Pl part of Raeburn Pl) and busy main rd out of town for Forth Rd Br and N, this is a tastefully converted Georgian town house. Informal, friendly, well-cared-for accom popular with academics and people we like. No smk. Vegn breakfast in conservatory. Jolly; nice people.
    7RMS JAN-DEC T/T XPETS CC KIDS GF MED.INX

77 **STUART HOUSE:** 557 9030. 12 E Claremont St. Nr the corner of main rd and
D1 pleasant walk up to Princes St (1.5km). Residential New Town st and family house decorated with taste and attention to detail – bonny flower gdn out front. Book well in advance. No smk.
    5RMS JAN-DEC T/T XPETS CC KIDS MED.EXP

78 **TEVIOTDALE HOUSE:** 667 4376. 53 Grange Loan, towards E end. Fecund
xD4 flower gdn out front in suburban southside house & comfortable better than your av B&B within. Mostly big beds (some 4-posters) & famously big b/fasts.
    5RMS JAN-DEC T/T XPETS CC KIDS MED.INX

THE BEST 'ECONOMY' HOTELS AND TRAVEL LODGES

Hotels/B&Bs below are included on grounds of price, convenience or just because we like them for some idiosyncratic reason.

79 **APEX EUROPEAN:** 474 3456. 90 Haymarket Terr. The western, more bedbox
C3 version of the Apex triumvirate. Apex City the grooviest (62/BOUTIQUE HOTELS) & the other, **APEX INTERNATIONAL,** which is adj in the Grassmarket, was once part of Heriot Watt Univ. International is a good location esp at Festival time. Rms with castle view, are more exp, but worth the extra. Ground-floor bar/restau **METRO** is a fairly fashionable watering hole. The European is cheaper. 67/168RMS JAN-DEC T/T XPETS CC KIDS EXP

80 **HILTON EDINBURGH AIRPORT:** 519 4400. At the airport, 10km W of city cen-
xA3 tre. No way 'economy', but a reliable travellers' tryst. An L-shaped box high-class transit camp; charming staff. You can virtually roll out of bed and check in. That smell over the airport by the way is due to some unconscionable thing they do to chickens in the factory nearby. Living Well health club has decent pool. 150RMS JAN-DEC T/T PETS CC KIDS LOTS

81 **TRAVEL INN:** 228 9819. 1 Morrison Link, nr Haymarket Stn. One of 5 in the city
B3 & see below. Likeable for the fact it makes no pretence to be anything other than a bed factory. Big, office-block dull but v cheap – as norm, flat charge. 7 rms specially adapted for wheelchair users. 281RMS JAN-DEC T/T XPETS CC KIDS CHP

82 **TRAVEL INN, LEITH:** 555 1570. Newhaven Pl which means off Commercial Rd,
xE1 along from Royal Yacht Britannia (signed) & Ocean Terminal. Regular box, but: easy parking, quiet location, sports complex adj (Next Generation incl open-air pool – get trial ticket) and for half of the rms a 'sea-view'. Otherwise formula incl Brewsters restau out front. 60RMS JAN-DEC T/T PETS CC KIDS MED.INX

83 **PREMIER LODGE:** 220 2299. 94-96 Grassmarket. Basic and boisterously locat-
C3 ed accom next to Biddy Mulligan's which is open to 1am, but levels 4/5 or at the back best. The Grassmarket is fairly full-on, so good for party animal business types on a budget. 44RMS JAN-DEC T/T XPETS CC KIDS MED.INX

84 **IBIS:** 240 7000. Hunter Sq. First in Scotland of the Euro budget chain (one
D3 other in Glas 523/LESS EXP HOTELS). Dead central behind the Tron so good for Hogmanay (or not). Serviceable and efficient. For tourists doing the sights, this is best bed box for location. 99RMS JAN-DEC T/T PETS CC KIDS MED.INX

85 **TAILORS HALL:** 622 6800. Cowgate. If you don't mind the racket (or want to
D3 be part of it), this is a clubby/young thing kind of hotel in the heart of the throbbing Cowgate area and above the hugely popular 3 Sisters pub. 3 bars to choose from (till 1am), 24 hr licence for residents. Can do 4 in a rm. Rms not above the courtyard best. 42RMS JAN-DEC T/T PETS CC XKIDS MED.EX

86 **TRAVEL LODGE:** 557 6281 (or central booking 0800 850950). 33 St Mary's St.
E3 Edin central version of national (often roadside) chain. All usual, formulaic facs but inx and nr Royal Mile (Holyrood end) and Cowgate for late-night action.
193RMS JAN-DEC T/T XPETS CC KIDS INX

Edin has some YHA hostels (nae drinking) and independents (young and Hoochy, open 24 hrs), also some handy univ halls of residence to let o/side term time. With all the independent hostels, it's best to turn up around 11/11.30am if you haven't booked. The SYHA is the Scottish Youth Hostels Association. 01786 891400.

87
D3, C3 ✓ ✓ **ROYAL MILE BACKPACKERS:** 557 6120. 105 High St. On the Royal Mile, nr the Cowgate with its late-night bars. Ideal central cheap 24 hr crash-out dormitory accom with all the facs for itinerant youth seeking a capital experience. The same company (who also run Mac backpackers tours) have the original hostel, **THE HIGH ST HOSTEL** (8 Blackfriars St): 557 3984, and the **CASTLE ROCK**, 15 Johnston Terr (225 9666) in the old Council Environmental Health HQ. Is huge (190 beds in various dorms, but no singles/doubles) and some gr views across the Grassmarket or to the castle which is just over there. Same folk (Mr Backpacker himself, Peter Macmillan) also have places in Ft William, Inverness, Oban, Pitlochry & Skye. CHP

88
A3 ✓ ✓ **S.Y. HOSTEL, EGLINTON:** 337 1120. 18 Eglinton Cres. From the stained glass over the main door to the tartan and wood entrance foyer, you know you're not in a typical hostel. Grand late-Victorian pile (shame about the lighting) in a quiet W End st with 150 beds – majority in dorms but some rms for 4 (single-sex dorms). Members only but you can join at reception. Booking recommended. Open 24 hrs. CHP

89
D3 ✓ **GLOBETROTTER INN:** 336 1030. Marine Drive, the Cramond foreshore. First venture of ambitious hostel chain. Former hotel in off-centre setting. Huge no of bunks (400), excl facs (spa, gym, internet, kitchen with battery of microwaves & shop). Only drawback is distance from downtown (half hour); last bus 11.20pm. Lawns & trees & riverside view do compensate. CHP

90
D3 ✓ **ST CHRISTOPHER INN:** 0207 407 1856. 9-13 Market St, behind Waverley Stn. Some good views from upper floors to Princes St. Couldn't be handier for the stn or city centre. This (with sister place in London) a hostel rather than hotel with bunk rms tho' there are 5 tw/dbl rms. Price depends on no sharing (£10–20 at TGP). Belushi's café-bar on ground floor open till 1am. A cheap, v central option, better than most other hostels (facs are en-suite). Internet access. 25RMS JAN-DEC X/X XPETS CC XKIDS CHP

91
A2 ✓ **BELFORD HOSTEL:** 225 6209. Douglas Gdns, nr Gallery of Modern Art (excellent café, 273/BEST TEAROOMS) and quaint Dean Village, but still fairly central. Bizarre concept – 98 beds in partitioned-off (un-soundproofed) 'rms' of 6-10 in a converted church. Top-bunk berth gets you a view of the vaulted wooden ceiling way above. Nice stained glass. Games rm, bar, MTV. Sister establishment **EDINBURGH BACKPACKERS HOSTEL**, 65 Cockburn St (220 1717), is closer to action. CHP

92
D2 **PRINCES ST BACKPACKERS EAST:** 556 6894. 5 W Register St. Behind Burger King at E end of Princes St. Incredibly central for cheap accom. Basic and attracts the usual international crowd. CHP

93
B3 **CALEDONIAN BACKPACKERS:** 226 2939. 3 Queensferry St. The city's biggest (accom for 300+) with a bar, kitchen. Doubles, triples & quads. CHP

94
xC4 **S.Y. HOSTEL, BRUNTSFIELD:** 447 2994. 7 Bruntsfield Cres. S of Tollcross about 10 min walk from W End. Reliable and secure hostel accom in a verdant corner of Bruntsfield. 130 beds but booking 2-3 months in advance essential at peak times. Again, members only, join at reception. No doubles. Doors cl 2am.CHP

95
D3 From July-Sep, SYHA also opens 3 temporary hostels in **ROYAL MILE/COW-GATE** area. All offer v central, single accom – a v good bet at peak time in the city. Phone HQ for info 01786 891400.

96
xD4 **ARGYLE BACKPACKERS HOTEL:** 667 9991. 14 Argyle Pl, in Marchmont area of up-market student flats. Quiet area though Argyle Pl the most happening st. 2 km to centre across 'The Meadows' (not advised for women at night). Nice gdn. CHP

97
MAP 3
D4

✔✔ **GREYWALLS, GULLANE:** 01620 842144. On coast 36km E of Edin off A198 just beyond golfers' paradise of Gullane. Prob best co house retreat o/side town. Full report 908/LOTHIANS.

98
MAP 3
B4

✔✔ **CHAMPANY INN:** 01506 834532. On A904, 3km Linlithgow on rd to Forth Rd Bridge and S Queensferry. Exemplary restau with rms some o/looking gdn. Legendary steaks (the meat hung for weeks) and seafood (258/RESTAUS FOR BURGERS AND STEAKS). B/fast in cosy dining kitchen excl with nice bacon. Extraordinary wine-list with dinner. But veggies best not venture here.

16RMS JAN-DEC T/T XPETS CC KIDS LOTS

99
MAP 3
D5

✔ **BORTHWICK CASTLE, NORTH MIDDLETON:** 01875 820514. On B6367, 3km off the A7, 18km bypass, 26km SE of centre. So this is a real Border castle, a big red one. Walls 30m high, this magnificent tower house knocks you off your horse with its authenticity – Mary Queen of Scots was blockaded here once and at night you expect to see her swishing up the spiral stairs. 8 rms in castle, 2 in gatehouse and the (v) grand banqueting hall is impressive but you came for the decor not the (EXP) dinner.

10RMS MAR-DEC T/X PETS CC KIDS LOTS

100
MAP A
xA3

✔ **NORTON HOUSE, INGLISTON:** 333 1275. Off A8 v close to airport, 10km W of city centre. Victorian country house in 55 acres of greenery close to airport. Pleasant to roam, good service but so-so food in restaurant & brasserie. Rms quite swish.

47RMS JAN-DEC T/T XPETS CC KIDS LOTS

101
MAP 3
C5

DALHOUSIE CASTLE, BONNYRIGG: 01875 820153. Just off B704 2km from the A7, 15km from bypass and 23km S of centre. The castle that tries too hard? It looks fantastic in its setting and some bits date way back to the 13th century; otherwise ersatz tho ideal for weddings. (Previous guests incl Edward I, Cromwell, Queen Victoria, some rock stars.) Multi-chambered Dungeon restau has 2AA rosettes.

34RMS JAN-DEC T/T PETS CC KIDS TOS LOTS

102
MAP 3
C4

HOUSTOUN HOUSE, UPHALL: 01506 853831. On A899 at end of Broxburn/Uphall Main St, 8km from r/bout at the start of the M8 Edin–Glas motorway. Airport 10km, 18km W of centre. Bits of this tower house date to the 16th century, in sharp contrast to shiny leisure facs (inc pool) which attracts local patronage. 4-posters in some rooms, blazing fires and 2 restaus (main has 3 dining areas & 2 AA rosettes), all in extensive greenery. Only quite posh hotel in barren hinterland of W. Lothian. Stuffed with farmers during Royal Highland Show week.

72RMS JAN-DEC T/T XPETS CC KIDS LOTS

103
MAP 3
C5

MARRIOTT DALMAHOY, KIRKNEWTON: 333 1845. On A71 (Kilmarnock rd) on edge of town – bypass 5km, 15km W of centre, airport 6km. Georgian house with distinctive rms and big modern annexe (6 turret suites best). Two internationally rated courses make this a golfing mecca. Plenty of other sports facs to while away the hours or improve your handicaps generally. V elegant surroundings. Good corporate choice.

215RMS JAN-DEC T/T XPETS CC KIDS LOTS

OPEN ARMS, DIRLETON: Report 949/LOTHIANS.

TWEEDDALE ARMS, GIFFORD: Report 951/LOTHIANS.

104 ✓✓ **MARTIN WISHART:** 553 3557. 54 The Shore. Discreet waterside
xE1 frontage for one of Edinburgh's most notable foody experiences.
Recently extended rm designed on simple lines; uncomplicated menu & wine-
list (no cheap plonk here). 2-Michelin-star chef Martin & a clutch of awards raise
expectation here, but prep, cooking & presentation are demonstrably a cut
above the rest. Martin just has that touch that we don't have, that brings a smile
as well as saliva to the lips when the plate appears. Mrs Wishart presides with
quiet elegance. Nae nonsense here, only the best meal in town. Gr vegn menu.
SD: Ravioli of lobster and truffle; Buccleuch beef. Lunch Tues-Fri, Dinner Tues-
Sat. LO 9.30pm
EXP

105 ✓✓ **THE ATRIUM:** 228 8882. Foyer of the Traverse Theatre (465/CULTURE),
C3 Cambridge St off Lothian Rd. After 10 yrs Andrew Radford's break-
thro restau still winning awards & still one of the most stylish venues in town
for biz lunch or supper with atmos. Many chefs have come & gone (& opened
their own restaus), but the kitchen & outfront combo of inspiration & efficiency makes the Atrium seem as fresh & new as ever. **SD:** Lamb and pork,
pithiviers, confits.
EXP

106 ✓✓ **THE TOWER:** 225 3003. Corner of Chambers St and George IV Br
D3 above the Museum of Scotland. Restaurant supremo James
Thomson's celebrated & celebrity-strewn restau atop the distinctive 'tower' on
the corner of the sandstone museum building (benefits from the much-
admired grand design and detail of Gordon Benson's architectural vision). It
feels that it could be anywhere, except for Edin rooftops and castle skyline outside the windows (in summer, the terrace is). Gr private dining-rm in the tower
itself. Kitchens far below in Prehistoric Scotland, but food everything one would
expect – Scottish slant on modern British. The steaks are good. 7 days. Lunch
and dinner. LO 11pm. W/end booking essential. Smokers to the balcony!   EXP

107 ✓✓ **THE WITCHERY:** 225 5613. Castlehill. At the top of the Royal Mile
C3 where the tourists come, many will be unaware that this is one of
the city's best restaus and certainly its most stylishly atmospheric. 2 salons,
the upper more witchery; in the 'secret gdn' downstairs, a converted school
playground, James Thomson has created a more spacious ambience for the
(same) elegant Scottish menu. Locals on a treat, many regulars & visiting
celebs pack this place out (although they do turn round the tables), so must
book. The new Witchery Apartments encapsulate this remarkable ambience
(70/LODGINGS). The wine-list is exceptional. Lunch and dinner. LO a v civilised
11.30pm. (296/LATE-NIGHT RESTAUS)
EXP

108 ✓ **OLOROSO:** 226 7614. 33 Castle St. Unassuming entrance and lift to this
C2 rooftop restau renowned for its terrace with views of the castle, the New
Town and Fife. Bar snacks are the best deal; main dining room exp but chef
Tony Singh excels esp with the meatier dishes. Despite winning recent
Restaurant Chef of the Year award, grumbles about food & service have taken
Oloroso down a tick from last edition. However, this is still a fashionable, foody
room at the top. **SD:** Highland beef carpaccio. Lunch and dinner 7 days. LO
10.30pm. Bar till 1am
EXP

109 ✓ **ROGUE:** 228 2700. 63 Morrison St thro très discreet, hardly marked door
C3 in the corner of the Scottish Widows building. The inimitable Dave
Ramsden's uptown bar & restau was fêted for food when it opened in 2001
but it's proven hard to keep up the thro'put in this corner of the so-called
financial district, even tho for this standard of food & service it's as chic as
chips (the austerity menu – £10 for 2 courses – was the best meal deal in town
at TGP). Mod-British menu with Conran approach & a gr take on comfort food.
SD: Buccleuch beef, sausage, egg and chips, jelly & fruit. Cl Sun. Lunch & LO
11pm.
MED

110 ✓ **NUMBER ONE PRINCES STREET, BALMORAL HOTEL:** 556 2414. Address
D2 with a certain ring for the principal restau of the Balmoral (47/BEST
HOTELS) entered through lobby or off st. Based apparently on the Mandarin
Grill, Hong Kong, these opulent subterranean salons have ample space
around the tables, but the lighting and lacquering do little to cosify the ritzi-
ness (and like many hotel restaus it's often not busy or buzzy – good to

remember when other top restaus may be full). Michelin starred 2003, but other reviews have varied. Attentive service. Scottish Chef of the Year (2003) Jeff Bland ensures that **HADRIAN'S BRASSERIE,** a peppermint lounge at st level, complements well. Cl Sat/Sun lunch. LO 10.30pm. EXP

111 ✔ **FISHER'S IN THE CITY:** 225 5109. 58 Thistle St. New, shiny, buzzy, uptown
C2 version of one of Leith's longest best eateries (179/SEAFOOD) & this place works on all its levels (we're talking mezzanine). Fisher fan staples ('favourites') all here – the fishcakes, the soup & the blackboard specials, excl wine-list combined with gr service Some vegn & meat (steaks a special). Open all day (reduced menu late aft). **SD:** fishcakes of course, and soup! 7 days.LO 10.30pm. MED

112 ✔ **THE GRILL ROOM at the SHERATON:** 229 9131. The fine dining rm at
C3 Edin's most corporate of top hotels. Sits alongside The Terrace which has the view (of Festival Sq) and Santini's, the Italian place out back (on Conference Sq). Not much 'Grill' about it, but a serious dining-out experience with an accoladed menu by long-standing chef Nicolas Laurent. Atmos minimal, food presentation minimalist (4 scallops, big plate loadsamoney starters), but much of the clientele are on expenses. Nevertheless, even for locals this is an estimable chef at the height of his powers. Lunch Mon-Fri & LO 10.30pm (cl Sun). **SD:** Rib of beef, miniature puds. MED

113 ✔ **MARTIN'S:** 225 3106. 70 Rose St N Lane. Quiet lane behind busy shop-
C2 ping precinct nr Princes St – odd place to find a decent restau but this is one of Edin's longstanding top eateries. Exemplary service, v high standard of contemporary cooking, delicate desserts and an unsurpassed (incl unpasteurised) Celtic cheeseboard. Good on game, duck and lovely breads, and Martin knows his wines. 3 AA rosettes. Lunch Tue-Fri, dinner Tue-Sat. LO 10pm. EXP

114 ✔ **VERMILLION:** 622 2814. North Bridge. The fine dining rm of the fabulous
D3 Scotsman Hotel (55/INDIVID HOTELS), deep in the baronial bowels of the building on N Bridge. Informal & intimate; no natural light so best for dinner à deux or a foody night out. Excl service, innovative menu. The new, smart place to eat (2003) & check for (classic) movie evenings combining dinner & the screening rm. Dinner only. LO 9.45pm. Cl Sun/Mon. EXP

115 ✔ **FORTH FLOOR, HARVEY NICHOLS:** 524 8350. St Andrews Sq. It is on the
D2 fourth floor (through deli & furnishings & HN souvenirs) & you can see the Forth from the balcony (superb outside dining on rare summer days, tho' somewhat in a row). The store & the restau often seem quiet, but all the better to come here where the food & service are reliably spot-on. You can partake of cheaper brasserie or more exp (but v similar) menus either side of the glass partition – dearer dining gets the view. All absolutely fabulous enough! Lunch 7 days, dinner Tues-Sat LO 10.30pm INX/MED

116 **THE MARQUE:** 466 6660. 19 Causewayside. Discreet southside bistro/restau
xD4 owned by chefs Glyn Stevens and John Rutter which spawned a satellite in Grindlay St nr the Lyceum called **MARQUE CENTRAL** (123/BISTROS) – John chefs there. The orig Marque seems more grown-up & restau-like tho' for atmos & lighter bites we still prefer Central. The Marque still hits the mark for a posher night out, with Scottish meets Med & Asian influences – the best meal on the S side! And the wine-list is superb. Lunch & LO 10pm (11pm w/ends). Cl Mon. MED

117 ✓✓ **FIRST COAST:** 313 4404. 99 Dalry Rd. Named after a place up N
A4 where brothers Hector & Alan McRae used to go their holidays, this
is a v grown-up & urban restau for 2 Highland lads. Food here is simply superb
value & full of integrity. May be beyond the pale for some but with this & the
Partenhope opp (170/TRUSTY TRATTS), it's destination Dalry for us in 2004.
Lunch Wed-Sat, dinner Mon-Sat LO 11pm.   INX

118 ✓✓ **BLUE:** 221 1222. Cambridge St. Upstairs in the Traverse Theatre
C3 building. From the makers of The Atrium (105/BEST RESTAUS), a
lighter, more informal menu which continues all day till late. Still the place you
think of when you want to graze. The menu, which changes every 6 wks, is mix
'n' match with 'light blue' snackier options. Sound levels high, but partly
because it's full of people with something to say. 12noon-3pm and 6pm-
10.30pm daily. Bar open to midnight (1am Sat). Cl Sun.   INX

119 ✓✓ **NORTH BRIDGE:** 622 2900. 20 North Bridge. The brasserie of the
D2 Scotsman Hotel (55/INDIVIDUAL HOTELS) with separate entrance
directly on to main rd. Formerly the foyer & public counter of the *Scotsman*
newspaper converted into excl bar/brasserie. Surrounding balcony reached
by rather intrusive metal staircase, but overall v sympathetic ambience for
exemplary brasserie-type menu with seasonal variations. Toilets are a find
when you find them. 7 days, all day LO 10 pm (10.30pm w/ends).   MED

120 ✓✓ **SKIPPERS:** 554 1018. 1a Dock Pl. In a corner of Leith off Commercial
xE1 Rd by the docks. Look for Waterfront (see below) and bear left into
adj cul-de-sac. The pioneer restau in Leith before it was a restau quarter. Quite
the best real bistro in town. V fishy, v quayside intimate and friendly. Look no
further out to sea. Lunch & dinner 7 days, LO 10pm.   MED

121 ✓✓ **THE OUTSIDER:** 226 3131 15 George IV Bridge. The downtown din-
D3 ing rm of the Apartment (below). Malcolm Innes, the notoriously
rude host, has once again created a sexy, contemp & inexpensive restau which
is always full. Minimalist design with surprising view of the castle. Innovative
contrasts in the menu. Big helpings! 7 days, noon-11pm.   INX

122 ✓✓ **THE APARTMENT:** 228 6456. 7 Barclay Pl, up from the King's Theatre.
C4 The first of Malcolm's hugely popular contemporary eating-out
experiences (see Outsider, above), now a Bruntsfield food fixture. Big helpings
of 'chunky, healthy' food, famously good salads. 7 days, dinner. Lunch Sat/Sun
only; LO 11pm. Best to book.   INX

123 ✓ **MARQUE CENTRAL:** 229 9859. 30b Grindlay St adj (& part of) the
C3 Lyceum. This Marque is offshoot of the original (116/RESTAUS). In the heart
of theatreland (betwixt Lyceum & Usher Hall nr Traverse & Filmhouse). It's
more informal here & the tone of everything esp the food & the pricing (v
good value lunch & pre-theatre menu) is just right. Some big tables, mellow
atmos. Lunch & LO 10pm (11pm w/ends). Cl Sun/Mon.   CHP/MED

124 ✓ **HOWIE'S:** 221 1777. 208 Bruntsfield Pl on the way to Morningside & at 10
xC4 Victoria St (225 1721), certainly one of the best in this st of many bistros.
Both are flagship outposts in Howie's urban village chain which serve the
locals, but are worth coming across the city for. Unpretentious, inexpensive,
contemp Scottish food. Can't say better than that. Bruntsfield is converted
church. All 7 days, lunch and dinner. LO 10/10.30pm. Lunch still, refreshingly
BYOB (with corkage) or unpretentious wine list. Also: INX

125 ✓ **HOWIE'S STOCKBRIDGE:** 225 5553. Glanville Pl by the br in Stockbridge.
B1 David Howie Scott's New Town restau with similar approach and menu to
D2 above: good-value contemporary food with some flair & no fuss. 7 days, lunch
& LO 10pm. **HOWIE'S WATERLOO:** 556 5766. 29 Waterloo Pl. 200 m east end
of Princes St (The Balmoral). Similar fare and service in beautiful lofty rm.
Never entirely sure of the changing art collection, but the food always reliable.
Easier to get tables than those above. 7 days LO 10.30pm. Both also BYOB. INX

126 ✓ **SWEET MELINDA'S:** 229 7953. 11 Roseneath St which is in deepest
xC4 Marchmont but round the corner from Argyle Pl where the good shops
are. Single not large rm on st with nice pics, catering v much for the neigh-

bourhood clientele but famous across the city. On Tues you can pay 'what you think the meal is worth'. Mainly fish (from estimable Eddie's across the rd), but meat & vegn. Home-made bread & gr touches. Everybody goes back. Good wines & fizz. Lunch & LO 10pm. Not Mon lunch; cl Sun.   MED

127   ✓ **BLONDE:** 668 2917. 75 St Leonard's St. Tucked away in the S side, a neigh-
E4   bourhood restau so relaxed, inexp & simply good you come back often. Handily nr Queens Hall & Pleasance (in Fringe time). Pale wood & spartan ie blonde set of rms & easy-eat food with quaffable wine (6 house wines under a tenner). Andy Macgregor presides; he chefs like Jamie O. Lunch (not Mon) & LO 10pm. 7 days.   INX

128   ✓ **HURRICANE BAR & GRILL:** 226 0770. 45 N Castle St. First venture of a
C2   projected chain, this is more a restau than a bar & way too styled to be a gastropub, but it does offer informal dining. Some have said more style than substance (v trendy at TGP), but the mod-Brit menu is well thought out & rather good. Lunch & LO 10.45pm (bar till 1am). Cl Sun.   INX

129   **ROCKSALT:** 226 1112. Hunter Sq nr Tron & Royal Mile. Contemp European &
D3   Asian food (it says here) in cool, mineral grey, blue salon with seats o/side. Some innovative combos in buzzy brazz atmos. Locals & tourists & open till the last one goes. 7 days 10am-late.   INX

130   **BROWNS:** 225 4442. 131 George St nr Charlotte Sq and **THE LIVING ROOM:**
C2   226 0880. 113 George St. The 2 best of many bar-eateries on re-invented George St & both northern outposts of small but carefully run UK chains that serve the late 90s/noughties version of the Menu-U-Like. Both noisy esp music in the L Room & both excl service. 7 days noon-10.45pm (Browns), till 11pm (LR & midnight w/ends).   INX

131   **BOUZY ROUGE:** 225 9594. 1 Alva St, nr corner with Queensferry St. Edin
B3   branch of the foody empire of the Brown family (def more style & integrity than most – see Roman Camp, Callendar, Bouzy Rouge & Rococo, Glasgow 907/CENTRAL HOTELS, 565/BISTROS, 549/GLAS RESTAUS). This Mediterraneo space is well thought out; accessible dining with some flair for the money – perfectly judged for the Jamie/Nigella generation. This basement can seem cramped (esp the seats), but reliable, contemporary and inx. 7 days, lunch and dinner, LO 9.30pm (Fri/Sat 10.30pm).   INX

132   **MALMAISON BRASSERIE:** 555 6969. Tower Pl at Leith dock gates. Restau and
xE1   café-bar of Malmaison (57/INDIVIDUAL HOTELS). Authentic brasserie atmos and menu, as in all Malmaisons, the expanding chain, with linen cloths, big windows & Paris meets NYC menu. Prix fixé (3 courses for £12.95 at TGP) is gr value. 7 days. Lunch and dinner. LO 10.45pm (Sun 10.15).   MED.INX

133   **LE SEPT:** 225 5428. 7 Old Fishmarket Close. The cobbled close winds steeply
D3   off the High St below St Giles. Wee o/side terr in summer and narrow, woody rm inside for nonsmokers (but smokey rm too). Crêpes, omelettes, plats du jour and Franco-bistro food. Cheerful, busy rendezvous that's been here forever – it worked then, it works now! 7 days lunch & LO 10.30pm (Sat 11, Sun 10pm).   INX

134   **A ROOM IN THE TOWN:** 225 8204. 18 Howe St, corner of Jamaica St. The room
C2   is in the New Town for these lads (Peter Knight & John Tindal) orig from the Highlands & reflects something of that legendary hospitality. So good value, friendly service; you can BYOB (a mere £1 corkage). Predom Scottish menu with twists. Their wicked banoffee pie however is as it comes. Same folk have **A ROOM IN THE WEST END** (226 1036) in William St with an upstairs bar **TEUCHTERS** (they love to be outsiders) & the restau downstairs. Similar menu. 7 days lunch & LO 10pm.   INX

It's a ghastly word, but since coined with reference to places like The Eagle or The Well in London's emerging East End, the Gastropub at least conveys the nature of those food destinations which are more pub than restaurant or 'café-bar'. The implication is that you can drink without eating. Many of these Edin examples are indeed exemplary & were here eons before the word was invented.

135
xE1
✓✓ **THE SHORE:** 553 5080. 3 The Shore, Leith. Long est as a 'gastropub'; prob one of the best in the UK – well, a personal favourite. Bar (often with live light folk or jazz) where you can eat from the same menu as the dining-rm/restau. Real fire and large windows looking out to the quayside – strewn with bods on warm summer nights. Food, listed on a blackboard, changes daily but is consistently good. Lots of fish, some meat, some vegn. No smk in restau/OK in bar. 7 days lunch & LO 10pm, bar till 12.   MED

136
xE1
✓✓ **KING'S WARK:** 554 9260. 36 The Shore, on the corner of Bernard St. Woody, candlelit, comfortable – a classic gastropub, ie emphasis on food. Bar & bistro dining rm. Pub-food classics & more adventurous even menu. Tho trad & dark rather than pale, light & modern, this is one of the best bets in Leith for the food we just love to eat. Scottish slant on the menu, with excellent fish incl beer batter and chips. Lunch and LO 10pm. Bar open to 11pm, 12midnight Fri-Sat.   INX

137
xC4
✓✓ **THE CANNY MAN:** 447 1484. 237 Morningside Rd (aka The Volunteer Arms) on the A702 via Tollcross, 7km from centre. Idiosyncratic renowned eaterie with a certain hauteur and a true, original 'gastropub'. Carries a complement of malts as long as your arm and a serious wine list. Excellent smorrebrod lunches (12noon-3pm) & evens 6.30-9.30pm. Salads & desserts with Luca's ice-cream (& alcohol). No loonies or undesirables are welcome (you may be tested) but this is a civilised pub; you could be in the Cotswolds. Till 12midnight Mon-Sat, 11pm Sun. (357/REAL-ALE PUBS)   INX

138
xD4
✓ **THE NEW BELL:** 668 2868. 233 Causewayside. Way down Causewayside in the s side, the New Bell is upstairs from the Old Bell; you may walk thro' the pub to find it. And it is a find! Woody, warm pubby atmos, nice rugs etc. Richard & Michelle Heller have got the rm and the Mod-British menu just right. Food & v decent vino well-priced for this sound quality & smart delivery. Dinner only. Tues-Sun LO 10.30pm.   INX

139
xE1
✓ **THE WATERFRONT:** 554 7427. 1c Dock Pl. Longest wine bar in this foody corner of the waterfront. The conservatory o/looks the backwater dock. It's *the* place to head in summer, but the warren of rms is cosy in winter. Food has wavered a bit over the yrs but v good again 2003 esp for fish & puds & of course, wine. Site, setting and gr friendly service are mostly what you come for. 7 days, Lunch & LO 9.30/10pm. Bar midnight.   MED

140
B3
✓ **HALO:** 539 8500. 3 Melville Pl (Queensferry St) ie main st W End. Out of place perhaps on this page (see also 379/STYLE BARS) like others below because this ain't publand & far from trad. Cool design, picture window; contemp spin on comfort food & Italian variants – chef Guy Hendry came from Cosmo (165/ITALIAN RESTAUS). Food 7 days 11am-4pm. Bar 1am.   INX

141
B3
indigo (yard): 220 5603. 7 Charlotte Lane. Food in bar area and in restau upstairs in converted and glazed-over yard behind the W End. Enormously popular, always buzzing & noisy later (you may not hear your wine pop nor your coin drop in the condom machine). Earlier therefore better for food. Contemp fusion food is better than café-bar standard. 7 days from 9am. Food all day LO 10pm. Bar till 1am. (383/STYLE BARS)   INX

142
C4
MONTPELLIERS: 229 3115. 159 Bruntsfield Pl. They call it 'Montpelliers of Bruntsfield' & it is almost an institution now S of the Meadows. Same ownership as above and similar buzz and noise levels, but more accent on food. From b/fast menu to late supper, they've thought of everything. All the contemp faves. Gets v busy. 7 days. LO 10pm. Bar till 1am.   INX

143
C2
RICK'S: 622 7800. 55a Frederick St. Basement bar/restau of Rick's Hotel (64/HOTELS) by same people as indigo (yard) & Montpelliers (above). They'll hate being called a gastropub but food more ambitious here and usually

works. Later on prob too noisy to enjoy food, so choose time & table carefully. Go-for-it crowd not as hip as they think (Nouveau Ricks? – a joke too cute not to mention again). Good cocktails. 7 days all day. LO 10pm (11pm w/ends). Bar 1am.   MED

143a   **THE DORIC:** 225 1084. 15 Market St. Opp the Fruitmarket Gallery and the back
D3   entrance to Waverley Stn. Upstairs boho bistro. Only locals know that this is quintessential Edinburgh & tho the food is neither remarkable nor cheap, we must still climb those creaking stairs from time to time for a civilised supper & a v excl bottle of vino. 7 days (not Suns in winter), lunch & LO 10.30pm. Bar midnight – there's also a downstairs Doric on street level, but we prefer up.

   MED

OUTSIDE TOWN

144 ✓ **THE WATERSIDE, HADDINGTON:** 01620 825674. 28km from town off A1.
MAP 3 ✓ Longest, landmark pub food watering hole. On riverside, esp ambient in
D4 summer. Can feel just like England. Upstairs restau and labyrinthine and v pub-like downstairs. Big helpings. Excellent food: pub menu with staples or upstairs à la carte even better. Lunch and supper. LO 9.30pm. Bar whenever!   INX

145 ✓ **DROVER'S INN, EAST LINTON:** 01620 860298. 5 Bridge St. Off the A1,
MAP 3 ✓ 35km E of city. Fair way to go for eats, but don't think about the A1, think
D4 about this welcoming pub with notable food (they run a courtesy bus if it goes on too long). A classic village pub with warmth and delicious meals in bistro beside bar or restau up top Thur-Sun. Beer gdn out back is o/looked and trains whoosh by, but on a sunny day, partake their excellent lunch here. Lunch and dinner (6-9.00pm); later w/ends.   INX

146 ✓ **HORSESHOE INN, EDDLESTON nr PEEBLES:** 01721 730225. 35km SW
MAP 3 ✓ on A703. Roadside hostelry (has 8 rms), but more a restau than a pub. 7
C5 days, 12noon-3pm and evenings to 9/9.30pm. All day Sun, incl their estimable roasts. See also 1420/PUB FOOD.   INX

THE BEST FRENCH RESTAURANTS

147 ✓ **LA GARRIGUE:** 557 3032. 31 Jeffrey St. Recent addition to top league of
D3 ✓ authentic French restaus in city, this more Languedoc than Left Bank (esp wine list). Chef/prop Jean Michel Ganffre brings the S of France to your plate. Simple food with flair and unusual touches. Best to book. Mon-Sat, lunch and LO 10pm   MED

148 ✓ **THE VINTNER'S ROOM:** 554 6767. 87 Giles St, Leith. Cobbled courtyard
xE1 ✓ to wine bar, with woody ambience and open fire. Vaults, formerly used to store claret (Leith was an important wine pt), also incl a restaurant lit by candlelight. New French props Laure & Patrice. Bar and restau have same classic evening menu (using fresh Scottish produce), but cheaper options at lunch in the bar and less formal. Excl cheeseboard and wine list. Mon-Sat lunch and 7-10pm.   MED

149 ✓ **DUCK'S AT LE MARCHE NOIR:** 558 1608. 2-4 Eyre Pl. Malcolm Duck pre-
C1 ✓ sides with meticulous attention to detail in his bistro/restau at the lower end of the New Town. In a residential neighbourhood, an easy-going but still business-like atmos. More Med than Midi, lighter than Lyonnaise, maybe less 'French' than formerly. Good-value wine list. Dinner 7 days, lunch Tues-Fri. LO 10-10.30pm (earlier Sun).   EXP

150 ✓ **CAFÉ SAINT-HONORÉ:** 226 2211. 34 Thistle St Lane, betw Frederick St
C2 ✓ and Hanover St. Suits a-plenty, New Town regulars and occasional lunching ladies all to be found in this busy, shiny bistro-cum-restau which oozes & even smells like Paris. Go on a rainy day when it feels esp warm & sweet & comforting. Lunch Mon-Fri, LO 10pm. Cl Sun. Veggies phone ahead.   EXP

151 ✓ **JACQUES:** 229 6080. 8 Gillespie Pl, Bruntsfield. Endearing French staff and
xC4 ✓ atmos. Hard-working wee rustic eaterie close to the King's Theatre. Innovative variations on the classics. Deals thro' even mean eating here is gr value. Excl affordable French wine list. Loyal following, book ahead. Refurb after fire at TGP. Lunch not Sun LO 11pm.   INX

152 ✓ **CAFÉ MARLAYNE:** 226 2230. 76 Thistle St. The third in the triumvirate of
C2 ✓ excl & authentic French eateries within 100m of another (Café St-Honoré,
La P'tite Folie), this is a wee gem (we do mean wee). Personal, intimate & v v
French. Food generally fab (tho not gr for veggies). Isla Fraser's in the kitchen.
This really is like a place you find in rural France on your hols. Lunch & LO
10pm. Cl Sun/Mon. INX

153 ✓ **PETIT PARIS:** 226 2442. 40 Grassmarket. On busy N side of st below cas-
C3 ✓ tle, teeming on w/end nights – get an outside table & watch: this could
be Montmartre apart from the inebriation. Good atmos & value with très typical menu. BYOB (not w/ends). 7 days lunch & LO late. Cl Mon in wint. INX

154 **DANIEL'S:** 553 5933. 88 Commercial Quay, off Dock Pl. Versatile with small
xE1 deli, takeaway and bistro. Main eaterie is housed in conservatory at back of
old bonded warehouse in Leith's 'restaurant row'. Clean lines, modern look
and v popular. Offers contemporary French menu with Alsace and external
influences that pack us in esp for 'tarte flambé' & casseroles (169/PIZZAS). Also
tables by the water 7 days, 10am-10pm. INX

155 **FRENCH CORNER BISTRO:** 226 1890. 17 Queensferry St upstairs & on corner
B3 of Alva St. 3 high-ceilinged Georgian rms usually full of people & buzz. Food
accessible French bistro fare, with good steaks, crêpes & cheese for example &
as French restaus go, not bad for veggies. You come back here, it's like a club.
Lunch & LO 10.30/11pm. Cl Sun. INX

156 **MAISON BLEUE:** 226 1900. 36 Victoria St. Contemp & unique spin on inx French
D3 food in intimate restau in Old Town. Grazing menu of 'bites' or 'bouchées' to mix
'n' match. Gr choice, très reasonable prices, but food often excl. Gr value set
lunch (2 bites & pud <£5). Lunch & LO 10.15pm. BYOB (not w/ends). INX

157 **LA CAMARGUE:** 554 9999. Corner at 23 Commercial St. Main rd to/from Leith nr
xE1 'Restaurant Row' & Dock Pl so one of many restaus to choose from. This v
French, incl atmos, menu & chef. Excl seafood & wine list. 7 days, dinner only LO
10pm (bar till 1am). INX

158 **LA P'TITE FOLIE** 225 7983. 61 Frederick St & Randolph Pl (225 7983). The word
C2 is unpretentious – mismatched furniture, inx French *plat du jour*. Relaxed eat-
ing-out in single New Town rm or Tudoresque 'maison' in W End cul de sac.
Cheap lunch. 7 days. LO 10/11pm. Cl Sun lunch. INX

159 **CAFÉ D'ODILE:** 225 5366. 13 Randolph Cres. A secret gdn and small cafeteria
B2 downstairs at the French Institute. Lunch only but can be booked for parties
at night (BYOB). Gr views over the New Town, simple French home-cooking,
patronised by ladies who lunch and students. Tue-Sat. CHP

✓ ✓ **PLAISIR DU CHOCOLAT:** 556 9524. Canongate. Principally a tearm,
but also serves excl pâtés, omelettes, onion soup. And chocolate!
Too French not to incl here. Full Report: 272/TEAROOMS.

✓ ✓ **RESTAURANT MARTIN WISHART:** 553 3557. The Shore, Leith. Best
in show! Report: 104/BEST RESTAUS.

162 ✓ **SANTINI:** 221 7788. Conference Sq by Conference Centre & back of the
C3 ✓ Sheraton (of which it's a part, below excl health club). Business-like Italian
restau & bistro created by Mr Santini himself who has brought the same clean
lines & stylish eating-out experience to London & Milan. Waiters & ingredients v
Italia. Restau is refined, exp & J & T. **SANTINI BIS** on sq itself is still smart but casual. Some recent murmurs about service. Both lunch & dinner LO 10.30pm. Cl
Sun.   MED/INX

163 ✓ **SCALINI:** 220 2999. 10 Melville Pl. Antithesis of Santini (above).
B3 ✓ Downstairs (*the scalini*) bistro restau in a low-ceilinged sliver of a basement has a straightforward and personal approach to Italian cooking – Silvio
will tell you what's good tonight and he'll be right. Pared-down menu; huge
collection of vintage Barolos, prob one for your birthday. Keep 'smoking'
upstairs. Cl Suns.   MED

164 ✓ **VALVONA & CROLLA:** 556 6066. 19 Elm Row. Cafe at the back of the leg-
E1 ✓ endary deli, and with all the flair and attention to detail that you would
expect. First-class ingredients, produce shipped in from Italy (fresh veg from
Milan markets) and gr Italian domestic cooking. One of the best & healthiest
b/fasts in town & fabuloso lunch (any wine in the shop for £4 corkage is a
deal) tho not so inx. This place is a treat without the trappings. May be queues.
No smk. Mon-Sat 8am-6pm.   INX

165 ✓ **COSMO:** 226 6743. 58 N Castle St (a no through rd). V much in the old, dis-
C2 ✓ creet style for those with some time and cash on their hands. Has been
the up-market Italian restau for yrs. The lighting and the music are soft, the
service impeccable and the (Italian) wine list exemplary. Menu pragmatically
brief; allow time to enjoy it in this not unpleasant time-warp. Cl Sun and Sat
lunch. LO 10.45pm.   EXP

166 ✓ **LA BRUSCHETTA:** 467 7464. 13 Clifton Terr. Extension of Shandwick Pl
B3 ✓ opp Haymarket Stn. Giovanni Cariello's Italian kitchen & tiny dining rm in
the W End. A modest & modern version of Cosmo (above) with a big following – so must book. The space does not cramp their style. Lunch & LO
10.30pm. Cl Sun/Mon.   INX

167 ✓ **TINELLI:** 652 1932. 139 Easter Rd. Edin regulars still swear by this small
E1 ✓ unassuming ristorante on unfashionable st that was serving carpaccio &
proper Italian food long before the pasta explosion. Still simple & uncompro-
mising. This is the real tiramisù. Lunch and LO 11pm. Cl Sun/Mon.   MED

168 **PREGO:** 557 5754. 38 St Mary's St. Small, airy, betw Royal Mile & Pleasance.
D3 Easy to overlook, but genuine non-regional Italian food complete with seen-
it-all grumpy manager/waiter. They call it 'cucina rustica' & it is v simply good.
Lunch & LO 10pm. Cl Sun.   INX

169 **LIBRIZZI'S:** 226 1155. Corner N Castle St and Queen St. Central under-
C2 estimated ristorante one block from George St. Sicilian chef and influence on
usual and unusual Italian fare. Esp good fish of the day. Good service and well
selected wines. Lunch & LO 10.30pm. Cl Sun.   MED

THE TRUSTY TRATTS

170 ✓ ✓ **LA PARTENHOPE:** 347 8880. 96 Dalry Rd. Food goddess Joanna B
A4 ✓ ✓ alerted us to this unlikely corner of Dalry (about 200m from
Haymarket) where the Sartore family have created a corner of Naples. Big
Rosario presides in the kitchen, with daily specials from market produce;
mainly fish. Expansion next door at TGP much needed – this place fills up fast.
So book.   INX

171 ✓ **BAR ROMA:** 226 2977. 39 Queensferry St. One of Edin's long-standing
B3 ✓ fave Italians, revamped so it almost looks like a Pizza Express from the
outside. Inside always bustling (this includes the menu) with Italian rudeboy
waiters as the floor show. 7 days, all day. LO 11.30pm (later w/ends).   INX

172 **VITTORIA:** 556 6171. Corner of Brunswick St & Leith Walk. Recently
E1 extended, excl tratt & caff that's a' things to a'body. Report 287/CAFÉS.

173 **GIULIANO'S:** 556 6590. 18 Union Pl, top of Leith Walk nr the main r/bout,
D2 opp Playhouse Theatre. No change at Giuli's but something sets it apart
as it's usually heaving with happy punters & their many birthdays! It's just
pasta and pizza but in a no-nonsense menu that appeals. The food is great,
the din is loud. Lunch and LO 2am daily – Giuli's is always late 'n' live. **–GIU-
LIANO'S on the SHORE:** 554 5272 on the corner of the bridge in Leith Central
has recently had a makeover but it's the same, reliable tratt menu. Some jazz
& esp good for kids (265/KID-FRIENDLY). Also 7 days, LO 10.30/11pm. INX

174 **LAZIO:** 229 7788. 95 Lothian Rd. One of the prerequisites of a 'Trusty Tratt' is
C3 that they're there where you want them to be. This W End stalwart is nr Usher
Hall, Filmhouse & many other destinations Best on these blocks & open v late.
Report 305/LATE-NIGHT RESTAUS. INX

175 **LA LANTERNA:** 226 3090. 83 Hanover St. One of several tratts sub street level
C2 in this block all family-owned. But this gets our vote. For 20 yrs the Zaino family have produced this straight-down-the-line Italian menu from their open
kitchen at the back of their no-frills restau with American soundtrack. 80% of
their customers are regulars and wouldn't go anywhere else. Well chosen wine-
list. Lunch & LO10pm. Cl Sun. INX

UMBERTO'S: 554 1314. Off Bonnington Rd. (262/KID-FRIENDLY PLACES).

GORDON'S TRATTORIA: 225 7992. 231 High St. (303/LATE-NIGHT RESTAUS).

THE BEST PIZZA

176 **L'ALBA D'ORO:** 557 2580. 5-11 Henderson Row. The t/away pizza section
C1 of the estimable fish 'n' chip shop, but this is def a slice above the rest. 3
sizes (incl indiv 7") & infinite toppings to go. Not thin but crispy/crunchy. Also
pasta, wine, fresh OJ. No ordinary chip shop! 7 days lunch & LO 12. CHP

177 **PIZZA EXPRESS:** 332 7229. 1 Deanhaugh St, Stockbridge. Ubiquitous nation-
B1 al chain, same formula everywhere, but what-the-hell, it's great design & the
UK standard pizza. Stockbridge branch best; award for architecture, in
refurbed bank with Water of Leith gurgling below. Simple, no-nonsense,
affordable pizza with good service. Edin W End branch, 225 8863, 32
Queensferry St. Also North Br, adj Calton Highland Hotel, 554 4332. Newest
branch on Shore in Leith. No-booking policy & late opening hrs (11.30, midnight on N Bridge) are worth remembering. INX

178 **MAMMA'S:** 225 6464. 30 Grassmarket. Brash, American style. Some alterna-
C3 tives to pizza, eg nachos, but you come to mix 'n' match – haggis, calamari and
BBQ sauce and 40 other toppings piled deep and so cheap for a filling meal.
7 days till 11pm/midnight. INX

179 **DANIEL'S BISTRO:** 553 5933. 88 Commercial St on 'restaurant row' in Leith. Gr
xE1 for the Tarte Flambé – v like a thin thin pizza made from milk bread dough
topped with onions, crème fraîche & lardons – an Alsace & house speciality.
There are other thin pizzas too (154/FRENCH RESTAUS). 7 days 10am-10pm. INX

180 **JOLLY'S:** 556 1588. 9 Elm Row (part of Leith Walk nr Valvona & Crolla
E1 1546/DELIS). Long-est (tho changed owners) tratt/ristorante well known
locally for their thinner-than-usual wood-fired pizza. Over 30 varieties. Good
family spot. Also t/away. 7 days. Lunch & LO 10.30pm. Cl Sun lunch. INX

181 ✓ **IGG'S:** 557 8184. 15 Jeffrey St, nr Royal Mile. Since 1989 this has been a
D3 corner of Spain in Scotland & one of the consistently best restaus in the
city. Warm south v much reflected in the excl wine-list, but food from well-
sourced Scottish ingredients more cosmo than merely Med. Some tapas but
see below. Good biz lunch spot. Lunch & LO 10.30. Cl Sun. MED

182 ✓ **OCHRE VITA:** 556 3636. 5 Learmonth Gardens. The conservatory restau-
B2 rant of Channings Hotel (51/BEST HOTELS) & with the same superb chef,
Hubert Lamort. Excl light Med food & wine for a fraction of downtown prices.
An odd, almost suburban outpost but well worth the detour – & free on-street
parking! 7 days. Lunch & LO 10pm. INX

183 ✓ **CAFÉ MEDITERRANEO:** 557 6900. 73 Broughton St. Discreet frontage to
D2 small, bright rms on busy little Broughton St. Brazilian owner Davi Bersi
keeps it fairly Mediterraneo (tho no pasta) with a mean espresso. This
café/bistro/restau serves many purposes from gorging to grazing & it's nice for
b/fast incl Suns (308/SUN B/FAST). 7 days 8am till 6pm, Fri-Sat LO 9pm. INX

184 ✓ **NARGILE:** 225 5755. 73 Hanover St. Not so much Mediterranean, most
C2 definitely Turkish. This is where to go to mess with the meze. All east of
the Med fares from houmous to shashlik with lots for veggies & good fish
choice. Some tables cramped but this is a night out with the mates or mate
kind of place. Buzbag as expected & fair selection of other Turkish & non
Turkish wines. Lunch & LO 10.30pm (11pm Fri/Sat). Cl Sun. INX

185 ✓ **TAPAS TREE:** 556 7118. 1 Forth St. Party night-out kind of restau with
D2 upbeat Spanish staff, gypsy/Cajun soundtrack & Flamenco live on Thurs.
Starter/main/pud is the heavier option but 3 well-chosen tapas (veg, fish and
something else) with some robust bread and a bottle of house red makes for
a v decent meal. Snappy service. Tapas in the £2 to £5 range, so not a pocket
buster. 11am-11pm. 7 days. INX

186 ✓ **DOMINICO:** 467 7266. 30 Sandport St. Leith's best kept secret, this tiny
xE1 restau with a loyal following has better food & is better value than most
in this quarter. Gr pastas & esp fresh fish. Lunch Mon-Fri, dinner Mon-Sat LO
10pm. INX

187 **BARIOJA:** 557 3622. 19 Jeffrey St. And after Igg's the restau (see above), the
D3 tapas bar next door – they are joined together in the basement. Small tables
and not much room to move upstairs; more space, less ambience down. Fairly
authentic tapas menu but no sideboard or counter full as in San Sebastian;
Spanish waiters and vino. 11am-11pm. 7 days. INX

188 **PHENECIA:** 662 4493. 55-57 W Nicolson St, on corner nr Edin Univ. N African
D4 Mohammed Sfina's unfussy and demonstrably yellow N African/Spanish
eaterie with couscous, lots of grilled meats and wide vegn choice. A culinary
odyssey thro' the warm south & one of the most eclectic menus in town. Poss
to eat v cheaply at lunch-time. Goodly portions. Lunch Mon-Sat & LO
10.30pm. They have the Château Musar. INX

189 **TAPAS OLÉ:** 556 2754. 8-10 Eyre Pl and 225 7069, 4 Forrest Rd, nr the Univ.
C1 Tapas restau/bar. Meat/vegn/seafood menus and the usual vinos. Good value
& authentic with Spanish proprietor and waiters. If in doubt, let them advise &
choose. Live music sometimes, live clientele always. An inx night out! We prefer Eyre Pl, the room is better. 7 days, lunch and LO 10pm. INX

190 **SANTORINI:** 557 2012. 32 Broughton St. Cheap, charming, authentic – what
D2 more could you ask from the only proper Greek restau in town. Start with
'mezedes' – small portions to share, then on to mousakka, stews, souvlakis.
Some sticky puds. Tues-Sun, 12-10.30pm. CHP

191 **RINCON DE ESPAÑA:** 313 3334. 63 Dalry Rd. New at TGP, but this we hear is
xE1 the city's most authentic taste of Spain. Phone for times. INX

THE BEST SEAFOOD RESTAURANTS

192
xE1
✓✓ **SKIPPERS:** 554 1018. 1a Dock Pl, Leith. Bistro with truly maritime atmos; mainly seafood. Best to book. Many would argue Skippers *is* still the best place to eat seafood in this town. Full report: 120/BEST BISTROS.

193
C2
✓✓ **FISHERS in the CITY:** 225 5109. 58 Thistle St. Separate entry to sister restau (below). Bigger & buzzier & one of the best all-rounders in the aforesaid city. (111/BEST RESTAUS).   MED

194
xE1
✓✓ **FISHERS:** 554 5666. Corner of The Shore and Tower St, Leith. At the foot of an 18th-century tower opp Malmaison Hotel and rt on the quay (though no boats come by). Seafood cooking with flair and commitment in boat-like surroundings where trad Scots dishes get an imaginative twist. Hugely popular, some stools around bar and tables o/side in summer (can be a windy corner). Often all are packed. Cheeseboard has some gr Brits if you have rm for a third course. 7 days. 12noon-10.30pm.   MED

195
D3
✓ **CREELERS:** 220 4447. 3 Hunter Sq. Tim & Fran's restau & smoke house near Brodick is also called Creelers. This corner of Arran in the city behind the Tron Church is just a short cast from the Royal Mile (tables alfresco in summer). Recent refresh for one of the best seafood spots in town (but with 2 meat & 1 vegn dish). Nice paintings, good atmos, not exp. Bistro at front, restau at back. Lunch and LO 10.30/11pm (not Tues/Wed lunch in winter).   MED

196
C2
✓ **THE MUSSEL INN:** 225 5979. 61 Rose St. Popular, populist. In the heart of the city centre where parking ain't easy, a gr little seafood bistro specializing in mussels and scallops (kings and queens) which the proprietors rear/find themselves. Also 'catch of the day' and a non-fish pasta option. Good chips. They're also in Glas (645/SEAFOOD RESTAUS). Lunch and dinner. LO 10pm.
INX

197
D2
✓ **CAFÉ ROYAL OYSTER BAR:** 556 4124. W Register St. One of the city's best rms & here forever but still a place for a flourish of indulgence or just to impress. Beluga caviar followed by Homard Newburg with a bottle of Bolly will cost you an arm and a leg. But you can also snack. Higher celeb quotient here for the classy surroundings with spillover atmos from adj bar. Tiles, linen, dark wood, v Victorian. Visitors usually find it all v groovy; locals lament that it ain't what it was. Lunch & LO 10pm. 7 days.   EXP

THE BEST FISH 'N' CHIPS

198
C1
✓ **L'ALBA D'ORO:** Henderson Row, nr corner with Dundas St. Large selection of deep-fried goodies, incl many vegn savouries. It's a lot more than your usual fry-up – as several plaques on the wall attest (incl *Scotland the Best!*) and the pasta/pizza counter next door is a real winner (176/PIZZAS). Open till 12midnight. Good wines to go with.   CHP

199
D2
✓ **THE RAPIDO:** 77 Broughton St. Fine chips. Popular with late-nighters stumbling back down the hill to the New Town, and the flotsam of the 'Pink Triangle'. Open till 1.30am (3.30am Fri-Sat).   CHP

200
E1
✓ **THE DEEP SEA:** Leith Walk, opp Playhouse. Open late and often has queues but these are quickly dispatched. The haddock has to be 'of a certain size'. Trad menu. Still one of the best fish suppers you'll ever feed a hangover with. Open till 2am (-ish) (3am Fri-Sat).   CHP

201
D2
YE OLD PEACOCK INN: 552 8707. Report: 267/KID-FRIENDLY & **KINGS WARK:** 554 9260. Report: 136/GASTROPUBS. Both excl for fish 'n' chips.   INX

202 ✓ ✓ **DAVID BANN'S:** 556 5888. St Mary's St. Foot of St Mary's St off Royal
D3 Mile – a bit off the beaten track, but always a busy restau & not only
with non-meaters. In fact this is one of the best restaus in town: mood lighting, non-moody staff & no dodgy stodge. A creative take on round-the-world
dishes. 7 days, lunch & LO 10pm (later w/ends) INX

203 ✓ **SUSIE'S DINER:** 667 8729. 51-53 W Nicolson St. Cosy, neighbourhood
D4 (the univ) self-service diner. Nice people behind and in front of the
counter. Mexican and Middle-Eastern dishes. Lotsa choice menu incl excl coffee. Licensed, also BYOB. Mon 9am-8pm, Tue-Sat 9am-9pm. Cl Sun. CHP

204 ✓ **HENDERSON'S:** 225 2131. 94 Hanover St. Edin's original and trail-blazing
C2 basement vegn self-serve café-cum-wine bar. Canteen seating to the left,
candles and live piano or guitar downstairs to the rt. Happy wee wine list and
organic real ales. Good cheese & some of those mains & puds will go on forever. 8am-10.30pm. Cl Sun. Also has the Farm Shop upstairs with a deli and
takeaway and the more bar-like **HENDERSON'S BISTRO** round the corner in
Thistle St. NOTE: Henderson's (organic) oatcakes are *the* best. CHP

205 ✓ **BLACK BO'S:** 557 6136. 57 Blackfriars St. Now long-est proper vegn
D3 restau, ie waiter service, foody approach to the food with some unpredictable often inspired vegn ideas and combos. Intimate & woody, laid-back
set-up. Adj bar has been cool for yrs. Restau now with meat & fish options
(sign of the times?) so you can go with all your bloody mates. Lunch Fri/Sat
only. Dinner 7 days. LO 10.30pm. INX

206 ✓ **KALPNA:** 667 9890. 2-3 St Patrick Sq. They say 'you do not have to eat
D4 meat to be strong & wise' & are they of course right. Maxim taken seriously in this long-est Indian restau on the S side. Thali gives a good overview
while bargain Wed buffet features regional cuisine. Lunch Mon-Sat, dinner
Mon-Sat, LO 10.30pm. (234/INDIAN RESTAUS). No smk. INX

207 ✓ **ANN PURNA:** 662 1807. 45 St Patrick Sq. Excellent vegn restau nr Edin
D4 Univ with genuine Gujarati/S Indian cuisine. Good atmos – old customers
are greeted like friends by Mr & Mrs Pandya. Indian beer, some suitable wines.
Lunch Mon-Fri, dinner 7 days, LO 10.30pm. (237/INDIAN RESTAUS) INX

208 **ENGINE SHED CAFÉ:** 662 0040. 19 St Leonard's Lane. Hidden away off St
E4 Leonard's St, this is a lunch-oriented vegn café where much of the work is
done by adults with learning difficulties on training placements, so worth
supporting. Simple, decent food and gr bread – baked on premises, for sale
separately. Nice stopping-off point after a tramp over Arthur's Seat. Lunch
only. Cl Sat/Sun. CHP

209 **CORNERSTONE CAFÉ:** 229 0212. Underneath St John's Church at the corner
C3 of Princes St and Lothian Rd. V central and PC self-service coffee shop in
church vaults. Home-baking and hot dishes at lunchtime. Some seats outside
in summer (in graveyard!) and market stalls during the Festival. One World
Shop adj is full of Third World-type crafts and v good for presents.
A respite from the fast-food frenzy of Princes St. Open 9.30am-4pm (later in
Festival). Cl Sun. CHP

210 **LEGUME:** 667 1597. 11 S College St. Off 'the Bridges' (& rel to Off the Wall –
D3 214/SCOTTISH RESTAUS) behind Univ old Quad building, discreet restau serving
seriously good vegn menu with French cuisine skill. Brief but exemplary
menu & service. Lunch & LO 9pm (9.30pm w/ends). Cl Sun. MED

211 **SURUCHI:** 556 6583. 14a Nicolson St. Excl Indian, esp good for vegn dishes.
D3 Report 231/INDIAN RESTAUS. INX

✓ ✓ **RESTAURANT MARTIN WISHART:** 553 3557. Not remotely a vegn
restau, but does have a special vegn menu. Food, ingredients & presentation are taken seriously here, so this is where to go for *the best* vegn food
in town. Report: 104/BEST RESTAUS. EXP

213 ✓ **FENWICK'S:** 667 4265. 15 Salisbury Pl. Tucked away in the depths of
xE4 Newington tho with plenty students and tourists from the drab hotel belt
to attract, this 90s kind of restau is what you call a 'hidden gem'. Excl value. The
cooking, with assorted international manoeuvres, offers local produce turned
out with style and honesty. Excl affordable wine list (from estimable
Villeneuve), but can BYOB. Lunch and LO 10.30pm. Cl Sun eve & Mon/Tues.   INX

214 ✓ **OFF THE WALL:** 558 1497. 105 High St. Not so much off the wall, but in
D3 the wall – a doorway off the tartan & tat Royal Mile & stairs up to this calm
first-floor rm. A discreet bistro often missed by the ravening foodies (but not
food critic Gillian G who raved… and if it's good enough for her…). Short, simple menu with Scottish stalwarts (salmon, venison, beef – and always haggis)
all nicely concocted with contemporary ingredients and twist. Chef David
Anderson was City Chef of the Year 2003. Mon-Sat, lunch and LO 10pm. Cl Sun.
MED

215 ✓ **DUBH PRAIS:** 557 5732. 123b High St. Slap bang (but downstairs) on the
D3 Royal Mile opp the Holiday Inn. Only 9 tables and a miniature galley
kitchen from which proprietor/chef James McWilliams and his team produce
a remarkably reliable à la carte menu & specials from sound and sometimes
surprising Scottish ingredients. Haggis is panfried, smoked haddock comes
with Ayrshire bacon. Athol Brose is as good as it gets. V regular clientele &
even some lucked-out tourists in this outpost of culinary integrity on the
Royal Mile. Cl Sun/Mon. Lunch & LO 10.30pm. Pron 'Du Prash'.   MED

216 **CHAMBERTIN:** 225 1251. 21 George St. Despite French title, a v Taste of
C2 Scotland menu in discreet, v professionally run main restau of George Hotel
(54/BEST HOTELS) an opulent salon where suits dine at lunch time and other
members of the Edin establishment compare chips (on the shoulder). More
relaxed in the eves. Knowledgeable sommelier will take you thro' excl wine
list. Lunch Mon-Fri, LO 10pm Mon-Sat. Cl Sun.   EXP

217 **HALDANE'S:** 556 8407. 39 Albany St. In basement of The Albany. Fine dining
D2 nr Brougton St and prob the best proper meal in the area. Scottish by nature
rather than hype. Everything done in a country house style, tho menu unpretentious. Lunch Mon-Fri, dinner 7 days LO 9.30pm.   MED

218 **STAC POLLY:** 229 5405. 8a Grindlay St. Opp Lyceum Theatre and not far from
C3, D2 Usher Hall, Traverse and cinemas. Dark wood and tartan interior is quietly
smart; service, too. Scottish beef, salmon, game well sourced. Cheeses come
from Iain Mellis. There's another **STAC POLLY** below-stairs at 29-33 Dublin St
in the New Town (556 2231). Similar menu but it feels clubbier. V fine. Both:
lunch Mon-Fri. Dinner 7 days LO 10pm.   MED

219 **THE GRAIN STORE:** 225 7635. 30 Victoria St. Regulars climb the stairs for the
D3 excl value grazing lunch menu or innovative à la carte at night. A laid-back
first-floor eaterie in a welcoming stone-walled labyrinth. Good for groups.
Perhaps more 'mod Brit' than simply 'Scottish'. Lunch and dinner LO 10 (11pm
Fri/Sat). 7 days.   MED

✓ ✓ **THE WITCHERY:** 225 5613. Top restau that really couldn't be anywhere else but Scotland. Report 107/BEST RESTAUS.   EXP

THE BEST MEXICAN (AND CENTRAL AMERICAN) RESTAURANTS

221 ✓ **VIVA MEXICO:** 226 5145. Anchor Close, Cockburn St. Since 1984 the pre-
D3 ✓ eminent Mexican bistro in town. Judy Gonzalez's menu still throws in
something innovative now and again, although all the expected dishes are
here, genuine originals & famously good calamares. Reliable venue for those
times when nothing else fits the mood but sour cream, fajitas and limey lager;
nice atmos downstairs. Lunch (not Sun) and LO 10.30pm (Sun 10pm).   INX

222 ✓ **MOTHER'S:** 662 0772. 107-109 St Leonard's St. Gr wee neighbourhood
E4 ✓ restau that manages to do the basics well (unlike many other Tex/Mexi-
cans in town). Burgers, excl fajitas and one or two departures. Simple décor,
good staff, proper coffee, home-made desserts. Bit of a southside institution
this place. Dinner only Wed-Sun, LO 10pm.   INX

223 **PANCHO VILLA'S:** 557 4416. 240 Canongate. This spartan cantina remains a
E3 reliable exponent of what we've come to regard as Mexican cooking with
nosh of the 'chilada, 'ajita, 'ichanga school. Plain décor, decent edibles, happy
place for parties. Lunch Mon-Sat (Fri/Sat 12 onwards) & dinner 7 days.   INX

224 **CUBA NORTE:** 221 1430. Morrison St (W End nr Haymarket Stn). Yes, we know
B3 it's not Mexican and perhaps not Cuban either, but this bar/restau with Latin
vibes has been a success since it opened during the late 90s Cuba wave. Bar
at front, tables upstairs through back serving Cuba-style cuisine (though we
know they don't have any food, never mind a cuisine) incl tapas & cocktails. DJ
salsa (various w/end nights) may drown out the flava later on, but a better
attempt at Havana than most. 7 days lunch and LO 10pm.   INX

225 **MARIACHI:** 538 0022. 72 Commercial Quay (the line of restaus off Dock Pl in
xE1 Leith, looking over to the Scottish Exec office – and car park). This place one of
the best is mostly, but not all Mexican (much like Mexico). However there are
Mexican waiters. Good for seafood variants. 7 days, LO 10.30pm/11pm.   INX

THE BEST JAPANESE & FUSION RESTAURANTS

226 ✓ **YO SUSHI:** 220 6040. 66 Rose St. This the full singing, dancing Edin ver-
D2 ✓ sion of the London lot. Street-level conveyor sushi & downstairs club
room full of cool gimmicks (karaoke waiters, DJs, massage, etc). Authentic
sushi/sashimi all rolled & precisely arranged in front of you. Assorted sets &
bentos to go (free delivery under 2 miles). 7 days 12-11pm, club till 1am. INX

227 ✓ **BONSAI:** 668 3847. 46 W Richmond St on discreet st on southside a Jap
D3 ✓ caff/bistro (good to graze) where Andrew & Noriko Ramage show a deft
hand in the kitchen. Freshly made sushi/yakitori & teppanyaki. No conveyor
belt in sight. More discreetly Nipponese. Teriyaki steaks, salads & crème brûlée
– great crème brûlée! 7 days noon-10pm (not Sun lunch).   INX

228 **IZZI:** 466 9888. 119 Lothian Rd. This boulevard of broken dreams an unlikely
C3 place for a Japanese restau never mlnd a good one, but this is high st Jap &
Chinese nosh where & when you want it. Some gr sushi, tempuras & teppa-
nyaki bar. Nice staff. 7 days 12-12.   INX

229 **YUMI:** 337 2173. 2 W Coates (continues from Haymarket Terr, W End). The
B3 classier and more polite of the capital's Japanese restaus – definitely old-style.
This is where visiting Japanese businessmen go (& stay, it is actually a hotel).
Many miles & yen away from Yo Sushi so not a lot of fun, but the real deal, com-
plete with tea ceremony & tatami room. Dinner only. LO 9.30pm. Cl Sun. EXP

230 ✓ **BRITANNIA SPICE:** 555 2255. 150 Commercial St on developing end of Leith
xE1 nr Ocean Terminal & Britannia (the **ROYAL YACHT**; 399/ATTRACTIONS). Widespread menu from the sub-continent served by mainly Nepali waiters in modern maritime setting. Some awards, some suits. 7 days, lunch LO 11.30pm. MED

231 ✓ **SURUCHI:** 556 6583. 14a Nicolson St. Upstairs opp Festival Theatre and
D3 ✓ **SURUCHI TOO** at 121 Constitution St, Leith (554 3268). Owner from Jaipur called Mr Rodriguez plus chefs from Bengal, Delhi and S India equals eclectic Indian menu written touchingly in Scots dialect (potatoes are tatties). Unfussy décor and food with light touch attracts students/academics from nearby univ as well as theatregoers. Loads for veggies. Better than av wines but can BYOB. Monthly food fests. Leith a little less compelling, but you can usually get a table in the airport-like lounge – both Suruchis are routinely praised to the skies. Lunch (not Sun) and LO 11.30pm daily. INX

232 ✓ **NAMASTE:** 466 7061. 41 W Preston St. Charming & mellow room, service
xD4 ✓ & food on the southside. Nomads' tent kind of decor & N Indian cuisine, tho many usual dishes. Nice light naans. Slightly heavy incense. But good vibes! Dinner 7 days. LO 10.30pm. INX

233 ✓ **KEBAB MAHAL:** 667 5214. 7 Nicolson Sq. Nr Edin Univ and Festival
D3 ✓ Theatre. Gr vegetable biryani and delicious lassi for under a fiver? Hence high cult status. Late-night Indo-Pakistani halal caff that attracts Asian families as well as students and others who know. Kebabs, curries and excellent sweets. One of Edin's most cosmopolitan restaus. 7 days noon-midnight (2am Fri/Sat). Prayers on Fri (1-2pm). No-alcohol zone. CHP

234 ✓ **KALPNA:** 667 9890. St Patrick Sq. The original Edin Indian veggie restau
D4 ✓ and still the business. Lighter, fluffier and not as attritional as so many tandooris. Wed buffet a bargain. Gujarati menu. Report: 206/VEGN RESTAUS. INX

235 ✓ **THE KHUKURI:** 228 2085. 8 W Maitland St. The W extension of Princes St
B3 ✓ & Shandwick Pl before Haymarket Stn. Here for 6 yrs, the unassuming Khukuri Nepalese restau is a quiet secret. Costumed, endlessly polite Nepali waiters. Chef Dharma Mahrajan routinely wins awards & brings the herbs himself from the mountains of Nepal. Despite massive menu & mellow atmos, meat-eaters will be happiest here. 7 days lunch & LO 11pm (cl Sun lunch). INX

236 **THE RAJ:** 553 3980. 89 Henderson St on S corner of The Shore, Leith. Nice loca-
xE1 tion for the irrepressible Tommy Miah's airy Indian/Bangladeshi restau here some yrs now, but still bustling & still changing (Goan dishes at TGP). Regular events (Bangladeshi New Year and Food/Culture Fest) add to the jollity; jars of things available to buy and take home, also recipe books. Tables best on the raised front area. Totally Raj, in the non-Irvine Welsh sense (in-joke for Edin readers). Lunch and LO 11.30pm, 7 days. INX

237 **ANN PURNA:** 662 1807. 45 St Patrick Sq. Friendly and family-run Gujarati/S
D4 Indian veggie restau with seriously value-for-money business lunch & lovely harmonious food at all times. Report: 207/VEGN RESTAUS. INX

238 **INDIAN CAVALRY CLUB:** 228 3282. Athol Pl, W End, just off the main Glas rd,
B3 about 250m from Princes St the upmarket one tho'. Bargain business lunch attracts the suits. Waiters uniformed at all times in keeping with officers' club theme now retro twice-over. Good buzz here & food always pukka. An unlikely carry-out place, but they do, and it's one of the best in town. Lunch and LO 11.30pm daily. INX

239 **THE ORIGINAL KHUSHI'S:** 667 0888. 26 Potterow. Long regarded as the only
D3 real Indian kitchen, this basic Punjabi café (no restau twiddly bits) has been drawing in students and others for cheap eats since Nehru was in his collar, or at least in the news. Recently moved to the centre of the Univ campus & considerably upmarket: both the menu & the prices have increased, authenticity not. 7 days lunch & dinner. LO 11pm. INX

240 **ZEST:** 556 5028. 115 N St Andrew St, close to St Andrew Sq and Harvey Nix.
D2 Light, modern Indian caff by the same people who have Eastern Spices (326/TAKEAWAYS). Also do home delivery (on orders above £10) so handy for New Town couch potatoes (or Aloos). 7 days lunch, LO 11pm INX

241 ✓✓ **DUSIT:** 220 6846. 49 Thistle St. In the recent proliferation of Thai
C2 restaus in Edin, this one gets the gold orchid. Elegant interior (back
from st), excl service & food good in any language that just happens to be
exquisite Thai cuisine. Tantalising combinations; decent wine list. The tops in
town at TGP. Lunch & dinner LO 10.30pm. Cl Sun.   MED

242 ✓ **THAI ORCHARD:** 228 4438. 44 Grindlay St. Opp Lyceum nr Filmhouse so
C3 handy location for excl Thai food in bright green room with one of the
best waiters in town (working the whole place singlehanded when we were
there). A family affair as is often best. Good seafood. Lunch Mon-Fri, dinner
Mon-Sat LO 10.45pm. Cl Sun.   INX

243 ✓ **THAI LEMONGRASS:** 229 2225. 40 Bruntsfield Pl. Another new & smart
xC4 Thai eatery, this by the people who have the estimable Jasmine (250/BEST
CHINESE). Nice, solid, woody ambience, charming waitresses (not so Thai) &
food that wavers from wonderful to not quite good enough, but popular &
rightly so (book w/ends). Can BYOB (£5 corkage) tho good wine list. Lunch
(Fri-Sun), dinner 7 days LO 11pm.   INX

244 ✓ **THAI ME UP IN EDINBURGH:** 558 9234. Picardy Pl by Playhouse Theatre
D2 nr top of Broughton St. Playful title & unobtrusive entrance belies surprisingly good & innovative Thai menu. Contemporary approach retaining
elegance of lofty Georgian rm. Good service. A welcome addition to the East
Village. 7 days lunch & dinner LO 10.30pm.   INX

245 ✓ **THAISAN UK:** 221 1231. 21 Argyle Pl. Your classic 'tucked-away' 'wee gem'
xD4 on residential st in student & mortgaged-to-the-hilt Marchmont.
Madame Ae offers healthy, fresh & authentic Thai food & other Asian specials.
This place is tiny so best book. BYOB (no wine list). 7 days dinner only. LO
10.30pm.   INX

246 **SIAM ERAWAN:** 226 3675. 48 Howe St. On corner of Stockbridge area, the first
C2 proper Thai to arrive in Edin and still thought by many to be the best – manages that quiet Eastern elegance v well, & those caverns have hosted many a
good night on the Thai. Food varies, good atmos. Lunch & dinner, LO 10.30pm.
7 days.   INX

247 **SONGKRAN:** 225 4804. 8 Gloucester St (behind Oddbins at the end of St
C1, B3 Stephen St) and 225 7889 24a Stafford St in West End. Latter in basement so
Stockbridge best for ambience. Food varies; the chefs alternate – you want to
get 'auntie'. Fresh prep & authentic – even the fishcakes are OK. Lunch (not
Sun) and LO 10.30pm.   INX

248 **AYUTTHAYA:** 556 9351. 14b Nicolson St, opp Festival Theatre. Decent
D3, C4 prospect pre- or post-show. Long, thin, a bit claustrophobic restau, but atten-
tive (and if necessary speedy) service, good vegn selection and a steady hand
in the kitchen. Under the same ownership is **SUKHOTHAI:** 229 1537. 23
Brougham Pl, Tollcross. Funkier eaterie with relaxed atmos tho dire decor.
Food adequate. Ayutthaya best. Both 7 days lunch & LO 10.30pm.   INX

249 **LANNA THAI CAFÉ, MUSSELBURGH:** 653 2788. 32 Bridge St opp Brunton
MAP 3 Hall. Unexpected Thai corner of city suburbs. Big local following who know
C4 that food here is a lot better than the look so must book w/ends. Not bad bet
if you're at the UCI cinema at Ford Kinnaird. Lunch (not Sun), LO 10.30pm. INX

250 ✓ **JASMINE:** 229 5757. 32 Grindlay St opp Lyceum. V Chinesey restau with
C3 big local following. Pre-post-theatre menus & good service to match.
Seafood a speciality (Cantonese style). BYOB (tho exp corkage). Often may
need to book or queue in tiny doorway. Some memorable dishes await. Mon-
Fri lunch, LO 11.30pm (12.30 on w/end, 2pm-11.30pm Sun).　　　MED

251 ✓ **JOANNA'S CUISINE:** 554 5833. 42 Dalmeny St. For yrs this was the
xE1 'Dalmeny St place', now it's the delightful & decorative eponymous
Joanna's. Tiny dining rm on ground floor of tenement off Leith Walk, nevertheless produces a menu of 200 Peking dishes. Home-made stocks rather
than MSG & other touches like specially imported teas make this a place people swear by, so book. Dinner only. LO 10.30pm (11.30 w/ends). Cl Mon.　MED

252 ✓ **KWEILIN:** 557 1875. 19 Dundas St. The here-forever New Town choice
C2 with imaginative Cantonese cooking (and other regions); v good seafood
and genuine dim sum in pleasant but somewhat uninspired setting.
(Makeover due, including much of the clientele.) Excl wine list. No kids
allowed in the evening – somewhere for grown-ups to eat their quail & v
good seafood in peace. Book. LO 10.45pm. Cl Mon.　　　MED

253 ✓ **DRAGON WAY:** 668 1328. 74 S Clerk St. Décor gloriously OTT in a
xE4 Crouching Tiger not so Hidden Dragon kind of a way and often described
as 'Hollywood film set'. Good food mind you, and service, so one of the more
interesting Chinese nights out. Cantonese with Peking & Szechuan as we like.
Seafood a speciality & vegn menu. Lunch Mon-Sat and LO 10.30.　　INX

254 ✓ **ORIENTAL DINING CENTRE:** 221 1288. 8 Morrison St, nr corner with
B3 Lothian Rd. An easily but not to be missed mini Chinatown comprising:
RAINBOW ARCH, the restau with excl rep & real dim sum and **HO HO MEI
NOODLE SHACK**, a stripped-down canteen upstairs, cash only (302/LATE
RESTAUS) – cheap eats & a beer under the bright lights – Mon-Sat 5.30pm-
1.30am. The Rainbow Arch is best by far in this neck of the W End. Clarissa
Dickson Wright can oft be seen ploughing thro' plates of unmentionable ani-
mal parts all deliciously & authentically prepared. The estimable Henry Tse
presides. **HENRY'S JAZZ CELLAR** is in the basement so you can make a v
good night of it. 12noon-midnight daily. (Henry's cl Mon.)　　　INX

255 ✓ **LOON FUNG:** 556 1781. 2 Warriston Pl, Canonmills. Upstairs (and down
C1 when it's crowded) the famous lemon chicken and crispy duck go round
forever tho the speciality here is Cantonese food. Now there's also crispy
monkfish in honey. Good dim sum. Mon-Fri noon-midnight, Sat 2pm-
12.30am, Sun 2pm-11.30pm.　　　INX

256 **NEW EDINBURGH RENDEZVOUS:** 225 2023. 10a Queensferry St. This old
B3 Chinese dining rm is easy to miss (upstairs, next door to travel agents) but it's
the real McCoy and serves dishes you won't find in any other Scottish Chinese
restaus, e.g. shredded sea blubber. Sound nice? Diehards say nobody does
better Peking food in this town. 7 days. Lunch and LO 11pm Mon-Sat, 1-11pm
Sun.　　　INX

257 **WOK & WINE:** 225 2382. 57a Frederick St. Basement restau recently refreshed;
C2 in fact complete rebranding of the estimable family-run Bamboo Garden
which was here for 20 yrs. New, lighter, less MSG feel to menu which has lots
of fish & veggie dishes. This is Edinburgh's chilled-out Chinese. 7 days. Lunch
& LO 11pm (Sun from 5.30pm).　　　INX

THE BEST RESTAURANTS FOR BURGERS AND STEAKS

258
xA2 ✓✓ **CHAMPANY'S:** 01506 834532. On A904, Linlithgow to S Queensferry rd (3km Linlithgow), but nr M9 at jnct 3. Accolade-laden restau (and 'Chop and Ale House') different from others below because it's out of town (and out of some pockets). Both surf 'n' turf with live lobsters on premises. Famously good Aberdeen Angus beef. Good service, huge helpings (Americans may feel at home). Top wine-list. Chop House 7 days, lunch and LO 10pm; restau lunch (not Sat) and LO 10pm. Cl Sun. Hotel rms adj (98/HOTELS O/SIDE TOWN)   INX/EXP

259
C1 ✓ **BELL'S DINER:** 225 8116. 7 St Stephen St, Stockbridge. Edin's small, but celebrated burger joint, the antithesis of the posh nosh. Now legendary, nothing has changed in 30 yrs except the annual paint job and (with an unusually low turnover) the staff. Some people go to Bell's *every* week in life & why? For perfect burgers, steaks, shakes and coincidentally, the best veggie (nut) burger in town. Sun-Fri 6-10.30pm, Sat 12noon-10.30pm.   INX

260
D4, B1 ✓ **BUFFALO GRILL:** 667 7427. 12-14 Chapel St opp Appleton Tower on the univ campus, and 1 Raeburn Pl, Stockbridge (332 3864). Although this diner trades on its reputation for steaks and such-like, there are some Mexican concessions to veggies. Both gr spots for easy-going nights out with chums so book and BYOB Lunch Mon-Fri, LO 10.15pm (Sun 10pm).   INX

261
D2 **SMOKE STACK:** 556 6032. 53-55 Broughton St. From the makers of The Basement (334/UNIQUE EDIN PUBS) came something equally reliably groovy across the rd – a burgundy and blue diner rather than an orange and blue bar. Modish décor has a soothing effect. Loads of burgers (Scottish beef or vegn), seared salmon, etc. jollied along by a gr staff. Proper menu available lunch and dinner, but food of some sort all day. Lunch Mon-Sat, dinner 7 days LO 10.30pm.   INX

262 ✓ **UMBERTO'S:** 554 1314. Bonnington Rd Lane off Bonnington Rd to E of
xE1   ✓ Newhaven Rd jnct.Whitewashed coach house hidden away in a v unlikely part of Leith. In contrast to some other 'kiddie' places, grown-ups would actually want to eat here too. Downstairs is a civilised restau, upstairs a theme area for kids where some booths form part of a big toy train and mobile youngsters can run in and out of the Wendy house. Excl Italian cooking with a Scottish twist. Upstairs open Mon-Fri noon-2pm then 5-10pm, Sat noon-10pm,Sun noon-6pm.   INX

263 ✓ **VITTORIA:** 556 6171. Corner of Brunswick St & Leith Walk. Excl Italian all-
E1   ✓ rounder that can seat 200 people incl outside on pavement corner. Report: 287/CAFÉS.

264 ✓ **LUCA'S:** 446 0233. 16 Morningside Rd. The ice cream kings (1532/ICE
xC4   ✓ CREAM) from Musselburgh opened this modern ice-creamerie and caff where kids with dads will enjoy their spag and their sundae. Big cups of capp. Crowded if not claustrophobic upstairs esp on w/ends. Excl for daytime snacks, family even meals & gorgeous ice-cream at all times. 9am-9.30pm. 7 days.   INX

265 ✓ **GIULIANO'S ON THE SHORE:** 554 5272. 1 Commercial St, by the br. The
xE1   ✓ Leith version of 'Gulies' (173/TRUSTY TRATTS) has all the trad Italian trappings despite its recent modern facelift, with cheerful pizza/pasta & waiters. Kids love it. For grown-ups nice antipasto, fish specials & decent wine list. Always a birthday party happening at w/ends. Luca's ice-cream (see above). Noon-10.30/11pm. 7 days.   INX

266 ✓ **CAFÉ HUB:** 473 2067. Castlehill, top of Royal Mile. Recently much
C3   ✓ improved food-wise restau for adults that also caters in a superior way for kids (special menu). This caff is within the International Festival Centre, so busy busy in Aug. Outside terrace a child-friendly zone (371/DRINKING OUTDOORS). 7 days 10am-10pm (Sun/Mon till 6pm).   INX

267 **YE OLDE PEACOCK INN:** 552 8707. Newhaven Rd nr Newhaven Harbour. One
xC1 of Edin's unsung all-round family eateries for yrs – you can take gran as well as the bairns. The fish here really is fresh, the menu is more adventurous than you'd think with lots that wee kids and we kids like. High tea is a treat. Lunch and LO 9.45pm. 7 days.   CHP

OUTSIDE TOWN

268 **CRAMOND BRIG:** 339 4350. At the R Almond as you hit Edin on the dual
xA2 carriageway from the Forth Rd Br. This inn has always put effort into attracting families, & altho there's no longer a kids' play area on the premises, there is one by the old brig itself, a pony field & a walk by the river. Food much better all round after recent major refurb. Lunch and LO 9.30pm, 7 days. Open from lunch straight through to close on Sat-Sun.   INX

269 **THE SUN INN, LOTHIANBURN:** 663 2456. On a bend of the A7 nr t/off for
MAP 3 Newtongrange, under mega viaduct, 18km S of city centre. Happy, homely
D4 pub in the unfashionable netherlands of Midlothian. Bistro-style food, lunch and LO 9pm (9.30 pm w/ends). Popular family spot (book w/ends).

270 **GOBLIN HA', GIFFORD:** 01620 810244. 35km from town in neat E Lothian
MAP 3 village. One of two hotels, this has the pub grub cornered. Lunch and supper
D5 (6-9pm, 9.30pm Fri-Sat). Gdn gets v busy in summer. Nice for kids.

271 **BRIDGE INN, RATHO:** 333 1320. 14km W of city centre via Sighthill & A71.
MAP 3 Report: 370/PUBS WITH GOOD FOOD.   INX

272 ✓✓ **PLAISIR DU CHOCOLAT:** 556 9524. 257 Canongate at bottom end of
E2 Royal Mile on tourist trek, but this is a real find. Chocolate yes but definitely for connoisseurs, and teas of which there is a huge & explicit list. Fabulous patisserie, home-made sourdough bread; also excl salads, omelettes, pâtés and innovative cuisine. Tables on the terrace and inside an Art Nouveau-ish rm. A top spot for that reviving cuppa & no coffee in sight. Tues-Sun 10am–6pm. There's a Plaisir outpost or salon up the st at 270 Canongate (opp side). Same hrs.

273 ✓✓ **GALLERY (OF MODERN ART) CAFÉ:** Belford Rd. Unbeatable on a
A2 fine day when you can sit out on the patio by the grass, with sculptures around, have some wine and a plate of Scottish cheese and oatcakes. Hot dishes are excellent – always 2 soups, meat/fish/vegn dish. Coffee and cake whenever. Art upstairs often questionable; this is always superb. 7 days 10am-4.30pm. (404/OTHER ATTRACTIONS). Lunch dishes usually gone by 2.30pm. **CAFÉ NEWTON** at the Dean Gallery (405/OTHER ATTRACTIONS) across the rd & the gardens from GOMA (above) is a smaller, more interior café by the same people. Soup, sandwiches & 2 hot lunch dishes. Coffee from mega machine. Same hrs as GOMA.

274 ✓✓ **QUEEN STREET CAFÉ:** National Portrait Gallery (403/OTHER ATTRAC-
C2 TIONS), Queen St, betw Hanover and St Andrew's Sq. And through the arched window … a civil slice of old Edin gentility. Serving seriously good light meals (same people as GOMA, above), tasteful sandwiches, coffee and cake – best scones in town, exquisite salads among other things. Self-s but you rarely wait long. Mon-Sat 10am-4.30pm, Sun 11am-4.30pm.

275 ✓ **CIRCUS CAFÉ-BAR & DELI:** 220 0333. Recent addition to chic New Town
B1 café society & no expense spared in conversion of former bank to chrome-&-leather eaterie upstairs & surprising deli hidden in the vaults. Grazing menu & specialising perhaps more in cocktails than cappuccino, but perfect for the upwardly mobile of Stockbridge.

276 ✓ **FRUITMARKET CAFÉ:** 226 1843. 29 Market St. Attached to the
D3 Fruitmarket Gallery, a cool spacious place for coffee, cake or a light lunch. Big salads & creative snacks, esp deli-sandwiches. Bookshop to browse with Andy Miller's lovely shelves, big windows to look out; good mix of tourists, Edin faithfuls and art seekers. Mon-Fri 11.30am-3pm, Sat till 4, Sun 12-4.

277 ✓ **G&T (GLASS & THOMPSON):** 557 0909. 2 Dundas St. Patrician New Town
C2 coffee shop and deli with contemporary food and attitude. A Clarissa Dickson-Wright kind of place: they love food. Gr *antipasti*, salads, sandwiches to go; and some cakes! 8.30am-5.30pm, Sun 11am-4.30pm. (320/TAKEAWAYS)

278 **AU GOURMAND:** 624 4666. 1 Brandon Terr at foot of Dundas St at
C1 Canonmills. V. French, v. New Town deli counter and caff in back with big windows onto garden. Deli selection small but select & making up main ingredients of the soup, salad, sandwich & crêpe menu. Restau menu at night (Tues-Sat). Coffee shop 7 days till 6pm.

279 **CAFÉ FLORENTIN:** 225 6267. 8 St Giles St. A true Edin-Franco original, tho no
D3, C2 longer what it was. Once they turned an entire generation of Edimbourgeois on to almond croissants and wicked tartelettes. Trading perhaps on past glory but still a funky caff with more French frou-frou than most. Open 8am-6.30pm daily. The other **FLORENTIN** at 5 NW Circus Pl, has diff ownership. It's nicely Stockbridge. 7am-7pm daily.

280 **KAFFE POLITIK:** 446 9873. 146-148 Marchmont Rd. All black and white and
xD4 wood and middle-Euro chic at another converted bank in the heart of student flat land. Recently taken over by Sweet Melinda's (126/BISTROS) – it's just up the rd. Damn fine cup of coffee, sodas, juice, soup 'n' sandwiches and Melinda-type hot dishes (menu under review at TGP). V good breakfasts (312/SUN BREAKFAST). Some o/side tables. 10am-9pm daily (but check hrs).

281 **BLACK MEDICINE COFFEE SHOP:** 622 7209. 2 Nicolson St, corner of
D3 Drummond St. Funky American-style coffee shop on busy Southside corner opp Festival Theatre and Univ Old Quad. Good place to take your book from

Blackwells; get a window seat! Good smell. Big bagels, cookies & fab smooth-ies. 7 days. 8am-8pm (Suns from 9am).

282 **CLARINDA'S:** 557 1888. 69 Canongate. Nr the bottom of the Royal Mile nr the
E2 Palace (and the new Parliament building). A small but total tearoom with hot dishes and snacks that may seem more of a sit-down stop on the tourist trail but has some of the best home-baking in town (esp the apple pie). V reason-able prices; run by good Edinburgh folk who slave over that stove. T/aways poss (I know I do). 7 days 9am-4.45pm (from 10am Sun).

283 **THE ELEPHANT HOUSE:** 220 5355. 21 George IV Br. Nr libraries and Edin Univ,
D3 a rather self-conscious but elephantine and well-run coffee shop with light snacks and big choice. J.K. Rowling (LITERARY PLACES) once sat here. Counter during day, waitress service evens. Big smoking section. Cakes/pastries are bought in but can be taken out. 7 days 8am-11pm. Same people have **ELEPHANTS & BAGELS** at Nicolson Sq. Soup 'n' a bagel t/away and sit-in. 7 days 8.30am-6pm (w/ends 9.30am-5pm).

284 **BOTANIC GARDENS CAFETERIA:** By 'the House' (where there are regular
xB1 exhibs), within the gdns (402/OTHER ATTRACTIONS). For café only, enter by Arboretum Pl. Disappointing catering-style food (in fact it can be ghastly) but the o/side tables & the view of the city is why we come. And the squirrels. 10am-5pm.

285 **CAFÉ GRANDE:** 228 1188. 182-184 Bruntsfield Pl. Coffee shop during the day,
xC4 more adventurous bistro menu at night (INX) – eclectic clientele & menu. In among assorted coffees and herbal teas, Bovril can be had. Occasional lapses (not all puds home-made) but a nice restful alternative to brash Montpelliers opp. 9am-11pm, till 12midnight Thu-Sat. Sun 10am-10pm.

286 **POLICE BOX COFFEE BARS:** 228 5001. Kiosks not caffs! Rose St (behind
E4, D3, Jenners), Morningside Park, Hope Park Cres (E of Meadows), top of Middle
D2 Meadow Walk (opp Forrest Rd) and outside John Lewis' dept store and St Andrew's Cathedral. Caffeine kiosks in former police boxes. Similar fare to Starbucks and Costas but these are home-grown and have, in their way, reclaimed the streets. Hrs vary but early-late. Gr coffee to go.

287 ✓ ✓ **VITTORIA:** 556 6171. Brunswick St, corner of Leith Walk. May get
E1 forgotten in the foody guides or the Italian round-up but for over 30 years Vittoria is one of the best, least pretentious Scottish-Italian scrans in town. Great fry-ups, omelettes and full Italian carbo variants. O/side tables on interesting corner always packed when the sun's out. 2003 refurb has extended restau with function rm to next corner. 7 days. 10am-11pm.

288 ✓ **NDEBELE:** 221 1141. 59 Home St, Tollcross. The Ndebele are a southern
C4 African people, but this café has dishes from all over the continent so get your ostrich, mielie bread and moi moi here – or just have a coffee. Loads of sandwiches, light meals and a good groovalong soundtrack. Brill for vegns. Africa distant and usually hot, this delightfully chilled. Daily 10am-10pm. T/away and sit-in.

289 ✓ **JUNIPER:** 225 1552. 121 Hanover St nr corner with Queen St. Restau &
C2 takeaway in legendary location (the former Laigh Coffee House) making its own solid rep for home cooking. Comfort food summed up, as they say, as 'soups, stews, salads & sweets'. Friendly, personal service. A cool drop-in. 8am-8/9pm. Cl Suns.

290 ✓ **BLUE MOON CAFÉ:** 557 0911. 1 Barony St on corner of Broughton St. (2
D2 entrances – lose the joke.) Longest-established gay café in Scotland and still evolving (1347/GAY EDIN). Straight-friendly & a good place to hang out from b/fast-late. All day b/fast. Female staff efficient, boys more spacey. Free condoms in the gents for the impecunious or impatient. 7 days 11am-1am. Food all day till 10pm (Fri/Sat till midnight), LO 15 mins before.

291 ✓ **LUCA'S:** 446 0233. 16 Morningside Rd. In town version of legendary ice
xC4 cream parlour in Musselburgh (1532/ICE CREAM). Ice cream and snacks d/stairs, more family food parlour up. Cheap and cheerful. Gr for kids. Report: 264/KIDS. 7 days.

292 **SPOON:** 556 6922. 15 Blackfriars St off Royal Mile opp the High St Hostel
D3 (87/BEST HOSTELS). Richard & Moira's friendly, off-high st, almost neighbourhood but modern, even minimalist caff. Counters service for snacks & hot dishes using selected ingredients & more TLC than usual. Big bowls of soup, nice coffee. Mon-Sat 8am-6pm. (7 days in July/Aug).

293 **ALWAYS SUNDAY:** No number at TGP. 170 High St. At last a caff on the Royal
D3 Mile that's trying & at least reflects contemp tastes. Deli-style counter offering 'healthy' b/fasts thro lunch to afternoon 'treats'. Home baking. 7 days 8am-6pm (Sat/Sun from 9am).

294 **LOST SOCK DINER:** 557 6097. Corner of E London St/Broughton St, adj
D1 Sundial laundrette. An innovation and caused a whirl when it opened – a café/restau attached to a laundrette where you could eat well while your washing spun. Several changes of chef and food policy since, still a cool place to snack with or without your powder. Big eclectic menu. 7 days. LO 4pm Mon, 10pm Tue-Sat. Sun 10am-5pm. Seats o/side in summer.

295 **FAVORIT:** 220 6880. 20 Teviot Pl, nr Univ and 30 Leven St nr King's Theatre (221
D3,C4 1800). Originally (changed hands 2003) by people who brought us indigo yard (369/STYLE BARS). All-day, all-round drop-in café in contemporary style. They've thought of everything. Great late (298/LATE BARS). Both 7 days, 8.30am/8am-3am. We think Leven St best.

KEBAB MAHAL: 667 5214. Nicolson Sq. Cult I. Report: 233/INDIAN.

296
C3
✓ ✓ **THE WITCHERY:** 225 5613. Castlehill, top of Royal Mile nr the Castle. Not open v late, but does take bookings up till 11.30pm, that crucial half hr beyond 11 that allows you to eat after the movies. Special after-theatre menu from 10.30pm has 2 courses for a tenner, a v good deal from one of the best restaus in town (107/BEST RESTAUS). 7 days, lunch and **LO 11.30pm.** MED

297
B1, B3
✓ **PIZZA EXPRESS:** Various branches (177/pizza) all open 11/11.30 but North Bridge (557 6411) **open till midnight** and no booking policy, so a good bet. New Leith branch on the shore (554 4332) is prob best chance of food after 11 in Leith. Report 177/BEST PIZZA. INX

298
D3, C4
✓ **FAVORIT:** 220 6880. 20 Teviot Pl and 30 Leven St (221 1800). New York diner-type café/restau – salads, pasta, wraps, Ben and Jerry's from dawn till almost dawn (295/BEST CAFFS, 310/SUNDAY BREAKFAST). **7 days till 3am.** MED

299
E1
✓ **GIULIANO'S:** 556 6590. 18 Union Pl, Leith walk opp Playhouse. Buzzing Italian tratt day and night. Report 162/TRUSTY TRATTS. **Handily open till 2am (2.30 w/ends).** INX

300
C2
✓ **LIVING ROOM:** 226 0880. 113 George St. Best of many for eats on 'stylish' George St & open later than similar others esp at w/ends. Full-on bar at front like Candy Bar downstairs; surprisingly large dining area at back. Mod-Brit menu with food better than you'd expect. V noisy & music too loud at w/ends, but service excl. Not a bad product from emerging UK chain. **7 days LO 11pm, midnight w/ends.** INX

301
D3
NEGOCIANTS: 225 6313. 45 Lothian St nr Univ & (esp at night) large student clientele. Diff ambiences & menu thro' day but special late-night fuel-up menu from 10pm-2.15am incl nachos, burgers, paninis. Don't hope for a quiet corner in which to graze – it rocks. **Till 2.15am incl Sun** but phone first if you're going v late, esp to eat. INX

302
B3
NOODLE SHACK: 221 1288. 8 Morrison St. 50m Lothian Rd corner opp rebuilt cinema complex. Upstairs from Rainbow Arch, a big bowl of noodles in a bright canteen. Limited booze, cash only. A post modern midnight. **Till 1am (cl Sun).** INX

303
D3
GORDON'S TRATTORIA: 225 7992. 231 High St. Although some late-night visitors mistake this for a kebab house, it's v definitely Italian. Best late-night spag in the Old Town. **Sun-Thu LO 12midnight, Fri-Sat 3am.** INX

304
B3
BAR ROMA: 226 2977. 39a Queensferry St, nr W End of Princes St. Buzzing day and night. An Edin institution even better after revamp. All the old standbys snappily served & lots of late night Italian jive. Best wine-list you'll find in W End after midnight. (See 171/TRUSTY TRATTS). **12noon-12midnight Sun-Thu; 12.45am Fri-Sat.** INX

305
C3
LAZIO: 229 7788. 95 Lothian Rd. Best of the Lothian Rd bunch by far, tho' you'd never know. Totally genuine Italian family restau (174/TRUSTY TRATTS). There's one guy always there eating at 1 in the morning when we're there. Now that's what we call 'a regular'. **Till 1.30am, 3am Fri/Sat.** INX

306 ✓ **HADRIAN'S:** 557 5000. 2 North Bridge, corner of & brasseries restau of
D2 Balmoral (47/HOTELS). Good daily (power) brunch place, but also Suns.
From 7am (Sun 7.30am). Not chp, but light (or lavish) & laid-back.

307 ✓ **THE BREAKFAST ROOM @ THE SCOTSMAN HOTEL:** 556 5565. 20 N
D3 Bridge. B/fast in Edin's top new boutique hotel (55/HOTELS). Many refs to
the morning paper this hotel replaces in the building, & this morning's is there
to read. Interior rm (adj Vermillion – 114/BEST RESTAUS), but an excl, leisurely
start to the day for guests & non-guests alike. **From 7-10.30am, 8-11.30
w/ends.**

308 ✓ **CAFÉ MEDITERRANEO:** 557 6900. 73 Broughton St. On busy st for b/fast
D2 (see below), this is the best choice for the non fry-up & easy start to the
day. From coffee/croissants to olive oil lunch in light surroundings (183/MED
RESTAUS). **From 9am (full b/fast from 10.30am).**

309 ✓ **RICKS:** 622 7800. 55a Frederick St. The cool café-bar (384/STYLE BARS) with
C2 rooms (64/INDIVIDUAL HOTELS) opens early & late, but an excl spot for laid-
back or power b/fast brunch 7 days, incl unusually early start on Suns. Eclectic,
contemp menu. **Open 7 days from 7am.**

310 **FAVORIT:** 221 1800. 30 Leven St. The all-people all-rounder. **Open 7 days**
C4 **from 8am.** Report: 295/BEST CAFFS and 298/LATE-NIGHT RESTAUS.

311 **NEGOCIANTS:** 45-47 Lothian St. Nr univ. Gr all-round pub (369/PUBS WITH
D3 GOOD FOOD), open v late and pretty early for Sun breakfast. **From 10am
(brunch till 6pm).**

312 **KAFFE POLITIK:** 446 9873. 146-148 Marchmont Rd. Good coffee in serenely
xD4 cerebral surroundings. B/fast & other menus under review by new owners (of
Sweet Melinda's) at TGP. **From 10am.** (280/BEST TEAROOMS)

313 **CITY CAFE:** Blair St. It's been here so long, it's easy to take for granted … but
D3 for that 'BIG' breakfast (carnivore or veggie), few places in the city beat the
content or American diner atmos. Not open exactly early as most of clientele
have been up v late. **From 11am.**

314 **KING'S WARK:** 554 9260. 36 The Shore on busy corner for traffic, but calm &
xE1 comforting inside. Dining rm or bar. No early start (**11am**), but a civilised
brunch on the waterfront.

315 **BLACK MEDICINE COFFEE SHOP:** 622 7209. 2 Nicolson St. Gr atmos
D3 American-style coffee with bagels/muffins type start to Sundays. 281/COF-
FEESHOPS. **From 9am.**

316 **ELEPHANT HOUSE:** 220 5355. 21 George IV Bridge. Another (this time exten-
D3 sive) coffee-house nr the Univ that's open early for caffeine & sustenance.
283/COFFEE SHOPS. **From 8am.**

317 **THE BROUGHTON ST BREAKFAST:** As well as top spots (see above), there's
D2, D1 lots of choice in the main st of Edin's East Village. (For late risers only in this
part of the world.) From the top down: **MATHER'S** the no-compromise drinking den does the trad fry-up from **12.30pm**, as does **THE OUTHOUSE** down
the lane but with veggie variants (& outside courtyard) & until 4pm.
BAROQUE also kicks in from **12.30pm** with similar nosh (slightly more
expensive). **THE BASEMENT** also does Tex-Mex brex from **noon** tho' it is a
basement. Further down on corner with people-watching windows is **THE
BARONY** with b/fast & the papers from 12.30-3.30 (gr live music Sun late aft).
THE LOST SOCK DINER is at the bottom and round the corner.
Neighbourhood caff **from 11am** (they also do laundry – see 294/CAFÉS).

318 **CAFÉ FLORENTIN:** St Giles St, off Royal Mile opp Cathedral. The first to open
D3 for a civilised start (or finish). The authentically French coffee shop with crois-
sants/pain au chocolat and whirly pastries. Caff now feels a bit rundown, perhaps like you do if you're still running on Sat night. **From 9am.** (279/BEST TEA-
ROOMS).

319 **indigo (yard):** 220 5603. 7 Charlotte Lane. Another fashionable spot (same
D3 org as Rick's above) & prob best brunch bet in W End. Details: 383/CAFÉ-BARS.
From 9am.

320 ✓ **G&T (GLASS & THOMPSON):** 557 0909. 2 Dundas St. Deli and coffee
C2 shop on main st in New Town, but also takeaway sandwiches/rolls in infinite formats using their drool-making selection of quality ingredients (breads,
cheeses, salamis, etc.). Take away to office, gdns or dinner party. Excellent sit-
in area and small terr for whiling away Edinburgh days. Mon-Sat 8.30am-
5.30pm, Sat 8.30am-5.30pm, Sun 11am-4.30pm. (277/BEST TEAROOMS)

321 ✓ **EMBO:** 652 3880. 29 Haddington Pl. Half way down Leith Walk & one of
E1 the reasons for going that far. Bespoke sandwiches, tortillas, etc. Excl cof-
fee & smoothies.'Panino Bar' & a couple of tables o/side the door. Nice baking.
Good to know. Mon-Fri 8am-3pm, Sat 10am-3.30pm. Cl Sun.

322 ✓ **THE GLOBE:** 558 3837. 42 Broughton St. A bright spot on the corner in
D2 the middle of the East Village. Open all day till 3/4pm for sand-
wiches/rolls and toasted focaccia. Big window for people-watching. Branches
at 23 Henderson Row, N Castle St & Bernard St, Leith (another busy shop on
the corner). Henderson Row branch the best for real b/fast. Cl Sun.

323 ✓ **JUNIPER:** 225 1552. 121 Hanover St, corner with Queen St. Basement
C2 t/away & diner (289/CAFFS). Self-serv counter for soups, stews & bespoke
s/wiches. Restau adj offers same menu. Comfort food with contemp twist. All-
day service 8am-8pm. Cl Suns.

324 ✓ **RUSHOUR:** 556 0050. Located at 20 Holyrood Rd, but this is a delivery
E3 service for city-centre postcodes – within 1 hr. Food not fab, but nice, serviceable pizza & limited Chinese/Indian menu. Also puds, wine, DVD & cigs.
Perfect for late-night couch potatoes. Sun-Thur 1pm-1.30am, Fri/Sat noon-
3.30am. £8 min charge. www.rushour.co.uk

325 **PRET À MANGER:** Shandwick Pl, Castle St, St Andrews Sq (& spreading like
B3, C2 mayo). Nice, but pity they sold out to McDonald's.

326 **EASTERN SPICES:** 558 3609. 2 Canonmills Br, by the clock. Long on the
C1 grapevine, this place is simply better than most – phone in your order or turn
up and wait. Also home delivery 2 ml radius. Full Indian menu from pakora to
pasanda and meals for one. 5-11.30 7 days. New, zestier menu due at TGP.

327 **TASTE GOOD:** 313 5588. 67 Slateford Rd. At last a 21st cent Chinese t/away
C1 unfortunately far from centre (they do deliver). Contemp look & presentation.
Tastes good too (also seating). 7 days 4.30-12midnight.

328 **L'ALBA D'ORO:** 557 2580. 5-11 Henderson Row. Excl pizza, pasta, wine as well
C1 as fish 'n' chips. Report 176/PIZZAS.

329 ✓✓ **PORT O' LEITH:** 58 Constitution St. The legendary Leith bar on busy
xE1 rd to what used to be the docks. The incorrigible & incorruptible
Mary Moriarty still puts up the odd sailor but it's mainly the rest of us from the
sea of life who frequent this unchanging neighbourhood pub full of warmth,
chat, good music & all the things we left behind. Truly a port in the storm. Go
find it. Till 12.45am.

330 ✓ **CAFÉ ROYAL:** Behind Burger King at the E end of Princes St, one of Edin's
D2 longest celebrated pubs. Unrelated to the London version, though there
is a similar Victorian/Baroque elegance. Through the partition is the Oyster
Bar (197/SEAFOOD RESTAUS). Central counter and often standing rm only. Open
to 11pm (later at w/ends).

331 ✓ **BENNET'S:** Leven St, by King's Theatre. Just stand at the back and watch
C4 light stream through the stained glass on a sunny day as it always did.
Same era as Café Royal and similar ambience, mirrors and tiles. Decent food at
lunch (348/PUB FOOD). Till 11.30pm Mon-Wed, 12.30am Thu-Sat, 11pm Sun.

332 ✓ **THE POND:** 467 3815. 2 Bath Rd, off Seafield Rd, Leith. Cool Edin bar on
xE1 the edge of dead dockland. They don't make 'em as understated or laid-
back as this anywhere except at the beach. Till 1am. (386/STYLE BARS).

333 **BARONY BAR:** 81 Broughton St. Real-ale venue with a mixed clientele & good
D2 vibe. Belgian and guest beers. Newspapers to browse over a Sun afternoon
b/fast or a (big) lunchtime pie. Bert's band on Sun aft/evens one of the best
pub nights in town. Till 12midnight Mon-Thu, 12.30am Fri-Sat, 11pm Sun.

334 **THE BASEMENT:** 109 Broughton St. Much-imitated, still crucial, this is a
D3 chunky, happening sort of, er, basement where you can have Mex-style food
during the day served by laaarvely staff in Hawaiian shirts. At night, the punters are well up for it – late, loud and lively. Till 1am daily.

335 **SHEEP'S HEID:** 656 6952. The Causeway, Duddingston Village. Not central, but
xE4 a pleasant and dramatic drive away behind Arthur's Seat in the Queen's Park.
Old coaching inn with good craic, some locals & ok grub in courtyard patio
(365/PUB FOOD). Food till 8.30pm, pub 11pm (12midnight Fri-Sat).

336 **KAY'S BAR:** 39 Jamaica St. The New Town – incl Jamaica St – sometimes gives
C2 the impression that it's populated by people who were around in the late
18th century. It's an Edinburgh thing (mainly male). They care for the beer
(358/REAL-ALE PUBS). Until 11.45pm (11pm Sun).

337 **MATHER'S:** 1 Queensferry St. Edin's W End has a complement of 'smart' bars
B3 that cater for people with tight haircuts and tight schedules. The alternative is
here – a stand-up space for old-fashioned pubbery, slack coiffure and idle talk
(350/'UNSPOILT' PUBS). Till 12midnight Mon-Thu, 1am Fri-Sat, 11pm Sun.

338 **ROBBIE'S:** Leith Walk, on corner with Iona St. Some bars on Leith Walk are
E1 downright scary – but not this one. Tolerant, good range of beer, TV will have
the football on (or not). Wild mix of Trainspotters, locals and the odd dodgy
character or 3, even a stray social worker (HQ is nearby). Always has the now
factor. (348/'UNSPOILT' PUBS). Till 12midnight Mon-Sat, 11pm Sun.

339 **CITY CAFÉ:** 220 0127. 19 Blair St. Seems ancient, but 15 yrs on, the retro
D3 Americana chic has aged gracefully. Pool tables, all-day food, decent coffee. A
hip Edin bar that has stood the test of mind-altering time. Music downstairs
w/ends courtesy of guest DJs (313/SUNDAY BREAKFAST). 11am-1am daily.

340 **BELUGA BAR:** 624 4545. 30a Chambers St. Token hip (well up to a point) in
D3 this section. Restau upstairs but we don't rate food. Down designery staircase
is vast cavern for drinking, debauchery, pub-grub etc. Places like this everywhere, but this one used to be a dental hospital. And that is unusual.

341 **THREE SISTERS:** Cowgate. Of the many booming bars in the Cowgate, we
D3 may as well select this one – one of Edinburgh's busiest bars. Nothing v special but good conversion of old warehouse and better than your av super bar
(3 atmospheres to choose from). Also has rms. 7 days, 11am-1am.

342 **THE DOME:** 624 8624. 14 George St. Edin's first megabar but not a chain.
C2 Former bank and grandiose in the way that only a converted temple to Mammon could be. Main part sits 15m under elegant domed roof with island bar and raised platform at back for determined diners. Staff almost impeccable, pricey menu; you come for the surroundings more than the victuals (MED). Lunch and LO dinner 10pm daily. Also snack menu for casual diners away from roped-off posh nosh area. Adj real-ale Art Deco bar Frazers is separate, more intimate, better for a blether. 'Garden' patio bar at back (in good weather) – enter via Rose St. Final bit, downstairs: Why Not? (494/ESS CULTURE/CLUBS), a nightclub for over-25s still lookin' for lurvv (Fri/Sat). Main bar Sun-Thu till 11.30pm, Fri-Sat till 1am.

343 **THE DORIC:** 225 1084. 15 Market St. More a bistro/restau than a mere pub, but
D3 the smaller rm by the bar is Edin in a nutshell (143a/BISTROS). Recent refurb downstairs but we always preferred upstairs looking over the town.

THE BEST OLD 'UNSPOILT' PUBS

Of course it's not necessarily the case that when a pub's done up, it's spoiled, or that all old pubs are worth preserving, but some have resisted change and that's part of their appeal. Money and effort are often spent to 'oldify' bars and contrive an atmos. The following places don't have to try.

344 ✓**THE DIGGERS:** 1 Angle Park Terr. (Officially the Athletic Arms.) Jambo
xA4 pub *par excellence*, stowed with the Tynecastle faithful before and after games. Still keeps a gr pint of McEwan's 80/-, allegedly the best in Edin. The food is basic ie pies. Till 11pm/midnight Mon-Sat, 11pm Sun.

345 ✓**THE ROYAL OAK:** Infirmary St. Tiny upstairs and not much bigger down.
D3 During the day, pensioners sip their pints (couple of real ales) while the cellar opens till 2am. Music up and down. Hell for non-smokers but they definitely don't make 'em like this any more. Gold carat pubness.

346 ✓**ROSEBURN BAR:** 1 Roseburn Terr, on main Glas rd out W from Haymarket
xA3 and one of the nearest pubs to Murrayfield Stadium. Wood and grandeur and red leather, bonny wee snug, fine pint of McEwan's and wall-to-wall rugby of course. Heaving before internationals. Till 11pm (midnight w/ends).

347 ✓**CLARK'S:** 142 Dundas St. A couple of snug snugs, red leather, brewery
C2 mirrors and decidedly no frills. Good McEwan's – just the place to pop in if you're tooling downhill from town to Canonmills. A local you might learn to love. Till 11pm (11.30pm Thu-Sat).

348 **ROBBIE'S:** Leith Walk, on corner of Iona St. Real ales and new lagers in a neigh-
xE1 bourhood howf that tolerates everyone from the wifie in her raincoat to multi-pierced yoof of indeterminate gender. More rough than smooth of course, but with the footy on the box, a pint and a packet of Hula Hoops – this is a bar to save or savour life. Till 12midnight Mon-Sat, 11pm Sun. (338/UNIQUE EDIN PUBS)

349 **OXFORD BAR:** 8 Young St, downhill from George St. No time machine need-
C2 ed – just step in the door to see an Edin that hasn't changed since yon times. Careful what you say; this is an off-duty cop shop poss incl Inspector Rebus (& Ian Rankin fans from far & wide). Some real ales but they're beside the point as the pies. Till 1am (midnight Sun).

350 **MATHER'S:** 1 Queensferry St. Not only a reasonable real-ale pub but almost
B3, D2 worth visiting just to look at the ornate fixtures and fittings – frieze and bar esp – they don't make 'em like that these days. Unreconstructed in every sense. Pies all day. Till 12midnight Mon-Thu, 1am Fri-Sat, 11pm Sun. (337/UNIQUE PUBS) There's another, unrelated, **MATHER'S** in Broughton St which is managing to keep its head in the city's grooviest thoroughfare by remaining pub-like and unpretentious. Football telly.

351 ✔ **THE CUMBERLAND BAR:** Cumberland St, corner of Dundonald St. After
C1 work this New Town bar attracts its share of suits, but later the locals reclaim it and Camra (Campaign for Real Ale) supporters seek it out too. Av of 9 real ales on tap. Nicely appointed, decent pub lunches, unexpected beer gdn. 7 days till 1am.

352 ✔ **STARBANK INN:** 64 Laverockbank Rd, Newhaven. On the seafront rd W of
xC1 Newhaven harbour. Usually 8 different ales on offer. Gr place to sit with pint in hand and watch the sun sink over the Forth. The food is good (363/PUB FOOD). Bar till 11pm Sun-Wed, 12midnight Thu-Sat.

353 ✔ **THE BOW BAR:** 80 W Bow, halfway down Victoria St. They know how to
D3 treat drink in this excellent wee bar. Huge selection ales & whiskies – no cocktails! One of the few places in the Grassmarket area an over 25-year-old might not feel out of place. Bliss. Till 11.30pm Mon-Sat, 11pm Sun.

354 ✔ **THE GUILDFORD ARMS:** 1 W Register St. Behind Burger King at E end of
D2 Princes St on same block as the Café Royal (330/UNIQUE PUBS). Forever in the same family. Lofty, ornate Victorian hostelry with loadsa good ales. There are some you won't find anywhere else in the city. Pub grub available on 'gallery' floor as well as bar. Sun-Wed till 11pm, Thu-Sat till 12midnight.

355 ✔ **BLUE BLAZER:** 2 Spittal St opp Point Hotel. No frills, no pretensions, just
C3 wooden fixtures and fittings, pies and toasties in this fine S&N-owned howf that carries a huge range of real ales. More soul than any of its competitors nearby even after recent refurb. All day till 12/12.30. Sun 12.30pm-11pm.

356 **BERT'S:** 29 William St. Rare ales, suits as well as casual crowd in this *faux*
B3, B1 Edwardian bar. Decent pies for carnivores or veggies alike and a good place to escape from office neurosis. Good range guest ales. Till 11pm Sun-Thu, 12midnight Fri-Sat. More local **BERT'S** at 2 Raeburn Pl, Stockbridge.

357 **THE CANNY MAN:** 237 Morningside Rd. Officially known as the Volunteer
xC4 Arms, but everybody calls it the Canny Man. Good smorrebrod at lunch time & evens (317/GASTROPUBS), a wide range of real ales & myriad malts. Casual visitors may feel that management have an attitude (problem) but this family has been here forever.

358 **KAY'S BAR:** 39 Jamaica St, off India St in the New Town. Go on an afternoon
C2 when gentlemen of a certain age talk politics, history and rugby over pints of real ale. The Poirot-moustached barman patiently serves. All red and black and vaguely distinguished bar with a tiny snug – The Library. Comfort food simmers in the window (lunch only). Till midnight (11pm Sun). (336/UNIQUE PUBS)

359 **CASK & BARREL:** 115 Broughton St. Wall-to-wall distressed wood, gr selection
D1 of real ales and mixed crowd at the bottom of groovy Broughton St. 'Cept here they prefer a good pint & the football. Till 12.30am Sun-Wed, 1am Thu-Sat.

360 **CLOISTERS:** 26 Brougham St, Tollcross. Nine real ales on tap (& 70 whiskies) in
C4 this simple and unfussy bar with its wooden panelling and laid-back app. Same owners as Bow Bar (*see above*). Basic pub grub at lunchtimes, bar closes 12midnight (12.30am Fri-Sat).

361 **CALEY SAMPLE ROOM:** 5-8 Angle Park Terr. Half-owned by the nearby (inde-
A4 pendent) Caledonian Brewery, the CSR sells all the expected Caledonian real ales and a couple of guests besides. A neighbourhood bar most of the time, a haven for home and away fans before and after games at Tynecastle/ Murrayfield. Basic pub lunches Mon-Fri, drink served till 12midnight Sun-Thu, 1am Fri-Sat.

362 **CALEDONIAN BEER FESTIVAL:** An annual event held around the first w/end
A4 in June at Edin's own – and independent – Caledonian Brewery, a red-brick Victorian pile at 42 Slateford Rd (on rt-hand side going out of town). It's a gr site, 50 real ales, food and music (esp jazz) on Fri & Sat evenings and Sun afternoon in a marquee and the brewery's own 'Festival Hall', a refurbed barley store. See local press for details or call 623 8066. The 'Festival Hall' also hosts ceilidhs. (477/CEILIDHS)

Also see GASTROPUBS, p. 35. These below are not so high-falutin foodwise, but nevertheless are worth going to for food as well as drink.

363 **STARBANK INN:** 552 4141. 64 Laverockbank Rd, the seafront rd in Newhaven.
xC1 Long-est family pub with real ales (352/REAL ALE PUBS) and excl value food, with big helpings. Gr seafood platter as well as mince 'n' tatties. 7 days lunch and dinner LO 9pm (Sun all day menu). Bar 11pm, midnight w/ends.

364 **OLD CHAIN PIER:** 552 1233. 1 Trinity Cres, on the Forth just W of Newhaven
xD1 Harbour. Rt on the waterfront nr Starbank (above), both nr Ocean Terminal. Well-kept real ale, gr bar snacks (Stilton with oatcakes, interesting toasties) and excellent-value bar meals. Some delays at busy times so be prepared to watch the sunset. LO food 9.45pm. Bar 11pm, 12midnight Thu-Sat.

365 **SHEEP'S HEID:** 656 6951. Causeway, Duddingston Village. An 18th-century
xE4 coaching inn 10km from centre behind Arthur's Seat and reached most easily through the Queen's Park. OK grub incl alfresco dining when poss. The village and the nearby wildfowl loch should be strolled around if you have time. Atmos rather than food is why we go. Food Lunch & 6.30-8pm, bar till 12.

366 **CRAMOND INN, CRAMOND VILLAGE:** 336 2035. Go west and down to the
xA1 sea. Appeal mainly as part of a stroll on the front (412/WALKS) but low ceilings, log fires, real ales make this a good escape from the city. Lotsa fish. Can snack or pack. Some complaints of late. More reports, please. Lunch and LO 9.30pm, 7 days. Bar open 11pm (12 w/ends).

367 **BENNET'S:** 229 5143. 8 Leven St, next to the King's Theatre. An Edin standby,
C4 listed for several reasons (331/UNIQUE PUBS), not least for its honest-to-goodness (and cheap) pub lunch. À la carte (sausage, fish, steak pie, etc.) and daily specials under the enormous mirrors. Lunch only, 12noon-2pm.

368 **THE ABBOTSFORD:** 225 5276. 3 Rose St. A doughty remnant of Rose St drink-
C2 ing days of yore, and still the best pub lunch nr Princes St. Fancier than it used to be but still grills and bread & butter pudding. Huge portions. Restau upstairs serves food in evening too – LO 9.45pm. Bar till 11pm. Cl Sun.

369 **NEGOCIANTS:** 225 6313. 45-47 Lothian St. (Pron 'Nigoshunts' by locals.)
D3 Mirrors, food, space and shooters (non-lethal variety) upstairs; dancefloor, DJs (every night), drink and more drink down. Range of clients from civilised bagel-nibblers mid-morning to dance fiends in the wee small hrs. Zanier and less pretentious than Iguana next door,– but just as studenty. Table service lacks pace – but hey! LO food 2.30am & that's worth remembering (301/LATE NIGHT RESTAUS). Bar 9am-3am daily.

OUTSIDE TOWN

370 **THE BRIDGE INN/THE POP INN, RATHO, W LOTHIAN:** 333 1320. 16km W of
MAP 3 centre via A71, turning rt opp Dalmahoy Golf Club. Large choice of comfort-
C4 ing food in canalside setting. Has won various awards, incl accolades for its kids' menu. Restau, bar food and canal cruises with nosh. Pop Inn 12noon-9pm daily. Restau lunch daily and LO 9pm Mon-Sat. Bar till 11pm, 12midnight Fri-Sat.

371 **THE (CAFÉ) HUB:** 473 2067. Castlehill. The café-bar of the International
C3 Festival Centre much improved for food 2003 & a gr enclosed terrace for people-watching. Brollies & heaters extend the possibilities.

372 **THE SHORE:** 553 5080. 3 The Shore, Leith. Excellent place to eat (135/GAS-
xE1 TROPUBS), some tables just o/side the door, but it's fine to wander over to the
dock on the other side of the st and sit with your legs over the edge. Do try
not to fall in. From 11am daily.

373 **THE WATERFRONT:** 554 7427. 1c Dock Pl. Another v good Leith eaterie
xE1 (139/GASTROPUBS) but with waterside tables and adj pontoon for those who
fancy a float. Gr wine list. From 12noon Mon-Sat, 12.30pm Sun.

374 **PEAR TREE:** 667 7533. 38 W Nicholson St. Adj to parts of Edin Univ so real stu-
D4 dent style with big (surprisingly floral) beer gdn and refectory-style food.
From noon Mon-Sat, 12.30pm Sun. Round the corner on main drag, the
opportunistically named **HUMAN BE-IN** spills out onto the wide pavement.

375 **THE OUTHOUSE:** 557 6668. 12a Broughton St Lane. Large enclosed patio out
D2 back, home to summer Sun afternoon barbecues. No view except of other
people. (381/STYLE BARS)

376 **THE PLEASANCE:** In The Pleasance. Open during the Festival only, this is one
E3 of the major Fringe venues, and has a large open courtyard. If you're here,
you're on the Fringe, so to speak.

377 **POPROKIT** 556 4272. 2 Picardy Pl. Catwalk café becomes sidewalk café in
D1 warm weather. Busy corner on major r/bout, but also the apex of the pink triangle and a traffic light system that never seems to go green so big people-
watching potential. (389/STYLE BARS)

General locations: **GREENSIDE PL** (**THEATRE ROYAL** and **CAFÉ HABANA**),
bars in **THE GRASSMARKET,** and **NEGOCIANTS** (369/PUBS WITH GOOD FOOD)
on **LOTHIAN ST.** All make a stab at pavement café culture when the sun's out.

THE BEST STYLE BARS

378 ✓ **OPAL LOUNGE:** 226 2275. 51a George St. Basement in Edin's fashion mile
C2 ✓ for latest and most ambitious 'lifestyle' project from the indigo yard stable (see below). Sunken and sexy lounges incl dancefloor and restau (fusion
menu tho not what they do best). Gr staff know how to serve cocktails. Big
door presence but Wills with St Andrews mates is a regular. Admn and queue
after 10pm. Open till 3am 7 days (food till 10pm).

379 ✓ **HALO:** 539 8500. 3 Melville Pl. Gt food till 4pm, then cool W End bar to
B3 ✓ hang out in with music & stuff. Report: 140/GASTROPUBS.

380 **FISHTANK:** 225 5364. 16a Queen St. Basement cellars nr corner with Hanover
C2 St made light with white walls & eponymous fish tank. Not the suity after-
work crowd like many on this page. More like **POND** life (see below). Usually
open.

381 **THE OUTHOUSE:** 557 6668. 12a Broughton St Lane. Happily mixed & unob-
D2 trusive modern bar off Broughton St 'in the lane' off the 'pink triangle'. Modish
food available 12noon-4pm for self-conscious business diners and a regular
Sun barbecue on the patio (not the greatest of views). Till 1am.

382 **PO NA NA:** 226 2224. 43b Frederick St. Still popular southern or eastern
C2 theme bar – part of the chain but not obtrusively. Functions as a bar till 11pm,
then it's more of a club with entry charge and DJs, and maybe a queue to get
in. 7 days till 3am. Cool for a long time now – who knows for how long!

383 **indigo (yard):** 220 5603. 7 Charlotte Lane, off Queensferry St. Tucked away in
B3 the W End, this spacious designer café-bar offers exposed brickwork, balcony
tables, booths and babes in blue of both genders serving good food and
drink. More Med than Mex cuisine with flexible menu, but poss too loud later
on for serious dining (141/GASTROPUBS). Bar till 1am daily. Same people have
OPAL LOUNGE (*above*) & **RICK'S** (*below*).

384 **RICK'S:** 622 7800. 55a Frederick St. New Town variant of the above. Another
C2 café-bar-restau but this time also with rms (64/HOTELS). Same problem with
the eating experience here as the others viz too much noise from the bar, tho'
prob best on this page. Bar service good & they know how to make cocktails.
Rocks from 10 onwards (till 1am). Also good early, ie b/fast.

385 **OXYGEN:** 557 9997. Infirmary St. By the people who brought us Baroque in
D3 Broughton St. This slightly off campus, off Grassmarket bar is cool but not too
cool – it's also the complete antithesis of The Oak next door (345/UNSPOILT
PUBS). Food improving '03.

386 **THE POND:** Corner of Bath Rd and Salamander St, Leith. Turn rt at the foot of
xE1 Constitution St past the warehouses. This bar is so cool it's the complete
opposite of a style bar, a million miles from George St (& hard to find). Run by
the people who do clubs like Soft (& formerly Going Places), Edinburgh Beige
Cricket Team and the fanzine, *Shavers Weekly*, The Pond is where you'll find the
people who don't want to be cool; they want to watch fish & swing in the bas-
ket chair. Open when you are.

387 **BERLIN BIERHAUS:** 467 7215. Queensferry St Lane. Labyrinthine bar/dance-
B3 club down W End alley. Up-for-it professional, but cooler than George St &
other chain bars. Happy hour (still happy at TGP) then louder. Mon-Sat 5pm-
3am (adm Sat after 11pm).

388 **CITY CAFÉ:** 220 0127. 19 Blair St. A true original that went from *the* hippest, to
D3 nowhere, and now back again with cool night people. Buzzing at the w/end,
downstairs the DJs play all kinds depending on the night. Pool tables never
stop. 11am-1am daily. then Sundays: 313/SUN BREAKFAST.

389 **POPROKIT:** 556 4272. 2 Picardy Pl. Corner glass box at the top of Broughton
D2 St and pink triangle for a be-seen crowd though, with DJs in the basement
open decks etc. Till 1am daily. Tables o/side but much human traffic and other
traffic besides. (377/DRINK OUTDOORS)

390
C3 ✓ ✓ ✓ **EDINBURGH CASTLE:** 225 9846. Go to Princes St and look up. Extremely busy AYR and yet the city's must-see main attraction does not disappoint. St Margaret's 12th-century chapel is simple and beautiful, the rolling history lesson that leads up to the display of Scotland's crown jewels is fascinating; the Stone of Destiny is a big deal to the Scots (though others may not see why). And, ultimately, the Scottish National War Memorial is one of the most genuinely affecting places in the country – a simple, dignified testament to shared pain and loss. Last ticket 45 min before closing. Apr-Sep 9.30am-6pm, Oct-Mar 9.30am-5pm. HS

391
xA1 ✓ ✓ ✓ **THE FORTH BRIDGE:** S Queensferry, 20km W of Edin via A90. First turning for S Queensferry from dual carriageway; don't confuse with signs for road br. Or train from Waverley to Dalmeny, and walk 1km. Knocking on now and showing its age (& true to legend takes forever to paint), the br was 100 in 1990. But still … Can't see too many private finance initiative wallahs rushing in to do anything of similar scope these days. And who would have the vision? An international symbol of Scotland, it should be seen, but go to the N side, S Queensferry's v crowded & sadly, very tacky these days (& shame on Tesco for spoiling the view from the road bridge approach).

392
E2 ✓ ✓ **PALACE OF HOLYROODHOUSE:** 556 5100. Foot of the Royal Mile. The Queen's N Brit time-share – she's here for a wee while late June/early July every yr. Large parts of the palace are dull (Duke of Hamilton's loo, Queen's wardrobes) so only a dozen or so rms are open, most dating from 17th century but a couple from the earlier 16th-century bit. Lovely cornices abound. Anomalous Stuart features, adj 12th-century abbey ruins quite interesting. Apr-Oct: 9.30am-5.15pm (last ticket), daily. Nov-Mar: 9.30am-3.45pm (last ticket) daily. Also… HS
THE QUEEN'S GALLERY: Recent addition to the foot of the Royal Mile (opp the Parliament building) with separate entrance & ticket from Holyroodhouse. By architect Ben Tindall (who also did the Hub at the top of the Royal Mile – this is better). Beautiful, contemp setting for changing exhibs from Royal Collection (opened with Da Vinci drawings) which will incl art, ceramics, tapestries, etc. Shop stuffed with monarchist mementoes. 7 days 9.30-6 (cl 4.30pm in wint).

393
C3
D3 ✓ ✓ **THE ROYAL MILE:** The High St, the medieval main thoroughfare of the capital following the trail from the volcanic crag of Castle Rock
E3 and connecting the 2 landmarks above. Heaving during the Festival but if on
E2 a winter's night you chance by with a frost settling on the cobbles and there's no one around, it's magical. Always interesting with its wynds and closes (Dunbar's Close, Whitehorse Close, the secret gdn opp Huntly House), but lots of tacky tartan shops too. Central block cl to traffic during Festival Fringe to create best street performance space in UK. See it on a walking tour – there are several esp at night (ghost/ghouls/witches, etc.). Some of the best actually take you under the st. Mercat Tours (557 6464), Witchery (225 6745) and City of the Dead (225 9044) are pretty good.

394
D3 ✓ ✓ **ROYAL MUSEUM:** 247 4422. Chambers St. From the skeletons to archaeological artefacts, stuffed animal habitats to all that we have done. Humankind and its interests encapsulated (and displayed) here. Building designed by Captain Francis Fowkes, Royal Engineers, and completed in 1888. Impressive galleried atrium (with coffee shop) often hosts dinners and parties. Mon-Sat 10am-5pm, Sun 12noon-5pm. Open till 8pm on Tue. FREE

395
D3 ✓ ✓ **MUSEUM OF SCOTLAND:** 247 4422. Chambers St. The story of Scotland from geological beginnings to Kirsty Wark's Saab Convertible, all housed in a marvellous, honey-sandstone building by Gordon Benson and Alan Forsyth. Opened in Dec '98, both it and the Royal (above) had admissions abolished in April 2001. World-class space with resonant treasures like St Filian's Crozier and the Monymusk Reliquary, said to contain bits of St Columba. Early peoples to famous recent ones. Mon-Sat 10am-5pm, Sun 12noon-5pm. Open till 8pm on Tue. **TOWER RESTAURANT** (own entrance) is on the top floor (106/RESTAURANTS). FREE

396 ✔✔ **OUR DYNAMIC EARTH:** 550 7800. Foot of Holyrood Rd. Edin's
E3 Millennium Dome, an interactive museum/visitor attraction, made
with Millennium money and a huge success since it opened summer '99. Now
within the orbit and campus of the Parliament building. Salisbury Crags rise
above. Vast restau, & outside an amphitheatre. Apr-Dec: 10am-6pm daily. Jan-
Mar: 10am-5pm Wed-Sun. Last admn 1 hr 10 mins before closing.   ADMN

397 ✔✔ **NATIONAL GALLERY OF SCOTLAND:** 624 6200. The Mound.
C3 Neoclassical buildings housing a superb collection of Old Masters in
a series of hushed salons. Many are world famous, but you don't emerge gog-
gle-eyed as you do from the National in London – more quietly elevated. The
building in front, the **ROYAL SCOTTISH ACADEMY**, reopened in Aug '03 after
a lengthy refurb. Daily 10am-5pm, Thurs 7pm. Extended hours during
Festival.   FREE

398 ✔✔ **EDINBURGH ZOO:** 334 9171. Corstorphine Rd. 4km W of Princes St,
xA3 buses from Princes St Gdns side. Whatever you think of zoos (see *Life of
Pi*, the 2003 Booker prize winner), this one is highly respected and its serious
zoology is still fun for kids (organised activities in Jul/Aug). The penguins waddle
out at 2.15pm daily over summer months, and the sad, accusing eyes of the
wolves connect with onlookers in a profoundly disconcerting manner. Open AYR
7 days, 9am-6pm Apr-Sept, 9am-5pm Nov-Feb, 9am-5.30pm Mar & Oct.
(1760/KIDS)   ADMN

399 ✔✔ **ROYAL YACHT BRITANNIA:** 555 5566. Ocean Dr, Leith, in the docks,
xE1 enter by Commercial St at end of Gr Junction St. Now finally berthed
outside Conran's shopping mall, the Ocean Terminal (incl famously unpopu-
lated shopping experience & 3 disappointing Conran food outlets). Done with
ruling the waves, the royal yacht has found a permanent home as a tourist
attraction (and prestigious corporate night out). Close up, the Art Deco lines
are surprisingly attractive, while the interior was one of the sets for our best-
ever soap opera. Apr-Sept 9.30am-4.30pm; Jan-Mar & Oct-Dec 10am-3.30pm;
Apr-May 9.30am-4pm. Booking advised in Aug.   ADMN

400 ✔ **ROYAL COMMONWEALTH POOL:** 667 7211. Dalkeith Rd. Hugely suc-
xE4 cessful pool complex which includes a 50m main pool, a gym, sauna/
steam rm/suntan suites, children's pool & play area, and a jungle of flumes.
Goes like a fair, morning to night. Some people find the water overtreated and
over noisy, but Edin has many good pools to choose from; this is the one that
young folk prefer. Some lane swimming. Mon-Fri 6am-9.30pm (cl 9-10am
Wed), Sat-Sun 10am-9pm. Sat-Sun 10am-4.30pm.

401 **THE SCOTTISH PARLIAMENT:** Front of the Royal Mile adj Holyrood & Our
E2 Dynamic Earth (above). At TGP this landmark building by Catalan architect
Enric Morales still showed no signs of opening. But it will within the lifetime
of this edn & given the controversy, delay & cost associated with it since the
first stone was laid, it should be a major attraction for locals & visitors alike, &
just possibly MSPs. I predict we will love it!

402 ✓✓✓ **ROYAL BOTANIC GARDEN:** 552 7171. Inverleith Row, 3km from
C1 Princes St. Enter from Inverleith Row or Arboretum Pl. 70 acres of
ornamental gdns, trees and walkways; a joy in every season. Tropical plant houses, landscaped rock & heath gdn and enough space just to wander. Chinese Gdn
coming on nicely, precocious squirrels everywhere. The 'Botanics' have talks,
guided tours, events (info 248 2968). They also look after other imp outstanding
gdns in Scotland. Gallery with occasional exhibs and café with outdoor terrace
for serene afternoon teas (284/BEST TEAROOMS). Total integrity & the natural high.
Open 7 days Nov-Feb 10am-4pm, Mar & Oct 10-6pm, Apr-Sept 10-7pm.   FREE

403 ✓✓ **SCOTTISH NATIONAL PORTRAIT GALLERY:** 624 6200. 1 Queen St. Sir
D2 Robert Rowand Anderson's fabulous & custom-built neo-Gothic pile
houses paintings and photos of the good, great and merely famous. Danny
McGrain hangs out next to Queen Mum and Nasmyth's familiar pic of Burns is
here. Good venue for photo exhibs, beautiful atrium with star-flecked ceiling &
frieze of (mainly) men in Scottish history from a Stone-Age chief to Carlyle.
Splendid. Gr café (274/BEST TEAROOMS). Mon-Sat 10am-5pm, 7pm on Thurs. FREE

404 ✓ **SCOTTISH NATIONAL GALLERY OF MODERN ART:** 624 6200. Belford
A2 Rd. Betw Queensferry Rd and Dean Village (nice to walk through). Best to
start from Palmerston Pl and keep left or see below (Dean Gallery). Former
school with permanent collection from Impressionism to Hockney and the
Scottish painters alongside. An intimate space where you can fall in love (with
paintings or each other). Important temporary exhibs. The café is excellent
(273/BEST TEAROOMS). Charles Jencks art in the landscape piece outside is stunning. Mon-Sat 10am-5pm, 7pm on Thurs. Extended hrs during Festival.   FREE

405 **DEAN GALLERY:** 624 6200. Belford Rd. Across the (busy) rd from GOMA.
A2 Relatively new addition to Edin art and life – sexy, intimate spaces, communal
coffee shop, gdns to wander. Superb 20thC collection; many surreal moments.
Gr way to app both galleries is by Water of Leith Walkway (410/WALKS IN THE
CITY). Mon-Sat 10am-5pm, 7pm on Thurs.   FREE

406 **MUSEUM OF CHILDHOOD:** 529 4142. 42 High St. Local authority-run shrine
D3 to the dreamstuff of tender days where you'll find everything from tin soldiers
to Lady Penelope on video. Full of adults saying, 'I had one of them!' Child-size
mannequins in upper gallery can be v spooky if you're up there alone. Mon-
Sat 10am-5pm. July & Aug Sun 12-5pm. (1760/KIDS)   FREE

407 **ST GILES' CATHEDRAL:** 225 9442. Royal Mile. Not a cathedral really, although
D3 it was once – the High Kirk of Edinburgh, Church of Scotland central and heart
of the city since the 9th century. The building is mainly medieval with Norman
fragments and all encased in a Georgian exterior. Lorimer's oddly ornate
Thistle chapel and the 'big new organ' are impressive. Simple, austere design
and bronze of John Knox set the tone historically. Holy Communion daily and
other regular services. Atmos coffee shop in the crypt. Summer: Mon-Fri 9am-
7pm, Sat 9am-5pm, Sun 1-5pm. Winter: Mon-Sat 9am-5pm, Sun 1-5pm.   FREE

408 **THE GEORGIAN HOUSE:** 225 2160. 7 Charlotte Sq. Built in the 1790s, this
B2 town house is full of period furniture and fittings. Not many rms, but the dining-rm and kitchen are drop-dead gorgeous – you want to eat and cook
there. Delightful ladies from the National Trust for Scotland answer your
queries. Apr-Oct 10am-5pm, Mar, Nov & Dec 11am-3pm. Cl Jan & Feb.   NTS

409 **LAURISTON CASTLE:** 336 2060. Cramond Rd S. 9km W of centre by A90, turn rt
xA1 for Cramond. Elegant architecture & gracious living. Largely Jacobean tower
house set in tranquil grounds o/looking the Forth. The liveability of the house &
preoccupations of the Reid family make you wish you could poke around but
exquisite decorative pieces & furniture mean it's guided tours only. Continue to
Cramond for the air (412/WALKS IN THE CITY). Apr-Oct 11.20am, 12.20pm, 2.20pm,
3.20pm, 4.20pm. Cl Fri. Nov-Mar 2.20pm & 3.20pm w/ends only.   ADMN

BUTTERFLY FARM, nr DALKEITH: Report: 1761/KIDS.

DEEP SEA WORLD, NORTH QUEENSFERRY: Report: 1767/KIDS.

ARTHUR'S SEAT: Report: 411/WALKS IN THE CITY.

THE PENTLANDS: Report: 414/WALKS OUTSIDE THE CITY.

THE SCOTT MONUMENT/CALTON HILL: Report: 432/430/BEST VIEWS.

See p. 12 for walk codes.

410
A2
B2
B1
C1
D1
✓ ✓ **WATER OF LEITH:** The indefatigable wee river that runs from the Pentlands through the city and into the docks at Leith can be walked for most of its length, though obviously not by any circular route. (A) The longest section from Balerno 12km o/side the city, through Colinton Dell to the Tickled Trout pub car park on Lanark Rd (4km from city centre). The 'Dell' itself is a popular glen walk (1-2km). All in all a superb urban walk.

START: (A) A70 to Currie, Juniper Green, Balerno; park by High School. (B) Dean Village to Stockbridge: enter through a marked gate opp Menzies Belford Hotel on Belford Rd (combine with a visit to the art galleries) (404/405/ATTRACTIONS). (C) Warriston, through the spooky old graveyard, to The Shore in Leith (plenty of pubs to repair to). Enter by going to the end of the cul-de-sac at Warriston Cres in Canonmills; climb up the bank and turn left. Most of the Walkway (A, B and C) is cinder track & good cycling.   12KM (OR LESS) XCIRC BIKE 1-A-1

411
xE3
✓ ✓ **ARTHUR'S SEAT:** Of many walks, a good circular one taking in the wilder bits, the lochs and gr views (431/BEST VIEWS) starts from St Margaret's Loch at the far end of the park from Holyrood Palace. Leaving the car park, skirt the loch and head for the ruined chapel. After 250m in a dry valley, the buttress of the main summit rears above you on the rt. Keeping it to the rt, ascend over a saddle joining the main route from Dunsapie Loch which appears below on the left. Crow Hill is the other peak crowned by a triangular cairn – both can be slippery when wet. From Arthur's Seat head for and traverse the long steep incline of Salisbury Crags. Paths parallel to the edge lead back to the chapel. Just cross the rd by the Palace & head up. No mt bikes.

PARK: There are car parks beside the loch and in front of the palace (paths start here too, across the rd).   5-8KM CIRC MT BIKE (RESTRICTED ACCESS) 2-B-2

START: Enter park at palace at foot of the High St. Cross main road or follow for 1km; the loch is on the rt.

412
xA1
CRAMOND: This is the charming village (tho not the suburb) on the Forth at the mouth of the Almond with a variety of gr walks. (A) To the rt along the 'prom'; the trad seaside stroll. (B) Across the causeway at low tide to Cramond Island (1km). Best to follow the tide out; this allows 4 hrs (tides are posted). People have been known to stay the night in summer, but this is discouraged. (C) Cross the mouth of the Almond in the tiny passenger boat which comes on demand (though beached at TGP so use alternative East Craigie gate to enter estate, to west of Cramond Brig Hotel) then follow coastal path to Dalmeny House which is open to the public in the afternoons (July & Aug, Sun-Tues); or walk all the way to S Queensferry (8km). (D) Past the boathouse and up the R Almond Heritage Trail which goes eventually to the Cramond Brig Hotel on the A90 and thence to the old airport (3-8km). Though it goes through suburbs and seems to be on the flight path of the London shuttle, the Almond is a real river with a charm and ecosystem of its own. The Cramond Bistro (312 6555) on the riverside is not a bad wee bistro – its gr cakes await your return. 7 days. **CRAMOND INN** (366/PUB FOOD) is another gr place to recharge.   1/3/8KM XCIRC BIKE 1-A-1

START: Leave centre by Queensferry Rd (A90), then rt following signs for Cramond. Cramond Rd N leads to Cramond Glebe Rd; go to end.

PARK: Large car park off Cramond Glebe Rd to rt. Walk 100m to sea.

413
xA2
CORSTORPHINE HILL: W of centre, a knobbly hilly area of birch, beech and oak, criss-crossed by trails. A perfect place for the contemplation of life's little mysteries and mistakes. Or walking the dog. It has a radio mast, a ruined tower, a boundary with the wild plains of Africa (at the zoo) and a vast redundant nuclear shelter that nobody's supposed to know about. See how many you can spot. If it had a tearoom in an old pavilion, it would be perfect.

START: Leave centre by Queensferry Rd and 8km out turn left at lights, signed Clermiston. The hill is on your left for the next 2km.

PARK: Park where safe, on or nr this rd (Clermiston Rd).   1-7KM CIRC XBIKE 1-A-1

NEWHAILES HOUSE: Report 1890/COUNTRY HOUSES.

414 ✓ **THE PENTLANDS:** A serious range of hills rising to almost 600m, remote
MAP 3   in parts and offering some fine walking. There are many paths up the var-
C5   ious tops and round the lochs and reservoirs. (A) A good start in town is made
by going off the bypass at Colinton, follow signs for Colinton Village, then the
left fork up Woodhall Rd. Second left up Bonaly Rd (signed Bonaly Scout
Camp). Drive/walk as far as you can (2km) and park by the gate leading to the
hill proper where there is a map showing routes. The path to Glencorse is one
of the classic Pentland walks. (B) Most walks start from signposted gateways
on the A702 Biggar Rd. There are starts at Boghall (5km after Hillend ski slope);
on the long straight stretch before Silverburn (a 10km path to Balerno); from
Habbie's Howe about 18km from town; and from the village of Carlops, 22km
from town. (C) The most popular start is probably from the VC behind the
Flotterstone Inn, also on the A702, 14km from town (decent pub lunch and 6-
10pm, all day w/ends); trailboard and ranger service. The remoter tops around
Loganlea reservoir are worth the extra mile. 1-20KM CAN BE CIRC MTBIKE 2-B-2

415 **HERMITAGE OF BRAID:** Strictly speaking, still in town, but a real sense of
MAP 3   being in a country glen and from the windy tops of the Braid Hills there are
C5   some marvellous views back over the city. Main track along the burn is easy
to follow and you eventually come to Hermitage House info centre; any paths
ascending to the rt take you to the ridge of Blackford Hill. In winter, there's a
gr sledging place over the first br up to the left and across the main rd.

START: Blackford Glen Rd. Go S on Mayfield to main T-jnct with Liberton Rd,
turn rt (signed Penicuik) then hard rt.   1-4KM CAN BE CIRC XBIKE 1-A-1

416 **ROSLIN GLEN:** Special: spiritual, historical and enchanting, with a chapel
MAP 3   (1915/CHURCHES), a ruined castle and woodland walks along the R Esk.
C5   **START:** A701 from Mayfield or Newington (or bypass, t/off Penicuik, A702 then
fork left on A703 to Roslin). Some parking at chapel (1915/CHURCHES), 500m
from corner of Main St/Manse Rd, or follow B7003 to Rosewell (also marked
Rosslynlee Hospital) and 1km from village the main car park is to the left.
1-8km XCIRC BIKE 1-A-1

417 **ALMONDELL:** A country park to W of city (18km) nr (and one of the best
MAP 3   things about) Livingston. A deep, peaceful woody cleft with easy paths and
B5   riverine meadows. Fine for kids, lovers and dog walkers. VC with teashop. Trails
marked.

START: Best app from Edin by A71 via Sighthill. After Wilkieston, turn rt for
Camp (B7015) then follow signs. Or A89 to Broxburn past start of M8. Follow
signs from Broxburn.   2-8KM XCIRC BIKE 1-A-1

418 **BEECRAIGS AND COCKLEROY HILL:** Another country park S of Linlithgow
MAP 3   with trails and clearings in mixed woods, a deer farm and a fishing loch. Gr
B4   adventure playground for kids. Best is the climb and extraordinary view from
Cockleroy Hill, far better than you'd expect for the effort – from Ben Lomond
to the Bass Rock; and the gunge of Grangemouth in the sky to the E.

START: M90 to Linlithgow (26km), through town and left on Preston Rd. Go
on 4km, park is signed, but for hill you don't need to take the left turn. The hill,
and nearest car park to it, are on the rt.   2-8KM CIRC MTBIKE 1-A-1

419 **BORTHWICK AND CRICHTON CASTLES:** Takes in 2 impressive castles, the
MAP 3   first a posh hotel (95/HOTELS O/SIDE TOWN) and the other an imposing ruin on
D5   a ridge o/looking the Tyne. A walk through dramatic Border Country steeped
in lore. Tricky route obvious at first in either direction, then peters out, but the
castle you're going to is always in view. Nice picnic spots nr Crichton.

START: From Borthwick: A7 S for 16km, past Gorebridge, left at N Middleton;
signed. From Crichton: A68 almost to Pathhead, signed then 3km.
7KM XCIRC XBIKE 1-B-2

420
MAP 3
C6
✓ **DAWYCK GARDENS, nr STOBO:** 01721 760254. 10km W of Peebles on B712 Moffat rd. Outstn of the Edin Botanics; a 'recent' acquisition, though tree planting here goes back 300 yrs. Sloping grounds around the Scrape Burn which trickles into the Tweed. Landscaped woody pathways for meditative walks. Famous for shrubs and blue Himalayan poppies. Apr-Sept 10am-6pm, Mar & Oct 10am-5pm, Feb 10am-4pm. 7 days. (Cl 17 Nov-13 Feb)   ADMN

421
MAP 3
C5
✓ **DALKEITH COUNTRY PARK:** 15km SE by A68. The wooded policies of Dalkeith House; enter at end of Main St. Along the river banks and under these stately deciduous trees, carpets of bluebells, daffs and snowdrops, primroses and wild garlic according to season. Most extensive preserved ancient oak forest in S Scotland. Excl adventure playground for kids.   ADMN

422
MAP 3
D5
HUMBIE WOODS: 25km SE by A68 t/off at Fala. Follow signs for church. Most open woods (beech) beyond car park. The churchyard is as reassuring a place to be buried as you could wish for; if you're set on cremation, come here and think of earth. Follow path from churchyard wall past cottage. After-hrs the sprites and the spirits must have a hell of a time.

423
MAP 3
D4
SMEATON NURSERY & GARDENS, EAST LINTON: 01620 860501. 2km from village on N Berwick rd (signed Smeaton). Up a drive in an old estate is this walled gdn going back to the early 19th century. An additional pleasure is the Lake Walk halfway down the drive through a small gate in the woods. A 1km stroll round a secret finger lake in magnificent woodland. Gdn hrs Mon-Sat 9.30am-4.30pm, Sun from 10.30am; phone for wint hrs. (2240/GARDEN CENTRES).

424
MAP 3
D4
WOODHALL DEAN, NR DUNBAR: From Spott r/bout on A1 by Dunbar, go to Spott village then follow sign for Woodhall & Elmscleugh SWT car park. Damp walk to ancient woodland. Few folk.

424a
MAP 3
D5
VOGRIE COUNTRY PARK, NR GOREBRIDGE: 25km S by A7 then B6372 6km from Gorebridge. Small country park well organised for 'recreational pursuits'. 9-hole golf course, tearoom and country ranger staff. May be busy on Sun, but otherwise a corral of countryside on the v edge of town.

425
MAP 3
C6
CARDRONA FOREST/GLENTRESS, nr PEEBLES: 40km S to Peebles, 8km E on B7062 and similar distance on A72. Cardrona on same rd as Kailzie Gdn. Tearoom (Apr-Oct). Forestry Commission woodlands so mostly regimented firs, but Scots pine and deciduous trees up the burn. Glentress (on A72 to Innerleithen) is mt bike central, but gr track also to walk. Consult at **THE HUB** (01721 721736) by car park (1480/GREAT CAFÉS).

426
MAP 3
D4
✓ **SEACLIFF:** The best: least crowded/littered; perfect for picnics, beachcombing and gazing into rock pools. Harbour good for swimming. 50km from Edin, off the A198 out of N Berwick, 3km after Tantallon Castle (1858/RUINS). At a bend in the rd and a farm (Auldhame) there is an unsigned rd off to the left. 2km on there's a barrier, costing £2 to get car through. Car park 1km then walk. From A1, take E Linton t/off, go through Whitekirk towards N Berwick, then same.

427
MAP 3
D4
PORTOBELLO: Edin's town beach, 8km from centre by London Rd. When sunny – chips, lager, bad ice cream. When miserable – soulful dog walkers. Arcades, mini-funfair, long prom and pool (439/SPORTS FACS). But if we have more summers like 2003, Portobello is set for a major comeback.

428
MAP 3
D4
YELLOWCRAIGS: Nearest decent beach (35km). A1 or bypass, then A198 coast rd. Left o/side Dirleton for 2km, park and walk 100m across links to fairly clean strand and sea. Gets busy, but big enough to share. Hardly anyone swims, but you can. Scenic. **GULLANE BENTS**, a sweep of beach, is nearby and reached from village main st. Connects westwards with **ABERLADY RESERVE**.

429
MAP 3
C4
SILVER SANDS, ABERDOUR: Over Forth Br on edge of charming Fife vill (1641/COASTAL VILLS). Can go by train from Edin. Caff, cliff walk. Nice!

430
E2 ✓ ✓ **CALTON HILL:** Gr view of the city easily gained by walking up from E end of Princes St by Waterloo Pl, to the end of the buildings and then up stairs on the left. The City Observatory and the Greek-style folly lend an elegant backdrop to a panorama (unfolding as you walk round) where the view up Princes St and the sweep of the Forth estuary are particularly fine. At night, the city twinkles. Popular cruising area for gays – take care if you do.

431
xE3 ✓ ✓ **ARTHUR'S SEAT:** W of city centre. Best app through Holyrood Park from foot of Canongate by Holyrood Palace. The igneous core of an extinct volcano with the precipitous sill of Salisbury Crags presiding over the city and offering fine views for the fit. Top is 251m; on a clear day you can see 100km. Surprisingly wild considering proximity to city. (411/WALKS IN THE CITY)

432
D2 **SCOTT MONUMENT:** 529 4068. East Princes St. Design inspiration for Thunderbird 3. This 1844 Gothic memorial to one of Scotland's best-kent literary sons rises 61.5m above the main drag and provides scope for the vertiginous to come to terms with their affliction. 287 steps mean it's no cakewalk; narrow stairwells weed out claustrophobics too. Those who make it to the top are rewarded with fine views. Underneath, a statue of the mournful Sir Walter gazes across at Jenners. Apr-Sept Mon-Sat 9am-6pm, Sun 10am-6pm; Oct-Mar, Mon-Sat 9am-3pm, Sun 10am-3pm. ADMN

433
C3 **CAMERA OBSCURA:** 226 3709. Castlehill, Royal Mile. At v top of st nr castle entrance, a tourist attraction that, surprisingly, has been there for over a century. You ascend through a shop, photography exhibs and interactive gallery to the viewing area where a continuous stream of small groups are shown the effect of the giant revolving periscope thingie. All Edin life is visible – amazing how much fun can be had from a pin-hole camera with a focal length of 8.6m. Apr-Oct 9.30am-6pm. Nov-Mar 10am-5pm. 7 days. ADMN

434
MAP 3
D4 **NORTH BERWICK LAW:** The conical volcanic hill, a beacon in the E Lothian landscape. **TRAPRAIN LAW** nearby is higher, tends to be frequented by rock-climbers, but has major prehistoric hillfort citadel of the Goddodin and a definite aura. BOTH 1-A-1

THE PENTLANDS/HERMITAGE: Reports: 414/415/WALKS O/SIDE CITY.

CASTLE RAMPARTS: Report: 390/MAIN ATTRACTIONS.

SWIMMING AND INDOOR SPORTS CENTRES

435
xE4
xD4
xE1
C1 ✓ ✓ **ROYAL COMMONWEALTH POOL:** 667 7211. Dalkeith Rd (400/MAIN ATTRACTIONS). The biggest, but Edin has many others. Recommended are **WARRENDER** (447 0052), Thirlestane Rd 500m beyond the Meadows S of centre; **LEITH VICTORIA** (555 4728), in Jnct Pl off the main st in Leith complete with crèche facilities; **GLENOGLE** (343 6376) in Stockbridge, the New Town choice, v friendly. All these pools are old and tiled, 25yd long, seldom crowded and excellent for lane swimming – at certain times. Also all have Pulse centres & fitness classes. Different sessions, phone to check.

436
C3 ✓ ✓ **ONE SPA, SHERATON HOTEL:** 229 9131. Actually a separate 4-storey building behind hotel, offering the 'height' of luxury with usual pool & a highly unusual outdoor one dangling over Conference Sq; spa & gym. Exotic hydrotherapy, whole-body mud encasement & treatments for anything & everything. Emphasis on pampering rather than sport. Treat yourself to a day or half-day ticket.

437
D2 ✓ **ESCAPE, SCOTSMAN HOTEL:** 556 5565. Enter thro' hotel or from Market St. Metallic, modern health club with all facs & excl service. Low-lit pool, floor of machinery. Sexy, almost cruisy. Best to look good *before* you get here!

438
D2 ✓ **HOLMES PLACE:** 550 1650. Greenside Pl, part of the Warners Omnicentre with its mediocre multiplex & tacky restaus. But Holmes Place, as elsewhere UK, has upmarket aspirations if High St realisation. This place v clean, corporate & well – cruisy. 25-lane pool, usual machinery. No day memberships, except if you're at the Glasshouse (60/INDIVIDUAL HOTELS).

439 **PORTOBELLO:** 669 6888. Portobello Esplanade (427/BEACHES). Similar to oth-
xE1   ers above. Recently refurbed, excellent Turkish baths still there, ladies-only,
gents-only and mixed days. Phone for details.

440 **AINSLIE PARK:** 551 2400. Pilton Dr, off Ferry Rd, N of centre, 5km from Princes
xC1   St. Has serious keep-fit side but all the usual spa, sauna, steam too. Mon-Thu
xE1   7.30am-10pm, Fri 7.30am-9pm, Sat & Sun 8am-5.30pm.

441 **NEXT GENERATION:** 554 5000. Newhaven Harbour. V much part of the regen-
xD1   eration of the waterfront, this sportsarama complex in the David Lloyd stable
(in fact son of, hence naff name). Courts, gym, 2 pools incl one outdoor o/look-
ing Forth (only in non-wet weather). Not cheap, but not as exp as some in
town. 7 days till 11.30pm. Day memberships tho not chp.

442 **MEADOWBANK:** 661 5351. London Rd. City athletics stadium with courts for
xE2   squash and badminton (often booked), Pulse centre, weights room, 13m indoor
climbing wall, all-weather football/hockey pitches and velodrome. No pool.

443 **MARCO'S:** 228 2141. 51 Grove St. Labyrinthine commercial centre with aero-
B3   bic classes, gym, squash and snooker. No pool. Little Marco's will look after
your kids while you sweat.

444 **UNIVERSITY GYM:** 650 2585. The Pleasance. No-nonsense complex, v cheap.
E3   The best in town for weights (all the right machinery) and circuit training.
Squash, badminton, indoor tennis, etc. Membership required (can be short-
term) but not during the quiet vac periods. For a reasonable fee, the Fitness
and Sports Injury Centre (FASIC) is an excellent alternative to the 'take 2
aspirin and go away' school of GP. Few fake suntans or lardarses here.

445 **DRUMSHEUGH BATHS CLUB:** 225 2200. 5 Belford Rd, W End. Private swim-
A2   ming club in elegant building above Dean Village that's more exclusive than
most. Gorgeous Victorian pool with rings and trapeze over the water, sauna,
multigym and bistro. Frequented by the quality. If you get to know a New
Town lawyer, get him to sign you in as a guest.

446 **BALMORAL SPA, BALMORAL HOTEL:** 556 2414. Health club for residents
D2   (47/HOTELS), members and visitors (half-day tickets). Pool, sauna, steam, gym.

GOLF COURSES

*There are several municipal courses (see phone directory under City of Edin
Council) and nearby, esp down the coast, some famous names that aren't open to
non-members.*

447 **BRAID HILLS:** 447 6666. Braid Hills app. 2 18-hole courses (no. 2 summer
MAP A only). Thought to be the best in town. Never boring; exhilarating views.
xC4   Booking usually not essential, except evenings & w/ends. Women welcome
(and that ain't true everywhere round here).

✓ ✓ **GULLANE NO. 1:** 01620 842255. The best of 3 courses in pretty village. Report: 2082/GOLF COURSES.

✓ ✓ **GLEN GOLF CLUB (AKA NORTH BERWICK EAST):** 01620 892726.
36 km from Edin, worth the drive. Report: 2083/GOLF COURSES.

MUSSELBURGH: 665 5438. Original home of golf. Report: 2084/GOLF COURSES.

GIFFORD: 01620 810591. Off the beaten track. Report: 2109/GOLF IN GREAT
PLACES.

OTHER ACTIVITIES

448 ✓ ✓ **THE ADVENTURE CENTRE, RATHO:** 229 3919. S Plate Hill, Ratho.
xA2   Follow signs from the M8 and A71. Still not open at TGP – it's been a
long climb! But ambitious and exciting facility designed to appeal to Joe
Public and elite athletes alike. Will incl: urban sports prk (BMX, skateboards,
etc), air park (a kind of assault course with ropes & trusses), National Judo
Academy, mountain bike tracks, scuba-diving pool and state-of-the-art
adventure sports gym, not to mention the **NATIONAL ROCK CLIMBING CEN-
TRE** – the best climbing arena in Europe in the roofed-off quarry. There's a
300-seater restau, internet café, 220-seater theatre, corporate facs, crèche &
retail sector (incl the excl Tiso). Open 7 days.

449 ✓ **SKIING:** Artificial slopes at **MIDLOTHIAN SKI CENTRE (HILLEND)** on
xC4 A702, 10km S of centre. 445 4433. Excellent fac with various runs. The
matting can be bloody rough when you fall and the chairlift is a bit of a dread
for beginners, but once you can ski here, Vale is all yours. Tuition available.
Open 9.30am-9pm (7pm Sun in summer). Snowboarders welcome but it ain't
Whistler.

450 **TENNIS:** There are lots of private clubs though only the **GRANGE** (332 2148)
xD4 has lawn tennis and you won't get on there easily. There are places you can
slip on (best not to talk about that), but the municipal centres (Edin resi-
dents/longer-stay visitors should get a Leisure Access card from any Edin
leisure centre allowing advance reservation) are: **THE MEADOWS:** (NE corner
by Univ Library). Just turn up. Many courts; **SAUGHTON:** 444 0422. Stevenson
Dr. 8km W of city centre. 2 astroturf courts and one other. Also used for football & hockey, so phone to book; **CRAIGLOCKHART:** 444 1969. Colinton Rd.
8km SW of centre via Morningside and Colinton Rd. 6 indoor courts, 7 outdoor
and a 'centre court' – best to check/book by phone. Other separate sports facs
incl squash, badminton and gym, 443 0101. Centre open Mon-Thu 9am-11pm,
Fri 10am-11 pm, Sat-Sun 9am-10.30pm.

451 **WORLD OF FOOTBALL:** 443 0404. Part of the 'Newmarket Leisure Village'
xA4 complex at the Corn Exchange, off Chesser Avenue. Newest of its type. 8 covered pitches. Can be booked between 9am-10.30pm daily.

452 **PONY-TREKKING: LASSWADE RIDING SCHOOL:** 663 7676. Lasswade exit
xE4 from city bypass then A768, rt to Loanhead 1km and left to end of Kevock Rd.
Full hacking and trekking facs and courses for all standards and ages.

453 **PENTLAND HILLS TREKKING CENTRE:** 01968 661095. At Carlops on A702
xE4 (25km from town) has sturdy, steady Icelandic horses who will bear you good-
naturedly into the hills. Exhilarating stuff. Cl Thur.

454 **ICE-SKATING: MURRAYFIELD ICE RINK:** 337 6933. Riversdale Cres, just off
xA3 main Glas Rd nr zoo. Cheap, cheerful and chilly. It has been here forever and
feels like a gr 1950s B movie … go round! Sessions daily from 2.30pm. Also …
WINTER WONDERLAND: E Princes St Gardens. Big open-air ice rink in the
gdns below the Scott Monument. Open late Nov-early Jan. 7 days. Mass fun!

455 **ALIEN ROCK:** 552 7211. Old St Andrew's Church, Pier Pl, Newhaven. Indoor
xD1 rock climbing in a converted kirk. Laid back atmos, bouldering rm and interesting 12m walls of various gnarliness to scoot up. Daily; phone for sessions.
Have a pint after in **THE STARBANK** or **THE OLD CHAIN PIER** nearby
(363/364/PUB FOOD).

THE BEST SMALL GALLERIES

456
E2
✓ ✓ **INGLEBY GALLERY:** 556 4441. 6 Calton Terr. Important chic gallery in a private house backing onto Calton Hill. Often shows work by significant contemporary UK artists, eg Scotland's Callum Innes & Alison Watt.

457
D3
✓ ✓ **THE FRUITMARKET GALLERY:** 225 2383. Market St opp City Art Centre. Under new direction, a smaller, warehousey space for contemporary work, retrospectives, installations, this is the space to watch. Excl bookshop. Always interesting. Café (276/BEST TEAROOMS) highly recommended for meeting & eating & once again watching the world go by.

458
D1
✓ **doggerfisher:** 558 7110. 11 Gayfield Sq. Susanna Beaumont's vital-to-Edin gallery in a converted garage in the heart of the 'East Village'. Not much wall space but always challenging new work. W/end viewing. Good openings.

459
C1
✓ **OPEN EYE GALLERY:** 557 1020 and **i2** (558 9872), both at 34 Abercromby Pl. Excellent 2 galleries in residential part of New Town. Always worth checking out for accessible contemporary painting and ceramics. Almost too accessible (take cheque book) – Tom Wilson will know what you want.

460
D1
✓ **THE PRINTMAKERS' WORKSHOP AND GALLERY:** 557 2479. 23 Union St, off Leith Walk nr London Rd r/bout. Workshops that you can look over. Exhibs of work by contemporary printmakers and shop where prints from many of the notable names in Scotland are on sale at reasonable prices. Bit of a treasure.

461
D3
THE COLLECTIVE GALLERY: 220 1260. 22 Cockburn St. Installations of Scottish and other young contemporary trailblazers. Members' work won't break the bank.

462
C2
THE SCOTTISH GALLERY: 558 1200. 16 Dundas St. Guy Peploe's influential New Town gallery on 2 floors. Where to go to buy something painted, sculpted, thrown or crafted by up-and-comers or established names – everything from affordable jewellery to original Joan Eardleys. Or just look.

463
D2
MERTZ: 558 8778. 87 Broughton St, corner of Broughton Pl. Friendly, neighbourhood (E Village) gallery, usually mixed work – a gr place to start buying art (Wed-Sat).

464
D1, D3
PHOTOGRAPHY: Edin is blessed with 2 contemporary photo-art venues. **STILLS:** 622 6200, 23 Cockburn St, with a café. **PORTFOLIO:** 220 1911, 43 Candlemaker Row, is a small 2-floor space in what used to be the city's left-wing bookshop.

ESSENTIAL CULTURE

For the current programmes of the places recommended below and all other venues, consult The List *magazine, on sale at most newsagents.*

UNIQUE VENUES

465
C3
THE TRAVERSE: 228 1404. Small but influential, dedicated to new work (though mainly touring companies) in modern Euro, v architectural 2-theatre premises in Cambridge St (behind Lyceum & Usher Hall). Good rendezvous café-bar upstairs (118/BEST BISTROS) plus excellent adj restau (105/BEST RESTAUS).

466
C3
DANCE BASE: 225 5525. 14-16 Grassmarket. Scotland's award-winning national centre for dance, in a new, purpose-built location. Classes & workshops AYR but check *The List* for dance performance in its larger studio. State of the art building, worth a visit on its own.

467
C4
THE CAMEO: 228 4141. Home St in Tollcross. 3 screens showing important new films and cult classics. Some late movies at w/ends. Good snug bar.

468
C3
FILMHOUSE: 228 2688. Lothian Rd, opp Usher Hall. 3 screens with everything from first-run art-house movies to subtitled obscurities and retrospectives. Home of the annual Film Festival; café-bar (till 11.30pm Sun-Thu, 12.30am Fri-Sat) is a haven from the excesses of Lothian Rd. Open to non-cinephiles.

469 THE QUEEN'S HALL: 668 2019. Clerk St. Converted church with good atmos
E4 and v varied prog. Your best bet if you want to go somewhere for decent
music. Café-bar & art exhibitions. Diverse (choral, jazz, art pop). Good atmos.

470 THE FESTIVAL THEATRE: 529 6000. Nicolson St. Edin's showcase theatre re-
D3 created from the old Empire with a huge glass frontage of bars and a stage
and screen dock large enough to accommodate the world's major companies. Eclectic programme AYR.

THE FESTIVALS

471 ✓ ✓ ✓ Edinburgh invented arts festivals (more than 50 years ago) &
D3 now can truly be called a Festival City. Most of the festivals listed below are world leaders.

EDINBURGH INTERNATIONAL FESTIVAL: 473 2000. Last 3 weeks of Aug.

EDINBURGH FESTIVAL FRINGE: 226 0026. 3 weeks in Aug.

EDINBURGH INTERNATIONAL FILM FESTIVAL: 229 2550. 2 weeks in Aug.

EDINBURGH INTERNATIONAL BOOK FESTIVAL: 228 5444. 2 weeks in Aug.

EDINBURGH MILITARY TATTOO: 08707 5551188. 3 weeks in Aug.

EDINBURGH INTERNATIONAL JAZZ & BLUES FESTIVAL: 467 5200. 1-2
weeks, end Jul/beginning Aug.

EDINBURGH INTERNATIONAL SCIENCE FESTIVAL: 220 1882. 1-2 weeks Apr.

SCOTTISH INTERNATIONAL CHILDREN'S FESTIVAL: 225 8050. 1 week end
May/beginning Jun.

EDINBURGH MELA: 557 1400. 2 days end Aug/early Sept.

EDINBURGH'S CAPITAL CHRISTMAS: 557 3900. 4 weeks. End Nov-Christmas
Eve. Mainly centred in E Princes St Gdns incl UK's biggest ice rink.

EDINBURGH'S HOGMANAY: 557 3990. 4 days, end of Dec-1st Jan.

JAZZ

472 HENRY'S JAZZ CELLAR: 467 5200. Morrison St opp cinema nr corner with
C3 Lothian Rd. Sounds of every stripe fill the tiny floor of this crowded basement.
W/ends and other nights. Gr vibe. Mellow crowd. Till 3am.

THE QUEEN'S HALL: 668 2019. See above.

FOLK MUSIC

473 SANDY BELL'S: 225 2751. Forrest Rd. Famous and forever. Sometimes you could
D3 look in and wonder why; other times you know you're in exactly the right place.

474 WEST END HOTEL: 225 3656. Palmerston Pl. A good place to stay or just to
B3 hang out with the Highlanders. Some trad folk live at w/ends and whenever.
(68/INDIVIDUAL HOTELS)

475 THE ROYAL OAK: 557 2976. Infirmary St. A folk institution. Locals drink in the
D3 tiny bar upstairs during the day. Live sessions kick-off downstairs every night
around 10pm with well-kent faces dropping in occasionally for the tunes and
singaround. Till 2am 7 days.

CEILIDHS

476 WEST END HOTEL: 225 3656. 35 Palmerston Pl. Edin's Heilan' hame hotel has
B3 occasional sessions of music/singing and storytelling (more like a trad ceilidh)
but no dancing. This is where to come (or phone) to find out where the others
are (occasional ceilidhs held in the church hall nearby). (68/INDIVIDUAL HOTELS)

477 CALEDONIAN BREWERY: 228 5688. 42 Slateford Rd. Ceilidhs most Sats in the
xA4 Festival Hall in the brewery 7pm-1am. Bands vary but the couple of hundred
heuchin' teuchin' punters have a good time regardless. (362/REAL-ALE PUBS)

LIVE ROCK & POP & BEST CLUBS

478 **INGLISTON EXHIB CENTRE & MURRAYFIELD STADIUM:** Rarely used, biggies
xA3 only (U2, the Stones, the Pope).

479 **PLAYHOUSE THEATRE:** 0870 6063424. Greenside Pl. Major theatre in
D2 Scotland, most regular programme, holds 3,000. More infrequent as concert
venue while they get through the musicals (apparently endless supply).

480 **USHER HALL:** 228 1155. Lothian Rd. Gr auditorium. Classier acts. Recently
C3 refurbed so looking good.

THE QUEEN'S HALL: 668 2019. See above (469/UNIQUE VENUES).

481 **THE CORN EXCHANGE:** 477 3500. Newmarket Rd. 8km SW of city centre. Used
xA4 to be the Edin slaughterhouse – say no more. It's now a multi-purpose
megabar and venue. Capacity of 2500 so you'd expect to see major touring
bands. Rough (tho not so rough) equivalent of Glasgow Barrowlands.

482 **BARONY BAR:** 557 0546. 81 Broughton St. Late Sun afternoon/eve perfect
D2 pub gig. 'Bert's band' includes many Edin musos and kent faces incl members
of The Proclaimers. A long-running Sun spot. (333/UNIQUE EDIN PUBS)

483 **NOBLE'S:** 554 2024. 44a Constitution St. Dependable bar food and real ales in
xE1 a fine-sized rm. Real mix of bands on a Fri/Sat.

484 **THE LIQUID ROOM:** 225 2564. Top of Victoria St. Probably the city's best
D3 turned-out venue for live music. Enter at st level and descend to watch bands
before they go on to greater things (or not). Also a major club venue.

485 **CABARET VOLTAIRE:** 220 6176. Bottom of Blair St. Basement bunker with
D3 selective, changing prog.

486 **THE HONEYCOMB:** 530 5540. 15 Niddry St. Another Old Town club in the war-
D3 ren of vaults below st. Deep house to deep funk.

487 **THE VENUE:** 557 3073. Calton Rd, behind Waverley Stn. Edin's major live
D3 venue at club level with well-established dance clubs among many. For live
music, it's on the club circuit, so often notable bands and the best of the
Scottish wannabes. Watch for posters & flyers.

488 **SUBWAY:** 225 6766. Cowgate, under George IV Bridge. Cavernous grungey
D3 rock 'n' roll. Fairly studenty, live music some nights, DJs on others playing
1960s to cheesy dance and chart. 5pm-3am daily. Also **SUBWAY WEST END**,
23 Lothian Rd – 229 9197. Glitzier than its Cowgate cousin. Nothing live. DJs
playing indie, 1970s, 1980s.

489 **CC BLOOM'S:** 556 9331. Greenside Pl. Late-night gay venue with bar upstairs
E1 (catch the floor show and eye contact generally). Report: 1344/GAY.

490 **EGO:** 478 7434. 14 Picardy Pl. One of the major Edin club venues hosting reg-
E2 ular big names such as **VEGAS, WIGGLE, DISCO INFERNO.** 2 floors in former
casino. Thu-Sun. And all tomorrow's parties.

491 **THE BONGO CLUB:** 558 7604. Moray House. A relatively new venue for the
E2 committed crowd who have created a club which is truly underground. No
isms here incl ageism. Thu-Sun.

492 **CAVENDISH:** 228 3252. W Tollcross. Upstairs it hosts the long-running
C4 **MAMBO CLUB** (Sat). 2 floors – African/reggae/generally good vibes music for
v mixed crowd – good for oldies who like to dance.

493 **MASSA:** 226 4224. 36-39 Market St. Probably Edinburgh's longest-running club
D3 venue. Recent revamp and an infusion of good club organisers means it's worth
checking out esp Trendy Wendy's legendary **TACKNO.**

494 **WHY NOT?:** 624 8311. 14 George St. Basement part of **THE DOME**
C3 (342/UNIQUE EDIN PUBS) – disco-mating venue for over-25s.

NEGOCIANTS: 225 6313. 45 Lothian St. Report: 369/PUBS WITH GOOD FOOD.

PO NA NA: 226 2224. 43b Frederick St. Report: 382/STYLE BARS.

SECTION 3

Glasgow

The telephone code for Glasgow is 0141
Refer to MAP B, *unless otherwise stated*

495 ✓✓ **ONE DEVONSHIRE GARDENS:** 339 2001. 1 Devonshire Gdns. Off Gr
xB1 Western Rd (the A82 W to Dumbarton). The original smartest hotel in town with refurbishment in progress. Though change in ownership, One Devonshire still engenders the design vision of its original owner Ken McCulloch (who went on to invent the Malmaison chain). Hotel occupies 4 out of the 5 townhouses on this elegant block set back from the busy rd west. Every rm is different but all have the things that we modern travellers look out for: DVD players, big beds, deep baths, thick carpets/towels/curtains. Many suites incl some doubles & super sumptuous. **TR:** 2, 4, 7, 9, 14 if you're Pavarotti-rich or just celebrating. Gordon Ramsay's Amaryllis restau a foodie experience in itself (539/BEST RESTAUS). 39RMS JAN-DEC T/T PETS CC KIDS LOTS

496 ✓ **RADISSON SAS:** 204 3333. 301 Argyle St. Bold, brash newcomer in
C4 emerging W end of Argyle St. Frontage makes major modernist statement, lifts the coolest in town. Leaning to minimalist, but rms have all you need. 2 restaus: **TAPAELL'YA** (634/SPANISH RESTAUS) more fun than Collage. **TR:** The 'Apartment' on the 6th (top) floor & corner suites on floors below. Fitness facs c/o LA Leisure Club in basement incl a pool. No parking. 247 RMS JAN-DEC T/T XPETS CC KIDS LOTS

497 ✓ **THE ARTHOUSE HOTEL:** 221 6789. 129 Bath St (style bar street), nr
D3 Sauchiehall Centre and above Sarti (584/ITALIAN RESTAUS), so gr coffee downstairs. Smart contemp town-house hotel with wide, tiled stairwell and funky lift to 3 floors of individual rms (so size, views & noise levels vary a lot). Fab gold embossed wallpaper in the hallways, notable stained glass & nice pictures. Grill downstairs has tepanyaki and other Mod Br dishes. Bar, a fashionable rendezvous for this, the sexiest hotel stopover in town. **TR:** 129 & 204/5/6 (the Velvet Suites). 63RMS JAN-DEC T/T XPETS CC KIDS MED.EXP

498 ✓ **LANGS:** 333 1500. Port Dundas Pl nr bus station and Concert Hall. Good-
D3 looking modern high-rise hotel with designs – from lofty atrium/bar to penthouse suites on 5th floor. Every surface, sink & self-conscious detail tones into Japanese. Some beds better to look at than sleep in (sunken in the suites not so good). Satellite TV/DVD & Playstations in all rms. Oshi restau on ground floor with oriental pretension (nice plates) & spa (no pool, but treatments). 'Californian cuisine' at Las Brisas on mezzanine. Langs tries v hard to please. Provided you get a rm you like, they will. **TR:** Duplexes on first floor. 100RMS JAN-DEC T/T XPETS CC KIDS LOTS

499 ✓ **THE MALMAISON:** 572 1000. 278 W George St. Sister hotel of the one in
C3 Edin and originally from the same stable and same team as One Devonshire (see above). This 'chain' of good design hotels has all the must-have features – well-proportioned rms (tho small), with CDs, cable, etc. – tho the location just off West End affords no gr views. However this is reliable stylish excellence. Cafe Mal downstairs contrasts with the woody clubbiness of The Brasseries (604/FRENCH RESTAUS). 72RMS JAN-DEC T/T XPETS CC KIDS EXP

500 ✓ **THE MILLENNIUM HOTEL:** 332 6711. 50 George Sq. Situated on the sq
D3 which is the municipal heart of the city and next to Queen St Stn (trains to Edin and pts N), Glasgow will be going on all about you and there's a conservatory terr, serving breakfast and afternoon tea, from which to watch. Bedrms vary greatly; some perhaps overdone and we think over dear but recent refurb has improved them greatly. Busy brasserie. 117RMS JAN-DEC T/T PETS CC KIDS LOTS

501 ✓ **CITY INN:** 240 1002. Finnieston Quay by the big crane on the riverside &
B4 nr the SECC. Recent block makes most of Clydeside location with deck & views. Designed by Andy Doulin of The Point in Edin (58/HOTELS), rms here are a cut above the usual tho not large. Uniformity is at least thought out. City Café on ground floor takes itself seriously as a restau. Recent price hike & improvements elevate from the economy travel lodge to the designer, almost boutique hotel. The river's the thing. 164RMS JAN-DEC T/T XPETS CC XKIDS EXP

502 **CARLTON GEORGE:** 353 6373. 44 W George St. Adj Queen St Stn and George
D3 Sq, this is a smart central option and apart from parking (a hike to car park behind the stn) a decent bet in the city centre for the business traveller. It's

more fun than that though with a huge Irish bar downstairs and airy rooftop restau up top (**WINDOWS**). Residents' lounge and drinks in rm all on the house. Good service and the usual comforts.

65RMS JAN-DEC T/T XPETS CC KIDS EXP

503 **GLASGOW HILTON:** 204 5555. 1 William St. App from the M8 slip rd or from
C4 city centre via Waterloo St. It has a forbidding Fritz Lang/*Metropolis* appear- ance and entrance via underground car park is grim. But hotel is one of the best in town with good service and appointments. Japanese people made esp welcome. Huge atrium. 20 floors with top 3 'executive'. Views from here to N are stunning so all **TR**. Cameron's, the hotel's main restau, is present and cor- rect, and the most highly Michelin-rated restau in town (though we don't agree). Minsky's bistro and Raffles bar are not so special. Shimla Pinks Indian cuisine makes a change. 319RMS JAN-DEC T/T PETS CC KIDS LOTS

504 **GLASGOW MARRIOTT:** 226 5577. 500 Argyle St, nr motorway. Modern and
C4 functional business hotel on 12 floors. Parking is a test for the nerves. Nevertheless, there's a calm, helpful attitude from the staff inside; for further de-stressing you can hypnotise yourself by watching the soundless traffic on the Kingston Br o/side; or there's a pool to lap and separate gym. Mediterraneo restau ain't bad. No-smk floors. 300RMS JAN-DEC T/T PETS CC KIDS LOTS

505 **HOLIDAY INN CITY CENTRE:** 352 8300. 161 W Nile St. Another block off the old
D3 block. In the city centre nr Concert Hall. Gym, but no pool, restau but not gr shakes. Holiday Inn Express adj is better value (25% less). Both rec here because of location & good set standard.

113/58RMS JAN-DEC T/T XPETS CC KIDS LOTS/MED.INX

506 **GLASGOW MOAT HOUSE:** 306 9988. Congress Rd. Beside the SECC, on the
B4 Clyde, this towering, glass monument to the 1980s feels like it's in a constant state of 'siege readiness'. Science Centre & Tower gleam & twinkle on the opp bank & there's a footbridge across. Some good river views from the 16 floors. The Marine Restau, in the lobby, has a good reputation and ring-side seating for river-gazing. Somewhat removed from city centre (about 3km, you would- n't want to walk), it's esp handy for SECC and Armadillo goings-on.

289RMS JAN-DEC T/T PETS CC KIDS LOTS

507 **THE QUALITY HOTEL CENTRAL:** 221 9680. Gordon St. Once (as the Central)
D3 the last word in gracious living, the elegance is now distinctly faded, although a certain atmos still remains in the sweep of the staircase and in the grandiose public rms. Rms (recently refurb) are individual, though may be small (and too hot). Many singles reflecting commercial traveller past. Corridors stretch for- ever but you're at the hub of a gr city. Leisure facs incl pool. Not so much 'qual- ity' as good value. 222RMS JAN-DEC T/T PETS CC KIDS EXP

INDIVIDUAL HOTELS

508 ✓ ✓ **SAINT JUDE'S:** 352 8800. 190 Bath St. Cool early 21st cent hotel now
C3 settled in. Upper floors more S/D & R&R than a book before bedtime (Ian Dury reference!), but both bar & esp restau (552/RESTAUS) have stood the test of recent times & are pop haunts of the Glasgow glitt & litt eratti. Rms more clever than comfy methinks, but excl service.

6RMS JAN-DEC T/T XPETS CC XKIDS MED.EXP

509 ✓ **THE PIPERS' TRYST HOTEL:** 353 5551. McPhater St. Visible from dual car-
D2 riageway nr STV HQ at Cowcaddens, but hard to get to the street in a car. Hotel upstairs from café-bar of the adj piping centre & whole complex a beau- tiful conversion of an old church & manse. Centre has course, conferences & a museum, so staying here is to get close to Highland culture.

8RMS JAN-DEC T/T XPETS CC KIDS MED.EXP

510 ✓ **THE INN ON THE GREEN:** 554 0165. 25 Greenhead St which is hard to
xE4 find (follow or get a taxi), but is close to Glas E End & Merchant City. Hotel & long-est restau on corner of Glas defining green place. Individually run & furnished with woody, tartan and even Gothic feel. Nice touches (picnic ham- pers in rms) though some furnishings perhaps a slat too far. Subterranean restau is both intimate & a group-night-out kind of place with piano player & occ singers. Carefully & caringly run. 18RMS JAN-DEC T/T PETS CC KIDS MED.INX

511 ✓ **THE TOWN HOUSE:** 357 0862. 4 Hughenden Terr. Quiet st off Gr Western
xB1 ✓ Rd via Hyndland Rd, o/looking rugby & cricket grounds. Same area as
One Devonshire (495/HOTELS) for a fraction of the price. Spacious rms faithfully restored – even if you don't happen to live in a well-appointed town house
on a gracious terr yourself, you'll feel at home. Close to the W End. Don't confuse with the Townhouse Hotel, Royal Cres.

10RMS JAN-DEC T/T XPETS CC KIDS MED.INX

512 ✓ **NUMBER 52 CHARLOTTE STREET:** Serviced apartments in superb con-
E5 ✓ version of the one remaining Georgian town house in historic (now dec-
imated) st betw the Barrows Market and Glas Green. Tobacco Merchant's
house by Robert Adam refurb by NTS. V good rates for bedrm/lounge/kitchen;
everything but breakfast. One-night lets poss, units sleep 1-5.

6APTS JAN-DEC X/T XPETS CC KIDS MED.INX

513 **THE BRUNSWICK HOTEL:** 552 0001. 104-108 Brunswick St. V contemporary,
E4 minimalist hotel in Merchant City. Bright and cheerful rms economically
designed to make use of tight space; low Japanese-style beds. Good base for
nocturnal forays into pub and club land. Restau has had mixed response, but
breakfast v pleasant. The penthouse suite is excl.

18RMS JAN-DEC T/T XPETS CC KIDS MED.EXP

514 **RAB HA'S:** 572 0400. 83 Hutcheson St. Rms above a pub in the urban heart of
E4 the Merchant City. Pub goes like a fair with good food and friendly folk so
noisy late night and if you lie in. Not a long-stay choice.

4RMS JAN-DEC T/T PETS CC XKIDS MED.INX

515 **THE MERCHANT LODGE:** 552 2424. 52 Virginia St. Conversion of the old
D4 Tobacco Merchant's house (in Merchant City) that has managed to retain the
original staircase (ask the porter to take your bags, there's no lift). Surprisingly
quiet area nr shops; in the gay zone (in case you didn't notice). Rms vary, look
first. 40RMS JAN-DEC T/T PETS CC KIDS INX

516 **BABBITY BOWSTER:** 552 5055. 16-18 Blackfriars St. This late 18th-century
E4 town house was pivotal in the redevelopment of the Merchant City and
famous for its bar (726/REAL-ALE PUBS, 739/PUB FOOD) and beer gdn,
Schottische restau upstairs & rms above with basic facs. A v Glasgow hostelry.

6RMS JAN-DEC T/X XPETS CC XKIDS MED.INX

517 **KIRKLEE HOTEL:** 334 5555. 11 Kensington Gate. In a city curiously short of
xB1 appealing & individual GHs here at least is one to rec – a tidy Edwardian
house and most notably a tidy gdn in a leafy suburb nr Botanics and Byres Rd.
Lots of pics. 9RMS JAN-DEC T/T XPETS CC KIDS MED.INX

518 **THE WHITE HOUSE:** 339 9375. 12 Cleveden Cres. Not a hotel, but self-cater-
xA1 ing apartments nr Botanics. A friendly hame from hame in this civilised crescent & a sensible alternative, esp if there are a few of you or you are staying a
week. Some quiet mews out back. 32UNITS JAN-DEC T/T PETS CC KIDS MED.INX

519 **THE OLD SCHOOL HOUSE:** 332 7600. 194 Renfrew St. Poss best option in row
D3 of GH uphill from Sauchiehall St & nr Art College. This house stands alone & is
less labyrinthine than the others – **THE VICTORIAN HOUSE** (332 0129) at no
212 (the most expansive) & the **RENNIE MACKINTOSH** (333 9992) at no 218
in which are displayed the worst excesses of cheap retro Mockintosh. All 3 are
similarly priced. Check rms first if poss.

16/52/24RMS JAN-DEC T/T PETS CC KIDS MED.INX

TRAVEL LODGES

520 ✓ **BEWLEYS:** 353 0800. 110 Bath St. In the downtown section of Bath St but
D3 ✓ nr the style bars & designer restaus, a bed block with more taste & character than most. Thought, for example, has gone into the choice of prints in
rms & halls. Loop, a credible restau on ground floor (578/BISTROS). Good accom
& facs at this price. 103RMS JAN-DEC T/T PETS CC KIDS MED.INX

521 **SOMERSET MERCHANT CITY:** 553 4288. Corner of Albion St & Argyle St.
E4 Large corner-block aparthotel with modern look befitting 'Merchant City'
moniker. Urban, understated, but no facs, bar, public spaces. Rms have
kitchens. Comfortable enough. Can book by night & share rms as you like.

102RMS JAN-DEC T/T XPETS CC KIDS EXP

522 **PREMIER LODGE:** 221 1000. 10 Elmbank Gdns, above Charing Cross Stn. Once
C3 an office block, now a vast city-centre budget hotel, with no frills and no pretence, but a v adequate rm for the night. Not a pile of charm and you would-
n't want to spend your holidays here, but its functionalism, anonymity and
urban melancholy may suit the lonesome traveller. M8 rms less quiet. Restau
& bar tho the excl Baby Grand is opp & open late (562/BISTROS). Rm rate a good
deal £50 at TGP.   278RMS JAN-DEC T/T XPETS CC KIDS MED.INX

523 **NOVOTEL:** 222 2775. 181 Pitt St. Branch of the French bed-box empire in quiet
C3 corner nr w end Sauchiehall St. Nothing much to distinguish, but brass/restau
is bright enough & Novotel beds are v good. Small bathrms. The 2- as opposed
to the 3-star **IBIS:** 225 6000 is adj. If it's merely a bed for the night you want,
it's much cheaper & hard to see what difference a star makes. They're both
pretty soulless.   139/141RMS JAN-DEC T/T PETS CC KIDS MED.INX/CHP

524 **EXPRESS BY HOLIDAY INN:** 548 5000. Corner of Stockwell and Clyde St (tho
D4 only 5 rms on the river). Functional bed-box that's still a good deal. All you do
is sleep here. Nr Merchant City so plenty of restaus, nightlife and other dis-
tractions and curiously midway betw 2 of Glasgow's oldest, funkiest bars, The
Scotia and Victoria (710/709/PUBS). Another Express adj Holiday Inn (City
Centre) but this one best (505/HOTELS).
          128RMS JAN-DEC T/T XPETS CC KIDS MED.INX

THE BEST HOSTELS

The SYHA is the Scottish Youth Hostel Association, of which you have to be a
member (or a member of an affiliated organization from another country) to stay
in their many hostels round Scotland. Phone 01786 451181 for details, or contact
any YHA hostel.

525 ✓ **SY HOSTEL:** 332 3004. 8 Park Terr. Close to where the old Glas hostel used
B2 ✓ to be in Woodlands Terr, in the same area of the W End nr the univ and
Kelvingrove Park. This building was converted in 1992 from the Beacons
Hotel, which was where rock 'n' roll bands used to stay in the 1980s. Now the
bedrms are converted into dorms for 4-6 (some larger) and the public rms are
common rms with TV, games, café, etc. Cl at TGP for renovation. Reopening
spring 2004. You must be a member of the YHA. *See above.*   150BEDS

526 ✓ **GLASGOW BACKPACKERS:** 332 9099. 17 Park Terr. Along from the SYH
B2 ✓ (*see opposite*), the funkier alternative. Mostly dorms (4-8 people) but
some twins available. Only open summer months. Close to W End thrills and
spills.   100BEDS

527 **MURRAY HALL, STRATHCLYDE UNIV:** 553 4148. Cathedral St. Modern, but
E3 not sterile block of single rms on edge of main campus and facing towards
Cathedral. Part of large complex (also some student flats to rent by the week)
with bar/shop/laundrette. Quite central, close to Merchant City bars. Vacs only.
          70BEDS

528 **EURO HOSTEL GLASGOW:** 222 2828. 318 Clyde St. A v central independent
D4 hostel block at the bottom of Union/Renfield St and almost o/looking the
river. Mix of single, twin or dorm accom, but all en-suite & clean. Breakfast
included in price but at TGP no café/kitchen facs. Games & TV room, laundry
& internet access. Open AYR.   365BEDS

Note: Both Strathclyde and Glasgow univs have several other halls of residence
available for short-term accom in the summer months. Phone: Glasgow 330 5385
or Strathclyde 553 4148 (central booking).

529
MAP 2
E4
✓ **CAMERON HOUSE HOTEL, NR BALLOCH, LOCH LOMOND:** 01389 755565. A82 dual carriageway through W End or via Erskine Br and M8. 45km NW of centre. Highly regarded mansion-house hotel complex with excellent leisure facs in 100 acres open grounds on the bonny banks of the loch. Sports incl 9-hole golf (& 10km L Lomond course – 2096/GOLF), good pool, tennis and a busy marina for sailing/windsurfing, etc. Notable restau (The Georgian Rm with 3 AA rosettes) and all-day brasserie. Many footballers & famous names have holed up here; it's a short helicopter hop to Glasg.
96RMS JAN-DEC T/T XPETS CC KIDS TOS LOTS

530
MAP 3
A4
✓ **THE BLACK BULL HOTEL, KILLEARN:** 01360 550215. 2 The Sq. A81 towards Aberfoyle, take the rt fork after Strathblane, and the hotel is at the top end of the village next to the church. Urban values, design and comforts in this notable pub/restau. Chef/prop Ian Macmaster. Clubby casual bistro & bar meals & finer dining conservatory restau (Sat only at TGP). Nice art on the walls. Garden. Rms tasteful, comfy & well priced.
12RMS JAN-DEC T/T PETS CC KIDS MED.INX

531
MAP 2
E4
✓ **GLEDDOCH HOUSE, LANGBANK, NR GREENOCK:** 01475 540711. Take M8/A8 to Greenock, then B789 signposted Langbank/Houston, then 2km – hotel is signed. 30km W of centre by fast rd. A château-like country-house hotel, formerly the home of the Lithgow shipping family. High above the Clyde estuary, there are spectacular views across to Dumbarton Rock and the Kilpatrick Hills. Rms not lavish but comfortable – only a few have the view. Reputable dining-rm strong on Scottish ingredients. 18-hole golf course (804/SPORTS FACS). New golf/health clubhouse; pool & new block of rms 2004.
79RMS JAN-DEC T/T PETS CC KIDS TOS LOTS

532
MAP 3
B5
✓ **NEW LANARK MILL HOTEL, LANARK:** 01555 667200. From Glasgow, take M74, then follow signs for Lanark and esp New Lanark, the conservation vill of Robert Owen (45 mins). Excl retreat from Glasgow, where you wake up on the banks of the Clyde and sleep to the sound of its running water. Serene spot tho' many visitors. Good walks up river (1686/WATERFALLS) and an excl restau in Lanark (10 mins), La Vigna (586/RESTAUS CLYDE VALLEY).
38RMS JAN-DEC T/T PETS CC KIDS MED.INX

533
MAP 2
E4
✓ **THE LODGE ON LOCH LOMOND:** 01436 860201. Edge of Luss on A82 N from Balloch. About 40 mins W End. Linear not lovely, but gr lochside setting. Rms above restau & wood-lined rms o/look the bonny banks with balconies & saunas, tho' Luss is not everybody's cup of tea (and sausage roll). Restau also has the view and terrace and is surprisingly good; booking may be necessary w/ends. From Apr 2004, extension to provide further rms plus leisure club with pool.
47RMS JAN-DEC T/T PETS CC KIDS MED.INX

534
MAP 3
A4
STRATHBLANE COUNTRY HOUSE HOTEL: 01360 770491. 20km N and only 20mins from Maryhill Rd on a good day (follow A81, the Milngavie rd, to Strathblane). A civilised lodging N of city with decent informal brasserie. Rms individual, reasonably well appointed.
11RMS JAN-DEC T/T PETS CC KIDS EXP

535
MAP 3
A5
BOTHWELL BRIDGE HOTEL, BOTHWELL: 01698 852246. Uddingston t/off from M74, 15km SE of centre. Main St nr castle (1851/RUINS). Comfortable, family-run hotel with an Italian ambience. V kid-friendly.
90RMS JAN-DEC T/T XPETS CC KIDS EXP

536
MAP 3
A4
CULCREUCH CASTLE HOTEL, FINTRY: 01360 860228. Off B818 in Campsie Fells, 32km N of centre via A81 Milngavie rd from Glas. Fintry is well kept and in a valley betw the Fells and the Fintry Hills. Some fine walking (780/WALKS O/SIDE THE CITY). Ancestral home of the Galbraiths with many old features, incl a half-tester bed. Dungeons converted into bar/bistro. Many weddings, so check w/ends.
13RMS JAN-DEC T/T PETS CC KIDS TOS MED.INX

537
MAP 2
E4
THE INVERKIP HOTEL, INVERKIP: 01475 521478. M8 from Glas then A8 and A78 from Pt Glas heading S for Largs. 50km W of centre. Rms above the pub in the main st.
5RMS JAN-DEC X/T PETS CC KIDS INX

538
MAP 2
E4
KIRKTON HOUSE, CARDROSS: 01389 841951. A814, past Helensburgh to Cardross village then N up Darleith Rd. Kirkton House is 1km on rt. 18th-century Scottish farmhouse that combines rustic charm with *every* mod con. Nr L Lomond.
6 RMS FEB-NOV T/T PETS CC KIDS MED.INX

539
xB1 ✓ ✓ **AMARYLLIS at ONE DEVONSHIRE GARDENS:** 337 3434. Glasgow's oldest boutique hotel (495/BEST HOTELS) boasts the Glas satellite of one of the UK's most controversial & Michelin-regarded chefs: Gordon Ramsay. Fine dining rm & less formal brasserie both under chef Colin Buchan. Menu studded with Ramsay staples. Food seductive & invariably perfectly turned out. Service from a flurry of waiters a tad overbearing in the dining rm & spectacularly exp wine list, tho inx for this level of cuisine. Brasserie: the good food for less tho not as informal as a busy brazz might be. **SD**: the Ramsay repertoire. Lunch Wed-Fri, dinner Wed-Sun. Cl Mon, Tues and LO 9.30pm. EXP

540
D3 ✓ ✓ **LE CHARDON D'OR:** 248 3801. 176 W Regent St. Brian Maule's (formerly head chef at the Roux brothers' famed Le Gavroche) Golden Thistle in French with contemp spin on Auld Alliance as far as the food's concerned – impeccable ingredients, French influence in preparation. Delightfully simple menu, tranquil rm. Glasgow fortunate to have these 2 (Amaryllis) temples to culinary excellence. **SD**: ham hock lentil salad with sherry vinaigrette. Braised lamb shank, port jus & pommes dauphinoise. Lunch Mon-Fri, LO 10.30pm. Cl Sun. EXP

541
C3 ✓ ✓ **GAMBA:** 572 0899. 225a W George St. Mellow minimalist seafood restau in basement at corner of W Campbell St. Straight-talking menu but here good fish/seafood speaks for itself so expect prawn cocktail, sole meunière. Fashionable rendezvous. Glas people love Gamba tho Michelin has failed to recognise. **SD** from chef Derek Marshall: fish soup, scallops with Thai dipping sauce & sticky rice. MED

542
A1 ✓ ✓ **THE UBIQUITOUS CHIP:** 334 5007. 12 Ashton Lane. A cornerstone of culinary Glasgow & still superb. 2-storey, covered courtyard draped with vines, off a bar-strewn cobbled lane in the heart of the W End, heaped with accolades over 30 yrs in residence. The main bit is still one of the most atmospheric of rms & the menu is exemplary – the best of Scottish seafood, game and beef and fine, original cooking. An outstanding wine list. Chip upstairs open w/ends but the simpler menu here is also avail in the courtyard. **SD**: Dishes with long list of ingredients, ea Scottish provenance noted eg the black pudding is Rothesay black pudding, raspberries from Blairgowrie. Daily lunch and 6.30-11pm. EXP

543
B2 ✓ ✓ **STRAVAIGIN:** 334 2665. 28-30 Gibson St. Constantly changing, innovative and consciously eclectic menu from award-winning chef Colin Clydesdale. Mixes cuisines, esp Asian and Pacific Rim. 'Think global, eat local'. Recent lighter look downstairs & pleasant café-bar upstairs is more continental. Excellent, affordable food without the foodie formalities and open later than most. **SD**: Ever-changing with precise long list of ingredients too long to mention here. Mon-Thu 5-11pm, Fri-Sat lunch & 5pm-12midnight, Sun 5pm-12midnight. Also **STRAVAIGIN 2:** 334 7165 (see 559/BISTROS) INX/MED

544
B3 ✓ ✓ **THE BUTTERY:** 221 8188. 652 Argyle St. Central but curious location for Glas's long-est and consistently top-end restau, refurbished & continually reinvented, the cosy old-style atmos retained. Prob the most gracious dining in the city, tho tables are close, service is unobtrusive. Dining fine from start to finish; chef Willy Deans sourcing sound Scottish ingredients, presenting them with some panache. Lunch & LO 10pm (not Sat lunch). Cl Sun/Mon. EXP

545
C3 ✓ **QUIGLEY'S:** 331 4060. 158 Bath St. John Quigley's big, v Glasgow operation on stylee Bath St with long, high-ceilinged restau upstairs, the **KELLY COOPER BAR** adj & vast bar (**LOWDOWN**) below street (747/STYLE BARS). Menu contemp Scottish with nice presentation & nae nonsense. Tapas & lighter bar menu avail in bars. Affordable wine-list. Chef: usually the man himself. In this manor & manner you have the complete Glasgow night out! MED

546
D4 ✓ **ÉTAIN:** 225 5630. The Glass House, Springfield Court off Queen St (enter by lift), but located in upper corner of Princes Sq, Glasgow's most interesting (small) shopping mall. This is a Conran restau & operates along with Zinc (563/BISTROS) in the new mallifying of our lives. Zinc may be more fun, but service and food here are excl & your lunch/evening will be an uncom-

promisingly urban experience. Chef Geoffrey Smeddle puts barely a foot or finger wrong. It all looks easily lovely! 7 days (cl Sat lunch, Sun dinner).   MED

547 ✔ **THE DINING ROOM:** 339 3666. 41 Byres Rd. *The List* says 'cosy & opulent'
A2 ✔ & could be right. Certainly small, this recent addition to Byres Rd menu takes itself & its food experience seriously. Voted New Restaurant of the Year 2003. Chef/prop Jim Kerr has created an exemplary contemp Scottish menu; service full-on in a tight space. Lunch Thurs/Fri only. Dinner LO 10.45pm. Cl Mon.   MED

548 ✔ **CORINTHIAN:** 552 1107. 191 Ingram St. Beautiful restau in a fabulous
E4 ✔ Merchant City building nr George Sq (and GOMA). Bars on same floor (706/GR GLAS PUBS), club below, but restau most impressive part. Vaulted rm in immaculate condition could be Vienna. 'Cosmopolitan, modern fusion cuisine' from chef Will Hay who also looks after the lite menu in the 'Lite Bar'. Good service – wines exp but overall an affordable de-luxe dining experience. 7 days. Cl Sat lunch. LO 10pm.   MED

549 ✔ **ROCOCO:** 221 5004. 202 W George St. corner of Wellington St and just
C3 ✔ along from Bouzy Rouge to which it is related (565/BISTROS). But this is the upmarket, fine dining and impeccable service version. Basement but light & relaxing. Excl contemp menu has the lot in the mix. Nice private dining area and smokers' courtyard o/side for post-prandial chat and coffee. Chef Mark Tamburrini. **SD:** Daube of beef with horseradish pommes purée. Lunch and LO 10pm, cl Sun.   MED

550 ✔ **ROGANO:** 248 4055. 11 Exchange Pl. Betw Buchanan St and Queen St. An
D3 ✔ institution in Glas since the 1930s. Décor replicating a Cunard ship, the *Queen Mary*, is the major attraction. *The* place to take visiting friends or clients, even if just for cocktails. Restau spacious, perennially fashionable, with fish and seafood the specialities tho fabulously exp for less than fabulous food. Downstairs has a lighter/cheaper menu, and though a bit sub-Rogano its informality is easier on the pocket. Restaurant: lunch and 6.30pm-10.30pm. Café Rogano: noon-11pm (Fri-Sat until 12midnight, Sun until 10pm). **SD:** lobster thermidor, oysters.   EXP.MED

551 ✔ **LA PARMIGIANA:** 334 0686. 447 Gr Western Rd. Simply the best Italian
B1 ✔ for many discriminating Glaswegians (convenient location nr Kelvin Br – usually parking nearby), the favourite posh place to eat pasta & vitello but that's just for starters. Main courses elaborate with Italian take on local provision. Lunch (good deal 'pre-theatre' menu). LO 11pm. Cl Sun. **SD:** char-grilled scallops with olive oil. (583/ITALIAN RESTAUS)   MED

552 ✔ **SAINT JUDE'S:** 352 8800. 190 Bath St. The restau of the boutique hotel in
C3 ✔ fashionable Bath St (508/INDIVID HOTELS) where food & service fit the urban, urbane surroundings. Bar in basement with snackier menu till 8pm (not Suns), but restau serves modern British menu in lofty, light retro-chic rm making it easy to eat here. New chef at TGP but David Sherry is still there. **SD:** market fish of the day, good steaks. Lunch Mon-Fri, dinner 7 days. LO 10/10.30pm.   MED

553 **THAI FOUNTAIN:** 332 2599. 2 Woodside Cres, Charing Cross. Same ownership
B2 as Amber Regent (*see below*), this is probably Glasgow's best Asian restau. Genuinely Thai and not at all Chinese. Innovative dishes with gr diversity of flavours and textures, so sharing several is best. Of course you will eat too much. Room v interior & rather dated now. Cl Sun. **SD:** weeping tiger beef. (617/FAR-EASTERN RESTAUS)   MED

554 **THE CABIN:** 569 1036. 996 Dumbarton Rd. Way down, follow Whiteinch.
xA2 Beautifully cooked fresh seafood and Scottish game with Irish twist incl home-made soda bread and delicious puds. Excl vegn choice. You'll probably have to linger after dinner, when Wilma, legendary waitress and *chanteuse*, does her diva thing. She and her unassuming parlour restau are Glasgow originals. BYOB (£3). Tue-Fri lunch, Tue-Sat dinner one sitting only 8pm.   MED

AMBER REGENT: 50 W Regent St. Report: 619/FAR-EASTERN.

555 ✓ **THE GIFFNOCK IVY:** 620 1003. 219 Fenwick Rd, Giffnock. Set in Glas S Side
xC5 ✓ & not London's W End, the joke is a good one (even if the name does refer
to the ivy in the doorway), but this place has big local rep & at w/ends it may be
just as difficult to get a table. Gr bistro atmos in small, busy rm; modest menu
with blackboard specials. V Scottish. 7 days, lunch & LO 9.30pm.   MED

556 ✓ **ARISAIG:** 552 4251. 24 Candleriggs. Just off main Candleriggs corner, a styl-
E4 ✓ ish, smartly presented Scottish bistro inspired by the area where Arisaig,
the village lies on the Road to the Isles (1718/ROUTES). Well sourced ingredients,
menu splits 'Sea and Land'. Good vegn choice. Big portions. Cool Scotland. 7
days, lunch w/ends only. LO 10.30pm.   INX

557 ✓ **MITCHELL'S:** 204 4312. 2 branches, W at 157 North St on the left bank of
B3, ✓ M8 at the Mitchell Library, next to the Bon Accord (724/REAL-ALE PUBS),
MAP 3 and S at Waterside Rd, Carmunnock (644 2255). Both have diff menus from
A5 individual chefs. North St is flagship & esp good for meat eaters. *The* place for
informal and v good food with a genuine bistro atmos. Lunch Tues-Fri & LO
10pm/10.30pm. Cl Sun/Mon. Southside cl Mon/Tues.   INX

558 ✓ **GORDON YUILL and COMPANY:** 337 1145. 2 Byres Rd. The eponymous
C3,A2 ✓ Mr Yuill has given up his city-centre restau & now concentrates his con-
siderable attentions on this hugely popular bistro on the corner of Byres Rd.
Mod-British menu that verges on comfort food with an easy ambience that is
just right. W/End brunches from 10am, otherwise Tues-Sun, lunch & LO
10.30pm.   INX

559 ✓ **STRAVAIGIN 2:** 334 7165. 8 Ruthven Lane. Just off Byres Rd thro' vennel
A1 ✓ opp underground stn. Off-shoot of **STRAVAIGIN** (543/BEST RESTAUS), one
of Glasgow's finest. Similar eclectic often inspirational but lighter menu somewhere betw the upstairs bar and downstairs finer dining of the mothership.
Smallish rms (upper brighter) & couple of tables in lane; book w/ends. 7 days all
day from 11/12 to 11pm.   INX

560 ✓ **NO. SIXTEEN:** 339 2544. 16 Byres Rd. Mags & Ronnie's tiny restau on 2
A2 ✓ postage stamp floors at the bottom end of Byres Rd now est as hugely pop
W End haunt – so you prob have to book. Winning combo is good bistro food,
no fuss and good value. Sublime puds. Lunch & LO 10pm, Sun 12.30-9pm. INX

561 ✓ **OTAGO:** 337 2282. 61 Otago St. Charming neighbourhood restau/café
B1 ✓ with a lighter daytime menu, giving way to the full meat/fish/game after
6pm. Mediterraneo slant & excl wine-list. Deli shelves from tasty tins to Tate &
Lyle like an art exhibit. Open 7 days 11am–10pm. LO 9pm.   CHP

562 ✓ **BABY GRAND:** 248 4942. 3-7 Elmbank Gdns. Inviting haven among high-
C3 ✓ rise office blocks opp hotel (522/LESS EXP HOTELS); a downtown-USA location. (Go behind the King's Theatre down Elmbank St, rt at gas stn and look for
the hotel.) Narrow rm with bar stools and banquettes, often with background
music from resident mad pianist. Char-grilled fish, steak & specials or you can
graze. Decent bottle of wine for £6 betw 5 & 7pm, & best late meal in town.
Daily 8am-midnight (2 on w/ends). (680/LATE RESTAUS)   CHP

563 ✓ **ZINC:** 225 5620. Princes Sq. Thro' the designer shopping centre & upstairs,
D4 ✓ the latest at TGP of Conran's Zinc café-bar chain, and adj to the more formal Étain (546/BEST RESTAUS). Grazing, groovy, busy, buzzy formula pioneered at
Mezzo now regionalised & in the mall rather than the quarter. At least the
menus are not formulaic; simple, good brasserie fare. Uncle Terry still knows
what we like! 7 days 11am, LO 10pm.   INX

564 ✓ **FRANGO:** 552 4433. 15 John St by the Italian Centre. With tables o/side at
E3 ✓ front on st & back in courtyard. Alan Tomkins' (Gamba, Papingo) Merchant
City venture & once again the quality of food & wine-list is excl – prob better
than it needs to be on a sunny day & discreetly so at night when the Merchant
City can be quiet. Mod British menu full of gr ideas. This is probably the best
casual food nr George Square. 7 days 9am-10.30pm (11pm w/ends).   INX

565 ✓ **BOUZY ROUGE:** 221 8804. 111 W Regent St. Key restau in the Bouzy
C3 ✓ Rouge chain, made by the enterprising Brown family & one of the few
chains we heartily endorse (also in Edin & Sheriffmuir, where they have a hotel

(908/CENTRAL HOTELS). An excellent bistro for eclectic, affordable contemporary food and wine. Good vegn choice. 7 days, lunch & LO 9.30pm (10.30pm w/ends). Also: INX

566 **BOUZY ROUGE SEAFOOD & GRILL:** 333 9725. 71 Renfield St. Diff emphasis
D3 but similar menu (tho' not all seafood). Beautiful room. 7 days, lunch & LO
10pm.   MED

567 ✓ **PAPINGO:** 332 6678. 104 Bath St. A bistro in a basement among many (in
D3 ✓ the streets round here) but as many Glaswegians know, food, service &
wine-list here are spot-on. Chef David Clunas' contemp Scottish menu in
Michelin & AA. A perennial fave. Lunch & LO 10/10.30pm. Cl Sun lunch.   MED

568 ✓ **THE SISTERS:** 434 1179. 1a Ashwood Gardens off Crow Rd, Jordanhill. Out
xA2 ✓ of the way but out of the ordinary, a gr modern-Scottish eaterie run by sisters Pauline & Jacqueline O'Donnell. Gr atmos, irresistible food from fine ingredients. Loyal clientele & a real find for the rest of us. Phone for directions. Tues-Sun lunch & dinner. LO 9.30pm.   INX

569 ✓ **SMITHS OF GLASGOW:** 552 6539. 109 Candleriggs. Adj City Merchant &
E4 ✓ another good food choice in bistro/brasserie style, this more 'French'.
Chef/prop Michael Smith shows flair & care that raises food from the ordinary.
Coffee-shop & lighter menu avail all day. 7 days from 9.30am. Tues-Sat till 10pm,
Sun/Mon till 5.30pm.   INX

570 ✓ **CITY MERCHANT:** 553 1577. 97 Candleriggs. One of the first restaus in the
E4 ✓ Merchant City & longevity in Glas attests to enduring appeal.'Seafood, game,
steaks' sums it up with daily & à la carte menus in warm bistro atmos. Good biz
restau or intimate rendezvous. 7 days lunch & dinner (not Sun lunch).   INX

571 **OPUS:** 204 1150. 150 St Vincent St. Office-block exterior & corporate feel
D3 inside make this a business-like diner tho' service can vary. Menu in bar & spacious dining area is Asian/fusion so some interesting combos.'Grand Dessert' a tasting & waist-expanding finale. Mon-Sat, lunch & LO 10.30pm. Bar till 3am.
This place is great late.   MED

572 **GONG:** 576 1700. 17 Vinicombe St which is off Byres Rd at the Botanics end.
A1 Seriously themed, some might say OTT remodelling of old cinema by the same people who have The Corinthian (above) & Arta (633/SPANISH RESTAUS). Bamboo-strutted dining area flanked by bars (one open non-diners) by United Designers (who did Met, London & Clarence, Dublin). Appearances however aren't everything & the food from the Easy Eating menu has been on occasion surprisingly good. Grazy, eclectic format to menu. Tibetan cool & cocktails. The West End like everywhere else, goes East. 7 days, lunch thro dinner, LO 10.30pm (till 2am 'supper' menu at weekends).   INX

573 **TUSK:** 649 9199. 18 Moss Side Rd, Shawlands (nr Cross). S Side version of Gong
xC5 (above) once again by United Designers. Buddha is still their god. Big in ambition & everything else; commentators suggested the S Side had arrived when it opened summer 2003. Well, maybe! Grazing menu incl 'supper' variant till 1am w/ends with good veggie choice, service & Glas vibe. 7 days. Lunch & LO 10.30pm (1am w/ends).   INX

574 **AIR ORGANIC:** 564 5200. 36 Kelvingrove St. Once much-applauded, media-
A3 friendly bar/café and upstairs restau in W End. Dated now (opened 99 but this was style before content & this is Glasgow); nevertheless still a cool place to eat. Food innovative fusion esp Pacific Rim: Bento Boxes (tuna best), tempura, sticky rice, miso soup – the works. Bar: food LO 9pm. Restau LO 11pm, 12midnight w/ends. (741/PUB FOOD).   INX

575 **LUX/STAZIONE:** 576 7576. 1057 Gr Western Rd. Nr Gartnavel Hospital, which for
xB1 non-Glaswegians means a long way down Gr Western Rd from the Botanic corner. Informal Italian bar/bistro & the rather more formal **LUX** (upstairs) in former station. Both have relaxed ambience. O/side tables in summer. Lux quite highly rated by some (Michelin 3 forks) & more relaxed than other city centre Mod-Brit eateries. 7 days, lunch and 5-11pm. Lux dinner only. Cl Sun/Mon.   MED/INX

576 **AD LIB:** 248 6645. 111 Hope St. Here for yonks, but cool as ever bar/restau &
D3 late-night DJ/club hangout. Narrow rm, eclectic menu, New York vibe. Food
noon-10pm, bar 2am.   INX

577 **COTTIER'S:** 357 5827. 93 Hyndland Rd. Off the top of Hyndland St nr
xA1 Highburgh Rd. Converted church that encompasses a theatre, a bar, etc; regular live music (841/ESS. CULTURE/CLUBS) and benches o/side. Restau with South/Central American menu made up of light, spicy dishes. Theatre stages range of music throughout the yr. A v broad church. (696/SUN BREAKFAST and other references.) 7 days. LO 10.30 (later w/ends). INX

578 **LOOP:** 572 1472. 64 Ingram St, Merchant City (main rd for traffic nr
E4 Fruitmarket venue) and 110 Bath St in Bewley's Hotel (354 7705). Contemp
D3 cafe-restau, light and stylish design, seems to meet with general Glaswegian approval (Bath St often packed). Menu hits all the right buttons for suits thro' to clubbers; risottos to club sandwich & fries. Lunch & LO 10.30 (Bath St from 7am for Bewley's b/fast). Ingram St cl Mon. MED

579 **ARTHOUSE GRILL:** 572 6002. 129 Bath St. Basement restau of excellent
D3 Arthouse Hotel (497/BEST HOTELS); enter through fab foyer or off st. Brasserie-type menu, incl lots of seafood and simple meat dishes alongside genuine (sit-round) tepanyaki grill (Thur-Sat). Sometimes food is not most fab, but popular spot on style street & good atmos. Good vegn menu. 7 days lunch & dinner. LO 10/10.30pm. INX

580 **CUL DE SAC:** 334 8899. 44 Ashton Lane, the main lane off Byres Rd with many
A1 restaus & bars & The Ubiquitous Chip (542/BEST RESTAUS). Perennially fashionable crêperie/diner now in Stefan King stable as Gong & Tusk (above), dedicated to serving good, simple food with flair, even wit. The atmos is relaxed and conversational, the burgers are famously good. (695/SUN BREAKFAST). All day till 10pm. CHP

581 **BAR BREL:** 342 4966. 39 Ashton Lane. Another Billy McAnnanie (Baby Grand,
A1 Cottier's) translation of an idea from elsewhere – in some ways this is his best yet. This is a Gallic bar/bistro across the lane from the Cul de Sac (*see above*). Flagstone floor, metal tables and enormous folding doors. No mistaking the Belgian influence in the cooking; fat, crispy chips served with large bowls of steaming mussels, or with steak. Belgian beers and ok wine list. Hugely pop bar in summer spreads thro back onto lawn. Absinthe can be partaken of. Daily 11am-10.30, bar midnight. INX

582 **TRON CAFÉ-BAR:** 552 8587. 63 Trongate. Attached to the important Tron
E4 Theatre, this buzzing bar/bistro has New Glas written all over it. Bar on st & 'Victorian' rm in back. Decent house wines and an eclectic menu. Not always the best grub in the city, but definitely up there for atmos and generally good vibes & good with kids. Food until 8pm Mon-Wed & Sun, 11 pm w/ends. CHP

✓ **FIREBIRD:** 334 0594. 321 Argyle St. Recently more bistrotastic than only pizza, for which it's renowned, but report: 597/BEST PIZZA.

✓ **CAFÉ GANDOLFI:** 552 6813. 64 Albion St. Last but right up there with the best. See Report: 650/BEST TEAROOMS.

583   ✓ **LA PARMIGIANA:** 334 0686. 447 Gr Western Rd. Sophisticated ristorante
B1   that blends trad service and contemporary Italian cuisine into a seamless performance. Carefully chosen dishes and wine list; solicitous service. Milano rather than Napoli. Expect to find Italians (who consider this to be one of the city's gr restaus – 551/BEST RESTAUS). Mon-Sat lunch and 6-11pm. Cl Sun.   MED

584   ✓ **FRATELLI SARTI:** 248 2228, 133 Wellington St, and 204 0440 (best num-
D3   ber for bookings), 121 Bath St. Glasgow's famed *emporio d'Italia* combining a **deli/wine shop** in Wellington St, **wine shop** in Bath St and **bistro** in each. Gr bustling atmos. Eating upstairs in deli has more atmos. Both may have queues at lunchtime. Good pizza, specials change every day, *dolci* and *gelati* in super-calorific abundance. 7 days 8am-10/11pm (Sun from noon) (601/PIZZA). The Sarti **restaurant** at 43 Renfield St (corner of W George St, 572 7000) is for finer Italian dining in elegant rm with exceptional marble tiling & wine-list. Same menu as others, but more ristorante specials. 7 days lunch & LO 10pm. To complete the pack there's a newer FS at 404 Sauchiehall St (572 3360) with t/away & b/fast counter & upstairs eating area. Under separate mngmt so some variations but still the flavour of Scotia Nostra. Hrs vary here but 7 days & late on Sat (681/LATE RESTAUS)   INX/MED/INX

585   ✓ **L'ARIOSTO:** 221 0971. 92 Mitchell St. Old-style ristorante but they'd not
D3   want to think of themselves as a tratt. Set in an indoor courtyard nr Buchanan St, this is full-blown Tuscan fare with flair & after 30 yrs still some passion. Notable for using only the right ingredients incl wild mushrooms. Dinner-dancing for those who do, this is old-style but real style. Gr wine list with good house. Lunch & LO 11pm. Cl Sun.   MED

586   ✓ **LA VIGNA, LANARK:** 01555 664320. 40 Wellgate. Not Glasgow, but
MAP 3   downtown Lanark 40km away – worth the drive for the authentic ris-
A5   torante, family-run for 20 yrs. 7 days, lunch & LO 10pm (Sun dinner only). MED

587   **LA FIORENTINA/LITTLE TUSCANY:** 420 1585. 2 Paisley Rd W. Not far from
B4   river and motorway over Kingston Br, but app from Eglinton St (A77 Kilmarnock Rd). It's at the Y-jnct with Govan Rd. Fiorentina has absorbed trad tratt Little Tuscany from next door. Fabulous, old-style rm & service, always busy. Usually seafood specials; lighter Tuscan menu. As Italian as you want it to be, enormous menu & wine list. Mon-Sat lunch and 5.30-11pm (though LO 9.30pm). Cl Sun.   MED

588   **PAPERINO'S:** 332 3800. 283 Sauchiehall St. Ordinary-looking though smart
C3   restau is better than the rest; down to the Giovanazzi brothers who also own La Parmigiana (*see above*) and The Big Blue (743/PUB FOOD). Perfect pasta and good service. 7 days. LO 11pm/12midnight.   INX

589   **ARIGO:** 636 6616. 67 Kilmarnock Rd, Shawlands. Smart but dating little Italian
xC5   joint on busiest stretch of this main drag. Spare, colour-tint décor. Some surprises on the menu. Friendly, efficient service & nice touches. **ARIGO CENTRO:** 353 6616. 85 Renfield St is more recent downtown addition. Mediterranean kind of menu, inexpensive with some integrity. Both 7 days, lunch & LO 10.30pm.   INX

Old style family-run restaurants (real Italians) with familiar pasta/pizza staples & the rest. There are many of these in Glasgow as elsewhere; these are the best.

590   ✓ **RISTORANTE CAPRESE:** 332 3070. 217 Buchanan St. Basement café nr
D3   the Concert Hall. Glaswegians (and footballers) love this place judging by the wall-to-wall gallery of happy smiling punters. Our fave too! Checked tablecloths and crooning in the background create the authentic 'mamma mia' atmos. Friendly service, totally reliable pasta 'n' pizza joint, usually busy. The antidote to Est Est Est! LO 10/11pm. Cl Sun. Book at w/ends.   INX

591   ✓ **TREVI:** 334 3262. 526 Gr Western Rd. Tiny family-run tratt with celebrity
B1   photos next to cool football memorabilia on the walls. The staff can get a bit distracted on international fixture nights. Loyal clientele lap up the pasta

(along with pollo, veal & other carne). Mama Donata does the sauces & the puds. Lunch: Mon-Fri. Dinner 7 days. LO 10.30/11.30pm. INX

592 ✓ **BATTLEFIELD REST:** 636 6955. 55 Battlefield Rd. On S Side nr Victoria
B1 Park & opp Infirmary in landmark pavilion building, former tram station. Family-run with gr pasta list & home-made puds & lovely thin bread. Small but light, this place always feels like you're on your holidays. 7 days 10am-10pm. Cl Sun. INX

593 ✓ **LA SCARPETTA, BALLOCH:** 01389 758247 Balloch Rd nr the bridge. Not
xB1 perhaps many reasons to linger in Balloch – the busy lochside (Lomond) here is not one of them, but this family–run restau is. Fave of writer A.L. Kennedy (she ain't easy to please) and now us. Gr service; integrity Italia when visiting Lomond shores (1/BIG ATTRACTIONS) out here! 7 days LO 10.30pm. INX

594 ✓ **ROMA MIA:** 423 6694. 164 Darnley Rd nr The Tramway on the S Side (& the
xC5 best option pre-/post-theatre). Expanded, v family-friendly tratt, members of 'Ciao Italia' (denoting a 'real' Italian restau). 7 days lunch & LO 10pm. INX

595 **BUONGIORNO:** 649 1029. 1012 Pollokshaws Rd nr Shawlands Cross. Ronaldo
xC5 follows parents' footsteps & recipe book. Pasta/pizza straight-up. Some home-made desserts. T/away menu. 7 days, lunch & LO 10/11pm. CHP

596 **MASSIMO'S:** 332 3227. 57 Elmbank St. Basement tratt opp King's Theatre,
C3 here for yonks but rel recent makeover has lightened it up a lot. Friendly staff serve up the usuals & some unusual Italian variants; good pizza. INX

THE BIG BLUE: 445 Gr Western Rd. Report: 598/PIZZA.

DI MAGGIO'S: Royal Exchange Sq & branches: 672/KIDS.

THE BEST PIZZA

597 ✓ **FIREBIRD:** 334 0594. 1321 Argyle St. Big-windowed, spacious bistro at
A3 the far W end of Argyle St. Mixed modern menu but notable for wood-smoked dishes, of which their light, imaginative pizzas are excellent. Noon-10/10.30pm (bar midnight/1am). INX

598 ✓ **BIG BLUE:** 357 1038. 445 Gt Western Rd on corner of Kelvinbridge & with
B1 terrace o/looking river. Bar & restau together so noise can obliterate meal & conversation later on. Lots of other dishes & morsels, but the big thin pizzas here are special. 7 days lunch & LO 9.45pm (w/ends 10.30pm). INX

599 **PIZZA EXPRESS:** 221 3333. 151 Queen St and 402 Sauchiehall St (332 6965).
D4, D3 The national chain who set the pizza standard, here in 2 well-situated and classy restaus. Always a reliable standby when pizza's the only thing you can agree on; it's sometimes handy that you can't book. 7 days LO 11pm (midnight w/ends). INX

600 **LITTLE ITALY:** 339 6287. 205 Byres Rd. Ready-made slices (well, slabs of pizza)
A1 and 3 sizes of made-to-order takeaway pies. Not the best pizza in your W End, but this is a Byres Rd fave esp the window seats, early & later. Mon-Thu 8am-10pm, Fri-Sat 8am-1am, Sun 10am-10pm. (704/TAKEAWAY) INX

601 **FRATELLI SARTI:** 248 2228. 133 Wellington St, 121 Bath St & 404 Sauchiehall
D3 St. Excellent, thin-crust pie, buffalo mozzarella and freshly-made *pomodoro*. 7 days, hrs vary. Full report: 584/ITALIAN RESTAUS. INX

602 **SANNINO:** 332 8025, 61 Bath St, and 332 3565, 61 Elmbank St and larger also
D3, C3 subterranean version at 61 Bath St (332 8025). Famous for its enormous 16" pizzas, made for sharing (there's also the 10"). You can half and half the toppings. 7 days, 12noon-10.30 (midnight w/ends). Elmbank (adj Kings Theatre) cl Sun. INX

603
D3 ✓ ✓ **LE CHARDON D'OR:** 248 3801. 176 W Regent St. Superlative French-style restau. Report: 540/BEST RESTAUS.

604
C3 ✓ **MALMAISON:** 221 6401. 278 W George St. The recently lightened brasserie in the basement of the hotel (499/BEST HOTELS) with the same setup as Edin & elsewhere and a v similar menu – based on the classic Parisian brasseries like La Coupole. Excellent brasserie ambience in meticulously designed woody salon. Seating layout and busy waiters mean lots of buzz; also private dining-rms and the adjacent Champagne Bar which serves lite bites (oysters, burgers, eggs benedict) thro'out the day. 7 days, lunch and LO 10.30pm.   MED

605
C2 ✓ **CAFÉ DU SUD:** 332 2054. 8 Clarendon St. Popular intimate restau tucked away behind St George's Cross. Mediterranean/French-style cooking from French husband and Glaswegian wife team who run it with an emphasis on the personal touch. Everything fresh and home-made incl the bread. Blackboard menu. Better book. Lunch: Fri/Sat only. Dinner LO 10pm. Cl Sun/Mon.   INX

606
D3 **78 ST VINCENT:** 221 7710. 78 St Vincent St. Based on century-old Le Chartier restau in Paris (on railway carriages in fact), this restau has more of a brasserie atmos than many who aspire tho' food more calculated than casual. Impressive split-level rm with a high ceiling and a big mural by Glas artist Donald McLeod. Stylish cuisine balancing the tried and tested with some originality. They say 'Scottish with a continental twist'. Slightly formal with an atmos of discreet efficiency. Not bad wines. Lunch (not Sun) and LO 10/10.30pm.   MED

607 ✓✓✓ **MOTHER INDIA:** 221 1663. 28 Westminster Terr. Legendary Glas
B3 restau for Indian home-cooking in a 2-floor laid-back but stylish setting & where the food rarely lets you down. Many faves & specialities by people who know how to work the flavours & textures. House wine & Kingfisher
beer but for 95p corkage you can BYOB. At w/ends & many other nights you
will have to book. Take-away too. Lots of vegn choice. V relaxed neighbourhood atmos. 7 days, lunch (not Sun-Tues) and LO 10.30/11pm. INX

608 ✓ **KILLERMONT POLO CLUB:** 946 5412. 2022 Maryhill Rd. After more than
xC1 a dozen yrs still one of the most refreshingly different Indian restaus in
Scotland. Within a hill-top restau at the Milngavie end of Maryhill Rd, you will
find courteous manners, attentive service and a clubby atmos in the front rm,
which is kept as a shrine to all things polo. The food is light, often experimental and the spices are sprinkled with care. Indian cuisine is taken seriously
though their excl Dum Pukht menu (slow cooked) is from Uzbekistan. 7 days
noon-11.30pm. INX/MED

609 ✓ **THE WEE CURRY SHOP:** 353 0777. 7 Buccleuch St nr Concert Hall & STV,
D3 & upstairs (above Jinty McGinty's) in Ashton Lane (357 5280). Tiny outpost of Mother India above, 2 neighbourhood home-style cooking curry
shops, just as they say. Cheap, always cheerful. Stripped-down menu in small,
if not micro rms. House red & white & Kingfisher but can BYOB (£2.50). Lunch
& LO 10.30pm. Cl Sun (Buccleuch St), Mon (W End). CHP

610 ✓ **SHISH MAHAL:** 339 8256. 68 Park Rd. First-generation Indian restau that
B1 still, after 30 yrs, remains one of Glasgow's faves. A major refurb brought
it back into the light. Myriad menu also completely recharged. Many different
influences in the cooking, & total commitment to the Glasgow curry. 7 days.
Till 11pm/12midnight. INX

611 ✓ **ASHOKA ASHTON LANE:** 357 5904. 19 Ashton Lane and the **ASHOKA**
A1, B3 **WEST END:** 339 0936. 1284 Argyle St. Part of the burgeoning Harlequin
Restaurants chain, they have always been good, simple and dependable
places to go for curry but have kept up with the times. Nothing surprising
about the menus, just sound Punjabi via Glasgow fare. Good takeaway service
(0800 195 3 195). Lunch & LO 11.30pm (not lunch W End Mon/Wed). Both 7
days, lunch and open till 12midnight (W End even later). INX

612 **THE DHABBA:** 553 1249. 44 Candleriggs. Mid-Merchant City curry house
E4 which presented itself as ground-breaking when it opened in 2003. It is at
least modern & enthusiastic. N Indian cuisine in big-window diner. We have
mixed feelings so not there yet with the Glas stalwarts ticked above. 7 days
noon-11pm. INX

613 **CRÈME DE LA CRÈME:** 221 3222. 1071 Argyle St. The biggest, the most flash
B3 (and God knows they love flash) restau in town – so *they* say. Former cinema,
feels like a dated disco and they even show movies (*sic*), incl cartoons
(675/KID-FRIENDLY). Frequently busy with office parties & leaving-dos. Behind
the flambé and the razzmatazz this is a restau that is run with some care and,
dare we say, determination. 7 days, lunch (not Sun) and LO midnight. MED

614 **CAFÉ INDIA:** 248 4074. 171 N St. Enormous brasserie, big on a glamour that
B3 seems a bit time-warped now, but the food is pretty good. Similar Crème de
la Crème (above, same owners). The extensive menu is busy with herbs and
spices and is not merely hot. A night on the town kind of joint. Buffet and à la
carte, Sun-Mon. 7 days, lunch and LO 11.30pm/12midnight. INX

615 **THE ASHOKA:** 221 1761. 108 Elderslie St. Confusingly, no relation to the
B3 Ashokas above. Designery interior but that old pink pakora sauce still runs
through the veins. Once voted No. 1 in the 'Best curry houses in Scotland' –
that's a matter of taste but the buffet is popular, esp the 'flame' specials. These
curries will run & run! Mon-Sat lunch, 7 days dinner. LO 12.30/1am. INX

616 **BALBIR'S:** 334 0084. 11 Hyndland St in Partick. Many fans of this fairly
xA2 nondescript but 'classic' Glas Punjabi restau. Gr detail in the dishes, some with
neither oils nor butter & lots for vegns. Real integrity here. Dinner only LO
11pm/midnight. INX

THAI

617
B2 ✓ **THAI FOUNTAIN:** 332 2599. 2 Woodside Cres. Charing Cross, nr M8, Mitchell Library, etc. Tho old-style now this is the best Thai in town (and probably in Scotland). Owned by Chinese Mr Chung but the Thai chefs know a green curry from a red. Tom yam excellent and weeping tiger beef v popular with those who really just want a steak. Lots of prawn and fish dishes and real vegn choice. Lunch and LO 11pm. Cl Sun.   MED

618
A3 ✓ **THAI SIAM:** 229 1191. 1191 Argyle St (W End side). Trad homely (if dimly lit) atmos but fashionable clientele who swear it has the prawniest crackers and greenest curry in town. Prop/chef Pawina Kennedy ensures authenticity and a packed house at w/ends. Lunch & LO 11pm. Cl Sun lunch.   MED

CHINESE

619
D3 ✓ **AMBER REGENT:** 331 1655. 50 W Regent St. Elegant Cantonese restau that prides itself on courteous service and the quality of its food, esp seafood. The menu is trad, the atmos too. Has v interior feel. Creditable wine list, quite romantic at night and a good business lunch spot. Only Glas Chinese restau in AA & Michelin. Lunch, LO 10.30pm w/ends 11/11.30pm. Cl Sun. MED

620
C3 ✓ **LOON FUNG:** 332 1240. 417 Sauchiehall St. For 35 yrs poss Glasgow's most 'respected' Cantonese, the place where the local Chinese community meet for lunch on a Sun/Mon/Tue. Pace is fast and friendly while the food, as you would expect, is fresh and authentic. Everybody on chopsticks. Even a noticeboard of Hong Kong/Beijing flights. 7 days, 12noon-11/11.30pm.   MED

621
D3 ✓ **PEKING INN:** 332 8971. 191 Hope St. Smart, urban kind of Chinese restau on busy corner (with W Regent St) but light, relaxing room. Famous for its spicy, Szechuan specials as well as Beijing cuisine; and nights on town. Lunch (not Sun), LO 11pm (w/ends 12).   MED

622
C2 ✓ **CHINA TOWN:** 353 0037. 42 New City Rd. Just off centre but nr Cowcaddens, under the m/way. Here you're in Hong Kong (almost). Endless food for lunch (esp Sun) or dinner. Divine dim sum. If you love Chinese food, you must come here. 7 days, noon-11.30pm.   INX

623
D4 **HO WONG:** 221 3550. 82 York St, in city centre nr river, betw Clyde St and Argyle St. Unlikely location for discreet, urbane Pekinese/Cantonese restau which relies on its reputation and makes few compromises. Décor dated now, but still up-market clientele; roomful of suits at lunch and champagne list. Notable for seafood and duck. Good Szechuan. Lunch (not Sun) and LO 11/11.30pm.   MED

624
D4 **CHOW:** 334 9818. 98 Byres Rd. Away from the other downtown Chinese restaus, this is the contemp, smarter & recent W End version. Broad menu incl speciality Singapore noodles & Szechuan dishes. Good vegn choice. T/away & delivery. 7 days lunch & dinner (Sun from 4.30pm). LO 10.30pm.   INX

625
C3 **GLASGOW NOODLE BAR:** 333 1883. 482 Sauchiehall St. Authentic, Chinese-style noodle bar, 100m from Charing Cross. Along with **CANTON EXPRESS** opp at 407 Sauchiehall St (332 0145), two gr fast food joints with genuine, made on the spot – in the wok – food late into the AM. Both shabby, but groovy in a W End way. 7days, 12noon-5am. (685/684/LATE-NIGHT RESTAUS) CHP

JAPANESE

626
D4 ✓ **OKO:** 572 1500. 68 Ingram St. On main st of Merchant City area, out east. The Japanese conveyor belt to the stars (local ex pop star Jim Kerr had a hand in setting this up). Reasonably authentic Japanese nibbles come past and can add up to quite a bill. Booths best. A good bet to lightly nosh when others may be booked or busy. Tues-Sun, all day. LO 10/11pm. Bar later.   MED

627
D4 **ICHIBAN:** 204 4200. 50 Queen St & 184 Dumbarton Rd (Partick). Noodle bar based loosely on the Wagamama formula. Fundamental food, egalitarian presentation, some technology. Ramen, udon, soba noodle dishes; also chow

meins, tempuras and other Japanese snacks. Long tables, eat-as-it-comes 'methodology'. Light, calm, hip. Lunch and LO 10pm (w/ends 10.30pm), Sun 1-10pm. The Partick Ichiban which is nr Byres Rd is prob the grooviest, certainly the healthiest caff in the quarter.   INX

FUSION

628 **OPUS:** 204 1150. 150 St Vincent St. Top-end contemp restau. Sound Scottish
C3 ingredients given Asian outing. Crisp service. Good & 'grand' desserts. Report: 571/BISTROS.   CHP

629 **MAO:** 564 5161. Corner of Brunswick and Wilson St in Merchant City. Bright, hip
E4 east-Asian restau transplanted not, of course, from Beijing but from Dublin. Good service, right-on wine-list. Asian beers & smoothies. Nice rice. Open all day. 7 days. LO 10/11pm (Sun 1pm-10pm).   INX

630 **YEN:** 847 0110. 28 Tunnel St in the Rotunda building nr the SECC so often busy
A4 with pre- or après-concert audiences. Upstairs café has Cantonese/Japanese/Thai noodle vibe, ground floor has more exp, more full-on teppanyaki restau with 8-course menus you sit & watch being prepared on the searing hobs. You might yearn for a quieter yen. 7 days, lunch & LO 10.30pm (cl Sun lunch).
                                                                                           INX/MED

631 **OSHI:** 333 5702. Pt Dundas Pl. The ground floor restau of Langs Hotel
D3 (498/HOTELS) with adj spa sees itself as an 'urban retreat'. It is a v nice space, ambient & urban. This reflected in menu where Euro meets Asia on almost equal split. Chef Pascale Eck sounds like a European painter or film director; he is a kitchen creature. 7 days noon-10pm.   INX

THE BEST SPANISH RESTAURANTS

632 ✓ **CAFÉ ANDALUZ:** 339 1111. 2 Cresswell Lane off Byres Rd. Basement on
A1 corner of Cresswell (the less heaving) lane where folks gather of an evening. Nice atmos encased in ceramica with wide choice tapas & mains (incl vegn). Owned by Di Maggio (Italian) chain so authentic más o menos (we mean more or less). 7 days LO 10.30/11pm.   CHP

633 ✓ **ARTA:** 552 2101. Old Cheesemarket, enter 62 Albion St. Not strictly speak-
E4 ing a restau but once you've negotiated the hugely OTT bar (usually packed), there's a cantina above (but not beyond) the mêlée. Catalan-style tapas-based menu with Italian pizzas thrown in. Good bread part of a grazing menu. You'd want to be up for it. Half-price menu Wed/Thur till 9pm. See also 707/UNIQUE PUBS. Wed-Sun 5pm-11pm, Fri/Sat till midnight (bar 1 hr later). INX

634 **TAPAELL'YA at the RADISSON HOTEL:** 225 2047. Robertson St at Argyle St.
C4 The walk-in restau of the audacious new Radisson (496/HOTELS) is not often busy so who knows if this formula will remain, but the paellas (3 of), tapas & excl Spanish wine selection are refreshingly particular in a Fusion-infused world. Mon-Fri 12-10.30pm, Sat 6-10.30pm. Cl Sun.   INX

635 **LA TASCA:** 204 5188. 39 Renfield St. Tapas bar chain thing, this was their first
D3 in Scotland. What Est Est Est has done for mass Italian food, this does for Spanish. Tapas here bear little relation to San Sebastian or Bilbao, but the ambience is OK when you're up for it. Packed at w/ends. Paella for two and some puds. 7 days, all day LO 10.30pm (Fri-Sat 11.30pm). Bar later.   CHP

MEXICAN

Glas has innumerable restaus and café-bars with Mexican choices on a menu that mixes food from all over (best to stick to the potato skins). The places below are close to genuine Mex (UK style):

636 **PANCHO VILLA'S:** 552 7737. 26 Bell St. Bright, colourful restau free of the clut-
E4   tered cantina stereotype, run by real, live Mexican, Maira Nunez. Menu in Spanish/ingredients in English. No burritos ('an American invention'). Plenty of veggie choices but you really have to try the *albondigas en salsa* (that's spicy meatballs). Mon-Sat lunch and 6-11pm, Sun 6-10.30pm.   INX

637 **SALSA:** 420 6328. 63 Carlton Pl. On S bank of river at end of Glasgow Bridge
D4   (pedestrian), an unlikely location perhaps since bright, spicy salsa lurks in a basement. Bar with rel small restau section, but some of the best Mexican sta- ples & lovely, imaginative mains in town. This place deserves to do well – cross that bridge when you come to it! Lunch & LO 10pm (bar later).   INX

CENTRAL AMERICAN

638 **CUBA NORTE:** 552 3505. 17 John St. Cavernous Cuban restau in mock Spanish
E3   rms underneath The Italian Centre, a rare example of appropriate pairing (eth- nic food & place – esp now Glasgow is twinned with Havana). Follows success of Edin version (224/CENTRAL AM RESTAUS), but this much bigger. Good at w/ends – eat, dance, get lively. Menu Central American-ish & better than you'd think (or know after a few Cuba Libres). Salsa classes Tue-Thur contribute to the weirdly authentic mix. 7 days lunch & LO 11pm (bar midnight/1am).   INX

GREEK

639 **CAFÉ SERGHEI:** 429 1547. 67 Br St, just over the Jamaica St (or the Glasgow)
D4   Br. Greek island evenings on a bleak rd heading S, a restau in an interesting conversion of a former bank with upstairs balcony beneath impressive cupo- la. In a tough world, this place has survived. Talkative waiters advise and dis- pense excellent Greek grub, incl vegn dishes. Fri is Greek party night. Lunch (not Sun) and 5-11pm, 7 days.   INX

640 **KONAKI:** 342 4010. 920 Sauchiehall St, w of M8 opp Kelvin Park Lorne Hotel.
A3   A paint job on the outside wouldn't go amiss here, but flaky façade is in keep- ing with no-frills, down-to-Greek-earth approach. This is back st Athens where the best caffs are – real, cheap, good Greek grub (incl pastas). 7 days, lunch & dinner (not Sun lunch). LO 11pm.   CHP

BELGIAN

641 **BAR BREL:** 342 4966. 39 Ashton Lane. Excl bar/bistro more fun than Brussels.
A1   Report: 581/BEST BISTROS.

642
C3
GAMBA: 572 0899. 225a W George St, in basement at corner of W Campbell St. A seafood bistro which happens to be one of the best restaus in the city (541/BEST RESTAUS). Fashionable clientele enjoy stylish setting and snappy service, as well as excellent fresh fish unfussily presented à la mode. Exemplary wine list. Unlike many, open on Mon (cl Sun). Lunch and dinner. LO 10.30pm but may serve later so check.   MED

643
A2
TWO FAT LADIES: 339 1944. 88 Dumbarton Rd. A landmark Glas restau now firmly reestablished after chef/prop change. Joanna B (food guru) complained that they didn't know where the fish came from, but there is real integrity here & everything *is* selectively sourced. The kitchen produces delicious dishes with a light touch. Lovely puds. 7 days (not Sun lunch).   MED

644
MAP 3
A4
GINGERHILL: 956 6515. Hillhead St, Milngavie. Upstairs above the chemist's at the end of the main st in this northern suburb of Glas (you are at the start of the W Highland Way), an excl but tiny neighbourhood restau. Chef/owner Alan Burns offers unpretentious seafood (meat/game options), occasionally adventurous. Those in the know know that life is easier here (esp if you don't have to drive home). Wed-Sun, dinner only. LO 9.30pm. BYOB (corkage £3.50).   INX

645
D3
MUSSEL INN: 572 1405. 157 Hope St. Downtown location for light, bright bistro (big windows) where seafood is serious, but fun. Mussels, scallops, oysters & vegn option, but mussels in variant concoctions & kilo pots are the thing. As in Edin (196/SEAFOOD), this formula is sound & the owners do know their oysters. 7 days, lunch & dinner (not Sun lunch).   INX

ROGANO: 11 Exchange Pl. Report: 550/BEST RESTAUS.

646
B2, C2
GRASSROOTS CAFÉ: 333 0534. 97 St George's Rd beneath St George's Studios nr Charing Cross. This is the caff offshoot of Grassroots (the deli) round the corner at 48 Woodlands Rd (1549/DELIS): serving proper vegn & vegan food. Nutritious, worthy – all this, but round the world dishes as vegn food should be and some simply splendid salads. Calming as well as healthy despite proximity of M8. 7 days. 10am-10pm.   CHP

647
E4
MONO: 553 2400. Kings Court opp carparks behind St Enoch's Centre. In odd no-man's land betw Merchant City & E End, a cool hangout in a forlorn mall by Craig Tannock who started 13th Note (below). Gr space with art, music, occ performance & interesting vegn food served by friendly staff. Organic ales/wines. No bullshit! 7 days noon-10pm (bar midnight).   CHP

648
E4
THE 13TH NOTE: 553 1638. 50-60 King St. Old-style veggie hangout – a good attitude/good vibes café-bar with live music downstairs. Big range menu from excellent vegeburgers to Indian and Greek dishes. All suitable for vegans. Organic booze on offer, but also normal Glasgow bevvy. 7 days, 12noon-12midnight. Food LO 10pm.

649
A3
STEREO: 576 5018. 11 Kelvinhaugh St off w extension of Argyle St beyond M8. More bar than caff, but vegan grub eg burgers, rashers. Gr selection of beers, organic wine. Food till 10pm 7 days, bar midnight.   CHP

Restaurants serving particularly good vegn food but not exclusively vegn:

THE UBIQUITOUS CHIP and **THAI FOUNTAIN**. Reports: 542/553/BEST RESTAUS.
BABY GRAND, FRANGO, ST JUDE'S, ARTHOUSE GRILL, ARISAIG and **TRON CAFÉ-BAR**. Reports: 562/564/BEST BISTROS, 552/BEST RESTAUS, 579/582/BEST BISTROS.
MOTHER INDIA. Report: 607/INDIAN RESTAUS.
CAFÉ GANDOLFI, TEMPUS, ARCAFFE. Report: 650/659/656/TEAROOMS.

650 ✓✓ **CAFÉ GANDOLFI:** 552 6813. 64 Albion St, Merchant City. For over 20
E4 yrs a definitive & landmark meeting/eating place – bistro menu, but casual ambience of a tearm or coffee shop. Bohemian, Europe-somewhere atmos. Stained glass and heavy, over-sized wooden furniture create a unique ambience that has stood the fashionability test. The food is light and imaginative and served all day. You may have to queue. 7 days, 9am-11.30pm, Sun from 12noon (689/SUN BREAKFAST). The much more recent Bar upstairs (734/BARFOOD) has added a new rm & a new dimension.

651 ✓✓ **TINDERBOX:** 339 3108. 189 Byres Rd, on busy corner with
A1 Highburgh Rd. Stylish, shiny, state-of-the-art neighbourhood coffee shop. Stuff for kids, stuff to buy. Snacks and Elektra, the good-looking coffee machine. Gr people-watching potential inside and out. 7 days, 7.45am-11pm (Sun from 8.45am).

652 ✓ **WHERE THE MONKEY SLEEPS:** 226 3406. 182 W Regent St adj Compass
D3 Gallery & in basement below Chardon D'Or (540/BEST RESTAUS): its commercial & spiritual opposite. Exhib space ie hanging as well as hanging out. Coffee, soups & picmix s/wiches. T/way & nearby delivery. Art students & what they turn into. 7 days. 7am-7pm. (Sat from 9am, Sun 11am).

653 ✓ **NORTH STAR:** 946 5365. 108 Queen Margaret Drive. Portuguese deli-
xB1 cum-espresso bar. Minimalist approach to design and product range but you always find something you must have. All home-made except bread. Yum tortilla. Can BYOB. 7 days Mon-Sat. 8am-7/8pm. Sun 11am-6pm.

654 ✓ **CAFÉ HULA:** 353 1660. 321 Hope St. Central, some say overlooked café
D3 opp Theatre Royal by people who have North Star (above). Simple, imaginative menu; good vegn choice. Live music some nights. 7 days 8.30am-10pm, Sun 11am-6pm.

655 **TCHAI-OVNA:** 357 4524. 42 Otago Lane off Otago St & round the back. A
B1 'house of tea' hidden away on the banks of the Kelvin with verandah & gdn terrace. A decidedly boho tearm which could be E Europe, N Africa or Kathmandu but not Glasgow. 70 kinds of tea, soup, organic s/wiches & cakes. Impromptu performances likely. A real find but suits not happy here. 7 days 11am-11pm.

656 **ARCAFFE:** 333 1333. 11 N Claremont St in W End beyond M8, behind Mitchell
B3 Library. Contemp dining rm (& sandwich t/away) with gr coffee-shop atmos & Italian pasta/pizza menu. Good vegn. Gets busy. Mon-Fri 9am-3pm. Cl Sat/Sun.

657 **THE WILLOW TEAROOMS:** 217 Sauchiehall St. On a balcony above a jewellery
C3, D4 & souvenir shop with a sister tearoom at 97 Buchanan St. Both celebrate the Rennie Mackintosh connection big time and under the discerning eye of proprietor Anne Mulhern, recreate the interiors of the original Miss Cranston's Tearooms he designed. 30 blends of loose-leaf tea, all manner of cakes, scones and sandwiches and now, hold on … a wee glass of wine. Mon-Sat 9am-4.30pm. Sun from noon. Buchanan St best by the way. (820/MACKINTOSH)

658 **CAFÉ SOURCE:** 548 6020. 1 St Andrews Sq. In a secret sq nr Saltmarket & Tron-
E4 gate below gorgeous St Andrews church, a secret caff with excl Scottish menu balancing old-style & new. 7 days lunch & dinner. LO 9pm (10pm Fri/Sat).

659 **TEMPUS:** 332 7959. 350 Sauchiehall St. The atrium café of the CCA, spectacu-
C3 larly refurbished 2002. Kind of like eating in a covered st. Stylish/contemp of course – the rm & the menu. 11am-9.30pm, Sun 11-4pm. Cl Mon.

660 **ART LOVER'S CAFÉ:** 353 4779. 10 Dumbreck Rd, Bellahouston Park. On the
xA5 ground floor of House for an Art Lover, a building based on drawings left by Rennie Mackintosh (822/MACKINTOSH). Bright rm more ambient than Willow Tearooms (above) and a counterpoint to the usual wrought iron, purply, swirly Mockintosh caffs elsewhere. This is unfussy & elegant. Garden views. Soup 'n' sandwiches & à la carte; a serious lunch spot. 7 days 10am-5pm.

661 **BRADFORDS:** 245 Sauchiehall St. Since 1924 the coffee shop/restau upstairs
C3 from the flagship shop of this local and estimable bakery chain. Familiar wifie waitresses, the macaroni cheese is close to mum's and the cakes and pies from downstairs represent Scottish bakery at its best. Mon-Sat 9am-5.30pm.

662
A2 ✓ ✓ **UNIVERSITY CAFÉ:** 87 Byres Rd. 'When your granny, in the lines of the well-known song, was "shoved aff a bus", this is where she was taken afterwards and given a wee cup of tea to steady her nerves. People have been coming here for generations to sit at the "kneesy" tables and share the salt and vinegar. Run by the Verecchia family who administer advice, sympathy and pie, beans and chips with equal aplomb." ' These astute words of Graeme Keiling describing a real Glasgow gem, still stand 2 editions later. Daily till 10pm (w/ends till 10.30pm). Cl Tue. Takeaway open later.

663
xC5 ✓ ✓ **THE UNIQUE:** 223 Allison St. Not exactly central, but if you're on the S-side you'll find the best fish 'n' chips in town here. Unspoiled, unaffected & unlike the University Café (above), uncelebrated. Through the curtain in the café they serve lunches, fish teas and spam fritters. Veg oil used. Old-fashioned hrs, viz 8am-7.30pm. Special 4-course lunch 11am-1.10pm: £2.50.

664
xE4 ✓ **COIA'S CAFÉ:** 473 Duke St. Since 1928, supplying this E End high st with ice cream, gr deal breakfasts and the kind of comforting lunch (they might call it dinner) café-bar places just cannot do. There's a telly in the corner lots of Glas chat at the tables. Sit-in or takeaway. Sweeties of all sorts; and Havana cigars. 7 days, 7.30am-9pm (LO 7.30pm); Sun from 10am.

665 ✓ **BROOKLYN CAFÉ:** 632 3427. 21 Minard Rd, corner of Frankfort St off Pollokshaws Rd. Whatever fancy café-bar Stefan King throws up on the S Side (573/BISTROS, Tusk), this caff here over 70 yrs will probably outlive the lot of them. More tratt perhaps than caff with pasta/pizza, 3 risottos, 6 salads, excl puds & gr ice-cream. Recent refurb but still & forever the real thing! 7 days 9am-10pm (Sat 11pm). Sun from 10am.

666 **GROSVENOR CAFÉ:** 31 Ashton Lane, behind Byres Rd nr Hillhead Stn. For
A1 over 30 yrs they've been cramming us in but 2 makeovers later the original cheery caff has become a bit more like every other café (with an 'é'). Still, nostalgia alone keeps it here & its Ashton Lane regulars happy. 7 days, hrs vary.

667 **CAFE D'JACONELLI:** 570 Maryhill Rd nr the Queen's Cross Church (815/MACK-
xC1 INTOSH). Neighbourhood caff with toasties, macaroni cheese and award-winning ice-cream to go that's been here for ever. This is the disappearing Glasgow, but used often as a film location (*Trainspotting, Carla's Song*). Get yourself a banquette. 7 days, 9am-10pm.

668 **CHOCOLATE THERAPY:** 632 5665. Abbot St off Pollokshaws Rd at Shawlands
xC5 Cross. Nr Brooklyn above but v different. A caff in a shack that celebrates chocolate with hot & cold varieties & ganache all over the place. Snacks, soups, b/fast, pancakes. Gr idea. Ok, the S Side is getting better! Daytime only.

669 **KOG:** 85 Parnie St. Backstreet of Merchant City, the interesting ungentrified bit
E4 nr Transmission Gallery. Boho coffee shop & hangout with free refills, homemade food, Cream o' Galloway ice-cream. Some live music. 9am-5pm (Fri till 11pm). Cl Sun.

670 **ALLAN'S SNACK BAR:** 6 Storie St, Paisley. Off the High St, a chip shop with
xA5 classic greasy spoon adj and a chips-with-everything menu in a Paisley days-gone-by atmos. Happy waitresses. Mon-Thu 11am-7pm, Fri-Sat 11am-8pm. Cl Sun.

671 **JACK McPHEE'S:** 285 Byres Rd. Jack McPhee Fresh from the Sea it says above
A1 the door of this trad tho' traded-up fish 'n' chip shop caff still frying up among the olive groves of Byres Rd. Mixed platters the thing, but a US-style Scottish b/fast (hash browns *and* potato scones) must be considered. 7 days 9am-10pm.

KID-FRIENDLY PLACES

672 **DI MAGGIO'S:** 334 8560. 61 Ruthven Lane, off Byres Rd, W End; 632 4194, 1038
A1 Pollokshaws Rd, on a busy corner S of the river; and 248 2111, 21 Royal
xC5 Exchange Sq. 'Our family serving your family' they say & they do. Bustling,
D4 friendly pizza joints with good Italian attitude to bairns. There's a choice to
defy the most finicky kid. High chairs, special menu. In summer, o/side tables
in Exchange Sq so the kids can run around. 7 days.

673 **TGI FRIDAY'S:** 221 6996. 113 Buchanan St. The Glas branch of the national
D3 chain adored by kids because of the way they get fussed over 2 menus (up to
& over 6). The food is from everywhere via America and when added, free-
hand, to the crayon drawings on the tablecloth, can look quite spectacular.
Huge range of cocktails available for parents who may need them. Face-
painter on Suns. 7 days, 11.30am-11.30pm, Sun till 11pm.

674 **HARRY RAMSDEN'S:** Paisley Rd W, beside M8 flyover – not far from centre,
B4 but difficult without a car. Not a bad branch of the national chain that caters
well for kids. Greasy, cooked in lard and in cheerfully tacky surroundings, the
chips and peas, sausage and fishcakes come in kids' portions and there's a
playground before you get back in the car.

675 **CRÈME DE LA CRÈME:** 221 3222. 1071 Argyle St. Big (huge), bustling Indian
B3 emporium which makes special allowances for kids (there are 40 high chairs
available!), incl cartoons on giant screens. Tempt them with a korma; there is
ice cream. 7 days, lunch and LO 11.30pm. (613/INDIAN RESTAUS)

676 **THE CANAL:** 954 5333. 380 Bearsden Rd. Nr Anniesland Cross, former micro-
xB1 brewery now a family pub with restau, bar, pool tables, terrace (o/side tables).
American-type Tex-Mex menu with kids' menu & diversions laid on. 7 days
noon-10pm (bar 11pm/1am).

677 **BROOKLYN CAFÉ & CHOCOLATE THERAPY:** 632 3427, 21 Minard Rd & 632
xC5 5665, Abbot St. 2 unassuming caffs on the S Side (off Pollokshaws Rd) where
families are v welcome. Reports: 665/668/CAFFS.

678 **ART LOVER'S CAFÉ** and **TEMPUS @ THE CCA:** 353 4779, Dumbreck Rd & 332
679 7959, 350 Sauchiehall St. 2 informal, light cafés with space for kids & parents
xA5 not to feel confined. Reports: 660/659/COFFEESHOPS.
C3

TRON CAFÉ: 552 8587. The Child-friendly Bar of the Year 2003. Report:
582/BISTROS.

THE BEST LATE-NIGHT RESTAURANTS

680 ✓ **BABY GRAND:** 248 4942. Elmbank Gardens by Charing Cross Stn &
C3 Premier Lodge skyscraper hotel (behind King's Theatre). Not easy for
strangers to find, but persevere – this is an excl bar/diner at any time of day
(562/BISTROS), but comes into its own after 10pm when just about everywhere
that's decent is closing. Char-grilled food & grazing contemp menu. Piano
player & night-time people. **Daily till midnight, Fri/Sat till 2am.**

681 ✓ **FRATELLI SARTI:** 572 3360. 404 Sauchiehall St. Towards W end of
C3 Sauchiehall St where the late people are, Karyn Neville's version of legendary Sarti's (584/ITALIAN RESTAUS) serving the best snacks & succour on the
strip. Gr pizzas. Usually open till 11pm (10pm Sun) but **till 2am Sat.**

682 ✓ **TIGER TIGER:** 553 4888. 20 Glassford St. UK chain superbar complex but
D4 stylish/contemp & full of options incl v late barfood. Restau o/looking st
till midnight & lighter menu till closing. **7 days, till 1am Sun-Wed, 2am Thur,
3am Fri/Sat.**

683 **SPICE GARDEN:** 492 4422. 11 Clyde Pl. Just over the river, under the Glasgow
C4 Br where trains go over, a restau that's long been a late-night destination. Now
most definitely Indian, it's for the late & last curry craving of the day. Pleasantly
light, food surprisingly good. **7 days 6pm-4am, Sun till 1am.**

684 **CANTON EXPRESS:** 332 0145. 407 Sauchiehall St. The first fast-food Chinese
C3 joint on this block; still the genuine Chinese article. Not as wok-tastic as once
was – a spruce-up might be good. **7 days, 12noon-4am.**

685 **GLASGOW NOODLE BAR:** 333 1883. 482 Sauchiehall St. Major competition to
C3 the above (even gets the edge in opening hrs). Authentic, Chinese fast food,
no frills (ticket service and eezee-kleen tables). The noodle is 'king' here; but
cooking *is* taken seriously. (625/FAR-EASTERN RESTAUS) **7 days, 12noon-5am.**

686 **SLEEPLESS ON SAUCHIEHALL:** 332 9290. 415 Sauchiehall St up the metal
C3 staircase & opp Garage club with a v post-pub/club clientele. Giant screen,
American diner menu, all-night b/fasts, good shakes. **7 days 8.30pm-5.30am
(1am Sun-Mon).**

687 **INSOMNIA @ THE BEARPIT:** Once Insomnia was the pioneering all-night caff
B2 on Woodlands Rd. Now it seems everyone's got work in the morning, but 'the
concept', tho' much reduced (w/ends only), has moved across the rd (corner of
Woodlands Rd leading up to Park Circus – still nr Charing Cross, it has
squeezed into the basement of the Bearpit bar. All-night b/fast & huge range
of cleansing teas. **Fri/Sat 11pm-8am.**

688 **STRAVAIGIN & STRAVAIGIN 2:** 334 2665 & 334 7165. Gibson St & Ruthven
B2, A1 Lane off Byres Rd. Worth remembering that both these excl restaus
(543/RESTAUS & 559/BISTROS) serve food to **11pm.**

PIZZA EXPRESS: Sauchiehall St/Queen St. (599/PIZZAS) **11.30pm.**

CRÈME DE LA CRÈME: 1071 Argyle St. Report: 613/INDIAN RESTAUS. **Midnight.**

ASHOKA ASHTON LANE: Ashton Lane. (611/INDIAN RESTAUS) **12.30am/1am
w/ends.**

GOOD PLACES FOR SUNDAY BREAKFAST

689 ✓ **CAFÉ GANDOLFI:** 552 6813. 64 Albion St. Atmospheric rm, with soft day-
E4 ✓ light filtering through stained glass and the comforting, oversized wooden
furniture. This is pleasant start to another Sun, that day of rest and more shopping made even better with some baked eggs, a pot of tea and the Sun papers
(650/BEST TEAROOMS). Bar upstairs has all-day menu. **Both from 12noon.**

690 ✓ **TINDERBOX:** 339 3108. Corner Byres Rd & Highburgh St. Gr café/diner
A1 ✓ open early to late (651/COFFEE SHOPS). **From 8.45am.**

691 ✓ **COIA'S CAFÉ:** 473 Duke St. They've been doing b/fast here for over 75 yrs
xE4 ✓ & it's still damned good. The full-fry monty lasts all day (incl vegn option).
Papers provided. This is the E End choice (664/CLASSIC CAFFS). **From 10am.**

692 **GRASSROOTS CAFÉ:** 97 St George's Rd at Charing X. An especially calm &
C2 healthy Sun thing (646/VEGN RESTAUS) and it **opens at 10am.**

693 **LOOP:** 354 7705. 110 Bath St the ground floor of Bewley's Hotel (520/TRAVEL
D3 LODGES) for whom it supplies daily b/fast hence early start. All the usual &
some contemp twists in mod restau surroundings. B/fast menu till 11am.
From 8am.

694 **BABBITY BOWSTER:** 552 5055. 16 Blackfriars St. The seminal Merchant City
E4 bar/hotel recommended for many things (739/PUB FOOD, 733/DRINKING OUT-
DOORS), but worth remembering as one of the best and earliest spots for Sun
breakfast. **From 10am.**

695 **CUL DE SAC:** 44 Ashton Lane, off Byres Rd. Kind of an institution in Glasgow's
A1 W End tho' recent change of ownership. But the relaxed boho brunch will continue. Fry-up includes potato scones and comes in a vegn version, and there
are the better-than-average burgers and exotic crêpes. Brunch **12.30pm-
4pm.** (580/BEST BISTROS)

696 **COTTIER'S:** 93 Hyndland St, off Hyndland Rd. Off the top of Hyndland St nr
xA1 Highburgh Rd. Deep in the hefty-mortgage belt of Hyndland, this converted
church probably gets more of a congregation now than it ever did. Eclectic
menu from fruit plate to the full monty and eggs benedict to cajun kedgeree.
Papers provided (577/BEST BISTROS). **12noon-4pm.**

697 **UPSTAIRS AT THE CHIP:** 334 5007. 12 Ashton Lane. 'Sair heid' or not, their
A1 Bloody Marys are the best in town and combined with a veggie breakfast (gr
potato crowdie), famously restorative. Selection of papers. Unhurried service.
(542/BEST RESTAUS). **From 12.30pm.**

698
A1 ✓ **HEART and BUCHANAN:** 334 7626. 308 Byres Rd. Deli & t/away but more what Fiona Buchanan describes as a 'traiteur', the French idea that excl food can be pre-prepared & you just take it home & reheat it. Certainly an extraordinary daily changing menu is produced in the kitchens downstairs according to a published menu of the week. Lots of other carefully selected goodies to go. Fiona puts her 'heart' into this place, it's a major plus to living around here. 7 days 8.30am-9.30pm. Suns 12-7pm.

699
xA2 ✓ **DELIZIQUE:** 339 2000. 66 Hyndland St on corner nr Cottiers. Serving the luvvies, loaded & long-term denizens of Hyndland & beyond, more an old-fashioned provisioner than spanking new deli. Fruit/veg o/side, cheese counter; the unusual alongside the dinner-party essentials. Gorgeous food to go. 7 days 8am-8pm (Suns from 9am).

700
A1 **NAKED SOUP:** 334 6200. 106 Byres Rd. First of the soup-to-go places. Nutritious but nice! Perhaps not best location for office lunches, but otherwise absolutely the right idea. 8 fresh (organic where poss) soups daily, gr salads (esp cous cous) & (perhaps too) thick smoothies. Sit-in or go. 7 days, 9am-5pm, Sun 12-5pm.

701
A2 **ANDREAS GREEK DELI:** 576 5031. 27 Old Dumbarton Rd. W End Greek & Cypriot deli/takeaway full of treats, eg almond & rose-water shortbread, aubergine pie, as well as more predictable moussakas. Mon-Sat 9.30am-9pm. Cl Sun.

702
D3 **PRÊT À MANGER:** 34 Sauchiehall St, St Vincent St, Bothwell St; possibly more on the way. Smart, formulaic but has wiped the floor with the more trad sandwich bars. So altho' we don't do many chains in this book, Prêt is still as good as sandwich bars get in Glasgow. Food comes with philosophy, tho' it didn't stop them selling out to McDonald's! Hrs vary.

703
B2 **GRASSROOTS:** 353 3278. 20 Woodlands Rd, Charing X. Food to go, but mainly big organic deli. Vegn ready meals, bespoke s/wiches. 7 days 8am-6/7pm, Sat 9.30-6pm, Sun 11-5pm.

704
A1 **LITTLE ITALY:** 339 6287. 205 Byres Rd. Basic, but a Byres Rd standby. Pizza focaccia and pasta (600/PIZZA), freshly-baked breads, ice cream, loadsa Italian wines and a no' bad (meaning 'not at all bad') cup of coffee. Mon-Thu 8am-10pm, Fri-Sat 8am-11.45pm, Sun 10am-10pm.

PHILADELPHIA FISH & CHICKEN BAR: 445 Gt Western Rd. Report: 1464/FISH 'N' CHIPS. The old W End standby!

705 ✓ ✓ **THE HORSESHOE:** 17 Drury St. A mighty pub since the 19th cent in
D3 the small st betw W Nile and Renfield Sts nr Central stn. Early example of this style of pub, dubbed 'gin palaces'. Island rather than horseshoe bar ('the longest in the UK'), impressive selection of alcohols and an upstairs lounge where they serve high tea. The food is amazing value (736/PUB FOOD). All kinds of folk. Daily till 12midnight.

706 ✓ ✓ **CORINTHIAN:** 191 Ingram St. Mega makeover of impressive listed
D4 building to form cavernous bar/restau, 2 comfy lounge/cocktail bars and a restau (548/BEST RESTAUS) nr George Sq and Gallery of Modern Art. Awesome ceiling in main rm recently transformed (again) into the 'Lite Bar' – better than megabars elsewhere. Food here ok, excl in restau. 7 days, till 12midnight. (Piano bar Thur-Sun).

707 ✓ ✓ **ARTA:** Old Cheesemarket, Walls St, Merchant City. Nr & rel to
E4 Corinthian (above) & similar scale of vision completely realised. This massive OTT bar/restau/club somewhere betw old Madrid & new Barcelona could prob only happen in Glasgow. Tapas type menu upstairs (633/SPANISH RESTAUS) & down the full-on Glas drinking, dressing up & chatting up experience. Go thro' that curtain into a dream or just possibly a nightmare. Wed-Sun from 5pm-1am (Thu/Fri/Sat till 3am).

708 ✓ **THE HALT BAR:** 160 Woodlands Rd. Edwardian pub largely unspoiled,
B2 unchanged tho paint job wouldn't go amiss. Original counter and snug intact. Always gr atmos – model of how a pub should look and feel. Live music and DJs Wed & w/ends. (832/ESS.CULTURE/LIVE MUSIC) Open till 11pm.

709 ✓ **VICTORIA BAR:** 157 Bridgegate. 'The Vicky' is in the 'Briggait', one of Glas's
D4 oldest streets, nr the Victoria Br over the Clyde. Once a pub for the fishmarket and open odd hrs, now it's a howf for all those who like an atmos that's old, friendly and uncontrived. Ales. Mon-Sat till 12midnight, Sun 11pm. (831/CULTURE.)

710 ✓ **SCOTIA BAR:** 112 Stockwell St. Nr the Victoria (*see above*), late-1920s
D4 Tudor-style pub with a low-beamed ceiling and intimate, woody 'snug'. Long the haunt of folk musicians, writers and raconteurs. Music and poetry sessions, folk and blues. Daily till 12midnight. (830/CULTURE)

711 ✓ **CLUTHA VAULTS:** 167 Stockwell St. This and the pubs above are part of
D4 the same family of trad Glas pubs. The Clutha (ancient name for the Clyde) has a Victorian-style interior and an even longer history. Known for live music. Mon-Sat till 12midnight, Sun till 11pm. (833/CULTURE)

712 **UISGE BEATHA:** 246 Woodlands Rd. 'Oo-i-skay Bay' (or something like that)
B2 means 'the water of life' and is a unique Highland outpost in the city. Shooting-lodge chic in 3 diff rms; some recent refurb. More than a mere draught of the Gael. Good grub at lunchtime. Sun-Thu till 11pm, Fri-Sat till 12midnight.

713 **BAR 10:** 10 Mitchell Lane, off Buchanan St. Opp new Lighthouse and nr the
D4 Tunnel, this was one of the orig 'cool' & pre-club bars before the Glas style-bar explosion. Dating now but remarkably resilient to fashionista trends, the Ben Kelly interior still looks good. Food till 4.30pm, then snax. Regular DJs at w/ends. (746/STYLE)

714 **REPUBLIK BIER HALLE:** 9 Gordon St. S side and Sauchiehall St branches
D3 developing at TGP. Beer cellar extraordinaire, the creation of well-known Glasg entrepreneur & mover/shaker Colin Barr. Huge list of Belgians, Czechs & incl Mongolian, Moroccan, Scottish beers. Stews, dogs & goulash to go with. You can smell the meat & the teen spirit. 7 days 12-12pm.

715 **LISMORE:** 206 Dumbarton Rd, main rd w after Byres Rd. Lismore/Lios mor
xA2 named after the long island off Oban. Gr neighbourhood (Partick) bar that welcomes all sorts. Gives good atmos, succour and malts. Daily till 12pm.

716 **BEN NEVIS:** Argyle St nr Crème de la Crème (613/RESTAUS). Owned by same
B3 people as Lismore (above). An excl makeover in contemp but not faux-Scottish style. Small & pubby, the Deuchars is spot-on. Live music Weds.

The following places don't have to pretend to be old. Open till 11pm/midnight.

HORSESHOE: 17 Drury St. Report: 705/UNIQUE PUBS.

HALT BAR: 160 Woodlands Rd. Report: 708/UNIQUE PUBS.

VICTORIA BAR: 157 Bridgegate. Report: 709/UNIQUE PUBS.

SCOTIA BAR: 112 Stockwell St. Report: 710/UNIQUE PUBS.

CLUTHA VAULTS: 167 Stockwell St. Report: 711/UNIQUE PUBS.

717
C3 ✓ **THE GRIFFIN (AND THE GRIFFINY AND THE GRIFFINETTE):** 266 Bath St. Corner of Elmbank St nr King's Theatre. Built 1903 to anticipate the completion of the theatre and offer the patrons a pre-show pie and a pint. Stand at the Edwardian Bar like generations of Glaswegians. Main bar still retains 'snug' with a posh, etched-glass partition; booths have been added but the atmos is still 'Old Glasgow'. Sun-Thu till 11pm, Fri-Sat till 12midnight. Amazingly cheap lunches (735/PUB FOOD).

718
xE4 **THE SARACEN'S HEAD:** Gallowgate, nr Barrowlands. An establishment of this name has existed in the neighbourhood since 1755, playing host to a multitude of characters; not least Boswell and Johnson, on the return leg of their grand Highland tour. This, the most recent incarnation, opened in 1905 and is famous for its lethal cider. The atmos is more 'wild west end' than E End, & Baird's across the st (see below) serves the stronger shot of culture, but the Sarrie Heid is still pure dead brilliant. 7 days, Cl 10.30pm weekdays.

719
E4 **STEPS:** 66 Glassford St. Tiny pub & barely noticed but has the indelible marks of better by-gone days. In no way celebrated like Rogano (550/RESTAUS), but also refers to the *Queen Mary* with stained glass & gr panelling. V typical, friendly Glasgow. Often, there are free snacks on the house. A real find.

720
xC5 **M J HERAGHTY:** 708 Pollokshaws Rd. More than a touch of the Irish here and easily more authentic than recent imports. A local with loyal regulars who'll make you welcome; old pub practices still hold in this howff in the sowff. Ladies' loos introduced in 1996! Sun-Thu till 11pm, Fri-Sat till 12midnight.

721
A5 **BRECHIN'S:** 803 Govan Rd. Nr jnct with Paisley Rd W and motorway overpass. Established in 1798 and, as they say, always in the same family. A former shipyard pub which is close in heart & soul to to Rangers FC. It's behind the statue of shipbuilder Sir William Pearce (which, covered in sooty grime, was known as the 'Black Man') and there's a feline 'rat-catcher' on the roof (making it a listed building). Unaffected neighbourhood atmos, some flute-playing. 7 days till 11pm, Fri/Sat midnight.

722
B4 **THE OLD TOLL BAR:** 1 Paisley Rd W. Opp the site of the original Parkhouse Toll, where monies were collected for use of the 'turnpikes' betw Glas and Greenock. Opened in 1874, the original interior is still intact; the *fin de siècle* painted glass and magnificent old gantry preserved under order. A 'palace pub' classic. Real ale and some single malts. 7 days till 11pm.

723
E4
xA5 **BAIRD'S BAR** and **THE DISTRICT:** 2 bars from opp sides of the gr divide. **BAIRD'S** in the Gallowgate adj Barrowlands is a Catholic stronghold green to the gills where, on days when Celtic play at home up the rd in Parkhead, you'd have to be in by 11am to get a drink. **THE DISTRICT,** 252 Paisley Rd W, Govan, nr Ibrox Park, is where Rangers supporters gather and rule in their own blue heaven. Both pubs give an extraordinary insight into what makes the Glas time-bomb tick. Provided you aren't wearing the wrong colours (or say something daft), you'll be very welcome in either.

Pubs on other pages may purvey real ale; the following take it seriously. All open 7 days till 11pm (midnight w/ends) unless stated.

724
B3 ✓ **BON ACCORD:** 153 N St. On a slip rd of the motorway swathe nr the Mitchell Library. One of the first real-ale pubs in Glas. Good selection of malts and up to 12 beers; always Theakstons, Deuchars & IPA plus many guest ales on hand pump. Food at lunchtime and light bites till 8pm. Light, easy-going atmos here, but they do take their ale seriously; there's even a 'tour' of the cellars if you want it. Mon-Sat till 12midnight, Sun till 11.00pm.

725
A1 **TENNENT'S:** 191 Byres Rd. Nr the always-red traffic lights at Univ Ave, a big, booming watering-hole of a place where you're never far away from the horseshoe bar and its several excellent hand-pumped ales, incl up to 9 guests. 'Tennent's is an institution' – some regulars do appear to live here. Basic bar meals till 9pm.

726
E4 **BABBITY BOWSTER:** 16 Blackfriars St. In a pedestrianised part of the Merchant City and just off the High St, a highly successful pub/restau/hotel (516/INDIVIDUAL HOTELS); but the pub comes first. Caledonian, Deuchars, IPA & well-chosen guests. Many malts & cask cider. Food all day (739/PUB FOOD), occasional folk music (esp Sun), o/side patio (733/DRINK OUTDOORS).

727
E4 **BLACKFRIARS:** 36 Bell St on corner of the Merchant City. Mixed crowd in this a' thing to a' body kind of pub (food till 7pm, then bites, also comedy & jazz programme). Ind Coope, Burton guest beers, bottled & draught Euro beers.

728
D3 **THE HORSESHOE:** 17 Drury St. Gr for lots of reasons (705/UNIQUE GLAS PUBS), not the least of which is its range of beers: Caledonian, Greenmantle, Maclays and Bass on hand pump.

729
D4 **VICTORIA BAR:** 157 Bridgegate. Another pub mentioned before (709/UNIQUE GLAS PUBS) where IPA, Maclays and others can be drunk in a dark woody atmos enlivened by occasional trad music (831/FOLK MUSIC).

730
xA1 **LOCK 27:** 1100 Crow Rd. At the very N end of Crow Rd beyond Anniesland, an unusual boozer for Glas: a canalside pub on a lock of the Forth and Clyde Canal (776/WALKS IN THE CITY), a touch English (a v wee touch), where of a summer's day you can sit o/side. Excellent bar food, always busy.

731
xA1 **COTTIER'S:** 357 5825. 93 Hyndland St. First on the left after the swing park on Highburgh Rd (going W) and the converted church is on your rt, around the corner. Gr place for many reasons (577/BEST BISTROS, 696/SUN BREAKFAST), but a cold beer on a hot day sitting in leafy shade is one of the best; or into the evening – it's a Hyndland kind of life!

732
A1 **ASHTON LANE:** As soon as the sun comes out, so do the punters. With the **CUL DE SAC** and **BAR BREL** at one end and **JINTY MCGINTY'S** at the other, benches suddenly appear and the whole lane becomes a cobbled, alfresco pub. It's the nearest Glas gets to Euro or even Dublin drinking.

733
E4 **BABBITY BOWSTER:** 552 5055. 16 Blackfriars St. Unique in the Merchant City for several reasons (726/REAL-ALE PUBS, 739/PUB FOOD), but in summer certainly for its napkin of gdn in an area bereft of greenery. Though enclosed by surrounding sts, it's a concrete oasis. Feels like Soho, Soho NYC? Naw, feels like Glas. Always good craic.

THE CANAL: 380 Bearsden Rd. Report: 676/KIDS.

734 ✔✔ **BAR GANDOLFI:** 552 6813. 64 Albion St above Café Gandolfi
E4 (650/TEARMS). Straight in at number 1 when it opened 2003. If
Glasgow could thole a gastropub (see Edinburgh p. 35), this would be it. Except
it has none of that pretence, just gr comfort food in a light, airy upstairs garret,
served all day till 11.30pm. Good veggie choice. All cool as … 7 days 9am–
11.30pm (Sun from noon).

735 ✔✔ **THE GRIFFIN:** 266 Bath St. On corner of Elmbank St across from
C3 King's Theatre. The Griffin rooms have always been there on that corner and your basic pie/chips/beans *and a pint* will not be bettered at this price
(£2.80 lunchtime, the equivalent 80 yrs ago of 8 old pence). Other staples available and a more elaborate menu in the lounge or the Griffinette next door.
Food: 12noon-2.30pm & evenings till 7pm. Pub till 12midnight. (717/'UNSPOILT'
PUBS)

736 ✔✔ **THE HORSESHOE:** 17 Drury St. This classic pub to be recommended
D3 for all kinds of reasons. But lunch is a particularly good deal with 3
courses for £2.80 (pie and beans still 80p), and old favourites on the menu like
mushy peas, macaroni cheese, jelly and fruit. Lunch 12noon-2.30pm and all
afternoon upstairs, incl high tea till 7pm (not quite the same atmos, but pure
Glas). Pub open daily till 12midnight. (705/UNIQUE GLAS PUBS)

737 ✔✔ **STRAVAIGIN:** 28-30 Gibson St. Excellent pub food upstairs from one
B2 of the best restaus in town. Doors open on to sunny Gibson St &
mezzanine above. Crowded maybe, but inspirational grub & no fuss. Nice
wines to go with. 7 days all day & LO 10pm. Report: 543/BEST RESTAUS.

738 ✔✔ **LOWDOWN:** 331 4061. 158 Bath St. Vast below street level bar
C3 underneath Quigley's (545/RESTAUS). Spacious & opening on to
sunken terrace with loungy furniture. Stylish look & clientele & easy eating
menu incl tapas by the irrepressible & eponymous Mr Quigley. Upstairs the
KELLY COOPER BAR serves a similar menu incl afternoon tea 2-5pm. The irrepressible & eponymous Ms KC Bar(r) may join you for a Kir royale if you're
famous enough (even locally). Food all day till 11pm.

739 ✔ **BABBITY BOWSTER:** 16 Blackfriars St. Already listed as a pub for real ale
E4 and as a hotel (there are rms upstairs), the food is mentioned mainly for
its Scottishness (haggis and stovies) and all-day availability. It's also pleasant
to eat o/side on the patio/gdn in summer. There is a restau upstairs (dinner
only Tues-Sat) but we prefer down. Also breakfast served from 8am (Sun
10am). (726/REAL-ALE PUBS, 516/INDIVIDUAL HOTELS)

740 ✔ **TIGER TIGER:** 553 4888. 20 Glassford St. Northern outpost of the UK
D4 chain whose multibar/room/decor formula aims to provide the complete night out. Certainly no expense spared here with 8 bars, 2 dancefloors,
a pretty good restau (not bistro) & themes that range across continents. Bar
food better than most & you could just about spend the night here. Food till
late (1am & 3am Fri/Sat).

741 **AIR ORGANIC:** 564 5200. 36 Kelvingrove St nr the park. Restau upstairs was
A3 once flavour of the month (2000), but snackier food in bar, e.g. Thai curry sandwiches, sushi boxes; still a hip place to graze. Open fire among cool minimal-
ism and music. 7 days, 11am–11pm. (574/BEST BISTROS)

742 **ELLIOTTS:** 248 2060. 203 Bath St. A basement bar among many at the w end
C3 of style street, but this is one where you eat or dine even. Italian influence, but
many specials. Modern as most. Lunch & dinner LO 10pm (not Sat Lunch). Cl
Sun. Bar midnight.

743 **THE BIG BLUE:** 445 Gr Western Rd. A modern bar/bistro in a gr uptown loca-
B1 tion literally on the (river) Kelvinside. Drinking may drown the eating later on,
but till mid/late-evening there's excellent Italian pasta/pizza pub grub. LO
10/10.30pm. Bar 12midnight.

744 **BLACKFRIARS:** 36 Bell St. Candleriggs is one of the focal points in the
E4 Merchant City. Gr Glas pub for all-round ambience, provision of real ale and
music, and food available all day (meals till 7pm, then 'bites') (but drinkers
loud after 9pm). 727/REAL ALES.

745 **FOX AND HOUNDS, HOUSTON:** On B790 village main st in Renfrewshire,
MAP 2   30km W of centre by M8 jnct 29 (A726), then cross back under motorway on
E5   B790. Village pub home to Houston brewery with gr ales, excl pubfood and
dining-rm upstairs for family meals and suppers. Folk come from miles
around. Sunday roasts. Lunch and 6-10pm (all day w/ends). Restau 01505
612448. Bar till midnight.

STRATA: 45 Queen St. Report: 750/STYLE BARS (below).

BREL: Ashton Lane. report: 581/BISTROS.

THE BEST STYLE BARS

746 ✓ **BAR 10:** 221 8353. 10 Mitchell Lane, halfway up Buchanan St pedestrian
D4   precinct on the left in the narrow lane that also houses the Lighthouse
design centre. There's an NYC look about this joint that is so loved by its
habitués, they still pack it at w/ends almost 10 yrs after it arrived. Ben Kelly
design has worn well. Food, DJs & pre-club preparations. 7 days till midnight.
(713/UNIQUE PUBS)

767 ✓ **LOWDOWN:** 331 4061. 158 Bath St Opened mid 2001 this, the lower
C3   down bar of Quigley's (545/BEST RESTAUS) quickly became an immensely
popular place to gather & graze (738/PUB FOOD) & for that matter gaze
(dressed-to-go crowd). **KELLY COOPER BAR** at street level, where a footballer
may meet or lose his wife, has extended the range.

748 ✓ **ARCHES:** 0901 022 0300 (box office). 253 Argyle St. The fab bar/café of the
B3   fab Arches Theatre, the club & experimental theatre space refurbished
with millennium money. Design by Timorous/Taller (see Strata below), this is
an obvious pre-club pre-theatre space, but works at any time. Food & DJs &
lots going on. Even if you're only in Glas for the w/end, you should come here.

749 ✓ **SAINT JUDE'S:** 352 8800. 190 Bath St. Further along Bath St (from
C3   Lowdown above), another bar below stairs that seems likely to outlive
the Bath St explosion. This, the bar of Saint Jude's (508/HOTELS, 552/BEST
RESTAUS) is minimalist but still fuzzy & friendly. Good cocktails. Food till drinking takes over & open till midnight 7 days.

750 **STRATA:** 221 1888. 45 Queen St. Was Style Bar of the Year, 2000, but we won't
D4   hold that against them. Nothing hugely obvious to distinguish this from a
clutch of others, but somehow it works. Done by Timorous Beasties & One
Food Taller (ubiquitous Glas design team), the room is not intrusive & the food
is better than most. Food till 10pm, bar midnight.

751 **BARGO:** 553 4771. 80 Albion St. In the Merchant City, this spacious, designer-
E4   theque is in demand for fashion shoots and, of course, high-glam posing on a
Sat night. Can be attractively, if not spookily, quiet during the week when sur-
prisingly OK food is served. Opens on to st in summertimes sometimes.

752 **CUL DE SAC:** 649 4717. 44 Ashton Lane. The upstairs bar and **ATTIC** is a peren-
A1   nial W End fave. Close to the underground for that last-minute dash into town
to beat club curfews. (580/BEST BISTROS)

753 **CANDY BAR:** 353 7420. 185 Hope St .Still stylee after all these years (well 6), a
D3   good place to look, linger and even eat (food till 8pm) – eclectic menu incl a
decent fish 'n' chips. Minimalist chic with the odd flourish. 7 days noon till midnight.

754 **POLO LOUNGE:** 553 1221. 84 Wilson St. Urbane and stylish bar/disco by the
E4   ubiquitous (tho hardly ever seen) Stefan King. Unmistakably gay in the heart
of the quarter (not him, it). Clubbable rather than clubby crowd (until later on)
arranged around the comfortable furniture; at w/ends you go downstairs to
disco. Mellow Sun afternoons; papers and jazz. (1358/GAY GLAS)

755 **BAR 91:** 552 5211. 91 Candleriggs. A better bar among many of this ilk here-
E4   abouts, food also is well-considered & put together, tho it stops at 6pm to
make way for pre-club ministrations (and till midnight).

756 **TOM TOM:** 205 Bath St. Latest addition at TGP in this boulevard of Glasgow
C3   dreams. Glass, wood, metal: it looks like an architect's office. Minimalist & of
the moment, we shall see if it's still on this page next edition. Food at front till
9pm, bar midnight.

AIR ORGANIC: 36 Kelvingrove St. Report: 741/PUB FOOD.

757 ✓ ✓ **KELVINGROVE ART GALLERY AND MUSEUM:** 287 2699. At westerly
A2 end of Argyle St & Sauchiehall St by Kelvingrove Park. Huge Victorian
sandstone edifice with awesome atrium. On the ground floor is a natural histo-
ry/ Scottish history museum. The upper salons contain the city's superb British
and European art collection. Closed for major refurb until Feb 2006 but majority of paintings can be seen until then at the **MACLELLAN GALLERIES**, 270
Sauchiehall St (331 1854). FREE

758 ✓ ✓ **THE BURRELL COLLECTION, POLLOK PARK & POLLOK HOUSE:** 287
xC5 2550. S of river via A77 Kilmarnock Rd (over Jamaica St Br) about 5km,
following signs from Pollokshaws Rd. Set in rural parkland, this award-winning
modern gallery was built to house the eclectic acquisitions of Sir William Burrell.
Showing a preference for medieval works, among the 8500 items the magpie
magnate donated to the city in 1944 are artefacts from the Roman empire to
Rodin. The building itself integrates old doorways and whole rms reconstructed from Hutton Castle. Self-serve café and restau on the ground floor (Mon-
Thurs, Sat 10am-5pm, Fri & Sun 11am-5pm). **POLLOK HOUSE** (NTS): 616 6410
and Gdns further into the park (with works by Goya, El Greco and William Blake)
is worth a detour and has, below stairs, the better tearooms & gds to the river.
Both open 7 days. 10am-5pm. (777/WALKS IN THE CITY) FREE/ADM

759 ✓ **GLASGOW CATHEDRAL/PROVAND'S LORDSHIP:** 552 6891/552 8819.
xE3 Castle St. Across the rd from one another they represent what remains of
the oldest part of the city, which (as can be seen in the People's Palace, *see
below*) was, in the early 18th century, merely a ribbon of streets from here to
the river. The present Cathedral, though established by St Mungo in AD 543,
dates from the 12th century and is a fine example of the v real, if gloomy,
Gothic. The house, built in 1471, is a museum which strives to convey a sense
of medieval life. Watch you don't get run over when you re-emerge into the
21st century and try to cross the st. In the background, the Necropolis piled
on the hill invites inspection and offers a viewpoint and the full Gothic perspective (tho' best not to go alone). Call for opening times. FREE

760 ✓ **THE PEOPLE'S PALACE:** 554 0223. App via the Tron and London Rd, then
xE5 turn rt into Glas Green. This has long been a folk museum *par excellence*
wherein, since 1898, the history, folklore and artefacts of a proud city have
been gathered, cherished and displayed. But this is much more than a mere
museum; it is the heart and soul of the city and together with the Winter Gdns
adj, shouldn't be missed, to know what Glasgow's about. Tearoom in the
Tropics, among the palms and ferns of the Winter Gdns. Opening times as
most other museums: Mon-Thurs, Sat 10am-5pm, Fri & Sun 11am-5pm. FREE

761 ✓ **GLASGOW SCIENCE CENTRE:** 420 5000/5010. On S Side of Clyde opp
A4 SECC, Glasgow's newest attraction built with Millennium dosh. App via
Kingston Br (from city) and Govan t/off, then rt fork at 'the angel', or walk from
SECC complex by 'Bell's Bridge'. Impressive titanium-clad mall, Imax cinema &
127m-high tower. 4 floors of interactive exhibs, planetarium & theatre. Rolling
story of the city with the science and the view. Separate tickets or combos
(only 20 people with 2 lifts at a time for the tower). 7 days. 10am-6pm. ADM

762 **ST MUNGO MUSEUM OF RELIGIOUS LIFE AND ART:** 553 2557. Part of the
xE3 lovely & not-cherished-enough cathedral precinct (see above), this houses art
and artefacts representing the world's 6 major religions arranged tactfully in
an attractive stone building with a Zen gdn in the courtyard. The dramatic
Dalí *Crucifixion* seems somehow lost, and the assemblage seems like a good
& worthwhile vision not quite realised. But if you like your spirituality shuffled
but not stirred, this is for you. Opening times as other museums (*above*). FREE

763 **HUNTERIAN MUSEUM AND ART GALLERY:** 330 4221/5431. Univ Ave. On
A1 one side of the st, Scotland's oldest museum with geological, archaeological
and social history displayed in a venerable building. The cloisters outside and
the **UNIVERSITY CHAPEL** should not be missed. Across the st, a modern
block contains part of Glasgow's exceptional civic collection – Rembrandt to
the Colourists and the Glas Boys, as well as one of the most complete collections of any artist's work and personal effects to be found anywhere, viz that
of Whistler. It's fascinating stuff, even if you're not a fan. There's also a print

gallery and the superb **MACKINTOSH HOUSE** (816/MACKINTOSH). Mon-Sat 9.30am-5pm (M. House closed daily 12.30-1.30pm). FREE

THE OTHER ATTRACTIONS

764 ✓✓ **MUSEUM OF TRANSPORT:** 287 2720. Off Argyle St behind the Kelvin
A2 Hall. May not seem your ticket to ride, but this is one of Scotland's most fascinating museums. Has something for everybody, esp kids. The reconstruction of a cobbled Glas st c1938 is an inspired evocation. There are trains, trams and unique collections of cars, motorbikes and bicycles. And model ships in the Clyde rm, in remembrance of a mighty river. Make a donation and the Mini splits in two. Mon-Thur, Sat 10am-5pm, Fri & Sun 11am-5pm. FREE

765 ✓✓ **BOTANIC GARDENS AND KIBBLE PALACE:** 334 2422. Gr Western
xB1 Rd. Smallish park close to R Kelvin with riverside walks (775/WALKS IN THE CITY), and pretty much the 'dear green place'. Kibble Palace (built 1873) is the distinctive domed glasshouse with statues set among lush ferns and shrubbery from around the (mostly temperate) world. A wonderful place to muse and wander. Gdns open till dusk; palace 10am-4.45pm (4.15pm in wint).

766 ✓✓ **GALLERY OF MODERN ART:** 229 1996. Queen St. Central, contro-
D4 versial and housed in former Stirling's Library, Glasgow's big visual arts attraction opened in a hail of art world bickering in 1996. Main pt is: does it reflect Glasgow's eminence as a provenance of cutting edge or conceptual work (all those Turner & Becks Prize nominees & winners?). Murmurs stilled of late by more representative exhibs. Leaving aside the quibbling it should def be on your Glasgow Hit list. Smart café up top. Same hrs as MOT (*above*). FREE

767 ✓✓ **THE BARROWS:** (pronounced 'Barras') The sprawling st and indoor
xE4 market area in the E End of the city around the Gallowgate. As with all gr markets, it's full of character and characters and it's still possible to find bargains and collectibles. Everything from clairvoyants to the latest scam. Purists, of course, point out that its glory days are well over & commercialisation has killed it, but it's still pure Glasgow. Sat and Sun only 10am-5pm.

768 **THE TENEMENT HOUSE:** 333 0183. 145 Buccleuch St. Nr Charing Cross but
C2 can app from nr the end of Sauchiehall St and over the hill. The typical 'respectable' Glas tenement kept under a bell-jar since Our Agnes moved out in 1965. She had lived there with her mother since 1911 and wasn't one for new-fangled things. It's a touch claustrophobic when busy and is distinctly voyeuristic, but, well … your house would be interesting, too, in 50 yrs time if the clock were stopped. Daily, Mar-Oct 2-5pm. ADMN

769 **SHARMANKA KINETIC GALLERY & THEATRE:** 552 7080. 2nd floor, 14 King St,
E4 Trongate. A small and intimate experience cf most others on this page, but an extraordinary one. The gallery/theatre of Russian emigre Eduard Bersindsky shows his meticulous & amazing mechanical sculptures. Mon-Sun 9.30am-5.30pm. Performances Thur 7pm, Sun 3pm & 6pm. Other times by arr. ADMN

770 **GREENBANK GARDENS:** 639 3281. 10km SW of centre via Kilmarnock Rd,
xC5 Eastwood Toll, Clarkston Toll and Mearns Rd, then signposted (3km). A spacious oasis in the suburbs; formal gdns and 'working' walled gdn, parterre and woodland walks around elegant Georgian house. V Scottish. Gdns open AYR 9.30am-dusk, shop/tearoom Apr-Oct 11am-5pm. NTS

771 **CITY CHAMBERS:** 287 4018. George Sq. The hugely impressive building along
D3 the whole E end of Glasgow's municipal central sq. This is a wonderfully over-the-top monument to the days when Glas was the second city of the empire. Guided tours Mon-Fri, 10.30am and 2.30pm. FREE

772 **FINLAYSTONE ESTATE:** 01475 540505. 30km W of city centre via fast M8/A8,
MAP 2 signed off dual carriageway just before Pt Glas. Delightful gdns and woods
E4 around mansion house with many pottering places and longer trails (and ranger service). Visitor centre & The Celtic Tree tearoom. Open Apr-late Sept 11am-5pm (VC also open wint w/ends). Spectacular bluebells. Slap bang in middle of the estate is **FERRINGTONS**, the largest complimentary therapy centre in Scotland (01475 540111). Sessions & classes in pilates, massage & – well, everything you can probably think of to feel better.

773 **THE PRIDE O' THE CLYDE:** 07711 250969. Amsterdam-style water-bus ferry-
C4 ing passengers between Glasgow (board at Broomielaw, Jamaica Bridge) and
Braehead Shopping & Leisure Centre (board at Maritime Heritage Centre). A
35-min journey incl commentary on the sights & history of the Clyde.
Refreshments avail. AYR. Also, while we're on the water…   ADMN

774 **THE WAVERLEY:** 0845 130 4647. 'The World's Last Sea-going Paddle Steamer'
B4 which plied the Clyde in the glorious 'Doon the Water' days is fresh from its
£7M lottery-funded refit. Def the way to see the W Coast. Sailings from Glas
Anderson Quay (by Kingston Br) on Fri-Mon to Rothesay, Kyles of Bute, Arran.
Other days leaves from Ayr or Greenock, many destinations. Call for complex
timetable.   ADMN

PAISLEY ABBEY: 15km from Glas. Report: 1848/ABBEYS.

BOTHWELL CASTLE, UDDINGSTON: 15km E, via M74. Report: 1851/RUINS.

THE BEST WALKS IN THE CITY

See p. 12 for walk codes.

775 **KELVIN WALKWAY:** A path along the banks of Glasgow's other river, the
B1 Kelvin, which enters the Clyde unobtrusively at Yorkhill but first meanders
through some of the most interesting parts and parks of the NW city. Walk
starts at Kelvingrove Park through the Univ and Hillhead district under Kelvin
Br and on to the celebrated Botanic Gdns (765/OTHER ATTRACTIONS). The trail
then goes N, under the Forth and Clyde Canal (*see below*) to the Arcadian
fields of Dawsholm Park (5km), Killermont (posh golf course) and Kirkintilloch
(13km from start). Since the river and the canal shadow each other for much
of their routes, it's possible, with a map, to go out by one waterway and return
by the other (e.g. start at Gr Western Rd, return Maryhill Rd).

START: Usual start at the Eildon St (off Woodlands Rd) gate of Kelvingrove
Park or Kelvin Br. St parking only.   2-13+KM XCIRC BIKE 1-A-1

776 **FORTH AND CLYDE CANAL TOWPATH:** The canal, opened in 1790, reopened
D2 2002 as the Millennium Link and once a major short cut for fishing boats and
xC1 trade betw Europe and America, provides a fascinating look round the back
of the city from a pathway that stretches on a spur from Pt Dundas just N of
the M8 to the main canal at the end of Lochburn Rd off Maryhill Rd and then
E all the way to Kirkintilloch and Falkirk (Falkirk Wheel: 01324 619888; 4/BIG
ATTRACTIONS), and W through Maryhill and Drumchapel to Bowling and the
Clyde (60km). Much of the route is through the forsaken or redeveloped
industrial heart of the city, past waste ground, warehouses and high flats, but
there are open stretches and curious corners and, by Bishopbriggs, it's a rural
waterway. More info from British Waterways (01324 671217).

START: (1) Top of Firhill Rd (gr view of city from Ruchill Park, 100m further on –
757/BEST VIEWS). (2) Lochburn Rd (*see above*) at the confluence from which to go
E or W to the Clyde. (3) Top of Crow Rd, Anniesland where there is a canalside
pub, Lock 27 (730/DRINK OUTDOORS), with tables o/side, real ale & food (12noon-
7/8pm). (4) Bishopbriggs Sports Centre, Balmuildy Rd. From here it is 6km to
Maryhill and 1km in other direction to the 'country churchyard' of Cadder or
3km to Kirkintilloch. All starts have some parking.   ANY KM XCIRC BIKE 1-A-1

777 **POLLOK COUNTRY PARK:** The park that (apart from the area around the
xC5 gallery and the house – 758/MAIN ATTRACTIONS) most feels like a real country
park. Numerous trails through woods and meadows. The leisurely guided
walks with the park rangers can be educative and more fun than you would
think (632 9299 for details). Burrell Collection and Pollok House and Gdns are
obvious highlights. There's a good restau & an 'old-fashioned' tearoom in the
basement of the latter serving excellent range of hot, home-made dishes,
soups, salads, s/wiches as well as usual cakes & tasties. Open 7 days 10am-
4.30pm (616 6410). Enter by Haggs Rd or by Haggs Castle Golf Course. By car
you are directed to the entry rd off Pollokshaws Rd and then to the car park in
front of the Burrell. Train to Shawlands or Pollokshaws W from Glas Central Stn.

778 MUGDOCK COUNTRY PARK: 956 6100. Not perhaps within the city, but one
MAP 3 of the nearest and easiest escapes. Park which incl Mugdock Woods (SSSI) and
A4 2 castles is NW of Milngavie. Regular train from Queen St Stn takes 20 min,
then follow route of W Highland Way for 4km across Drumclog Moor to S
edge of park. In summer, shuttlebus will meet the trains at Milngavie Stn and
take you right into park. By car to Milngavie by A81 park is 5km N. Well signed.
5 car parks, main one incl Craigend Visitor Centre, Stables Tearoom (10am-
5pm daily), discovery room & theatre. Many trails marked out and further
afield rambles. This is a godsend betw Glas and the Highland hills.

5-20KM CAN BE CIRC BIKE 1-A-2

779 CATHKIN BRAES: S edge of city with views. Report: 786/BEST VIEWS.
xA5

<hr>

EASY WALKS OUTSIDE THE CITY

See p. 12 for walk codes.

780 CAMPSIE FELLS: Range of hills 25km N of city best reached via Kirkintilloch
xC1 or Cumbernauld/Kilsyth. Encompasses area that includes the Kilsyth Hills,
Fintry Hills and Carron Valley betw. (1) Good app from A803, Kilsyth main st up
the Tak-me-Doon (*sic*) rd. Park by the golf club and follow path by the burn. It's
poss to take in the two hills to left as well as Tomtain (453m), the most east-
erly of the tops, in a good afternoon; views to the E. (2) Drive on to the jnct
(9km) of the B818 rd to Fintry and go left, following Carron Valley reservoir to
the far corner where there is a forestry rd to the left. Park here and follow track
to ascend Meikle Bin (570m) to the rt, the highest peak in the central
Campsies. (3) The bonny village of Fintry (536/HOTELS O/SIDE TOWN) is a good
start/base for the Fintry Hills and Earl's Seat (578m). (4) Campsie Glen – a sliver of glen in the hills. App via Clachan of Campsie on A81 (decent tearoom) or
from viewpoint high on the hill on B822 from Lennoxtown-Fintry. This is the
easy Campsie intro.   10KM+ CAN BE CIRC XBIKE 2-B-2

781 GLENIFFER BRAES, PAISLEY: Ridge to the S of Paisley (15km from Glas) has
MAP 3 been a favourite walking-place for centuries. M8 or Paisley Rd W to town cen-
A5 tre then: (1) S via B775/A736 towards Irvine or (2) B774 (Causeyside St then
Neilston Rd) and sharp rt after 3km to Glenfield Rd. For (1) go 2km after last
houses, winding up ridge and park/start at Robertson Park (signed). Here
there are superb views and walks marked to E and W. (2) 500m along Glenfield
Rd is a car park/ranger centre (0141 884 3794). Walk up through gdns and formal parkland and then W along marked paths and trails. Eventually, after 5km,
this route joins (1).   2-10KM CAN BE CIRC MTBIKE 1-A-2

782 GREENOCK CUT: 45km W of Glas. Can app via Pt Glas but simplest route is
MAP 2 from A78 rd to Largs. Travelling S from Pt Glas take first left after IBM, brown-
E4 signed L Thom/Cornalees. Lochside 5km up winding rd. Park at Cornalees Br
Centre (01475 521458). Walk left along lochside rd to Overton (5km) then path
is signed. The Cut, an aqueduct built in 1827 to supply water to Greenock and
its 31 mills, is now an ancient monument. Gr views from the mast along the
Cut. Another route to the rt from Cornalees leads through a glen of birch,
rowan and oak to the Kelly Cut. Both trails described on board at the car park.

15/16KM CIRC MTBIKE 1-B-2

783 MUIRSHIEL: General name for vast area of 'Inverclyde' W of city, incl Greenock
MAP 2 Cut (*see above*), Lochwinnoch, Castle Semple Country Park and Lunderston
E4 Bay, a stretch of coastline nr the Cloch Lighthouse on the A770 S of Gourock
for littoral amblings. Best wildish bit is around Muirshiel Centre itself, Muirshiel
Country Park (01505 842803), with trails, a waterfall and Windy Hill (350m).
Nothing arduous, but a breath of air. From M8 jnct 28A, take A737
Lochwinnoch, then B786 to top of Calder Glen Rd. Follow brown signs.

784 THE WHANGIE: On A809 N from Bearsden about 8km after last r/bout and
MAP 3 2km after the Carbeth Inn, is the car park for the Queen's View (756/BEST VIEWS).
A4 Once you get to the summit of Auchineden Hill, take the path that drops down
to the W (a half-rt-angle) and look for crags on your rt. This is the 'back door' of
The Whangie. Carry on and you'll suddenly find yourself in a deep cleft in the
rock face with sheer walls rising over 10m on either side. The Whangie is more
than 100m long and at one pt the walls narrow to less than 1m. Local

mythology has it that The Whangie was made by the Devil, who lashed his tail in anticipation of a witchy rendezvous somewhere in the N, and carved a slice through the rock, where the path now goes.   5KM CIRC XBIKE XDOGS 1-A-1

785 **CHATELHÉRAULT, nr HAMILTON:** Jnct 6 off M74, well signposted into
MAP 3   Hamilton, follow rd into centre, then bear left away from main rd where it's
A5   signed for A723. The gates to the 'château' are about 3km o/side town. A drive leads to the William Adam-designed hunting lodge of the Dukes of Hamilton, set amid ornamental gdns with a notable parterre and extensive grounds. Tracks along the deep, wooded glen of the Avon (ruins of Cadzow Castle) lead to distant glades. Good walks and ranger service (01698 426213). House open 10.30am-4.30pm, walks at all times.   2-7KM CIRC BIKE 1-A-2

THE BEST VIEWS OF THE CITY AND BEYOND

786 **CATHKIN BRAES, QUEEN MARY'S SEAT:** The southern ridge of the city on
C5   the B759 from Carmunnock to Cambuslang, about 12km from centre. Go S of river by Albert Br to Aikenhead Rd which continues S as Carmunnock Rd. Follow to Carmunnock, a delightfully rural village, and pick up the Cathkin Rd. 2km along on the rt is the Cathkin Braes Golf Club and 100m further on the left is the park. Marvellous views to N of the Campsies, Kilpatrick Hills, Ben Lomond and as far as Ben Ledi. Walks on the Braes on both sides of the rd.

787 **QUEEN'S VIEW, AUCHINEDEN:** Not so much a view of the city, more a per-
MAP 3   spective on Glasgow's Highland hinterland, this short walk and sweeping vista
A4   to the N has been a Glaswegian pilgrimage for generations. On A809 N from Bearsden about 8km after last r/bout and 2km after the Carbeth Inn, a v decent pub to repair to. Busy car park attests to popularity. The walk, along path cut into ridgeside, takes 40-50 min to cairn, from which you can see The Cobbler (1994/HILLS), that other Glas favourite, Ben Ledi and sometimes as far as Ben Chonzie 50km away. The fine views of L Lomond are what Queen Victoria came for. Further on is The Whangie (784/EASY WALKS).   1-A-1

788 **RUCHILL PARK:** An unlikely but splendid panorama from this overlooked but
xC1   well-kept park to the N of the city nr the infamous Possilpark housing estate. Go to top of Firhill Rd (past Partick Thistle football ground) over Forth and Clyde Canal (776/WALKS IN THE CITY) off Garscube Rd where it becomes Maryhill Rd. Best view is from around the flagpole; the whole city among its surrounding hills, from the Campsies to Gleniffer & Cathkin Braes (*see above*), becomes clear.

789 **BAR HILL AT TWECHAR, nr KIRKINTILLOCH:** 22km N of city, taking A803
xE2   Kirkintilloch t/off from M8, then the 'low' rd to Kilsyth, the B8023, bearing left at the 'black-and-white br'. Next to Twechar Quarry Inn, a path is signed for Bar Hill and the Antonine Wall. Steepish climb for 2km, ignore strange dome of grass. Over to left in copse of trees are the remains of one of the forts on the wall which was built across Scotland in the 2nd century AD. Ground plan explained on a board. This is a special place with strong history vibes and airy views over the plain to the city which came a long time after.   1-A-2

790 **BLACKHILL, nr LESMAHAGOW:** 28km S of city. Another marvellous outlook,
MAP 3   but in the opp direction from above. Take jnct 10/11 on M74, then off the B7078
A5   signed Lanark, take the B7018. 4km along past Clarkston Farm, head uphill for 1km and park by Water Board mound. Walk uphill through fields to rt for about 1km. Unprepossessing hill which unexpectedly reveals a vast vista of most of E central Scotland.   1-A-2

791 **PAISLEY ABBEY:** M8 to Paisley; frequent trains from Central Stn. Abbey Mon-Sat
MAP 3   10am-3.30pm. Every so often on Abbey 'open days', the tower of this amazing
A5   edifice can be climbed. The tower (restored 1926) is 50m high and from the top there's a grand view of the Clyde. This is a rare experience, but phone TIC (889 0711) or Abbey itself (889 7654, am) for details; could be your lucky day. (1848/GREAT ABBEYS)

792 **LYLE HILL, GOUROCK:** Via M8 W to Greenock, then round the coast to rela-
MAP 2   tively genteel old resort of Gourock where the 'Free French' worked in the
E4   yards during the war. A monument has been erected to their memory on the top of Lyle Hill above the town, from where you get one of the most dramatic views of the gr crossroads of the Clyde (Holy L, Gare L and L Long). Best van-tage-point is further along the rd on other side by trig pt. Follow British Rail

stn signs, then Lyle Hill. There's another gr view of the Clyde further down the water at **HAYLIE, LARGS**, the hill 3km from town reached via the A760 rd to Kilbirnie and Paisley. The island of Cumbrae lies in the sound and the sunset.

CAMPSIE FELLS and **GLENIFFER BRAES:** 780/781/WALKS O/SIDE THE CITY.

THE BEST OF THE SPORTS FACILITIES

PUBLIC SWIMMING & INDOOR SPORTS CENTRES

793 **WHITEHILL POOL:** 551 9969. Onslow Dr parallel to Duke St at Meadowpark St
xE4 in the E End nr Alexandra Park (not open to all at all times, so phone for times). 25m pool with sauna/multigym (Universal).

794 **NORTH WOODSIDE LEISURE CENTRE:** 332 8102. Braid Sq. Not far from St
B2 George's Cross nr Charing Cross at the bottom of Gr Western Rd. In a rebuilt area; follow AA signs. Modern pool (25m) and sauna/steam/sun centre plus the usual fitness suite & classes. Mon 10am, Tue & Thur 9.30am, Wed & Fri 7.30am all till 9pm; Sat/Sun 10am-4pm.

795 **POLLOK LEISURE CENTRE:** 881 3313. Cowglen Rd. Not a do-your-lengths
xA5 kind of a pool – more a family water outing. Mon-Fri 9.30am (Tue 10am)-9pm (Wed 5pm), Sat/Sun 10am-4pm.

796 **GOUROCK BATHING POOL:** 01475 631561. On rd S, an open-air heated pool
xA5 on the Clyde. Gr prospect for summers like they used to be. May-Sept. (2134/SWIMMING POOLS)

797 **KELVIN HALL INTERNATIONAL SPORTS ARENA:** 357 2525. Argyle St by
A2 Kelvingrove Museum (757/MAIN ATTRACTIONS). Major venue for international indoor sports competitions, but open otherwise for weights/ badminton/tennis/athletics/climbing. Book hr-long sessions. No squash. Mon, Fri, Sat, Sun 9am, Tue & Thurs 7.30am, Wed 10am all to 10.30pm (6.30pm Sat).

798 **SCOTSTOUN LEISURE CENTRE:** 959 4000. Danes Dr. Huge state-of-the-art
xA2 sports multiplex. 10 lane pool, indoor halls and outdoor pitches. Mon, Wed, Fri 7.30am-10pm, Tue 9am-10pm, Thur 10am-10pm, Sat 9am-6pm, Sun 9am-10pm. (2129/LEISURE CENTRES)

799 **TOLLCROSS PARK LEISURE CENTRE:** 763 2345. Wellshot Rd, Tollcross.
xE4 Another biggie. 10-lane pool, indoor halls, split-level fitness suite. Mon-Fri 7am (Thu 10am)-10pm, Sat 9am-5pm, Sun 9am-9pm.

800 **ALLANDER SPORTS COMPLEX:** 942 2233. Milngavie Rd, Bearsden, 16km N of
xC1 centre via Maryhill Rd. Best by car. Squash (2 courts), sports halls, snooker, badminton, swimming pool, fitness suite. Mon-Fri 7.30am-11pm, Sat/Sun 9am-10pm.

GOLF COURSES

Glas has a vast number of parks and golf courses. The following clubs are the best open to non-members.

801 **CATHKIN BRAES:** 634 0650. Cathkin Rd, SE via Aikenhead Rd/Carmunnock Rd
xC5 to Carmunnock village, then 3km. Best by car. Civilised hilltop course on the S edge of the city. Non-members Mon-Fri (though probably not Fri am).

802 **HAGGS CASTLE:** 427 3355. Dumbreck Rd nr jnct 22 of the M8; go straight on
xC5 to clubhouse at first r/bout. Part of the grounds of Pollok Park; a convenient course, perhaps overplayed. Non-members Mon-Fri.

803 **POLLOK GOLF CLUB:** 632 1080. On the other side of the White Cart Water and
xC5 Pollok House and rather more up-market. Well-wooded parkland course, flat and well kept but not cheap. Women permitted to play but call for specific timeslots!

804 **GLEDDOCH, LANGBANK:** 01475 540704. Excellent 18-hole course adj and
xA5 part of Gleddoch House Hotel (531/HOTELS O/SIDE TOWN). Restricted play.

TENNIS

805 Public courts (Apr-Sep), membership not required: **KELVINGROVE PARK** 6 courts, **QUEEN'S PARK** 6 courts, **VICTORIA PARK** 6 courts. 12noon-8pm.

THE BEST SMALL GALLERIES

*Apart from those listed previously (*MAIN ATTRACTIONS, OTHER ATTRACTIONS*) the following galleries are always worth looking into. The Glasgow Gallery Guide, free from any of them, lists all the current exhibs.*

806 ✓ ✓ **GLASGOW PRINT STUDIO:** 552 0704. 22 & 25 King St. Influential and
E4   accessible upstairs gallery with print work on view and for sale from many of Scotland's leading and rising artists. Cl Sun & Mon. Print Shop over rd.

807 ✓ ✓ **TRANSMISSION GALLERY:** 552 4813. 28 King St. Cutting edge and
E4   often off-the-wall work from contemporary Scottish and international artists. Reflects Glasgow's increasing importance as a hot spot of conceptual art. Stuff you might disagree with. Cl Sun & Mon.

808 ✓ ✓ **THE MODERN INSTITUTE:** 248 3711. 73 Robertson St. Not really a
C4   gallery – more a concept. International rep for cutting-edge art ideas and occasional events. Shows at London's Frieze Art Fair.

809 ✓ ✓ **THE GLASGOW ART FAIR:** George Sq in tented pavilions. Held
D3   every yr in mid-Apr. Most of the galleries on this page and many more are represented; highly selective and good fun. (2211/WHERE TO BUY ART)

810 ✓ **COMPASS GALLERY:** 221 6370. 178 W Regent St. Glasgow's oldest estab-
C3   lished commercial contemporary art gallery. Their 'New Generation' exhib in Jul-Aug shows work from new graduates of the art colleges and has heralded many a career. Combine with the other Gerber gallery (*see below*). Cl Sun.

811 ✓ **CYRIL GERBER FINE ART:** 221 3095. 148 W Regent St. British paintings
C3   and esp the Scottish Colourists and 'name' contemporaries. Gerber, the Compass (*see above*), and Art Exposure (*see below*) have Christmas exhibs where small, accessible paintings can be bought for reasonable prices. Cl Sun.

812 **ART EXPOSURE GALLERY:** 552 7779. 19 Parnie St. Behind the Tron Theatre.
E4 Showcase gallery with a friendly, down-to-earth attitude exhibiting the work of contemporary/graduate Scottish artists. Sort of 'affordable'. Cl Sun.

813 **SHARMANKA KINETIC GALLERY:** 552 7080. Report: 769/OTHER ATTRACTIONS.
E4

THE MACKINTOSH TRAIL

The gr Scottish architect and designer Charles Rennie Mackintosh (1868–1928) had an extraordinary influence on contemporary design.

814 ✓ ✓ ✓ **GLASGOW SCHOOL OF ART:** 353 4526. 167 Renfrew St.
C2   Mackintosh's supreme architectural triumph. It's enough almost to admire it from the st (and maybe best, since this is v much a working college) but there are guided tours at 11am & 2pm (Sat 10.30am, 11.30am, 1pm & more in summer) of the sombre yet light interior, the halls and library. You might wonder if the building itself could be partly responsible for its remarkable output of acclaimed painters. Temp exhibitions in the Mackintosh Gallery. The Tenement House (768/OTHER ATTRACTIONS) is nearby.

815 ✓ ✓ **QUEEN'S CROSS CHURCH:** 870 Garscube Rd, where it becomes
xC1   Maryhill Rd (corner of Springbank St). Built 1896-99. Calm and simple, the antithesis of Victorian Gothic. If all churches had been built like this, we'd go more often. The HQ of the Charles Rennie Mackintosh Society (946 6600), which was founded in 1973. Mon-Fri 10am-5pm, Sun 2-5pm. Cl Sat. DONATION

816 ✓ ✓ **THE MACKINTOSH HOUSE:** 330 5431. Univ Ave. Opp and part of the
A1   Hunterian Museum (763/MAIN ATTRACTIONS) within the univ campus. The Master's house has been transplanted and methodically reconstructed from the next st (they say even the light is the same). If you've ever wondered what the fuss is about, go and see how innovative and complete an artist, designer and architect he was, in this inspiring yet habitable set of rms. Mon-Sat 9.30am-5pm (cl 12.30-1.30pm & Sun). FREE

817 ✓ ✓ **SCOTLAND STREET SCHOOL MUSEUM:** 287 0500. 225 Scotland St.
B5   Opp Shields Rd u/ground and best app by car from Eglinton St (A77

Kilmarnock Rd over Jamaica St Br). Entire school (from 1906) preserved (and recently renovated) as museum of education through Victorian/ Edwardian and wartimes. Original, exquisite Mackintosh features, esp tiling, and powerfully redolent of happy school days. This is a uniquely evocative time capsule. Café and temporary exhibs. Mon-Thur, Sat 10am-5pm, Fri & Sun 11am-5pm.   FREE

818 ✓ **THE LIGHTHOUSE:** 221 6362. Mitchell Lane, off Buchanan St. Glasgow's
D4 legacy from its yr as UK City of Architecture and Design. Changing exhibs in Mackintosh's 1893–5 building for *The Glasgow Herald* newspaper. Also houses a shop with cool design stuff, a café-bar & an interpretation centre on the gr architect with fantastic rooftop views from the corner tower. Mon-Sat 10.30am-5.30pm (Tue 11am), Sun 12-5pm.   ADM

819 ✓ **THE HILL HOUSE, HELENSBURGH:** 01436 673900. Upper Colquhoun St.
MAP 2 Take Sinclair St off Princes St (at Romanesque tower and TIC) and go 2km
E4 uphill, taking left into Kennedy Dr and follow signs. A complete house incorporating Mackintosh's typical total unity of design, built for Walter Blackie in 1902-4. Much to marvel over and wish that everybody else would go away and you could stay there for the night. There's even a library full of books to keep you occupied. Tearoom; gdns. Apr-Oct 1.30-5.30pm. Helensburgh is 45km NW of city centre via Dumbarton (A82) and A814 up N Clyde coast.   ADMN

820 **THE WILLOW TEA ROOMS:** 332 0521. Sauchiehall St & Buchanan St. A café he
D3, D4 designed (or what's left of it); where to go for a break on the trail (657/TEAROOMS).

821 **MARTYR'S PUBLIC SCHOOL:** 287 8955. Parson St. Latest renovation and pub-
xE3 lic access to another spectacular Mackintosh building. Check those roof trusses.   FREE

822 **HOUSE FOR AN ART LOVER:** 353 4770. Bellahouston Park. 10 Dumbreck Rd.
xA5 Take the M8 W, then the M77, turn rt onto Dumbreck Rd and it's on your left. These rms were designed, nearly a century ago, specifically, it would seem, for willowy women to come and go, talking of Michelangelo. Detail is the essence of Mackintosh, and there's plenty here, but the overall effect is of space and light and a complete absence of clutter. Design shop and Café (660/BEST TEA-ROOMS) on the ground floor. Phone for opening times.   ADMN

ESSENTIAL CULTURE

UNIQUE VENUES

823 ✓✓ **THE CITIZENS' THEATRE:** 429 0022. Gorbals St, just over the river.
D5 Fabulous main auditorium and 2 small studios. Drama at its v best. One of Britain's most influential theatres, esp for design. Refurbished with lottery funds. Love the theatre, love this theatre.

824 ✓✓ **THE TRAMWAY:** 422 2023. 25 Albert Dr on S side. Studio, theatre
xC5 and vast performance & exhibition space. Dynamic and widely influential with an innovative and varied programme from all over the world, tho' slated to be the home of Scottish Ballet at TGP. Secret Garden behind (1612/GARDENS). Worth a visit.

825 ✓ **CCA:** 332 7521. Centre for Contemporary Arts, 350 Sauchiehall St. Major
C3 refurb of central arts-lab complex for all kinds of performance & visual arts presentation. Impressive atrium/courtyard houses cool café/restau called Tempus. Watch press for CCA programme.

826 ✓ **THE ARCHES:** 221 4001. 253 Argyle St. Experimental and vital theatre on
D4 a tight budget in the railway arches under the tracks of Central Stn. Director Andy Arnold's gong must surely be in the post! Opening times vary. W/end clubs among the best (843/ESS. CULTURE/CLUBBING IT). Bar/café cool place to hang & even talk.

827 **THE TRON THEATRE:** 552 4267. 63 Trongate. Contemporary Scottish theatre
E4 and other interesting performance, esp music. Gr café-bar with food before and *après* (582/BEST BISTROS).

828 **GLASGOW FILM THEATRE:** 332 6535. Rose St at downtown end of
C3 Sauchiehall St. Known affectionately as GFT, has café/bar and 2 screens for essential art house flicks.

829 ✓✓✓ **BARROWLAND BALLROOM:** 552 4601. Gallowgate. When its
xE4 lights are on, you can't miss it. The Barrowland is world-famous
and for many bands one of their favourite gigs. It's tacky and a bit run-down,
but distinctly venerable; and with its high stage and sprung dance floor, perfect for rock 'n' roll. The Glas audience is 'the best in the world'.

FESTIVALS

THE WEST END FESTIVAL: 341 0844. 2 weeks in June. Neighbourhood and
arts fest that incl parade in Byres Rd and a lot of drinking.

GLASGOW INTERNATIONAL JAZZ FESTIVAL: 552 3552. 1 week in July.
Scotland's most credible jazz (in its widest sense) prog over diff venues.

GLASGOW ART FAIR: 552 6027. 4 days in Apr. (2211/WHERE TO BUY ART)

CELTIC CONNECTIONS: 353 8000. 3 weeks in Jan.

HOGMANAY: 552 6027. 31 December. Not on the same scale as Edin. Usually
a stage in George Sq (ticketed) at least.

JAZZ MUSIC

CAFÉ SOURCE: 548 6020. St Andrews on the Square.

BLACKFRIARS: 552 5924. 36 Bell St.

FOLK MUSIC

830 ✓ **SCOTIA BAR:** 552 8681. 112 Stockwell St. The folk club and writers' retreat
D4 and all things non-high cultural. A mixed programme but always the
'right folk' here. (710/UNIQUE GLAS PUBS)

831 ✓ **VICTORIA BAR:** Briggait. Nr the Scotia (*see above*) and a similar set-up. Fri
D4 & Sat night sessions of Irish/Scottish trad music. (709/UNIQUE GLAS PUBS)

832 ✓ **THE HALT BAR:** 564 1527. Woodlands Rd. Among a mixed music pro-
B2 gramme, always some folk for the kind of folk who inhabit the bar.
(708/UNIQUE GLAS PUBS)

833 ✓ **CLUTHA VAULTS:** 552 7520. 167 Stockwell St. E end nr Clyde. Gr atmos for
D4 the drink and the music. Mixed programme: readings, bluegrass, open
mic slot. (711/UNIQUE GLAS PUBS)

ISLAY INN: 334 1055. Argyle St. Fri-Sun. More squeeze-box Scottish than folk.

CEILIDHS

834 **THE RIVERSIDE:** 248 3144. Fox St, off Clyde St. The place that started the
D4 ceilidh revival in Glas. Upstairs in quiet st, the joint is jumping. Fri-Sat from
8pm, fills up quickly. Good bands. Good, mixed crowd.

LIVE ROCK & POP AND BEST CLUBS

835 **SECC:** 248 3000/0870 040 4000. Finnieston Quay beyond the city centre and,
A3 for many, beyond the pale as far as concerts are concerned (big shed, not big
on atmos), but there are 3 different-sized halls for mainly arena-sized acts and
everyone from pop to Pav and U2 have played here (but not Madge).

836 **CLYDE AUDITORIUM, aka THE ARMADILLO:** Adj to the SECC. A smaller the-
A3 atre space, a belter for concerts, but not big enough for the megas.

BARROWLANDS BALLROOM: The dancehall! See Unique Venues, above.

837 **KING TUT'S WAH WAH HUT:** 221 5279. 272 St Vincent St. Every bit as good as
C3 its namesake in Alphabet City used to be; the room for interesting new bands,
make-or-break atmos and cramped. Bands on the club circuit play to a damp
and appreciative crowd. See flyers. Doors open 8.30pm. Tickets at bar or Tower
Records, Argyle St.

838 **NICE 'N' SLEAZY:** 333 9637. 421 Sauchiehall St at the W End. Not esp sleazy
C3 and fairly rock 'n' roll. Popular art school hang-out. Every flavour of alco-pop
and voddie to drink. Good indie jukebox and PlayStation for hire. Bands

downstairs (esp Thu-Sun) with a nominal entrance charge. Usually from 9pm. All over before midnight.

839 **THE CATHOUSE:** 248 6606. 15 Union St, and **THE GARAGE:** 332 1120.
D4, C3 Sauchiehall St, W End (same owners). Live rock clubs with mixed programme on various nights depending on availability of touring bands (other 'clubs' on other nights).

840 **THE 13TH NOTE:** 553 1638. CAFE 60 King St and CLUB, Clyde St (243 2177).
E4 The vegn restau in King St (648/VEGN RESTAUS) and the gig thing down nr the river. Various combos of the indie or merely hip in both. These are the ones to watch. Most nights 8pm-midnight. Clubs on 4 times a week till 3am. Tue-Sun 8pm-3.30am.

841 **COTTIER'S:** 357 5825. 93 Hyndland St. In the densely populated quadrant
xA1 betw Dumbarton Rd and Byres Rd. A neighbourhood atmos to this converted church (off Hyndland St nr Highburgh Rd). Restau upstairs (577/BEST BISTROS). Bar and theatre, on the ground level, serve as a platform for local talent and cult-ish acts from abroad.

BLACKFRIARS, THE HALT, SCOTIA BAR, THE CLUTHA VAULTS: See above in Folk. All have varied programme of live music incl 'open mic' spots. Free.

842 **GLASGOW ROYAL CONCERT HALL:** 353 8000. 2 Sauchiehall St. Full prog of
D3 mainly classical music but also a civilised theatre for more thoughtful pop.

CLUBBING IT

843 **CLUBS AT THE ARCHES:** 0901 022 0300. At the Arches Theatre, Argyle St (see
D4 above), w/ends only. Glasgow's finest. 2/3 vaulted archways, serious sound system and v up-for-it crowd. Best clubs: Colours, Inside Out, Slam one-offs.

844 **THE SUB CLUB:** 248 4600. 22 Jamaica St. Sub street right enough for long-est
D4 dance culture club.

845 **THE TUNNEL:** 204 1000. 84 Mitchell St. Once defined club culture in Glas. Still
D4 high-glam quotient and designer ambience with vogue-ish crowd. W/ends (Ark and Triumph) and student nights. On same circuit as Liverpool's Cream so big-name DJs every month.

846 **CUBE:** 226 8990. 34 Queen St. Sliver of doorway leads to underground beat-
D4 box for boy/girl ravers. (Gay Mon.)

847 **TRASH:** 572 3372. 197 Pitt St. Mega disco thing in city centre. Student-ish
C3 crowd so not teensy. Clubs vary, till 3am.

848 **ARCHAOS:** 204 3189. 25 Queen St. Dance emporium on 3 floors, incl Betty's
D4 Mayonnaise. Central dance floor has state-of-the-art lighting. Balconies upstairs.

849 **MAS:** 221 7080. 23 Royal Exchange Sq. Colin Barr's drinking and dancin' club
D4 upstairs opp Gallery of Modern Art. Hot local & often interesting imported DJs. Best clubs: Subculture & Optimo. Wed-Mon 11pm-3am.

SECTION 4

Regional Hotels and Restaurants

THE BEST HOTELS AND RESTAURANTS IN ARGYLL

See also 2250/BEST OF OBAN. *Refer to Map 2.*

850
D2
✓ ✓ **ISLE OF ERISKA:** 01631 720371. 20km N of Oban. Report: 1210/COUNTRY-HOUSE HOTELS.

851
D3
✓ ✓ **ARDANAISEIG, LOCH AWE:** 01866 833333. Report: 1216/COUNTRY-HOUSE HOTELS.

852
D2
✓ ✓ **AIRDS HOTEL, PORT APPIN:** 01631 730236. 32km N of Oban 4km off A828. For a long time one of the foremost hostelries in the N & a legendary gourmet experience. Recent new owners Shaun & Jenny McKivragan keep chef Paul Burns & seem determined not to change too much tho perhaps make it less formal. Conservatory restau on roadside with 3 AA rosettes firmly in place. Pt Appin one of Scotland's most charming places. Lismore passenger ferry 2km away (2305/MAGIC ISLANDS).

12RMS (+4) FEB-DEC T/T XPETS CC KIDS LOTS/MED.EX

EAT One of the best meals you will find in the N (and S, E and W). EXP

853
C4
✓ ✓ **CRINAN HOTEL, CRINAN:** 01546 830261. 8km off A816. On coast, 60km S of Oban (Lochgilphead 12km) at head of the Crinan Canal which joins L Fyne with the sea. O/side on the quay is the boat which has landed those massive prawns, sweet clams and other creatures with legs or valves, which are cooked v simply and brought on heaped tureens to your table. Inside a choice of the 'Westward' dining rm on the ground floor or Lock 16 the top floor bistro with a stunning view of the Sound of Jura (latter not always open) or pub grub in the cosier bar. This hotel has long housed one of the gr seafood restaus in the UK. Nick Ryan presides; his wife's (the notable artist, Frances MacDonald) pictures are fitting & for sale.

22RMS JAN-DEC T/T PETS CC KIDS MED.EX

854
D4
✓ **THE ROYAL HOTEL AT TIGHNABRUAICH:** 01700 811239. Roger and Bea McKie & daughter Clare in the kitchen continue to transform this one of many mansions on the seafront into one of the best hotels in the W of Scotland. Lovely rms, many looking over to Bute, comfy furnishings & pictures. Dining rm & bar with conservatory restau. Bea leads gr out-front service & Clare McKie is a chef to watch. Doon the Water was never as good as this. Bar meals 7 days, dining cl Sun/Mon. 11RMS JAN-DEC T/T PETS CC XKIDS MED.EX

855
D3
✓ **GEORGE HOTEL, INVERARAY:** 01499 302111. Main st of interesting town on L Fyne with credible attractions (2356/HOLIDAY CENTRES). Ancient inn (1770) still in the capable and friendly hands of the Clark family with real atmosphere in bar. Rms recently refurb & tastefully so in a Highland chic kind of way. Open fire, gr grub & locals in the bar. This hotel is exceptionally good value. 15RMS JAN-DEC T/T PETS CC KIDS MED.INX

856
C3
✓ **LUNGA HOUSE, CRAOBH HAVEN:** 01852 500237. Signed off A816. Family seat of the Lindsay-Macdougalls, welcomes B&B & advance dinner bookings. Here you are in the family home – portraits, ephemera. Rooms retain ancestral air. Colin and Sarah entertain with charm and a little post-sixties eccentricity. Self-cat avail. 4RMS JAN-DEC T/T PETS CC KIDS INX

857
D3
✓ **TAYCHREGGAN, KILCHRENAN:** 01866 833211. Signed off A85 just before Taynuilt, 30km from Oban and nestling on a bluff by L Awe in imposing countryside. Quay for the old ferry to Portsonachan is nearby with boats available. With a spruce refurb & new rooms, rowan tree at the door and water lapping at gnds' edge, this hostelry suffers a tad from absentee landlord. But fine dining in restau enjoyed near & far. Gr pub 1 km walk away (1379/PUBS). 19RMS JAN-DEC T/T PETS CC KIDS LOTS

858
D4
KILFINAN HOTEL, KILFINAN: 01700 821201. 13km from Tighnabruaich on B8000. A much-loved hotel that's been thro' bewildering changes of ownership in the last few yrs tho' charming Madalon is always there. Now Mick & Tricia Cressdee preside over this classic, quiet getaway inn (quiet as the graveyard adj) with long-standing rep for food in bar and dining rm. For a MED. EX retreat on a quiet peninsula, this is still a good bet.

11RMS JAN-DEC T/T PETS CC KIDS MED.EX

859 **LOCH FYNE HOTEL, INVERARAY:** 01499 302148. Another surprisingly ok
D3 hotel in this charming town. On main A83 towards Lochgilphead o/looking
loch. Part of British Trust Hotels; this one of their best. Pleasing & simple
design makeover with a touch of tartan. Pool & facs. They do take coach
parties. 80RMS JAN-DEC T/T PETS CC KIDS MED.INX

860 **STONEFIELD CASTLE HOTEL, TARBERT (ARGYLL):** 01880 820836. Just
D4 o/side town on the A83, a castle which evokes the 1970s more than preced-
ing centuries. Splendid luxuriant gdns leading down to L Fyne. Dining-rm
with baronial splendour and staggering views. Friendly, flexible staff; overall,
it seems quintessentially Scottish and ok, esp for families (1225/KIDS) though
the style police would have words. Most deals incl dinner too. (MED).
33RMS JAN-DEC T/T PETS CC KIDS TOS MED.EX

861 **WEST LOCH HOTEL, TARBERT (ARGYLL):** 01880 820283. Picturesque 1710
D4 former coaching inn on the cusp of Kintyre, just o/side of Tarbert on A83.
Within easy reach of ferries to Islay, Gigha and Arran. Lovely views of loch over
rd, nice staff, relaxed atmos, coaching inn character remains. Good food in
conservatory restau. You can feel at home here & we'll forgive the Jack
Vettrianos. (1262/INNS) 7RMS FEB-DEC X/T PETS CC KIDS MED.INX

862 **COLUMBA HOTEL, TARBERT:** 01880 820808. New owners of this ideal bud-
D4 get hotel on water front in this perfect Argyll town. Bar v popular with
yachties and locals. Meals till 9pm. Some refurb of rms wouldn't go amiss.
10RMS JAN-DEC T/T PETS CC KIDS TOS MED.INX

863 **DUN NA MARA, BENDERLOCH:** 01631 720233. Off A828 Oban–Ft William rd,
D2 12km N of Oban. Contemp conversion of seaside mansion. Good reports.
7RMS JAN-DEC X/T XPETS CC KIDS MED.INX

864 **BARRIEMORE, OBAN:** 01631 566356. Corran Esplanade. This hotel, the v last
D2 one in a st full of them along the coast to Ganavan, is a good bet if you're in
Oban. Front rms have excellent views of Kerrera and Lorne. Recently opened
for dinners (JAN-DEC). 13RMS MAR-OCT X/T PETS CC KIDS INX

RESTAURANTS

865 ✓ **INVER COTTAGE, STRATHLACHLAN, L FYNE:** 01369 860537. S of
D4 Strachur on B8000, the scenic south rd by L Fyne, a cottage bar/bistro
o/looking loch & ruins of Castle Lachlan. Home baking & cooking at its best.
Comfort food & surroundings. Lovely walk before or after. A real find! Apr-Oct.
All-day menus till 6pm (9pm in summer). INX

866 ✓ **CHATTERS, DUNOON:** 01369 706402. 58 John St next to Safeway. Rosie
E4 Macinnes' excellent restau in town rather than on esplanade is, by itself,
a good reason for getting the ferry. The Cowal peninsula awaits your explorations (and Benmore Gdns 1590/GARDENS). Bar menu and à la carte, and a
small gdn for drinks or lunch on a good day. All delightful. Wed-Sat only, lunch
and dinner. MED

867 **CREGGANS INN, STRACHUR:** 01369 860279. 2km N Strachur on A815 to
D3 Cairndow, a busy rd in summer along L Fyne. Road house bar/restau and more
formal dining-rm in a place once notable as the fiefdom of Sir Fitzroy & Lady
Maclean, but now the Robertsons'. 14 rms upstairs with some fine views of
loch. CHP/MED/EXP

See also 2244/AYR. Refer to Map 2 except where indicated.

868
E6 ✔ ✔ **THE WESTIN TURNBERRY RESORT, TURNBERRY:** 01655 331000. Not just a hotel on the Ayrshire coast, more a way of life centred on golf. Looks over the 2 courses which are difficult to get on unless you're a guest (2078/GREAT GOLF). All that should be expected of a world-class hotel except, perhaps, the buzz; but plenty of golf chat and time moving slowly. The spa complex adj has state-of-the-art 'treatments', even exercise – with deals for day visitors & nice pool. Colin Montgomerie 'Golf Academy' takes all sorts. Brasserie here has excl 'light' all day menus; main dining-rm looks over the courses to Ailsa Craig beyond – dinner only, and epic Sun lunch. New lovely lodges down the hill.   221RMS JAN-DEC T/T PETS CC KIDS LOTS

EAT The Terrace Brasserie is the light place to eat; pastas, risottos, etc. Main restau has 2 AA rosettes.   MED/EXP

869
MAP 1 ✔ ✔ **GLENAPP CASTLE, by BALLANTRAE:** 01465 831212. New upmar-
A2 ket jewel in the crown for S Ayrshire (full report: 1213/SUPERLATIVE COUNTRY HOUSE HOTELS).

870
E6 ✔ **CULZEAN CASTLE, nr MAYBOLE:** 01655 760615. 18km S of Ayr (coast rd most pleasant), this is accom in the suites of Culzean, the house itself (1825/CASTLES) so a bed for the night rarely comes as posh as this (includes the famous Eisenhower suite). Rates are exp, but incl afternoon tea. Dinner (incl wine) is avail. The cliff-top setting, the gdns & the vast grounds are superb. Programme of events thro'out yr incl major concert in May; many weddings.   6 SUITES APR-OCT T/T XPETS CC KIDS LOTS

871
E4 ✔ **GLEDDOCH HOUSE, LANGBANK, nr GREENOCK:** 01475 540711. 35km from Glas by fast rd – M8/A8 t/off marked Langbank/Houston after jnct 31, follow Houston then signs. Set in extensive grounds (including 18-hole golf course), with commanding view of Clyde by Dumbarton Rock (but only from a few rms). Leisure club adj with a 15km pool. Excellent conservatory and dining-rms. Most civilised place to stay close to Glas tho' some recent com-plaints about service. New block of rms 2004; main house best.
                38(40+)RMS JAN-DEC T/T PETS CC KIDS MED.EX

EAT Excellent restau with 2 AA rosettes. Scottish accents.   EXP

872
E6 ✔ **THE IVY HOUSE, AYR:** 01292 442336. North Park on the Alloway Rd, almost feels like the country. Cosy, well-appointed rms with bathrms bordering on the lavish. Seriously good restau makes this the best stopover Ayr/Alloway way.   5RMS JAN-DEC T/T PETS CC KIDS MED.EX

EAT One of the best meals in Ayrshire, tho at a price.   EXP

873 **ENTERKINE HOUSE, nr ANNBANK, by AYR:** 01292 521608. 10km Ayr in
E6 beautiful grounds tho Annbank (2km) not the loveliest of vills. Self-con-sciously upmarket with pleasant tho' not so modern public rms. Chef Douglas Smith v good indeed Whether you like the ambience or not, go eat.
                6RMS JAN-DEC T/T XPETS CC XKIDS LOTS

874 **PIERSLAND HOTEL, TROON:** 01292 314747. Craig End Rd opp Portland Golf
E6 Course which is next to Royal Troon (2079/GREAT GOLF). Mansion house of some character and ambience much favoured for weddings. Wood-panelling, open fires, lovely gdns only a 'drive' away from the courses (no preferential booking on Royal, but Portland usually poss) and lots of gr golf nearby. 2 AA rosettes for the food.   30RMS JAN-DEC T/T PETS CC KIDS EXP

875 **LOCHGREEN HOUSE, TROON:** 01292 313343. Part of the Bill Costley empire
E6 in this neck of the woods, Lochgreen (adj to Royal Troon Golf Course) the most full-on upmarket – new extension gives 40 rms. Good restau with a Costley in the kitchen. The **BRIG O' DOON** at Alloway is the romance-and-Rabbie Burns hotel (01292 442466), lots of weddings and only 5 rms, while **HIGHGROVE** (01292 312511) is that bit more intimate, just outside Troon. Major refurb 2003. All operate at a very acceptable standard – Highgrove has 2 AA rosettes, Lochgreen has 3. These Costleys also have a good roadside inn – the **COCHRANE** at Gatehead, nearby (1411/PUB FOOD).

876 THE PARK HOTEL, KILMARNOCK: 01563 545999. Rugby Park ie adj
E5 Kilmarnock's football stadium. Contemp business & family hotel much better
than chains of travelodge ilk. Good café/restau. Sports facs at the ground opp.
50RMS JAN-DEC T/T PETS CC KIDS MED.INX

877 SHIELDHILL CASTLE, QUOTHQUAN, nr BIGGAR: 01899 220035. Well S of the
MAP 3 Clyde, Glasgow & anywhere, a countryside retreat just off the B7016 Biggar-
B5 Carnwath. Mostly dates from late 16thC but older bits go back to 1199.
Famous guests have included a certain Mr Mandela. Pick yr rm carefully and
you get a 4-poster and a jacuzzi. 2 AA rosettes for the food.
16RMS JAN-DEC T/T PETS CC KIDS EXP/LOTS

878 WILDING'S HOTEL & RESTAURANT, MAIDENS: 01655 331401. Maidens is
E6 coastal vill in S Ayrshire, S of Maybole & lovely Culzean (1825/CASTLES), so a
good base. Run by Brian Sage, restaurateur, this is perhaps more a restau with
rms. Many o/look serene harbour but are more motel than seaside inn.
10RMS JAN-DEC T/T PETS CC KIDS MED.INX

EAT May be a drive for dinner, but a beautiful spot & excl menu. Food LO 9pm.
They come from all over the county (& Turnberry) so book w/ends.   MED

RESTAURANTS

879 ✓ FOUTERS, AYR: 01292 261391. 2a Academy St. Off Sandgate. The best
E6 ✓ meal in town. Laurie and Fran Black 25 yrs in their cellar bistro caring
about food and wine and Scotland's efforts to do better. Creative cooking and
here the phrase 'best local ingredients' means what it says. Mon-Sat lunch &
LO 10pm. Sun: dinner only.   MED

880 ✓ BRAIDWOODS, nr DALRY: 01294 833544. First find Dalry; near the Esso
E5 ✓ garage take the small rd to Saltcoats and the restau is discreetly signed
around a mile out that rd. Once you find Keith and Nicola's place, you'll be glad
you made the effort. Michelin star, 3 AA rosettes, nice people, great food. Best
meal in the shire. Wed/Sun lunch and Tues-Sat dinner.   MED

881 ✓ MACCALLUMS, THE HARBOUR, TROON: 01292 319339. Harbourside
E6 ✓ seafood bistro. Report: 1438/SEAFOOD.   MED/INX

882 ✓ RISTORANTE LA VIGNA, LANARK: 01555 664320. 40 Wellgate. Famously
MAP 3 ✓ good Italian restau in a back st in Lanark. Unexpected, and quite a find if
B5 you're lost in the badlands. Superb Italian wine-list. Lunch Mon-Sat, dinner 7
days.   MED

883 RESTAURANTS in STRATHAVEN: This Lanarkshire vill (pron *Straven*) S of E
MAP 3 Kilbride & W of Lanark & the Clyde Valley, has 3 good restaus. The **STEAYBAN:**
A5 01357 523400 is a bar/restau in Glassford, 2km from Strathaven & serves excl
suppers (Wed-Sat) & Sun lunch. The **TRATTORIA da MARIO**, 01357 522604, is
a fine Italian tratt comparable with any in the city, & The **CABIN** is a good-
value family restau. Both in the centre of Strathaven, a foody oasis in the
southern hinterland of Glasgow.   ALL INX

884 THE WHEATSHEAF, SYMINGTON, nr AYR & PRESTWICK: 01563 830307. Off
E6 main A77 (2km), just N of main Prestwick r/about. Roadside & village inn
tucked away off main rd with big local rep for wholesome pub grub. Their
steak pie is famous. No fuss, gr service. Report 1401/PUB FOOD. LO 9.30pm.

885 PAPILLONS, GOUROCK: 01475 633998. Main st above the trad Victoria pub;
E4 still not in the foodie guides but big local reputation. German owner. Lunch
Tues-Sun, dinner Tues-Sat.   INX

886 FINS, FAIRLIE, nr LARGS: 01475 568989. 8 km S of Largs on A78. Excellent
E5 seafood bistro. Report: 1447/SEAFOOD RESTAUS.   MED

THE BEST HOTELS AND RESTAURANTS IN THE SOUTH-WEST

See also 2347/BEST OF DUMFRIES. Refer to Map 1.

887 **✓✓ KNOCKINAAM LODGE, PORTPATRICK:** 01776 810471. Tucked away
A3 on dream cove, historic country house full of fresh flowers, gr food, sea air and informal, but v good service. New owners Sian & Diana Ibbotson are planning improvements. (1212/COUNTRY-HOUSE HOTELS)

10RMS JAN-DEC T/T PETS CC KIDS LOTS

EAT Best meal in the S. from outstanding chef, Tony Pierce. Fixed menu – lots of unexpected treats. Michelin Star.　　　　　　　　EXP

888 **✓ CORSEWALL LIGHTHOUSE HOTEL, STRANRAER:** 01776 853220. A718
A2 to Kirkcolm 3km, B738 to Corsewall 6km (follow signs). Wild location on cliff top. Cosily furnished clever but cramped (or snug) conversion. Best with a suite and a close personal friend. The adj fully functioning lighthouse (since 1817) makes for surreal evenings. New owners the Ward family are hoping to expand.　　　　9RMS (+ SUITES) JAN-DEC T/T PETS CC KIDS EXP

889 **✓ CAVENS, KIRKBEAN:** 01387 880234. 20km S Dumfries via A710, Cavens
D2 signed from Kirkbean 2km to Carse Bay. We haven't stayed in this elegant mansion (once home to tobacco baron Sir Richard Oswald) in 6 landscaped acres, but readers & others heartily recommend. Fine dining, fine views. Angus & Jane Fordyce will pamper most of your whims apparently.

8RMS JAN-DEC T/T XPETS CC KIDS MED.EX

890 **KIRROUGHTREE HOTEL, NEWTON STEWART:** 01671 402141. On A712. Built
B2 1719, Rabbie Burns was once here. Extensive country house newly refurb with heavy drapes and plush atmos. Original panelled hall and stairs, spacious rms. Food here gets 3 AA rosettes and is probably the main reason for coming. New man in kitchen – Ralph Mueller, formerly at the Kilfinan on Cowal consolidating rep for food.　　　17RMS FEB-DEC T/T PETS CC KIDS LOTS

891 **BALCARY BAY, AUCHENCAIRN, nr CASTLE DOUGLAS:** 01556 640311. 20km
C3 S of Castle Douglas and Dalbeattie. Off A711 at end of shore rd and as close to the water as you can get without getting wet. Ideal for walking and bird watching. Andrew Lipp, new in the kitchen, continues a strong committment to local produce.　　　　20RMS MAR-NOV T/T PETS CC KIDS MED.EXP

892 **CLONYARD HOUSE, COLVEND, nr ROCKCLIFFE, nr DALBEATTIE:** 01556
D3 630372. On Solway Coast rd nr Rockcliffe and Kippford (1639/COASTAL VILLAGES; 2071/ COASTAL WALKS) but not on sea. Later extension to house provides bedrms adj to patio gdn with own private access and … aviary! Friendly family, decent pub grub.　　　17RMS JAN-DEC T/T PETS CC KIDS MED.INX

893 **GOOD SPOTS IN KIRKCUDBRIGHT:** pronounced 'cur-coo-bree'; a gem of a
C3 town. On a street filled with posh B&Bs the **GLADSTONE HOUSE** stands out (High St 01557 331734). **SELKIRK ARMS** (yup, High St, 01557 330402) is much more your 'proper hotel'; new owners John & Sheila Shearer in May 2003.

894 **ANCHOR, KIPPFORD:** 01556 620205. Seaside hotel in cute vill 3km off main
C2 A710. New owners making waves. More reports please.

7RMS (+ COTT) JAN-DEC X/T PETS CC KIDS INX

895 **ABBEY ARMS & CRIFFEL INN, NEW ABBEY, nr DUMFRIES:** 01387
D2 850489/850244. Opp each other on village sq, comfy rms above village inns with loads of atmos nr Sweetheart Abbey and Criffel (2000/HILLS) 12km S of Dumfries.　　　　　　　　　　　　　　　　　　CHP

896 **BEECHWOOD COUNTRY HOUSE HOTEL, MOFFAT:** 01683 220210. O/look
D1 Moffat with dreamy, bucolic views W over valley to gentle upland sheep pastures. Much travelled new owners Stavros & Cheryl Michaelides run a relaxed, welcoming hotel. Good food, & we liked the beds!

7RMS FEB-DEC T/T PETS CC KIDS MED.EX

RESTAURANTS

897 ✔ ✔ **THE PLUMED HORSE, CROSSMICHAEL, nr CASTLE DOUGLAS:**
C2 01556 670333. Just N of Castle Douglas on A713. Amazing find in
unexpected surroundings – serious food by inimitable chef/prop/even waiter,
Tony Borthwick. Firmly est on foodie map of Scotland. Michelin star & other
food guides routinely praise it to the skies. Expect first-class ingredients and
real flair. Lunch Tues-Fri and Sun, dinner Tues-Sat (7 or 8pm).   MED.EXP

898 ✔ **LIME TREE RESTAURANT, MOFFAT:** 01683 221654. High St. Raved about
D1 by Joanna B, Scotland's most get-around food critic, this newish venture
has become a destination restau in this historic spa town. Mat & Artemis
Seddon aim to serve good food at sensible prices – but this is an understate-
ment – it's fantastic value. Tues-Sat 6.30-9.30pm, Sun 12.30-2.30pm.   MED

899 **THE CROWN, PORTPATRICK:** 01776 810261. Harbourside hotel/pub restau
A3 with better than your av pub-grub. Goes like a fair in summer. Lounge and
conservatory. Most excl chips. 7 days. LO 10pm. Competition next door from
the **WATERFRONT** 01776 810800. Crown is the better pub, newcomer has
more mod rms.   INX

900 **CAMPBELLS, PORTPATRICK:** 01776 810314. Further round harbour from
A3 Crown, above. More upmarket but medium-range seafood bistro.
Unpretentious fishy fare (some pork/lamb/beef/duck/chicken dishes ie some-
thing for everyone). 7 days lunch and LO 10pm.   INX

901 **THE AULD ALLIANCE, KIRKCUDBRIGHT:** 01557 330569. Solway scallops and
C3 salmon, etc. 7 nights. Franco-Scottish flavour. Open Easter-Oct for dinner only
(and Sun lunch) but the quieter it gets, the less they open so call and book.
MED

902 **CARLO'S, CASTLE DOUGLAS:** 211 King Street, 01556 503977. Curiously,
C2 Castle Douglas is Scotland's food town. Not much to write home about but
this. Bustling atmos in small rm with odd green phone box. Best Italian food
in S. Open Tues-Sun from 6.30pm – until 9.30 in winter, until you stop eating
in summer.   INX

903 **HULLABALOO, DUMFRIES:** 01387 259679. At the Robert Burns Centre, W side
D2 of the river and which also houses the local art-house cinema. Wraps, steaks,
burgers & superior soup; oh and sandwiches. Cl time varies acc to movie
times, but usually 11am-9/10pm (wint Tues-Sat only).   INX

904 **KIRKPATRICK'S, KIRKCUDBRIGHT:** 01557 330888. Scottish restau opened in
C3 2002 & doing good business with vistors & locals alike. LO 9.15pm. Cl Mon &
Jan.

905 **THE MASONIC ARMS, GATEHOUSE OF FLEET:** 01557 814335. New owners
C2 Chris & Sue Walker & chef Paul Somerville, all formerly of Creebridge Hotel, are
determined to make their mark on the culinary map. Not yet open at TGP but
looks very promising & we wish them all the best! Great local bar. Apr-Oct
Noon-2pm, 6-9pm. Nov-Mar closed Mon-Tues.   MED

THE BEST HOTELS AND RESTAURANTS IN CENTRAL SCOTLAND

See also 2252/BEST OF STIRLING. *Refer to Map 3 except where indicated.*

906
B4
✓ ✓ **CROMLIX HOUSE, DUNBLANE:** 01786 822125. 3km from A9 and 4km from town on B8033; first follow signs for Perth, and then Kinbuck. A long drive through an old estate with splendid mature trees to this spacious country mansion both sumptuous and comfortable (fabulous bathrooms). Ailsa and David Assenti have a firm but not formal touch with gr attention to detail & service. No leisure facs – this is a place for rest & respite. Walk the 3000 sylvan acres & fishing lochs. The House Loch nearby comes complete with swans and solitude. The house has its own chapel! Paul Devonshire's 2 AA rosette menu.

14RMS (8 SUITES) FEB-DEC T/T PETS CC KIDS LOTS

EAT Non-residents: drive that drive for dinner (or Sun lunch)! Gr conservatory.

EXP

907
A3
✓ ✓ **THE ROMAN CAMP, CALLANDER:** 01877 330003. Behind the main st (at E or Stirling end), away from the tourist throng and with extensive gdns on the R Teith; another, more elegant world. Roman ruins nearby, but the house was built for the Dukes of Perth and has been a hotel since the war. Rms low-ceilinged and snug; period furnishings; some rms small, many magnificent. In the old building corridors do creak. Delightful drawing rm and conservatory. Oval dining-rm v sympatico. Private chapel should a prayer come on and, of course, many weddings. Rods for fishing – the river swishes past the lawn. More rooms may be added at TGP.

14RMS JAN-DEC T/T PETS CC KIDS LOTS

EAT Dining-rm effortlessly the best food in town (with chef Ian McNaught).

EXP

908
B4
✓ **BOUZY ROUGE at the SHERIFFMUIR INN, SHERIFFMUIR nr DUNBLANE:** 01786 823285. On old rd across the moor (app from A9 or via Dunblane or Bridge of Allan). Old coaching inn at crossroads transformed by Bouzy Rouge of Edin/Glas fame (565/GLAS BISTROS) into contemp restau with rms. Now the smartest stopover in the area & v much worth the short detour into the back of beyond. Gr swimming spot nearby (1756/SWIMMING HOLES).

4RMS JAN-DEC T/T PETS CC KIDS MED.INX

909
B4
STIRLING HIGHLAND, STIRLING: 01786 475444. Reasonably sympathetic conversion of former school (with modern accom block) in the historic section of town on rd up to castle. Serviceable businessy hotel in prime location; light 17m pool. 'Sophisticated' Scholars restau up top (2 AA rosettes). Best in-town choice mainly because of location.

96RMS JAN-DEC T/T PETS CC KIDS MED.EX/EXP

910
B4
QUEENS HOTEL, BRIDGE OF ALLAN: 01786 833268. Main st of pleasant town (good shops & restaus). Surprisingly & self-consciously 'stylish' & modern with cool interiors & art (tho' main picture odd choice). Groovy restau (Jekyll's) & bar.

5RMS JAN-DEC T/T PETS CC KIDS MED.EXP

911
A4
LAKE HOTEL, PORT OF MENTEITH: 01877 385258. A v lake side hotel on the Lake of Menteith in the purple heart of the Trossachs. Good centre for touring and walking. The Inchmahome ferry leaves from nearby (1962/MARY, CHARLIE AND BOB). 5 rms o/look lake (and are more exp, but worth the extra). Conservatory for sunset supper. Makeover due but for clean air and/or dirty w/end, this is a romantic spot.

16RMS JAN-DEC T/T PETS CC KIDS MED.EX

912
B4
HILTON DUNBLANE HYDRO, DUNBLANE: 01786 822551. One of the huge hydro hotels left over from the last health boom, many bought & now tarted up by Hilton (tho far from modern). Nice views for some and a long walk down corridors for most. Exercise in Living Well gym and the pool. It's a dinner-dance and wedded world.

210RMS JAN-DEC T/T PETS KIDS CC EXP

913
MAP 2
E3
INVERARNAN HOTEL/THE DROVER'S INN, INVERARNAN: 01301 704234. N of Ardlui on L Lomond and 12km S of Crianlarich on the A82. Much the same as it was when it began in 1705; bare floors, open fires and heavy drinking

(1374/BLOODY GOOD PUBS). Highland hoolies here much recommended. Bar staff wearing kilts look like they mean it. Rms not Gleneagles but highly individual. A wild place in the wilderness. Expect atmos not service. They also own the Stagger Inn across the road (704274). 16 en suite rms & restau.

12RMS JAN-DEC X/X PETS CC KIDS CHP

914 **THE PRIORY, CALLANDER:** 01877 330001. Bracklinn Rd off Main St (500m).
A3 Victorian mansion in nice garden (one of many, but better than most). Gets Michelin mention. Teddy bears & attentive hosts.

8RMS APR-OCT X/T PETS CC KIDS MED.INX

915 **HOTELS IN KILLIN:** Killin is a v Highland sort of a place, famous for the Falls of
A3 Dochart, the rocky course of the river that runs through the town. Mighty Ben Lawers is nearby and is a good gateway for pts N & W. There are 2 good inexp hotels. **THE KILLIN HOTEL:** 01567 820296. V Scottish, tartan everywhere, old-fashioned feel; conservatory on front. **DALL LODGE:** 01567 820217. Smaller, more personal, many *objets* and 4 Tourist Board whatsits (Killin only 2). Both hotels on main st.

32/10RMS JAN-DEC T/T PETS CC KIDS MED.INX

916 **GEAN HOUSE, ALLOA:** 01259 720101. Former hotel now part of Inglewood
B4 Conference Centre but the Edwardian mansion designed by Lutyens is stunning and rms available depending on their calendar. Stylish comfort, terraced gdns. Most elegant B&B for mls (and evening meals). Phone for details.

RESTAURANTS

917 ✓ **BLACK BULL, KILLEARN:** 01360 550215. Good-looking village, 30mins N
A4 of Glasgow betw L Lomond (Drymen) and the Campsies. Excellent bistro food and restau, 'Poachers'. Stylish makeover of long-est inn prob best out-of-city stay, & menu under Ian MacMaster worth the drive (530/HOTELS OUTSIDE TOWN). Bar/bistro lunch & LO 9.30. Poachers Sat only at TGP. In Killearn for a run, check also **THE OLD MILL** (1412/PUB FOOD). MED

918 ✓ **UNICORN, KINCARDINE:** 01259 739129. Excise St but follow signs. Real
B4 find in Forth shores wasteland, a bistro with gr food & seafood dining upstairs in the Red Room. Tony & Liz Budde run a tight & classy shop. Go find! Cl Mon & Sun evens. Red Room Fri/Sat dinner only. INX/MED

919 ✓ **CREAGAN HOUSE, STRATHYRE:** 01877 384638. End of the village on
A3 main A84 for Crianlarich. Creagan House is the place to eat in Rob Roy country and at TGP one of only 4 Michelin Bib Gourmand restaus in Scotland & the only one with accom. They have 5 inexp rms and the Gunns are a congenial bunch. Gordon Gunn is also an innovative and individualist chef and ingredients do come local, incl the gdn. You eat in a pleasant baronial dining-rm. There are many hills to walk (1996/HILLS). Cl Feb. MED

920 ✓ **CROSS KEYS HOTEL AND BAR, KIPPEN:** 01786 870293. Main st of couthie
A4 town 15km W of Stirling by A811. Award-winning pubfood in bars and restau setting (same menu). Gr for families and generally for informal unpretentious approach & atmos. A wee treasure. 1404/PUB FOOD. LO 9pm. INX

921 ✓ **THE ALLAN WATER CAFÉ, BRIDGE OF ALLAN:** Caff that's been here for
B4 ever at end of the main st in Bridge of Allan. Original features, gr feel, gr fish 'n' chips and, of course, the ice cream (1477/CAFÉS). 7 days, 9am-9pm. CHP

922 ✓ **BOUZY ROUGE at the SHERIFFMUIR INN, SHERIFFMUIR nr DUN-**
B4 **BLANE:** 01786 823285. Old Sheriffmuir rd behind Dunblane (& Br of Allan). Trad coaching inn given Bouzy Rouge treatment (see above). 'Casual gourmet dining' in bar & surprisingly large restau. LO 9/10 pm. Book w/ends. Tables o/side o/look the bare hills. 4RMS JAN-DEC T/T PETS CC KIDS MED.INX

923 **GLENSKIRLIE HOUSE, BANKNOCK:** 01324 840207. On A803 Kilsyth-
B4 Bonnybridge rd, J4 off A80 Glas-Stirling rd, not far (15 mins) Stirling or Falkirk. Edwardian elegant mansion house serving bar lunches and serious dining in stylish surroundings. Mod British menu with good Scottish ingredients.

CHP/EXP

924 **ATRIUM, CALLANDER:** 01877 331611. Main St above CCW (Caledonian) out-
A3 door shop. Unprepossessing approach thro' shop & upstairs to light, spacious mezzanine self/s restau prob best choice in stopover town. Home-made comfort food. Daytime only (till 5pm). CHP

See also 2248/BEST OF THE BORDER TOWNS, p. 310. *Refer to Map 3.*

925
E6 ✓ ✓ **ROXBURGHE HOTEL, nr KELSO:** 01573 450331. *The* best country-house hotel in the Borders. Owned by the Duke and Duchess of Roxburghe, who have a personal input. Rms distinctive, all light with green views. Reliable wine list (by the Duke) and menu (safe and satisfying). The 18-hole golf course has broadened appeal – it's challenging and championship standard and in a beautiful riverside setting. Non-res can play (2097/GOLF). Compared with other country-house hotels, the Roxburghe is good value. Personal, not overbearing service. 22RMS JAN-DEC T/T PETS CC KIDS EXP

EAT Where to go for fine dining and wining in the E Borders. Chef Keith Short. Also Fairways Brasserie o/looking golf course open w/ends. EXP

926
C5 ✓ **CRINGLETIE HOUSE, PEEBLES:** 01721 730233. Country house 5km from town just off A703 Edin rd (35km). Late 19th-century Scottish baronial house in 28 acres under new ownership 2003. Comfortable & civilised. Conservatory does light lunches and nice aft tea (reservations only). Walled gdn being restored at TGP. Tennis. 14RMS JAN-DEC T/T PETS CC KIDS LOTS

EAT Gracious dining (o/looking) conservatory & gdn. Friendly escape. EXP

927
D6 ✓ **BURTS, MELROSE:** 01896 822285. In Market Sq/main st, some (double-glazed) rms o/look. Busy bars, esp for food, The dining-rm is *where to eat* in this part of the Borders. Trad, but comfortably modernised small town hotel, though some rms also feel small. Convenient location. Good service (1953/ABBEYS; 2011/HILL WALKS; 1603/GARDENS). Where to stay for the Sevens, but try getting in! 20RMS JAN-DEC T/T PETS CC KIDS MED.EX

EAT Jolly and busy bar; more refined dining-rm has 2 AA rosettes. EXP

928
E6 ✓ **EDENWATER HOUSE, EDNAM, nr KELSO:** 01573 224070. Find Ednam on Kelso–Swinton rd B6461, 4 km. Discreet manse-type house beside old kirk and o/look graveyard and tranquil green countryside. You have the run of the home of Jeff & Jacqui Kelly & Jacqui's superb cooking. Good wines, good life. Even a smoking rm. 4RMS JAN-DEC X/T XPETS CC KIDS MED.INX

929
E5 ✓ **CHURCHES, EYEMOUTH:** 01890 750401. Albert Rd on corner of rd down to harbour surrounded by churches. Surprising boutique hotel in fishing town that's seen some hard times. Modern Habitat decor with some flourish-es. Stylish dining rm & conservatory & tables o/side in summer. Only a short detour (5km) from A1. 6RMS JAN-DEC T/T PETS CC KIDS MED.EXP

EAT Fresh and creative menu. Lots of seafood. EXP

930
D5 ✓ **LODGE at CARFRAEMILL, nr LAUDER:** 01578 750750. On A68 r/bout 8km N of Lauder. Old coaching type lodging. This sure beats a motel! Old-style Aga-type cooking, a good stop on the rd for grub & a gateway to the Borders. Nice for kids. 10RMS JAN-DEC T/T PETS CC KIDS MED.INX–EXP

931
D6 **DRYBURGH ABBEY HOTEL, nr ST BOSWELLS:** 01835 822261. Secluded, ele-gant 19th-century house in Abbey grounds banking R Tweed. Peaceful atmos; good tho small swimming pool. Lovely riverside walks. Abbey pure romance by moonlight. 38RMS JAN-DEC T/T PETS CC KIDS EXP

932
D6 **PHILIPBURN, SELKIRK:** 01750 720747. 1km from town centre on A707 Peebles Rd. Excl hotel for families, walkers, weekend away from it all. Selkirk is a good Borders base. Restaurant and bar-bistro and rare outdoor pool (with 2 gdn rms o/looking). Comfy rms & then, luxury rms. Best vegn food for miles around. 17RMS JAN-DEC T/T PETS CC KIDS EXP

933
D6 **JEDFOREST COUNTRY HOTEL, nr JEDBURGH:** 01835 840222. On A68 about 12km from the border at Carter Bar (the first hotel in Scotland!) and 5km from Jedburgh, my home town. Refurb rms and notable restau (French chef, 2 AA rosettes). You must walk down to that river Jed. 8RMS JAN-DEC T/T XPETS CC KIDS MED.INX

934
E6 **EDNAM HOUSE, KELSO:** 01573 224168. Just off town sq, o/look R Tweed; a majestic Georgian mansion with v old original features incl some of the

guests! Dated in a comfy way, fishing regalia dotted around; the restau's river view is , however, the main attraction. *The* place to stay when fishing these parts. 32RMS JAN-DEC T/T PETS CC KIDS TOS MED.INX

935 **CLINT LODGE, ST BOSWELLS:** 01899 860274. Lovely Arts & Crafts house on
D6 A72 nr Biggar. Bob Hunter is excl chef & host. César Scottish GH of the Year 2003. 5RMS MAR-DEC X/T PETS CC KIDS MED.INX

936 **SKIRLING HOUSE, SKIRLING:** 01835 822027. Phone for directions. On B6356
C5 (1713/SCENIC ROUTES). Small country GH in gr border country with tranquil views from rms. V good home cooking. 5RMS JAN-DEC X/T PETS XCC KIDS MED

937 **CADDON VIEW, INNERLEITHEN:** 01896 830208. Pirn Rd. Hotel in the doctor's
C6 house, comfy & tasteful rms. Excl restau dinner & b/fast from French chef/prop. Many glowing recs from readers. 8RMS EASTER-DEC X/T PETS CC KIDS MED.INX

938 **FAUHOPE, MELROSE:** 01896 823184. Borders house in sylvan setting o/looking
D6 Tweed. Only 3 rms but run by Sheila Robson who also has Marmions (see below), so worth a stopover. Highly awarded. 3RMS JAN-DEC T/X PETS CC KIDS INX

HART MANOR, ESKDALEMUIR: 01387 373217. Report: 1294/GET-AWAY HOTELS.

AND 1 SUPERB & 5 GOOD COUNTRY INNS

WHEATSHEAF, SWINTON: 01890 860257. (1401/PUBFOOD)

HORSESHOE INN, EDDLESTON: 01721 730225. (1420/PUBFOOD)

AULD CROSSKEYS INN, DENHOLM: 01450 870305. (1421/PUBFOOD)

TRAQUAIR ARMS, TRAQUAIR: 01896 830229. (1270/ROADSIDE INNS)

THE CRAW INN, AUCHENCROW: 01890 761253. (1269/ROADSIDE INNS)

CROSSKEYS INN, ETTRICKBRIDGE: 01750 52224. (1259/ROADSIDE INNS)

RESTAURANTS

EATING IN MELROSE (the Borders' best bet):

939 ✓ **MARMION'S:** 01896 822245. Buccleuch St nr the abbey. Local fave bistro,
D6 now going a long time, but on our last visit it was better food-wise than ever. Lunch and dinner. Cl Sun. INX

940 ✓ **KING'S ARMS:** 01896 822143. High St. Excl bar food in 17th cent coach-
D6 ing inn. The locals' choice. LO 9pm (9.30pm Sat).

941 ✓ **CHAPTERS, GATTONSIDE, nr MELROSE:** 01896 823217. Over the R
D6 Tweed (you could walk by footbridge as quick as going round by car). Kevin & Nicki Winsland's surprising bistro – a bit of a find. Huge choice from à la carte and specials. Expanding at TGP. Tues–Sat dinner only. MED

942 **THE HOEBRIDGE INN, GATTONSIDE, nr MELROSE:** 01896 823082. Award-
D6 winning chef. Fresh and bright. Mostly n/s superior & imaginative pub fd with flair. Book for w/end. INX

BURTS and **CRINGLETIE** (*see above*): Burts for best dining hereabouts, Cringletie for country treat (Cringletie is nr Peebles).

All the inns listed above for accomm also serve great food (some esp noted).

943 **SUNFLOWER RESTAURANT, PEEBLES:** 01721 722420. Bridgegate off Main St
C5 at Veitches corner. Long-standing spot for restau, but good again. Cafe menu during day & nice for kids. Thu/Fri/Sat for dinner 7–9 pm. Cl Suns. INX

944 **LAZEL'S, PEEBLES:** 01721 730233. Restaurant in the bowels of the Hydro
C5 (1224/FAMILY HOTELS), but real chef so good for lunch if passing thro' or Fri/Sat dinner. Modern makeover & menu, but well below stairs. INX/MED

945 **CULTER MILL, nr BIGGAR:** 01899 220950. A respite from the frustration of
B6 crawling along in a convoy on the A702 (the main Edin – S route). Neatly con-verted mill – fuel for the rd. Bistro daily 12-8pm, restau 6.30-10pm. In Coulter, just S of Biggar. INX

GIACOPAZZI'S & OBLO'S, EYEMOUTH: 01890 752527. Gr fish 'n' chips & ice-cream plus new upstairs bistro nr harbour of this fishy & friendly town. 1469/FISH 'N' CHIPS. INX

See Section 2 for Edin. Refer to Map 3.

946
D4 ✓✓ **GREYWALLS, GULLANE:** 01620 842144. On the coast, 36km E of Edin off A198 just beyond Gullane towards N Berwick. O/looks Muirfield, the championship course (no right of access) and nr Gullane's 3 courses and N Berwick's 2 (2082/2083/GREAT GOLF). No grey walls here but warm sandstone and light, summery public rms in this Lutyens-designed manor with gdns attributed to Gertrude Jekyll. It's the look that makes it special and the roses are legendary. Occasional literary lunches and sculpture gdns. Library like a London club, and service. Golf ain't everything but it helps.
23RMS APR-OCT T/T PETS CC XKIDS LOTS

EAT Fine and subtle dining in elegant rm adj course; experienced chef Simon Burns is a confident player. Wine list has depth and character. EXP

947
B4 ✓✓ **CHAMPANY INN nr LINLITHGOW:** 01506 834532. Excl restau with rms nr M9 jnct 3 (Edinburgh-Stirling), 30rms Edin city centre, 15 mins airport. Convenient high standard hotel adj nationally famous restau (98/EDIN RESTAUS) esp if you love your meat well-hung. Separate b/fast rm. Superlative wine-list, esp S African vintages. 16RMS JAN-DEC T/T XPETS CC XKIDS LOTS

EAT As much mentioned, the best meal in West Lothian. INX/EXP

948 **MARINE HOTEL, NORTH BERWICK:** 01620 892406. The old seaside hotel of N
D4 Berwick reeks of holidays gone by – you almost expect to see Margaret Rutherford on the putting green. A £10M refit expected in late 2003 courtesy of Macdonald Hotels, with good leisure facs to come too. Watch this space. O/looks Links and Fidra. Good for kids and golf.
83RMS JAN-DEC T/T PETS CC KIDS EXP

949 **OPEN ARMS, DIRLETON:** 01620 850241. Dirleton is 4km from Gullane
D4 towards N Berwick. Comfortable, pricey and rather precious hotel in centre of village, opp ruins of castle. Location means it's a golfers' haven and special packages are available. Deveaus Restau has one wee AA rosette.
10RMS JAN-DEC T/T PETS CC KIDS LOTS

950 **THE OLD ABERLADY INN:** 01875 870503. Main St. Straightforward drop inn
D4 with simple, well-kept rms, a good farmhouse-style bistro with interesting menu and a trad howf for drinks and bar food 6–9.30 pm. Popular with golfers – OK for anyone. 8RMS JAN-DEC T/T PETS CC KIDS MED.INX

951 **TWEEDDALE ARMS, GIFFORD:** 01620 810240. One of two inns in this heart
D5 of E Lothian village 9km from the A1 at Haddington, within easy reach of Edin. Set among rich farming country, Gifford is conservative and couthy. Some bedrms small, but public rms pleasant if chintzy. Has been here forever, like some of the guests. 16RMS JAN-DEC T/T PETS CC KIDS MED.INX

RESTAURANTS

952 ✓ **THE WATERSIDE, HADDINGTON:** 01620 825674. 115 Waterside. On the
D4 river, opp side of the pedestrianised old br from St Mary's (1931/CHURCHES). Upstairs restau is more of a pink-napkin affair, bistro/bar down has various rms. Separate vegn menu. This was the pioneer bistro in these parts, now owned by major brewery. Daily lunch/supper, LO 10pm (Sun 9pm). INX

953 ✓ **DROVER'S INN, EAST LINTON:** 01620 860298. Bridge St, middle of neat
D4 vill just off A1. Pub with good atmos; bistro downstairs and more elaborate dining up. Beer gdn out back. Lunch and dinner all areas, LO 9.30pm Pub till 11pm, 1am w/ends. Courtesy buses so … Don't drink and drove now!
INX/MED

954 ✓ **LIVINGSTON'S, LINLITHGOW:** 01506 846565. Thro arch at E end of High
B4 St opp PO. Cottage conversion with conservatory and gdn – a quiet bistro with imaginative modern Franco-Scottish cuisine. 2 AA rosettes. Polite and formal but easily the best in town. Tues-Sat, lunch and dinner. Cl Jan. INX

955 **THE OLD BAKEHOUSE, WEST LINTON:** 01968 660830. Jens and Anita Steffen
C5 – no strangers to this book – opened this place early in 2000. Just a place that feels really cared for. Everything made on the premises, and a nice line in smorrebrod too. Lunch and dinner, Wed-Sun. MED

956 **MUSEUM OF FLIGHT CAFE, nr HADDINGTON:** 01620 880308. Café in Nissen
D4 Hut run by home-cooking locals. Scones, sandwiches and soup and excl bacon sarnies to keep you going on your sortie. Easter-Oct 10.30am-5pm daily; in winter phone for times. ☕ INX

957 **BONAR'S, HADDINGTON:** 01620 822100. Douglas Bonar has been in this
D4 book before with eateries in Gifford and Edinburgh. Now he's doing his ostentatious French thing in Haddington, in the old mill on the road out to Gifford. Accomplished and polite. Wed-Sun, lunch and dinner. MED/EXP

958 **CREEL, DUNBAR:** 01368 863279. In Lamer St by harbour. New prop since early
D4 '03: Gavin Howat, formerly at Greywalls (946/BEST LOTHIAN HOTELS). Still small & intimate and the best for aways around. Tues-Sun lunch & dinner. INX-MED

959 **THE OLD CLUBHOUSE, GULLANE:** 01620 842008. E Links Rd behind main st,
D4 on corner of Green. Large woody clubhouse; a bar/bistro serving food all day till 9.45pm. Gr busy atmos. Surprising wine selection. INX

960 **MARYNKA, LINLITHGOW:** 01506 840123. Couple of doors down from 4
B4 Marys. Stylish, bright, modern town restaurant with bistro-cool lunches and serious dinners. Small New World wine list & Iain Mellis cheese to end. Tues-Sat 12-2pm, 6–11.30pm. INX–MED

961 **TIGH BALLA, nr TORPHICHEN, nr BATHGATE:** 01506 652133. 1 km west of
B4 village off A801. Oasis of Scottish trad cuisine in rural setting. Modern bungalow among old Scots pines serving excellent range of dishes. Unfashionable decor but owners enthuse. Lunch & dinner 7 days. MED

962 **LA POTINIÈRE, GULLANE:** 01620 843214. It's back! On the main street, the
D4 restau that once defined fine eats in the Lothians has reopened. Not eaten yet but Mary Runciman and Keith Marley look like they're dong a fine, well-kempt and upmarket job. Reports? Wed-Sun lunch & dinner LO 9pm. MED

963 **DRAGON WAY, PORT SETON:** 01875 813551. 27C Links Rd. E Lothian country
D4 cousin of the DW in town (253/BEST CHINESE). Near the local caravan park and often packed. This is the E Lothian t/away. CHP

THE BEST HOTELS AND RESTAURANTS IN FIFE

See also 2348/BEST OF DUNFERMLINE AND KIRKCALDY, *p. 307*; 2357/HOLIDAY CENTRES: ST ANDREWS, *p. 319. Refer to Map 3.*

964
D3 ✓ ✓ **OLD COURSE, ST ANDREWS:** 01334 474371. This world-famous hotel is the one you come to first on the A91 from N or W. Unlike many de luxe hotels in the UK, this has lightness to it and accessibility – it is after all surrounded by greens and full of golfers coming and going. Most rms o/look the famous course and sea (immaculate and tastefully done with no fac or expense spared), as do the Sands Brasserie and less informal Road Hole Grill up top. Bar here also for lingering views and whisky in the glass. Truly gr for golf, but anyone could unwind here, towelled in luxury. Spa well appointed. Small but beautiful pool.   134RMS JAN-DEC T/T PETS CC KIDS TOS LOTS

EAT Rd Hole Grill for spectacular dinner esp in late light summer. Sands on ground floor for lighter and later food. Both excl.   EXP/MED

965
C3 ✓ **BALBIRNIE HOUSE, MARKINCH:** 01592 610066. Signed from the rd system around Glenrothes (3km) in surprisingly sylvan setting of Balbirnie Country Park. One of the most sociable and comfortable country-house hotels in the land, with high standards in service and décor that's easy to be at home with. Library Bar leads on to tranquil gdn. Orangery restau has 2 AA rosettes and good wine list. Their 'pamper breaks' – incl tea on arrival – are a gr deal *à deux*. No leisure facs, but good golf in the park. Wake to the thwack of balls!   30RMS JAN-DEC T/T PETS CC KIDS TOS LOTS

EAT An elegant hotel for lunch and dinner. 2 AA rosettes.   EXP

966
D3 ✓ **RUFFLETS, ST ANDREWS:** 01334 472594. 4km from centre via Argyle St opp W Pt along Strathkinness Low Rd past univ playing fields. Serene feel to this country-house hotel on edge of town. The celebrated gdns are a joy. Garden restau fine dining with 2 AA rosettes and more informal bar/brasserie. Cosy rms incl garden suites.   24RMS JAN-DEC T/T PETS CC KIDS TOS EXP

967
D3 ✓ **ST ANDREWS BAY nr ST ANDREWS:** 01334 837000. 8km E on A917 to Crail o/looking eponymous bay. Modern edifice in rolling greens. Soulless perhaps but every fac a golfing family could need. Brasserie-type restau in immense atrium. Fine dining with award-winning chef Graeme Nesbit on its way at TGP.   209RMS JAN-DEC T/T PETS CC KIDS EXP

968
D3 ✓ **OLD STATION nr ST ANDREWS:** 01334 880505. On B9131 (Anstruther rd) off A917 from St Andrews round St Andrews Bay (3km). Fab makeover of old station with contemp look, almost boutique rms. Conservatory dining rm, comfy lounge with log fire. 2 'suites' are in a railway carriage!   8RMS JAN-DEC X/T PETS CC XKIDS MED.INX

969
D3 **KILCONQUHAR CASTLE ESTATE, nr ELIE:** 01333 340501. On B942 nr Colinburgh, 3km from Elie (that famously nice town). Mainly time-share villas (newer ones seem fairly naff), but 'club rms' available in castle itself with access to all facs incl pool, tennis, golf and esp riding. Daily rates poss. Bistro & posher dining rm in baronial setting. 9RMS JAN-DEC T/T PETS CC KIDS MED.INX

970
D3 **CAMBO ESTATE, nr CRAIL:** 01333 450313. 2km E of Crail on A917. Huge country pile in glorious gdns on the coastal rd betw St Andrews and Crail. Only few flats (and 2 cotts), but this is self/c in the grand manner. Rms vary greatly. Grds are superb. Rattle around, pretend you're house guests and be grateful you don't have to pay the bills.   4&2COTTS JAN-DEC X/X PETS CC KIDS MED.INX

971
D4 **THE SHIP INN, ELIE:** 01333 330246. 6 basic rms in rock View adj pub notable for food and good life (1410/PUB FOOD) close to beach in an excellent neuk of Fife. Summer only.   6RMS JAN-DEC X/X PETS CC KIDS CHP

972
D3 **THE FOSSIL HOUSE, ST ANDREWS:** 01334 850639. 12 Main St so v central. B&B house & cottage built round courtyard (guests have private access). Celebrated b/fast buffet (10 main courses), everything from garden or market & home-made.   4RMS JAN-DEC X/T XPETS CC KIDS INX

973
C4 **WOODSIDE HOTEL, ABERDOUR:** 01383 860328. Refurb inn in main st of pleasant village with prize-winning rail stn, castle and church (1923/CHURCHES),

coastal walk and nearby beach. This is where to come from Edin (by train, of course) with your bit on the side. 20RMS JAN-DEC T/T PETS CC KIDS MED.INX

INN ON NORTH STREET, ST ANDREWS: 01334 474664. Cool place tho more for students than their parents (busy bar/restau below). Report: 2357/ST ANDREWS.

SANDFORD HILL: 01382 541802. 7km S of Tay Br. Underrated country-house hotel in N Fife nr Dundee. Report: 1217/COUNTRY-HOUSE HOTELS.

PEAT INN nr CUPAR: 01334 840206. The definitive 'restaurant with rooms' (*see below*).

RESTAURANTS

974
D3
✓✓ **THE PEAT INN, nr CUPAR and ST ANDREWS:** 01334 840206. At a crossroads of the county, the hamlet of Peat Inn (signed from all over), for 30 years one of the gr Scottish restaus and David Wilson our first and still outstanding chef. Standards have improved immeasurably and now you don't need to go 50 miles to be sure of superb food. But on occasion come here – it is still an epicurean experience with classic cuisine on a no-nonsense menu and superb wine-list. 8 cottage rms for staying the night. 3 AA rosettes. Tues-Sat 1-3pm and 7-9.30pm. EXP

975
D3
✓✓ **THE CELLAR, ANSTRUTHER:** 01333 310378. This classic bistro serves some of the best fish you'll eat in Scotland or anywhere. Off courtyard behind Fisheries Museum in this busy E Neuk town (1640/COASTAL VILLAGES) – you'd never think this was a restau from the entrance. It's a family affair – even the crabs want to come here. Peter Jukes sources only the best produce. One meat dish, excl complementary wine-list. Pure, simple food & atmos. Fri–Sun lunch, 6.30-9.30 7 days. Times may change. (1435/SEAFOOD RESTAUS) MED

976
C3
✓✓ **OSTLER'S CLOSE, CUPAR:** 01334 655574. Down a close of the main st, Amanda and Jimmy Graham run a bistro/restau that has Cupar on the gastronomic map (for 20 yrs). Intimate, cottagy rms. Amanda out front also does puds, Jimmy a star in the kitchen. Often organic, big on mushrooms and other wild things. Fri/Sat lunch & Tues–Sat 7-9.30pm. MED

977
978
D3, D4
✓✓ **THE SEAFOOD RESTAURANTS, ST ANDREWS:** 01334 479475 **and ST MONANS:** 01333 730327. Both excl, unpretentious restaus by the Butler family & both in perfect settings. Reports: 1437/1440/SEAFOOD RESTAUS. INX

979
C3
THE GREENHOUSE, FALKLAND: 01337 858400. St on corner of main st of delightful mid-Fife vill (1826/CASTLES, 2010/HILL WALKS, 2042/GLEN WALKS). Light and friendly cafe-bistro serving supper (Wed-Sun) & Sun brunch (summer hrs may extend). All home-made, mostly organic (incl wine-list). Cl Mon/Tues. LO 9.00pm. INX

980
C4
OLD RECTORY, DYSART: 01592 651211. 2km E of Kirkcaldy (5km centre); still worth the drive from town or anywhere W Fife. Loyal regulars wouldn't go anywhere else. Tues-Sat lunch and dinner. MED

981
C4, D3
FISH 'N' CHIPS IN FIFE: VALENTE'S, KIRKCALDY & THE ANSTRUTHER FISH BAR: 2 gr fish 'n' chip shops with queues every day. Famously good, that's why! (1457/1467/FISH AND CHIPS). CHP

982
D4
WOK & SPICE, ST MONANS: 01333 730888. On main A917 rd turning past St Monans. Not a caff but a takeaway. Sizzling woks, proper rice, a taste of real Malaysian food (forget the chips). This would work in Edin or Glas. When in Fife, order here (they deliver betw N. Largo & Crail). 7 days 4.30 til whenever. CHP

THE GRANGE INN, ST ANDREWS: 01334 472670. Report: 1409/PUB FOOD.

THE SHIP INN, ELIE: 01333 330246. Report: 1410/PUB FOOD.

BEST RESTAURANTS IN ST ANDREWS: See p. 319–320.

See also DUNDEE HOTELS AND RESTAURANTS, p. 146–147; 2352/CENTRES: PERTH, p. 314; and 2355/HOLIDAY CENTRES: PITLOCHRY, p. 318. Refer to Map 3.

983
C2
✓✓ **BALLATHIE HOUSE, nr PERTH:** 01250 883268. 20km N of Perth and more fully reported in the town section (2352/PERTH), but a true country-house hotel on the Tay that you fall in love with. Good dining, good fishing; good for the w/end away. New riverside rms are pretty nice.

42RMS JAN-DEC T/T PETS CC KIDS TOS LOTS

EAT Award-winning chef Kevin MacGillivray. Gr local produce esp beef/lamb.

EXP

984
C2
✓ **KINLOCH HOUSE, nr BLAIRGOWRIE:** 01250 884237. 5km W on A923 to Dunkeld. The Allen family, formerly at Airds Hotel, Port Appin, have been much praised in this book. Since the last edition they've moved to Kinloch House. Still finding their feet & guests' reports vary. Country house with good views, walled garden and decent pool. Graeme is an accomplished chef. Once they've settled in, so will we. 18RMS JAN-DEC T/T PETS CC KIDS TOS LOTS

985
C3
✓ **KINFAUNS CASTLE, PERTH:** 01738 620777. A90 Dundee rd (Perth 7km). Sumptuous country-house hotel in convenient v central location nr Perth and motorway. Glorious staircase, ceilings and wood panelling and 16 spacious suites. Bags of history and many oriental artefacts (owner used to work in the Far East). The 'dragon bar' is quite a feature. Restau open to non res consistently gets 2 AA rosettes. 16RMS FEB-DEC T/T PETS CC KIDS LOTS

986
B2
✓ **HILTON DUNKELD HOUSE, DUNKELD:** 01350 727771. Former home of Duke of Atholl, a v large impressive country house on the banks of the R Tay in beautiful grounds (some time-share) just outside Dunkeld. Leisure complex with good pool etc and many other activities laid on. V decent menu. Fine for kids. Pleasant walks. Not cheap but often good deals available. No jeans after 6.30pm! 96RMS JAN-DEC T/T PETS CC KIDS LOTS

987
B3
✓ **ROYAL HOTEL, COMRIE:** 01764 679200. Central sq of cosy town, a sympathetic and stylish if trad small-town hotel. Excellent restau with good light and superb pub out back with real ale and atmos (1389/REAL ALES). Exquisite rugs and pictures. A pleasing bit of style in the county bit of the country. Delightful restau & bar meals. Originally an 18thC coaching inn.

11RMS JAN-DEC T/T XPETS CC KIDS MED.EX

988
D2
✓ **GORDON'S, INVERKEILOR, nr ARBROATH:** 01241 830364. Halfway betw Arbroath and Montrose on the main st. A restau with rms (3) which has won loadsa accolades incl 2 AA rosettes. It's been here for more than 18 years! Splendid people doing good Franco-Scot cooking. Lunch Tues-Fri & Sun; dinner Tues-Sat LO 8.45pm. Advisable to book. MED

989
B2
FARLEYER RESTAURANT & ROOMS, nr ABERFELDY: 01887 820332. Out the same Dull (*sic*) road as Castle Menzies (1835/CASTLES). A welcome return for Farleyer, under new management (Jake and Kim Schamrel). Cosmopolitan mod-Euro bistro and bar, with boutique hotel rms. Unusually cool for round here & nr Glen Lyon (1666/GLENS). 6RMS JAN-DEC T/T XPETS CC KIDS TOS MED.EX

990
C3
HUNTINGTOWER HOTEL, nr PERTH: 01738 583771. 3km from town, 1km ring rd (direction Crieff). Serviceable, good looking hotel in gdns close to Perth and the rds north and west. Report: (2352/PERTH).

34RMS JAN-DEC T/T XPETS CC KIDS TOS EXP

991
C2
CASTLETON HOUSE, EASSIE, nr GLAMIS: 01307 840340. 13km W of Forfar, 25km N of Dundee. App from Glamis, 5km SW on A94. Family-run country-house hotel with good restau. Castleton House piling up the accolades lately and now has 2 AA rosettes for food; an Angus leader.

6RMS JAN-DEC T/T PETS CC KIDS TOS EXP

992
B2
PINE TREES HOTEL, PITLOCHRY: 01796 472121. A safe haven in visitor-ville – it's above the town and above all that (there are many mansions here). Take Larchwood Rd off W end of main st. Woody gdns, woody interior. Piano-player at Sat dinner. Scots owners. With some taste (nice rugs).

20RMS JAN-DEC T/T XPETS CC KIDS MED.EX

993 **KILLIECRANKIE HOTEL, KILLIECRANKIE:** 01796 473220. 5km N of Pitlochry.
B2 Village inn ambience; cosy rms of individual character. Carefully run. Gr food
and all the better since new owner (late '01).

10RMS MAR-DEC T/T PETS CC KIDS EXP

EAT Lunch and dinner in the conservatory but also a fine dining rm with 2 AA
rosettes. Good for vegetarians. EXP/INX

994 **KENMORE HOTEL, KENMORE:** 01887 830205. Ancient coaching inn (16thC)
B2 in quaint conservation village. Excellent prospect for golfing (at Taymouth
Castle adj, 2108/GOLF IN GREAT PLACES) and fishing. On river (Tay) itself with ter-
race and restau o/looking. Comfy rms. Front area of hotel best with real fires.

40RMS JAN-DEC T/T PETS CC KIDS MED.INX

995 **GLEN CLOVA HOTEL:** 01575 550350. Nr end of Glen Clova, one of the gr
C1 Angus Glens (1670/GLENS), on B955 25km N of Kirriemuir. A walk/climb/coun-
try retreat hotel; v comfy. Superb walking nearby. Often full. Also CHP bunkhouse accom. 10RMS JAN-DEC T/T XPETS CC KIDS MED.INX

996 **COLL EARN HOUSE, AUCHTERARDER:** 01764 663553. Signposted from main
B3 st. Extravagant Victorian mansion with exceptional stained glass. Comfy rms,
huge beds. Pleasant gdn. 8RMS JAN-DEC T/T XPETS CC KIDS EXP

997 **GUINACH HOUSE, ABERFELDY:** 01887 820251. On A826 Crieff rd and among
B2 the famous 'Birks' (2057/WOODLAND WALKS). Small country house in pleasant
gdn. Chef prop Bert MacKay always has 2 AA rosettes. Best place to eat in this
town. 7RMS JAN-DEC X/T PETS CC KIDS TOS MED.EX

998 **ATHOLL ARMS, BLAIR ATHOLL:** 01796 481205. Main st opp castle, the major
B1 attraction hereabouts (1828/CASTLES), close to estate & Glen Tilt. Magnificent
lofty dining rm (former ballroom). Bothy Bar out the back with local cask ales
& adj station. Gt special offers in winter. 31RMS JAN-DEC T/T PETS CC KIDS INX

999 **DALMUNZIE HOUSE, SPITTAL O' GLENSHEE, nr BLAIRGOWRIE:** 01250
C1 885224. 3 km from Perth–Braemar rd close to Glenshee ski slopes & good
base for Royal Deeside without Deeside prices. 9 hole golf-course for fun.
Food adequate (1 AA rosette). Hills all around. Fire to come home to.

16RMS JAN-DEC T/T PETS CC KIDS TOS MED.INX

1000 **BIRNAM WOOD HOUSE by DUNKELD:** 01350 727782. Perth rd in Birnam vill
B2 off rd to Dunkeld 2 mins A9. Edwardian house restored & furnished in keeping. We haven't stayed but excl reports. Chef Bob Merriman has good rep for
cooking. 4RMS JAN-DEC X/X PETS CC KIDS INX

GLENEAGLES: 01764 662231 (1211/COUNTRY-HOUSE HOTELS).

KINNAIRD HOUSE: 01796 482440 (1209/COUNTRY-HOUSE HOTELS).

CRIEFF HYDRO, CRIEFF: 01764 655555. Superb for many reasons, esp kids.
Quintessentially Scottish (1220/KIDS).

ARDEONAIG, LOCH TAY nr KILLIN: 01567 820400 (1285/GET AWAY FROM IT ALL).

RESTAURANTS

1001 ✓ ✓ **ANDREW FAIRLIE at GLENEAGLES:** 01764 694267. The 'other'
B3 restau apart from main dining rm in this de-luxe resort hotel
(1211/CO HOUSE HOTELS) & comfortably the best meal to be had in this & many
other counties. Mr Fairlie comes with big rep, a Michelin star & good PR.
Understated opulence in interior rm and confident French food of a v superi-
or nature. Andrew has recently lambasted the parlous state of Scottish cooking – come spot the difference. Mon-Sat dinner only. LO 10 pm. EXP

1002 ✓ ✓ **LET'S EAT, PERTH:** 01738 643377. Corner of Kinnoull St. Tony Heath
C3 and Shona Drysdale's perfect county town eaterie. Cuisine without
the trappings, but all the rt trimmings. Extremely good value and many
awards. MED

1003 ✓ ✓ **63 TAY STREET, PERTH:** 01738 441451. 63 Tay St on the new river-
C3 side rd and walk. Award winning young chef Jeremy Wares in
kitchen, Shona out front running a small tight ship. Contemp light rm and
Modern Brit cuisine with hand-picked ingredients. A cut above the newer
competition hereabouts. Tues–Sat lunch, LO 9 pm. Book w/ends. MED

1004 ✓ **THE BUT 'N' BEN, AUCHMITHIE, nr ARBROATH:** 01241 877223. 2km off
D2 A92 N from Arbroath, 8km to town or 4km by cliff-top walk. Village perched on cliff top where ravine leads to small cove and quay. Adj cottages converted into cosy restau. Cl Tues all day and Sun eve but otherwise 11am-9.30pm for lunches, high tea & dinner. Menus vary but all v Scottish and informal with emphasis on fresh fish/seafood. Brilliant value – Margaret Horn continues to provide a Scottish experience for her ain folk and all others for 27 years and counting! INX

1005 **LOCHSIDE LODGE, BRIDGEND OF LINTRATHEN:** 01575 560340. 9km from
C2 Alyth towards Glenisla on B954 past Reekie Linn (1687/WATERFALLS), or via Kirriemuir. Deep in watery countryside. Converted stone steading nr loch; gr setting, good food. Accom (4rms). Lunch/dinner LO 9pm. Cl Sun even. MED

1006 **CARGILLS, BLAIRGOWRIE:** 01250 876735. Cosy wine bar ambience, busy à la
C2 carte menu and blackboard. Serviceable, reliable and a bit of a hidden gem. Unprepossessing frontage, but on river side. Adj coffee shop/gallery. The place to eat in this corner of the country. Mon-Sat lunch & dinner until 10pm, Sun brunch 12.30-4.30pm. INX

1007 **OLD ARMOURY, PITLOCHRY:** 01796 474281. On rd from main st that winds
B2 down to Salmon Ladder attraction. Old Black Watch armoury gives spacious, light bistro ambience and nice terrace/tea gdn. All things to all people: fish & chips for lunch, afternoon tea outdoors, and decent dinner with good veggie options. Decor kitsch in places, eats excellent at times. Mar-Nov, food all day LO 9.30pm. Weekends only in winter. INX/MED

1008 **THE LOFT, BLAIR ATHOLL:** 01796 481377. Off the A9, in vill turn left at Bridge
B1 of Tilt Hotel. Odd kind of location (corner of a caravan park) for this solidly reputable restau which has 2 AA rosettes. Hearty food with a good combo of new and traditional touches in lofty setting. Bistro & finer dining menus. Lunch and LO 9.30pm. INX

1009 **THE BANK, CRIEFF:** 01764 656575. 32 High St opp TIC and town clock. Prob
B3 best food in cosy Crieff (you may want a meal out from the Hydro) in former bank. Chef/prop Bill McGuigan's modern Scottish cooking. Lunch Tues-Sun, dinner Mon-Sat. MED

1010 **PORT-NA-CRAIG, PITLOCHRY:** 01796 472777. Just by the Pitlochry Theatre,
B2 new owners in '02 and now a bright, modern bistro in a 17thC inn. Informal and friendly with a mod-Euro menu.

1011 **GROUSE AND CLARET, KINROSS:** 01577 864212. On the west side of the
C3 M90, follow the sign to and from Kinross services, it's only 1km away. Popular, pleasant restau on fishing lochans at Heatheryford; a better lunch than the service station, of course. Lunch Tues-Sun, dinner Mon-Sat. INX

1012 **DEIL'S CAULDRON, COMRIE:** 01764 670352. 27 Dundas St on bend of A85
B3 main rd thro' town and rd to Glen Lednock. Cottage restau with simple, effective menu like haggis and neeps or tiger prawns. Lunch Tues-Sun, dinner Tues-Sat. INX

KERACHER'S, PERTH: 01738 449777 (2352/PERTH) MED

ROYAL HOTEL, COMRIE: 01764 679200 (see above) MED

THE BEST HOTELS AND RESTAURANTS IN THE NORTH-EAST

Excludes city of Aberdeen (see pp. 141–45). See 2358/ROYAL DEESIDE. *Refer to Map 4.*

1013
C3 ✓✓ **DARROCH LEARG, BALLATER:** 01339 755443. On main A93 at edge of town. The Franks maintain their standards at this Deeside mansion esp for food (long in the family). With a relaxed ambience and an excellent dining-rm, it is the best in this hotel-studded town. Three AA rosettes; other Deeside hoteliers aspire to its good standards. Comfortable, informal with attentive and considerate staff. No bar, but civilised drinks before and *après*. Good base for touring. They also run the Station Restau (see below).

17RMS FEB-DEC T/T PETS CC KIDS TOS LOTS

EAT Conservatory dining-rm and one of best restaus in NE; Chef David Mutter continues to hit the heights. Nice gdn view, fab food. EXP

1014
D3 ✓✓ **RAEMOIR HOUSE, BANCHORY:** 01330 824884. 5km N from town via A980 off main st. Mansion in the country just off the Deeside conveyor belt which gets everything right Old-fashioned comfy rms given contemporary details. Flowers everywhere. 9-hole golf and tennis. Stable annex and self-cat apts. The Bishop-Milnes run a popular and friendly house; great things expected from new chef Grant Walker. Watch this space.

21RMS & SELF-CAT JAN-DEC T/T PETS CC KIDS TOS LOTS

1015
B2 ✓ **CRAIGELLACHIE HOTEL, CRAIGELLACHIE:** 01340 881204. The quintessential Speyside hotel, off A941 Elgin to Perth and Aber rd by the br over Spey. Esp good for fishing, but well placed for walking (Speyside Way runs along bottom of gdn, see 2028/LONG WALKS) and distillery visits (1585/WHISKY). Informal; some fab rms. The food is well regarded but the bar could keep a whisky lover amused for years. Simply one of the best places in Scotland for a dram. 25RMS JAN-DEC T/T XPETS CC KIDS TOS MED.EX

1016
D2 ✓ **PITTODRIE HOUSE, PITCAPLE:** 01467 681444. Large 'family' mansion house on estate in one of the best bits of Aberdeenshire with Bennachie above. 40km Aber but 'only 30mins from airport' via A96. Follow signs off B9002. Lots of activities available on the estate, croquet lawn, billiards and lots of comfortable rms. Exquisite walled gdn 500m from house. Macdonald Hotels have an interest here and huge 60-rm extensions plus leisure facs coming in the next year or two. 27RMS JAN-DEC T/T PETS CC KIDS LOTS

1017
E2 ✓ **UDNY ARMS, NEWBURGH:** 01358 789444. A975 off A92. Village pub with gr food and character run by the Craig family for many yrs. Rms tasteful and individually furnished. Folk come from Aber (22km) to eat here. Golf course Cruden Bay (2087/GREAT GOLF) 16km N and walks beside Ythan estuary (1813/WILDLIFE). 26RMS JAN-DEC T/T XPETS CC KIDS TOS MED.INX

EAT Excellent grub in bar or dining-rm. Good ambience and the Cullen Skink is wonderful. Lunch; LO 9.30pm. They say that this was where Sticky Toffee Pudding was invented & the lady is still around. MED

1018
C3 ✓ **HILTON CRAIGENDARROCH, BALLATER:** 013397 55858. On the Braemar rd (A93). Part of a country-club/time-share operation with elegant dining, good leisure facs and discreet resort-in-the-woods feel. 2 restaus: an informal one by the pool, and the more self-conscious Oaks. Lodges can be available on short lets, a good idea for a group holiday or w/end. Barbacoa, an outside bar-b-que, is v pleasant when the weather permits.

45RMS JAN-DEC T/T XPETS CC KIDS LOTS

1019
D2 **MELDRUM HOUSE, OLDMELDRUM:** 01651 872294. 1km from village, 30km N of Aber via A947 Banff rd. Immediately impressive and solid establishment – Scottish baronial style. Set amid new 18-hole golf course (private membership, but guests can use) landscaped & managed to high standard (gr practice range). Rms have atmos & nice furnishing – many orig antiques & chosen pictures. New lodge had added bedspace and good things are expected of chef Simon Gosling. 14RMS (5 IN LODGE) JAN-DEC T/T PETS CC KIDS LOTS

1020 **SEAFIELD HOTEL, CULLEN:** 01542 840791. On the main Brae; an activity-ori-
C1 ented hotel with lots to do on nearby Seafield estate (hunt, shoot, fish). Single
rms can be a bit pokey but there's a comfortable lounge with a fair range of
malts. Restau good for fresh fish. Mr and Mrs Cox run an enduring and exemplary family hotel. 20RMS JAN-DEC T/T PETS KIDS CC MED.INX

1021 **THE MANSION HOUSE, ELGIN:** 01343 548811. Strangely hard to find but
B1 near the big Tesco store. Comfortable and elegant town house in a comfortable and gentle town with 'leisure facs', incl small pool/gym and drop-in (v
small) bistro. Nice dining-rm. 23RMS JAN-DEC T/T XPETS CC KIDS EXP

1022 **BANCHORY LODGE HOTEL, BANCHORY:** 01330 822625. Cheek-by-jowl with
D3 the Dee, this is a very neat and suburban country house and not the 'wellies
& rods' place you'd expect next to the river. (But they can arrange fishing and
shooting.) Fight for a window table at dinner.
22RMS JAN-DEC T/T PETS CC KIDS EXP

1023 **DELNASHAUGH INN, BALLINDALLOCH, nr GRANTOWN ON SPEY:** 01807
B2 500255. Road-side and Speyside (actually the Avon, pron 'Arn') inn, comfy,
unpretentious. On bend of A95 betw Craigellachie and Grantown nr confluence of main rds and rivers. Laura Ashley/Sarah Churchill décor, not minimalist, but simple. Food also. Much ado about fishing, and golf.
9RMS JAN-DEC T/T PETS CC KIDS INX

1024 **CASTLE HOTEL, HUNTLY:** 01466 792696. Behind Huntly Castle ruin; app from
C2 town through castle entrance and then over R Deveron up impressive drive.
Former dowager house of the Dukes of Gordon, taken over by the Meiklejohn
family in '01. Not bad value for the grandeur/setting – tourists and business
travellers keep it busy. Meiklejohns steadily making their mark.
18RMS JAN-DEC T/T PETS CC KIDS MED.EX

1025 **ARCHIESTOWN HOTEL, ARCHIESTOWN:** 01340 810218. Main st of small vil-
B2 lage in heart of Speyside nr Cardhu Distillery (1587/WHISKY). A village inn with
comfortable rms and celebrated food in bistro setting (LO 8.30pm). Fishers
and locals. 8RMS FEB-SEPT T/T PETS CC KIDS MED.EX

1026 **WATERSIDE INN, PETERHEAD:** 01779 471121. Edge of town on A952 to
E2 Fraserburgh on tidal R Ugie. Standard, well-run modern hotel, recommended
for its service and convenience and because it's the best option around. Good
for kids (1161/KIDS). 109RMS JAN-DEC T/T PETS CC KIDS MED.EX

1027 **GRANT ARMS, MONYMUSK:** 01467 651226. The village inn on a remarkable
D3 small square, a good centre for walking (1876/HILLS), close to the 'Castle Trail'
(1838/CASTLES; 1896/COUNTRY HOUSES) and with fishing rts on the Don. Rms in
hotel & (9) round courtyard are v basic, but the food esp in the bar, is why we
come. 17RMS JAN-DEC T/T PETS CC KIDS INX

EAT Best pub food for miles, and dining. Daily lunch, 6.30-9pm. INX

1028 **TANNOCHBRAE, DUFFTOWN:** 01340 820541. 22 Fife St. Twee-named (older
MAP 3 readers will remember *Dr Finlay's Casebook*) GH in Speyside centre. Conscien-
C2 tiously run accom & à la carte restau. Readers have recced; we haven't stayed.
6RMS JAN-DEC X/T XPETS CC KIDS INX

1029 **BRAEMAR LODGE, BRAEMAR:** 013397 41627. Down-home granite country
C1 house where the owners won't look down their nose at muddy walkers. Few
frills but a haven after a long day in the Cairngorms with a wee dram. Log cabins for hire out back and now a bunkhouse. Sleeps 12 but you can have breakfast in the hotel (CHP). 7RMS JAN-DEC X/T PETS CC KIDS MED.INX

RESTAURANTS

1030 ✓**LAIRHILLOCK, nr STONEHAVEN:** 01569 730001. 15km S of Aber off A92.
D3 Excellent country pub and restau, good for kids. Full report 1111/ABER
RESTAUS; 1399/PUB FOOD.

1031 ✓**TOLBOOTH, STONEHAVEN:** 01569 762287. Excl location on Stonehaven
E1 Harbour. New owners give great lobster. Report: 1446/SEAFOOD RESTAUS.

1032 ✓**THE OLD MONASTERY, nr BUCKIE:** 01542 832660. Leave A89 at Buckie
C1 jnct for Drybridge, 4 km, restau at top of hill & consequently has brilliant
views. Also v good food, still with 2 AA rosettes in long-established setting.
Good atmos. Tues-Sat Lunch and LO 8.30/9pm (cl Sun, Mon). EXP

1033   ✓ **MILTON RESTAURANT:** 01330 844566. On main A93 Royal Deeside rd
D3   ✓ 4km E of Banchory opp the entrance to Crathes (1592/GARDENS; 1897/COUNTRY HOUSES). Roadside and surprisingly contemporary restau in old steading adj craft vill of varying quality. Light and exceedingly pleasant space. Menu from brunch-lunch-aft tea (till 5pm)-supper, then dinner so they cater for everything (& rather well). Tues-Sat LO 9pm, Sun & Mon lunch only. A design statement on Deeside.   INX

1034 **STATION RESTAURANT, BALLATER:** 01339 755050. Centre town in the old
C3 station. Restoration of Victorian tearm in v capable hands of the Franks who have Darroch Learg (see above) so you know the food will be good. Open for b/fast (bacon sarnie to pain au chocolat) through to supper with gr cream teas in betw (all home-baking). Daily 10am-5pm.   INX

1035 **THE GREEN INN, BALLATER:** 01339 755701. Victoria Rd. Officially a restau
C3 with a few rooms (INX) but under new management lately: the O'Halloran family, with Chris in the kitchen cooking up a French-slanted menu. Dinner only Mon-Sat 7-9pm.

1036 **HORSEMILL RESTAURANT, CRATHES CASTLE, nr BANCHORY:** 01330
D3 844525. Adj magnificent Crathes (1897/COUNTRY HOUSES; 1592/GARDENS) so lots of reasons to go off the Deeside rd (A93) & up the drive. More tearm than restau but some hot dishes eg haggis tart with red-onion marmalade and excl home-baking mm … meringues. Open AYR lunch/aft tea till 5pm.   INX

1037 **FAGINS, WHITEHILLS nr BANFF:** 01261 861321. Loch St on rt as you app this
C1 coastal village 3km W of Banff off B9139. Long-standing local reputation for surf 'n' turf suppers cooked in galley kitchen in corner of dining-rm above an unpromising pub (although the barmaid has cute tattoos). Honest to goodness food with some flair but don't expect a Gordon Ramsay experience. Wed-Sat dinner, LO 9pm. Lunch Sun only.   INX

1038 **LA FAISANDERIE, DUFFTOWN:** 01340 821273. The Whisky Trail gets a French
C2 restau! A small Franco-Scots affair, corner of The Square and Balvenie St, nr the TIC. A welcome departure for these parts – let's hope it stays the course. Lunch & dinner dailly LO 9pm (except cl all day Tues & Wed lunch).   INX

1039 **THE COUNTY HOTEL, BANFF:** 01261 815353. Francophile dining options in
D1 dear sleepy Banff. Bistro & bar downstairs (lunches & bar suppers Mon-Sat); posh evening meals upstairs (daily 7-9pm, booking advisable). Quite a find and there's a beer garden with an apple tree.   CHP/EXP

THE BLACK-FACED SHEEP, ABOYNE: 01339 887311. Report: 1490/TEARMS.

THE BEST HOTELS AND RESTAURANTS IN THE HIGHLANDS

See also Ft William, p. 309; Skye, p. 295; Western Isles, p. 297.

1040
MAP 5
C2
✓✓ **INVERLOCHY CASTLE, FORT WILLIAM:** 01397 702177. 5km from town on A82 Inverness rd, Scotland's flagship Highland (*Relais et Châteaux*) hotel. Less stuffy than it used to be, still stuffed with sumptuous furnishings, objects and occasional film stars, luminaries and royalty. Everything you expect of a 'castle'; the epitome of grandeur and service. Huge colourful, comfortable rms, set in acres of rhododendrons with rainbow trout in the lake (lovely terrace) and the big Ben over there. Eat in tho this is not a drop-in kind of a dining rm (3 AA rosettes for chef Matthew Gray).

17RMS JAN-DEC T/T PETS CC KIDS LOTS

1041
MAP 5
E1
✓✓ **THE BOATH HOUSE, AULDEARN, nr NAIRN:** 01667 454896. Signed from the main A96 3km E of Nairn. A small country-house hotel in a classic & immaculately restored mansion - Don & Wendy Matheson's family home; well chosen pics for sale. Add chef Charlie Lockley (3AA) & you're in for a memorable stay. Spa/gym in basement, massage on hand & delightful grounds with walled garden in restoration (& beautiful Brodie nearby – 1824/CASTLES) with a lake.

7RMS JAN-DEC T/T PETS CC KIDS LOTS

EAT Consummate chef, ambience. All the ingredients just right. MED

1042
MAP 6
A3
✓✓ **POOL HOUSE HOTEL, POOLEWE:** 01445 781272. Formerly owned by Osgood MacKenzie who founded the gdns up the road (1591/GARDENS). The Harrisons have transformed this Highland home into one of the most stylish stopovers in the land. Only 4, but fabulously themed suites (& 1 single rm). Huge bathrooms. Gr dining with chef John Moir; bar has great malt collection. Simultaneously special and personable. This is the new destination hotel in the N.

5RMS MAR-DEC T/T XPETS CC XKIDS LOTS

1043
MAP 5
D2
✓✓ **CULLODEN HOUSE, INVERNESS:** 01463 790461. 5km E of town nr A9, follow signs for Culloden village, not the battlefield. Hugely impressive, Georgian mansion and lawn a big green duvet on edge of suburbia and, of course, history. The most conscientiously de luxe hotel hereabouts. Lovely big bedrooms o/looking the policies. Some fab gdn suites, and elegant dining.

28RMS JAN-DEC T/T PETS CC KIDS LOTS

1044
MAP 5
E3
✓ **THE CROSS, KINGUSSIE:** 01540 661166. Off main st at traffic lights, 200m uphill then left into glen. Tasteful hotel & superb restau in converted tweed mill by river which gurgles o/side most windows. New owners David & Katie Young less precious than previous & Becca still in the kitchen.

8RMS FEB-DEC T/X XPETS CC KIDS EXP

EAT To stay, you're expected to eat; you'd be mad not to. Open non-res for the best restau in the ski-zone. Fixed 3-choice menu. Cl Sun/Mon.

1045
MAP 5
D1
✓ **DOWER HOUSE, nr MUIR OF ORD:** 01463 870090. On A862 between Beauly and Dingwall, 18km NW of Inverness and 2km N of village. Charming, personal place; you are a house guest so best to fit in. Cottagey-style small country house, with comfy public rms. Also self-cat lodge house.

8RMS JAN-DEC T/T PETS CC XKIDS EXP

EAT Consummate chef Robyn Aitchison, simple, sophisticated. Fixed menu. MED

1046
MAP 5
D2
✓ **DUNAIN PARK, INVERNESS:** 01463 230512. 6km SW town on A82 Ft William rd. Mansion-house just off the rd, a quiet, civilised and old-style alternative to hotels in town, esp for those on business. Some good deals out of season. Nice gdns, small pool and sauna; real countryside beyond. Notable restau/dining-rm with sound Scottish menu; lots of creamy puds. Excellent wine and malt list. Nice people who care, and enviro-friendly gdn.

11(+2 COTT)RMS JAN-DEC T/T PETS CC KIDS EXP

EAT Ann Nicholl's no-nonsense menu and sideboard of delicious puds. MED

1047
MAP 5
D2
✓ **GLENMORISTON TOWN HOUSE HOTEL, INVERNESS:** 01463 223777. One of the many mansions/hotels on the riverside below the castle, but this unquestionably the best; poss the best in town. New owners & many changes (incl absorption of adj townhouse) afoot at TGP. Hotel opp Eden

Court Theatre (2285/THEATRES)so handy for most Invernusion things, but also Ness Island walks for peace & quiet. 15RMS (+15 NEW) JAN-DEC T/T PETS CC KIDS MED.EXP

EAT Restau (open non-res) **LA RIVIERA** for best Italian dining in town at TGP; see above (MED).

1048   ✓ **THE SUMMER ISLES HOTEL, ACHILTIBUIE:** 01854 622282. 40km from
MAP 6   Ullapool with views over the isles; Stac Polly and Suilven are close by to
B3   climb. For 20 years Mark & Gerry Irvine's famous for dining romantic retreat, seeming a tad old-style now. Adj pub offers similar quality food at half the price.   13RMS APR-OCT T/X PETS CC XKIDS EXP

EAT Formal dining: don't be late! (Very) fixed, no-choice menu. Trolleys of puds & cheese, the big moment. Sunsets nice. Bar better value & ambience.   MED.EX

1049   ✓ **LOCH TORRIDON HOTEL, L TORRIDON, nr KINLOCHEWE:** 01445
MAP 5   791242. At the end of Glen Torridon in immense scenery. Highland Lodge
C1   atmos, big hills to climb. Report: 1279/GET-AWAY-FROM-IT-ALL
           20RMS JAN-DEC T/T XPETS CC XKIDS LOTS

1050   **BUNCHREW HOUSE, nr INVERNESS:** 01463 234917. On A862 Beauly rd only
MAP 5   5km from Inverness yet completely removed from town; on the wooded
D2   shore of the Beauly Firth. Dining-rm and some bedrms o/look water; you might see Ben Wyvis. Gr club bar, esp for late dram. Graham and Janet Cross have really built the wedding business. Afternoon tea on the lawn when sunny is unmissable.   14RMS JAN-DEC T/T PETS CC KIDS EXP

1051   **COUL HOUSE, CONTIN, nr STRATHPEFFER:** 01997 421487. Comfortable
MAP 5   country-house hotel on the edge of the wilds with some elegant public rms,
D1   partic the octagonal lounge. Well-kept lawns where a piper plays in summer (Fri evenings). V Taste of Scotland menu. New owners at TGP. Some titivations would not go amiss.   20RMS JAN-DEC T/T PETS CC KIDS MED.EX

1052   **GOLF VIEW, NAIRN:** 01667 452301. Seafront on Inverness side of town. Not so
MAP 4   much golf, more beach view but nr the famous course (2088/GOLF). Well
A1   appointed, refurb rms with conservatory restau & leisure facs incl good pool for kids.   44RMS JAN-DEC T/T PETS CC KIDS MED.EX

1053   **ROYAL GOLF, DORNOCH:** 01862 810283. Sits on golf course nr small town sq.
MAP 6   Recent, tasteful refurb to boutique hotel style, nice sunny rm, gr malts & of
C3   course… gr golf (2089/GOLF).   25RMS JAN-DEC T/T PETS CC KIDS MED.EX

1054   **POLMAILY HOUSE, DRUMNADROCHIT, LOCH NESS:** 01456 450343. 5km
MAP 5   from Drumnadrochit on A831 to Cannich in Glen Urquhart and awesome
D2   Glen Affric (1665/GLENS). Unpretentious country-house retreat in lived-in unmanicured grounds. Many walks; tennis, riding and covered-in pool. Small, comfy public rms, individual bedrms. Sensible dinner and wine list. Everything on hand for kids (1223/KIDS), but ok for those without. The house and the glen are yours.   10RMS JAN-DEC T/T PETS CC KIDS EXP

1055   **LODGE ON THE LOCH, ONICH:** 01855 821237. In my view the best hotel in
MAP 2   this strip S of Ft William (16km) and that of the Freedom of the Glens group
D1   tho' this privately owned. Notable relaxed ambience, colour scheme, furnishings etc. Hydrotherapy massage, showers, double jacuzzis, mature hippy colour scheme in parts, posh toiletries, and CD players. The inimitable Jackie Burns in charge.   19RMS MAR-OCT T/T PETS CC XKIDS TOS MED.EX-EXP

1056   **ONICH HOTEL, ONICH, by FORT WILLIAM:** 01855 821214. As above 16km S
MAP 2   on main A82, one of many roadside and in this case, loch side hotels which are
D1   more attractive than many in Ft William. Onich is the best value and some of its rms o/look L Linnhe. Busy bars, grassy terrace & nice garden.
           25RMS JAN-DEC T/T PETS CC KIDS MED.EX

1057   **HOLLY TREE, KENTALLEN, ARGYLL:** 01631 740292. On A828 Ft William
MAP 2   (Ballachulish) – Oban rd, 8km S of Ballachulish Bridge. On road & sea & once the
D2   railway; formerly a station. A slightly idiosyncratic hotel with decor of mixed taste (incl Mockintosh), but fab views from bdrms and dining rm. Superb location, gd seafd restau. Nice for kids.   10RMS JAN-DEC T/T PETS CC EXP

ACKERGILL TOWER, nr WICK: 01955 603556 (1337/HOUSE PARTIES).

HOUSE OVER BY, SKYE: 01470 571258 (2306/ISLAND HOTELS).

EILEAN IARMAIN, SKYE: 01470 833332 (2311/ISLAND HOTELS).

KINLOCH LODGE, SKYE: 01470 833333 (2308/ISLAND HOTELS).

SCARISTA HOUSE, S HARRIS: 01859 550238 (2312/ISLAND HOTELS).

● **CLIFTON HOUSE, NAIRN:** 01667 453119. Seafield St off A96 to Inverness. Now closed. J Gordon MacIntyre hotellier of the decades – lang may yer lum reek & your garden grow.

RESTAURANTS

1058
MAP 5
C2

✓✓ **OLD PINES, nr SPEAN BRIDGE:** 01397 712324. Medium-priced dining in inexp hotel, still one of the best meals in the Highlands (with big table and crocks). How Sukie Barber does it with all those kids, God knows, but the food can be brilliant. Essentially an award-winning restau with rms (Rural Chef of the Year 2003). Kids may eat with theirs. Carefully selected & reasonable wine list. New smokehouse so expect smoky menu. Cl Sun eve and Mon, but phone to check. No smk. See also 1063/LESS EXP HIGHLAND HOTELS.　MED

1059
MAP 6
C3

✓✓ **2 QUAIL RESTAURANT, DORNOCH:** 01862 811811. Castle St. Unassuming townhouse on rd into centre conceals best restau N of Inverness. Tiny rms (lounge & library/dining rm). 4 tables so book! 3-choice menu. The Carrs do everything to make you feel comfortable. Rms above (1065/LESS EXP HOTELS). Dinner only Tues-Sat.　MED

✓✓ **THREE CHIMNEYS, SKYE:** 01470 511258. Report: 2322/ISLAND RESTAUS.

BEST RESTAURANTS IN INVERNESS see pp. 149–150. Especially:

ROCPOOL: 01463 717274 Ness Walk, corner of main bridge.

THE MUSTARD SEED: 01463 220220 Bank St.

LA RIVIERA at GLENMORISTON HOTEL: 01463 223777. Ness Bank.

GOOD LESS EXPENSIVE HOTELS IN THE HIGHLANDS

1060
MAP 6
B3

✓✓ **THE CEILIDH PLACE, ULLAPOOL:** 01854 612103. Jean Urquhart's oasis of hospitality, craic & culture in the Highlands. What started out in the 1970s as a coffee/exhibition shop in a boat shed, has spread along this row of cottages now comprising a restau, bookshop, café/bar (& performance) area, and bdrms upstairs. In winter food is served in front of the roaring fire in the Parlour Bar. Bunkhouse across the rd offers cheaper accom but is not a substitute for the hotel. Live music and events throughout the yr, or you can simply sit in the lounge upstairs with honesty bar or on the terrace overlooking gorgeous Ullapool.　11RMS+BUNKS JAN-DEC T/X PETS CC KIDS EXP

EAT Restau & coffee shop/bistro 8am-11pm. Restau service sometimes slips when busy, but we'll come back here forever.　MED

1061
MAP 6
B2

✓✓ **THE ALBANNACH, LOCHINVER:** 01571 844407. 2km up rd to Baddidarach as you come into Lochinver on the A837 at the br. Lesley & Colin have created a unique and comfortable haven in their 18thC house. The suite adj used to be a byre & looks over 'the croft' with Stac Polly peeping while house rms & terrace look to Suilven. Expansion of dining rm imminent at TGP to allow more non-res to sample excl 5-course dinner using local ingredients & incl Colin's perfect puds.
　5RMS MAR-DEC T/X XPETS CC XKIDS MED.INX

EAT When in farflung Assynt, eat at the far-out, in-front Albannach.　MED

1062
MAP 5
E2

✓ **AUCHENDEAN LODGE, DULNAIN BRIDGE, nr GRANTOWN ON SPEY:** 01479 851347. An urbane enclave in an area of stunning scenery nr Aviemore skiing and Whisky Trail. Tastefully and cosily furnished Edwardian lodge with log fires, good malts and cellar, and books. Food with flair and imagination with many ingredients from the kitchen gdn. TOS award for using local produce. Esp good with mushrooms. Home-made bread. Intimate dinner can turn into a house party as Ian patiently serves: Eric takes care of the kitchen. Plans to close wint months at TGP so phone.

5RMS (& FLAT) JAN-DEC X/T PETS CC KIDS TOS GF MED.EX

EAT Most imaginative menu in wide area of S Speyside, incl Aviemore. MED

1063
MAP 5
C2
✓ **OLD PINES, nr SPEAN BRIDGE:** 01397 712324. 3km Spean Br via B8004 for Garlochy at Commando Monument. This award-winning 'restau with rms' is a home from home. Open-plan pine cabin with log fires, games, enough books for a public library, neat bedrooms and a huge new polytunnel (where bits of yr dinner come from). Enjoy Sukie Barber's exceptional cooking and the ducks on the stream. Handy for Nevis Range skiing. (1221/KIDS; 1058/HIGHLAND HOTELS). 8RMS JAN-DEC X/X XPETS CC KIDS TOS MED.INX

EAT It's a restau first; worth drive from Fort William. MED

1064
MAP 5
E2
✓ **BOAT HOTEL, BOAT OF GARTEN:** 01479 831258. Centre of vill o/looking the steam train line & golf course (2102/GOLF). Gr old style (Victorian/ 1920s) hotel refurb with good restau, The Capercaillie, where chef Tony Allcott has 2 AA rosettes. Bar the locals use & hotel bar with good bar meals. This hotel an excl alternative to Aviemore. 32RMS JAN-DEC T/T PETS CC KIDS MED.INX

1065
MAP 6
C3
✓ **2 QUAIL, DORNOCH:** 01862 811811. Castle St as you arrive from S. Rms above restau (1059/HIGHLAND RESTAUS), only 3 but every bit as much detail & elegance as the food below. 3RMS JAN-DEC X/X XPETS CC XKIDS MED.INX

1066
MAP 5
C2
✓ **GLENFINNAN HOUSE HOTEL, GLENFINNAN:** 01397 722235. Victorian mansion with lawns down to L Shiel and the Glenfinnan Monument over the water. No shortbread-tin twee or tartan carpet here; instead a warm welcome from the MacFarlanes & new managers the Gibsons (much improved dining). You are piped into dinner and the refurbed bar has gr atmos. A cruise on this stunning loch or your own rowboat a must (01687 470322 for cruise)! (1321/SCOTTISH HOTELS). 17RMS APR-OCT X/X PETS CC KIDS MED.INX-EXP

1067
MAP 5
D3
GLENGARRY CASTLE, INVERGARRY: 01809 501254. A family-run hotel in the Highlands for over 40 yrs, now in the charge of young Donald MacCallum. Lichen on the balustrades, honeysuckle as you walk to the loch and a ruined castle in the grounds. Perhaps better for romance and atmos than fine dining.

26RMS MAR-NOV T/T PETS CC KIDS MED.EX

1068
MAP 5
D1
KINKELL HOUSE nr DINGWALL: 01349 861270. 15 km n of Inverness, 2km from main A9 taking B9169 E signed Easter Kinkell. Mansion house in farming country (the Black Isle) with rms o/look the Firth & Ben Wyvis. Gr local rep for food. 9RMS JAN-DEC T/T PETS CC KIDS MED.INX

EAT Best in the Black Isle. Local produce. Book w/ends. MED

1069
MAP 5
B2
THE PLOCKTON INN, PLOCKTON: 01599 544222. Neat village inn and seafood restau in neat little seaside vill (1633/COASTAL VILLAGES). Some good cask ale (Burton's, London Pride etc). Simple, quiet tasteful rms. Bar and bistro, mainly seafood. Tables on terrace in summer, back gdn for kids.

9RMS JAN-DEC T/T PETS CC KIDS MED.INX

Also in Plockton & nearby, **THE HAVEN** (01599 544223) is more refined & **THE PLOCKTON HOTEL** (01599 544274) on the water's edge has 11 nice rms above the pub & excl grub (it goes like a fair). Report: 1261/INNS.

1070
MAP 5
C1
LOCH MAREE HOTEL, TALLADALE: 01445 760288. On A832 15km from Kinlochewe and rt by the loch side (1692/LOCHS). A Highland fishing hotel catering for discriminating tourists (incl Queen Victoria – her rm slightly more exp, but has the view) since 1872. But the aristos have gone and so have many of the fish. Not all though. Good for Torridon walking; near Inverewe (1591/GARDENS). 20RMS MAR-NOV T/T PETS CC KIDS MED.INX

1071
MAP 5
C1
OLD MILL HIGHLAND LODGE: 01445 760271. Across the rd from L Maree Hotel (above) so similar views, this highly individual place comes recommended by readers. Simple, honest & superb cooking. Pinemartins come to the kitchen window. 6RMS MAR-OCT X/X XPETS XCC XKIDS INX

1072
MAP 6
C1
TONGUE HOTEL, TONGUE: 01847 611206. One village, more than one hotel – which is best? At the moment we reckon this one has the edge. Former Duke of Sutherland hunting lodge – and he'd probably still like it.

19RMS APR-NOV T/T PETS CC KIDS TOS MED.EX

1073 **TIGH-AN-EILEAN, SHIELDAIG:** 01520 755251. Lovely freshly-furnished hotel
MAP 5 on waterfront o/look Scots Pine island on loch. The Fields run a pleasant
B1 house – the locale has that serene otherness. Chris is a folk-buff so poss music
in the adj pub. Dinner or seafd supper in bar. The view remains fab, just like a
Colin Baxter postcard. 11RMS APR-OCT X/X PETS CC KIDS EXP

1074 **EDDRACHILLES HOTEL, nr SCOURIE:** 01971 502080. New, friendlier broom
MAP 6 (Fiona & Graham Deakin) since last we stayed in this excellent location hotel
B2 on Badcall Bay. Conservatory & woody walk to sea. Excl value retreat. Handy
for Handa (1792/BIRDS) or for walks on many shorelines.
11RMS MAR-OCT T/T XPETS CC XKIDS MED.INX

1075 **SUTHERLAND ARMS HOTEL, GOLSPIE:** 01408 633234. Roadside inn at N end
MAP 6 of town nr Dunrobin Castle and Big Burn Walk (2043/GLEN WALKS). First coach-
D3 ing inn in Scotland: a stopover on the way north. Reports please.
14RMS JAN-DEC T/T PETS CC KIDS INX

1076 **DORNOCH CASTLE HOTEL, DORNOCH:** 01862 810216. Atmos 16th-century
MAP 6 castle in main st. Complete with dungeons (huge stone fireplace) and drinks
C3 upstairs in the turreted bar o/look cathedral. New restau extension at TGP.
Bdrms in old part and new wing. Beach and golf nearby (2089/GREAT GOLF).
Rolling refurb in progress. On the Madonna trail, so lively with other weddings
at w/ends. 18RMS JAN-DEC T/T PETS CC KIDS MED.EX

1077 **LOVAT ARMS, BEAULY:** 01463 782313. Best hotel of many in main st of mar-
MAP 5 ket town 20km from Inverness. Relaxed, welcoming family-run hotel with gr
D2 bar meals and comfy public rms. Much tartan upstairs. Locals also rec the
Priory bar meals. 28RMS JAN-DEC T/T PETS CC KIDS TOS MED.EX

1078 **TOMICH HOTEL, TOMICH, nr DRUMNADROCHIT:** 01456 415399. The inn of
MAP 5 a quiet conservation village, part of an old estate on the edge of Guisachan
D2 Forest. Nr fantastic Plodda Falls (1677/WATERFALLS) and Glen Affric
(1665/GLENS). Basic facs, but use of pool nearby in farm steading (9am-9pm);
esp good for fishing holidays. 25km drive from Drum by A831.
8RMS JAN-DEC T/T PETS CC KIDS MED.INX

1079 **PORT-NA-CON, nr DURNESS:** 01971 511367. Ken and Lesley Black's guest-
MAP 6 house on this idyllic shore is gr value. New conservatory since last time, bril-
B1 liant for browsing the extensive library or just gazing at the Bens (Loyal and
Hope). Seafood from the loch often on the dinner menu (INX). Non-residents
should book. If they're full, Lesley might be able to find you a rm at her mum's
house in Durness. 4RMS JAN-DEC X/X PETS CC KIDS CHP

1080 **THE OLD SMIDDY, LAIDE:** 01445 731425. This book doesn't feature many
MAP 6 B&Bs, but after those readers' letters … Kate MacDonald's place in jolie Laide
A3 (Gruinard Bay, Wester Ross on the A832) is one of the superior examples. She's
a fine cook and does serious dinners (book then BYOB) for res only. 3 rms (and
self-cat cottages out the back). 3RMS JAN-NOV X/T PETS XCC XKIDS MED.EX

1081 **CORRIECHOILLE LODGE, by SPEAN BRIDGE:** 01397 712002. Around 3 river-
MAP 5 side kms out of Spean Bridge on the small rd by the station. Justin & Lucy
C2 Swabey getting 4-star acclaim from all over. Beautiful corner of the country
with spectacular views towards the Grey Corries & Aonach Mor. Lovely dinner,
cosy rms. 2 turf-roofed self-cat chalets face the hills. Gt walks begin here. Also
1290/GET AWAY HOTELS. 5RMS MAR-OCT X/T XPETS CC KIDS INX

1082 **GARRAMORE, S MORAR:** 01687 450268. On main A830 (rd to the Isles) betw
MAP 5 Arisaig & Mallaig, opp Camusdaroch (the *Local Hero*) beach. We haven't stayed
B3 but this antique-filled GH in a lush garden, well away from the rd, comes
heartily rec. B&B (dinner) & P&Q (peace & quiet).
7RMS JAN-DEC X/X PETS CC KIDS INX

GLENELG INN, GLENELG: 01599 522273 (1255/INNS).

TOMDOUN HOTEL, nr INVERGARRY: 01809 511218 (1268/INNS).

OLD LIBRARY LODGE, ARISAIG: 01687 450651. Report 1090/INX HIGHLAND
RESTAUS.

1083
MAP 6
B2
✓✓ **DRUMBEG HOTEL & RESTAURANT:** 01571 833236. Half-way round the spectacularly scenic B869 off the A894 NW coast rd from Scourie to Lochinver (1710/SCENIC ROUTES). Tiny township inn with rms run by chef patrons Michel & Carolyn Hédoin. French panache, first-class locally sourced (& direct from family in France) ingredients – literally no supermarket in sight. Gr Islay malt list & wines. Lunch & dinner AYR. A fabulous find. **MED**

1084
MAP 5
B2
✓ **THE SEAFOOD RESTAURANT, KYLE OF LOCHALSH:** 01599 534813. Gt atmos bistro nr (and still an actual station platform) the busy port, off the rd to Skye and with that bridge in the distance. Seafood from Kyle/Mallaig/Skye ie v local, and vegn selection. Apr-Oct: lunch Mon-Sat 10am-3pm; dinner 7 days 6.30-9pm. V popular. Phone to book & check opening hrs (may vary edge of season). **MED**

1085
MAP 5
B2
✓ **OFF THE RAILS, PLOCKTON:** 01599 544423. On the platform of this working railway stn; but no droopy sandwiches here, just good home cooking. Snacks in the day then blackboard specials and evening menu later. 10am-9.30pm in summer. Weekends only in winter. Brilliant faraway bistro atmos. Take the trail! (Also 1633/COASTAL VILLAGES). **INX**

1086
MAP 6
D2
✓ **LA MIRAGE, HELMSDALE:** 01431 821615. Dunrobin St nr the Br Hotel. A little piece of Las Vegas in Sutherland; this glitterati parlour is a novelty in this wee village by the sea. Snacks of every kind all day; with life-size photos of the inimitable proprietor Nancy Sinclair and various celebs gracing the walls. Up for sale for ages and at TGP, sad to say. Great fish and chips while it survives and we hope it does cause we love Nancy to bits. **INX**

1087
MAP 5
E2
✓ **THE ECCLEFECHAN, CARRBRIDGE:** 01479 841374. Opp estimable Landmark Centre (1784/KIDS), a main st bistro, family-run, proper chef, excl ingredients. Lunch Sat/Sun only, dinner Wed-Mon. **INX**

1088
MAP 5
E3
HAMBLETTS & CAFÉ MAMBO, AVIEMORE: 01479 810300 & 01479 811670. Main st (s end). At last some decent café/restaus in benighted Aviemore. Hamblett's better food with Mambo more attitude & après ski, good music & food all day (till 7.30/8.30pm). Both middle of the strip nr the stn. All-day menu, supper at night. Nice rms, light food. LO 10pm (maybe earlier in wint). For eats in Aviemore see also **THE OLD BRIDGE INN** (1407/PUBFOOD).

1089
MAP 5
E3
THE BOATHOUSE, KINCRAIG: 01540 651394. 2km from village towards Feshiebridge along L Insh. Part of L Insh Water sports (2149/WATER SPORTS), a balcony restau o/look beach and loch. Fine setting and ambience, friendly young staff (but they come and go). Some vegn. Salmon from the loch. You're in competition with the ospreys. Bar menu and home-baking till 6pm; supper till 8.30pm, bar 11pm. Apr-Oct. But check opening hrs. **CHP**

1090
MAP 5
B3
OLD LIBRARY LODGE, ARISAIG: 01687 450651. Nr the end of the infamous 'Road to the Isles' just as they start to hove into view. Converted stables with 6 bedrms (MED.INX) above and behind. Hot and cold lunch snacks (INX) 11.30am-2.30pm. Good selection of not only seafood but also meat and veg for the evening table d'hôte (MED) 6.30-9.30pm, booking advisable. Quay and beach nearby (with boats to Rum, Eigg and Muck), bask in the sunset behind them. Cl Tues. **INX**

1091
MAP 6
C3
CARRON RESTAURANT, STRATHCARRON: 01520 722488. On A890 rd round L Carron (joins A87 Kyle of Lochalsh rd) just S of Strathcarron. Peter & Michelle Teago's roadside diner & grill a welcome stop in these parts. Apr-Nov, 10.30am-9pm. Cl Sun. **INX**

1092
MAP 6
B1
OLD SCHOOL, INSHEGRA, nr KINLOCHBERVIE: 01971 521383. B801 Betw Rhiconich and Kinlochbervie. Not exactly converted but *adapted*, which is what makes it atmos (the huge ruler on the wall helps). The world map from 1945 is not the only nostalgia. Gourmet it is not, but you're usually glad you stopped. Dinner daily 6-8pm, Easter-Sept. **INX**

1093
MAP 4
A1
THE CLASSROOM, NAIRN: 01667 455999. Cawdor St – ask directions. Ambitious, stylish makeover in this conservative, golfy town. Contemp bar/ restau menu. 7 days.

1094 **RIVERSIDE BISTRO, LOCHINVER:** 01571 844356. On way into town on A837.
MAP 6 Self-serve during day; vast array of Ian Stewart's home-made pies and calorif-
B2 ic cakes. You can eat in or take away. Conservatories out front & back. Bistro on
riverside serves v popular meals at night; using local seafood, venison, vegn –
something for everyone incl, apparently, Michael Winner (though don't let
that put you off). Food 10am-8pm although bistro menu kicks in at 6.30pm
MED

1095 **THE OYSTERCATCHER, PORTMAHOMACK, nr TAIN:** 01862 871560. On
MAP 6 promontory of the Dornoch Firth (Tain 15km) this hidden seaside village
C3 could bring back childhood memories (even somebody else's). Seafd menu,
snackier during day. Fish tanks inside, fishy waters o/side. Tues-Sun July & Aug,
Wed-Sun rest of season. Cl Mar-Oct. LO 9.30pm but best to book.   CHP

1096 **MORANGIE HOUSE, TAIN:** 01862 892281. On way into/out of Tain from A9.
MAP 6 Popular locally for its food; nicely kept hotel with 26 rms (EXP). A very TOS
C3 menu, but you're in very TOS environment. Wynne family run a good house.
Lunch and 6-9.30pm.   MED/INX

1097 **FALLS OF SHIN VISITOR CENTRE:** Self-serve café/restau in VC & shop across
MAP 6 rd from Falls of Shin on the Achany Glen rd 8km S of Lairg (1691/WATERFALLS).
C3 Good basic food in an unlikely emporium of Harrods (Mohammed al Fayed's
Highland estate is here). They come from miles at Xmas for hampers! 9.30am-
6pm AYR.

1098 **KYLESKU HOTEL, nr KYLESTROME:** 01971 502231. On A894; tucked down
MAP 6 beside L Glencoul where the boat leaves to see Britain's 'highest waterfall'
B2 (1682/WATERFALLS). Small quayside pub/hotel (8 rms) serving gr seafood in
seafood setting with mighty Quinag behind. Noon-9pm AYR (see also
1408/PUB FOOD).   INX

GOOD INEXPENSIVE RESTAURANTS IN INVERNESS see p. 149. Especially:

CAFÉ ONE: 01463 226200. Castle St. (1196/INVERNESS RESTAUS.)

LA TORTILLA ASESINA: 01463 709809. Castle St. (1203/INVERNESS RESTAUS.)

RIVER CAFÉ: 01463 714884. Bank St. (1198/INVERNESS RESTAUS.)

CASTLE RESTAURANT: The legendary caff. Castle St. (1474/CAFÉS.)

BEST INEXPENSIVE RESTAURANTS IN THE ISLANDS

LOCHBAY SEAFOOD, SKYE: 01470 592235 (1422/SEAFOOD RESTAUS).

THAI CAFÉ, STORNOWAY: 01851 701811 (2342/WESTERN ISLES).

TIGH MEALROS, LEWIS: 01851 621333 (2342/WESTERN ISLES).

APPLECROSS INN, APPLECROSS: 01520 744262 (1286/GET AWAY HOTELS).

GLENELG INN, GLENELG: 01599 522273 (1255/INNS).

CRANNOG, FT WILLIAM: 01397 705589 (1451/SEAFOOD RESTAUS).

THE BEST PLACES TO STAY IN AND AROUND ABERDEEN

It's been said before, but in oil city, hotels are expensive. But remember, though full during the week, many places offer surprisingly good w/end deals. Refer to Map 4 except where indicated.

1099 ✓✓ **MARCLIFFE OF PITFODELS:** 01224 861000. N Deeside Rd (en route
D3 to Royal Deeside 5km from Union St). 10 yrs on & still unquestionably Aberdeen's premiere hotel. On the edge of town, a successful mix of the intimate and the spacious, the old (mansion house) and the new (1993 refurb). Personally run by the Spence family, the sort of hoteliers whom no detail or guest's face escapes. 2 excellent restaus, breakfast in light conservatory. Nice courtyard & terrace o/looking gardens. Friendly Aberdonian service.
42RMS JAN-DEC T/T PETS CC KIDS TOS LOTS

1100 ✓ **MARYCULTER HOUSE HOTEL, MARYCULTER:** 01224 732124. Another
D3 out-of-town hotel, in the same direction as Ardoe below but 7km further on. Excellent situation on banks of Dee with river side walks and an old graveyard and ruined chapel. Newer annex; 8/9 rms o/look river. Poacher's Bar (best) and dining-rm. Many weddings here, so be prepared if over w/end. Hotel on site of 13th C preceptory. Also loads of Christmas promos.
23RMS JAN-DEC T/T XPETS CC KIDS EXP

1101 **ARDOE HOUSE, BLAIRS:** 01224 867355. 12km SW of centre on the S Deeside
D3 (it's poss to turn off the A92 from Stonehaven and the S at the first br and get to the hotel avoiding the city). The Dee is on other side of rd from hotel, but nearby. A granite chunk of Scottish Baronial with few, but more individual rms and an annex where most rms have pleasant countryside views. Restau gets 2 AA rosettes. Leisure facs & all-round fairly reliable biz hotel.
110RMS JAN-DEC T/T PETS CC KIDS TOS LOTS

1102 **THE PATIO HOTEL:** 01224 633339. Beach Boulevard. Accom in the Beach pleasure zone, slightly apart from both the dire mall-type development & the beautiful long seafront that it dominates. Serviceable biz hotel wins no architectural plaudits from the o/side, but is comfortable and contemporary in its inner courtyard. Lightsome though bedrms have curiously wee windows. Own pool etc. Not far to Silver Darling for dinner (1110/ABER RESTAUS).
124RMS JAN-DEC T/T PETS CC KIDS EXP./ LOTS

1103 **CALEDONIAN THISTLE HOTEL:** 01224 640233. Victorian edifice on Union Terr. Of several city centre hotels just off Union St, this always seems the most easy to deal with, the most calm and efficient. Dining rm & refurb bar/brasserie. Some nice suites o/looking the Gardens. 80RMS JAN-DEC T/T PETS CC KIDS TOS LOTS

1104 **SIMPSON'S HOTEL:** 01224 327777. 59 Queen's Rd. V late 90s hotel (peach & turquoise thro' out) which tries hard to please. Huge bar & brasserie/restau adj is hugely pop – they say it 'evokes a Roman bath house'. 'Classic', 'Executive' rms & suites have same decor but diff sizes. Modern people will prob like all this; take your sunglasses. 50RMS JAN-DEC T/T XPETS CC KIDS TOS MED.EXP/LOTS

1105 **ATHOLL HOTEL:** 01224 323505. 54 King's Gate, a busy rd in w towards Hazelhead. An Aberdeen stalwart, the sort of place you sort out for your rellies and join them for dinner or a bar meal. I've never stayed, but people say this is the best among many mansions. They say it's 'in a class of its own'.
35RMS JAN-DEC T/T XPETS CC KIDS MED.EX

1106 **THE BRENTWOOD HOTEL:** 01224 595440. 101 Crown St. In an area of many hotels and guesthouses to the S of Union St, this one's somewhat garish tho flower-covered appearance belies a surprisingly commodious hostelry that is a better prospect than most. An adequate business hotel on a budget. Close to Union St and bars/restaus. Bar meals in subterranean 'carriages' recommended; the ale is real. 65RMS JAN-DEC T/T PETS CC KIDS MED.INX

1107 **TRAVELODGE:** 01224 584555. 9 Bridge St tho' actually o/looking Union St bang in the middle which is why it's incl here. Usual conversion of office block into serviceable bedbox, but given Abd prices, this is a v reasonable billet.
97RMS JAN-DEC T/T XPETS CC KIDS CHP

1108 **THE CULTS HOTEL, CULTS:** 01224 867632. 9km from centre on A93 Deeside
D3 rd so well-placed for touring/Castle Trail. Fine roadside pub/hotel with local
following and quite comfortable. They were adding rooms at TGP. Bar full of
ale & golf.   10+RMS JAN-DEC T/T PETS CC KIDS MED.INX

1109 **HOSTELS: SYHA:** 8 Queen's Rd, an arterial rd to W. Grade 1 hostel 2km from
centre (plenty buses). No café. Rms mainly for 4 to 6 people. You can stay out
till 2am. Other hostels and self-catering flats c/o Univ, of which the best is
probably the **ROBERT GORDON'S**, 01224 2621344. Campus in Old Aberdeen
which is good place to be though 2km city centre has univ halls accom 01224
272664. Vacs only.

THE BEST RESTAURANTS IN ABERDEEN

THE TOPS

1110 ✓ ✓ **SILVER DARLING:** 01224 576229. Didier Dejean's breakthrough
bistro still going strong in this perfect spot poss the best location of
any seafood (or other) restau in the land. Not so easy to find – head for Beach
Esplanade, the lighthouse and harbour mouth (Pocra Quay). The light winks and
boats glide past. Upstairs dining-rm not large (best to book) & you want to be
by the window. Mostly chargrilled; the smell pleasantly pervades. Different
menu for lunch and dinner, changes seasonally and depends on the catch. Ap-
posite wines, wicked desserts. Mon-Fri lunch, Mon-Sat dinner 7-9.30pm.   EXP

1111 ✓ ✓ **THE LAIRHILLOCK INN:** 01569 730001. Not in the city at all, but a
D3 roadside inn at a country crossroads to the S, reached off either the
rd to Stonehaven or the S Deeside Rd W. Easiest is: head S on main A92, turn
off at 'Durris' then 5km. Long-famous for its pub food (1399/PUB FOOD), informal atmos and posher restau, new owners determined to keep the rep. Restau
now called 'Crynoch'. Likely to remain notable for good atmos, cheeseboard &
malt selection & still worth the drive from town. Restau: dinner and Sun lunch.
Cl Tues. LO 9.30pm. Inn: 7days lunch and LO 10pm.   MED/INX

1112 ✓ **SHISO:** 01224 624324. 8 Golden Sq. Not often one can try a place before
it officially opens (at TGP) & know it's a tick (or two) in the making, but
Robbie Robertson's ambitious 3-story food townhouse seems set for gr things.
Fine dining up top, brasserie at st level & bar/deli kind of thing below stairs. Gr
young team & food with care, maybe chutzpah. 7 days. LO 9.45pm.   INX/MED

1113 ✓ **THE FOYER:** 01224 582277. 82a Crown St. Remarkable in that this busy,
contemporary restau with good mod-British seasonal menu & gr service
is part of a local charity org who help homeless & disadvantaged people. No
hint of charity here, but you can satisfy your conscience as well as your
appetite for food & tasteful surroundings. Can't help thinking there should be
more places like this. Lunch onwards LO 9.30pm. Cl Sun/Mon.   INX

1114 ✓ **OLIVE TREE:** 01224 208877. 32 Queen's Rd. A late 90s addition to smart
dining in the Granite City and Mike Reilly certainly made sure it had the
look & the good management. Fine dining bistro & **BLACK OLIVE** brasserie in
conservatory annex. Service and presentation tip top. The Olive Branch adj is
curiously more Spar than special. Mon-Sat L and LO 10pm, BO till 11pm.   EXP

1115 **THE SQUARE:** 01224 646362. 1 Golden Sq, enter by S Silver St off Union St nr
Music Hall. Spacious, modern rm (nice windows) & contemp menu (3 diff thro'
day). Gd service & relaxing ambience. Lunch & dinner LO 10/11pm. Cl
Sun/Mon.   INX

SEAFOOD

✓ ✓ **SILVER DARLING:** 01224 576229. The Tops (*see above*).

1116 ✓ **ATLANTIS at the MARINER HOTEL:** 01224 591403. 349 Gr Western Rd.
Those that know where to go in Aber for excellent fish and seafood may
not necessarily go to Silver Darling, but come here. Hotel dining-rm atmos is
not too evident (tables in conservatory) and the fish v good. Moderately
priced wines. Lunch (not Sat) and dinner LO 9.30pm.   MED

1117 **BISTRO VERDE:** 01224 586180. The Green (down steps from Union St at Virgin megastore). Unpretentious fish restau (one steak, one chicken dish) with blackboard daily catch. Nice place. Lunch & LO 10pm. cl Sun/Mon. INX

1118 **THE ASHVALE:** 01224 596981. 46 Gt Western Rd nr Union St and branches (incl Elgin, Br of Don, Inverurie and Brechin). The famous Ashvale fish 'n' chip shop, the NE equivalent of Harry Ramsden's, but we'd all say better, esp here at original branch. Sit in (room for 300) or take away. Long, varied menu; you'd be daft not to have fresh fried fish (1458/FISH AND CHIPS). INX

ITALIAN

1119 ✓ **RUSTICO:** 01224 658444. Corner of Union Row & Summer St 50m from Union St. Small, typico but actually better than your average tratt. S Italian & Sicilian influences; some serious dishes. Lunch & LO 10.30pm. Cl Sun. INX

1120 ✓ **LITTLE ITALY:** 01224 572240. 79 Holburn St nr W end of Union St. The authentic good-fun and esp late-night Italian eaterie. Usual pasta/pizza mix. Can be raucous. Small & gets crowded. Prop Bono (no relation) does love to get in the picture! 7 days LO 11.15pm. MED

1121 ✓ **VIA MILANO:** 01224 593222. Bon Accord St, part of the 'Galleria' mall thing. Large, modern Italian retau – Est Est Est-like, but not part of a chain. Lunch & LO 10pm. 7 days (not Sun lunch).

1122 **BORSALINO:** 01224 732902. Peterculter on main A93 (after Rob Roy Br), 15km
D3 W of city centre but famously worth the drive. For over 20yrs Franco's unlikely cantina in a roadside cottage. Looking a little tired now, but a corner of Tuscany on a sunny day. Lunch & dinner Tues-Sun. MED

1123 **POLDINO'S:** 01224 647777. 7 Little Belmont St. Enduring haunt of Aberdonians in search of pasta etc. Good Italian home-cooking, incl puddings. City centre, always buzzy. Mon-Sat lunch and 6-10.45pm. INX

1124 **CARMINE'S PIZZA:** 01224 624145. 32 Union Terr. This tiny slice of a rm for the best pizza in town & on the wall, a few famous faces who've eaten them. Take away (to the Gardens opp). Real authentic pasta in basic spag/tag & penne variants. Noon-6.45pm. Cl Sun. CHP

EASTERN

1125 **THE ROYAL THAI:** 01224 212922. Crown Terr (off Crown St which is off Union St). The first and still one of the best of the welcome Asian invasion. 'Banquets' with sample dishes are a good idea. Good service, moody lighting. Daily lunch and LO 11pm. MED

1126 **JEWEL IN THE CROWN:** 01224 210288. Way down (145) Crown St, on corner with Affleck. Gr N Indian food all home-made & authentic. Prob best curry in town. Lunch & LO 11pm. 7 days.

1127 **BLUE MOON:** 01224 589977. 11 Holburn St. Contemp curry house, long thin & quite blue. Trad menu incl kids'. 7 days, lunch & LO 1am (a good late bet in a city that tucks up early).

1128 **YU:** 01224 580318. 347 Union St. Central, stylish, airy and relaxed and now long-standing Peking Chinese. Good fish; light sauces. Daily lunch & 7-11pm. MED

1129 **NARGILE:** 01224 636093. 77 Skene St. Turkish survivor that made its regulars happy for 20 yrs. Turkish owner, who also has t/away **MEZE CAFÉ** at 3 Rose St caff-style but open late for t/aways and another **NARGILE** in Edin (184/BEST MED FOOD). Doric staff, reliable meze, kebabs, swordfish etc. Dinner only LO 11pm. Cl Sun. MED

BISTROS & CAFÉS

1130 ✓ **THE VICTORIA:** 01224 621381. Upstairs at 140 Union St. Not a bistro as such, more a luncheon & tearm, but too good not to mention. Same staircase & foyer as adj jewellery & gift emporium so an odd alliance. Gr light menu, everything home-made & terribly well incl the bread & the biscuits & in July, a lemonade. 9am-5pm (6.30pm Thur). Cl Sun. INX

1131 ✓ **HOWIE'S:** 01224 639500. 50 Chapel St. Foll successful formula in Edin (124/BISTROS) & elsewhere in classic/contemp bistro style, this discreetly fronted restau presses all the right Aberdonian buttons (yes, incl price!). 7 days, lunch & LO 10.30pm. INX

1132 **THE LEMON TREE:** 01224 642230. 5 W North St. From E end of Union St heading for beach, W North St is off King St. Excellent arts centre with café-bar/restau. Food ok rather than fantastic, but gr ambience. Lunch only Tues-Sun. INX

1133 **LA BONNE BAGUETTE:** 01224 644445. Off Union St down steps at side of graveyard. Très popular and quite French café. Pâtisserie, snacks (baguettes, etc.) and specials. Daytime only 8.30am-5pm (Thur 7.30pm). Cl Sun. CHP

1134 **LA BAMBA:** 01224 590088. Crown Terr. Tex-Mex with attitude. Good buzz. A party place but passable grub too. People do salsa after the salsa. 7 days 5.30pm-LO 10pm. INX

1135 **CAFÉ 52:** 01224 590094. 52 The Green (opp Bistro Verde, above). A sliver of a cosy bistro with outside tables & light, contemp food incl tapas (4-7pm). 12-9.30pm (bar midnight). Till 6pm Suns. Cl Mon. CHP

1136 **BEAUTIFUL MOUNTAIN:** 01224 645353. 11 Belmont St. In area of many bars & eateries, this unpretentious caff stands out. Few tables, much t/away. Gr combos & ingredients – just better! 7 days till 5pm (Sun 4pm). CHP

1137 **MOONFISH:** 01224 644166. New t/away & café (at TGP) along from Bonne Baguette & by the same people who have Bistro Verde (both above). Light food Euro-style: meze, tapas, salads etc. Hrs vary. Cl Sun/Mon. CHP

THE BEST PUBS AND CLUBS IN ABERDEEN

PUBS WITH ATMOSPHERE

1138 ✓ **THE PRINCE OF WALES:** 7 St Nicholas Lane, just off Union St at George St. An all-round gr pub always mentioned in guides and one of the best places in the city for real ale: Old Peculier, Caledonian 80/- and guest beers. V cheap self-service food at lunchtime. Lots of wood, flagstones, booths. Large area but gets v crowded. 7 days, 11am-midnight (11pm Sun).

1139 ✓ **UNDER THE HAMMER:** 11 N Silver St. Basement bar along the st from above, v intimately Aberdonian and a good place to meet them. Slightly older and mixed crowd. Only open evenings (till midnight) and best late on. My kind of place. Every time I go there seems to be a single, beautiful girl reading a book hence methinks: a v civilised bar!

1140 ✓ **THE LEMON TREE:** 5 W North St. A theatre (upstairs) and a spacious bar/restau on st level where there's lunchtime food (1132/ABER RESTAUS) and a mixed programme of entertainment. Phone (01224 642230) or watch for fliers, but prog will include comedy, jazz, folk, pop and cabaret. This is one of the best live rooms in the land.

1141 **THE BLUE LAMP:** Gallowgate. Snug pub with nice ambience and long-established clientele and up the st large stone-floored lounge (The Blue Lampie) with gr atmos and often gr live music w/ends (so open 1am). Pub has pics of that '83 team and a jukebox unchanged forever.

1142 **MA CAMERON'S INN:** Little Belmont St. The 'oldest pub in the city' (though the old bit is actually a small portion of the sprawling whole – but there's a good snug). No nonsense oasis in buzzy street. Food: lunch and early evening.

1143 **THE GLOBE:** 13 N Silver St. Urban and urbane bar in single rm – a place to drink coffee as well as lager, but without self-conscious, pretentious 'café-bar' atmos. Known for its food at lunch and 5-7.45pm (not w/ends) and for live music – jazz and blues in the corner.

CONTEMPORARY PUBS

1144   **COLLEGE:** Alfred Pl at W end of Union St. Hugely popular 'sports' and MTV kind of bar with stylish interior. Screens hanging everywhere for the footie, boxing, and other bodies disporting and competing as they do around the bar.

1145   **THE PRIORY:** Belmont St. Excl conversion of town centre church. If churches were like this we'd all go back.

1146   **PARAMOUNT:** Bon Accord St. Designer café-bar looking a little worn now, but v popular and gr place to check out the club scene (flyers etc). You wouldn't want to eat here. Till midnight.

1147   **BLUE:** Bon Accord St adj Via Milano & actually in the mini-shopping mall (bouncers at the entrance on the st). Difficult to see the appeal here, but it was still pumping autumn '03. 7 days till midnight.

1148   **ILLICIT STILL:** Betw Broad St and Netherkirkgate. Studenty, wooden real ale labyrinth with brews from Tomintoul among others. Also bar food. Not a bad mix. 7 days till midnight.

1149   **JUSTICE MILL LANE and WINDMILL BRAE:** Many pubs to choose from. JM Lane has bigger selection and slightly older age gap. All loud and lively. For the up-for-it crowd (& the oil workers).

1150 **THE APEX:** 01382 202404. West Victoria Dock Rd. The Apex chain landed on Dundee waterfront in spring '03 & was a palpable hit. Huge, wooden designer edifice with spa facs and good rep for food in its Metro restau. More style than the HIlon adj, we'll see how it weathers. A big hit, though.

153RMS JAN-DEC T/T XPETS CC KIDS MED.INX/MED.EXP

1151 **HILTON:** 01382 229271. On riverside adj Olympic Centre nr Discovery Point. Serviceable, mainly business hotel with little charm but reasonable facs. Living Well leisure centre with ok pool. The rms facing south have some great Tay views. 129RMS JAN-DEC T/T PETS CC KIDS EXP

1152 **THE QUEEN'S HOTEL:** 01382 322515. 160 Nethergate. Not much charm but convenient location bang in the middle nr Arts Centre. Some back rms o/looking distant R Tay are best. 47RMS JAN-DEC T/T PETS CC KIDS MED.EX

1153 **THE SHAFTESBURY:** 01382 669216. 1 Hyndford St just off Perth Rd (about 3km from city centre). A suburban (jute baron's) mansion converted into a comfortable hotel with neat back gdn. All rms different; loungeable lounge. Decent food courtesy of chef Bill Morrison.

12RMS JAN-DEC T/T PETS CC KIDS MED.INX

1154 **FISHERMAN'S TAVERN:** 01382 775941. Broughty Ferry, Fort St nr the river/sea. 17thC fisherman's cottage converted to a pub in 1827. Rms much more recent! Excl real ales, but also nearby Ship Inn (1159/PUBS WITH BEST FOOD) preferred for eats. 14RMS (5 EN-SUITE) JAN-DEC T/T PETS CC KIDS INX

1155 **HOTEL BROUGHTY FERRY, BROUGHTY FERRY:** 01382 480027. 16 W Queen St. On main rd into the 'Ferry' (*see below*). Cleanly refurb inside, with conservatory. Pool and sauna rm lurking surprisingly in the basement. On busy corner, but calm inside. Bar and Bombay Brasserie serving Indian & à la carte that was good enough for Michelin 2003. 16RMS JAN-DEC T/T XPETS CC KIDS MED.INX

1156 **WOODLANDS, BROUGHTY FERRY:** 01382 480033. In the 'burbs between 3F and Monifieth, signposted up Abercromby St opp the Esso garage. Highfalutin' house in substantial acreage. Recent refurb & good disabled access. Popular out-of-town wedding venue quite complete with small swimming pool and gym. 38RMS JAN-DEC T/T PETS CC KIDS MED.INX

1157 **SANDFORD HILL:** 01382 541802. Excellent rural retreat over the water 7km S of Tay Br via A92/914 (1217/COUNTRY-HOUSE HOTELS).

1158 **SWALLOW HOTEL:** 01382 641122. Modern, all-purpose chain hotel on town ring rd, but good for families (1229/KIDS).

HOSTELS: There is no S.Y.H. in the area, although in summer months univ hall accom is available – info from TIC. 01382 527527. **THE RIVER VIEW** 127 Broughty Ferry Rd (01382 450565) caters for backpackers.

1159 ✓ **THE SHIP INN:** 01382 779176. On front at Broughty Ferry. Weathered by the R Tay since the 1800s, this cosy pub has sustained smugglers, fishermen and foody folk alike. Bar and upstairs restau; no-nonsense Scottish menu and picture windows o/look the Tay. Lunch & 5-9pm, w/ends noon-9pm. CHP

1160 ✓ **HOWIE'S:** 01382 200399. 25 South Tay St. The estimable Howie's with 3 notable easy-eating establishments in Edin has come N to Aber (1131/ABER RESTAUS) & here in Dundee's emerging 'cultural quarter'. Here there's a bar/café, 2 floor restau & 4 rms. Happily familiar and seems to be established now, so we're thankful for that. Lunch & dinner daily LO 9.30pm. INX

1161 ✓ **DIL SE:** 01382 221501. 99-101 Perth Rd. Dundee gets a designer Bangldeshi restau; on two floors even. Food from all over the subcontinent really but massive hit with locals. Lunch & dinner Sun-Thurs, open all day Fri & Sat. Until late! MED

1162 ✓ **JUTE at DUNDEE CONTEMPORARY ARTS:** 01382 909246. Perth Rd. The bar/cafe/restau of the arts centre which is Dundee's most contemporary space and menu. Also gallery, cinema, classy craft shop. A good rendezvous. Snacks during day. Good coffee. 7 days 10.30am-midnight. Lunch and dinner LO 9/9.30pm. Clientele changes dramatically from b/fast thro' late-night. CHP

1163 ✓ **THE SOCIAL:** 01382 202070. 10 South Tay St. Dundee's top style bar. Clean lines and pre-club vibe, but also one of those more eclectic style-bar menus. LO food 9.30pm. MED

1164 ✓ **THE AGACAN:** 01382 644227. 113 Perth Rd. Fabled bistro for Turkish eats and wine. OTT frontage and much art on the walls. Bohemian ambience & you smell the meat (veggies go meze). Cl Mon. INX

1165 **VISOCCHI'S:** 01382 779297. 40 Gray St, Broughty Ferry. More of a café than the original Kirriemuir branch caff. After almost 70yrs they're still making mouthwatering Italian flavoured ice creams (amaretto, cassata etc.) alongside home-made pasta and snacks. CHP

1166 **CAFE MONTMARTRE:** 01382 739313. 289 Brook St, Broughty Ferry. Charming and genuine bistro with extensive menu. French/N African cuisine incl N African wines. Gr value. Lunch 12-2 Thurs-Sat, dinner Mon-Sat LO 9.45pm. CHP

1167 **CAFÉ BUONGIORNO:** 01382 221179. 11 Bank St. Fairly authentic Italian job behind shopping centre. Prob best Italian in town. Excl pasta. LO 9pm. Cl Suns. MED

1168 **ROYAL OAK:** 01382 229440. 167 Brook St. Only a few minutes from the West Port but oddly hard to find (ask a Dundonian). A pub that serves curry & other East Asian specials. Mon-Fri until 7pm. Dundee's funky find. INX

1169 **BARRIO:** 01382 201500. Corner of Tay St & Nethergate. The more populist style bar (ie it has a kids' menu). LO food 9.45pm, bar until 11.45pm. INX

1170 **GULISTAN HOUSE:** 01382 738844. Queen St in Broughty Ferry (on main rd in/out) in converted church. Perennially popular curry in a church. In many curry guides & with many hygiene certificates on display. With adj snooker hall? The alternative is Spice in Erskine Lane (739291). INX

1171 **JAHANGIR:** 01382 202022. 1 Session St at West Port. Another Dundee fave with taste only in the curry. Many pubs nearby so 10 pints then a tikka masala? Until midnight daily (1am Fri & Sat). Cl Sun lunch. INX

1172 **BYZANTIUM:** 01382 228866. Corner of Session St on busy Hawkhill. A pebbledash box opp Jahangir (above). Italian and more generally Med cooking. Joanna B not impressed, nor me but makes a change from curry or pizza. INX

1173 **MANDARIN GARDEN:** 01382 227733. 40 Tay St. V acceptable Chinese. Low key décor, peaceful atmos; food is the thing. Excellent seafood and different meats covered sauce-u-like but also MSG. Dinner only 5-11pm. INX

1174 **FISHER & DONALDSON:** Whitehall St off Nethergate. Trad bakers among v best in Scotland (1520/BAKERS) with elevated tearm. Snacks & all their fine fare. Mon-Sat LO 4.45pm. CHP

... AND DRINK

1175 **THE FISHERMAN'S TAVERN:** 12 Fort St, Broughty Ferry. Good pub lunches here, but notable for real ales. Listed 17th-century fisherman's cottage, snug portside atmos. Also accom (1154/HOTELS). 11am-midnight (1am Thur-Sat).

1176 **LAING'S:** Roseangle, off Perth Rd. V popular with 20s-30s crowd. Beer gdn gets crowded in summer, typical pub food to fill you up and the *de rigeur* Banoffee pie. 11am-midnight, LO food 8pm.

1177 **TAYBRIDGE BAR:** 129 Perth Rd. Legendary drinking place. Est 1867: the smoke-filled gloom of a Dundee afternoon. When Peter Howson runs out of Glaswegian gnarled heads, he might come here. Women are present, but usually accompanied by their 'man'.

1178 **PUBS IN THE WEST PORT: TALLY-HO, THE GLOBE, BAR PIVO, etc:** Popular student and 20-something hang-outs in W Port (end of S Tay St & off Marketgait; behind univ). Seats outside at some.

1179 **CULLODEN HOUSE:** 01463 790461 (1043/HIGHLANDS HOTELS). LOTS

1180 **DUNAIN PARK HOTEL:** 01463 230512 (1046/HIGHLANDS HOTELS). EXP

1181 **BUNCHREW HOUSE:** 01463 234917 (1050/HIGHLANDS HOTELS). LOTS

1182 **GLENMORISTON:** 01463 223777. Ness Bank. Scottish country house feel meets Italian influence. An expanding (at TGP), smart establishment with excl restau (see below). 15RMS(+15ADJ) JAN-DEC T/T XPETS CC KIDS EXP

1183 **ROYAL HIGHLAND HOTEL:** 01463 231926. Academy St. Formerly the Station Hotel but big refurb & new owners. Well-chosen pics incl Michael Forbes – a surreal start to the day in the b/fast rm. V much in the centre of things with all mod cons. 75RMS JAN-DEC T/T PETS CC KIDS EXP

1184 **THE HEATMOUNT:** 01463 235877. Kingsmills, then centre (from Eastgate Mall). Surprisingly groovy boutique-style hotel with pop bar/restau (chef has growing rep). Lotsa detail in the dark decor upstairs.
7RMS JAN-DEC T/T XPETS CC XKIDS MED/INX

1185 **MARRIOTT HOTEL:** 01463 237166. Culcabock Rd. In suburban area S of centre nr A9. Modern, v well-appointed with pleasant gdn. Chain hotel but dependable. 82RMS JAN-DEC T/T PETS CC KIDS EXP

1186 **RAMADA JARVIS:** 08457 303040 (central booking). Church St. V central & some rms o/look river. Better than av bunk for the night. Ok restau & bar. Leisure facs with pool. 106RMS JAN-DEC T/T XPETS CC KIDS MED/INX

1187 **ARDMUIR/BRAENESS/FELSTEAD:** 01463 231151/712266/231634. 3 hotels on Ness Bank, along the river opp Eden Court and v central. Felstead got Landlady of the Year 2003. All family-run, basic. Many other hotels in this st. These ones are decent value. 11/7RMS VARIES X/T PETS CC KIDS MED.INX

1188 **MOYNESS HOUSE:** 01463 233836. 6 Bruce Gardens. Multi-accolade-gathering guest house in the 'burbs. Neil Gunn used to live here! MED.INX

1189 3 **GOOD HOSTELS. S. Y. HOSTEL:** 01463 231771. Victoria Drive; Large official hostel. More funky are the **STUDENT HOSTEL:** 236556. 8 Culduthel Rd, and 3 doors down **BAZPACKERS** 717663.

1190 **CAMPING AND CARAVAN PARKS:** Most central (2km) at **BUGHT PARK,** 01463 236920. Well-equipped and large-scale municipal site on flat river meadow. Many facs. App via A82 Ft William rd.

THE BEST PLACES TO EAT IN INVERNESS

1191 ✓✓ **BOATH HOUSE, AULDEARN:** 01667 454896. Well out of town, but worth drive. Just off A96 3km E of Nairn. 30mins from Inverness. Chef Charlie Lockely accumulating AA rosettes & rep. Report: 1041/HIGHLAND HOTELS. MED

1192 ✓ **THE MUSTARD SEED:** 01463 220220. Bank St. Cool restau in spectacular riverside rm attests (with Rocpool below) to Inverness's new confidence & city status. Contemp menu, ok wine. Service can vary, but a restau that would not be out of place in any European city. 7 days 12-4pm, 6-10pm. INX

1193 ✓ **ROCPOOL:** 01463 717274. Ness Walk. Corner of main br over river. Excl modern diner with accent on tapas-grazing daytime & eclectic even menu. Joanna B (whom we love) gave it 9/10! 7 days. Cl Sun lunch. INX

1194 ✓ **GLEN MORISTON HOTEL:** 01463 223777. Ness Bank. On rd along river. Comfortable elegant dining-rm with effective Italian menu well known as the place to eat Mediterraneo in this town. MED

1195 ✓ **DUNAIN PARK HOTEL:** As above. 3 adj elegant dining-rms; drawing rm for avant/après. The country-house hotel on the L Ness edge of town where the good burghers come for Ann Nicholl's honest-to-goodness cookery and wish they'd left more rm for the puds. Excl wines; and malt list.   MED

1196   ✓ **CAFÉ ONE:** 01463 226200. 10 Castle St nr the Castle. Contemporary décor and cuisine in hands of good team. Menu changes monthly, carefully sourced ingredients – salmon wild all summer – reasonably priced for this standard of food and service. Another restau for Inverness to be pleased about. Lunch, dinner LO 9.30pm. Cl Sun.   MED

1197   **RIVERHOUSE RESTAURANT:** 01463 222033. Greig St, over the pedestrian bridge. Intimate restaurant with contemp food from open kitchen. Gets busy so can feel cramped but excl rep. LO 10pm. Cl Mon.   MED

1198   **RIVER CAFÉ:** 01463 714884. Bank St on town side of river nr pedestrian br. Small, friendly café/restau. Solid & unpretentious even menu. 7 days LO 8.30 (Sun/Mon 7.30pm).   INX

1199   **SHAPLA:** 01463 241919. 2 Castle Rd on town side of main rd br. Indian restau with the usual menu served in upstairs lounge with river views. Open late (LO 11.30pm).   INX

1200   **PALIO:** 01463 711950. Serviceable town centre Italian (26 Queensgate). 7 days (cl Sun lunch). LO 10pm.   INX

1201   **RED PEPPER:** 01463 237111. 74 Church St. Recent cooler coffee-shop by the people that brought the Mustard Seed (above). Daytime caffeine hit with s/wiches etc. 7.30am-4.30pm. Cl Mon.   INX

1202   **THE LEMON TREE:** 18 Ingle St, pedestrianised town centre st and other entrance from behind M&S. Unlikely high st location for unpretentious family-run café with home-bakes, own burgers, etc. Mon-Sat 8.30am-5.45pm.   CHP

1203   **LA TORTILLA ASESINA:** 01463 709809. Top of Castle St nr castle & hostels (see above). Things looking up in Inverness – another tapas bar! This one with authentic Spanish owners & authentic laid-back feel. Also open Spanish hrs (till midnight/1am at TGP).   INX

1204   **PIZZA EXPRESS:** 01463 709700. Below stn nr Eastgate mall. Ubiquitous chain with formula menu. Room not as designer-chic as usual. 7 days. LO 10pm. INX

   ✓ **CASTLE RESTAURANT:** Castle St. Legendary caff of the Highlands. Hardest-working tearm in the N turns out all the things with (crinkly) chips we love. Report: 1474/CAFÉS.

   KINKELL HOUSE: off A9N. 01349 861270. Report 1068/HIGHLAND RESTAUS.

SECTION 5

*Particular Places to Eat and Stay
throughout Scotland*

1206
MAP 3
B4
✓ ✓ **CROMLIX HOUSE, DUNBLANE:** 01786 822125. Full report (906/CENTRAL HOTELS), but one of the best country-house hotels in the UK. Vast and fabulously sylvan grounds, fastidious service, excellent food. Go rest!

1207
MAP 4
D3
✓ ✓ **RAEMOIR HOUSE, BANCHORY:** 01330 824884. 5 km N from town via A980. A gem in the NE. Historical with contemp comforts & excl dining. Report 1014/NE HOTELS.

1208
MAP 3
E6
✓ ✓ **THE ROXBURGHE HOTEL nr KELSO:** 01573 450331. Report: 925/BORDERS. The pre-eminent hotel in the green, rolling Borders. Fewer facs than some on this page, but excl golf course.

1209
MAP 3
B2
✓ ✓ **KINNAIRD, DUNKELD:** 01796 482440. 12km N of Dunkeld (Perth 35km) via A9 and B898 for Dalguise. In Kinnaird estate, a bucolic setting beneath woody ridge of Tay Valley, this country house envelops you with good taste and comfort. Good, unobtrusive service from friendly arrival to sad departure. You get a teddy on your bed and there's a stylish 'K' on everything. Gr snooker rm and drawing rm warmed by open fires. J/T preferred. Elegant dining; chef Trevor Brooks gets 3 AA rosettes. Silently beyond the grounds and river, endless traffic ploughs N and S on the A9. One day you'll have to join it again. Until then, live Kinnaird. Also 8 superb individual cottages (esp 'Castle Peroch') for more privacy. 9RMS (8 COTT) JAN-DEC T/T PETS CC KIDS LOTS

1210
MAP 2
D2
✓ ✓ **ISLE OF ERISKA, LEDAIG:** 01631 720371. 20km N of Oban (signed from A85 nr Benderloch Castle). As you drive over the Victorian iron br onto the isle (a real island), you enter a more tranquil and gracious world. Its 300 acres are a sanctuary for wildlife; you are not the only guests. The famous badgers, for example, come almost every night to the door of the bar for their milk. Comfortable baronial house with fastidious service and facs. Highly picturesque 9 hole golf, gr 17m pool (and gym) (excl in summer when it opens on to the gdn). Also putting, tennis and clay shooting; it's all there if you feel like action, but it's v pleasant just to stay still (and aromatherapy is avail). Dining, with a Scottish flavour and impeccable local ingredients from a rich backyard and bay, has 3 AA rosettes under chef Robert MacPherson – Hotel Chef of the Year 2003.
17RMS FEB-DEC T/T PETS CC KIDS LOTS

1211
MAP 3
B3
✓ ✓ **GLENEAGLES, AUCHTERARDER:** 01764 662231. Off A9 Perth-Stirling rd and signposted. Scotland's truly luxurious resort hotel. For facs on the grand scale others pale into insignificance; it is an international destination. Only the sun may be missing, but the famous golf (3 courses), the Equestrian Centre, Shooting School, Falconry Centre and Country Club make up for the climate. The Club has 2 pools and outdoor tubs. The new & refurb bedrms by Amanda Rosa are esp contemporary & elegant. Strathearn Restau is a foodie heaven but fabulously expensive. Also Club bistro lighter and brighter. Andrew Fairlie's intimate dining rm is considered by many to offer the best dining in Scotland. Report 1001/PERTHSHIRE RESTAUS. When you are in love and rich go here; there are no cheap w/ends.
276RMS JAN-DEC T/T PETS CC KIDS LOTS

1212
MAP 1
A3
✓ ✓ **KNOCKINAAM LODGE, PORTPATRICK:** 01776 810471. An ideal place to lie low; an historic Victorian house nestled on a cove. The Irish coastline is the only thing on the horizon, apart from discreet service and excellent food (chef Tony Pierce excels with a fixed menu which is full of surprises). Now with new owners; we'll see if they live up to previous high standards. Reports, please. 15km S of Stranraer, off A77 nr Lochans.
10RMS MAR-DEC T/T PETS CC KIDS TOS LOTS

1213
MAP 1
A2
✓ ✓ **GLENAPP CASTLE, nr BALLANTRAE:** 01465 831212. Luxury manor S of Ballantrae. V discreet entrance (phone for directions). Home of Inchcape family for most of 20thC, opened as a hotel in first year of 21st. Run by Graham and Fay Cowan (Fay's family has other hotels in the SW). Fabulous restoration on a house that fell into disuse in the 1990s. Excellent and studied service, good food (3 AA rosettes), impeccable environment. Quality costs but the price is inclusive of just about everything, so relax and join this effortless house party. Tennis, lovely walks. A southern secret! 17RMS EASTER-OCT T/T PETS CC KIDS LOTS AND LOTS

1214 ✓ **ARDSHEAL HOUSE, KENTALLAN:** 01631 740227. On A828 Oban-
MAP 2 ✓ Ballachulish rd (7km S of bridge), signposted then 2km rough track. Neal
D2 & Philippa Sutherland's small, elegant co house in lovely grounds o/looking L
Linnhe. Good brekkie, tho dinner only in wint. A gorgeous B&B.

3RMS MAR-NOV T/T XPETS CC KIDS TOS MED.EX

1215 ✓ **BALLATHIE HOUSE, KINCLAVEN, nr BLAIRGOWRIE and PERTH:** 01250
MAP 3 ✓ 883268. Superb situation on R Tay; culinary delights, comfortable, relax-
C2 ing: a chance to enjoy the finer things in (Perthshire) life. Merits longer mention than this, but because it is handy for Perth and probably the best place
to stay nr the town; full report and codes: 2251/PERTH.

1216 ✓ **ARDANAISEIG, LOCH AWE:** 01866 833333. 16km from Taynuilt signed
MAP 2 ✓ from main A85 to Oban down beautiful winding rd and 7km from
D3 Kilchrenan. In sheltered landscaped gdns dotted with funny faux Roman stat-
uary and sculptures that burst from the rhododendrons. Rambling gothic
mansion o/looking loch – stop in all times of day. Gr trees. Genuine 'faux'
grand that works. O/side by the loch, deer wander and bats flap at dusk. Pure
romance. Chef Gary Goldie deserves some plaudits too.

16RMS MAR-DEC T/T PETS CC KIDS TOS LOTS

1217 ✓ **SANDFORD HILL, nr WORMIT (nr DUNDEE & ST ANDREWS):** 01382
MAP 3 ✓ 541802. 7km S of Tay Bridge via A92 and A914, 100m along B946 to
D3 Wormit. In an unpromising landscape of quarries and pigfarms, a civilised
withdrawal from the jams of Dundee and bunkers of St Andrews. An austere
mansion with unusual layout and mullioned windows looking out to gorgeous gdns. Wild but romantic tennis court (someday they must get it back in
use), pub lunches. 750 acres adj farmland of 'activities' – clay-pigeon shooting,
fishing in Farm Loch, off-road driving.

16RMS JAN-DEC T/T PETS CC KIDS TOS EXP

1218 ✓ **FLODIGARRY COUNTRY HOUSE, SKYE:** 01470 552203. Nr Staffin, 32km
MAP 5 ✓ N of Portree. Set on the face of a hill with amazing views across Staffin
B1 bay and the mighty Quirang behind. Gr craic in the bar (good backpacker
meals) and the lounge; the piano is often played. Flora MacDonald's cottage
in the grounds with its tastefully refurbished bedrooms offers a rare opportunity actually to stay in a romantic place redolent of this island's history. Great
sky and great Skye all around you.

19RMS (7 IN COTT) JAN-DEC T/X PETS CC KIDS EXP

1219 ✓ **CORROUR HOUSE, AVIEMORE:** 01479 810220. Small country house 3km
MAP 5 ✓ from Aviemore on Coylumbridge rd, handy for the ski slopes. Without airs
E3 but not without graces, this family-run hotel is good value. Young deer in the
gdn at daybreak, fine-size rms, the best deal for miles.

8RMS JAN-DEC T/T PETS CC KIDS TOS MED.INX

 BALLACHULISH HOUSE, BALLACHULISH: 01855 811266. Report:
1318/SCOTTISH HOTELS.

1220 ✓ ✓ **CRIEFF HYDRO, CRIEFF:** 01764 655555. A national institution and
MAP 3 still a family business; your family is part of theirs. App via High St,
B3 turning off at Drummond Arms Hotel uphill then follow signs. Vast Victorian
pile with activities for everybody from bowlers to babies. Still run by the
Leckies from hydropathic beginnings but with continuous refurbs, incl the
fabulous winter gdns moving graciously with the times (fine coffee shop).
Formal dining rm & the Brasserie (best for food Med-style; open all day). Gr
tennis courts, riding school, Lagoon Pool. Tiny cinema shows family movies;
nature talks, donkey rides. Kids endlessly entertained (even while you eat). The
chalets in grounds are certainly among the best in Scotland. Gr for family get-
togethers.   225RMS JAN-DEC T/T PETS CC KIDS TOS MED.INX

1221 ✓ ✓ **OLD PINES, nr SPEAN BRIDGE:** 01397 712324. 3km Spean Br via
MAP 5 B8004 for Gairlochy at Commando Monument. Bill and Sukie Barber
C2 have 8 kids so will be unfazed by the demands of yours. Amazing value. One
level pine log cabin – all bedrms individually furnished; bunk beds with wee
teddies to cuddle and take home. Playrm with books, videos and games for
kids of all ages, and the Barber brood are also on hand to play with. Menagerie
of animals around the stream (many ducks) and Sukie's legendary cooking.
Kids can eat separately (not pizza and chips). (1058/BEST HIGHLANDS RESTAUS).
                                         8RMS JAN-DEC X/X XPETS CC KID TOS MED.INX

1222 ✓ **GLENFINNAN HOUSE, GLENFINNAN:** 01397 722235. Just off the 'Road
MAP 5 to the Isles' (the A830 from Ft William to Mallaig). V large Highland 'hoose'
C2 with so many rms and such large gdns you can be as noisy as you like. Great
intro to the Highland heartland; music, scenery and local characters. Cruise of
the loch leaves from the foot of the lawn. (1066/INEXP HIGHLAND HOTELS). Note:
this is not posh accom.   17RMS APR-OCT X/X PETS CC KIDS MED.INX-EXP

1223 **POLMAILY HOUSE, nr DRUMNADROCHIT:** 01456 450343. 5km from main L
MAP 5 Ness rd at Drumnadrochit via A831 to Cannich (and glorious Glen Affric;
D2 1665/GLENS), a good country-house hotel for adults that is excellent for kids.
The Whittington-Davis's have 4 themselves. Their lucky kids and yours have
lots to do in the gdns – trout pond where older kids can fish, pet rabbit run,
bikes, indoor swimming pool, pool room. Tree house and swing up the back
esp popular. Separate kids' meal time; special rates.
                                     10RMS + 2SUITES JAN-DEC T/T PETS CC KIDS MED.EX

1224 **PEEBLES HYDRO, PEEBLES:** 01721 720602. Innerleithen Rd. One of the first
MAP 3 Victorian hydros, now more Butlins than Bath. Huge grounds, corridors (you
C5 get lost) and floors of rms where kids can run around. Pool & leisure facs.
Entertainment and baby-sitting services. V traditional and refreshingly
untrendy. Rms vary. Dining rm is vast and hotel-like. Lazels bistro downstairs
is light, contemp and refreshingly good (944/BORDER EATS).
                                      137RMS JAN-DEC T/T PETS CC KIDS TOS MED.INX/EXP

1225 **STONEFIELD CASTLE HOTEL, TARBERT:** 01880 820836. O/side Tarbert on
MAP 2 A83 on slopes of L Fyne with wonderful views. A real castle with 60 acres of
D4 woody grounds to explore. Full report and codes: 860/ARGYLL HOTELS.

1226 **ISLES OF GLENCOE HOTEL, BALLACHULISH:** 01855 811602. Beside the A82
MAP 2 Crianlarich to Ft William: a modern hotel and leisure centre jutting out onto L.
D2 Leven. Adventure playground o/side and nature trails. Conservatory restau
o/looking the water. Lochaber Watersports next door have all kind of boats
from pedalos to kayaks & bikes. Snacks in the restau all day. Glencoe and 2 ski
areas nearby.   59RMS JAN-DEC T/T PETS CC KIDS MED.INX/EXP

1227 **HILTON COYLUMBRIDGE, nr AVIEMORE:** 01479 810661. 8km from Aviemore
MAP 5 Centre on B970 rd to ski slopes and nearest hotel to them. 2 pools of decent
E3 size, sauna, flume, etc. Plenty to do in summer and winter (1782/KIDS) and certainly where to go when it rains. Best of the often-criticised Aviemore corporate hotels, the most facs, huge new shed with kids' play area (the 'Funhouse'),
staff wandering around in animal costumes and kids' diner.
                                175 (INCL FAMILY)RMS JAN-DEC T/T PETS CC KIDS LOTS

1228 **WATERSIDE INN, PETERHEAD:** 01779 471121. Edge of town on A952 to
MAP 4 Fraserburgh. Modern hotel with pool etc and some activities for kids. Aden
E2 Country Park nearby (1779/KIDS). Kids' menu and meal times and family rms.
Ugie and Deedee (the bears) are a gr success, but you wouldn't want to take
them to bed. Adventure playground. Go-karts. Sometimes special family
w/ends.   109(16 FAMILY)RMS JAN-DEC T/T PETS CC KIDS TOS MED.EX

1229 **SWALLOW HOTEL, DUNDEE:** 01382 631200. Conveniently placed on the edge
MAP 3 of town, just off ring rd system and the rd in from Perth. A link in the com-
D3 mercial chain; but pleasantly sprawling with surprisingly lush gdns, nature
trails and leisure facs. Deals available.   107RMS JAN -DEC T/T PETS CC KIDS EXP

THE BEST HOSTELS

For hostels in EDINBURGH, *see p. 29; for* GLASGOW, *see p. 78. SYHA Info: 01786*
891400. Central reservations (SYHA) 01541 553255.

1230 ✔ ✔ ✔ **CARBISDALE CASTLE, CULRAIN, nr BONAR BRIDGE:** 01549
MAP 6 421232. The flagship hostel of the SYHA, an Edwardian castle in
C3 terraced gdns o/looking the flood plain of a river on the edge of the Highlands.
Once the home of the exiled King of Norway, it still contains original works of
art (nothing of gr value though the sculptures are elegant). The library, ballrm,
lounges are all in use and it's only a few quid a night. Shared dorms as usual
but no chores. Kitchens and café. Bike hire in summer; lots scenic walks. Stn
(from Inverness) 1km up steep hill. Buses: Inverness/Thurso/Lairg. 75km
Inverness, 330km Edin. 189 beds.

1231 ✔ **STIRLING:** 01786 473442 Fax 445715. Modern conversion in gr part of town,
MAP 3 close to castle, adj ancient graveyard and with fine views from some rms.
B4 One of the new hotel-like hostels with student-hall standard and facs. Many
oldies & internat tourists. B'fast incl or self-catering. Access till 2am. 126 beds.

1232 ✔ **LOCH LOMOND S.Y.H.:** 01389 850226 Fax 850623. Alexandria,
MAP 2 Dumbarton. Built in 1866 by George Martin, the tobacco baron (as
E4 opposed to the other one who produced the Beatles), this is hostelling on the
grand scale. Towers and turrets, galleried upper-hall, space for banqueting
and a splendid view across the loch, of where you're going tomorrow. 30km
Glas. Stn (Balloch) 4km. Buses 200m. Access till 2am. 160 beds.

1233 ✔ **AVIEMORE BUNKHOUSE, AVIEMORE:** 01479 811181. Nr main rd into Avie-
MAP 5 more from S (A95) off Coylumbridge rd to Cairngorm & by the river. Part of
E3 Old Inn (1407/PUBFOOD) so gr food adj. En-suite rms for 6/8 & family rms avail. AYR.

1234 ✔ **INCHNADAMPH LODGE, ASSYNT:** 01571 822218. 25km N Ullapool on
MAP 6 A837 rd to Lochinver & Sutherland. Well appointed mansion house for
B2 individs or groups in geologist-gazing, hill-walking, mountain-rearing Assynt.
Kitchen, canteen, annex with smoking rm. Some twins.

1235 ✔ **POTTERY BUNKHOUSE, LAGGAN BRIDGE nr A9:** 01528 544231. On rd
MAP 5 E-W nr L Laggan, 12km from A9 at Dalwhinnie. Homely bunkhouse & gt
D3 home-bake caff (1491/TEARMS). Lounge o/look hills, wood stove, hot tub on
deck. AYR.

1236 ✔ **GLEN FESHIE, nr AVIEMORE:** 01540 651323. Privately run hostel in farm-
MAP 5 house by the rd-side in Glen Feshie, signed Achlean from Feshiebridge
E3 on the B970. A walkers' refuge which has a genuine, friendly atmos. Store sells
basics; free porridge, but also meals provided. Good base for Cairngorm walking (2035/SERIOUS WALKS). 4 places incl 3 rms for 4. Open AYR.

1237 **THE BORDERS** *There are some ideal wee hostels in this hill-walking tract of*
MAP 3 *Scotland (where it all began). These 2 are esp good, one grand, one very small.*
D6
MELROSE: 01896 822521. Grade 1, 90 beds, v popular. Well-appointed man-
sion looking across to the Abbey; student-hall standard.

BROADMEADOWS: 8km from Selkirk off A708, the first hostel in Scotland
(1931) is a cosy howff with a stove and a view.

1238 **INVERNESS STUDENT HOSTEL:** 01463 236556. Indep hostel at 8 Culduthel Rd
MAP 5 opp the SYH, uphill from town centre (some dorms have views). Run by same
D2 folk who have the great Edin one (87/HOSTELS), with similar laid-back atmos and
camaraderie. Hostels seem to be springing up all over. If this is full ask at the TIC.

1239 **ROWARDENNAN, LOCH LOMOND:** 01360 870259. The hostel at the end of
MAP 2 the rd up the E (less touristy) side of L Lomond from Balmaha and Drymen.
E3 Large, well managed and modernised and on a water-side site. On W
Highland Way and obvious base for climbing Ben Lomond (2016/MUNROS).
Good all-round activity centre and lawns to the loch of your dreams.
Rowardennan Hotel boozer nearby.

1240 **HOSTELLING IN THE HEBRIDES:** Simple hostelling in the crofting communi-
ties of Lewis, Harris and the Uists. Run by a trust to maintain standards in the
spirit of Highland hospitality with local crofters acting as wardens. Lewis,
Harris and one each in N and S Uist. No advance bookings necessary or
accepted (suggests they will always fit you in). No smk and no Sun arrival or
departure. Check local TICs for details (2342/WESTERN ISLES). Also:

1241 **AM BOTHAN, HARRIS:** 01859 520251. At Leverburgh in the S of S Harris a
MAP 7 bunkhouse handbuilt & personally run – a bright, cool building with contemp
B3 feel. Good disabled facs. Caff, shop nearby. 18 spaces & camping nearby. One
of 8 hostels in Scotland given 5 Stars by visitscotland. Check also 2247/MUSE-
UMS for the new hostel in a Blackhouse a little further N (N Lewis).

1242 **LAGANDORAIN, IONA:** 01681 700781. At north tip of island on John
MAP 2 Maclean's farm. This feels like the edge of the world looking over to Staffa and
B3 beyond on the spiritual isle. Open AYR.

1243 **TOBERMORY, MULL:** 01688 302481. Looks out to Tobermory Bay. Central rel
MAP 2 high standard hostel v busy in summer. 39 places 7 rms (4 on front). Kitchen.
B2 Internet. Nr ferry to Ardnamurchan main Oban ferry 35km away (1637/VILLS).

1244 **LOCHRANZA YOUTH HOSTEL, LOCHRANZA:** 01770 830631. On left thro' vil-
MAP 2 lage – Vict house o/looking fab bay & ruined castle. Swans dip at dawn. Full
D5 self-cat facs. Comfortable sitting rm & lots of local books. Mar-Nov.

1245 **GLENCOE:** 01855 811219. Deep in the glen itself, 3km off A82/4km by back rd
MAP 2 from Glencoe village and 33km from Ft William. Modern timber house nr
D2 river; especially handy for climbers and walkers. Clachaig pub, 2km for good
food and craic. (Also 1704/SCENIC ROUTES; 1982/SPOOKY PLACES; 1957/BATTLE-
GROUNDS; 1378/PUBS; 2118/SKIING; 2032/SERIOUS WALKS.)

1246 **RATAGAN:** 01599 511243. 29km from Kyle of Lochalsh, 3km Shiel Br (on A87).
MAP 5 A much-loved Highland hostel on the shore of L Duich and well situated for
C2 walking and exploring some of Scotland's most celebrated scenery e.g. 5
Sisters of Kintail/Cluanie Ridge (2034/SERIOUS WALKS), Glenelg (1705/SCENIC
ROUTES; 1882/PREHISTORIC SITES), Falls of Glomach (1676/WATERFALLS). From
Glenelg there's the short and dramatic crossing to Skye through the Kylerhea
narrows (continuous, summer only), quite the best way to go.

1247 **KINLOCH CASTLE, RUM:** 01687 462037. The hostel below stairs in one of the
MAP 5 most opulent castle-fantasies in the Highlands. Currently subject to grant-aid
A3 to restore to former glory, the hostel operates to allow visitors to experience
the rich natural wildlife, grandeur & peace of Rum. Self-cat, but also a 'bistro'
Apr-Oct. For ferry details see Rum: 2298/ISLANDS.

1248 **INDEPENDENT HOSTELS IN SKYE: DUN FLODIGARRY, nr STAFFIN:** 01470
MAP 5 552212. In far N 32km from Portree beside Flodigarry Country-House Hotel,
B1 whose pub is one of the best on the island and has great ceilidhs (2341/SKYE),
and amidst big scenery. O/looks sea. Bunkrms for 2-6 & 4 singles (holds up to
54) and great refectory. Open AYR.

1249 **SKYE BACKPACKERS GUEST HOUSE, KYLEAKIN:** 01599 534510. Convenient
MAP 5 guest house with mainly 4-bunk rms and smallish gantry/lounge nr br for last/
B2 first stop on what used to be the island. Open AYR. There are many other in-
dependent hostels on Skye incl 2 in Portree. This has laundry service & internet.

1250 **THE BURGH LODGE, FALKLAND:** 01337 857710. Back Wynd behind main st
MAP 3 of Fife's most charming inland village (1826/PALACE, 2042/WALKS). Refurb,
C3 friendly, linen provided, log fire. Gr organic restau round corner (979/RESTAU).
Run by local community. Ideal for walking in Lomond Hills. 9 rms incl 2 twins.

1251 **MOUNT COLDINGHAM SANDS YOUTH HOSTEL, COLDINGHAM off A1:**
MAP 3 01890 771298. Impressive position & views over N Sea, N of Berwick. Usual
E5 ascetics of hostel life (SYH) but vill has some facs. Gr surfing & kayaking spot.
Cl Oct-Mar.

THE BEST ROADSIDE, SEASIDE AND COUNTRYSIDE INNS

1252
MAP 5
A2
✓✓ **THE THREE CHIMNEYS, COLBOST, SKYE:** 01470 511258. 7km W of Dunvegan on B884 to Glendale. Rms in a new build across the yard from the excl, long-established and much-awarded Three Chimneys restau (2322/ISLAND RESTAU) called **THE HOUSE OVER-BY**. Roadside tho few cars and within sight and smell of the sea. Exceptionally high standard split-level rms with own doors to the sward. Breakfast lounge, s/serv v healthy buffet. A model of its kind in the Highlands, hence often full. And be sure to book for dinner! 8RMS JAN-DEC T/T PETS CC KIDS LOTS

1253
MAP 6
B2
✓ **DRUMBEG HOTEL, NW SUTHERLAND:** 01571 833236. On spectacular B869 coast rd (1710/SCENIC ROUTES). Roadside inn in tiny township with more than a touch of French éclat esp in the kitchen (1083/HIGHLAND RESTAUS). Miles from anywhere except some of the best hill & coastal scenery on earth. Rms vary. 6RMS JAN-DEC X/X PETS CC KIDS INX-EXP

1254
MAP 3
B4
✓ **BOUZY ROUGE at the SHERIFFMUIR INN:** 01786 823285. Narrow Sheriffmuir rd off A9 but also app via Dunblane or more scenically from Bridge of Allan. Historic coaching inn with stylish makeover by the people with the hugely popular restau chain (565/GLASGOW). Boutique hotel standard rms and contemp dining. Excl value and restful location (908/CENTRAL HOTELS). 4RMS JAN-DEC T/T PETS CC KIDS MED.INX

1255
MAP 5
B2
✓ **GLENELG INN, GLENELG:** 01599 522273. At the end of that gr rd over the hill from Shiel Br on the A87 (1705/SCENIC ROUTES)…well, not quite the end because you can drive further round to ethereal L Hourn, but this halt is the civilised hostelry of the irrepressible Chris Main. Decent food, good drinking, snug lounge. Gdn with tables and views. Charming rms. Chris's wife's pictures adorn the walls & his boat *Blossom* may take you to Sandaig or elsewhere on this mystic coast. Yvonne cooks Tues-Sat. Adj cottage (rm7) avail. From Glenelg, take the best route to Skye (7/FAVOURITE JOURNEYS). 6RMS (+1) APR-OCT X/X PETS XCC KIDS MED.EXP

1256
MAP 2
B3
✓ **ARGYLL HOTEL, IONA:** 01681 700334. On beautiful, turquoise bay betw Iona & Mull on rd betw ferry & abbey. Daytrippers come & go but here you can really chill and roam this remarkable island. Cosy rms (1 suite), good food (esp vegn) fresh from the organic garden. The real peace & quiet and that's just sitting on the bench outside – this is Colourist country & this is where they would have stayed. 16RMS EASTER-OCT X/X PETS CC KIDS MED.INX

1257
MAP 6
A3
✓ **OLD INN, GAIRLOCH:** 01445 712006. Southern app on A832, tucked away by river and 'old bridge'. Excl pub for food, music (trad & contemp nights incl legendary Martin Stephenson when I was there). A recent 'pub of the year'. Nice, simple rms. 15RMS JAN-DEC T/T PETS CC KIDS MED.INX

1258
MAP 5
B2
✓ **THE APPLECROSS INN:** 01520 744262. The legendary end of the rd, seaside inn on the shore opp Applecross. Report 1286/GET AWAY HOTELS. 15RMS JAN-DEC T/T PETS CC KIDS MED.INX

1259
MAP 3
D6
CROSS KEYS INN and COURTYARD COTTAGES, ETTRICKBRIDGE nr SELKIRK: 01750 52224. Well not that nr Selkirk, but 12 km down beautiful B7009 & the historic valley of the Ettrick. James Hogg country excl for walking, fishing, getting away. 2/3 bedrm houses adj pub are light & spacious. Pub cosy & cluttered but choose food carefully. New props at TGP. 5RMS JAN-DEC X/T PETS CC KIDS MED.INX

1260
MAP 5
A1
THE STEIN INN, WATERNISH, SKYE: 01470 592362. Off B886 the Dunvegan-Portree rd, about 10km Dunvegan. In row of cottages on waterside. The 'oldest inn on Skye' with gr pub (open fire, good grub) & comfortable small rms above. Gr value in a special spot. Excl seafood restau adj (1442/SEAFOOD RESTAUS). 5RMS JAN-DEC X/X PETS CC KIDS CHP

1261
MAP 5
B2
PLOCKTON HOTEL, PLOCKTON: 01599 544274. On shoreline of one of Scotland's most picturesque vills (1633/COASTAL VILLS). Dreamy little bay. Many visitors & this pub gets busy, but food is great & rms upstairs are recently refurb & not without charm. 11RMS JAN-DEC T/T XPETS CC KIDS MED.INX

1262 **WEST LOCH HOTEL, TARBERT:** 01880 820283. Beside A83 just W of Tarbert;
MAP 2 ideal stopover en route to the islands. Comfortably furnished; with original
D4 features sympathetically retained. Board games and books dotted around,
children welcome in relaxed, friendly atmos. Good value, but roadside rms
may be noisy. And doesn't that staff member suit her leather trousers…?
8RMS JAN-DEC X/T PETS CC KIDS MED.INX

1263 **KILBERRY INN nr TARBERT, ARGYLL:** 01880 770223. Half-way round the
MAP 2 Knapdale peninsula on the single-track B8024, the long way to Lochgilphead.
C5 Homely roadside inn with excl cooking. A gem.
3RMS JAN-DEC X/T PETS CC KIDS MED.INX

1264 **PIER HOUSE, PORT APPIN:** 01631 730302. An inn at the end of the rd (the
MAP 2 minor rd that leads off the A828 Oban to Ft William) and at the end of the
D2 'pier', where the tiny passenger ferry leaves for Lismore (2305/MAGIC ISLANDS).
Bistro restau with decent seafood (1454/SEAFOOD RESTAUS) in gr setting. Comfy
motel-type rms o/look the sea & island & conservatory restau & lounge. Gr
place to take kids.   12RMS JAN-DEC T/T XPETS CC KIDS MED.EX

1265 **GLENISLA HOTEL, KIRKTON OF GLENISLA:** 01575 582223. 20km NW of
MAP 3 Kirriemuir via B951 at head of this secluded story-book glen. A home from
C2 home: hearty food, real ale and local colour. Fishers, stalkers, trekkers and
walkers all come by. Miles from the town literally and laterally. Neat rms; con-
vivial bar.   6RMS JAN-DEC X/X PETS CC KIDS INX

1266 **BRIDGE OF ORCHY HOTEL, BRIDGE OF ORCHY:** 01838 400208. Unmissable
MAP 2 on the A82 (the rd to Glencoe, Ft William and Skye) 11km N of Tyndrum. Old
E2 inn extensively refurbished and run as a stopover hotel. Simple, quite stylish
rms. Hearty pub grub and dining. Good spot for the malt on the W Highland
Way (2026/LONG WALKS). Also 54-bed bunkhouse (v chp).
10RMS JAN-DEC T/T PETS CC KIDS MED.INX

1267 **CLUANIE INN, GLENMORISTON:** 01320 340238. On main rd to Skye 15km
MAP 5 before Shiel Br, a trad inn surrounded by the mt summits that attract walkers
C3 and travellers – the 5 Sisters, the Ridge & the Saddle (2034/SERIOUS WALKS). Club
house adj has some group accom while inn rms can be high-spec – one with
sauna, one with jacuzzi! Bar food LO 9pm. New management finding its feet
might review bunkhouse prices & rms do vary. Friendly staff.
12RMS+BUNKHOUSE JAN-DEC T/X PETS CC KIDS INX-MED.EX

1268 **TOMDOUN HOTEL, nr INVERGARRY:** 01809 511218. 20km from Invergarry,
MAP 5 12km off the A87 to Kyle of Lochalsh. A 19th-century coaching inn that
D3 replaced a much older one; off the beaten track but perfect (we do mean perfect) for fishing, walking (L Quoich and Knoydart have been waiting a long
time for you) and naturalising. Superb views over Glengarry and Bonnie
Prince Charlie's country. House-party atmos & nice dogs.
10RMS JAN-DEC X/X PETS CC KIDS INX

1269 **CRAW INN, AUCHENCROW, nr RESTON:** 01890 761253. 5 km A1 and well
MAP 3 worth short detour into Berwickshire countryside. Quintessential inn with
E5 cosy pub & dining rm. Funky furniture, simple rms. Food so-so, wines a sur-
prise.   3RMS JAN-DEC X/X PETS CC XKIDS INX

1270 **TRAQUAIR ARMS, INNERLEITHEN:** 01896 830229. 100m from the A72
MAP 3 Gala–Peebles rd towards Traquair, a popular village and country inn that
C6 caters for all kinds of folk (and, at w/ends, large numbers of them). Notable for
bar meals, real ale and family facs. Rms recently refurb. Nice gdn out back. All
food v home-made.   15RMS JAN-DEC T/T PETS CC KIDS MED.INX

1271 **THE KAMES HOTEL, TIGHNABRUAICH:** 01700 811489. Frequented by pass-
MAP 2 ing yachtsmen who moor alongside and pop in for lunch. Good base for all
D4 things offshore; marine cruises or a nostalgic journey on a 'puffer', with a gr
selection of malts to warm you up before or after. Hotel on a rolling refurb,
keen to be seen as an inn with rms. Great bar tho' the famous lock-ins may be
over.   10RMS JAN-DEC X/T PETS CC KIDS MED.INX

1272 **BRIDGE OF CALLY HOTEL, BRIDGE OF CALLY:** 01250 886231. Wayside pub
MAP 3 on a bend of the road betw Blairgowrie and Glenshee/Braemar (the ski zone
C2 and Royal Deeside). Cosy and inexpensive betw gentle Perthshire and the
wilder Grampians. Newish owners.   9RMS JAN-DEC T/T PETS CC KIDS MED.INX

1273 **CLACHAIG INN, GLENCOE:** 01855 811252. Basic accom but you will sleep
MAP 2 well, esp after walking/climbing/drinking, which is what most people are
D2 doing here. Gr atmos both inside and out. Food avail bar/lounge and dining
rm. 4 lodges out back. Harry Potter & crew drunk here 2003.

20RMS JAN-DEC X/T XPETS CC KIDS INX

1274 **MOULIN HOTEL, PITLOCHRY:** 01796 472196. Kirkmichael Rd; at the landmark
MAP 3 crossrds on the A924. Rms above and beside notable pub for food and esp
B2 ales – they brew their own out the back. (1338/REAL ALES).

16RMS JAN-DEC T/T MED.INX

1275 **CULFAIL HOTEL by KILMELFORD:** 01852 200274. On A816 20 km S of Oban
MAP 2 and nr a gr bit of W Highland coast that includes Seil Island, Luing etc. A trad
D3 roadside hostelry incl the 'Tartan Puffer' Bar B Q restau. A gantry full of choice
single malt whiskies and bar food provided as and when. A friendly hotel with
a lounge that speaks of time and travellers gone by.

12RMS JAN-DEC X/T PETS CC KIDS MED.INX

1276 **GALLEY OF LORNE, ARDFERN:** 01852 500284. Roadside/seaside inn in
MAP 2 yachty haven of Ardfern. Salts, locals and other worthies mingle at the bar.
C3 We'd like this place better but it needs some TLC.

JAN-DEC X/T PETS CC KIDS INX

1277 **GLENMORISTON ARMS HOTEL, INVERMORISTON, LOCH NESS:** 01320
MAP 5 351206. On main A82 betw Inverness (45km) and Ft Augustus (10km) at the
D2 Glen Moriston corner, and quite the best corner of this famous loch side to
explore. Busy local bar, fishermen's tales. Bistro over-by (LO 8.30pm) table
o/side in summer. Bar meals look ok and extensive malt list – certainly a good
place to drink them. 8RMS JAN-DEC T/T PETS CC KIDS MED.INX

✓ **THE HARBOUR INN** 01496 810330, **THE PORT CHARLOTTE HOTEL**
01496 850360, **ISLAY** Reports: 2310/2309/ISLAND HOTELS

✓ **THE ROYAL at TIGHNABRUAICH:** 01700 811239. More hotel perhaps
than inn (tho gr pub meals), but top service & attention to detail in glorious seaside setting. Report: 854/ARGYLL HOTELS

✓ **ARDEONAIG, LOCH TAY:** 01567 820400. On tiny lochside rd, a haven with
improvements afoot. Report: 1285/GET AWAY FROM IT ALL

ANCHOR HOTEL, KIPPFORD: 01556 620205. Report: 894/SW HOTELS/RESTAUS

THE OLD ABERLADY INN: 01875 870503 Report: 950/LOTHIANS HOTELS

1278
MAP 6
C3
✓✓✓ **SKIBO CASTLE, DORNOCH:** 01862 894600. A vast estate once home to the formidable Carnegies (those halls in NYC, Dunfermline, etc.). They declared it to be 'heaven on earth' which may be your sentiment too. Now like an Edwardian 'gentleman's' club you can sample the atmos once, but to return you join the club. Some club! de Savery moved on but the sumptuous castle retains its original furnishings (silk wallpaper, panelling, etc.) and the service from your discreet 'hosts' is exemplary. Lodges in the grounds offer more privacy, with the obligatory golf course, spa, gym and beach, all oases of relaxing indulgence – vintage Rolls Royces take you around. You get the feeling they weren't that bothered about the publicity boost when Maddy got married here. Phone for details. LOTS AND LOTS

1279
MAP 5
C1
✓ **LOCH TORRIDON, GLEN TORRIDON, nr KINLOCHEWE:** 01445 791242. Impressive former hunting lodge on lochside, surrounded by majestic mts. A comfortable but cosy baronial house with very relaxed atmos. For all that, it's been focusing on outdoor activities lately like clay-pigeon shoots, mountain bikes or fishing. Lots of walking possibilities and Diabeg nearby (1643/COASTAL VILLAGES). Gr malts in the dwindling day (WHISKY, p. 193).
19RMS JAN-DEC T/T XPETS CC XKIDS TOS LOTS

1280
MAP 3
A3
✓ **MONACHYLE MHOR, nr BALQUHIDDER:** 01877 384622. Not so very remote, but seems so once you've negotiated the thread of rd alongside Loch Voil from Balquhidder (only 11km from the A84 Callander-Crianlarich rd) and Rob Roy's now famous grave (1942/GRAVEYARDS). Farmhouse o/looking L Voil from the magnificent Balquhidder Braes. Friendly, cosy and inexp; a place to relax in summer or winter. Rms in courtyard annex are best (5), but all have character. Fishing. Food fairly fab, well-sourced ingredients, 2 AA rosettes. Tastefully done, gr informal atmos.
5+5RMS+2 COTT JAN-DEC T/T PETS CC KIDS TOS MED.INX

1281
MAP 2
B2
✓ **TIRORAN HOUSE, ISLE OF MULL:** 01681 705232. SW corner on rd to Iona from Craignure then B8035 round Loch na Keal. 1 hr Tobermory but you don't ever have to go there. Family-friendly small co house in gr gdns by the sea. Excl food from sea & kitchen gdn – almost Himalayan gdn setting. Lovely rms (esp the gdn one). Wolsey Lodge but you don't have to eat together. Find this place!
6RMS+2COTT MAR-NOV X/X XPETS CC KIDS MED.EXP

1282
MAP 2
B3
✓ **ARGYLL HOTEL, IONA:** 01681 700334. Quintessential island hotel on the best of small islands just large enough to get away for walks & explore (2296/ISLANDS). You can hire bikes (or bring). Abbey is nearby (1946/ABBEYS). 3 lounges (1 with TV, 1 with sun) & 1 lovely suite (with wood-burning stove). Gd home-grown/made food.
15RMS(1SUITE) APR-OCT X/X PETS CC KIDS MED.INX

1283
MAP 3
B4
✓ **BOUZY ROUGE at the SHERIFFMUIR INN:** 01786 823285. The old rd across the moor app via A9, from Dunblane or Bridge of Allan (see The Ochils: 2012/HILLS). Excl food in pub or restau by the BR people (565/GLAS BISTROS) & 4 stylish rms, a real surprise in this isolated spot (though only 20 mins from Stirling). Not many walks adj but a real sense of being at the crossroads to nowhere.
4RMS JAN-DEC T/T PETS CC KIDS MED.INX

1284
MAP 1
A3
✓ **CORSEWALL LIGHTHOUSE HOTEL nr STRANRAER:** 01776 853220. Only 15mins from Stranraer (via A718 to Kirkcolm) and follow signs, but way up on the peninsula and as it suggests a hotel made out of a working lighthouse. Gordon Ward took over in 2000 and doing well. Romantic and offbeat, decent food too, and there are attractions nearby (Portpatrick 30 mins).
7RMS (+ SUITES IN GROUNDS) JAN-DEC T/T PETS CC KIDS EXP

1285
MAP 3
A2
✓ **ARDEONAIG, LOCH TAY:** 01567 820400. On narrow and scenic S Loch Tay rd midway betw Kenmore and Killin. An airy roadside inn by the water opp Ben Lawers. New owners 2003 with good plans. We always liked this location & expect this hotel to become an excl retreat. Friendly staff. Cosy public rms and bar. Upstairs library with cool books and dreamy view of the Ben. Good food. Love that loch!
16RMS FEB-DEC T/X PETS CC KIDS MED.EX

1286
MAP 5
B2
✓ **APPLECROSS INN, APPLECROSS:** 01520 744262. At the end of the rd (the Pass of the Cattle which is often snowed up in winter, so you can really disappear) N of Kyle of Lochalsh and W of Strathcarron. After a spectacular journey, this waterside inn is a haven of hospitality. Buzzes all seasons. Rms small (1+7 best). Judy Fish & a gr team & a real chef look after you. Poignant VC (2252/HERITAGE), walled garden, lovely walks and even a real pizza hut (1504/COFFEE SHOPS) to keep you happy in Applecross for days.

7RMS JAN-DEC X/X PETS CC KIDS INX

1287
MAP 4
A1
GLENMORANGIE HOUSE: 01862 871671. Cadboll, by Fearn, nr Tain. On the little peninsula E of Tain – phone to ask for directions. Owned by the whisky people since '89, they decided to open it up in '98. Still used for corporate entertainment by Glenmorangie and other companies – Sting stayed here when Madonna got hitched at Skibo. Chef has good rep. Class not just in the glass.

9RMS JAN-DEC T/X XPETS CC XKIDS EXP

1288
MAP 5
B3
THE PIER HOUSE, INVERIE, KNOYDART: 01687 462347. Currently the only restau on this far-away peninsula, though good grub at the pub nearby (1376/BLOODY GOOD PUBS). Accessible on foot (sic) from Kinlochourn (25km) or Bruce Watt's boat from Mallaig (Mon, Wed, Fri). Friendly couple offer warm hospitality in their home and surprisingly good cooking for somewhere so remote; rovers often return. Some say the better and certainly remoter option is the **DOUNE STONE LODGE** 01687 462667; 5km up the single rd. We couldn't stay, but it comes much recommended.

4RMS MAR-OCT X/X XPETS XCC KIDS TOS CHP

1289
MAP 3
C1
CLOVA, GLEN CLOVA HOTEL, nr KIRRIEMUIR: 01575 550350. Well, not that nr Kirriemuir; 25km N to head of glen on B955 and once you're there there's nowhere else to go except up. Rms all en-suite. Walkers' bar. Superb walking hereabouts (e.g. L Brandy and the classic path to L Muick). A v pleasant getaway tho lots of families drive up on a Sun for lunch. Also has (CHP) bunkhouse.

10RMS JAN-DEC T/T XPETS CC KIDS MED.INX

1290
MAP 5
C3
CORRIECHOILLE LODGE by SPEAN BRIDGE: 01397 712002. 3km from S Bridge via rd by station. Lovely rd & spectacularly situated when you arrive. Justin & Lucy share their perfect retreat with you in house & chalets outs back. Report 1081/HIGHLAND HOTELS.

5RMS MAR-OCT X/T XPETS CC KIDS INX

1291
MAP 5
D2
TOMICH HOTEL nr CANNICH: 01456 415399. 8km from Cannich which is 25km from Drumnadrochit. Fabulous Plodda Falls are nearby (1677/WATERFALLS). Cosy country inn in conservation village with added bonus of use of swimming pool in nearby steading. Good base for outdoorsy w/end. Glen Affric across the way.

8RMS JAN-DEC T/T PETS CC KIDS MED.INX

1292
MAP 6
B1
CAPE WRATH HOTEL, nr DURNESS: 01971 511212. 3km S Durness just off A838; on rd to Cape Wrath Ferry (2069/COASTAL WALKS) which takes you to Britain's farthest-flung corner and the Cliffs of Clo Mor. O/looking the loch, the sparsely furnished hotel is popular with fisherman; passing tourists also shoal up for lunch. Fishing on 2 rivers including the celebrated Dionard and lochs. Durness Golf nearby (2112/GOLF) and there's some of Britain's most spectacular and undisturbed coastline to wander. Excl views from some rms down Kyle of Durness; like a setting for something morose by Ibsen. 14RMS JAN-DEC X/X PETS CC KIDS MED.INX

1293
MAP 1
B1
LADYBURN, MIDDLE OF NOWHERE, AYRSHIRE: 01655 740585. On the B741 Girvan to Crosshill, find the turnoff 2 miles from Crosshill marked for campsite/caravan park. Ladyburn's around a mile up there. Small and discreet country house with AA rosette and sense of decorum.

5RMS EASTER-OCT T/T XPETS CC XKIDS LOTS

1294
MAP 1
E1
HART MANOR, ESKDALEMUIR: 01387 373217. A pleasant old house outside the village with views along the valey. Clean, fresh, calm & home-made.

6RMS JAN-DEC X/T PETS CC KIDS MED.INX

1295
MAP 3
E5
SPRINGBANK COTTAGE, ST ABBS: 018907 71477. Centre of the village next to St Abbs harbour, 5km from the A1. Not a hotel, certainly a B&B but definitely a gr place to get away. Small and friendly cottage (no smk) with an outdoors tea gdn open all year, popular with divers – bring a wetsuit when raining. Walk in St Abb's Head nature reserve (1812/WILDLIFE RESERVES). Few rms so often full in summer.

3RMS FEB-DEC X/T PETS CC KIDS CHP

PARTICULAR PLACES TO EAT AND STAY 161

1296 **TUSHIELAW INN, ETTRICK VALLEY:** 01750 62205. Further down the valley
MAP 3 (15 miles Selkirk) a cosy retreat. Only 3 rms, but good value. Both this country
C6 inn and the Cross Keys, below, are in wildly beautiful James Hogg country
(1979/LITERARY PLACES) about 1 hr from Edinburgh. Nice walks from here incl S
Upland Way (2027/LONG WALKS).   3RMS JAN-DEC X/T PETS CC KIDS CHP

1297 **MOOR OF RANNOCH HOTEL, RANNOCH STATION:** 01882 633238. Beyond
MAP 2 Pitlochry and the Trossachs and far W via L Tummel and L Rannoch (B8019
E2 and B8846) so a wonderful journey to the edge of Rannoch Moor. Literally the
end of the road but an exceptional find in the middle of nowhere. Quirky
rooms, great restau (open to non-residents). Many readers rave about this
place.   5RMS JAN-DEC X/X PETS CC KIDS MED INX

ALSO ...

✓ ✓ **KNOCKINAAM LODGE, nr PORTPATRICK:** 01776 810471. Report:
887/SW BEST HOTELS

✓ ✓ **THREE CHIMNEYS, SKYE:** 01470 511258. Report: 1252/ROADSIDE
INNS, 2322/ISLAND RESTAU.

✓ ✓ **ACKERGILL TOWER, nr WICK:** 01955 603556. Report: 1337/HOUSE
PARTIES.

✓ **DRUMBEG HOTEL, SUTHERLAND:** 01571 833236. Report: 1253/ROAD-
SIDE INNS.

STEIN INN, SKYE: 01470 59232 (report: 1260/ROADSIDE INNS).

GLENELG INN, GLENELG: 01599 522273 (report: 1255/ROADSIDE INNS).

CROSS KEYS, ETTRICKSHAWS: 01750 52224 (report: 1259/ROADSIDE INNS).

In Scotland the Best we don't do caravan life style. In fact, because we spend a lot of time behind them on Highland roads, WE HATE CARAVANS, but wild camping is a different matter. Although probably irresponsible to encourage it, it's a good and inexp way to experience Scotland, provided you are sensitive to the environment and respect the rights of farmers and other landowners.

1298 **KINTRA, ISLAY:** Bowmore-Port Ellen rd, take Oa turn-off then follow signs
MAP 2 7km. Long beach one way, wild coastal walk the other. Camping (room also for
B5 a few caravans) on grassy strand looking out to sea; not a formal site but facs available.

1299 **LOCHAILORT:** A 12km stretch S from Lochailort on the A861, along the
MAP 5 southern shore of the sea loch itself. A flat, rocky and grassy foreshore with a
B3 splendid seascape and backed by brooding mtns. Nearby is L nan Uamh where Bonnie Prince Charlie landed (1969/MARY, CHARLIE AND BOB). Once past the salmon farm laboratories, you're in calendar scenery; the Glenuig Inn at the southern end is a pub to repair to. No facs except the sea.

1300 **MULL:** Calgary Beach 10km from Dervaig, where there are toilets; also S of
MAP 2 Kilchronan on the gentle shore of L Na Keal where there is nothing but the sky
B2 and the sea. Ben More is in the background (2019/MUNROS).

1301 **GLEN ETIVE, nr BALLACHULISH and GLENCOE:** One of Scotland's gr unoffi-
MAP 2 cial camping grounds. Along the rd/river side in a classic glen (1668/GLENS)
E2 guarded where it joins the pass into Glencoe by the awesome Buachaille Etive Mor. Innumerable grassy terraces and small meadows on which climbers and walkers have camped for generations, and pools to bathe in (1743/SWIMMING HOLES). The famous Kingshouse Pub is 2km from the foot of the glen for sustenance, malt whisky and comparing midge bites.

1302 **GLENELG:** Nr the vill of Glenelg itself which is over the amazing hill from Shiel
MAP 5 Bridge (1705/SCENIC ROUTES). Vill has gr pub, the Glenelg Inn (1255/INNS) & cof-
B2 fee shop (1497/COFFEE SHOPS) for sustenance & a shop. Best spots 1km from vill on rd to Skye ferry (1705/JOURNEYS) on the strand.

1303 **OLDSHOREMORE, nr KINLOCHBERVIE:** 3km from vill and supplies.
MAP 6 Gorgeous beach (1649/BEACHES) & **POLIN**, next cove. On the way to
B1 Sandwood Bay where the camping is legendary (but you have to carry everything 7km).

1304 **ARCHMELVICH, nr LOCHINVER:** Signed off the fabulous Lochinver to
MAP 6 Drumbeg rd (1712/SCENIC ROUTES) or walk from vill 3km via Ardroe (& a gr spot
B2 to watch otters that have been there for generations). There is an official campsite, but anywhere on this rd might do.

1305 **ON THE ROAD TO APPLECROSS:** The rd that winds up the mountain from
MAP 5 the A896 that takes you to Applecross (1706/SCENIC ROUTES) is one of the most
B2 dramatic in Scotland or anywhere. At the plateau before you descend to the coast, the landscape is lunar & the views to die for. Camp here (wind permitting) with the gods. Lay-by & Applecross Inn (1258/INNS) 8km downhill & proper campsite with caff (see next page).

CAMPING WITH THE KIDS

Caravan sites and camp grounds that are especially kid-friendly, with good facilities and a range of things to do (incl a good pub).

Key: HIRE *Caravans for rent* XHIRE *No rental caravans available* X CVAN *Number of caravan pitches* X TENT *Number of tent pitches*

1306 **GLEN MORE CAMP SITE, nr AVIEMORE:** 01479 861271. 9km from Aviemore on
MAP 5 the road to the ski slopes, the B970. Across the road from the Glen More Visitor
E3 Centre and adj to L Morlich Watersports Centre (2150/WATER SPORTS). Extensive grassy site on loch side with trees and views of the mountains. Loads of activities include watery ones esp the reindeer (1782/KIDS) and at the Coylumbridge Hotel (1227/HOTELS THAT WELCOME KIDS) where there's a pool and The Fun House – a separate building full of stuff to amuse kids of all ages (soft play, mini golf, etc). Well stocked shop at site entrance. DEC-OCT XHIRE 240TENT

1307 **TAYMOUTH HOLIDAY CENTRE, KENMORE:** 01887 830226. On the A827 road
MAP 3 leading out of picturesque vill at the end of L Tay. The campsite is part of a
B2 centre which also includes cottages to rent as well as numerous facs. Close to Croft-Na-Caber Water Sports (2151/WATER SPORTS) which has everything that you can do on a boat, board, etc and the Crannog Centre (1868/PREHISTORIC SITES). Kenmore Hotel (994/HOTELS TAYSIDE) good for pub food – the kids can run about on the terraces. MAR-OCT XHIRE MANY TENT

1308 **CARFRAEMILL CAMPING & CARAVANNING SITE:** 01578 750697. Just off
MAP 3 A697 where it joins the A68 near Oxton. Small, sheltered and friendly camp-
D5 site in the green countryside with trickling burn. 4 chalets for hire on site. Good gateway to the Borders (Melrose 20km). The Lodge (or Jo's Kitchen as it is also known) adj has gr family restau where kids made v welcome (play area and the food they like, etc). MAR-OCT XHIRE 60TENT

1309 **APPLECROSS CAMPSITE:** 01520 744268. First thing you come to as you app
MAP 5 the coast afther your hair-raising drive over the bealach, the mountain pass.
B2 Grassy meadow in farm setting 1km sea. Usual facs & Flower Tunnel bakery & café (1504/COFFEE SHOPS). Safe haven. APR-OCT XHIRE CVAN/TENT

1310 **SANDS HOLIDAY CENTRE, GAIRLOCH:** 01445 712152. On L Gairloch with
MAP 6 views to the islands, a large park with its own sandy beach. Kids' play area but
A3 plenty to do & see in Gairloch itself – & gr pub, the Old Inn, for adults (1257/ROADSIDE INNS) – plus walking, fishing, etc. APR-OCT HIRE 100CVAN 200TENT

1311 **BOAT OF GARTEN CARAVAN PARK:** 01479 831652. In vill itself, a medium-
MAP 5 sized, slightly regimented site tailored to families with play area for the kids
E2 and even cots available to rent for the very wee. Cabins if the Scottish weather gets too much. Not the most rural or attractive site in the Highlands, but lots on doorstep to keep the kids happy, incl brilliant Landmark Centre (1784/KIDS) and Loch Garten ospreys (1799/BIRDS). AYR HIRE 37TENT

1312 **OBAN DIVERS CARAVAN PARK, OBAN:** 01631 562755. 1.5 miles out of Oban.
MAP 2 Quiet, clean and friendly ground with stream running through. All sorts of
D2 'extras' such as undercover cooking area, BBQ, adventure playground. In case of severe downpours, you can always escape to the 6-berth bunk room. No dogs. A good base for day trips incl Rare Breeds Farm and Sealife Centre (1788/KIDS). MAR-OCT XHIRE 30CVAN 32TENT

1313 **SHIELING HOLIDAYS, CRAIGNURE, MULL:** 01680 812496. 35km from
MAP 2 Tobermory but right where the ferry comes in. Gr views and a no-nonsense,
C2 thought-of-everything camp park. Self-catering shielings or hostel beds if you prefer. Loads to do & see, incl nearby Torosay & Duart Castles (1832/ 1831/CASTLES) and fun & novel Mull Light Railway. APR-OCT XHIRE 30CVAN 30TENT

1314 **CASHEL CARAVAN AND CAMPSITE, ROWARDENNAN:** 01360 870234.
MAP 2 Forestry Commission site on the quieter shores of L Lomond in Queen Elizabeth
E3 Forest Park. Excellent facilities and tons to do in the surrounding area which incl Ben Lomond and plootering by the loch. MAR-OCT XHIRE 100CVAN 135TENT

1315 **SCOUTSCROFT HOLIDAY CENTRE, COLDINGHAM:** 01890 771338. Massive
MAP 3 coastal park with every fac under the sun, incl restau, burger bar, cabaret bar,
E5 sports bar. Not everyone's cup of tea but kids will love it and adults will love the kids' activity prog (summer only) & play area. MAR-NOV HIRE 30CVAN 60TENT

1316
MAP 6
B3

✓ ✓ **THE CEILIDH PLACE, ULLAPOOL:** 01854 612103. Off main st near pt for the Hebrides. Inimitable Jean Urquhart's place which more than any other in the Highlands, encapsulates Scottish trad culture and hospitality and interprets it in a contemporary manner. Caters for all sorts: there's an excellent hotel above (with a truly comfortable lounge – you help yourself to drinks) and a stylish if not punctilious restau below. A bar with occasional live music and gr bar meals. A bunkhouse across the way with cheap and cheerful (though thin-walled) accom and a bookshop where you can browse through the best new Scottish literature. Scottish-ness is all here and nothing embarrassing in sight. Nothing more to say, Jean! 23RMS JAN-DEC T/X PETS CC KIDS EXP/CHP

1317
MAP 6
B2

✓ ✓ **THE ALBANNACH, LOCHINVER:** 01571 844407. 2km up rd to Baddidarach as you come from S into Lochinver on A837, at the br. Lovely 18th-century house in one of Scotland's most scenic areas, Assynt, where the mtns can take your breath away even without going up them (1991/1992/FAVOURITE HILLS). Colin & Lesley have created a quite exceptional Highland retreat. The outbuilding o/looking the croft gives extra privacy & space. You unwind in tasteful, informal surroundings. The food is the best for miles. Gr walk behind house to Archemelvich beach – otters on the way. No smk. 5RMS MAR-DEC T/X XPETS CC XKIDS MED.INX

1318
MAP 2
D2

✓ ✓ **BALLACHULISH HOUSE, BALLACHULISH:** 01855 811266. On A828 nr south side of the bridge, not to be confused with the nearby hotel house thro' the golf course! Marie McLaughlin in charge will make you v welcome & chef Allan Donald goes from strength to strength (3AAs certainly due). Gr b/fast to fuel Glencoe walking. Sometimes piper with dinner. This small co house hotel is best bet nr Ft William. House v Scottish and makes much more of its historical background (Appin murder, Glencoe etc) – tasteful update of 17thC laird's place. 8RMS JAN-DEC T/X XPETS CC KIDS MED.EX/EXP/LOTS

1319
MAP 4
C3

✓ **KILDRUMMY CASTLE HOTEL, nr ALFORD, ABERDEENSHIRE:** 01975 571288. 60km W of Aberdeen via A944, through some fine bucolic scenery and the green Don valley to this spectacular location with the real aura of the Highlands. Well placed if you're on the 'Castle Trail', this comfortable chunk of Scottish Baronial has the redolent ruins of Kildrummy Castle on the opposite bluff and a gorgeful of gdns betw. Some rms small, but all v Scottish. Romantic in autumn when the gdns are good. J/tie for dinner. 16RMS FEB-DEC T/T PETS CC KIDS TOS LOTS

1320
MAP 5
B3

✓ **EILEAN IARMAIN, SKYE:** 01471 833332. Sleat area on S of island, this snug Gaelic inn nestles in the bay and is the classic island hostelry. A dram in your rm awaits you; from the adj whisky company. Bedrms in hotel best but cottage annex quieter. New suites in adj steading more exp. Food real good in d-rm or pub. Mystic shore walks. Gallery with selected exhibs and shop nearby. 12RMS+4SUITES JAN-DEC T/T PETS CC KIDS EXP/LOTS

1321
MAP 5
C2

✓ **GLENFINNAN HOUSE, GLENFINNAN:** 01397 722235. Off the Road to the Isles (A830 Ft William to Mallaig). The MacFarlanes have been running their legendary hotel in this historic house for nigh 30 yrs (1970/MARY, CHARLIE AND BOB). Some refurb without losing its charm, the huge rms remain intimate and cosy with open fires. Impromptu sessions and ceilidhs wherever there's a gathering in the house and you get piped into dinner. Solitude still achievable in the huge grounds, or fishing or dreaming on L Shiel (boat available 01687 470322). Day trips to Skye and small islands, nearby. New chef & management '03 – same owners. 17RMS APR-OCT X/X PETS CC KIDS MED.INX-EXP

1322
MAP 2
E6

✓ **SAVOY PARK, AYR:** 01292 266112. 16 Racecourse Rd. In a street and area of many indifferent hotels this one, owned and run by the Henderson family for over 40 yrs, is a real Scottish gem. Many weddings here. Period features, lovely gdn, not too much tartan, but a warm cosy lived-in atmos. Round one of the fireplaces, 'blessed be God for his giftis'. Good place to stop for the Burns Festival (21/EVENTS). 15RMS JAN-DEC T/T PETS KIDS MED.INX

CRIEFF HYDRO, CRIEFF: 01764 655555. The quintessential Scottish family hotel. (1220/HOTELS FOR KIDS).

STONEFIELD CASTLE, TARBERT: 01880 820836 (860/ARGYLL HOTELS).

1323
MAP 1
E1
✓ ✓ ✓ **SAMYE LING, ESKDALEMUIR, nr LOCKERBIE/DUMFRIES:** 01387 373232. Bus or train to Lockerbie/Carlisle then bus (Mon-Sat) to Boreland (0345 090510) or taxi (01576 470480). 2km from village, community consists of an extraordinary and inspiring temple incongruous in these border parts. The complex comprises main house (with some accom), dorm and guesthouse blocks many single rms, a café (open 7 days 9am-5pm) and shop. Further up the hill, real retreats – months and years – in some annexes. Much of Samye Ling, a world centre for Tibetan Buddhism, is still under construction under the supervision of Tibetan masters, but they offer daily and longer stays (£15-25) and courses in all aspects of Buddhism, meditation, tai chi, Alexander Technique, etc. Daily timetable, from prayers at 6am and work period. Breakfast/lunch and soup, etc. for supper at 6pm; all vegn. Busy, thriving community atmos; some space cases and holier-than-thous, but rewarding and unique and thriving. This is Buddhism with no celebrity, pure & simple. See also World Peace Centre (below).

1324
MAP 4
B1
✓ ✓ **PLUSCARDEN, between FORRES and ELGIN:** Fax: 01343 890258. Signed from the main A96 (11km from Elgin) in a sheltered glen S-facing with a background of wooded hillside, this is the only medieval monastery in the UK still inhabited by monks. It's a deeply calming place. The (Benedictine) community keep walled gdns and bees. 8 services a day in the glorious chapel (1947/ABBEYS) which visitors can attend. Retreat for men (14 places) and women (separate, self-catering) with 2 week max and no obligatory charge. Write to the Guest Master, Pluscarden Abbey, by Elgin IV30 8VA; no telephone bookings. Men eat with monks (mainly vegn). Restoration/building work always in progress (of the abbey and of the spirit).

1325
MAP 4
B1
✓ ✓ **FINDHORN COMMUNITY, FINDHORN, nr FORRES:** 01309 690311. The world-famous spiritual community (now a foundation) begun by Peter Caddy and Dorothy Maclean in 1962, a village of mainly caravans and cabins on the way into Findhorn on the B9011. Open as an ordinary caravan park and visitors can join the community as 'short-term guests' eating and working on-site but probably staying at recommended B&Bs. Full programme of courses and residential workshops in spiritual growth/dance/healing, etc. Accom mainly at Cluny Hill College in Forres. Many other aspects and facs available in this cosmopolitan and well-organised new-age township. Excl shop (1555/DELIS) and cafe – the Green Room (1424/VEGN).

1326
MAP 3
A3
✓ **LENDRICK LODGE, BRIG O' TURK:** 07774 263544. On A821 scenic rd thro' the Trossachs, 15km from Callander. Nr rd but in beautiful grounds with gurgling river. An organised retreat & get away from it all 'yoga and healing' centre. Yoga/reiki & shamanic teaching thro'out yr. Indiv rms & full board if reqd.

1327
MAP 2
D5
COLLEGE OF THE HOLY SPIRIT, MILLPORT, ISLAND OF CUMBRAE: 01475 530353. Continuous ferry service from Largs (hourly in winter), then 6km bus journey to Millport. Off main st through gate in the wall, into grounds of the Cathedral of the Isles (1685/CHURCHES) and another more peaceful world. A retreat for the Episcopal Church since 1884, there are 16 comfortable rms, all renovated 2003, some ensuite, in the college next to the church with B&B (around £20). Also half/full board. Morning and night prayer each day, Eucharist on Sun and occasional concerts in summer. Warden available for direction and spiritual counselling. Fine library. Bike hire available on island. Phone the warden. Try the island's gr café (1478/CAFÉS).

1328
MAP 2
D6
THE WORLD PEACE CENTRE, HOLY ISLAND: 01387 373232. Take a ferry from Lamlash on Arran to find yourself part of a Tibetan (albeit contemporary) mystery. Escape from the madding crowd on the mainland and compose your spirit or just refresh the parts that need it. Built by Samyeling Abbot on this tiny Celtic refuge, the centre offers a range of activities to help purge the soul or restore the faith. Day trippers to the island welcome. Sleeps 50 and conf centre, too, so phone ahead. Only 1 boat a week in winter.

1329
MAP 3
C4
CARBERRY TOWERS, MUSSELBURGH, nr EDINBURGH: 0131 665 3135. Sitting in extensive, well-kept grounds 3km S of Musselburgh, parts of this fine old house date back to the 15th century. Now a Christian residential and

conference centre, most accom is in new block 50m away; student-hall standard. Courses for church workers/group weekends which visitors may sometimes join. Not a quiet retreat but inexp for a break; high on 'renewal', low on rock 'n' roll.

1330 **NUNRAW ABBEY, GARVALD, nr HADDINGTON:** 01620 830228. Cistercian
MAP 3 community earning its daily bread with a working farm in the land surround-
D4 ing the abbey – but visitors can come and stay for a while and get their heads together in the Sancta Maria Guesthouse (a house for visitors is part of their doctrine). Payment by donation. V Catholic monastic ambience throughout. Guesthouse is 1km from the monastery, a modern complex built to a trad Cistercian pattern. Services open to visitors.

1331 **SALISBURY CENTRE, EDINBURGH:** 0131 667 5438. 2 Salisbury Rd.
MAP B 'Community and creative resource' in Georgian house on capital's Southside,
xE4 est 1973 by Dr Winifred Rushforth, psychotherapist and dream specialist. Not a retreat in the isolated sense, although 'w/end retreats' are possible. Classes during week and w/end workshops in meditation, healing, aromatherapy, massage, yoga, shiatsu, tai chi and pottery. Organic gdn, therapy rm, some basic accom.

1332 **CAMAS ADVENTURE CENTRE, MULL:** 01681 700367. Part of Iona
MAP 2 Community (2 others on Iona; this one is aimed at yoof and youth) near to
B3 Fionnphort in S of island (good bus service). No electricity, cars, TV or noise except the waves and the gulls. Outdoor activities (e.g. canoeing, hillwalking). 2 dorms; share chores. Week-long stays. You'll probably have to relate.

Places you can rent for families or friends & have to yourself.

1333 **MYRES CASTLE:** 01337 828350. 2 km Auchtermuchty on Falkland rd. Well-
MAP 3 preserved castle/family home in stunningly beautiful gdns. High country life
C3 though at a price. 9 rms individually & recently refurb to exceptional standard.
Formal dining rm, funky kitchen and impressive billiard rm. The perfect set-
ting for a murder mystery shindig. Central to all Fife attractions esp Falkland &
St Andrews. £250 per person per night, can take 18. Dinners up to 20.

1334 **CARBISDALE CASTLE, CULRAIN, NR BONAR BRIDGE:** 01549 421232.
MAP 6 Another castle and hugely impressive but on a per head basis, v inexpensive.
C3 Carbisdale is the flagship hostel of the SYHA (1230/BEST HOSTELS gives directions). From Nov-Feb you can hire the whole place so big Highland hoolies
over Xmas/Hogmanay are an option. More than 150 people can be accom in
the 32 rms (varying from singles to 12-bed dorms). Per night price £1200-
1500. Bring your own chef or muck in. You get the whole place to yourself.
Other SYHA hostels can be hired Oct-May. Check 0870 1553255.

1335 **GLEN FESHIE HOSTEL, nr AVIEMORE:** 01540 651323. At other end of scale
MAP 5 from above, a friendly, independent hostel in the superb walking countryside
E3 nr Cairngorm and Aviemore. A max of 15 people in dorms of 4, twins and a
single. Meals provided or self-cater. Main report 1236/BEST HOSTELS.

1336 **ON SKYE: GRESHORNISH HOUSE:** 01470 582266. Fairly remote and on its
MAP 5 own peninsula, o/look L Greshornish, a small co house hotel that you could
A1 have for yourself. Billiard rm and open fires. Food to order. Report 2341/SKYE.
STEIN INN, WATERNISH: 01470 592362. In N W off Dunvegan-Portree rd in
ribbon of houses by the sea. 5 rms above atmos pub adj gr seafood cottage
(2341/SKYE RESTAUS). Easy to feel at home here and very Skye.

1337 **ACKERGILL TOWER, nr WICK:** 01955 603556. Deluxe retreat in distant north.
MAP 6 Totally geared for parties and groups (mostly corporates). 6 times a year, eg
E1 Valentines/Hogmanay, you can join their 'House Parties'. Fixed price (3 nights
minimum stay) all inclusive. You'll prob have to mingle.

1338 **MELDRUM HOUSE, OLDMELDRUM:** 01651 872294. Of several small/med co
MAP 4 house hotels that might be taken over, this is a good one and highly individ.
D2 Lovely open fires everywhere. Stuffed with antiques, selected pics and atmos.
Can accom up to 18 in main house (all twins and doubles). Also 5 rm lodge.
Esp good for golfers with 18-hole course/prof/practice range in grounds.
Doubtless a deal can be struck. Report 1019/BEST HOTELS NE.

1339 **CAVENS, KIRKBEAN nr DUMFRIES:** 01387 880234. Off A710, the Solway
MAP 1 Coast rd 20km S Dumfries. Well-appointed mansion in gorgeous grounds nr
D2 the beach. Up to 14 guests accom with exclusive use & service. (889/SW
HOTELS).

1340 **GLENN HOUSE, TRAQUAIR:** 01896 830210. On A709 4km from vill in stun-
MAP 3 ning Border scenery, the notable family home of the Tennants (Colin Tennant
C6 the man who made Mustique and host to royalty). House reeks of atmosphere
and echoes of swinging parties gone by. Hire complete (incl Princess
Margaret's bedroom), ballroom, snooker room, etc. for up to 40 people. £4K
per 48 hrs, meals extra but you can BYOB. Live like they did! 22 rms.

1341 **CASTLE LACHLAN, LOCH FYNE:** 01369 860669. For directions see Inver
MAP 2 Cottage, the tearm on the estate (865/ARGYLL RESTAUS). Stunning setting in
D4 heart of Scotland scenery, the 18thC ancestral home of the Clan Maclachlan.
Beautiful library, snooker rm – you are guests of Lisa & Evan Maclachlan.
Sumptuous surroundings for rock stars & the rest of us.

National Trust for Scotland *have many interesting properties they rent out for
w/ends or longer. 0131-243 9331 for details.*

EDINBURGH

BARS AND CLUBS

1342
MAP A
D2
✓ **NEW TOWN BAR:** 538 7775. 26 Dublin St. Basement and underground club. Tends to be watering hole for older crowd. No twinkies. Downstairs bar open weekend nights for more shady corners and dance action. Open 7 days till 1am, w/ends 2am. Mixed crowd.

1343
MAP A
D2
✓ **PLANET OUT:** 524 0061. Traditionally the pre-club, pre-CCs hangout. Now has loyal following of bright-er, younger things. Handy too for the Playhouse & the Hull; it has an unthreatening vibe. You could take your mum. 7 days till 1am.

1344
MAP A
D2
✓ **CC BLOOM'S:** 556 9331. Next to Playhouse. Bar up, disco down. Now an institution, this is where everybody eventually ends up. Busy bar with karaoke upstairs & club below. It's stuffed (489/ESSENTIAL CULTURE/CLUBS) at weekends. 7 days 7pm-3am (your second-last chance!).

1345
MAP A
C2
FRENCHIE'S: 225 7651. Rose St Lane N nr Castle St. Intimate bar quite removed from the East End Pink Triangle. Hence more intimate but no less trashy. Fun before age (or beauty) so suits all. 7 days till 1am. (Sun midnight.)

1346
MAP A
E2
STAG AND TURRET: 478 7231. 1 Montrose Terr, Abbeyhill nr well-known cruising area. Friendly local. Pool table. 7 days till 1am.

OTHER PLACES

1347
MAP A
D2
✓ **BLUE MOON CAFÉ:** 556 2788. 36 Broughton St. Always busy, the boys and girls serve quick & cool in this all-day café. Attracts lively mixed (& earnest) crowd for food & drink and chat. Exhibitions and 'Out of the Blue' gay accessories shop next door in Barony St. If you are arriving in Edin and don't know anybody, come here first. Food 7 days till 10ish; bar 11/11.30pm. (290/CAFÉS)

1348
MAP A
D2
✓ **SALA:** 478 7069. 60 Broughton St. Tapas bar run by Spanish dykes. Hence the bravas & chorizo autentico & atmos Euro – great vibe – non-smoking rest at rear. Open Tues-Sun 11am-11pm.

1349
MAP A
D1
CLAREMONT BAR & RESTAURANT: 556 5662. 133 East Claremont St. Small and cheery wee bar handy for sauna. Own crowd and occasional fetish nights. Bulkies and furries have nights too. Food 7 days till 10pm. Bar 7 days till 1am.

1350
MAP A
E1
NO. 18: 553 3222. 18 Albert Pl. Sauna for gentlemen. Discreet doorway halfway down Leith Walk. Mon–Sat 12noon-10pm. Sun 2-10pm.

1351
MAP A
D1
TOWNHOUSE HEALTH CLUB: 556 6116. 51 E Claremont St, just down from Broughton St. Move 'upmarket' and move downstairs (up & down, up & down they go). It's all quite civilised really. Sauna steam; nice lounge.

1352
MAP A
D2
STEAMWORKS: 477 3567. Broughton Market which is at the end of Barony St off Broughton St at the Blue Moon. Modern, Euro-style wet & dry areas. Cubies. 7 days 11am-11pm.

HOTELS

1353
MAP A
xE4
✓ **SOUTHSIDE GH:** 668 4422. 8 Newington Rd nr Commonwealth Pool. Not too far away and (72/EXCL LODGINGS) Well-appointed GH. Mixed so not cruisy. No smk.   7RMS JAN-DEC X/T XPETS CC KIDS INX

1354
MAP A
xE1
✓ **ARDMOR HOUSE:** 554 4944. 74 Pilrig St. Quiet mix of contemporary & original design meet in this stylish GH run by nice boys who have a nice dog called Lola. Family room so straightfriendly. No smk.
    5RMS JAN-DEC X/T PETS CC KIDS MED.EXP

1355
MAP A
D2
MANSFIELD HOUSE: 556 7980. 57 Dublin St. Small New Town guest house and OK gay stay. Candelabra in the hall, various other camperie. Breakfast on a tray. No public rms – you'll have to leave your door open. New Town Bar (*see above*) up the st.   5RMS JAN-DEC X/X XPETS XCC XKIDS MED.INX

1356
MAP A
xE1
GARLANDS: 554 4205. 48 Pilrig St. Quiet st of many other GH – a stroll to the scene (but nr sauna). No smk.   6RMS JAN-DEC X/T PETS CC KIDS CHP

GLASGOW
BARS AND CLUBS

1357
MAP B
D4
✓ **DELMONICA'S:** 552 4803. 68 Virginia St. Newly refurbed stylish pub with long bar and open plan in quiet lane in Merchant City. Open-plan bar in gay quarter. Pleasant and airy during day but busy and 'sceney' at night, esp w/ends. As they say in Scots Gay – 'nice if your face fits'. 7 days till 12midnight.

1358
MAP B
D4
✓ **POLO LOUNGE:** 553 1221. 84 Wilson St. Great venue with stylish refurb decor, period furnishings. Something like gents' club meets Euro-lounge. Downstairs disco (Fri-Sun) with 3am licence; otherwise till 1am (one of the few pubs in town serving after midnight). (754/STYLE BARS)

1359
MAP B
C4
WATERLOO BAR: 221 7539. 306 Argyle St. Scotland's oldest gay bar and it tells. But an unpretentious down-to-earth vibe so refreshing in its way. Old-established bar and clientele. Not really for trendy young things. You might not fancy anybody but they're a friendly old bunch. 7 days till 12 midnight.

1360
MAP B
E4
CANDLE BAR: 564 1285. 20 Candleriggs. Newly refurb bar, funky design with purples and lilacs attracts the v fashion conscious younger set. Something on every night. Every day till 12 midnight.

1361
MAP B
E4
COURT BAR: 552 2463. 69 Hutcheson St, centre of Merchant City area. Long-going small bar that's straight till mid-evening then turns into a fairy. 7 days till midnight.

1362
MAP B
D3
SADIE FROST'S: 332 8005. 8 W George St, in front of Queen St Stn, hence catches all the passing trade and well placed for the brief encounter. Gets jumpy nr closing time. Pool room for sporty girls. 7 days till midnight.

1363
MAP B
D4
BENNET'S: 552 5761. 80 Glassford St. In the beginning & in the end... Bennet's. Relentless, unashamed disco fun without attitude on 2 floors. Wed-Sun 11pm-3am, Tue is 'traditionally' straight night.

1364
MAP B
E4
REVOLVER: 553 2456. 6a John St in basement opp Italian Centre. Civilised subterranea. Gr free juke box, pool, ale. Some uniform nights. 7 days all day to midnight.

OTHER PLACES

1365
MAP B
D4
GGLC (GLASGOW GAY & LESBIAN CENTRE): 221 7203. 11 Dixon St in a car-park zone. Café-bar drop-in centre with newspapers, info, 'garden of reflec-tion', art gallery. Good spot! Daily 11am-midnight.

1366
MAP B
C4
CLUB EROS: 0845 4562310. 1 Bridge St, first building on left crossing the Jamaica St Br. 3-floor sauna, spa & caff. Dark room. 7 days till 10pm.

1367
MAP B
C4
THE LANE: 221 1802. 60 Robertson St, nr Waterloo (*see above*) opp side of Argyle St, lane on rt. You 'look for the green light'. Sauna and private club. You wouldn't call it upmarket, that cabin fever! 7 days, afternoons till 10pm.

1368
MAP B
B1
ALBION HOTEL: 339 8620. 405 N Woodside Rd, off Gr Western Rd. Currently Glasgow's only prospect is gay-friendly (ie they advertise in gay mags) rather than gay. From the window, prospect is of treelined River Kelvin and handy for West End restaus etc.   16RMS   JAN-DEC   T/T   XPETS   CC   KIDS   INX

ABERDEEN

Gay scene in Aberdeen in disarray at TGP.

1369
MAP 4
D3
OUT: 01224 212527. 7 Crown St. Longest-running gay venue in a city as hard as granite in gay-friendly terms. Regular PAs. Thur-Sun 11pm-2/3am.

DUNDEE

1370
MAP 3
D3
CHARLIE'S BAR: 01382 226840. 75 Seagate nr Yates Wine Lodge. Okay gay-friendly pub, small-city scene, but if you're in Dundee for the night, you might. 7 days till 11pm/midnight.

1371
MAP 3
D3
OUT: 01382 200660. 124 Seagate. Along from the above so follows on. Bar and dancefloor. Everybody knows everybody else, but not you. This may have its advantages. Wed-Sun till 2.30am. Also ...

1372 **BROOKLYN BAR:** 01382 200660. St Andrews Lane. Behind and above Out.
MAP 3 Small bar, a pre-club bar on disco nights (reduced tickets avail at bar). Wed-
D3 Sun till midnight (11pm Sun).

HOTELS ELSEWHERE

Not many, but Auchendean more than just 'gay-friendly'.

1373 **AUCHENDEAN LODGE, DULNAIN BRIDGE:** 01479 851347. A Highland
MAP 4 retreat in an area with lots of outdoorsy things to do. Innovative cooking. (Eric
A2 and Ian well on the case; 1062/INEXP HIGHLAND HOTELS). This is still the place to
take your other half away from it all. Romance and more. Tho E & I are thinking of getting more well-earned rests in the future so phone to check out-of-
season opening.   7RMS   JAN-DEC   X/T   PETS   CC   KIDS   TOS   MED.EX

SECTION 6

Good Food and Drink

Pubs in EDIN, GLAS, ABER *and* DUNDEE *are listed in their own sections.*

1374
MAP 2
E3
✓ ✓ **DROVER'S INN, INVERARNAN:** A famously Scottish drinking den/hotel on the edge of the Highlands just N of Ardlui at the head of L Lomond and 12km S of Crianlarich on the A82. Smoky, low-ceilinged rooms, open ranges, whisky in the jar, stuffed animals in the hall and kilted barmen; this is nevertheless the antithesis of the contrived Scottish tourist pub. Also see 913/HOTELS CENTRAL.

1375
MAP 2
B2
✓ ✓ **THE MISHNISH, TOBERMORY:** The Mish has had its refit, but it's still the real Tobermory. 7 days till late. Usually live music from Scot trad to DJs and indie. Gr pub grub, open fire.

1376
MAP 5
B3
✓ **OLD FORGE, INVERIE, KNOYDART:** 01687 462267. A warm haven for visitors to this remote peninsula. Suddenly you're part of the community, real ales and real characters, excl pub grub. Stay along the rd. (1288/GET-AWAY-FROM-IT-ALL)

1377
MAP 2
C3
✓ **TIGH-AN-TRUISH, CLACHAN, ISLE OF SEIL:** 01852 300242. Beside the much-photographed 'Bridge over the Atlantic' which links the 'Isle' of Seil with the 'mainland'. On B884, 8km from B816 and 22km S of Oban. Country pub with 2 apartments above (with views of br). A place where no one cares how daft your hair looks after a hard day's messing about on boats. Food LO 8.30pm. (Mar-Oct)

1378
MAP 2
D2
✓ **CLACHAIG INN, GLENCOE:** 01855 811252. Deep in the glen itself down the rd signed off the A82, 5km from Glencoe village. Both the pub with its wood-burning stove and the lounge are woody and welcoming. Real ale and real climbers and walkers. Handy for hostel 2km down rd. Decent food (in bar/lounge or dining rm) and good, inexp accom incl 4 lodges. Clachaig now deep in Harry Potter country. They have beerfests – Oct one is quite a biggie.

1379
MAP 2
D3
KILCHRENAN INN, KILCHRENAN, LOCH AWE: On the corner where the wonderful, woody rd that winds along the N bank of the long loch from Ford turns N to Taynuilt. Nr Taychreggan Hotel (857/ARGYLL HOTELS) & Ardanaiseig (1216/CO HOUSE HOTS), but much cheaper grub & a friendly alternative to country house ways. Food LO 8.45pm.

1380
MAP 7
A5
CASTLEBAY BAR, BARRA: Adj Castlebay Hotel. Brilliant bar. All human life is here. More Irish than all the Irish makeovers on the mainland. Occasional live music, conversations with strangers.

1381
MAP 5
D2
PHOENIX, INVERNESS: 108 Academy St. Trad horseshoe bar. Always lively. The lounge is the place to relax with robust food (macaroni cheese & chips) and a pint of Deuchars IPA. However, **BLACKFRIARS** on Academy St also has its fans – inc researchers for this book! Good cask ale and regular live music.

1382
MAP 5
C2
CLUANIE INN: 01320 340238. On A87 at head of L Cluanie 15km before Shiel Br on the long rd to Kyle of Lochalsh. A wayside inn with good pub food, a restau and the accom walkers want. Good base for climbing/ walking (esp the Five Sisters of Kintail, 2034/SERIOUS WALKS). A cosy refuge. LO 9pm for food.

1383
MAP 3
C6
TIBBIE SHIELS INN: Off A708 Moffat-Selkirk rd. Occupies its own particular place in Scottish culture, esp literature (1979/LITERARY PLACES) and in the Border hills SW of Selkirk where it nestles between 2 romantic lochs. On Southern Upland Way (1685/WATERFALLS) a good place to stop and refuel.

1384
MAP 1
C2
THE MURRAY ARMS and THE MASONIC, GATEHOUSE OF FLEET: 2 adj, unrelated pubs that just fit perfectly into the life of this gr wee town. New owners at the Masonic Arms are upping the ante food-wise but the bar reeks atmos; masonic symbols still on the walls of the upstairs rms.

1385
MAP 5
D3
LOCK INN, FORT AUGUSTUS: Busy canalside (Caledonian Canal which joins L Ness in the distance) pub for locals and visitors. Good grub (you should book for the upstairs restau) The Gilliegorm, reasonable malts. Food LO 9.30pm. Some live music.

GREAT PUBS FOR REAL ALE

*For pubs in **EDINBURGH**, see p. 56–61, **GLASGOW** p. 98–102.*

1386
MAP 3
D3
✓ **FISHERMAN'S TAVERN, BROUGHTY FERRY:** In Dundee, but not too far to go for gr atmos and the best collection of ales in the area. In Fort St near the seafront. Regular ales and many guests. Low-ceilinged and friendly (1131/DUNDEE PUBS). Inx accom adj (1154/DUNDEE HOTS).

1387
MAP 3
D4
✓ **THE PHEASANT, HADDINGTON:** On corner where main st divides. Old-style, real-ale howff claiming to have the best selection in E Lothian. No arguments from us. Rare guests on tap, and local Belhaven brewed along the road in Dunbar. Busy market-town atmos; pool and frequent live music. Mind the parrot and 'spirited' locals at weekend.

1388
MAP 3
B2
✓ **MOULIN INN/HOTEL, PITLOCHRY:** 2km uphill from main st on rd to Br of Cally, an inn at a picturesque crossrds since 1695. Some rms and restau, but notable mainly for cosy (partly smoky) bar and brewery out back from which comes 'Moulin Light', 'Ale of Atholl' & others. Live music some Sun. Food LO 9.30pm.

1389
MAP 3
B3
✓ **ROYAL HOTEL, COMRIE:** Main sq; public bar is behind hotel. Distressed-wood & stone-walled howf behind hotel on main st (987/PERTHSHIRE HOTELS). Cask ales & beer garden. Good stop, v pleasant in summer.

1390
MAP 3
B4
✓ **THE FOUR MARYS, LINLITHGOW:** Main st nr rd up to palace so handy for a pint after schlepping around the historical attractions. Mentioned in most beer guides. Half a dozen ales on tap incl various guests. Beer festivals May and Oct. Notable malt whisky collection and popular locally for lunches (daily) and evening meals (Thurs-Sat, LO 8.45pm). Open 7 days.

1391
MAP 2
D5
✓ **THE PORT ROYAL, PORT BANNATYNE nr ROTHESAY:** Seafront on Kames Bay in Bute. A 'Russian' tavern with latkas & sauerkraut with your stroganoff. Some live music. 5 rms upstairs & a gr selection of ales. Brill atmos.

1392
MAP 3
B4
THE TAPPIT HEN, DUNBLANE: By the cathedral. Good ales (usually 5 guests & many malts), atmos and live music. A real find in these parts.

1393
MAP 3
E1
MARINE HOTEL, STONEHAVEN: Popular local on great harbour front with seats o/side; juke box and bar meals inside. Youngish crowd. Has won awards for its cask ales – various on tap. Lounge/restau upstairs. Open all day.

1394
MAP 3
B4
THE WOOLPACK, TILLICOULTRY: Via Upper Mill St (signed 'Mill Glen') from main st on your way to the Ochils. They come far and wide to this ancient pub. Bar food and a changing selection of ales which they know how to keep. Sup after stroll.

1395
MAP 5
D2
CLACHNAHARRY INN, INVERNESS: On A862 Inverness-Beauly rd just outside Inverness o/looking firth with beer gdn. Long list of regulars posted, 5/6 on tap when we visited, also Clachnaharry Village Ale, and three Tomintouls 'from the wood'. Local fave for pub food.

1396
MAP 4
C1
THE SHORE INN, PORTSOY: Down at the harbour so good atmos (& ales). Food all day in summer, weekends only in winter. The place to drink when you come for the Trad Boats fest (27/EVENTS)

1397
MAP 6
A3
THE OLD INN, GAIRLOCH: Southern app on A832 nr golf course, an 'old inn' across an old br; a goodly selection of malts. Some real ales in the cellar. Tourists and locals mix in season, live music some nights. Tasteful Origin Studio Gallery adj. Rms above make this an all-round good reason to stop in Gairloch (1257/ROADSIDE INNS).

1398
MAP 3
C4
BETTY NICOL'S, KIRKCALDY: 297 High St at the E end. Innkeepers who know and love their ales. Gr selection with usually 8 posted. Check also the FEAURS ARMS in this town (2348/BEST KIRKCALDY). Open 7 days.

Pubs in EDIN, GLAS, ABER *and* DUNDEE *are listed in their own sections.*

1399 ✓ ✓ **LAIRHILLOCK, nr NETHERLEY, STONEHAVEN:** 01569 730001.
MAP 4 Known forever for gr pubfood and more gourmet restau: open
D3 evenings – LO 9.30pm – and Sun lunch (1111/ABER RESTAUS). Inn (7 days lunch & dinner) more informal and downright friendly. Fine for kids. Superb cheese selection, notable malts and ales. Can app from S Deeside Rd, but simplest direction for strangers is: 15km S of Aber by main A92 towards Stonehaven, then signed Durris, go 5km to country crossrds.

1400 ✓ ✓ **BOUZY ROUGE at the SHERIFFMUIR INN:** 01786 823285.
MAP 3 Sheriffmuir rd 'behind' Dunblane and Bridge of Allan or from A9.
B4 Contemp food unexpectedly stylish at this far flung crossrds and tasteful rms upstairs. Report: 908/CENTRAL HOTELS.

1401 ✓ ✓ **THE WHEATSHEAF, SWINTON, betw KELSO and BERWICK:** 01890
MAP 3 860257. A hotel pub in an undistinguished village about halfway
E5 betw the 2 towns (18km) on the B6461. In deepest, flattest Berwickshire, Alan and Julie Reid serve up the best pub grub you've had since England. AA pub fd of the yr. 7 rms adj. An all-round excl hostelry. Lunch, 6-9.30pm. Cl Mon.

1402 ✓ **LION & UNICORN, THORNHILL, TROSSACHS:** 01786 850204. On A873
MAP 3 off A84 rd betw the M9 and Callander & nr Lake of Menteith. On main rd
A4 thro' nondescript vill. They come from mls around. Cosy dining areas & gdn. Changing menu, not fancy. 7 days. LO 9pm.

1403 ✓ **THE INN at KIPPEN, KIPPEN:** 01786 871010. The new place in town (well,
MAP 3 village) & country, reports here have put this place immediately on the
A4 foodie map. Gr value & excl special menu for kids. Suddenly Kippen is the rural food capital of central Scotland. 3 rms (MED. INX). 7 days, lunch & LO 9pm.

1404 ✓ **THE CROSS KEYS, KIPPEN:** 01786 870293. Here forever in this quiet
MAP 3 backwater town off the A811 15km W of Stirling. Bar meals by coal fire, à
A4 la carte and family restaus. A real pub food haven, for a'body. LO 9pm.

1405 ✓ **THE BYRE, BRIG O' TURK:** 01877 376292. Off A821 at Callander end of the
MAP 3 village adj Dundarroch Hotel and L Achray. Ann Parks back in this country
A3 inn in deepest Trossachs. Blackboard table d'hôte in bar or (no smk) restau. Best pub food for a long way in any direction. Lunch and 6-9pm.

1406 ✓ **WHEATSHEAF INN, SYMINGTON, nr AYR:** 01563 830307. 2km A77.
MAP 2 Pleasant village off the unpleasant A77 with this busy coaching inn
E6 opposite church. Folk come from miles around to eat (book at w/ends) honest-to-goodness pub fare in various rms (roast beef every Sunday). Menu on boards. Beer gdn. LO 9.30pm.

1407 ✓ **OLD BRIDGE INN, AVIEMORE:** Off Coylumbridge rd at S end of Aviemore
MAP 5 as you come in from A9 or Kincraig. 100m main st but sits in hollow. An
E3 old inn like it says with basic à la carte and more interesting blackboard spe-cials. Three cask ales on tap. Kids' menu that is not just pizza & chips, ski-bums welcome. Lunch and 6-9pm. In summer, tables over rd go down to river. New hostel adj (1233/HOSTELS). LO 9.30pm.

1408 ✓ **KYLESKU HOTEL, KYLESKU:** 01971 502231. Off A894 betw Scourie and
MAP 6 Lochinver in Sutherland. A hotel and pub with a gr quayside location on
B2 L Glencoul where boats leave for trips to see the 'highest waterfall in Europe' (1682/WATERFALLS, 1098/INEXP HIGHLAND RESTAUS). A friendly atmos with local fish, seafood (esp with legs) and yummy desserts. Noon-9pm.

1409 ✓ **THE GRANGE INN, ST ANDREWS:** 01334 472670. 4km out of town off
MAP 3 Anstruther/Crail rd A917. Perenially pop, almost Englishy pub with cosy
D3 rms & comfort food with flair. Lunch & dinner (not Sat lunch) LO 8.30pm. Must book w/ends.

1410 ✓ **SHIP INN, ELIE:** Pub on the bay at Elie, the perfect toon in the
MAP 3 picturesque East Neuk of Fife (1640/COASTAL VILLAGES). Bar and rm
D4 through back, but food mainly in refurbished boathouse next door and bistro above (good view, book w/ends). Same menu throughout and blackboard specials. Real popular place esp in summer when terrace o/looking the beach goes like Bondi. LO 9pm. Also has 6 chp rms adj in summer (01333 330246).

1411   ✔ **COCHRANE INN, GATEHEAD:** 01563 570122. Part of the Costley hotel
MAP 2   empire (840/HOTELS IN AYRSHIRE). A trim and cosy ivy-covered inn – most
E6   agreeable. On the A759 Troon to Kilmarnock & 2km A71 Kilmarnock-Irvine rd.
Excl gourmet pub with huge local rep – must book w/ends. Lunch & LO 9pm.

1412   **OLD MILL, KILLEARN:** 01360 550068. Main St. The 'other' gr pub in Killearn
MAP 3   (Black Bull more upscale 530/HOTELS OUTSIDE TOWN) but this is cosy, friendly, all
A4   an old pub should be (old here is from 1774). Pub & restau. Log fires, nice for
kids. Garden. 7 days 12-9.30pm, Sun from 12.30.

1413   **HUNTING LODGE HOTEL, FALKLAND :**01337 857226. Main st of much visit-
MAP 3   ed town in central Fife, opp the fabulous Palace (1826/CASTLES). All day menu
C3   of mainly stalwarts like 80/- ale steak pie and macaroni cheese. Beer gdn a bit
removed. Open 7 days. LO 8pm.

1414   **GOBLIN HA' HOTEL, GIFFORD:** 01620 810244. Twee village in the boondocks;
MAP 3   one of 2 hotels (951/LOTHIANS HOTELS). This, the one with the gr name, serves a
D5   decent pub lunch and supper (6-9pm; 9.30pm on Fri and Sat) in lounge and
more basic version in the pub. Conservatory and gdn; kids' play area.

1415   **DROVER'S INN, E LINTON:** 01620 860298. A village off A1, 35km from Edin. A
MAP 3   notable & hospitable E Lothian hostelry within reach of city. Restau upstairs,
D4   bistro with blackboard specials down. Can eat alfresco in summer with trains
whooshing by (145/EDIN PUBS WITH GOOD FOOD). LO 9.30pm.

1416   **TORMAUKIN INN, GLENDEVON:** 01259 781252. On A823 through wooded
MAP 3   Glen to Auchterarder, 36km NE of Stirling, 16km W of M90 at jnct 6/7. An 18thC
B3   drovers' inn with very pleasant accom (12 rms/MED.EX), à la carte restau and
fine pub meals. Vegn dishes. W/ends busy. Lunch and 5.30-9.30pm. All day
Sun.

1417   **ARCHIESTOWN HOTEL, ARCHIESTOWN:** 01340 810218. On square of small
MAP 4   Speyside vill, more a bistro perhaps than a mere pub, but mentioned here
B2   because it is top quality, unpretentious pub grub & so you don't miss it. See
also 983/NE HOTELS.

1418   **THE CROWN, PORTPATRICK:** 01776 810261. Hugely popular pub on harbour
MAP 1   with tables o/side in summer. Light, airy conservatory at back serving freshly
A3   caught fish. 12rms above. Locals and Irish who sail over for lunch (sic). Excl
chips LO 10pm.

1419   **THE SHIP INN, BROUGHTY FERRY:** Excellent seafront (Tay estuary) snug pub
MAP 3   with food upstairs and down (best tables at window upstairs). Famous for
D3   clootie dumpling (but not in summer). 7 days, lunch and 5-9pm (1159/DUNDEE
EAT AND DRINK).

1420   **HORSESHOE INN, EDDLESTON, nr PEEBLES:** 01721 730225. 5km N on A703
MAP 3   to Edin, this rdside inn is more a restau than just a pub. Lunch & dinner LO
C5   11pm bar, 9pm food (Sun all day till 8pm). A hostelry worth a stop-over, there
are 8 bedrms out-back by the church.

1421   **THE AULD CROSS KEYS INN, DENHOLM, nr HAWICK:** 01450 870305. Not a
MAP 3   lot to recommend in Hawick, so Peter and Heather Ferguson's village pub
D6   with rms is worth the 8km journey on the A698 Jedburgh rd. On the Green,
with pub and dining lounges through the back. Blackboard menu, heaps of
choice. Real fire & candles. Sun carvery until 3pm. Open late Thur-Sat (Sun
11pm). 3 rms if you want to stay (CHP).

FOX AND HOUNDS, HOUSTON: 01505 612448. (745/GLAS PUBS WITH GOOD
FOOD)

OLD CLUBHOUSE, GULLANE: 01620 842008. Report: 959/LOTHIANS HOTELS.

OLD INN, GAIRLOCH: 01445 712006. AA Pub of the Year 2003. Report:
1257/ROADSIDE INNS.

THE BEST VEGETARIAN RESTAURANTS

Not surprisingly, perhaps, there are precious few completely vegetarian restaus in Scotland. But there are lots in EDIN *(see p. 42) and some in* GLAS *(see p. 92).*

1422
MAP 2
C3
✓ **KILMARTIN HOUSE CAFE, KILMARTIN:** 01546 510278. Attached to early peoples museum (2110/MUSEUMS) in Kilmartin Glen & on main rd N of Lochgilphead. Organic garden produce incl tisanes for the revitalising that the gr range of home-made lunches & teas don't fix. 7 days, hot food till 3pm, cakes till 5pm. CHP

1423
MAP 2
D4
✓ **PINTO'S, LOCHGILPHEAD:** 01546 602547. So unlikely (in Lochgilphead!) this has to be a gr find – 1 Argyll St nr main rd thro' town. Chef/prop Ian Ward bravely bringing vegn food to the wild west. Vegan options. Tues-Sat, Lunch & LO 9pm.

1424
MAP 4
B1
✓ **GREEN ROOM at FINDHORN COMMUNITY, FINDHORN:** You will go a long way in the N to find real vegn food, so it may be worth the detour from the main A96 Inverness–Elgin rd, to Findhorn and the famous commune (1247/RETREATS) where there is a gr deli (1325/DELIS) and a pleasant caff by the 'Hall'. 7 days till 5pm and evens if event in the hall. CHP

1425
MAP 2
D2
✓ **CAFE NA LUSAN, OBAN:** 01631 567268. 9 Craigard Rd nr main st (uphill & nr the Studio restau). Groovy caff in any part of the world, with internet facs & import-label record shop downstairs. Rhona & Marie bring some funk to Oban & cook gr organic food. 7 days. 11.30-9.30pm (till 3.30pm Sun/Mon). INX

1426
MAP 5
A2
AN TUIREANN, PORTREE, SKYE: Off Uig (then Struan) rd (at the Co-op). Excl gallery cafe and restau with contemp menu; salads, hot meals, snacks. Prob best coffee on Skye and soups. 10am-4.30pm. Cl Sun. Changing exhibs. CHP

1427
MAP 6
A3
THE MOUNTAIN RESTAURANT, GAIRLOCH: 01445 712316. Vegn-friendly restau with conservatory and tables outside with mt view. Bookshop and adj Nature Shop with every kind of spiritual whatsits you may want. We've had complaints about the price of tea and scones – but look at the size of them! Self-serv food all day. All seems kinda American & v welcome this far N. AYR till 6pm (later July/Aug). INX

THE BEST VEGETARIAN-FRIENDLY PLACES

EDINBURGH *and* GLASGOW *cafés and restaus are mentioned in their own sections, see p. 42 and p. 92.*

1428 **HIGHLANDS**
MAP 5

THE CEILIDH PLACE, ULLAPOOL: 01854 612103 (1060/INEXP HIGHLAND HOTELS).

CAFÉ NUMBER ONE, INVERNESS: 01463 226200 (1196/INVERNESS).

BOOKSHOP CAFE, INVERNESS: 01463 239947. Church Street.

THREE CHIMNEYS, SKYE: 01470 511258 (2322/ISLAND RESTAUS).

OLD SCHOOL, DUNVEGAN, SKYE: 01470 521421 (2341/SKYE)

THE SEAFOOD RESTAURANT, KYLE OF LOCHALSH: (1084/INEXP HIGHLAND RESTAUS).

RIVERSIDE BISTRO, LOCHINVER: 01571 844356 (1094/INEXP HIGHLAND RESTAUS).

PLOCKTON HOTEL: 01599 544274 (1261/ROADSIDE INNS).

CAFÉ BEAG, FORT WILLIAM: 01397 703601 (2349/FT WILLIAM).

1429 **NORTH EAST**
MAP 4

THE FOYER, ABERDEEN: 01224 582277 (1113/ABER RESTAUS).

LEMON TREE, ABERDEEN: 01224 642230 (1132/ABER RESTAUS).

MILTON RESTAURANT, CRATHES: 01330 844566 (1033/NE HOTELS)

ARGYLL

INVER COTTAGE: 01369 860537 (865/ARGYLL RESTAUS).

THE GREEN WELLY STOP, TYNDRUM: 01838 400271.

THE ROYAL at TIGHNABRUAIGH: 01700 811239 (854/ARGYLL HOTELS).

JULIE'S COFFEE HOUSE, OBAN: 01631 565952. (2351/OBAN).

FIFE AND LOTHIANS

THE GREEN HOUSE, FALKLAND: 01337 858400 (979/FIFE RESTAUS).

PILLARS OF HERCULES nr FALKLAND: 01337 857749 (1493/BEST TEARMS).

OSTLER'S CLOSE, CUPAR: 01334 655574 (976/FIFE RESTAUS).

THE VINE LEAF, ST ANDREWS: 01334 477497 (2357/ST ANDREWS).

BRAMBLES, ST ANDREWS (1517/TEAROOMS).

WATERSIDE BISTRO, HADDINGTON: 01620 825674 (952/LOTHIANS RESTAUS).

DROVER'S INN, EAST LINTON: 01620 860298 (145/EDIN PUB FOOD).

CENTRAL:

LET'S EAT, PERTH: 01738 643377 (1002/PERTHSHIRE RESTAUS).

BOUZY ROUGE at the SHERIFFMUIR INN: 01786 823285 (908/PUB FOOD).

MONACHYLE MHOR nr BALQUHIDDER: 01877 384622 (1280/GET-AWAY-FROM-IT-ALL).

KILLIECRANKIE HOTEL BAR, KILLIECRANKIE: 01796 473220 (993/PERTHSHIRE HOTELS).

THE OLD ARMOURY, PITLOCHRY: 01796 474281 (1007/PERTHSHIRE RESTAUS).

SOUTH AND SOUTH WEST:

MARMIONS, MELROSE: 01896 822245 (939/BORDERS EATS).

PHILIPBURN, SELKIRK: 01750 20747 (932/BORDERS HOTELS).

ORKNEY

WOODWICK HOUSE, EVIE, ORKNEY: 01856 751330. B&B, seals, music and woodland. (2344/ORKNEY)

For seafood restaus in EDINBURGH, *see p. 41; for* GLASGOW, *see p. 92.*

1435
MAP 3
D3
✓ ✓ **THE CELLAR, ANSTRUTHER:** 01333 310378. V poss the best seafood restau in Scotland right now tho' it's been here for yrs. Behind Fisheries Museum in busy East Neuk of Fife town. Fish & shellfish from only the best waters, some meat options. Cosy French bistro atmos. Report: 975/FIFE RESTAUS. MED

1436
MAP 4
D3
✓ ✓ **SILVER DARLING, ABERDEEN:** 01224 576229. Down by harbour. For many yrs one of the best restaus in the city and the NE. Exquisite chargrilled seafood. Report: 1110/ABER RESTAUS. MED

1437
MAP 3
D3
✓ ✓ **THE SEAFOOD RESTAURANT, ST ANDREWS:** 01334 479475. Opened autumn '03 & effortlessly became top spot. Landmark position o/looking Old Course & building – glass-walled pavilion. Chef/prop Craig Millar is brilliant with (esp) white fish & the little things that make it zing. Gr wines, rich puds. 7 days lunch & dinner LO 10pm. MED

1438
MAP 2
E6
✓ ✓ **MACCALLUM'S OF TROON OYSTER BAR:** 01292 319339. Right down at the quayside, so follow the signs for Seacat & look out for Ailsa. 3km from centre. Red brick building with discreet sign, so eyes peeled. Lovely fish, great atmos, unpretentious and worth the trip even from Glasgow. Tues-Sat lunch and LO 9pm. Sun lunch only. MED

1439
MAP 2
D4
✓ ✓ **THE ANCHORAGE, TARBERT:** 01880 820881. Daft that this discreet, quayside bistro isn't recognised by more food guides. Clare Johnson gets it so right! Unpretentious, effortless (well probably not) seafood from local & selected suppliers. Best place to eat in these peninsulas. Daily menu. Lunch & LO 9pm (9.30pm summer). Cl Jan. MED

1440
MAP 3
D4
✓ **THE SEAFOOD RESTAURANT, ST MONANS, FIFE:** 01333 730327. West end of East Neuk Village. As St Andrews (above), Butler family offer simple title & no fuss in the menu either. Conservatory & terrace o/looks sea, waves lap, gulls mew etc. Bar menu lunch & dinner LO 10pm Cl Sun even & Mon. MED

1441
MAP 2
D2
✓ **EE-USK, OBAN:** 01631 565666. New build on the north pier by the indefatigable Macleod's. This is Riviera/urban seafood chic like you've never seen this far north before. The food leaps straight from the boats to your plate. And a gr wee wine list. LO 10pm 7 days. ·

1442
MAP 5
A1
✓ **LOCHBAY SEAFOOD, SKYE:** 01470 592235. 12km N Dunvegan; A850 to Portree, B886 Waternish peninsula coastal route. A scenic Skye drive leads you to the door of this small cottage at end of the village row. O/looks water where your scallops, prawns & oysters have surfaced. Main dishes served unfussily with puds from clootie dumpling to crème brûlée. Simply v good – you'll need to book. Apr-Oct; lunch & LO 8.30ish. Cl Sun & Sat except dinner in season. MED

1443
MAP 6
D1
✓ **THE CAPTAIN'S GALLEY, SCRABSTER:** 01847 894999. At last somewhere good to eat on the N coast. All local produce (from 50 ml radius). No tuna here, just what they catch (conservation ethos in menu). Nice rm, nice guy (Jim Cowie): even the fish would approve. Home-made bread, ice-cream, etc. C'mon food reviewers, make that journey. 7 days dinner 2 sittings (but check). MED

1444
MAP 2
E3
✓ **LOCH FYNE SEAFOOD AND SMOKERY:** 01499 600264. On A83 the L Lomond to Inveraray rd, 20km Inveraray/11km Rest and Be Thankful. Landmark roadside restau and all-round seafood experience on the way out west. Tho now a huge UK chain this is the original. This restau not actually in the chain – a separate entity after management buy-out. People come from afar for the oysters & the smokery fare, esp the kippers. Spacious, though the booths can seem cramped. House white (other whites & whisky) well chosen. Same menu all day; LO 8.30pm. Shop sells every conceivable packaging of salmon, etc.; shop 8pm. INX

1445
MAP 2
D2
✓ **THE WATERFRONT, OBAN:** 01631 563110. On the waterfront at the station. Upstairs from unimposing entrance a light, airy rm which is poss serving the best food in town. Blackboard specials change daily. At last somewhere in Oban to linger on the way to the ferry. Mar-Dec. L and LO 9pm. MED

1446 ✔ **THE TOLBOOTH, STONEHAVEN:** 01569 762287. On corner of harbour,
MAP 3 long one of the best restaus in the area in a great setting – oldest build-
E1 ing in town. Upstairs bistro with new owner Robert Cleaver in '03 determined
to keep up the fresh-with-flair rep. Wed-Sun lunch & dinner, LO 9pm. MED

1447 ✔ **FINS, FAIRLIE, nr LARGS:** 01475 568989. On main A78 S of Fairlie a
MAP 2 seafood bistro, smokery (Fencebay), shop and craft/cookshop. Roadside
E5 fish farm bistro, best place to eat for miles in either direction. Chefs Jane &
Gary use exemplary restraint and the wine list is similarly to the point. Lunch
& dinner LO 8.30pm. Cl Mon. New conservatory. INX

1448 ✔ **CREELERS, BRODICK, ARRAN:** 01770 302810. Just outside Brodick on rd
MAP 2 N to castle in uninspiring plastic gift plaza. Excl seafood bistro – gr food,
D5 fun staff. But phone ahead, this is Arran. Easter-Oct. Cl Mon. MED

1449 **CAMPBELL'S, PORTPATRICK:** 01776 810314. Friendly, harbourside restau of
MAP 1 recent origin ('99). Some meat dishes, but mainly seafood. Sardines were nice.
A3 7 days lunch and LO 10pm. Cl Jan-Mar and Mons. MED

1450 **KERACHER'S, PERTH:** 01738 449777. Corner of South St and Scott St. Seafood
MAP 3 bar at street level, designery restau upstairs. Keracher's are major fish whole-
C3 salers & supply most of the best hotel dining rms in Perthshire, so they know
their mullet. Lunch Tues-Sat, dinner Mon-Sat LO 10pm. INX/MED

1451 **CRANNOG, FORT WILLIAM:** 01397 705589. Long-established as the best
MAP 2 restau in Ft William, Finlay Finlayson's bistro on the quay in the middle of the
D1 waterfront – one day maybe the middle of a great waterfront. In meantime a
reliable, unpretentious resau with home- & locally produced seafood fare.
AYR. Lunch & dinner. LO 10pm (earlier in wint). INX

1452 **SEAFOOD CAFÉ, TARBET, nr SCOURIE:** 01971 502251. Charming conserva-
MAP 6 tory restau on cove where boats leave for Handa Island bird reserve
B2 (1663/BIRDS). Julian catches your seafood from his boat (he'll also take you on
a cruise) and Jackie cooks it; they have the Rick Stein seal of approval.
Cheesecake for dessert. Located at end of unclassified rd off the A894
between Laxford Br and Scourie; best phone to check openings. Apr-Sept:
Mon-Sat 12-8pm. Some Sun in summer. Licensed. INX

1453 **KISHORN SEAFOOD BAR:** 01520 733240. On A896 at Kishorn on rd betw
MAP 5 Lochcarron (Inverness) and Sheildaig nr the rd over the hill to Applecross
B2 (1583/ROUTES). Fresh local seafood in a roadside diner. Light, bright and a real
find in the middle of beautiful nowhere. Oysters, scallops & queenies courtesy
of the enthusiastic Viv Rollo. Apr-Oct daily 10-5pm. Sun 12-5pm. MED

1454 **THE PIERHOUSE, PORT APPIN:** 01631 730302. At the end of the minor rd and
MAP 2 3km from the A828 Oban–Ft William rd in Pt Appin village rt by the tiny 'pier'
D2 where the passenger ferry leaves for Lismore. Locally caught seafood (Lismore
oysters, Mallaig flatfish, hand-dived shellfish) is handed over fresh to the door
by boat. Lively atmos, wine and wonderful view. (1264/INNS) INX

1455 **APPLECROSS INN:** 01520 744262. The inn at the end of the rd with excl fresh
MAP 5 seafd & classic fish 'n' chips. Report: 1286/GETAWAY HOTELS.
B2

THE BEST FISH AND CHIP SHOPS

1456 ✔✔ **L'ALBA D'ORO, EDINBURGH:** Henderson Row, nr corner with Dundas
MAP A St. Large selection of deep-fried goodies, incl many vegnsavouries.
C1 Inexpensive proper pasta, real pizzas and superb, surprising Italian wine to go.
This is the chip shop of the future. Open until midnight. (176/EDIN PIZZA)

1457 ✔✔ **VALENTE'S, KIRKCALDY:** 01592 651991. 73 Overton Rd (not down-
MAP 3 town version). Ask directions to this superb chippy in E of town;
C4 worth the detour and worth the queue when you get there. Phone if you're
lost. Lard used. Till 11pm. Also branch at 73 Henry St 01592 203600. Cl Wed.

1458 ✔✔ **THE ASHVALE, ABERDEEN, ELGIN, INVERURIE and BRECHIN:**
MAP 4 Original restau (1985) at 46 Gt Western Rd nr Union St, and 2 other
B1, D3 city branches. Restau and takeaway complex à la Harry Ramsden (they stick to
MAP 3 dripping but veg oil supplied on request). Various sizes of haddock, sole,
D2 plaice. Home-made stovies, etc., all served fresh & fast though you may wait.
Open 7 days, noon-1am; restau noon-11pm Sun-Thu; till midnight Fri/Sat.

1459 ✓ ✓ **THE NEW DOLPHIN, ABERDEEN:** Chapel St. Despite the pre-emi-
MAP 4 nence of the Ashvale, many would rather swear by this small, always
D3 busy place just off Union St. Few tables, superb takeaway. Till 1am; 3am w/ends.

1460 ✓ **THE RAPIDO, EDINBURGH:** 77 Broughton St. Legendary chippie. Popular
MAP A with late-nighters stumbling back down the hill to the New Town, and
D2 the flotsam of the 'Pink Triangle.' 1.30am (3.30am Fri/Sat).

1461 ✓ **THE DEEP SEA, EDINBURGH:** Leith Walk, opp Playhouse. Open late and
MAP A often has queues but these are quickly dispatched. The haddock has to
E1 be 'of a certain size'. Trad menu. Still one of the best fish suppers you'll ever
feed a hangover with. 2am-ish (3am Fri/Sat).

1462 ✓ **THE UNIQUE, GLASGOW:** 223 Allison St. Not exactly central, but if you're
MAP B on the S-side you'll find the best fish 'n' chips in town here. Through the
xC5 curtain in the café, they serve lunches, fish teas and spam fritters. Veg oil used.
Old-fashioned hours, viz 8.15am-1.15pm, 3.45-9pm. That's right, 9pm – closed.

1463 ✓ **DEEP SEA, DUNDEE:** 81 Nethergate at bottom end of Perth Rd; v central.
MAP 3 The Sterpaio family have been serving the Dundonians excellent fish 'n'
D3 chips since 1939; gr range of fish in veg oil. Café with aproned waitress service
is a classic. so v trad, so very tasty. Mon-Sat, 11.30am-6.40pm (7pm carry-out).

1464 ✓ **PHILADELPHIA, GLASGOW:** 445 Gt Western Rd. Adj Big Blue (598/PIZZA)
MAP B & La Parmagiana (551/BEST RESTAUS), owned by same family. Since 1930, a
B1 Glas fixture & fresher fryer than most. 7 days noon-12 (Fri/Sat 3am).

1465 ✓ **PEPPO'S, ARBROATH:** 51 Ladybridge St next to the harbour where those
MAP 3 fish come in. Fresh as that and chips in dripping. Peppo has been here
D2 since 1951; John and Frank Orsi are carrying on the gr family trad and feeding
the hordes. Tues-Fri 4-10pm, Sat-Mon till 8pm. Smell the smokies outside.

1466 ✓ **THE BERVIE CHIPPER, INVERBERVIE, ARBROATH and STONEHAVEN:**
MAP 3 Main st Inverbervie. Sit-in area up and downstairs and take-away. Gets
E1 through enormous amounts of haddock and cod. Lard used. Newer opening
in Stoney on David St the rd to Aberdeen has queues out the door on Sat
nights. All open noon-10pm 7 days.

1467 ✓ **THE ANSTRUTHER FISH BAR:** On the front in Fife seaside town
MAP 3 (1640/COASTAL VILLAGES). They say best F&C UK 2000; the continuous
D3 queue suggests they may be right. Lard used. Eating in is cramped (cardboard
trays etc) so takeaway best (walk round the harbour). 7 days 11.30-10.30pm.

1468 ✓ **WEST END, ROTHESAY:** 1 Gallowgate. Winner of awards but time to get
MAP 2 the early nineties off the windows and unmissable if you're on Bute
D5 despite the ticket system. Only haddock, but wide range of other fries and
fresh pizza. Uses expensive groundnut oil. We can't make head nor tail of their
hrs, but they're mostly open!

1469 ✓ **GIACOPAZZI'S, EYEMOUTH:** Harbour by the fishmarket (or what's left of
MAP 3 it). A caff & takeaway with the catch on its doorstep. Dispensing excl F&C
E5 & their award-winning ice-cream quietly here in the far-flung SE corner of
Scotland since 1900. 7 days 11am-9pm. Upstairs to **OBLO'S BISTRO** 01890
752527. Sun-Thur 10am-midnight, Fri & Sat 10am-1am.

1470 **BALMORAL, DUMFRIES:** Balmoral Rd. Seems as old and essential as the Bard
MAP 1 himself. Now using groundnut oil, hence the best chip in the south. Out the
D2 Annan rd heading E, 1km from centre. Daily.

1471 **FISH & CHIP VAN, TOBERMORY:** Parked on Fisherman's Quay on the harbour
MAP 2 this really is a moveable feast – fresh-landed & popped in the frier. Prince Charles
B2 loves 'em (so he told us).

1472 **SANDY'S, STONEHAVEN:** Market Sq. The established Stoney Chipper, dealing
MAP 3 well with the recent competition (*see above*). Daily, LO 10pm, 9pm Sun. Big
E1 haddock like the old days.

1473 **CORVI'S, BO'NESS:** Old-style fryer on rd out of town – a fine fish supper, and
MAP 3 gr home-made ice cream (1544/ICE CREAM).
B4

For cafés in EDINBURGH, *see p. 52,* GLASGOW, *p. 94.*

1474
MAP 5
D2
✓✓ **THE CASTLE RESTAURANT, INVERNESS:** On rd that winds up to the castle from the main st, nr the TIC and the hostels. No pandering to tourists here, but this great caff has been serving chips with everything for 40 years (crinkle chips). Pork chops, prawn cocktail, perfect fried eggs. They work damned hard. In Inverness or anywhere, there is no better deal than this! 8am-8.30pm. Cl Sun.

1475
MAP 6
B3
✓ **THE TEA STORE, ULLAPOOL:** Argyll St parallel to & one up from the waterfront. Laurie Chilton's excl, unpretentious café serving all-day fry-ups & other snacks. Gr home baking incl strawberry tarts in season. Best in Ullapool (or Lewis where you might be heading). AYR. 8am-5pm.

1476
MAP 2
E5
✓ **NARDINI'S, LARGS:** 01475 674555. The Esplanade, Glas side. An institution. The epitome of the seaside cafeteria and all the nostalgia of Doon the Watter days, now seems to be going doon the tubes. The airy brasserie, the light fittings still the true originals but nothing lasts forever. In 2001 Nardini's passed out of the hands of the Nardini family and at TGP the biz had sunk into the hands of the receivers. We will want to see if this seaside icon can be restored.

1477
MAP 3
B4
✓ **ALLAN WATER CAFÉ, BRIDGE OF ALLAN:** Henderson St (main st) beside the eponymous br. Real whiff of nostalgia along with the fish'n'chips and the ice cream, which are the best around. Worth coming over from Stirling (8km) for a takeaway or a seat in the comforting woody caff – and a reminisce of the life before the mall and the burgering of your high st. 7 days, 8am-8pm.

1478
MAP 2
D5
✓ **THE RITZ CAFÉ, MILLPORT:** See Millport, see the Ritz. Since 1906 and now in its fourth generation, the classic café on the Clyde. Somewhat overshadowed by Nardini's (*see above*) and a short ferry journey away (from Largs, continuous; then 6km), but it should be an essential part of any visit to this part of the coast, and Millport is not entirely without charm. Toasties, rolls, the famous 'hot peas', home-made ice cream (esp with melted marshmallow). Something of 'things past'. 7 days, 10am-10pm in season. Other hrs vary.

1479
MAP 2
E6
✓ **TOGS, TROON:** Templehill nr main crossrds. There are more caffs in Troon than any other toun (the pleasingly named Venice Café is also good), but this is the one that did it for me – it even smells like a café should. Fairy drops and vanilla fudge & the rest! 7 days 9am-6 or 8pm (from 10am on Sun).

1480
MAP 3
C6
✓ **THE HUB, GLENTRESS nr INNERLEITAN:** 01721 721736. At entranceway to Glentress Forest Park on A72 5km from Peebles. Glentress is mt bike mecca so this US-style caff in a shack serves shorts- & lycra-clad allsorts with big appetites. Frys & baking. Outdoor terrace. Cool spot. 7 days (daytime only).

1481
MAP 6
C3
LUIGI'S, DORNOCH: Main st as you arrive (Castle St) adj 2 Quail (1059/HIGH-LAND RESTAUS). Recent recreation of seaside caff with gr sandwiches & toasties, home-made cakes & movenpick ice-cream. AYR till 5.30pm (later in July/Aug).

1482
MAP 3
A3
THE CAFÉ IN BRIG O'TURK IN THE TROSSACHS: 01877 376267. Hanging baskets of flowers o/side this shack are what you notice from the rd (the A821 12km W of Callander) in the heart of the afternoon tea belt of the Trossachs. Under new management at TGP.

1483
MAP 3
A3
BEN LEDI CAFE, CALLANDER: Main st nr sq. Fish teas, and a sq meal. Unprepossessing frontage, but here is the genuine, ungentrified article – who needs an internet cafe? Take away or sit in. The best ice-cream for miles around tho' we're told many locals now favour 'the other chip shop'. Cl Thu.

1484
MAP 2
E5
THE MELBOURNE, SALTCOATS: 72 Hamilton St. A tatty 1950s leftover with good coffee, good panini, breakfasts, filled rolls etc. Juke box nearly as cool as the lassies behind the counter! Used as a film location (*Late Night Shopping*). Damned fine! Daily until 5pm.

THE BEST TEAROOMS AND COFFEE SHOPS

For EDINBURGH, *see p. 50; for* GLASGOW, *p. 93.*

1485
MAP A
E2
✓✓ **PLAISIR DU CHOCOLAT, EDINBURGH:** All other Edin places on p. 50, but this must feature here. A celebration of tea, France & the good life. Report 272/TEARMS.

1486
MAP B
E4
✓✓ **CAFÉ GANDOLFI, GLASGOW:** Glas's definitive tearm, long-standing & a formula that has not been bettered. Report 650/TEARMS. Also in Glasgow the more recent and decidedly new wave **TCHAI-OVNA**. No chintz nor cream teas here, just good tchai and chat. Report 655/TEARMS.

1487
MAP 2
E6
✓✓ **TUDOR RESTAURANT, AYR:** 8 Beresford Terr, nr Odeon and Burns Monument Sq. High tea from 3.15pm, breakfast all day. Roomy, well-used, full of life. Bakery counter at front (fab cream donuts and bacon butties as they're supposed to be) and disdainful nippy waitresses in the body of the kirk. 9am-8pm Mon-Sat, 9pm July and Aug. Open Sun in season.

1488
MAP 3
B4
✓✓ **THE POWMILL MILKBAR, nr KINROSS:** On the A977 Kinross (on the M90, jnct 6) to Kincardine Br rd, a real milkbar and a real slice of Scottish craic and cake. Apple pie and moist fly cemeteries – an essential stop on any Sunday run (but open every day). The paper plates do little justice to the confections they bear, but they are part of the deal, so don't complain! Hot meals and salads. Good place to take kids. 7 days, 9am-6pm (8pm summer, earlier in winter). (2039/GLEN AND RIVER WALKS)

1489
MAP 2
E2
✓✓ **THE GREEN WELLY STOP, TYNDRUM:** On A82, a strategically placed pit-stop on the drive to Oban or Ft William (just before the rd divides), with a Scottish produce shop and the gas stn (open later). Self-service comfort food to break the journey. Much home-made, v Scottish & a whole lot better than you'd expect. Shop stuffed wth everything you do & don't need. 7 days, 8.30am-5.30pm.

1490
MAP 4
C3
✓✓ **THE BLACK-FACED SHEEP, ABOYNE:** 01339 887311. Nr main Royal Deeside rd through Aboyne (A93) and TIC, this excellent coffee shop/gift shop is well-loved by locals (and regulars from all over) but is thankfully missed by the bus parties hurtling towards Balmoral. Home-made breads and cakes, snacks; good coffee (real capp & espresso from Elektra machine). 10am-5pm, Sun from 11am.

1491
MAP 5
D3
✓ **LAGGAN COFFEESHOP nr LAGGAN:** On A889 from Dalwhinnie on A9 that leads to A86, the rd W to Spean Bridge & Kyle. Former pottery. Craft shop & bunkhouse (1235/HOSTELS) but gr home baking, esp carrot cake & lemon drizzle. Nr gr spot for forest walks & river swimming (1746/HOLES). 7 days till 6pm.

1492
MAP 4
C2
✓ **THE TEAROOM at CLATT, nr ALFORD and INVERURIE:** In the village hall in the hamlet of Clatt where local ladies display gr home-made Scottish baking – like a weekly sale of work. Take A96 N of Inverurie, then B9002 follow sign for Auchleven, then Clatt. Gr countryside. W/ends May-Sept 1pm-5pm. One of the gr tea & scone experiences in the world.

1493
MAP 3
C3
✓ **THE PILLARS OF HERCULES nr FALKLAND:** 01337 857749. Tearm on organic farm on A912 rd 2km from vill towards Strathmiglo & m/way. Excl, homely place & fare & all PC. Home-made cakes, soup etc. 7 days 10am-5.30pm.

1494
MAP 1
C2
✓ **KITTY'S TEAROOM, NEW GALLOWAY:** Main St of town in the forest. Absolutely splendid. Sylvia Brown's steady hand in the kitchen, great cakes, good tea, and conversations between local ladies that are totally Alan Bennett. 11am-7pm, Easter-Oct. Tues-Sun.

1495
MAP 2
E4
✓ **THE COACH HOUSE, LUSS, LOCH LOMOND:** In the heart of Take The High Road country & this vill still throngs with visitors. Gary & Rowena Grove's much (self) publicised success story also goes like the proverbial fair. Not all home-made but they'd need v big ovens. Nice loos, some o/side seating. 7 days 10am-5pm.

1496
MAP 2
C5
✓ **NORTH BEACHMORE FARM RESTAURANT, nr MUASDALE:** on A83 Tarbert–Campbeltown rd. Signposted up a steep track, 2km off the rd and into the hills. Matt and Eileen McInnes' home-cooking is hugely popular locally; you see why. Stunning views of the Sound of Gigha, (and on a clear day Ireland). Food excl too. 10am-10pm. Cl in wint.

1497
MAP 5
B2
✓ **GLENELG CANDLES, GLENELG:** As you come into the vill after the spectacular mountain pass rd from Shiel Bridge, a candle-making studio & craft shop (2185/SHOPPING) & café/restau in fab modern, woody conservatory with grass roof. All home-made; garden. Apr-Oct 9.30-5.30 & dinner Thur-Sun.

1498
MAP 2
B2
✓ **THE GLASS BARN, TOBERMORY, MULL:** Up the hill at the edge of town 500m off Dervaig rd, 2km centre. Run by (and part of) the Reades' dairy farm the people who make the excellent Mull cheddar, but that's not the reason I'm recommending it. Rather, it's just gr what they've done with it – go see! A glass barn full of plants, hearty soup, farm bakes. Walk from the village – it will do you good. May-Sep; Mon-Fri (Cl Sun) 10am-4pm.

1499
MAP 2
B2
✓ **GLENGORM FARM COFFEE SHOP nr TOBERMORY:** 01688 302321. First right on Tobermory-Dervaig rd. Organic food served in well refurbed stable block. Soups, cakes, venison burgers… all you need after a walk in the grounds of this gr estate.

1500
MAP 2
D5
✓ **THE LIGHTHOUSE, PIRNMILL, ARRAN:** 01770 850240. On rd W looking on to Mull of Kintyre. Perfect pit-stop for giant scones & cakes looking over bay. Full menu avail in unaffected squeaky-clean decor. 7 days 10am-9pm Jan-Dec.

1501
MAP 3
A3
✓ **LIBRARY TEAROOM, BALQUHIDDER:** Centre of vill opp church (1942/GRAVEYARDS) where many walks start incl gr view (1735/VIEWS) & nr long walk to Brig o' Turk (2038/GLEN WALKS). Excl bakes: carrot cake, cheese scones, soup & BLT. Only 4 tables. Apr-Oct, 10am-4.30pm.

1502
MAP 3
C3
✓ **KIND KYTTOCK'S KITCHEN, FALKLAND:** Folk come to Falkland (1826/CASTLES; 2010/HILL WALKS) for many reasons, not least for afternoon tea. Several choices, this the longest established and most regarded. Omelettes, toasties, baked potatoes, baking. Good service. 10.30am-5.30pm. Cl Mon.

1503
MAP 3
B4
✓ **PUDDLEDUCKS, BLAIRLOGIE, nr STIRLING:** On main A91 in tiny village. Hot dishes at lunch & snacks and a cabinet of delicious cakes, and I do mean delicious. Stock up on the way to the Ochils. There's a pavilion in the extensive gdn (in fine weather). Garden always good for a stroll while you wait to be called to your tiny table. 7 days 10.30-4.30pm.

1504
MAP 5
B2
THE FLOWER TUNNEL, APPLECROSS: In campsite (1309/CAMPING WITH KIDS) as you arrive in Applecross after amazing journey (2010/SCENIC ROUTES). Bakery & coffee-shop in greenhouse full of plants & outdoor seating. Famous pizzas. Apr-Oct. 7 days, supper only high season.

1505
MAP 3
B3
TULLY BANNOCHER FARM RESTAURANT: 2km W on A85 to Lochearnhead. Recommended roadside coffee shop/self-service diner with fairly trad hot dishes, salads, some baking. Handy for the delights of Comrie. Tables o/side. Open till 8pm Mar-Oct (earlier if they're quiet!).

1506
MAP 3
D5
FLAT CAT GALLERY COFFEE-SHOP, LAUDER: 2 Market St opp Eagle Hotel. Speeding thro' Lauder (note speed camera at Edinburgh end) you might miss this cool coffee spot & serious gallery. Always interesting work & ethnic things. Home-baking natch. 7 days till 5pm.

1507
MAP 3
C5
SILVER SPOON, PEEBLES: Innerleithen Rd at end of main st adj Green Tree hotel. Mumsy, definitely not funky tearoom, but with good attitude to baking (& mums). Perfectly Peebles! 7 days. 9-4.30pm (Sun 11-4pm).

1508
MAP 3
E5
THE RIVERSIDE and ABBEY ARTEFACTS, ABBEY ST BATHANS: 01361 840312. By the trout farm, nr R Whiteadder in the middle of this rustic hamlet on the Southern Upland Way. A welcome place for a restau & gallery. Seasonal menu. Light or 3-course lunches incl savoury flans, steaks, local seafood. Cream teas. Tues-Sun 11am-5pm (4pm Oct-Easter). Cl Mons.

1509
MAP 3
D6
SELKIRK GLASS: 01750 20954. Off A7 north of town. Good soup, bread, salads & home baking. Mon-Sat 9-5pm, Sun 11-5pm.

1510
MAP 1
D2
THE OLD BANK, DUMFRIES: 95 Irish St, off High St. Coffee shop in converted bank (revolving doors and cornices remain) on st where Burns lived. Delicate snacks, good puds and cakes. Mon-Sat 10am-4.30pm.

1511 **THE (ART DECO) CARRON RESTAURANT, STONEHAVEN:** 01569 760460. 20
MAP 3 Carron St off main st nr the sq. They use 'art deco' in the title, but you couldn't
E1 miss the reference in this fantastic period piece faithfully restored & embellished. Open for b/fast thro lunch, aft tea & high teas until 7pm (Sat 9pm, Sun 8pm). Cl Mon.

1512 **THE HARBOUR CAFE, ROTHESAY:** 01700 505166, East Princes St. Internet
MAP 2 and espresso come to Bute. This urban outpost offers coffee/chat/snacks &
D5 the 21st C to sleepy seasidey Rothesay. Licensed. And dinner at w/ends. Mon-Thur 11am-5pm, Fri/Sat till 4.30pm then dinner. Suns in summer.

1513 **GARDEN ROOM TEASHOP, ROCKCLIFFE:** On main rd in/out of this seaside
MAP 1 cul de sac. Best on sunny days when you can sit in the gdn. Snacks and cakes
D3 (though not all home-made). 10.30-5pm. Cl Mon & Tues.

1514 **COZY KNITS, STRONTIAN:** At beginning of walk in Ariundle Woods
MAP 2 (2055/WOODLAND WALKS) in wonderful Ardnamurchan. Bungalow tearm with
C1 knits & nick nacks. Hot dishes, home bakes. AYR incl dinner in summer.

1515 **COFFEE HOUSE, GRANTOWN-ON-SPEY:** 35 High St. Surprisingly authentic
MAP 4 Italian café with genuine Italian cakes, ice cream and espresso. They serve
B2 stew, pasta and gr ice-cream. Nice people run this place. Till 5pm.

1516 **THE PANTRY, CROMARTY:** In great wee town in Black Isle 45km NE of
MAP 5 Inverness (1635/COASTAL VILLAGES) on corner of Church St. Good home baking
E1 and the best cup of coffee for miles. Easter-end Oct. 10.30am-4pm. Cl Fri.

1517 **BRAMBLES, ST ANDREWS:** 5 College St off Middle St. Small (incl entrance-
MAP 3 way) & always busy. Home-bakes & good vegn. 7 days till 5.30pm.
D3 **NORTHPOINT, ST ANDREWS:** 24 North St. Bagels, brunches, pancakes & vegn soups in this bright, busy café in univ town. 7 days till 5.

1518 **DUN WHINNY'S, CALLANDER:** Off main st at Glas rd, a welcoming wee (but
MAP 3 not twee) tearoom; not run by wifies. Banoffee pie kind of thing and clootie
A3 dumpling. There's a few naff caffs in Callander. This one still OK in my book. 7 days till 5pm.

1519 **ABBEY COTTAGE, NEW ABBEY:** Literally over the lane from Sweetheart
MAP 1 Abbey, this place serves a decent double espresso and fruit pie for a sunny
D2 afternoon when all you want to do is sit out and gawp at Devorguilla's pile opp (1952/ABBEYS). Apr-Oct 7 days; Mar, Nov, Dec w/ends.

THE BEST SCOTCH BAKERS

1520 ✓✓ **FISHER & DONALDSON, DUNDEE/ST ANDREWS/CUPAR:** Main or
MAP 3 original branch in Cupar and 3 in Dundee. Superior contemporary
C3, D3 bakers along trad lines (born 1919) – surprising (and a pity) that they haven't gone further, although they do supply a few selected outlets (e.g. Jenners in Edin with pastries and the most excellent Dr Floyd's bread which is as good as anything you could make yourself). Main sq, Cupar; Church St, St Andrews; Whitehall St, 300 Perth Rd and Lochee, Dundee, which is v well served with decent bakers (see below). Dundee Whitehall has good tearm (1174/DUNDEE).

1521 ✓ **GOODFELLOW AND STEVEN:** The other bakers in this neck of central
MAP 3 Scotland. G&S have several branches in Dundee, Perth and Fife. Good
D3 Scotch baking with the kind of cakes your mum used to have for a treat.

1522 ✓ **BRADFORD'S:** 245 Sauchiehall St, Glas, and suburban branches in select-
MAP B ed areas, i.e. they have not over-expanded; for a bakery chain, some lines
C3 seem almost home-made. Certainly better than all the industrial 'home'-bakers around. Individual fruit pies, for example, are uniquely yummy, and the all-important Scotch pie pastry is exemplary. (661/TEAROOMS.)

1523 ✓ **ALEXANDER TAYLOR'S, STRATHAVEN, nr LANARK:** 01357 521260.
MAP 3 Specialising in huge array of savoury breads: sunflower, Bavarian, sour-
A5 dough, black bun and, at Christmas, stollen. Also make all their shortbreads and oatcakes. Good & wholesome! Mon-Sat 8am-5.30pm (Sat from 7am!).

1524
MAP 3
A3
✓ **SCOTCH OVEN, CALLANDER:** W end of main st in busy touristy town and one of the best things about it. Good bread, rolls, cakes, the biggest, possibly the best, tattie scones and sublime doughnuts. Also featuring what may be the perfect Scotch pie pastry. Adj caff at side much less convincing. Better to picnic on the Braes or by the river. Open 7 days.

1525
MAP 2
E4
✓ **BLACK'S OF DUNOON:** aka Cowal Cottage Bakery at 144 Argyll St, the main st of Dunoon. Popular for aeons, easily found opp the masonic lodge; loads of doughnuts and muffins. The old favourites shortbread, potato scones and the like still draw the queues & they've reintroduced the gr Scottish morning roll.

1526
MAP 5
E1
CROMARTY BAKERY, CROMARTY: Bank St. One of the many reasons to visit this picturesque seaside town. Abundance of speciality cakes, organic bread, rolls & pies, baked daily on premises. Also tea, coffee, hot savouries & takeaway. Mon, Tue, Thu, Fri 8.30am-5.30pm; Wed 8.30am-4pm; Sat 8.30am-4 pm.

1527
MAP 3
B2
BREADALBANE BAKERY, ABERFELDY: 37 Dunkeld St. On rd out of town to Grandtully opp petrol stn. Home of Aberfeldy Whisky Cake (a rich fruit job with single malt flavour) and Holyrood Tarts (no, not Hollywood). Nice biscuits, nice cheese 'n' onion pasties. Nice.

1528
MAP 6
C3
THE DORNOCH BAKERY, DORNOCH: Behind cathedral, a busy town bakery with a couple of tables in front of the ovens. Great selection of pies (esp fruit pies) and bread (esp milk bread). Often has queues.

1529
MAP 3
C4
PILLANS AND SONS, KIRKCALDY: Nr Harbour and end of High St. Poss one of the oldest family-run businesses in Scotland. Here for 120 yrs turning out their Scottish rolls and cakes and famous unconventional Scotch pies. Nostalgia and good Scots baking. Long may they remain Pillans, the Pie Shop.

1530
MAP 3
D3
ADAMSON'S IN PITTENWEEM: 12 Routine Row. Bakers since 1887, they had branches all over Fife till recently. Now old Mr Adamson just does his famous oatcakes. Supplied all over UK, they can be purchased here. 01333 311336.

1531
MAP 3
D2
McLAREN'S, FORFAR: Town centre next to Queens Hotel and in Kirriemuir. The best in town to sample the famous Forfar bridie, a meaty shortcrust pastie that'll keep you going all the way to Aber. **SADDLER'S** North St make an excl meringue.

THE BEST ICE-CREAM

1532
MAP 3
C4
✓✓ **LUCA'S, MUSSELBURGH, nr EDINBURGH (and EDINBURGH):** 32 High St. Queues out the door in the middle of a Sun afternoon in February are testament to the enduring popularity of this almost-legendary ice-cream parlour. 3 classic flavours (vanilla, choc and strawberry) and pure ingredients attract folk from Edin (14km) though there is now a branch in Edin at 16 Morningside Rd, a more designery Italian version (291/CAFÉS). In café thro the back, still basic after recent refurb, sundae, snacks, and you might have to wait. In Edin café upstairs more pizza/pasta and smart sandwiches. Mon-Sat 9am-10pm, Sun 10.30am-10pm. Edin hrs: 7 days 9am (10.30 Sun)-10pm. Luca's (wholesale) now spreading everywhere so look out for the sign.

1533
MAP 2
E6
✓✓ **MANCINI'S, THE ROYAL CAFÉ, AYR:** 11 New Rd, the rd to Prestwick. Ice cream that's taken seriously, entered for competitions and usually wins. Family biz for aeons. Massive no. of flavours at their disposal, always new ones. Home-made ice-cream cakes. Café recent refurb. Their sorbets taste better than the fruit they're made from. They were first with the ice-cream toastie and diabetic ice-cream. These Mancinis are the kings of ice cream. 9.30am-11.00pm; cl Thu in winter.

1534
MAP 3
B6
✓ **THE CHOCOLATE BOX, BIGGAR:** Christine White's little sweetie and ice-cream shop, under her charge since '92. (Mr White makes the ice-cream in a factory by Lanark). Daily until 5pm. Sweet sustenance on the rd from/to Edinburgh (or you know, if you live there!).

1535
MAP 3
D3
✓ **JANETTA'S, ST ANDREWS:** 31 South St. Family firm since 1908. There are two Janetta's, but the one to adore is top end South St. Once only vanilla, Americans at the Open asked for other flavours. Now there are 52, & numerous awards. Also frozen yogs. Janetta's is another good reason for being a student at

St Andrews. Good café adj, family fare, o/side tables. LO 5/5.30pm. 7 days til 5/5.30pm.

1536 ✓ CALDWELL'S, INNERLEITHEN: On the High St in this ribbon of a town
MAP 3 between Peebles and Gala they've been making ice cream since 1911.
C6 Purists may bemoan the fact that they've succumbed to fancy flavours in the 21st cent, but their vanilla is still best. The shop still sells everything from Blue Nun to bicycles. Mon-Fri till 8.30pm, Sat/Sun 7.30pm.

1537 ✓ CREAM O' GALLOWAY, RAINTON, nr GATEHOUSE OF FLEET: 01557
MAP 1 814040. A75 take Sandgreen exit 2km, then left at sign for Carrick.
C3 Originally a dairy farm producing cheese, now you can watch them making the creamy concoctions which you find all over in 'good shops'. Nature trail, absolutely fab kids adventure play area (1775/KIDS), and decent organic café. Open AYR 10am-5pm; 8pm summer, 4pm winter.

1538 VISOCCHI'S, BROUGHTY FERRY/KIRRIEMUIR: Orig from St Andrews; ice-
MAP 3 cream makers for 50 years and still with the café they opened in Kirriemuir in
C2, D3 1953. On the main drag of the Angus town (1670/GLENS), it's the local caff (v basic menu, no chips). Broughty Ferry (Dundee's seaside suburb) more middle-class, with a contemporary menu; home-made pasta as well as the peach melba. But whatever comes and goes, the ice cream will go on forever. 7 days (1165/DUNDEE EAT AND DRINK).

1539 THE ALLAN WATER CAFÉ, BRIDGE OF ALLAN: An old-fashioned café in an
MAP 3 old-fashioned town, near the eponymous br in the main st since 1902.
B4 Fabulously good fish 'n' chips and ice cream. The former now dispensed from a modernised shop next door. Ice cream in the old woody atmos. One of the few that's not succumbed to flavours (only vanilla). 7 days, 8am-8pm.

1540 COLPI'S, MILNGAVIE, GLASGOW: Opp Marks & Spencer in Milngavie centre
MAP 3 (pron Mullguy) and there since 1928. Many consider this to be Glas's finest.
A4 Only vanilla at the cone counter but strawb/choc flake/amaretto/honeycomb to take home. There's another branch in Clydebank. Till 9pm, 7 days.

1541 TORTOLANO'S, UDDINGSTON: 29 Main St. 15km E of city via M74,
MAP 3 Uddingston t/off, at the lights where you turn for Bothwell Castle
A5 (1851/RUINS). Tiny confectioners/ice-cream shop with proper biscuit cones as an option and fab flavours (try the 'caramel shortcake') all home made and rather fantastic. Their loss, definitely our weight gain.

1542 NARDINI'S, LARGS: On the Esplanade. No longer owned by the Nardini fam-
MAP 2 ily, we doubt the ice cream will be any different. Some summers back I had an
E5 epiphany over a pistachio and vanilla on the esplanade. All became right with the world. In 2001, Keith said the comfort & the nostalgia was still there. Long may it linger. (1476/GREAT CAFÉS). Nardini's no longer what it was, but the ice-cream will linger on our lips forever.

1543 DRUMMUIR FARM, COLLIN, nr DUMFRIES: 5km off A75 (Carlisle/Annan) rd
MAP 1 E of Dumfries on B724 (nr Clarencefield). A real farm producing real ice cream
D2 – still does supersmooth original and honeycomb, seasonal specials; on a fine day, sit out and chill. Easter-Sept daily to 5.30pm; Oct-Dec Sat-Sun until 5pm; Jan-Mar closed.

1544 CORVI'S, BO'NESS 'THE SEAVIEW CAFÉ': Seaview Pl, opp car park with
MAP 3 tourist info. Downhome fish 'n' chip shop that serves home-made vanilla and
B4 strawberry ice cream in premises that look like an extended version of someone's parlour. Eat in or take away – the fish supper is the local choice. Mon-Tues 11am-6.30pm, Thurs-Sat 11am-7.30pm (seated area cl 4.30pm).

1545 CAPALDI'S, BRORA: Rosslyn St. Here since 1936 & never seems to change –
MAP 6 all kinds of inventive flavours, the crème caramel was pretty good last time we
D3 passed. Daily until 8pm. Also avail locally at selected outlets and at the beach in Dornoch.

BEN LEDI CAFÉ, CALLANDER: Main St (1483/CAFÉS).

1546
MAP A
E1

✓ ✓ ✓ **VALVONA AND CROLLA, EDINBURGH:** 19 Elm Row, nr top of Leith Walk. Since 1934, an Edin institution, the shop you show visitors. Full of smells, genial, knowledgeable staff and a floor-to-ceiling range of cheese (Ital/Scot, etc.), meats, oils, wines and more. Fresh veg trucked in from Milan markets, on-premises bakery, great café/bar (164/ITALIAN RESTAUS). Also demos, tastings, Fringe venue. Second to none and we can't say better than that! 8am-6.30pm (Sun 11-5pm). Gr website (valvonacrolla.com).

1547
MAP A
D3
xC4 B1
MAP B
B1

✓ ✓ **I.J. MELLIS, EDINBURGH, GLASGOW & ST ANDREWS:** 3 branches in Edin – Victoria St, Bruntsfield & Stockbridge; Kelvinbridge in Glas & St Andrews. Started out as the cheese guy, now more of a v select deli for food that's good & 'slow'. Coffees, hams, sausages, olives & seasonal stuff like apples & mushrooms (branches vary), so smells mingle. Irresistible! 7 days tho' times vary. See also 1573/CHEESES.

1548
MAP A
C2

✓ **GLASS & THOMPSON, EDINBURGH:** 2 Dundas St. Exemplary and contemporary New Town provisioner. Selective choice of Mediterranean – style goodies to eat or take away and bread/pâtisserie; also those all-important New Town dinner party essentials. Report: 277/TEAROOMS.

1549
MAP B
B2

✓ **GRASSROOTS ORGANIC, GLASGOW:** 48 Woodlands Rd, nr Charing Cross. First-class vegn food and provisions store, everything chemically unaltered and environmentally-friendly. Gr breads and sandwiches for lunch and the best organic fruit/veg range in town. Vegn restau round the corner (646/GLAS VEGN). 7 days 8am-8pm (Sat 9am-6pm, Sun 11am-5pm).

1550
MAP 3
C5

✓ **COOK'S FINE FOODS, PEEBLES:** 25 High St in midst of Peebles where people like a good bit of cheese. Here the selection is exemplary & they make bread, savouries & continental-type bakes. Sit-in for snacks; they also do outside catering. A place you'd expect to find in Edinburgh New Town. Tues-Sat 10am-6pm.

1551
MAP B
D3

✓ **SARTI'S, GLASGOW:** 113 Wellington St. Definitive corner of little Italy – a deli/tratt here and another eating place/wine shop in Bath St (584/ITAL-IAN RESTAUS). Feels like Italy.

1552
MAP B
A1

✓ **HEART and BUCHANAN, GLASGOW:** 380 Byres Rd. Gr deli & first-rate t/away. Report 698/T/AWAY.

1553
MAP B
xA1

✓ **DELIZIQUE, GLASGOW:** 66 Hyndland St nr Cottier's bar & theatre. Excl neighbourhood deli for the affluent Hyndlanders & others who roam & graze round here. Gr prepared meals (in-house chef) & hand-picked goodies incl oils, hams, flowers & Mellis cheeses. 7 days 8am-8pm (9am-8pm Sun).

1554
MAP 3
B4

✓ **CLIVE RAMSAY, BRIDGE OF ALLAN:** Main St. Here for yrs, but just gets better. New café/restau adj with gr coffee & eats. Deli gr for fruit/veg, cheese, olives, seeds & well-chosen usuals incl own-brand. 7 days 7am-7pm.

1555
MAP 4
B1

✓ **PHOENIX FINDHORN COMMUNITY, FINDHORN:** Serving the new age township of the Findhorn Community and therefore pursuing a conscientious app, this has become an exemplary and v high quality deli, worth the detour from the A96 Inverness-Elgin rd even if you have apprehensions about their 'thing'. Packed and carefully selected shelves; as much for pleasurable eating as for healthy. Till 6pm. (W/ends 5pm.) Cl Tue am.

1556
MAP 5
D2

GOURMET'S LAIR, INVERNESS: 81 Union St. Inverness is a city & now it has delis of which this is the best. Huge selection of cheeses. Shelves & baskets & cold counter all stuffed with good things. 8.30am-5pm. Cl Sun.

1557
MAP A
C4
MAP B
B1

LUPE PINTOS, EDINBURGH & GLASGOW: 24 Leven St nr King's Theatre & 313 Gt Western Rd. Unusual Latin deli (ie Mexican, Central American, Spanish). Where to go for chorizo, manchego and 20 kinds of tequila. T/away incl homemade burritos and the usual Tex-Mex. Every kind of chili & gr Riojas. 10am-6pm. Cl Suns.

1558
MAP B
xE4

GARLIC, GLASGOW: 793 Shettleston Road. 0141 763 0399. A foody oasis in the unfashionable E End, the fame of this little emporio Italiano has spread to the Merchant City and beyond. The usual meats and cheeses are represented, with a gr Italian wine range (incl org) and beer, and a superb choice of home-made and fresh foods. Giovanna's pasta dishes supply city-centre restaurants, but the shop offers a wider and ever-changing range, such as pumpkin risot-to, and a daily special. Have a coffee while you peruse.

1559 **PECKHAM'S, GLASGOW (inc LENZIE & NEWTON MEARNS) & EDINBURGH:**
MAP B Scotland's most prolific deli chain, but ea shop v individually run. Hyndland (43
xA1, Clarence Dr) & Merchant City (61 Glassford St) are exemplary. Always service-
D4 able & loads of choice from staples to fine wines and cheeses, and a good range
MAP A of up-market nibbles and quick meals. The better Edin branch is at 155
B1 Bruntsfield Pl which is packed with goodies, tables o/side in summer. Peckham's
Underground is the restaurant under the shop. LO 10pm. Also at 48 Raeburn Pl.

1560 **BUTLER & CO, ST ANDREWS:** 10 Church St. Excl deli by the people who have
MAP 3 the seafood restau in St Monans (1440/SEAFOOD RESTAUS). Good range of
D3 Scottish and other cheeses. Cl Suns.

1561 **GORDON AND MACPHAIL, ELGIN:** South St. Purveyors of fine wines, cheeses,
MAP 4 meats, Mediterranean goodies, unusual breads and other epicurean delights
B1 to the good burghers of Elgin for nigh on a century. Traditional shopkeeping,
in the style of the 'family grocer'. G & M are widely known as bottlers of lesser-known high-quality malts ('Connoisseurs' range) – on sale here. Some rare real
ales by the bottle too. Mon-Sat 9am-5.15pm.

1562 **TERROIR, ABERDEEN:** 22 Thistle St. Small but well-formed & thought-out deli
MAP 4 with not much competition in Aberdeen. Cold counter selective dry goods.
D3 Usually a nice soundtrack. Mon-Sat 9am-5.30pm.

1563 **JACQUES & LAWRENCE, HADDINGTON:** 37 Court St. Ex-Masterchef & École
MAP 3 Culinaire caterers have teamed up to bring latest (local & far-flung) fine deli
D4 foods to E Lothian punters. Fast food of the home-made pasta & Thai green
curry variety.

1564 **THE OLIVE TREE, PEEBLES:** 7 High St. Small emporium packed with wide
MAP 3 selection of European groceries plus local delicacies: beer, honey, cheese ad
C5 infinitum – specialises in farmhouse and unpasteurised cheeses.

1565 **LURGAN FARM SHOP, DRUMDEWAN, ABERFELDY:** 01887 829303 for direc-
MAP 3 tions. Shop on the Murrays' farm with big local rep for meat, organic fruit 'n'
B2 veg, ready-made meals & bakery. Other unexpected goodies. Cl Suns. Not vis-ited, we got it on the grapevine.

1566 **MULL or TOBERMORY CHEDDAR:** From Sgriob-Ruadh Farm (pron 'Skibrua'). Comes in big 50lb cheeses and 1lb truckles. Good, strong cheddar, one of the v best in the UK.

1567 **DUNSYRE BLUE/LANARK BLUE:** Made by Humphrey Errington at Carnwath. Next to Stilton, **DUNSYRE** (made from the unpasteurised milk of Ayrshire cows) is the best blue in the UK. It is soft, rather like Dolcelatte. **LANARK,** the original, is Scotland's Roquefort and made from ewes' milk. Both can vary but are excellent. Go on, live dangerously – unpasteurise your life.

1568 **LOCHARTHUR CHEESE:** Anything from this SW creamery is worth a nibble: the cheddar, CRIFFEL (mild), KEBBUCK (shaped like a dinosaur's tooth, semi-soft).

1569 **BONNET:** Hard goat's milk cheese from Anne Dorwood's farm at Stewarton in Ayrshire. Also a v good cheddar (& sheep's-milk cheddar).

1570 **WESTER LAWRENCETON FARM CHEESES, FORRES:** Pam Rodway's excl organic cheeses: CAROLA, CALIFER (goat's milk) & the hard-to-get SWEETMILK CHEDDAR. On sale Findhorn shop & Gordon & MacPhail (1561/DELIS).

1571 **HIGHLAND FINE CHEESES:** From the Stone family in Tain. 6 cheeses incl **CROWDIE** (trad curd cheese), **CABOC** & **STRATHDON BLUE** (recent award winner).

1572 **CAIRNSMORE:** A hard, tangy, cheddary cheese from Sorbie in Wigtownshire surprisingly made from ewes' milk, smoked or unsmoked.

AND WHERE TO FIND THEM

All the delis mentioned previously will have good selections (esp Valvona's and Delizique). Also:

1573
MAP A
D3xC4
MAP B
xB1
✓✓ **I.J. MELLIS, EDINBURGH, GLASGOW & ST ANDREWS:** 30a Victoria St, 205 Bruntsfield Pl and Baker's Pl, Stockbridge (Edin), 492 Gr Western Rd (Glas), 149 South St, St Andrews. A real cheesemonger. Smell and taste before you buy. Cheeses from all over the UK in prime condition. Daily and seasonal specials. (1547/DELIS)

1574
MAP A
B1
✓ **HERBIE, EDINBURGH:** 66 Raeburn Pl & William St. Excellent selection – everything here is the right stuff. Gr bread, bagels etc from independent baker, home-made hummus & with Scottish cheeses, it's practically impossible here to find a Brie or a blue in less than perfect condition. All too moreish.

✓ **COOK'S FINE FOODS, PEEBLES:** Report: 1550/DELIS

1575
MAP 3
C2
✓ **MACDONALD'S CHEESE SHOP, RATTRAY nr BLAIRGOWRIE:** 2km Blairgowrie on rd to Glenshee and Braemar. Discreet 'shack' you could easily miss, but don't! Extraordinary selection of cheese esp Scottish and Swiss – only shop selling complete wheels of gruyère in Scotland. New owners '03; now even more choice, veg too. 7 days till 6pm (early closing Thur).

1576
MAP 2
D5
ISLAND CHEESES, ARRAN: 5km Brodick, rd to castle and Corrie. Excellent selection of their own (the well-known cheddars but many others esp crowdie with garlic and hand-rolled cream cheeses) and others. See them being made. 7 days.

1577
MAP 5
B2
WEST HIGHLAND DAIRY, ACHMORE, nr PLOCKTON: 01599 577203. Mr and Mrs Biss still running their great farm dairy shop selling their own cheeses (ewe and cow milk), yoghurt, ice cream and cheesecake. Mar-Dec dawn to dusk! Signed from village. If you're making the trip specially, phone first to check they're open.

HOUSE OF BRUAR, nr BLAIR ATHOLL: Roadside emporium (2170/SHOPPING).

FALLS OF SHIN VISITOR CENTRE nr LAIRG: The Harrods of the North (2180/SHOPPING).

PETER MACLENNAN, FORT WILLIAM: 28 High St.

SCOTTISH SPECIALITY FOOD, NORTH BALLACHULISH: By Leven Hotel.

JENNERS DEPARTMENT STORE, EDINBURGH: Princes St, top-floor.

THE BEST DISTILLERY TOURS

The process is basically the same in every distillery, but some are more atmospheric and some have more interesting tours, like these:

1578
MAP 2
B4, B5

THE ISLAY MALTS: Plenty to choose from incl the recently re-introduced **BRUICHLADDICH**, back in production after a hiatus of several yrs. Three tours daily Mon-Fri, twice daily on Sat (01496 850221). Elsewhere on Islay you can visit several of Scotland's most impressive distilleries and sample their gr malts. The distilleries here look like distilleries ought to. **LAGAVULIN** (01496 302400) and **LAPHROAIG** (01496 302418) are both nr Pt Ellen. They offer fascinating tours where your guide will lay on the anecdotes as well as the process and you get a feel for the life and history as well as the product of these world-famous places. At Laphroaig you can join their 'Friend' scheme (free) and own a piece of their hallowed ground. Lagavulin tours Mon-Fri only, Laphroaig same. For the two nr Port Askaig, call **BUNNAHABHAIN** on 840646 & **CAOL ILA** on 840207. **BOWMORE** (810441) has professional, more commercial, 1hr tours regularly (incl video show & the usual dram). **ARDBEG** (nr Port Ellen) is perhaps the most visitor-oriented and has a really good café (2340/ISLAY RESTAUS) where if you blunder in at mid morning and ask for toast, they make you some toast (302244). All these distilleries are in settings that entirely justify the romantic hyperbole of their advertising. Worth seeing from the o/side as well as the floor.

1579
MAP 4
C1

STRATHISLA, KEITH: 01542 783044. The oldest working distillery in the Highlands, literally on the strath of the Isla river and methinks the most evocative atmos of all the Speyside distilleries. The refurb made this an even classier halt for the malt. Used as the 'heart' of Chivas Regal, the malt not commonly available is still a fine dram. Feb-Easter, Mon-Fri 9.30am-4pm, Easter-Nov Mon-Sat 9.30am-4pm, Sun 12.30-4pm.

1580
MAP 5
A2

TALISKER, CARBOST, ISLE OF SKYE: From Sligachan-Dunvegan rd (A863) take B8009 for Carbost and Glen Brittle along the S side of L Harport for 5km. Skye's only distillery; since 1830 they've been making this classic after-dinner malt from barley and the burn that runs off the Hawkhill behind. A dram before the informative 40min tour. Good VC. Apr-Oct 9.30am-5pm (2-5pm wint). Gr gifts nearby (2183/CRAFT SHOPS).

1581
MAP 3
D5

GLENKINCHIE, PENCAITLAND, nr EDINBURGH: 01875 342004. Only 25km from city centre (via A68 and A6093 before Pathhead), so popular. Founded in 1837 in a peaceful, pastoral place (it's 3km from the village) with its own bowling green; a country trip as well as a whisky tour. State-of-the-art VC. Summer daily till 5pm. Wint cl w/ends.

1582
MAP 3
B2

EDRADOUR, nr PITLOCHRY: Claims to be the smallest distillery in Scotland, producing single malts for blends since 1825 and limited quantities of the Edradour (since 1986) as well as the House of Lords' own brand. Guided tour of charming cottage complex every 20min. 4km from Pitlochry off Kirkmichael rd, A924; signed after Moulin village. Mar-Oct daily until 5pm. Nov-Dec Mon-Sat until 4pm cl Jan-Feb.

1583

HIGHLAND PARK, KIRKWALL, ORKNEY: 01856 874619. 2km from town on main A961 rd S to S Ronaldsay. The whisky is great and the award-winning tour one of the best. The most northerly whisky in a class and a bottle of its own. You walk through the floor maltings and you can touch the warm barley and fair smell the peat. Good combination of the industrial and trad. Tours every half hour Apr-Oct 10am-5pm (w/ends in summer only 12-5pm). Nov-Mar 2pm tour only w/days.

THE BEST OF THE SPEYSIDE WHISKY TRAIL: *Well signposted but bewildering number of tours, though by no means at every distillery. Many are in rather featureless industrial complexes and settings. These are the best along with Strathisla (see above):*

1584
MAP 4
B2

THE GLENLIVET, MINMORE: 01542 783220. Starting as an illicit dram celebrated as far S as Edin, George Smith licensed the brand in 1824 and founded this distillery in 1858, registering the already mighty name so that anyone else had to use a prefix. After various successions and mergers, independence was lost in 1978 when Seagrams took over. The famous Josie's Well, from which the water springs, is underground and not shown, but small parties and a walk-through which is not on a gantry make the tour as satisfying and as popular, esp with Americans, as the product. Excellent reception centre with bar/restau and shop. Apr-Oct, 10am-4pm. Sundays 12.30-4pm.

1585 **GLENFIDDICH, DUFFTOWN:** O/side town on the A941 to Craigellachie by the
MAP 4 ruins of Balvenie Castle. Well-oiled tourist operation and the only distillery
C2 where you can see the whisky bottled on the premises; indeed, the whole process from barley to bar. Also the only major distillery that's free (incl dram). Also now runs own artists-in-residence scheme with changing shows over the summer: 01340 821565 for details. AYR 9.30am-4.30pm not w/ends in winter. On the same rd there's a chance to see a whisky-related industry/craft that hasn't changed in decades. The **SPEYSIDE COOPERAGE** is 1km from Craigellachie. You watch those poor guys from the gantry (no chance to slack). AYR Mon-Fri 9.30am-4.30pm.

1586 **GLEN GRANT, ROTHES:** In Rothes on the A941 Elgin to Perth rd. Not the most
MAP 4 picturesque but a distillery tour with an added attraction viz the gdns and
B2 orchard reconstructed around the shallow bowl of the glen of the burn that runs through the distillery. Tour vouchers can be used there to take a dram in the delightful Dram Pavilion. Apr-Oct 10-4pm, from 12.30pm on Sun.

1587 **CARDHU, CARRON:** Off B9102 from Craigellachie to Grantown through
MAP 4 deepest Speyside, a small if charming distillery with its own community, a
B2 millpond, picnic tables, etc. Owned by United Distillers, Cardhu is the 'heart of Johnnie Walker' (which, amazingly, has another 30 malts in it). July-Sept daily 10am-5pm Mon-Fri, 12-4pm Sun. Otherwise open at least weekdays – call 01340 872555 for details.

1588 **DALLAS DHU, nr FORRES:** Not really nr the Spey (3km S of Forres on B9010)
MAP 4 and no longer a working distillery (ceased 1983), but instant history provided
B1 by HS and you don't have to go round on a tour. The wax workers are a bit spooky; the product itself is more life-like. Apr-Sept 9.30-6.30, restricted hrs in wint (01309 676548).   HS

1589 **SCOTCH WHISKY HERITAGE CENTRE, EDINBURGH:** 0131 220 0441. On Castle-
MAP 2 hill on last stretch to castle (you cannot miss it). Not a distillery of course, but a
D4 visitor attraction to celebrate all things a tourist can take in about Scotland's main export. Shop has huge range. 7 days 10-5pm (extended hrs in summer).

PROMOTIONAL TOURS: GLENTURRET nr CRIEFF, and ABERFELDY: A recent and not entirely welcome trend has been to makeover distilleries into inter-active ads for certain brands of blends. The quaint old Glenturret distillery by Crieff is now the Famous Grouse Experience (daily AYR 08450 451800) while Aberfeldy distillery is now Dewar's World of Whisky (AYR, call for times 01887 822010). The branding density is tiresome but the production tours are super-professional. Watch out for Andy Garcia in Aberfeldy!

WHERE TO FIND THE BEST SELECTION OF MALTS
EDINBURGH

✓ ✓ **SCOTCH MALT WHISKY SOCIETY:** The Vaults, 87 Giles St, Leith & 28 Queen St (from spring 2004). Your search will end here. More a club (with membership) and visitors must be signed in.

BENNET'S: 8 Leven St by King's Theatre.

KAY'S BAR: 39 Jamaica St.

THE BOW BAR: 80 West Bow.

CADENHEAD'S: 172 Canongate. The shop with the lot.

CANNY MAN'S: 237 Morningside Rd.

BLUE BLAZER: Corner Spittal & Bread St (355/REAL ALE PUBS).

GLASGOW

✓ ✓ **THE POT STILL:** 154 Hope St. Over 150 separate bottlings.

THE BON ACCORD: 153 North St (724/REAL ALE).

THE LISMORE: 206 Dumbarton Rd (715/UNIQUE PUBS).

UBIQUITOUS CHIP: Ashton lane. Restau, bistro & gr bar on the corner.

BEN NEVIS: Argyle St (far W end) (716/UNIQUE PUBS).

REST OF SCOTLAND

√ √ **LOCHSIDE HOTEL, BOWMORE, ISLAY:** More Islay malts than you ever imagined in friendly local near the distillery.

√ √ **LOCH TORRIDON HOTEL nr KINLOCHEWE:** Classic Highland hotel & 300 malts shelf by shelf. And the mountains! 1279/GET AWAY HOTELS.

√ √ **CLACHAIG INN, GLENCOE:** Over 100 malts to go with the range of ales & the range of folk that come here to drink after the hills (1378/BLOODY GOOD PUBS).

√ √ **THE DROVER'S INN, INVERARNAN:** Same as above, with around 75 to choose from and the rt atmos to drink them in (1374/BLOODY GOOD PUBS).

√ **THE BAR AT THE CRAIGELLACHIE HOTEL:** Whiskies arranged around cosy bar of this essential Speyside hotel & the river below (1015/NE HOTELS).

√ **ARISAIG HOTEL, ARISAIG, nr MALLAIG:** Small, civilised lounge and busy local. 100 malts move betw the bars.

√ **KNOCKINAAM LODGE, PORTPATRICK:** Comfortable country-house hotel; esp good lowland selection incl the (extinct) local Bladnoch (853/SW HOTELS).

√ **DUNAIN PARK HOTEL, INVERNESS:** After dinner in one of the best places to eat hereabouts, there's a serious malts list to mull over (1046/HIGHLAND HOTELS).

√ **HOTEL EILEAN IARMAIN, SKYE:** Also known as the Isleornsay Hotel (2311/ ISLAND HOTELS); not the biggest range but one of the best places to drink (it).

CROMLIX HOUSE HOTEL, DUNBLANE: Excl and not overly expensive whisky list after dinner in civilised setting (906/CENTRAL HOTELS).

KINLOCH HOUSE HOTEL nr BLAIRGOWRIE (984/PERTHSHIRE BEST HOTELS).

FOX 'N' HOUNDS, HOUSTON: 745/PUBFOOD.

OBAN INN, OBAN: Good mix of customers, whisky and ale.

FISHERMAN'S TAVERN, BROUGHTY FERRY: (1154/DUNDEE EAT AND DRINK).

LOCK INN, FORT AUGUSTUS: Canalside setting, good food & plenty whisky.

THE TAPPIT HEN, DUNBLANE: By the Cathedral (1392/REAL ALE).

KNOCKOMIE HOTEL: S of Forres on A940.

SLIGACHAN HOTEL, SKYE: 01478 650204. On A87 (A850) 11km S of Portree. 71 malts in Seamus' huge cabin bar. Good ale selection; Apr/Sept festivals.

FORSS HOUSE, THURSO: The dram of the far N (2354/THURSO).

PITTODRIE HOUSE HOTEL, PITCAPLE: In the snug (1016/NE HOTELS).

THE LAIRHILLOCK nr STONEHAVEN: Public bar (1399/PUB FOOD).

GORDON & MACPHAIL, ELGIN: The whisky provisioner and bottlers of the Connoisseurs brand you see in other shops and bars all over. From these humble beginnings over 100yrs ago, they now supply their exclusive and rarity range to the world. Mon-Sat till 5.15pm (5pm Wed). Cl Sun.

THE WHISKY SHOP, DUFFTOWN: The whisky shop in the main st (by the clock-tower) at the heart of whisky country. Within a few miles of numerous distilleries and their sales operations, this place stocks all the product (incl many halfs). 10am-5pm Mon-Sat, 2-4pm Sun.

PETER MACLENNAN, FORT WILLIAM: Main st, long-established emporium with big whisky section.

LOCH FYNE WHISKIES, INVERARAY: Beyond the church on the A83 a shop with 400 malts to choose from in various sizes & disguises; and whisky ware.

THE BEST MALTS AND WHEN TO DRINK THEM

Obviously, opinions vary. The following list is compiled from the consensus of several whisky buffs and 'authorities', but mainly Charlie Maclean who has several books under his belt. Vintages make a discernible difference to the connoisseur; the whiskies here are fine in any of their readily available forms.

BEFORE DINNER

Glenkinchie	(LOWLAND)	*Old Pulteney*	(HIGHLAND)
Glenmorangie	(SPEYSIDE)	*Rosebank*	(LOWLAND)

AFTER DINNER

Ardbeg	(ISLAY)	*Mortlach*	(SPEYSIDE)
Glenfarclas	(SPEYSIDE)	*Springbank*	(CAMPBELTOWN)
Highland Park	(ORKNEY)	*Strathisla*	(SPEYSIDE)
Lagavulin [1]	(ISLAY)	*Talisker*	(SKYE)
Macallan	(HIGHLAND)		

ANYTIME

Aberlour	(SPEYSIDE)	*Glenlivet*	(SPEYSIDE)
Bunnahabhain [2]	(ISLAY)	*Glen Ord*	(HIGHLAND)
Clynelish	(HIGHLAND)	*Oban*	(HIGHLAND)
Cragganmore	(SPEYSIDE)	*Tamdhu* [3]	(SPEYSIDE)
Dalwhinnie	(HIGHLAND)		

[1] pronounced 'Laga-voolin'
[2] pronounced 'Boona-have-en'
[3] pronounced 'Tam-doo'

SECTION 7

Outdoor Places

1590
MAP 2
D4
✔✔ **THE YOUNGER BOTANIC GARDEN, BENMORE:** 12km Dunoon on the A815 to Strachur. An 'outstation' of the Royal Botanic in Edin, gifted to the nation by Harry Younger in 1928, but the first plantations dating from 1820. Walks clearly marked through formal gdns, woody grounds and the 'pinetum' where the air is often so sweet and spicy it can seem like the v elixir of life. Redwood avenue, terraced hill sides, views; a gdn of different moods and fine proportions. Good walk, 'Puck's Glen', nearby (2053/WOODLAND WALKS). Café. Mar-Oct 10-6pm. ☕ ADMN

1591
MAP 6
A3
✔✔ **INVEREWE, POOLEWE:** on A832, 80km S of Ullapool. The world-famous gdns on a promontory of L Ewe. Begun in 1862, Osgood Mackenzie made it his life's work in 1883 and it continues with large crowds coming to admire his efforts. Helped by the ameliorating effect of the Gulf Stream, the 'wild' gdn became the model for many others. The guided tours (1.30pm Mon-Fri Apr-Sept) are probably the best way to get the most out of this extensive gdn. Gardens AYR till dusk – go in the evening when it's quiet! Shop, VC till 5pm. ☕ ADMN

1592
MAP 4
D3
✔✔ **CRATHES, nr BANCHORY, ROYAL DEESIDE:** 25km W of Aber and just off A93. One of the most interesting tower houses (1897/COUNTRY HOUSES) surrounded by exceptional topiary and walled gdns of inspired design and tranquil atmos. Keen gardeners will be in their scented heaven. The Golden Garden (after Gertrude Jekyll) works particularly well and there's a wild gdn beyond the old wall that many people miss. All in all, a v *House and Garden* experience. Grounds open AYR 9am-sunset. ☕ NTS ADMN

1593
MAP 3
B5
✔✔ **LITTLE SPARTA nr DUNSYRE:** 01899 810252. Nr Biggar SW of Edin off A702 (5km), go thro vill then signed. House in bare hill country the home of conceptual artist & national treasure, Ian Hamilton Finlay. Gardens lovingly created over yrs, full of thought-provoking art/sculpture/perspectives. Unike anywhere else. A privilege to visit. Easter-Sept, Fri & Sun 2.30-5pm only.

1594
MAP 3
B3
✔✔ **DRUMMOND CASTLE GARDENS, MUTHILL, nr CRIEFF:** Signed from A822, 2km from Muthill and then up a long avenue, the most exquisite formal gdns viewed first from the terrace by the house. A boxwood parterre of a vast St Andrew's Cross in yellow and red (esp antirrhinums and roses), the Drummond colours, with extraordinary sundial centrepiece; 5 gardeners keep every leaf in place. 7 days May-Oct 2-5pm (last adm). House not open to the public. ADMN

1595
MAP 1
A3
✔✔ **LOGAN BOTANICAL GARDENS, nr SANDHEAD, S of STRANRAER:** 16km S of Stranraer by A77/A716 and 2km on from Sandhead. Remarkable outstation of the Edin Botanics amongst sheltering woodland in the mild SW. Compact and full of pleasant surprises. Less crowded than other 'exotic' gdns. Their 'soundwands' giving commentary on demand make it all v interesting. Salad bar not bad. The Gunnera Bog is quite extraterrestrial. Mar-Oct; 7 days, 10am-5pm. ☕ ADMN

1596
MAP 2
D3
✔✔ **CRARAE, INVERARAY:** 16km SE on A83 to Lochgilphead. Famed & fabulous. Recntly taken over by NTS so difficulties in staying open resolved. The wooded banks of L Fyne with gushing burn are as lush as the jungles of Borneo. Dawn till dusk. Vis centre till 5pm . NTS

1597
MAP 1
C2
✔ **THREAVE nr CASTLE DOUGLAS:** 64 acres of magnificent Victorian landscaping in incomparable setting overlooking Galloway coastline. Don't miss the walled kitchen garden. Horticulturally inspiring; and daunting. Open Feb-Dec 10-4pm. ☕

1598
MAP 3
C6
✔ **DAWYCK, STOBO, nr PEEBLES:** On B712 Moffat rd off the A72 Biggar rd from Peebles, 2km from Stobo. Another outstation of the Edin Botanics; a 'recent' acquisition, though tree planting here goes back 300 yrs. Sloping grounds around the gurgling Scrape burn which trickles into the Tweed. Landscaped woody pathways for meditative walks. Famous for shrubs and blue Himalayan poppies. The chapel is closed. Gr walk on Drovers rd, 2km on Stobo Rd before entrance. Tiny basic tearoom. Mar-Oct 10am-5pm. ADMN

1599
MAP 2
D2
✔ **ANGUS' GARDEN, TAYNUILT:** 7km from village (which is 12km from Oban on the A85) along the Glen Lonan rd. Take first rt after Barguillen Gdn Centre. A gdn laid out by the family who own the centre in memory of their son Angus, a soldier, who was killed in Cyprus. On the slopes around a small loch brimful of lilies and ducks. Informal mix of tended and uncultivated (though wild prevails), a more poignant remembrance is hard to imagine as you while an hr away in this peaceful place. Open AYR.   HONESTY BOX

1600
MAP 2
C3
✔ **ARDUAINE GARDEN, nr KILMELFORD:** 28km S of Oban on A816, one of Argyll's undiscovered arcadias gifted to the NTS and brought to wider attention. Creation of the microclimate in which the rich, diverse vegetation has flourished, influenced by Osgood Mackenzie of Inverewe and its restoration a testimony to 20yrs hard labour by the Wright brothers. Enter/park by L Melfort hotel, gate 100m. Until dusk.   NTS

1601
MAP 2
C5
✔ **ACHAMORE GARDENS, ISLE OF GIGHA:** 1km from ferry. Walk or cycle from ferry (bike hire at post office at top of ferry rd); an easy day trip. The 'big house' on the island set in 65 acres. For sale at TGP, but public access will remain. Lush tropical plants mingle with rhodies that flourish early (Feb-March): all due to the mild climate and the devotion of only 2 gardeners. 2 marked walks (40mins/2hrs) start from the walled gdn (green route takes in the sea view of Islay and Jura). Density and variety of shrubs, pond plants and trees revealed as you meander around this enchanting spot. Leaflet guides at entrance. Open AYR. (2299/MAGICAL ISLANDS)   ADMN

1602
MAP 2
D5
ASCOG HALL FERNERY, ROTHESAY: Outside town on rd to Mt Stewart (1886/CO HOUSES), worth stopping here at this small garden & Victorian Fern House. Green & lush & dripping! Easter-Oct, 10-5pm. Cl Mon/Tues. (& don't miss the Victorian loos in Rothesay itself.)   ADMN

1603
MAP 3
D6
PRIORWOOD, MELROSE: Next to Melrose Abbey, a tranquil secret gdn behind high walls which specialises in growing flowers and plants for drying. Picking, drying and arranging is continuously in progress. Samples for sale. Run by enthusiasts on behalf of the NTS, they're always willing to talk stamens with you. Also includes an historical apple orchard with trees through the ages. Heavenly jelly on sale. Mon-Sat 10am-5pm; Sun 1.30-5pm. Cl 4pm wint. Dried flower shop.   NTS ADMN

1604
MAP 3
C5
KAILZIE GARDENS, PEEBLES: On B7062 Traquair rd. Informal woodland gdns just out of town; not extensive but eminently strollable. Old-fashioned roses and wilder bits. Some poor birds in cages and the odd peacock. Courtyard teashop. Kids' corner. Fishing pond popular. Apr-Oct.   ADMN

1605
MAP 4
D2
PITMEDDEN GARDEN, nr ELLON: 35km N of Aber and 10km W of the main A92. Formal French gdns recreated in 1950s on site of Sir Alex Seaton's 17th-century ones. The 4 gr parterres, 3 based on designs for gdns at Holyrood Palace, are best viewed from the terrace. Charming farmhouse 'museum' seems transplanted. For lovers of symmetry and an orderly universe only (but there is a woodland walk). May-Sept 10am-5.30pm. ☕   NTS ADMN

1606
MAP 4
D2
PITTODRIE HOUSE nr INVERURIE: An exceptional walled gdn in the grounds of Pittodrie House Hotel at Chapel of Garioch in Aberdeenshire (1016/NE HOTELS). 500m from house and largely unvisited by most of the guests, this secret and sheltered haven is both a kitchen gdn and a place for meditations and reflections (and possibly wedding photos).

1607
MAP 2
E3
ARDKINGLAS WOODLAND, CAIRNDOW: Off the A83 L Lomond to Inveraray rd. Through village to signed car park and these mature woodlands in the grounds of Ardkinglas House on the southern bank nr the head of L Fyne. Fine pines include the 'tallest tree in Britain'. Magical at dawn or dusk. 2km Loch Fyne Seafood (1444/SEAFOOD RESTAUS) where there is also a tree-shop gdn centre esp for trees & shrubs (2233/GARDEN CENTRES).   ADMN

1608
MAP 2
B5
JURA HOUSE WALLED GARDEN: Ardfin, Jura. Around 8km from the ferry on the only rd. Park opp & follow track into woods. Walled garden only part of walk that takes you to coast & ultimately (tho steep) to the beach & the 'Misty Pools'. Beautiful in rain (frequent) or shine! Open AYR.   ADMN

1609
MAP 5
C2
ATTADALE GARDENS, STRATHCARRON: On A890 from Kyle of Lochalsh & A87 just S of Strathcarron. Lovely W Highland house & gardens nr L Carron. Exotic specials, water gardens, sculpture, gr rhodies May/June. Nursery & kitchen gdn. Good restau nearby (1091/HIGHLAND RESTAUS). Apr-Oct 10am-5.30pm.   ADMN

1610　**THE HYDROPONICUM, ACHILTIBUIE:** The 'Garden of the Future'; a weird
MAP 6　indoor waterworld. Geraniums cluster round the pond by the café and other
B3　plants thrive in the microclimates. Apr-Sep. Tours: hourly. Limited hrs in Oct.
Growing kits to buy (strawberries at Christmas?) 01854 622202.　　ADMN

1611　**ARD-DARAICH HILL GARDEN, ARDGOUR:** 3 km S Ardgour at Corran Ferry
MAP 2　(8/JOURNEYS) on A861 to Strontian. Private, labour of love 'hill' and wild gdn
D1　which you are at liberty to wander in. Specialising in rhodies, shrubs, trees.
Nursery/small gdn centre. 01855 841248. Open AYR, 7 days.

1612　**THE HIDDEN GARDENS, GLASGOW:** This garden oasis in the asphalt jungle
MAP B　of Glasgow's S side opened in the disused wasteland behind The Tramway
xA5　performance & studio space in 2003. A project of environmental theatre
group nva working with landscape architects City Design Co-operative, this is
a v modern approach to an age-old challenge – how to make & keep a sanctuary in the city! It works so far. Open 10am-8pm (wint hrs vary). Cl Mon.

ROYAL BOTANIC GARDEN, EDINBURGH: 402/OTHER ATTRACTIONS.

BOTANIC GARDEN and KIBBLE PALACE, GLASGOW: 765/ATTRACTIONS.

THE BEST COUNTRY PARKS

1613　✓✓ **DRUMLANRIG CASTLE, THORNHILL, nr DUMFRIES:** 01848 330248.
MAP 1　On A76, 7km N of Thornhill in the W Borders in whose romance and
D1　history it's steeped, much more than merely a country park; spend a good day,
both inside the castle and in the grounds. Apart from THAT art collection
(Rembrandt, Leonardo, Holbein) and the Craft Courtyard (2198/CRAFT SHOPS),
the delights include: a stunning tearoom, woodland and riverside walks, an
adventure playground, the 'Working Forge' and bike hire for further afield
explorations along the Nith etc. Open May-Aug, Mon-Sun 11am-4pm.

1614　✓ **MUIRSHEIL, nr LOCHWINNOCH:** Via Largs (A760) or Glas (M8, jnct 29
MAP 2　A737 then A760 5km S of Johnstone). N from village on Kilmacolm rd for
E5　3km then signed. Muirshiel is name given to wider area, but park proper
begins 6km on rd along the Calder valley. Despite proximity of conurbation
(Pt Glas is over the hill), this is a wild and enchanting place for walking/picnics
etc. Trails marked to waterfall and summit views. Extensive 'events' programme: www.clydemuirsheil.co.uk Escape!

1615　**JOHN MUIR COUNTRY PARK, nr DUNBAR, EAST LOTHIAN:** Named after the
MAP 3　19th-century conservationist who founded America's National Parks (and the
D4　Sierra Club) and who was born in Dunbar. This swathe of coastline to the W of
the town (known locally as Tyninghame) is an important estuarine nature
reserve but is good for family walks and beachcombing. Can enter via B6370
off A198 to N Berwick or by 'cliff-top' trail from Dunbar (1815/WILDLIFE).

1616　**STRATHCLYDE PARK, between HAMILTON and MOTHERWELL:** 15km SE of
MAP 3　Glas. Take M8/A725 interchange or M74/jnct 5 or 6. Scotland's most popular
A5　country park, esp for water sports. From canoeing to parascending; you can
hire the gear (2011/WATER SPORTS). Also; excavated Roman bath house, playgrounds, sports pitches and now that the trees are maturing, some pleasant
walks. Nearby Baron's Haugh (2148/BIRDS) and Dalzell Country Park more
notable for their nature trails and gdns. (1902/MONUMENTS.)

1617　**FINLAYSTONE ESTATE, LANGBANK nr GREENOCK:** A8 to Greenock,
MAP 2　Houston direction at Langbank, then signed. Grand mansion home to Chief of
E4　Clan Macmillan set in formal gdns in wooded estate. Lots of facs ('Celtic' tearm,
craft shop etc), leafy walks, walled gdn. Rare magic. Oct-Mar w/ends only, Apr-
Sep daily until 5pm. ☕

1618　**ALMONDELL, nr EAST CALDER:** 12km from Edin city bypass. Well-managed
MAP 3　park in R Almond valley set amidst area of redundant industry. If you've just
C5　spent light yrs trying to exit from Livingston's notorious rd system, you'll need
this green oasis with its walks in woods, meadows and along cinder tracks. Picnic
sites, VC with refreshments, kids' areas. From Edin take A71 from bypass
(Kilmarnock rd), then B7015 (Camp) for 7km. Park on rt just into E Calder. Walk
ahead to woods.

1619 **HIRSEL COUNTRY PARK, COLDSTREAM:** On A697, N edge town. 3000 acres
MAP 3   grounds of Hirsel House (not open public). 2-4km walks thro' farmland &
E5   woods incl lovely lake. Museum, crafts, tearm. Quieter park than most.

1620 **MUIRAVONSIDE COUNTRY PARK:** 4km SW of Linlithgow on B825. Also sign-
MAP 3   posted from J4 of the M9 Edin/Stirling. Former farm estate now run by the
B4   local authority providing 170 acres of woodland walks, parkland, picnic sites
         and a VC for school parties or anyone else with an interest in birds, bees and
         badgers. Ranger service does guided walks Apr-Sep. Gr place to walk off that
         lunch at the not-too-distant Champany Inn (258/BURGERS).

1621 **EGLINTON nr IRVINE:** Beside main A78 Largs to Ayr rd signed from
MAP 2   Irvine/Kilwinning intersection. Spacious lungful of Ayrshire nr new town
E5   nexus and traffic tribulations. Visitor centre with interpretation of absolutely
         everything. Much made of the Eglintons' place in Scottish history. Park open
         all the time, VC Easter-Oct. Network of walks.

✓✓ **CULZEAN CASTLE PARK:** Superb & hugely pop (1825/CASTLES).

✓ **HADDO HOUSE, ABERDEENSHIRE:** Beautiful grounds (1885/CO HOUSES).

MUGDOCK COUNTRY PARK, nr MILNGAVIE: Marvellous park close to Glas (5
car parks around the vast site). Report 778/CITY WALKS.

TENTSMUIR, nr TAYPORT: Estuarine; John Muir, on Tay (1818/WILDLIFE).

ADEN, MINTLAW, nr PETERHEAD: 1779/KIDS.

KELBURNE COUNTRY CENTRE, LARGS: 1766/KIDS.

THE BEST TOWN PARKS

1622 **PRINCES ST GARDENS, EDINBURGH:** S side of Princes St. The green-
MAP A   ery that launched a thousand postcards – millions probably – it's Edin.
C3   This former loch – drained around the time the New Town was built – is divid-
         ed by the Mound. The eastern half has pitch and putt, Winter Wonderland and
         the Scott Monument (432/BEST VIEWS), the western has its much-photographed
         fountain, open-air café and space for locals and tourists to sprawl on the grass
         when sunny. You'll also find the the Ross Bandstand here – heart of Edinburgh's
         Hogmanay (39/BEST EVENTS) and the International Festival's gobsmacking fire-
         works concert (471/ANNUAL EVENTS). Louts with lager, senior citz on benches,
         Italian teens with daft wee rucksacks – all our lives are here. Till dusk.

1623 **HAZELHEAD PARK, ABERDEEN:** Via Queens Rd, 3km centre.
MAP 4   Extraordinary park where the mysterious gardening skills of the
D3   Aberdonians are magnificently in evidence. Many facs incl a maze, mini-zoo,
         wonderful tacky tearoom and there are lawns, memorials and botanical splen-
         dours aplenty esp azalea gdn in spring and roses in summer. Gr sculpture.

1624 **DUTHIE PARK, ABERDEEN:** Riverside Dr along R Dee from the br carry-
MAP 4   ing main A92 rd from/to Stonehaven. The other large well-kept park with
D3   duck pond, bandstand, hugely impressive rose gdns in summer, carved sculp-
         tures and the famous, though now somewhat shabby Winter Gdn of subtrop-
         ical palms/ferns etc (10am-7.30pm summer, wint at dusk).

1625 **PITTENCRIEFF PARK, DUNFERMLINE:** The extensive park alongside the
MAP 3   Abbey and Palace ruins gifted to the town in 1903 by Carnegie. Open
C4   areas, glasshouses, pavilion (more a function rm) but most notably a deep ver-
         dant glen criss-crossed with pathways. Lush, full of birds, good after rain.

1626 **BEVERIDGE PARK, KIRKCALDY:** Also in Fife, another big municipal park with
MAP 3   a duck and boat pond, wide-open spaces and many amusements (e.g. bowling,
C4   tennis, putting, paddling). Ravenscraig a coastal park on the main rd E to Dysart
         is an excellent place to walk. Gr prospect of town and Firth, coves and skerries.

1627 **WILTON LODGE PARK, HAWICK:** Hawick not overfull of visitor attractions, but
MAP 3   it does have a nice park with facs and diversions enough for everyone e.g. the
D6   civic gallery, rugby pitches (they quite like rugby in Hawick), a large kids' play-
         ground, a café and lots of riverside walks by the Teviot. Lots of my school
         friends lost their virginity in the shed here. All-round open-air recreation cen-
         tre. S end of town by A7.

1628 **DEAN CASTLE PARK, KILMARNOCK:** A77 S first t/off for Kilmarnock then
MAP 2 signed; from Ayr A77 N, 3rd t/off. Surprising green & woody oasis in suburban
E5 Kilmarnock; lawns & woods around restored castle & courtyard. Riding centre.
Burns rose garden.

1629 **ROUKEN GLEN AND LINN PARK, GLASGOW:** Both on S side of river. Rouken
MAP B Glen via Pollokshaws/Kilmarnock rd to Eastwood Toll then rt. Good place to
xC5 park is second left, Davieland Rd beside pond. Across park from here (or
beside main Rouken Glen rd) is main visitor area with info centre, gdn centre,
a Chinese restau, kids' play area and woodland walks (0141 577 3913 for info).
Linn Park via Aikenhead and Carmunnock rd. After King's Park on left, take rt
to Simshill Rd and park at golf course beyond houses. A long route there, but
worth it; this is one of the undiscovered Elysiums of a city which boasts 60
parks. Ranger Centre (0141 637 1147) – activities, wildlife walks, kids' nature
trails, horse-riding (0141 637 3096).

1630 **CAMPERDOWN PARK, DUNDEE:** Calling itself a country park, Camperdown
MAP 3 is the main recreational breathing space for the city and hosts a plethora of
D3 distractions (a golf course, a wildlife complex, mansion house etc). Situated
beyond Kingsway, the ring-route; go via Coupar Angus rd t/off. Best walks
across the A923 in the Templeton Woods. **BALGRAY PARK** also excl.

1631 **GRANT PARK, FORRES:** Frequent winner of the Bonny Bloom competitions
MAP 4 (but not recently, so spruce up, Forres!) with its balance of ornamental gdns,
B1 open parkland and woody hill side, this is a carefully tended rose. Good munic-
ipal facs like pitch and putt, playground. Cricket in summer and topping topiary.
Through woods at top of Cluny Hill, a tower affords gr views of the Moray and
Cromarty Firths and surrounding forest from which the town takes its name.

1632 **CALLANDER PARK, FALKIRK:** Park on edge of town centre, signed from all
MAP 3 over. O/looked by high-rise blocks & nr busy rd system, this is nevertheless a
B4 beautiful green space with a big hoose (heritage museum), woods & lawns.
Comes alive in May as venue for Big in Falkirk (22/EVENTS).

THE MOST INTERESTING COASTAL VILLAGES

1633 ✓ **PLOCKTON, nr KYLE OF LOCHALSH:** A Highland gem of a place 8km
MAP 5 over the hill from Kyle, clustered around inlets of a wooded bay on L
B2 Carron. Cottage gdns down to the bay and palm trees! Some gr walks over
headlands. Plockton Inn prob best bet for reasonable stay and eats (1069/LESS
EXP HIGHLAND HOTELS). Haven Hotel (01599 544223) also good place to eat.
Plockton Hotel (1261/ROADSIDE INNS CHP, pub grub). It's not hard to feel con-
nected with the village.

1634 ✓ **STROMNESS, ORKNEY MAINLAND:** 24km from Kirkwall and a different
kettle of fish. Hugging the shore and with narrow streets and wynds, it
has a unique atmos, both maritime and European. Some of the most singular
shops you'll see anywhere and the Orkney folk going about their business.
Park nr harbour and walk down the cobbled main st if you don't want to
scrape your paintwork (2344/ORKNEY; 2280/GALLERIES).

1635 ✓ **CROMARTY, nr INVERNESS:** At end of rd across Black Isle from Inverness
MAP 5 (45km NE), but worth the trip. Village with dreamy times-gone-by atmos,
E1 without being twee. Lots of kids running about and a pink strand of beach.
Delights to discover include: the east kirk, plain and aesthetic with countryside through the windows behind the altar; Hugh (the geologist) Miller's cot-
tage/Courthouse museum (2359/BEST HISTORY AND HERITAGE); The Pantry
(1516/TEAROOMS); Cromarty Bakery (1526/BEST SCOTCH BAKERS); the shore and
cliff walk (2075/COASTAL WALKS) and of course the dolphins (1811/DOLPHINS).

1636 **CULROSS, nr DUNFERMLINE:** By A994 from Dunfermline or jnct 1 of M90
MAP 3 just over Forth Rd Br (15km). Old centre conserved and being restored by NTS.
B4 Mainly residential and not awash with craft and coffee shops. More historical
than merely quaint; a community of careful custodians lives in the white, red-
pantiled houses. Footsteps echo in the cobbled wynds. Palace and Town
House open Easter-Sept 10-6pm, Oct 1-5pm. Interesting back gdns and lovely church at top of hill (1924/CHURCHES). Pamphlet by Rights of Way Society
available locally, is useful.

1637 **TOBERMORY, MULL:** Not so much a village or setting for a kids' TV show (the
MAP 2 brilliant *Balamory*), rather the main town of Mull, set around a hill on superb
B2 Tobermory Bay. Ferry pt for Ardnamurchan, but main Oban ferry is 35km away
at Craignure. Usually a bustling harbour front with quieter streets behind; a
quintessential island atmos. Some good inexp hotels (and quayside hostel)
well situated to explore the whole island. (2343/MULL; 2314/ISLAND HOTELS;
1243/BEST HOSTELS.)

1638 **PORT CHARLOTTE, ISLAY:** A township on the 'Rhinns of Islay', the western
MAP 2 peninsula. By A846 from the pts, Askaig and Ellen via Bridgend. Rows of white-
B5 washed, well-kept cottages along and back from shoreline. On rd in, there's an
island museum and a coffee/bookshop. Also a 'town' beach and one between
PC and Bruichladdich (and esp the one with the war memorial nearby). Quiet
and charming, not quaint. (2340/ISLAY; 2309/ISLAND HOTELS; 1820/WILDLIFE
CENTRES)

1639 **ROCKCLIFFE, nr DUMFRIES:** 25km S on Solway Coast rd, A710. On the
MAP 1 'Scottish Riviera', the rocky part of the coast around to Kippford (2071/COASTAL
D3 WALKS). A good rock-scrambling foreshore tho not so clean, and a village with
few houses and Baron's Craig hotel; set back with gr views. Tearm at Rockcliffe
(1513/TEAROOMS).

1640 **EAST NEUK VILLAGES:** The quintessential quaint wee fishing villages along
MAP 3 the bit of Fife that forms the mouth of the Firth of Forth, **CRAIL, ANSTRUTHER,**
D3 **PITTENWEEM, ST MONANS** and **ELIE** all have different characters and attractions esp Crail and Pittenweem harbours, Anstruther as main centre and home
of Fisheries Museum (see also 1467/FISH AND CHIPS; FIFE HOTELS; 1795/BIRDS)
and perfect Elie (2163/WINDSURFING; 970/971/FIFE HOTELS; 1410/BEST FOOD;
2092/GREAT GOLF). Or see ST ANDREWS. Cycling good, traffic in summer not.

1641 **ABERDOUR:** Betw Dunfermline and Kirkcaldy and nr Forth Rd Br (10km E
MAP 3 from jnct 1 of M90) or, better still, go by train from Edin (frequent service:
C4 Dundee or Kirkcaldy); delightful station. Walks round harbour and to headland, Silver Sands beach 1km (429/EDIN BEACHES), castle ruins. (1923/CHURCHES;
932/933/FIFE HOTELS.)

1642 **MORAY COAST FISHING VILLAGES:** From Speybay (where the Spey slips into
MAP 4 the sea) along to Fraserburgh, some of Scotland's best coastal scenery and
C1, D1 many interesting villages in cliff/cove and beach settings. Esp notable are
PORTSOY with 17thC harbour – and see 27/EVENTS; **SANDEND** with its own
popular beach and a fabulous one nearby (1648/BEACHES); **PENNAN** made
famous by the film *Local Hero* (the hotel/pub is cosy and cheap: 01346
561201); **GARDENSTOWN** with a walk along the water's edge to **CROVIE**
(pron 'Crivee') the epitome of a coast-clinging community; and **CULLEN,**
which is more of a town and has a gr beach. (1020/NE HOTELS.)

1643 **DIABEG, WESTER ROSS:** On N shore of L Torridon at the end of the unclassi-
MAP 5 fied rd from Torridon on one of Scotland's most inaccessible peninsulas.
B1 Diabeg (pron 'Jee-a-beg') is simply beautiful. Fantastic rd there and then walk!

1644 **ISLE OF WHITHORN:** Strange faraway village at end of the rd, 35km S Newton
MAP 1 Stewart, 6km Whithorn (1879/PREHISTORIC SITES). Mystical harbour where low
B3 tide does mean low, saintly shoreline, a sea angler's pub (Steam Packet) v
good pub grub. Ninian's chapel round the headland not so uplifting but en
route you'll see the *Solway Harvester* memorial by the ruins of the 19thC
lifeboat house.

1645 **CORRIE, ARRAN:** Last but not least, the bonniest bit of Arran, best reached by
MAP 2 bike from Brodick (2339/ARRAN). I'd like a memorial bench on that shoreline.
D5

1646 **✓ ✓ KILORAN BEACH, COLONSAY:** 9km from quay and hotel, past
MAP 2 Colonsay House: parking and access on hill side. Described as the
B4 finest beach in the Hebrides, it does not disappoint, even in the rain. Craggy
cliffs on one side, negotiable rocks on the other and, in betw, tiers of grassy
dunes. The island of Colonsay was once bought as a picnic spot. This beach
was probably the reason why.

1647 **✓ ✓ MACHRIHANISH:** At the bottom of the Kintyre peninsula 10km
MAP 2 from Campbeltown. Walk N from Machrihanish village or golf
C6 course, or from the car park on the main A83 to Tayinloan and Tarbert at pt
where it hits/leaves the coast. A joyously long strand (8km) of unspoiled
orange-pink sand backed by dunes and facing the 'steepe Atlantic Stream' all
the way to Newfoundland (2099/GOLF IN GREAT PLACES).

1648 **✓ ✓ SANDWOOD BAY, KINLOCHBERVIE:** This mile-long sandy strand
MAP 6 with its old 'Stack', is legendary, but therein lies the problem since
B1 now too many people know about it and you may have to share in its glorious isolation. Inaccessibility is its saving grace, a 7km walk from the sign off
the rd at Balchrick (nr the cattle grid), 6km from Kinlochbervie; allow 3hrs
return plus time there. More venturesome is the walk from the N and Cape
Wrath (2069/COASTAL WALKS). Managed by John Muir Trust. Go easy & go in
summer! Also:

1649 **✓ OLDSHOREMORE:** The beach you pass on the rd to Balchrick, only 3km
MAP 6 from Kinlochbervie. It's easy to reach and a beautiful spot: the water is
B1 clear and perfect for swimming, and there are rocky walks and quiet places.
POLIN, 500m N, is a cove you might have to yourself. (1303/CAMPING)

1650 **✓ ISLAY: SALIGO, MACHIR BAY and THE BIG STRAND:** The first two are
MAP 2 bays on NW of island via A847 rd to Pt Charlotte, then B8018 past L Gorm.
A5 Wide beaches; remains of war fortifications in deep dunes, Saligo perhaps the
nicer. They say 'no swimming' so paddle with extreme prejudice. The Big
Strand on Laggan Bay: along Bowmore-Pt Ellen rd take Oa t/off, follow Kintra
signs. There's camping and gr walks in either direction, 8km of glorious sand
and dunes (contains the Machrie Golf Course). An airy amble under a wide
sky. (2098/GOLF IN GREAT PLACES; 2067/COASTAL WALKS.)

1651 **✓ OSTAL BEACH/KILBRIDE BAY, MILLHOUSE, nr TIGHNABRUAICH:** 3km
MAP 2 from Millhouse on B8000 signed Ardlamont, a track to rt before white
D4 house (often with a chain across to restrict access). Park and walk 1.5km, turning rt after lochan. You arrive on a perfect white sandy crescent known locally as Ostal and, apart from the odd swatch of sewage, in certain conditions, a
mystical secret place to swim and picnic. The N coast of Arran is like a Greek
island in the bay.

1652 **✓ SOUTH UIST:** Deserted but for birds, an almost unbroken strand of beach
MAP 7 running for miles down the W coast; the machair at its best early summer.
A4 Take any rd off the spinal A865; usually less than 2km. Good spot to try is t/off
at Tobha Mor; real black houses and a chapel on the way to the sea.

1653 **✓ SCARISTA BEACH, SOUTH HARRIS:** On main rd S of Tarbert (15km) to
MAP 7 Rodel. The beach is so beautiful that people have been married there.
B3 Hotel over the rd is worth staying just for this, but is also a gr retreat
(2312/ISLAND HOTELS). Golf course on links (2105/GOLF IN GREAT PLACES). Fab in
early evening. The sun also rises.

1654 **✓ LUNAN BAY, nr MONTROSE:** 5km from main A92 rd to Aber and 5km of
MAP 3 deep red crescent beach under a wide northern sky. But'n'Ben,
D2 Auchmithie, is an excellent place to start or finish (1004/PERTHSHIRE EATS) and
good app (from S), although Gordon's restau at Inverkeilor is closer
(988/PERTHSHIRE EATS). Best viewpoint from Boddin Farm 3km S Montrose and
3km from A92 signed 'Usan'. Often deserted.

1655 **JURA, LOWLANDMAN'S BAY:** Not strictly a beach (there is a sandy strand
MAP 2 before the headland) but a rocky foreshore with ethereal atmos; gr light and
C4 space. Only seals break the spell. Go rt at 3-arch br to first group of houses
(Knockdrome), through yard on left and rt around cottages to track to
Ardmenish. After deer fences, bay is visible on your rt, 1km walk away.

1656 **VATERSAY, OUTER HEBRIDES:** The tiny island joined by a causeway to Barra.
MAP 7   Twin crescent beaches on either side of the isthmus, one shallow and shel-
A5   tered visible from Castlebay, the other an ocean beach with rollers.
Dunes/machair; safe swimming. There's a helluva hill betw Barra and Vatersay
if you're cycling.

1657 **BARRA, SEAL BAY:** 5km Castlebay on W coast, 2km after Isle of Barra Hotel
MAP 7   through gate across machair where rd rt is signed Taobh a Deas Allathasdal.
A5   A flat, rocky Hebridean shore and skerries where seals flop into the water and
eye you with intense curiosity. The better-beach beach is next to the hotel.

1658 **WEST SANDS, ST ANDREWS:** As a town beach, this is hard to beat; it domi-
MAP 3   nates the view to W. Wide swathe not too unclean and sea swimmable. Golf
D3   courses behind. Consistently gets 'the blue flag', but beach buffs may prefer
Kinshaldy (1819/WILDLIFE), Kingsbarns (10km S), or Elie (28km S).

1659 **MORAY COAST:** Many gr beaches along coast from Spey Bay to Fraserburgh,
MAP 4   notably **CULLEN** and **LOSSIEMOUTH** (town beaches) and **NEW ABERDOUR**
B1,   (1km from New Aberdour village on B9031, 15km W of Fraserburgh) and
C1,   **ROSEHEARTY** (8km W of Fraserburgh) both quieter places for walks and pic-
D1   nics. One of the best-kept secrets is the beach at **SUNNYSIDE** where you walk
past the incredible ruins of Findlater Castle on the cliff top (how did they build
it? A place, on its grassed-over roof, for a picnic) and down to a cove which on
my sunny day was simply perfect. Take a left going into Sandend 16km W of
Banff, follow rd for 2km, turn rt, park in the farmyard. Walk from here past
dovecote, 1km to cliff. Also signed from A98. *See also* 2074/COASTAL WALKS.

1660 **NORTH COAST:** To the W of Thurso, along the N coast, are some of Britain's
MAP 6   most unspoiled and unsung beaches. No beach bums, no Beach Boys. There
C1, D1 are so many gr little coves, you can have one to yourself even on a hot day, but
those to mention are: **STRATHY** and **ARMADALE** (35km W Thurso), **FARR** and
TORRISDALE (48km) and **COLDBACKIE** (65km). My favourite (which may be
called Ceannabeinne after the hill above it, but **PETE'S BEACH** is easier to
remember) is further along where L Eriboll comes out to the sea and the rd
hits the coast again 7km E of Durness. It's a small 100m cove flanked by walls
of oyster-pink rock and shallow turquoise sea; perfect. Excl inx GH nearby –
Port-Na-Con (1079/INX HIGHLAND HOTELS).

1661 **SANDS OF MORAR, nr MALLAIG:** 70km W of Ft William and 6km from
MAP 5   Mallaig by newly improved rd, these easily accessible beaches may seem
B3   overpopulated on summer days and the S stretch nearest to Arisaig may have
one too many caravan parks, but they go on for miles and there's enough
space for everybody. The sand's supposed to be silver but in fact it's a v pleasing pink. Lots of rocky bits for exploration. One of the best beachy bits is (coming from Mallaig) the next bay after the estuary signed 'Camusdaroch' (where
Local Hero was filmed), further from rd, is quieter and a v good swathe of sand.
Traigh, the golf course makes good use of the dunes (2114/GOOD GOLF). Gr inx
place to stay nearby – Garramore (1082/INX HIGHLAND HOTELS).

1662 **THE BAY AT THE BACK OF THE OCEAN, IONA:** Easy 2km walk from frequent
MAP 2   ferry from Fionnphort, S of Mull (2296/MAGICAL ISLANDS) or hire a bike from the
B3   store on your left as you walk into the village (01681 700357). Paved rd most
of way. John Smith, who is buried beside the abbey, once told me that this was
one of his favourite places. There's a gr inx hotel on Iona, The Argyll (1282/GET
AWAY FROM IT ALL).

1663 **DORNOCH and EMBO BEACHES:** The wide and extensive sandy beach of
MAP 6   this pleasant town at the mouth of the Dornoch Firth famous also for its golf
C3   links. 4km N, Embo Sands starts with caravan city, but walk N towards Golspie.
Embo is twinned with Kaunakakai, Hawaii!

1664 **PORT OF NESS, ISLE OF LEWIS:** Also signed Port Nis, this is the beach at the
MAP 7   end of the Hebrides in the far N of Lewis. Just keep driving. There are some
C1   interesting stops on the way (2209/ART, 2247/2248/MUSEUMS) – until you get
to this tiny bay & harbour down the hill at the end of the rd. Anthony
Barbour's Harbour View Gallery full of his own work (which you find in many
other galleries & even postcards) is worth a visit (10am-5pm, cl Sun).

1665
MAP 5
C2
✓ ✓ ✓ **GLEN AFFRIC:** Beyond Cannich at end of Glen Urquhart A831, 20km from Drumnadrochit on L Ness. A dramatic gorge that strikes westwards into the wild heart of Scotland. Superb for rambles (2037/GLEN AND RIVER WALKS), expeditions, Munro-bagging (further in, beyond L Affric) and even just tootling through in the car. Shaped by the Hydro Board, L Benevean nevertheless adds to the drama. Cycling good (bike hire in Cannich 01456 415251) as is the detour to Tomich and Plodda Falls (1677/WATERFALLS). Stop at Dog Falls (17053/PICNICS).

1666
MAP 3
A2
✓ ✓ ✓ **GLEN LYON, nr ABERFELDY:** One of Scotland's crucial places both historically and geographically, much favoured by fishers/walkers/Munro-baggers. Wordsworth and Tennyson, Gladstone and Baden Powell all sang its praises. Site of ground-breaking theatre 'The Path' in 2000. The Lyon is a classic Highland river tumbling through corries, gorges and riverine meadows. Several Munros are within its watershed and rise gloriously on either side. Rd all the way to the loch side (30km). Eagles soar over the remoter tops at the head of the glen. Pity we've lost Invervar Lodge.

1667
MAP 2
D1
✓ ✓ **GLEN NEVIS, FORT WILLIAM:** Used by many a film director; easy to see why. Ben Nevis is only part of magnificent scenery. Many walks and convenient facs (1683/WATERFALLS; 2033/SERIOUS WALKS). W Highland Way emerges here. Vis centre & cross river to climb Ben Nevis. Good caff in season (2349/FT WILLIAM). This woody glen is a national treasure.

1668
MAP 2
E2
✓ ✓ **GLEN ETIVE:** Off from more exalted Glencoe (and the A82) at Kingshouse, as anyone you meet in those parts will tell you, this truly is a glen of glens. And, as my friends who camp and climb here implore, it needs no more advertisement. (1301/CAMPING, 1743/POOLS)

1669
MAP 6
C3
STRATHCARRON, nr BONAR BRIDGE: You drive up the N bank of this Highland river from the br o/side Ardgay (pron 'Ordguy') which is 3km over the br from Bonar Br. Rd goes 15km to Croick and its remarkable church (1829/CHURCHES). The river gurgles and gushes along its rocky course to the Dornoch Firth and there are innumerable places to picnic, swim and stroll further up. Quite heavenly on a warm day.

1670
MAP 3
C1
THE ANGUS GLENS: Glen Clova/Glen Prosen/Glen Isla. All via Kirriemuir. Isla to W is a woody, approachable glen with a deep gorge, on B954 nr Alyth (1687/WATERFALLS) and the lovely Glenisla Hotel (1265/INNS). Others via B955, to Dykehead then rd bifurcates. Both glens stab into the heart of the Grampians. 'Minister's Walk' goes betw them from behind the kirk at Prosen village over the hill to B955 before Clova village (7km). Glen Clova is a walkers' paradise esp from Glendoll 24km from Dykehead; limit of rd. Viewpoint. 'Jock's Rd' to Braemar and the Capel Mounth to Ballater (both 24km). Good hotel at Clova (995/PERTHSHIRE HOTELS) and famous 'Loops of Brandy' walk (2hrs, 2-B-2); stark and beautiful.

1671
MAP 2
D4
GLENDARUEL: The Cowal Peninsula on the A886 betw Colintraive and Strachur. Humble but perfectly formed glen of R Ruel, from Clachan in S (a kirk and an inn) through deciduous meadowland to more rugged grandeur 10km N. Easy walking and cycling. W rd best. Kilmodan carved stones signed. Inver Cottage on L Fyne a gr coffee/food stop (865/ARGYLL RESTAUS). 2-B-2

1672
MAP 2
D2
GLEN LONAN, nr TAYNUILT: Betw Taynuilt on A85 and A816 S of Oban. Another quiet wee glen, but all the rt elements for walking, picnics, cycling and fishing or just a run in the car. Varying scenery, a bubbling burn (the R Lonan), some standing stones and not many folk. Angus' Garden at the Taynuilt end should not be missed (1599/GARDENS). No marked walks; now get lost! 2-B-2

1673
MAP 1
B2
GLEN TROOL, nr NEWTON STEWART: 26km N by A714 via Bargrennan which is on the S Upland Way (1894/LONG WALKS). A gentle wooded glen of a place around L Trool. One of the most charming, accessible parts of the Galloway Forest Park. (1971/MARY, CHARLIE, BOB.) Start of the Merrick climb (2001/HILLS).

1674
MAP 3
B3
THE SMA' GLEN, nr CRIEFF: Off the A85 to Perth, the A822 to Amulree and Aberfeldy. Sma' meaning small, this is the valley of the R Almond where the Mealls (lumpish, shapeless hills) fall steeply down to the rd. Where the rd turns away from the river, the long distance path to L Tay begins (28km). Sma' Glen, 8km, has good picnic spots, but they get busy and midgy in summer.

1675 **STRATHFARRAR, nr BEAULY or DRUMNADROCHIT:** Rare unspoiled glen
MAP 5 accessed from A831 leaving Drumnadrochit on L Ness via Cannich (30km) or
D2 S from Beauly (15km). Signed at Struy. Arrive at gatekeeper's house. Access
restricted to 25 cars per day (Cl Tue and Sun till 1.30pm). For access Oct-Mar
01463 761260; you must be out by 6pm. 22km to head of glen past lochs.
Good climbing, walking, fishing. The real peace & quiet!

THE MOST SPECTACULAR WATERFALLS

One aspect of Scotland that really is improved by rain. All the walks to these falls
are graded 1-A-1 unless otherwise stated (see p. 12 for walk codes).

1676 ✔✔ **FALLS OF GLOMACH:** 25km Kyle of Lochalsh off A87 nr Shiel Br, past
MAP 5 Kintail Centre at Morvich then 2km further up Glen Croe to br. Walk
C2 starts other side; there are other ways, (e.g. from the SY Hostel in Glen Affric),
but this is most straightforward. Allow 5/7 hrs for the pilgrimage to one of
Britain's highest falls. Path is steep but well trod. Glomach means gloomy and
you might feel so, peering into the ravine; from precipice to pool, it's 200m.
But to pay tribute, go down carefully to ledge. Vertigo factor and sense of
achievement both fairly high. (1246/HOSTELS.) Consult *Where to Walk in Kintail,*
Glenelg & Lochalsh, sold locally for the Kintail Mt Rescue Team.   2-C-3

1677 ✔✔ **PLODDA FALLS, nr TOMICH, nr DRUMNADROCHIT:** A831 from L
MAP 5 Ness to Cannich (20km), then 7km to Tomich, a further 5km up
D2 mainly woodland track to car park. 200m walk down through woods of Scots
Pine and ancient Douglas Fir to one of the most enchanting woodland sites
in Britain and the Victorian iron br over the brink of the 150m fall into the
churning river below. The dawn chorus here must be amazing. Freezes into
winter wonderland (ice climbers from Inverness take advantage). Good hotel
in village (1078/HIGHLANDS HOTELS).

1678 ✔ **FALLS OF BRUAR, nr BLAIR ATHOLL:** Close to the main A9 Perth-
MAP 3 Inverness rd, 12km N of B Atholl nr House of Bruar shopping experience.
B1 (2170/CRAFT SHOPS). Consequently, the short walk to lower falls is v consumer-
led but less crowded than you might expect. The lichen-covered walls of the
gorge below the upper falls (1km) are less ogled and more dramatic. Circular
path is well marked but steep and rocky in places. Tempting to swim on hot
days (1753/SWIMMING HOLES). ☕

1679 ✔ **GLENASHDALE FALLS, ARRAN:** 5km walk from br on main rd at Whiting
MAP 2 Bay. Signed up the burn side, but uphill and further on than you think, so
D6 allow 2hrs (return). Series of falls in a rocky gorge in the woods with paths so
you get rt down to the brim and the pools. Swim here, swim in heaven!   1-B-1

1680 **EAS FORS, MULL:** On the Dervaig to Fionnphort rd 3km from Ulva Ferry; a
MAP 2 series of cataracts tumbling down on either side of the rd. Easily accessible.
B2 There's a path down the side to the brink where the river plunges into the sea.
On a warm day swimming in the sea below the fall is a rare exhilaration.

1681 **LEALT FALLS, SKYE:** Impressive torrent of wild mt water about 20km N of
MAP 5 Portree on the A855. There's a car park on a bend on rt (going N). You can walk
A2 to grassy ledges & look over or go down to beach.
KILT ROCK, a viewpoint much favoured by bus parties, is a few km further
(you look over & along the cliffs). Also…
EAS MOR Glen Brittle nr end of rd. 24km from Sligachan. A mt waterfall with
the wild Cuillins behind and views to the sea. App as part of a serious scramble or merely a 30-min Cuillin sampler. Start at the Memorial Hut, cross the rd,
bear rt, cross burn and then follow path uphill.   2-C-2

1682 **EAS A' CHUAL ALUINN, KYLESKU:** 'Britain's highest waterfall' nr the head of
MAP 6 Glencoul, is not easy to reach. Kylesku is betw Scourie and Lochinver off the
B2 main A894, 20km S of Scourie. There are 2hr cruises at 11am/2pm May-Sept
(and 3pm Fri) outside hotel (1098/INEXP HIGHLAND RESTAUS). Falls are a rather distant prospect, but you may be able to alight and get next boat. The captain's rap
will keep you going. There's also a track to the top of the falls from 5km N of the
Skiag Br on the main rd (4hrs return), but you will need to take directions locally. The water freefalls for 200m, which is 4 times further than Niagara (take pinch
of salt here). There is a spectacular pulpit view down the cliff, 100m to rt. 2-C-3

1683 **STEALL FALLS, GLEN NEVIS, FORT WILLIAM:** Take Glen Nevis rd at r/bout
MAP 2 o/side town centre and drive 'to end' (16km) through glen. Start from the sec-
D1 ond & final car park, following path marked Corrour, uphill through the woody
gorge with R Ness thrashing below. Glen eventually and dramatically opens
out and there are gr views of the long veils of the Falls. Precarious 3-wire br for
which you will also need nerves of steel. Always fun to see the macho types
bottle out of doing it!   3-A-3

1684 **CORRIESHALLOCH GORGE/FALLS OF MEASACH:** Jnct of A832 and A835,
MAP 6 20km S of Ullapool; possible to walk down into the gorge from both rds. Most
B3 dramatic app is from the car park on the A832 Gairloch rd. Staircase to swing
br from whence to consider how such a wee burn could make such a deep
gash. V impressive. A must-stop on the way to Ullapool.

1685 **THE GREY MARE'S TAIL:** On the wildly scenic rd betw Moffat and Selkirk, the
MAP 3 A708. About halfway, a car park and signs for waterfall. 8km from Tibby Shiels
C6 Inn. The lower track takes 10/15mins to a viewing place still 500m from falls;
the higher, on the other side of the Tail burn, threads betw the austere hills
and up to L Skene from which the falls overflow (45/60mins). Mountain goats.

1686 **THE FALLS OF CLYDE, NEW LANARK, nr LANARK:** Dramatic falls in a long
MAP 3 gorge of the Clyde. New Lanark, the conservation village of Robert Owen the
B5 social reformer, is signed from Lanark. It's hard to avoid the 'award-winning'
tourist bazaar, but the riverbank has… a more natural appeal. The path to the
Power Station is about 3km, but the route doesn't get interesting till after it, a
1km climb to the first fall (Cora Linn) and another 1km to the next
(Bonnington Linn). Swimming above or below them is not advised (but it's gr).
Certainly don't swim on an 'open day', when they close the station and divert
all the water back down the river in a mighty surge (twice a year when we
asked; details from TIC: 01555 661661). There is a gr Italian restau in Lanark
and one of the mills is now a hotel (532/HOTELS O/SIDE GLASGOW). The strange
uniformity of New Lanark is better when the other tourists have gone home.

1687 **REEKIE LINN, ALYTH:** 8km N of town on back rds to Kirriemuir on B951 betw
MAP 3 Br of Craigisla and Br of Lintrathen. A picnic site and car park on bend of rd
C2 leads by 200m to the wooded gorge of Glen Isla with precipitous viewpoints
of defile where Isla is squeezed and falls in tiers for 100ft. Can walk further
along the glen. Loch side restau nearby (1005/PERTHSHIRE EATS) and tearoom.

1688 **FALLS OF ACHARN nr KENMORE, LOCH TAY:** 5km along S side of loch on
MAP 3 unclass rd. Walk from nr bridge in township of Acharn; falls are signed.
A2 Steepish start then 1km up side of gorge; waterfalls on other side. Can be cir-
cular route.

1689 **FALLS OF ROGIE, nr STRATHPEFFER:** Car park on A835 Inverness-Ullapool
MAP 5 rd, 5km Contin/10km Strathpeffer. Accessibility makes short walk (250m)
D1 quite popular to these hurtling falls on the Blackwater R. Br (built by T Army)
and salmon ladder (they leap in summer). Woodland trails marked, include a
circular route to Contin (2064/WOODLAND WALKS).

1690 **FOYERS, LOCH NESS:** On southern route from Ft Augustus to Inverness, the
MAP 5 B862 (1716/SCENIC ROUTES) at the village of Foyers (35km from Inverness). Park
D2 next to shops and cross rd, go through fence and down steep track to viewing places (slither-proof shoes advised). R Foyers falls 150m into foaming
gorge below and then into L Ness throwing clouds of spray into the trees (you
may get drenched).

1691 **FALLS OF SHIN, nr LAIRG, SUTHERLAND:** 6km E of town on signed rd, car
MAP 6 park and falls nearby are easily accessible. Not quite up to the splendours of
C3 others on this page, but an excellent place to see salmon battling upstream
(best June-Aug). Visitor centre with extensive shop; the café/restau is ok
(1097/INX RESTAUS) & you can leave with some junk in a Harrods bag. ☕

1692 ✓ ✓ **LOCH MAREE:** A832 betw Kinlochewe and Gairloch. Dotted with
MAP 6 islands covered in Scots pine hiding some of the best examples of
A3 Viking graves and apparently a money tree in their midst. Easily viewed from
the rd which follows its length for 15km. Beinn Eighe rises behind you and the
omniscient presence of Slioch is opposite. Aultroy Vistor Centre (5km
Kinlochewe), fine walks from car park further on, good accom at L Maree
Hotel (1070/INEXP HIGHLAND HOTELS).

1693 ✓ ✓ **LOCH AN EILEAN:** An enchanted loch in the heart of the
MAP 5 Rothiemurchus Forest (2054/WOODLAND WALKS *for directions*).
E3 There's a good VC. You can walk rt round the loch (5km, allow 1.5hrs). This is
classic Highland scenery, a landscape of magnificent Scots pine.

1694 ✓ **LOCH ARKAIG:** 25km Ft William. An enigmatic loch long renowned for its
MAP 5 fishing. From the A82 beyond Spean Br (at the Commando Monument)
C2 cross the Caledonian Canal, then on by single track rd through the Clune
Forest and the 'Dark Mile' past the 'Witches' Pool' (a cauldron of dark water
below cataracts), to the loch. Bonnie Prince Charlie came this way before and
after Culloden; one of his refuge caves is marked on a trail.

1695 **LOCH LUBHAIR, nr CRIANLARICH:** The loch you pass (on the rt) on the A85
MAP 2 to Crianlarich (4km), in Glen Dochart, the upper reaches of the Tay water sys-
E3 tem. Small, perfect, with bare hills surrounding and fringed with pines and
woody islets. Beautiful scenery that most people just go past in the car heading for Oban or Ft William. Enquire locally for kayak hire.

1696 **LOCH ACHRAY, nr BRIG O' TURK:** The small loch at the centre of the
MAP 3 Trossachs betw **LOCH KATRINE** (on which the *SS Sir Walter Scott* makes thrice-
A3 daily cruises, 2 on Wed: 01877 376316) and **LOCH VENACHAR.** The A821 from
Callander skirts both Venachar and Achray (picnic sites). Ben Venue and Ben
An rise above: gr walks (1995/HILLS) and views. A one-way forest rd goes round
the other side of L Achray thro Achray Forest (enter and leave from the Duke's
Pass rd betw Aberfoyle and Brig O'Turk). Details of trails from forest VC 3km N
Aberfoyle. Bike hire at L Katrine/Callander/Aberfoyle – it's the best way to see
these lochs.

1697 **GLEN FINGLAS RESERVOIR, BRIG O' TURK:** And while we're on the subject
MAP 3 of lochs in the Trossachs (see above) here's a hidden gem. Although it's man-
A3 made it's a real beauty surrounded by soft green hills & the odd burn bubbling in. App 'thro' Brig O'Turk houses (past the caff; 1482/CAFFS) and park 2km
up road. Walk to right (not 'the Dam' rd although this an interesting 1km diversion on the way back). 5 km walk to head of loch or poss make the loop round
it & back to dam (no path, lots of scrambling, boots only) or go further to
Balquhidder – a walk across the heart of Scotland (2038/GLEN WALKS).

1698 **LOCH MUICK, nr BALLATER:** At head of rd off B976, the S Dee rd at Ballater.
MAP 3 14km up Glen Muick (pron 'Mick') to car park, VC and 100m to loch side.
C1 Lochnagar rises above (2021/MUNROS) and walk also begins here for Capel
Mounth and Glen Clova (1670/GLENS). 3hr walk around loch and any number
of ambles. The lodge where Vic met John is at the furthest pt (well it would
be). Open aspect with grazing deer and not too much forestry.

1699 **LOCH ERIBOLL, NORTH COAST:** 90km W of Thurso. The long sea loch that
MAP 6 indents into the N coast for 15km and which you drive rt round on the main
C1 A838. Deepest natural anchorage in the UK, exhibiting every aspect of loch
side scenery including, alas, fish cages. Ben Hope stands nr the head of the
loch and there is a perfect beach (my own private Idaho) on the coast
(1660/BEACHES). Walks from Hope.

1700 **LOCH TROOL, nr NEWTON STEWART:** The small, celebrated loch in a bowl of
MAP 1 the Galloway Hills reached via Bargrennan 14km N via A714 and 8km to end
B2 of rd. Woodland VC/café on way. Good walks but best viewed from Bruce's
Stone (1971/MARY, CHARLIE AND BOB) and the slopes of Merrick (2001 /HILLS). An
idyllic place.

1701 **LOCH MORAR, nr MALLAIG:** 70km W of Ft William by the A850 (a wildly
MAP 5 scenic and much improved route). Morar village is 6km from Mallaig and a sin-
B3 gle track rd leads away from the coast to the loch (only 500m but out of sight)
then along it for 5km to Bracora. It's the prettiest part with wooded islets,
small beaches, loch side meadows and bobbing boats. The rd stops at a turning place but a track continues from Bracorina to Tarbet and it's poss to connect with a post boat and sail back to Mallaig on L Nevis around 3.30pm
(check TIC). L Morar, joined to the coast by the shortest river in Britain, also has
the deepest water. There is a spookiness about it and just possibly a monster
called Morag. Nice GH (Garramore) nearby (1082/INX HIGHLAND HOTELS).

1702 **LOCH TUMMEL, nr PITLOCHRY:** W from Pitlochry on B8019 to Rannoch (and
MAP 3 the end of the rd), L Tummel comes into view, as it did for Queen Victoria, scin-
B2 tillating beneath you, and on a clear day with Schiehallion beyond
(1734/VIEWS). This N side has good walks (2061/WOODLAND WALKS), but the S rd
from Faskally just o/side Pitlochry is the one to take to get down to the
lochside to picnic etc.

1703 **LOCH LUNDAVRA, nr FORT WILLIAM:** Here's a secret loch in the hills, but not
MAP 2 far from the well-trodden tracks through the glens and the sunny streets of Ft
D1 William. Go up Lundavra Rd from r/bout at W end of main st, out of town, over
cattle grid and on (to end of rd) 8km. You should have it to yourself; good
picnic spots and gr view of Ben Nevis. W Highland Way comes this way
(2026/LONG WALKS).

LOCH LOMOND: The biggest, maybe not the bonniest (1/BIG ATTRACTIONS)
with major VC & retail experience, **LOMOND SHORES**, at S end nr Balloch.

LOCH NESS: The longest; you haven't heard the last of it (3/BIG ATTRACTIONS).

1704
MAP 2
D2
✓ ✓ ✓ **GLENCOE:** The A82 from Crianlarich to Ballachulish is a fine drive, but from the extraterrestrial L Ba onwards, there can be few rds anywhere that have direct contact with such imposing scenery. After Kingshouse and Buachaille Etive Mor on the left, the mts and ridges rising on either side of Glencoe proper are truly awesome. The new VC, more discreet than the former nr Glencoe village, sets the topographical and historical scene. (1378/BLOODY GOOD PUBS; 2032/SERIOUS WALKS; 1957/BATTLEGROUNDS; 1982/SPOOKY PLACES; 1245/HOSTELS.)   NTS

1705
MAP 5
B2
✓ ✓ **SHIEL BRIDGE–GLENELG:** The switchback rd that climbs from the A87 (Ft William 96km) at Shiel Br over the 'hill' and down to the coast opp the Sleat Peninsula in Skye (short ferry to Kylerhea). As you climb you're almost as high as the surrounding summits and there's the classic view across L Duich to the 5 Sisters of Kintail. Coming back you think you're going straight into the loch! It's really worth driving to Glenelg (1497/COFFEE SHOPS, 1302/CAMPING, 1255/INNS) and beyond to Arnisdale & ethereal L Hourn (16km).

1706
MAP 5
B2
✓ ✓ **APPLECROSS:** 120km Inverness. From Tornapress nr Lochcarron for 18km. Leaving the A896 seems like leaving civilisation; the winding ribbon heads into monstrous mts and the high plateau at the top is another planet. It's not for the faint-hearted and Applecross is a relief to see with its campsite/coffee shop and a faraway inn: the legendary Applecross Inn. 1286/GET-AWAY-FROM-IT-ALL. Also see 1504/COFFEE SHOPS, 1305/1309/CAMPING. This hair-raising rd rises 2000' in 6 mls. See how they built it at the Applecross Heritage Centre (2252/HERITAGE).

1707
MAP 5
C1
✓ ✓ **GLEN TORRIDON:** The A896 which follows the glen to Kinlochewe. Starting in delightful Diabeg (1643/COASTAL VILLS) allows views of staggering Ben Alligin, but either side of L Torridon is impressive. Excl hotel (1049/HIGHLAND HOTELS). Towards Kinlochewe there's Liatach & Beinn Elghe (1724/VIEWS). Much to climb, much to merely amaze.

1708
MAP 2
D5
✓ ✓ **ROTHESAY–TIGHNABRUAICH:** A886/A8003. The most celebrated part of this route is the latter, the A8003 down the side of L Riddon to Tighnabruaich along the hill sides which give the breathtaking views of Bute & the Kyles, but the whole way, with its diverse aspects of lochside, riverine and rocky scenery, is supernatural. Includes short crossing betw Rhubodach and Colintraive. Gr hotel/retau at Tighnabruaich (854/ARGYLL HOTELS).

1709
MAP 7
B3
✓ **THE GOLDEN ROAD, SOUTH HARRIS:** The main rd in Harris follows the W coast, notable for bays and sandy beaches (1653/BEACHES). This is the other one, winding round a series of coves and inlets with offshore skerries and a treeless rocky hinterland – the classic Hebridean landscape, esp Finsbay. Tweed is woven in this area; you can visit the crofts but it seems impolite to leave without buying some tweedy token (2226/TWEED).

1710
MAP 6
B2
✓ **LOCHINVER–DRUMBEG–KYLESTROME:** The coast rd N from Lochinver (35km) is marvellous; essential Assynt. Actually best travelled N-S so that you leave the splendid vista of Eddrachilles Bay and pass through lochan, moor and even woodland, touching the coast again by sandy beaches (at Stoer a rd leads 7km to the lighthouse and the walk to the Old Man of Storr, 2070/COASTAL WALKS) and app Lochinver (poss detour to Ardmelvich and beach) with one of the classic long views of Suilven. Excl hotel & restau at Drumbeg half-way round (1253/INNS).

1711
MAP 6
B2
LOCHINVER–ACHILTIBUIE: And S from Lochinver Achiltibuie is 40km from Ullapool; so this is the route from the N; 28km of winding rd/unwinding Highland scenery; through glens, mts and silver sea. Known locally as the 'wee mad rd' (it is maddening if you're in a hurry). Passes Achin's Bookshop (2188/CRAFT SHOPS), the path to Kirkaig Falls and the mighty Suilven.

1712
MAP 5
B3
SLEAT PENINSULA, SKYE: The unclassified rd off the A851 (main Sleat rd) esp coming from S, i.e. take rd at Ostaig nr Gaelic College (gr place to stay nearby: 2341/SKYE); it meets coast after 9km. Affords rare views of the Cuillins from a craggy coast. Returning to 'main' rd S of Isleornsay, pop into the gr hotel pub there (2311/ISLAND HOTELS).

1713 **LEADERFOOT–CLINTMAINS, nr ST BOSWELLS:** The B6356 betw the A68
MAP 3 and the B6404 Kelso–St Boswells rd. This small rd, busy in summer, links Scott's
D6 View and Dryburgh Abbey (1950/ABBEYS; best found by following Abbey
signs) and Smailholm Tower, and passes through classic Border/Tweedside
scenery. Don't miss Irvine's View if you want to see the Borders (1732/VIEWS).
Nice GH (936/BORDER HOTELS).

1714 **BRAEMAR–LINN OF DEE:** 12km of renowned Highland river scenery along
MAP 3 the upper valley of the (Royal) Dee. The Linn (rapids) is at the end of the rd, but
C1 there are river walks and the start of the gr Glen Tilt walk to Blair Atholl
(2035/SERIOUS WALKS). Deer abound.

1715 **BALLATER–TOMINTOUL:** This is the ski road to the Lecht (1982/SKIING), the
MAP 4 A939 which leaves the Royal Deeside rd (A93) W of Ballater before it gets real-
C3 ly royal. A ribbon of road in the bare Grampians, past the sentinel ruin Corgarff
(open to view, 250m walk) and the valley of the trickling Don. Rd proceeds
seriously uphill and main viewpoints are S of the Lecht. There is just nobody
for miles. Walks in Glenlivet estates S of Tomintoul.

1716 **FORT AUGUSTUS–DORES, nr INVERNESS:** The B862 often single-track rd
MAP 5 that follows and, for much of its latter length, skirts L Ness. Much quieter and
D2 more interesting than the main W bank A82. Starts off in rugged country and
follows the extraordinary straight rd built by Wade to tame the Highlands.
Reaches the loch side at Foyers (1690/WATERFALLS) and goes all the way to
Dores (15km from Inverness). There are paths to the shore of the loch.
Fabulous untrodden woodlands nr Errogie (marked) and the spooky grave-
yard adj Boleskin House where Aleister Crowley did his dark magic and Jimmy
Page of Led Zeppelin may have done his. 35km total; worth taking slowly.

1717 **THE DUKE'S PASS, ABERFOYLE–BRIG O'TURK:** Of the many rds through the
MAP 3 Trossachs, this one is spectacular though gets busy; numerous possibilities for
A3 stopping, exploration and gr views. Good viewpoint 4km from L Achray Hotel,
above rd and lay-by. One-way forest rd goes round L Achray. Good hill walking starts (1995/1996/1997/FAVOURITE HILLS) and L Katrine Ferry (2km) 3 times
a day Apr-Oct (01877 376316). Bike hire at L Katrine, Aberfoyle and Callander.

1718 **GLENFINNAN–MALLAIG:** The A830, Road to the Isles. Through some of the
MAP 5 most impressive and romantic landscapes in the Highlands, splendid in any
C2 weather (it does rain rather a lot) to the coast at the Sands of Morar
(1661/BEACHES). This is deepest Bonnie Prince Charlie country (1970/MARY,
CHARLIE AND BOB) and demonstrates what a misty eye he had for magnificent
settings. A full-throttle bikers' dream. The rd is shadowed for much of the way
by the West Highland Railway, which is an even better way to enjoy the
scenery (11/FAVOURITE JOURNEYS). Rd recently improved, esp Arisaig–Mallaig.

1719 **LOCHAILORT–ACHARACLE:** Off from the A830 above at Lochailort and turn-
MAP 2 ing S on the A861, the coastal section of this gr scenery is superb esp in the
C1 setting sun, or in May when the rhodies are out. Glen Uig Inn is rough & ready!
This is the rd to Castle Tioram, which should not be missed (1646/RUINS), & glo-
rious Ardnamurchan.

1720 **AMULREE–KENMORE:** The unclassified single track and often v narrow rd
MAP 3 that leads from the hill-country hamlet of Amulree to cosy Kenmore signed
B2 Glen Quaich. Past L Freuchie, a steep climb takes you to a plateau ringed by
magnificent (distant) mts to L Tay. Steep descent to L. Tay and Kenmore. Don't
forget to close the gates.

1721 **PURE PERTHSHIRE, MUTHILL–COMRIE:** A route which takes you through
MAP 3 some of the best scenery in central Scotland and ends up (best this way
B3 round) in Comrie with its teashops and other pleasures (1505/TEAROOMS;
1751/PICNICS). Leave Muthill by Crieff rd turning left (2km) into Drummond
Castle grounds up a glorious avenue of beech trees (gate open 2-5pm). Visit
gdn (1594/GARDENS) then continue through estate. At gate, go rt, following
signs for Strowan. V quiet rd; we have it to ourselves. First jnct, go left following signs (4km). At T-jnct, go left to Comrie (7km). Best have a map, but if not,
who cares – it's all bonny!

1722 **THE HEADS OF AYR:** The coast rd S from Ayr to Culzean (1825/CASTLES) &
MAP 2 Turnberry (868/AYRSHIRE HOTELS) incl these headlands, gr views of Ailsa Craig &
E6 Arran & some horrible caravan parks. The Electric Brae S of Dunure vill is
famously worth stopping on (your car runs the opp way to the slope). Culzean
grounds are gorgeous.

For views of and around EDINBURGH *and* GLASGOW *see p. 68 and p. 107. No views from hill or mt tops are included here.*

1723
MAP 5
A1
✓ ✓ ✓ **THE QUIRANG, SKYE:** Best app is from Uig direction taking the rt-hand unclassified rd off the hairpin of the A855 above and 2km from town (more usual app from Staffin side is less of a revelation). View (and walk) from car park, the massive rock formations of a towering, contorted ridge. Solidified lava heaved and eroded into fantastic pinnacles. Fine views also across Staffin Bay to Wester Ross. (2335/ISLAND WALKS.)

1724
MAP 6
B3
✓ ✓ ✓ The views of **AN TEALLACH** and **LIATHACH:** An Teallach, that gr favourite of Scottish hill walkers (40km S of Ullapool by the A835/A832), is best viewed from the side of Little L Broom or the A832 just before you get to Dundonald.
The classic view of the other great Torridon mts (**BEINN EIGHE** and **LIATHACH** together, 100km S by rd from Ullapool) in Glen Torridon (1707/SCENIC ROUTES) 4km from Kinlochewe. This viewpt is not marked but it's on the track around L Clair which is reached from the entrance to the Coulin estate off the A896, Glen Torridon rd (be aware of stalking). Park o/side gate; no cars allowed, 1km walk to lochside. These mts have to be seen to be believed.

1725
MAP 5
B2
✓ ✓ From **RAASAY:** There are several fabulous views looking over to Skye from Raasay, the small island reached by ferry from Sconser (2192/MAGICAL ISLANDS). The panorama from Dun Caan, the hill in the centre of the island (444m) is of Munro proportions, producing an elation quite incommensurate with the small effort required to get there. Start from the rd to the 'N End' or ask at the Activity Centre in the big house: the Dolphin Café (& bar). 2-B-2

1726
MAP 2
E3
✓ ✓ **THE REST AND BE THANKFUL:** On A83 L Lomond-Inveraray rd where it's met by the B828 from Lochgoilhead. In summer the rest may be from driving stress and you may not be thankful for the camera-toting masses, but this was always one of the most accessible, rewarding viewpoints in the land. Surprisingly, none of the encompassing hills are Munros but they are nonetheless dramatic. There are mercifully few carpets of conifer to smother the grandeur of the crags as you look down the valley.

1727
MAP 5
B2
✓ **ELGOL, SKYE:** End of the rd, the B8083, 22km from Broadford. The classic view of the Cuillins from across L Scavaig and of Soay & Rum. Cruises (Apr-Oct) in the *Bella Jane* (0800 731 3089) or the more rockin' *AquaXplore* (same no.) to the famous corrie of L Coruisk, painted by Turner, romanticised by Walter Scott; 3 hrs with 90mins ashore or 2 hrs with 1 hr on the *Aqua*. A journey you'll remember.

1728
MAP 6
B3
✓ **THE SUMMER ISLES, ACHILTIBUIE:** The Summer Isles are a scattering of islands seen from the coast of Achiltibuie (and the lounge of the Summer Isles Hotel 1048/HIGHLANDS HOTELS) and visited by boat from Ullapool. But the best place to see them, and the stunning perspective of this western shore is on the road to Altandhu, possibly to the pub there. On way to Achiltibuie, turn rt thro Polbain, on about 2.5km. There's a bench. Sit on it. You're alive!

1729
MAP 2
C1
CAMAS NAN GEALL, ARDNAMURCHAN: 12km Salen on B8007. 4km from Ardnamurchan's Natural History Centre (1791/KIDS) 65km Ft William. Coming esp from the Kilchoan direction, a magnificent bay appears below you, where the rd first meets the sea. Almost symmetrical with high cliffs and a perfect field (still cultivated) in the bowl fringed by a shingle beach. Car park viewpoint and there is a path down. Amazing Ardnamurchan!

1730
MAP 5
D3
GLENGARRY: 3km after Tomdoun t/off on A87, Invergarry-Kyle of Lochalsh rd. Lay-by with viewfinder. An uncluttered vista up and down loch and glen with not a house in sight (pity about the salmon cages). Distant peaks of Knoydart are identified, but not L Quoich nestling spookily and full of fish in the wilderness at the head of the glen. Bonnie Prince Charlie passed this way.

1731
MAP 3
D6
SCOTT'S VIEW, ST BOSWELLS: Off A68 at Leaderfoot Br nr St Boswells, signed Gattonside. 'The View', old Walter's favourite (the horses still stopped there long after he'd gone), is 4km along the rd (Dryburgh Abbey 3km further; 1950/ABBEYS). Magnificent sweep of his beloved Border country, but only in one direction. If you cross the rd and go through the kissing gate and head up the hill towards the jagged standing stone that comes into view, you reach ...

1732 **IRVINE'S VIEW:** The full panorama from the Cheviots to the Lammermuirs.
MAP 3 This, the finest view in southern Scotland, is only a furlong further (than
D6 Scott's View, above). This is where I'd like my bench – unfortunately some bas-
tard has erected a horrible phone mast up there (not that I hardly go anywhere without a moby – but maybe not here).

1733 **THE LAW, DUNDEE:** Few cities have such a single good viewpoint. To N of the
MAP 3 centre, it reveals the panoramic perspective of the city on the estuary of the
D3 silvery Tay. Best to walk from town; the one-way system is a nightmare, tho
there are signposts.

1734 **QUEEN'S VIEW, LOCH TUMMEL, nr PITLOCHRY:** 8km on B8019 to Kinloch
MAP 3 Rannoch. Car park and 100m walk to rocky knoll where pioneers of tourism,
B2 Queen Victoria and Prince Albert, were 'transported into ecstasies' by the view
of L Tummel and Schiehallion (1702/LOCHS; 2061/WOODLAND WALKS). Their
view was flooded by a hydro scheme after WW2, but you get the idea.

1735 **THE RALLYING PLACE OF THE MACLARENS, BALQUIDDER:** Short climb
MAP 3 from behind the church (1942/GRAVEYARDS), signed Creag an Tuire, steep at
A3 first. Superb view down L Voil, the Balquhidder Braes and the real Rob Roy
Country & gr caff with home-baking on your descent (1501/COFFEE SHOPS).

1736 **CALIFER, nr FORRES:** 7km from Forres on A96 to Elgin, turn rt for 'Pluscarden',
MAP 4 follow narrow rd for 5km. Viewpoint is on rd and looks down across Findhorn
B1 Bay and the wide vista of the Moray Firth to the Black Isle and Ben Wyvis.
Fantastic light.

1737 **THE MALCOLM MEMORIAL, LANGHOLM:** 3km from Langholm and signed
MAP 1 from main A7, a single-track rd leads to a path to this obelisk raised to cele-
E2 brate the military and masonic achievements of one John Malcolm. The eulo-
gy is fulsome esp compared with that for Hugh MacDiarmid on the cairn by
the stunning sculpture at the start of the path (1910/MEMORIALS). Views from
the obelisk, however, are among the finest in the S, encompassing a vista from
the Lakeland Fells and the Solway Firth to the wild Border hills. Path 1km.

1738 **DUNCRYNE HILL, GARTOCHARN, nr BALLOCH:** Gartocharn is betw Balloch
MAP 2 and Drymen on the A811, and this view, was recommended by writer and out-
E4 doorsman Tom Weir as 'the finest viewpoint of any small hill in Scotland'. Turn
up Duncryne rd at the E end of village and park 1km on left by a small wood
(a sign reads 'Woods reserved for Teddy bears'). The hill is only 470ft high and
'easy', but the view of L Lomond and the Kilpatrick Hills is superb.

1739 **BLACKHILL, LESMAHAGOW, nr GLASGOW:** 28km S of city. Another marvel-
MAP 3 lous outlook, but in the opp direction from above. Take jnct 10/11 on M74,
B6 then off the B7078 signed Lanark, take the B7018. 4km along past Clarkston
Farm, head uphill for 1km and park by Water Board mound. Walk uphill
through fields to rt for about 1km. Unprepossessing hill which unexpectedly
reveals a vast vista of most of E central Scotland.   1-A-2

1740 **TONGUE:** From the causeway across the kyle, or following the minor rd to
MAP 6 Talmine on the W side, look S to the ben, or north to the small islands off the
C1 coast.

1741 **CAIRNPAPPLE HILL nr LINLITHGOW:** Volcanic geology, neolithic henge, E
MAP 3 Scottish agriculture, the Forth plain, the Bridges, Grangemouth industrial
B4 complex & telecoms masts: not all pretty, but the whole of Scotland at a
glance. For directions see 1871/PREHISTORIC SITES.

Care should be taken when swimming in rivers; don't take them for granted. Kids should be watched. Most of these places are trad local swimming and picnic spots where people have swum for yrs, but rivers continuously change their course and their nature. Wearing sandals or old sports shoes is a good idea.

1742
MAP 5
A2
✓ ✓ **THE FAIRY POOLS, GLEN BRITTLE, SKYE:** On a hot day, this is one of the best places on Skye to head for; swimming in deep pools with the massif of the Cuillins around you. One pool has a stone br you can swim under. Head off A863 Dunvegan rd from Sligachan Hotel (2341/SKYE) then B8009 and Glenbrittle rd. 7km down just as rd begins to parallel the glen itself, you'll see a river coming off the hills. Park in lay-by on rt. 1km walk, follow this up. Lady Clair Macdonald recs also, the pools at Torrin nr Elgol.

1743
MAP 2
E2
✓ ✓ **THE POOLS IN GLEN ETIVE:** Glen Etive is a wild, enchanted place where people have been camping for yrs to walk and climb in the Glencoe area. There are many grassy landings at the river side as well as these perfect pools for bathing. The first is about 6km from the main Glencoe rd, the A82 at Kingshouse, but just follow the river and find your own. Take midge cream for evening wear. Lots.

1744
MAP 5
E3
✓ ✓ **FESHIEBRIDGE:** At the br itself on the B970 betw Kingussie and Inverdruie nr Aviemore. 4km from Kincraig. Gr walks here into Glen Feshie and in nearby woodland, but under br a perfect spot for Highland swimming. Go down to left from S. Rocky ledges, clear water. One of the best but cold even in high summer.

1745
MAP 3
B2
✓ ✓ **RUMBLING BRIDGE & THE BRAAN WALK nr DUNKELD:** Excl stretch of cascading river with pools, rocky banks & ledges. Just off A9 heading N opp first turning for Dunkeld, the A822 for Aberfeldy, Amulree. Car park on rt after 4km. Connects with forest paths (the Braan Walk) to the Hermitage (2058/WOODLAND WALKS) – 2km. Fab picnic & swimming spot tho take gr care. This is the nearest Highland-type river to Edin (about 1 hr).

1746
MAP 5
D3
✓ ✓ **STRATHMASHIE, nr NEWTONMORE:** On A86 Newtonmore-Dalwhinnie (on A9) to Ft William rd 7km from Laggan, watch for Forest sign. Car parks on either side of the rd. Gr swimming spot, but often campers. Viewpoints, waterfall, pines. If people are here don't despair – there are gr forest walks (see boards) & foll river, there are many other gr pools. Gr café with home-baking 5km towards A9 (1491/TEAROOMS).

1747
MAP 2
E3
✓ ✓ **ROB ROY FALLS, nr INVERARNAN:** A82 N of Ardlui and 3 km past The Drover's Inn (1374/BLOODY GOOD PUBS). Sign on the rt (Picnic Area), height restriction so watch your Landcruiser. Park, then follow the path to the main waterfall where you'll be able to glimpse a secluded upper pool, through the trees. There's an overhanging rock face on one side and smooth slabs at the edge of the falls. Natural suntrap in summer, but the water is 'Baltic' at all times.

1748
MAP 3
C5
✓ **NEIDPATH, PEEBLES:** 2km from town on A72, Biggar rd; sign for castle. Park by Hay Lodge Park or poss the lay-by past the castle track (sometimes by the castle itself). Idyllic setting of a broad meander of the Tweed, with medieval Neidpath Castle, a sentinel above. Two 'pools' (3m deep in av summer) linked by shallow rapids which the adventurous chute down on their backs. Usually a rope-swing at upper pool. TAKE CARE. Also see (2045/GLEN AND RIVER WALKS).

1749
MAP 4
A2
✓ **RANDOLPH'S LEAP nr FORRES:** Spectacular gorge on the mythical Findhorn which carves out some craggy scenery on its way to a gentle coast. This secret glade and fabulous swimming hole are behind a wall and it's difficult to describe how to find them succinctly (*see* 2051/WOODLAND WALKS *for directions*), but it's S of Forres and Nairn and nr Logie Steading, a courtyard of good things (a board there maps out walks). One Randolph of course once leapt here; we just bathe & lie under the trees dreaming of gods (and maybe satyrs).

1750
MAP 5
C2
DOG FALLS, GLEN AFFRIC: Half-way along Glen Affric rd from Cannich before you come to the loch, a well-marked picnic spot and gr place to swim in the peaty waters surrounded by the Caledonian Forest (with trails). Birds well

sussed to picnic potential – your car covered in tits – Hitchcock or what? (2037/GLEN AND RIVER WALKS).

1751
MAP 3
B3
Nr COMRIE: 2 great pools of different character nr the neat little town in deepest Perthshire. **THE LINN**, the town pool: go over humpback br from main A85 W to Lochearnhead, signed The Ross. Take left fork then after 2km there's a parking place on left. River's relatively wide, v pleasant spot. For more adventurous, **GLENARTNEY** is past Cultybraggan training camp (follow signs), (5km) and then MoD range on left until a ruined cottage on rt. Park and walk down to river in glen. What with the twin perils of the Army and the Comrie Angling Club, you might feel you have no right to be here, but you do and this stretch of river is marvellous. Respect the farmland. Follow rd further for more gr picnic spots. Comrie has gr pub/hotel bistro (987/PERTHSHIRE HOTELS) & tearm (1505/TEAROOMS).

1752
MAP 2
D5
NORTH SANNOX BURN, ARRAN: Park at the North Sannox Bridge on the A841 (rd from Lochranza to Sannox Bay) and follow the track W to the deer fence and treeline (1km). Just past there you will find a gt pool with small waterfall, dragonflies and perhaps even an eagle or two above.

1753
MAP 3
B1
FALLS OF BRUAR, nr BLAIR ATHOLL: Just off A9, 12km N of Blair Atholl. 250m walk from **HOUSE OF BRUAR** car park and shopping experience (2170/CRAFTS) to lower fall (1678/WATERFALLS) where there is an accessible large deep pool by the br. Cold, fresh mt water in a woody gorge. The proximity of the 'retail experience' can make it all the more daring.

1754
MAP 1
B2
THE OTTER'S POOL, NEW GALLOWAY FOREST: A clearing in the forest reached by a track, 'The Raider's Rd', running from 8km N of Laurieston on the A762, for 16km to Clatteringshaws Loch. The track, which is only open Apr-Oct, has a toll of £2 and gets busy. It follows the Water of Dee and halfway down the rd – the Otter's Pool. A bronze otter used to mark the spot (it got nicked) and it's a place mainly for kids and paddling; but when the dam runs off it can be deep enough to swim. Rd closes dusk. (2062/WOODLAND WALKS.)

1755
MAP 3
D6
ANCRUM: A secret place on the quiet Ale Water (out of village towards Lilliesleaf, 3km out 500m from farm sign to Hopton – a recessed gate on the rt before a bend and a rough track). A meadow, a Border burn, a surprisingly deep pool to swim. Arcadia!

1756
MAP 3
B4
PARADISE, SHERIFFMUIR, nr DUNBLANE: A pool at the foot of an unexpected leafy gorge on the moor betw the Ochils and Strathallan. Here the Wharry Burn is known locally as 'Paradise', and for good reason. Take rd from 'behind' Dunblane or Br of Allan to the Sheriffmuir Inn (908/PUB FOOD); head downhill (back) towards Br of Allan and park 1km after the hump back br. Head for the pylon nearest the river & you'll find the pool. Swim/picnic then back to the pub. It can be midgy and it can be perfect.

1757
MAP 4
C3
POTARCH BRIDGE & CAMBUS O'MAY on the DEE: 2 places on the 'Royal' Dee, the first by the reconstructed Victorian br (and nr the hotel) 3km E of Kincardine O'Neill. Cambus another stretch of river E of Ballater (6km). Locals swim, picnic on rocks, etc, and there are forest walks on the other side of rd. The brave jump off the bridge at Cambus – best just to watch. Gr tearm nearby – The Black Faced Sheep in Aboyne (1490/TEAROOMS).

1758
MAP 5
D2
INVERMORISTON: On main L Ness rd A82 betw Inverness and Ft Augustus, this is the best bit. R Moriston tumbles under an ancient br. Perfectly Highland. Ledges for picnics, invigorating pools, ozone-friendly. Nice beech woods. Tavern/bistro nearby (1277/INNS).

1759
MAP 4
A2
DULSIE BRIDGE, nr NAIRN: 16km S of Nairn on the A939 to Grantown, this locally revered beauty spot is fabulous for summer swimming. The ancient arched br spans the rocky gorge of the Findhorn (again) and there are ledges and even sandy beaches for picnics and from which to launch yourself or paddle into the peaty waters.

STRATHCARRON, nr BONAR BRIDGE: Pick your spot (1669/GLENS).

CENTRAL:

1760
MAP A
xA3
✓✓ **EDINBURGH ZOO:** 0131 334 9171. Corstorphine Rd. 4km W of Princes St. A large and long-established zoo, where the natural world from the poles to the plains of Africa is ranged around Corstorphine Hill. Enough huge/exotic/ghastly creatures and friendly, amusing ones to fill an overstimulated day. The penguins and the seals do their stuff at set times. More familiar creatures hang out at the 'farm'. Café and shop stocked with PC toys and souvenirs. Open AYR 7 days. Apr-Sept 9am-6pm, Nov-Feb 9am-5pm, Mar & Oct 9am-5.30pm.

✓✓ **OUR DYNAMIC EARTH, EDINBURGH:** 0131 550 7800. Holyrood Rd. Edinburgh's major kids' attraction. Report 396/ATTRACTIONS.

✓✓ **MUSEUM OF CHILDHOOD, EDINBURGH:** 0131 529 4142. 42 High St. An Aladdin's cave of toys for all ages. 406/ATTRACTIONS.

1761
MAP 3
C5
✓ **EDINBURGH BUTTERFLY FARM & INSECT WORLD, nr DALKEITH and EDINBURGH:** 0131 663 4932. On A7, signed Eskbank/Galashiels from ring rd (1km). Part of a gdn centre complex and the swish **BIRDS OF PREY CENTRE** (flying displays; kids can handle some of the birds, phone for details 0131 654 1720). As for the bugs, the butterflies are delightful but kids will be far more impressed with the scorpions, locusts and other assorted uglies on show. Red-kneed tarantula not for the faint-hearted. 7 days, 9.30am-5.30pm (10am-5pm in winter).

1762
MAP B
✓ **GLASGOW SCIENCE CENTRE:** 0141 420 5000. Glasgow's newest and most flash attraction. State-of-the-art interactive, landmark tower & Imax. Report 761/MAIN ATTRACTIONS.

1763
MAP A
GORGIE CITY FARM, EDINBURGH: 0131 337 4202. 57 Gorgie Rd. A working farm on busy rd in the heart of the city. Friendly domestic animals, garden & café. AYR 9.30m-4.30pm (4pm in wint). Free.

1764
MAP A
D3
THE EDINBURGH DUNGEON: 0131 204 1000. 31 Market St. Multimillion très contrived experience takes you thro a ghoulish history of Scottish nasties. Hammy of course, but kids will love the monorail. 7 days 10am-7pm summer, 10am-5pm wint.

1765
MAP 3
B3
AUCHINGARRICH WILDLIFE CENTRE, nr COMRIE: 4km from main st turning off at br then signed. Sympathetic corralling in picturesque Perthshire Hills. Excl for kids. Huge playbarn. Daily hatchings & lots of baby fluffy things, some of which you can hold. Don't ask what happens to them when they grow up! Good place to start sex education. Emus and meerkats especially weird. Apr-Oct(ish) 10am-dusk. Coffee shop till 5pm.

1766
MAP 2
E5
KELBURN COUNTRY CENTRE, LARGS: 2km S of Largs on A78. Riding school, gdns, woodland walks up the Kel Burn and a central visitor/consumer section with shops/exhibits/cafés. Wooden stockade for clambering kids; commando assault course for exhibitionist adults and less doddering dads. Falconry displays (and long-suffering owl). 'The Plaisance' indeed a pleasant place. Combine with Vikingar (2126/LEISURE CENTRES) for an exhausting day. Stock up at Nardini's (1542/ICE CREAM). 7 days 10am-6pm. Apr-Oct. Grounds only in wint 11-5pm.

✓✓ **FALKIRK WHEEL, FALKIRK:** Report: 4/MAIN ATTRACTIONS.

FIFE AND DUNDEE:

1767
MAP 3
C4
✓ **DEEP SEA WORLD, N QUEENSFERRY:** 01383 411411. The aquarium in a quarry which may be reaching its swim-by date. Park'n'ride system and buses from Edin, or better still by *Maid of the Forth* from S Queensferry (9/FAVOURITE JOURNEYS). Habitats are viewed from a conveyor belt where you can stare at the fish and diverse divers teeming around and above you. Maximum hard sell to this all-weather attraction, but kids like it even when they've been queueing for aeons (ask about the 'fast track' route). Cafe is fairly awful, but nice views. Open AYR 7 days: summer 10am-6pm; winter 11am-5pm.

1768
MAP 3
D3
✓ **SENSATION, DUNDEE:** 01382 228800. Greenmarket across r/bout from Discovery Pt and adj DCA (2273/GALLERIES). Purpose-built indoor kids info-tainment attraction. With basis in Dundee's 'Discover Yourself' & 'Scientific Centre of Excellence' claims, this is an innovative and v interactive games room with a message. We all learn something. 7 days 10am-5pm.

1769
MAP 3
D3
✓ **VERDANT WORKS, DUNDEE:** 01382 225282. West Henderson's Wynd nr Westport. Heritage museum that recreates workings of a jute mill. Sounds dull, but brilliant for kids and grown-ups. Report: 2246/MUSEUMS. ☕

1770
MAP 3
D3
✓ **CRAIGTON PARK, ST ANDREWS:** 01334 473666. 6km SW of St Andrews on the Pitscottie rd. An oasis of fun: bouncy castles, trampolines, putting, crazy golf, boating lake, a train thro the grounds, adventure playgrounds and glasshouses. A perfect day's amusement esp for nippers. 10.30am-5.30pm (wint: w/ends only).

1771
MAP 3
D3
CAMPERDOWN PARK, DUNDEE: The large park just off the ring-road system (the Kingsway and via A923 to Coupar Angus) with a wildlife centre and a nearby play complex. Animal-handling at w/ends. 'Over 80 species'. Open AYR, but centre 10am-4.30pm, earlier in winter (1630/TOWN PARKS).

SOUTH AND SOUTH WEST:

1772
MAP 2
E5
✓ **THE BIG IDEA, IRVINE:** 08708 404030. Opened in 2000 but closed at TGP wtih funding issues. Well worth a visit if it re-opens (check TIC). TBI bills itself as the world's first inventor centre. Enough going on to fill 3-4 hrs easily.

1773
MAP 2
E6
✓ **KIDZ PLAY, PRESTWICK:** 01292 475215. Off main st at Station rd, past stn to beach and to rt. Big shed soft play area for kids. Everything that the little blighters will like in the throwing-themselves-around department. Shriek city. Sun-Thur 9.30am-7pm. Fri-Sat 9.30am-7.30pm.

1774
MAP 3
A6
✓ **LOUDOUN CASTLE, nr GALSTON:** Theme park with big ambitions S of Glas. Off A71 Kilmarnock-Edin rd (go from Glas via A77 Kilmarnock rd). Behind the ruins of the said Loudon Castle (burned out in 1941), a fairground which includes the 'largest carousel in Europe' and 'chairy plane', has been transplanted in the old walled gdn. Nice setting. Big plans afoot for Loudoun at TGP. Open Easter-Sep.

1775
MAP 1
C3
✓ **CREAM O' GALLOWAY, RAINTON:** Famously good ice-cream factory but much more: adventure playground with '3D maze', 5km of child-friendly nature trails & then the ice-cream. Report 1537/ICE CREAM.

1776
MAP 3
A4
PALACERIGG COUNTRY PARK, CUMBERNAULD: 01236 720047. 6km E of Cumbernauld. 740 acres of parkland; ranger service, nature trails, picnic area and kids farm. 18-hole golf course and putting green. Exhib area with changing exhibits about forestry, conservation etc. Open AYR: 7 days; daylight hrs. Visitor centre and tearoom till 6pm in summer, 4.30pm winter.

1777
MAP 3
D6
HARESTANES COUNTRY VISITOR CENTRE: 01835 830306. Lovely old farm converted into café, art gallery with great child's play equip. Adventure playground, woodland walks. Many ranger-led activities and seasonal events.

✓✓ **DRUMLANRIG CASTLE, nr DUMFRIES:** 1613/COUNTRY PARKS.

NORTH EAST

1778
MAP 4
D1
✓ **MACDUFF MARINE AQUARIUM:** On seafront E of the harbour, a family attraction for this under-rated Moray Firth port. Under-rated perhaps because neighbouring Banff gets more attention from tourists, but Duff House (2278/GALLERIES) gets fewer visitors than this user- and child-friendly sea-life centre. All the fish seem curiously happy with their lot and content to educate and entertain. Open AYR 10-5pm.

1779
MAP 4
E2
✓ **ADEN, MINTLAW, nr PETERHEAD:** (pron 'Ah-den'). Country park just beyond Mintlaw on A950 16km from Peterhead. Former grounds of mansion with walks and organised activities and events. Farm buildings converted into Heritage Centre (kids free), café etc. Adventure playground. AYR.

1780
MAP 4
D3
✓ **STORYBOOK GLEN, nr ABERDEEN:** Fibreglass fantasy land in verdant glen 16km S of Aber via B9077, the S Deeside rd, a nice drive. Characters from every fairy tale and nursery story dotted around 20-acre park. Their fixed

manic stares give them a spooky resemblance to people you know. Older kids may find it tame – no guns, no big technology but nice for little 'uns. Indoor play area. 7 days, 10am-4pm weather permitting.

1781 ✓ **SATROSPHERE, ABERDEEN:** Nr beach (off Beach Boulevard, nr Patio
MAP 4 Hotel), Scotland's 'original interactive science centre'. Hands on, it is!
D3 Granny will learn as much as she can take in. AYR. 7 days 10am-5pm.

HIGHLANDS & ISLANDS

1782 ✓ **THE CAIRNGORM REINDEER HERD nr AVIEMORE:** 01479 810363. Stop
MAP 5 at Centre (shop, exhibition) to buy tickets and follow the guide in your
E3 vehicle up the mountain. From here, 20 min walk. At Glenmore Forest Park on rd from Coylumbridge 12km from Aviemore. Real reindeer aplenty in reasonably authentic free-ranging habitat (when they come down off the cloudy hillside in winter with snow all around). They've come a long way from Sweden (in 1952). 1hr 30min trip. They are so …small. 11am AYR plus 2.30pm in summer. Wear appropriate footwear and phone if weather looks threatening.

1783 ✓ **LEAULT FARM nr KINCRAIG:** On the main A9, but easier to find by look-
MAP 5 ing for sign 1km S of Kincraig on the B9152. Working farm with daily
E3 sheepdog trials where Neil Ross demonstrates his extraordinary facility with dogs and sheep (and ducks). A gr spectacle and totally authentic in this setting. Usually noon and 4pm (May-Oct, also 10 and 2pm July/Aug). Cl Sat.

1784 ✓ **LANDMARK CENTRE, CARRBRIDGE:** 01479 841614. A purpose-built
MAP 5 tourist centre with audiovisual displays and a gr deal of shopping. Gr for
E2 kids messing about in the woods on slides, in a 'maze' etc, in a large adventure playground, Microworld or (esp squealy) the Wildwater Coaster. The Tower may be too much for Granny but there are fine forest views. Open AYR 7 days till 6pm.

1785 **THE HIGHLAND WILDLIFE PARK, KINCRAIG:** On B9152 betw Aviemore and
MAP 5 Kingussie. Large drive-through 'reserve' run by Royal Zoological Society with
E3 wandering herds of deer, bison etc and pens of other animals. 'Habitats', but mostly cages. Must be time to bring back bears, let the wolves go free and liven up the caravan parks. Open 10-6pm (July/Aug 7pm, wint 4pm).

1786 **ISLAY WILDLIFE INFO & FIELD CENTRE, PORT CHARLOTTE:** 01496 850288.
MAP 2 Fascinating wildlife centre, activities and day trips. (1820/WILDLIFE; 2340/ISLAY).
B5

1787 **WINGS OVER MULL, CRAIGNURE, MULL:** 01680 812594. Whatever you think
MAP 2 about falconry, this is a wonderful place for the Balamory bairns to see these
C2 elusive birds of prey up close. Regular flying displays and birds on perches – not by choice we suppose. Meanwhile swallows flit above them. Check out the bald eagle & Soo & Boo the owls. Apr-Oct 7 days.

1788 **THE SCOTTISH SEALIFE SANCTUARY, OBAN:** 01631 720386. 16km N on the
MAP 2 A828. On the shore of L Creran this one of the oldest of a number of UK water-
D2 worlds still the best (another in **ST ANDREWS**). Environmentally conscientious they 'rescue' seals and house numerous aquatic life. The new, multi-level viewing otter enclosure is spectacular. Café/shop/adventure playground. Open summer, 10am-6pm. Call for winter hrs.

1789 **RARE BREEDS FARM, OBAN:** 4km from town via Argyll Sq, then S (A816),
MAP 2 bearing left at church, past golf course. Weird and wonderful collection of ani-
D2 mals in hill side pens and runs and a touchy-feely barn, who seem all the more peculiar because they're versions of familiar ones. Leaving the caging questions aside, it's a funny farm for kids and the creatures seem keen enough for the attention and crumbs from the tearoom table. New owners. 7 days in season.

1790 **ARGYLL WILDLIFE PARK, INVERARAY:** 4km W of town on A83. Another zoo-
MAP 2 type place, but with many native animals in more or less their natural habitat.
D3 Lots of them just wander and waddle about. Set amongst pinewoods on the braes of L Fyne, there are probably even a few animals e.g. mink and foxes, trying to get in. (They recently got some of the wallabys.) Many badgers, wildcats, deer and multifarious wildfowl. AYR, 10-5pm, 7 days.

1791 **NATURAL HISTORY CENTRE, ARDNAMURCHAN:** 01972 500209. A861
MAP 2 Strontian, B8007 Glenmore 14km. Photographer Michael McGregor's award
C1 winning interactive exhib; under new owners. Kids will enjoy, adults may be impressed. Tearoom. Mon-Sat; 10.30am-5.30pm. Sun; 12-5.30pm.

THE BEST PLACES TO SEE BIRDS

See p. 222 for WILDLIFE RESERVES, *many of which are good for bird-watching.*

1792
MAP 6
B2
✓ ✓ **HANDA ISLAND, nr SCOURIE, SUTHERLAND:** Take the boat from Tarbet Pier 6km off A894 5km N of Scourie and land on a beautiful island run by the Scottish Wildlife Trust as a sea bird reserve. Boats (Apr-mid Sept though fewer birds after Aug) are continuous depending on demand (01971 502347). Crossing 30mins. Small reception hut and 2.5km walk over island to cliffs which rise 350m and are layered in colonies from fulmars to shags. Allow 3 to 4hrs. Perhaps you can persuade the boatman to go to see the cliffs and the formidable stack from below. Though you must take care not to disturb the birds, you'll be eye to eye with seals and bill to bill with razorbills. Eat at the seafood café on the cove when you return (1452/SEAFOOD RESTAUS). Mon-Sat only (some Suns in summer).

1793
MAP 1
D2
✓ ✓ **CAERLAVEROCK, nr DUMFRIES:** 17km S on B725 nr Bankend, signed from rd. The WWT Caerlaverock Wetlands Centre (01387 770200) is an excellent place to see whooper swans, barnacle geese and more (countless hides, observatories, viewing towers). Has Fair Trade café as well as farmhouse-style accom for up to 14 (INX). More than just birds too: natterjack toads, badgers so not just for twitchers. Eastpark Farm, Caerlaverock. Centre open daily AYR 10am-5pm.   ADMN

1794
MAP 2
B2
✓ ✓ **LUNGA and THE TRESHNISH ISLANDS:** Off Mull. Sail from Iona or Fionnphort or Ulva ferry on Mull to these uninhabited islands on a 5/6hr excursion which probably takes in Staffa and Fingal's Cave. Best months are May-July when birds are breeding. Some trips allow 3hrs on Lunga. Razorbills, guillemots & a carpet of puffins oblivious to your presence. This will be a memorable day. Boat trips (01688 400242) or ring Tobermory TIC (01688 302182) who will advise of other boatmen. All trips dependent on sea conditions.

1795
MAP 3
D4
✓ ✓ **ISLE OF MAY, FIRTH OF FORTH:** Island at mouth of Forth off Crail/Anstruther reached by daily boat trip from Anstruther Harbour (01333 310103), May-Oct 9am-2.30pm depending on tides. Boats hold 40-50; trip 45mins; allows 3hrs ashore. Island (including isthmus to Rona) 1.5km x 0.5km. Info centre and resident wardens. See guillemots, razorbills and kittiwakes on cliffs and shags, terns and thousands of puffins. Most populations increasing. This place is strange as well as beautiful. The puffins in early summer are, as always, engaging.

1796
MAP 3
C4
✓ **THE LAGOON, MUSSELBURGH:** On E edge of town behind the racecourse (follow rd round, take turn-off signed Levenhall Links), at the estuarine mouth of the R Esk. Waders, sea birds, ducks aplenty and often interesting migrants on the mudflats and wide littoral. The 'lagoon' itself is a man-made pond behind with hide and attracts big populations (both birds and binocs). This is the nearest diverse-species area to Edin (15km) and in recent yrs has become one of the most significant migrant stopovers in the UK.

1797
MAP 3
E1
✓ **FOWLSHEUGH, nr STONEHAVEN:** 8km S of Stonehaven and signed from A92 with path from Crawton. Sea-bird city on 2km of red sandstone cliffs up to 200' high; take gr care. 80,000 pairs of 6 species esp guillemots, kittiwakes, razorbills and also fulmar, shag, puffins. Poss to view the birds without disturbing them and see the 'layers' they occupy on the cliff face. Or go by boat thrice weekly in summer from Stonehaven Harbour (check TIC for details 01224 288828). Best seen May-July.

1798
MAP 3
B2
✓ **LOCH OF THE LOWES, DUNKELD:** 4km NE Dunkeld on A923 to Blairgowrie. Properly managed (Scottish Wildlife Trust) site with double-floored hide and permanent binocs. Main attractions are the captivating ospreys (from early Apr-Aug/Sept). Nest 100m over loch and clearly visible. Their revival is well documented, including diary of movements, breeding history etc. Also otters and pine martens. Hide 10am-5pm.

1799
MAP 5
E2
✓ **LOCH GARTEN, BOAT OF GARTEN:** 3km village off B970 into Abernethy Forest. Famous for the ospreys and so popular that access may be restricted until after the eggs have hatched. 2 car parks: the first has nature trails through Scots pine woods and around loch; other has the main hide 300m away. Extraordinary palaver considering there's only one pair and there

are no fish in the loch so they don't feed there (anyhow fish farms are easier). Och, but they are magnificent.

1800
MAP 2
B4

✓ **ISLAY, LOCH GRUINART, LOCH INDAAL:** RSPB reserve. Take A847 at Bridgend then B8017 turning N and rt for Gruinart. The mudflats and fields at the head of the loch provide winter grazing for huge flocks of Barnacle and Greenland geese. They arrive, as do flocks of fellow bird-watchers, in late Oct. Hides and good vantage points near rd. The Rhinns and the Oa in the S sustain a huge variety of bird life.

1801

✓ **MARWICK HEAD, ORKNEY MAINLAND:** 40km NW of Kirkwall, via Finstown and Dounby; take left at Birsay after L of Isbister cross the B9056 and park at Cumlaquoy. Spectacular sea bird breeding colony on 100m cliffs and nearby at the Loons Reserve, wet meadowland, 8 species of duck and many waders. Orkney sites include the Noup cliffs on Westray, North Hill on Papa Westray and Copinsay, 3km E of the mainland. The remoter, the merrier.

1802
MAP 2
B2

ISLE OF MULL: Sea eagles. Since the reintroduction of these magnificent eagles, there is now a hide with CCTV viewing. By appt only. Site changes every yr. Contact Forest Enterprise (01631 566155) or ask at TIC.

1803

ORKNEY PUFFINS: 'Wildabout' tour's dusk puffin patrol (01856 851011). Or go solo at Costa Head, Brough of Birsay and Westray; check Kirkwall TIC for latest.

1804
MAP 3
D4

THE BASS ROCK, off NORTH BERWICK: 01620 892838. 'Temple of gannets'. A gr-guano encrusted spaceship take-off ramp sticking out of the Forth and where Davie Balfour was imprisoned in RLS's *Catriona* (aka *Kidnapped II*). Weather-dependent boat trips available May-Sep courtesy of Chris Marr & the *Sula II*, from N Berwick harbour (also to nearby Fidra). Phone for details.

1805
MAP 3
D4

SCOTTISH SEABIRDS CENTRE, N BERWICK: 01620 890202. Award-winning, interactive visitor attraction nr Harbour o/looking Bass Rock and Fidra. Video and other state-of-the-art technology makes you feel as if the birds are next to you. Viewing deck for dramatic perspective of gannets diving (140kmph!) St Kilda link-up in offing at TGP. 10am-6pm (4pm wint/5.30pm w/ends).

1806
MAP 3
E2

MONTROSE BASIN WILDLIFE CENTRE: 1.5km south of Montrose on the A92 to Arbroath. V accessible Scottish Wildlife Trust centre, opened in '95, overlooks the estuarine basin that hosts various residents and migrants. Good for twitchers and kids. And autumn geese. Apr-Oct daily 10.30am-5pm. Wint hrs, ring 01674 676336.

1807
MAP 6
D2

FORSINARD NATURE RESERVE: By road, 44km from Helmsdale on the A897, or the train stops on route to Wick/Thurso. RSPB reserve, acquired in '95 following public appeal. 17,500 acres of flow country and the birds that go with it: divers, plovers, merlins and hen harriers. Reserve open AYR; VC Apr-Oct daily 9am-6pm.

1808
MAP 3
C2

LOCH OF KINNORDY, KIRRIEMUIR: 4km W of town on B951, an easily accessible site with 3 hides o/look loch and wetland area managed by RSPB. Geese in late autumn, gulls aplenty; always tickworthy.

1809
MAP 3
C2

PIPERDAM GOLF & COUNTRY PARK, FOWLIS by DUNDEE: 01382 581374. This expensive housing development o/looking loch also attracts the upwardly mobile osprey. Gd viewing centre. Other upmarket residents inc short-eared owls & reed buntings (cheers, Anthony, for the tip-off!).

1810
MAP 4
E1

STRATHBEG, nr FRASERBURGH: 12km S off main Fraserburgh-Peterhead rd, the A952 and signed 'Nature Reserve' at Crimond. Wide, shallow loch v close to coastline, a 'magnet for migrating wildfowl' and from the (unmanned) reception centre at loch side it's poss to get a v good view of them. Marsh/fen, dune and meadow habitats. In winter 30,000 geese/widgeon/mallard/swans and occasional rarities like cranes and egrets. Binocs in centre and other hides (new Towerpool hide is 1km walk).

✓ ✓ *The coast around the N of Scotland offers some of the best places in Europe from which to see whales and dolphins and, more ubiquitously, seals. You don't have to go on boat trips, though of course you get closer, the boat-man will know where to find them and the trip itself can be exhilarating. Good operators are listed below. Dolphins are most active on a rising tide esp May-Sept.*

MORAY and CROMARTY FIRTHS, nr INVERNESS and CROMARTY:

The best area in Scotland. The population of bottlenose dolphins in this area well exceeds 100 and they can be seen AYR.

THE DOLPHINS AND SEALS OF THE MORAY FIRTH CENTRE: 01463 731866. Just N of the Kessock Br on the A9 and adj the TIC (01463 731505). Underwater microphones pick up the chatterings of dolphins and porpoises and there's always somebody there to explain. They keep an up-to-date list of recent sightings and all cruises available. Summer only Mon-Sat 9.30am-4.30pm (Wed 4.15pm), Sun 10am-4.30pm.

CROMARTY: Any vantage around the town is good esp S Sutor for coastal walk and an old lighthouse cottage has been converted into a research station run by Aberdeen Uni. **CHANONRY POINT, FORTROSE,** E end of pt beyond lighthouse is the *best* place to see dolphins from land in Britain. Occasional sightings can also be seen at **BALINTORE,** opp Seaboard Memorial Hall; **TAR-BERT NESS** beyond **PORTMAHOMACK,** end of path through reserve further out along the Moray Firth poss at **BURGHEAD, LOSSIEMOUTH** and **BUCKIE, SPEY BAY** and **PORTKNOCKIE.**

NORTH WEST

On the W coast, esp nr Gairloch the following places may offer sightings of orcas, dolphins and minke whales mainly in summer.

RUBHA REIDH nr GAIRLOCH: 20km N by unclassified rd beyond Melvaig. Nr the Carn Dearg Youth Hostel W of Lonemore where rd turns inland is good spot.

GREENSTONE POINT N of LAIDE on the A832 nr Inverewe Gardens and Gruinard Bay. Harbour porpoises here Apr-Dec and minke whales May-Oct.

RED POINT of GAIRLOCH: by unclassified rd via Badachro. High ground looking over N Minch and S to L Torridon. Harbour porpoises often along this coast.

RUBHA HUNISH, SKYE: The far NW finger of Skye. Walk from Duntulm Castle or Flodigarry (2341/SKYE). Dolphins & mink whales in autumn.

OTHER PLACES

MOUSA SOUND, SHETLAND: 20km S of Lerwick (1867/PREHISTORIC SITES).

ARDNAMURCHAN, THE POINT: The most westerly point (and lighthouse) on this wildly beautiful peninsula. Go to end of rd or park nr Sanna Beach and walk round. Sanna Beach is worth going to just to walk the strand. Visitor centre with tearoom and toilets.

STORNOWAY, ISLE OF LEWIS: Heading out of town for Eye Peninsula, at Holm nr Sandwick S of A866 or from Bayble Bay (all within walking distance).

DOLPHIN ECOSSE, CROMARTY: 01381 600323. Intimate and informative tours, but pricey. 2 trips per day AYR. Booking essential.

MORAY FIRTH CRUISES, INVERNESS: 01463 717900. 4 trips per day Apr-Oct.

SUMMER ISLES CRUISES: 01854 622200. Seals & seabirds abound round these beautiful islands. 2 trips per day plus all day special.

WILDLIFE CRUISES, JOHN O' GROATS: 01955 611353. Puffins, seabirds, seals. 2.30pm daily June-Sept. Also all-day trips to Orkney from John o' Groats & Inverness.

SEA.FARI ADVENTURES: Based in **EDINBURGH** (0131 331 5000), **OBAN** (01852 300003) and **SKYE** (01471 833316). Sealife adventure boating specialists. Range of eco-tours & trips in fast, inflatable boats. Same product at 3 locations.

ON THE ISLANDS

SEA-LIFE SURVEYS, MULL: 01688 400223. Various packages from relaxed four hour trip to the more intense eight hour. Small groups on comfortable boat. Good percentage of dolphin & whale sightings.

TURUS MARA, MULL: 08000 858786. Daytrips from Ulva Ferry. Various itineraries taking in bird colonies of Treshnish Isles, Staffa & Iona. Dolphins, whales, puffins & seals. Booking essential.

SHETLAND WILDLIFE & THE COMPANY OF WHALES, SHETLAND: 01950 422483. From day trips to 7-day wildlife holidays. Sealife, birds, whales & otters.

BRESSABOATS, SHETLAND: 01595 693434. Award-winning wildlife adventure cruises.

ISLAND CRUISING, LEWIS: 01851 672381. Wildlife, birdwatching and diving cruises around the Western Isles and St Kilda.

ISLAY MARINE CHARTERS, ISLAY: 01496 850436. Trips on Sound of Islay, round Jura, Colonsay. Fishing & whale watching.

STROND WILDLIFE CHARTERS, HARRIS: 01859 520204. From one hour to full day boat trips to see seals & birdlife of the Sound of Harris. Pay per boat, not per person.

There are two glass-bottom boat companies offering trips in **SKYE. FAMILY'S PRIDE II** (0800 7832175) operate from Broadford Bay and concentrate on the reefs round the local islands. **SEAPROBE ATLANTIS** (0800 9804846) are based on the mainland at Kyle (just over the bridge) and stay around Kyle of Lochalsh area. Sit underwater in the 'gallery' so better viewing advantage.

WILDLIFE TOURS

ISLAND ENCOUNTER WILDLIFE SAFARIS, MULL: 01680 300441. All-day tour with local expert. Possible sightings of otters, eagles, seals and falcons. Numerous pick-up points. Book in advance.

WILDABOUT, ORKNEY: 01856 851011. Various trips with experienced guides. Wildlife plus history & folklore.

OUT & ABOUT TOURS, LEWIS: 01851 612288. Ex-countryside ranger leads groups of all sizes on guided walks and day trips of Lewis and Harris. Experience the landscape, culture and wildlife of the islands.

Otters can be seen all over the NW Highlands in sheltered inlets, esp early morning and late evening and on an ebb tide. Skye is one of best places in Europe to see them. Go with:

INTERNATIONAL OTTER SURVIVAL FUND, BROADFORD: 01471 822487 organise guided walks for all wildlife and might pt you in the rt direction.

OTTER HAVEN, KYLERHEA: Basically a viewing hide with CCTV, binoculars and a knowledgeable warden (not always there). Seabirds & seals too and a forest walk. 500m walk along a track from car park signposted on road out of Kylerhea (& from the ferry from Glenelg – 7/JOURNEYS).

These wildlife reserves are not merely bird-watching places. Most of them are easy to get to from major centres; none requires permits.

1812
MAP 3
E5
✓✓ **ST ABB'S HEAD, nr BERWICK:** 22km N Berwick, 9km N Eyemouth and only 10km E of main A1. Spectacular cliff scenery (2072/COASTAL WALKS), a huge sea bird colony, rich marine life and a varied flora make this a place of fascination and diverse interest. Good view from top of stacks, geos and cliff face full of serried ranks of guillemot, kittiwake, razorbill etc. Hanging gdns of grasses and campion. Behind cliffs, grassland rolls down to the Mire L and its varied habitat of bird, insect and butterfly life and vegetation. Superb.

1813
MAP 4
E2
✓✓ **SANDS OF FORVIE and THE YTHAN ESTUARY, NEWBURGH:** 25km N of Aber. Cross br o/side Newburgh on A975 to Cruden Bay and park. Path follows Ythan estuary and, bearing N, enters the largest dune system in the UK undisturbed by man. Dunes in every aspect of formation. Collieston, a 17/18th-century fishing vill arranged in terraces on the cliffs, is 5km away. These coastal habitats support the largest population of eiders in UK (esp June) and huge numbers of terns. Plenty to see even from main rd lay-bys; also hides. It's easy to get lost here, so get lost!

1814
MAP 5
C1
✓ **BEINN EIGHE:** Bounded by the A832 and A896 W of Kinlochewe, this first National Nature Reserve in Britain includes one of the remaining fragments of old Caledonian pinewood on the S shore of Loch Maree and rises to the rugged mountain tops with their spectacular views & varied geology. Excellent woodland and mountain trails. Best app via Glen Torridon (1707/SCENIC ROUTES). Start from roadside car park (on A832 4km from Kinlochewe). 3km nearer the village on this road is a VC.

1815
MAP 3
D4
JOHN MUIR COUNTRY PARK, DUNBAR: The vast park betw Dunbar and N Berwick named after the naturalist/explorer who was born in Dunbar and who, in founding Yellowstone National Park in the US, is regarded as the father of the Conservation movement. Includes estuary of the Tyne (park also known as Tyninghame), cliffs, sand spits and woodland, it covers a wide range of habitats. Many bird species (e.g. 30 waders), crabs, lichens, sea and marsh plants. Enter at E extremity of Dunbar at Belhaven, off the B6370 from A1; or off A198 to N Berwick 3km from A1. Or better, walk from Dunbar by 'cliff top trail' (2km).

1816
MAP 2
E5
LOCHWINNOCH: 30km SW of Glas via M8 jnct 28A then A737 past Johnstone onto A760. Also from Largs 20km via A760. Reserve is just o/side village on loch side and comprises wetland and woodland habitats. A serious 'nature centre' incorporating an observation tower. Hides and marked trails; and a birds-spotted board. Shop and coffee shop. Good for kids. Centre open daily 10am-5pm (cl Thurs).   RSPB

1817
MAP 5
E3
INSH MARSHES, KINGUSSIE: 4km from town along B970 (after Ruthven Barracks, 1859/RUINS), 2500 acres of Spey floodplain run by RSPB. Trail (3km) marked out through meadow and wetland and a note of species to look out for (including 6 types of orchid, 7 'red list' birds & half the UK population of goldeneye). Also 2 hides (250m and 450m) high above marshes, vantage points to see waterfowl, birds of prey, otters and deer. Declared a National Nature Reserve in 2003.

1818
MAP 3
D3
TENTSMUIR, betw NEWPORT and LEUCHARS: The northern tip of Fife at the mouth of the Firth of Tay, reached from Tayport or Leuchars via the B945. Follow signs for Kinshaldy Beach taking rd that winds for 4km over flat and then forested land. Park amongst Corsican pine plantation (car park closes 9pm in summer) and cross dunes to broad strand which many consider to be a better beach than the W Sands, St Andrews. Walks in both direction: W back to Tayport, E towards Eden Bird Sanctuary. Also 4km circular walk of beach and forest. Hide 2km away at Ice House Pond. Seals often watch from waves and bask in summer. Lots of butterflies. Waders aplenty and, to E, one of UK's most significant populations of eider. Most wildfowl offshore on Abertay Sands.

1819
MAP 3
C4
VANE FARM: RSPB reserve on S shore of L Leven, beside and bisected by B9097 off jnct 5 of M90. Easily reached and v busy VC with observation lounge and education/orientation facs. Hide nearer loch side reached by tunnel under rd. Nature Trail on hill behind through heath and birchwood (2km circ). Good place to introduce kids to nature watching. Events: 01577 862355.

1820 **ISLAY WILDLIFE INFO & FIELD CENTRE, PORT CHARLOTTE:** Jam-packed
MAP 2 info centre that's v 'hands-on' and interactive. Up-to-date displays of geology,
B5 natural history (rocks, skeletons, sealife tanks). Recent sightings of wildlife,
flora and fauna lists, video rm, reference library. Kids' area and activity days
when staff take you on a tour around the surrounding area. Quietly attractive
staff. Check TIC for opening hours.

1821 **BALRANALD, NORTH UIST, WESTERN ISLES:** W coast of N Uist reached by
MAP 7 the rd from Lochmaddy, then the Bayhead t/off at Clachan Stores (10km N).
A3 We have listened for the corncrake, this being one of its last strongholds but
so far not a cheep. However here and there they are…

SECTION 8

Historical Places

NTS: Under the care of the National Trust for Scotland. Hrs vary. HS: Under the care of Historic Scotland. Standard hrs are: Apr-end Sept Mon-Sat 9.30am-6.30pm; Sun 2-6.30pm. Oct-Mar Mon-Sat 9.30am-4.30pm; Sun 2-4.30pm.

1822
MAP 3
B4
✓✓✓ **STIRLING CASTLE:** Dominating the town and the plain, this like Edin Castle is worth the hype and the history. And like Edin, it's a timeless attraction that can withstand waves of tourism as it survived the centuries of warfare for which it was built. Despite this primary function, it does seem a v civilised billet, with peaceful gdns and rampart walks from which the views are excellent (esp the aerial view of the Royal Gdns, 'the cup and saucer' as they're known locally). Incls the Renaissance Palace of James V and the Great Hall of James IV recently restored to full magnificence. Some rock legends also play here in summer (Van Morrison in 2003). The Costa caff is a bit of a letdown in these historical circumstances (but it does hot food). HS

1823
MAP A
C3
✓✓✓ **EDINBURGH CASTLE:** City centre. Impressive from any angle and all the more so from inside. Despite the tides of tourists and time, it still enthralls. Superb perspectives of the city and of Scottish history. Stone of Destiny & the Crown Jewels are the Big Attractions. Café and restau (superb views) with efficient, but uninspiring catering operation; open only castle hrs and to castle visitors. Report: 390/MAIN ATTRACTIONS. HS

1824
MAP 4
A1
✓✓ **BRODIE CASTLE, nr NAIRN:** 6-7km W of Forres off main A96. More a (Z-plan) tower house than a castle, dating from 1567. In this century & like Cawdor nearby, the subject of family feuding. With a minimum of historical hocum, this 16/17th-century, but mainly Victorian, country house is furnished from rugs to moulded ceilings in the most excellent taste. Every picture (v few gloomies) bears examination. The nursery and nanny's rm, the guest rms, indeed all the rms, are eminently habitable. I could live in the library. There are regular musical evenings and other events (01309 641371 for event programme). Tearoom and informal walks in grounds. An avenue leads to a lake; in spring the daffodils are famous. Apr-Sept 12-4pm (cl Fri/Sat May, June, Sept); Sun 1.30-5.30pm. W/ends in Oct. Grounds open AYR till sunset. NTS

1825
MAP 2
E6
✓✓ **CULZEAN CASTLE, MAYBOLE:** 24km S of Ayr on A719. Impossible to convey here the scale and the scope of the house and the country park. Allow some hrs esp for the grounds. Castle is more like a country house and you examine from the other side of a rope. From the 12th century, but rebuilt by Robert Adam in 1775, a time of soaring ambition, its grandeur is almost out of place in this exposed cliff-top position. It was designed for entertaining, and the oval staircase is magnificent. Wartime associations (esp with President Eisenhower) plus the enduring fascination of the aristocracy. 560 acres of grounds including cliff-top walk, formal gdns, walled gdn, Swan Pond (a must) and Happy Valley. Harmonious home farm is VC with café, exhibits and shop etc. Open Apr-Oct 11am-5.30pm. Many special 'events'. Culzean is pron 'Cullane'. And you can stay (870/AYRSHIRE HOTELS). ☕ NTS

1826
MAP 3
C3
✓✓ **FALKLAND PALACE, FALKLAND:** Middle of farming Fife, 15km from M90 jnct 8. Not a castle at all, but the hunting palace of the Stewart dynasty. Despite its recreational rather than political role, it's one of the landmark buildings in Scottish history and in the 16th century was the finest Renaissance building in Britain. They all came here for archery, falcony and hunting boar and deer on the Lomonds; and for Royal Tennis which is displayed and explained. Still occupied by the Crichton-Stewarts, the house is dark and rich and redolent of those days of 'dancin and deray at Falkland on the Grene'. Mar-Oct 10-6pm. Sun 1-5.30pm. Ambitious events programme. 979/FIFE RESTAUS. Gr walks from village (2010/HILL WALKS). (2042/GLEN WALKS). NTS

1827
MAP 4
A1
✓ **CAWDOR CASTLE, CAWDOR, nr NAIRN and INVERNESS:** The mighty Cawdor of Macbeth fame. The famously feuding family clear off for the summer and leave their romantic yet habitable castle, sylvan grounds and gurgling Cawdor Burn to you. Pictures from Claude to John Piper and Conroy, a modern kitchen as fascinating as the enormous one of yore. Even the 'tartan passage' is nicely done. The burn is the colour of tea. An easy drive (25km) to Brodie (above) means you can see 2 of Scotland's most appealing castles in one day. Gdns are gorgeous. May-early Oct, 7 days, 10am-5.30pm, 9-hole golf.

1828 ✔ **BLAIR CASTLE, BLAIR ATHOLL:** Impressive from the A9, the castle and
MAP 3 the landscape of the Dukes of Atholl (present duke not present); 10km N
B1 of Pitlochry. Hugely popular; almost a holiday camp atmos. Numbered rms
chock-full of 'collections': costumes, toys, plates, weapons, stag skulls, walking
sticks – so many things! Upstairs, the more usual stuffed apartments including the Jacobite bits. Walk in the policies (incl 'Hercules Gdn' with tranquil
ponds). Apr-Oct 9.30am-5pm daily.

1829 ✔ **GLAMIS, FORFAR:** 8km from Forfar via A94 or off main A929, Dundee-
MAP 3 Aber rd (t/off 10km N of Dundee, a picturesque app). Fairy-tale castle in
C2 majestic setting. Seat of the Strathmore family (Queen Mum spent her childhood here) for 300 yrs; every rm an example of the interior of a certain period. Guided tours (continuous/50mins duration). Restau/gallery shop haven
for tourists. Easter-mid Oct, 10.30am. Last admn 4.45pm. Italian Gdns & nature
trail well worth 500m walk.

1830 ✔ **BRODICK CASTLE, ARRAN:** 4km from town (bike hire 01770 302868/
MAP 2 302009). Impressive, well-maintained castle, exotic formal gdns and
D5 extensive grounds. Goat Fell in the background and the sea through the trees.
Dating from 13th century and until recently home of the Dukes of Hamilton.
An over-antlered hall leads to liveable rms with portraits and heirlooms, an
atmos of long-ago afternoons. Tangible sense of relief in the kitchens now all
the entertaining is over. Robert the Bruce's cell is not so convincing. Easter-Oct
daily until 4pm (last adm). Marvellous grounds open AYR.   NTS

1831 ✔ **DUART CASTLE, MULL:** 13th-century ancestral seat of the Clan Maclean
MAP 2 who take up residence for the summer and clan gatherings. Quite a few
C2 modifications over the centuries as methods of defence grew in sophistication
but with walls as thick as a truck and the sheer isolation of the place it must
have made any prospect of attack seem doomed from the outset. Of course
the only attacking that gets done these days is on scones in the tearoom but
some scent of the old bloodthirst still remains. May-Oct 10.30am-6pm. ☕

1832 **TOROSAY CASTLE, MULL:** 3km from Craignure and the ferry. A Victorian
MAP 2 *arriviste* in this strategic corner where Duart Castle has ruled for centuries. Not
C2 many apartments open but who could blame them – this is a family home,
endearing and eccentric esp their more recent history (like Dad's Loch Ness
Monster fixation). The heirlooms are valuable because they have been cher-
ished and there's a human proportion to the house and its contents which is
rare in such places. The gdns, attributed to Lorimer, are fabulous, esp the
Italianate Statue Walk, and are open AYR. The Mull Light Railway from
Craignure is one way to go, woodland walk another. Tearoom. Mar-Oct 10am-
6pm. Gardens AYR.

1833 **DUNVEGAN CASTLE, SKYE:** 3km Dunvegan village. Romantic history and
MAP 5 setting, though more baronial than castellate, the result of mid-19th-century
A2 restoration that incorporated the disparate parts. Necessary crowd management leads you through a series of rms where the Fairy Flag, displayed above
a table of exquisite marquetry, has pride of place. Gdns down to the loch,
where boats leave the jetty 'to see the seals'. Busy café and gift shop at gate
side car park. Open AYR, facs Mar-Oct.

1834 **EILEAN DONAN, DORNIE:** On A87, 13km before Kyle of Lochalsh. A calendar
MAP 5 favourite, often depicted illuminated; and with the balloon hovering above,
C2 an abiding image from the BBC promo. Inside it's a v decent slice of history for
the price. The Banqueting Hall with its Pipers' Gallery must make for splendid
dinner parties for the Macraes. Much military regalia amongst the bric-a-brac,
but also the impressive Raasay Punchbowl partaken of by Johnson and
Boswell. Mystical views from ramparts. Mar-Nov, 10-5.30pm.

1835 **CASTLE MENZIES, WEEM, nr ABERFELDY:** In Tay valley with spectacular
MAP 3 ridge behind (there are walks here in the Weem Forest, part of the Tummel
B2 Valley Forest Park; separate car park). On B846, 7km W of Aberfeldy, through
Weem. The 16th-century stronghold of the Menzies (pron 'Ming-iss'), one of
Scotland's oldest clans. Sparsely furnished with odd clan memorabilia, the
house nevertheless conveys more of a sense of Jacobite times than many
more brimful of bric-a-brac. Bonnie Prince Charlie stopped here on the way to
Culloden. Open farmland situation, so manured rather than manicured
grounds. Apr-Oct 10.30am-5pm, Sun 2-5pm. Tearoom.

1836 SCONE PALACE, nr PERTH: On A93 rd to Blairgowrie and Braemar. A 'great
MAP 3 house', the home to the Earl of Mansfield and gorgeous grounds. Famous for
C3 the 'Stone of Scone' on which the Kings of Scotland were crowned, and the
Queen Vic bedroom. Maze and pinetum. Many contented animals greet you
and a plethora of peacocks. Easter–Oct 7days 9.30am-4.45pm (last adm.) Fri
only in wint 10am-4pm.

1837 KELLIE CASTLE, nr PITTENWEEM, FIFE: Major castle in Fife. Dating from 14th
MAP 3 century restored by Robert Lorimer, his influence evidenced by magnificent
D3 plaster ceilings and furniture. The gdns, nursery and kitchen recall all the old
Victorian virtues. The old-fashioned roses still bloom for us. Apr-Sept 1-5pm.
Grounds open AYR.   ADMN

1838 CRAIGIEVAR, nr BANCHORY: 15km N of main A93 Aber-Braemar rd betw
MAP 4 Banchory and Aboyne. A classic tower house, perfect like a porcelain miniature.
C3 Random windows, turrets, balustrades. Set amongst sloping lawns & tall trees.
Limited access to halt deterioration (only 8 people at a time) means you are
spared the shuffling hordes, but don't go unless you are respecter of the NTS
conservation policy. Apr-Sept, Fri-Tues only 12-5.30pm (last adm 4.45pm). NTS

1839 DRUM CASTLE (the IRVINE ANCESTRAL HOME), nr BANCHORY: 1km off
MAP 4 main A93 Aberdeen-Braemar rd betw Banchory and Peterculter and 20km
D3 from Aberdeen centre. For 24 generations this has been the seat of the
Irvines. Our lot! Gifted to one William De Irwin by Robert the Bruce, it
combines the original keep, a Jacobean mansion and Victorian expansionism.
I have twice signed the book in the Irvine Rm and wandered through the
accumulated history hopeful of identifying with something. Hugh Irvine, the
family 'artist' whose extravagant self-portrait as the Angel Gabriel raised eye-
brows in 1810, seems more interesting than most of my soldiering forebears.
Give me a window seat in the library! Grounds have a peaceful walled rose
gdn (Apr-Sept 10-6pm). House: Easter-Sept 12.30-5.30 (from 10am June-Aug).
Tower can be climbed for gr views.   NTS

1840 BALMORAL, nr BALLATER: On main A93 betw Ballater and Braemar. Limited
MAP 4 access to the house (i.e. only the ballrm – public functions are held here when
B3 they're in residence) so grounds (open Apr-July) with Albert's wonderful trees
are more rewarding. For royalty rooters only, and if you like
Landseers …Crathie Church along the main rd has a good rose window, an
altar of Iona marble. John Brown is somewhere in the old graveyard down
track from VC, the memorial on the hill is worth a climb for a poignant
moment and the view of the policies. The Crathie services have never been
quite the same Sunday attraction since Di and Fergie on a prince's arm. Daily
10-5pm, Easter-July.

1841 CASTLE of MEY, CAITHNESS: Off A836 betw Wick & Thurso on the N coast.
MAP 6 The historical home of the Queen Mother, her retreat since 1952. Now with
E1 Prince Charles in charge. Nice, unfussy gardens in dramatic bare north. More
habitable than many on this page, more poignant since the Queen Mum's
passing. End of May-mid Oct, cl 2-13 Aug, but check local TIC. Cl Mon.

1842 DUNROBIN CASTLE, GOLSPIE: The largest house in the Highlands, the home
MAP 6 of the Dukes of Sutherland who once owned more land than anyone else in
C3 the British Empire. It's the first Duke who occupies an accursed place in Scots
history for his inhumane replacement, in these vast tracts, of people with
sheep. His statue stands on Ben Bhraggie above the town (1906/MONUMENTS).
Living the life of English grandees, the Sutherlands transformed the castle
into a *château* and filled it with their obscene wealth. Once there were 100
servants for a house party of 20 and it had 30 gardeners. Now it's all just history. The gdns are still fabulous. The castle and separate museum are open
Apr-mid Oct. Check 01408 633177 for times.   ADMN

CRATHES, nr BANCHORY: 1592/GARDENS; 1897/COUNTRY HOUSES.

FYVIE, ABERDEENSHIRE: 1896/COUNTRY HOUSES.

FASQUE, nr STONEHAVEN: 1887/COUNTRY HOUSES.

FLOORS CASTLE, KELSO: 1852/COUNTRY HOUSES.

TRAQUAIR, INNERLEITHEN: 1889/COUNTRY HOUSES.

THIRLESTANE, LAUDER: 1895/COUNTRY HOUSES.

THE MOST INTERESTING RUINS

HS: *Under the care of Historic Scotland. Standard hrs are: Apr-end Sept 7 days 9.30am-6.30pm. Oct-Mar Mon-Sat 9.30am-4.30pm, Sun 2-4.30pm. Some variations with individual properties; call 0131 668 8831 to check. 'Friends of Historic Scotland' membership: 0131 668 8600 or any of the manned sites (annual charge but then free admn).*

1843
MAP 3
B4
✔ ✔ ✔ **LINLITHGOW PALACE:** Impressive from the M9 and the S app to this most agreeable of W Lothian towns, but don't confuse the magnificent Renaissance edifice with St Michael's Church next door, topped with its controversial crown and spear spire. From the Gr Hall, built for James V, with its huge adj kitchens, & the North Range with loch views, you get a real impression of the lavish lifestyle of the court. Apparently 'underperforms' as an attraction for Historic Scotland, so King's Fountain under wraps for glam restoration (expected back 2005).   HS

1844
MAP 1
D2
✔ ✔ **CAERLAVEROCK, nr DUMFRIES:** 17km S by B725. Follow signs for Wetlands Reserve (1795/BIRDS), but go past rd end. Fairy-tale fortress within double moat and manicured lawns, the daunting frontage being the apex of an uncommon triangular shape. Since 1270, the bastion of the Maxwells, the Wardens of the W Marches. Destroyed by Bruce, besieged in 1640; now with siege engine and AV voiced by Time Team's Tony Robinson. The whole castle experience.   HS

1845
MAP 3
E1
✔ **DUNNOTTAR CASTLE, nr STONEHAVEN:** 3km S of Stonehaven on the coast rd just off the A92. Like Slains further N, the ruins are impressively and precariously perched on a cliff top. Historical links with Wallace, Mary Queen of Scots (the odd night) and even Oliver Cromwell, whose Roundheads besieged it in 1650. Mel Gibson's *Hamlet* was filmed here (bet you don't remember that) and the Crown Jewels of Scotland were once held here. 400m walk from car park. Can walk along cliff top from Stonehaven (2km). Mar-Oct 9am-6pm, Sun 2-5pm. Nov-Mar weekdays only 9-dusk.

1846
MAP 2
C1
✔ **CASTLE TIORAM, nr ACHARACLE:** Romantic ruin where you don't need the saga to sense the place, and maybe the mystery is better than the history. 5km from A861 just N of Acharacle. A sign on the foreshore says 'Don't get stranded'; the walk across a short causeway adds to the experience. Future of this ruin still under review at TGP. Pron 'Cheerum'. Musical beach at nearby Kentra Bay (2073/COASTAL WALKS).

1847
MAP 4
B1
✔ **ELGIN CATHEDRAL, ELGIN:** Follow signs in town centre. Set in a meadow by the river, a tranquil corner of this busy market town, the scattered ruins and surrounding graveyard of what was once Scotland's finest cathedral. The nasty Wolf of Badenoch burned it down in 1390, but there are some 13th-century and medieval renewals. The octagonal chapterhouse is especially revered, but this is an impressive and evocative slice of history. Guided tours are v good. Around the corner, there's now a biblical gdn planted with species mentioned in the Bible. (May-Sept, 10am-7.30pm daily).   HS ADMN

1848
MAP 4
C3
✔ **KILDRUMMY CASTLE, nr ALFORD:** 15km SW of Alford on A97 nr the hotel (1391/SCOTTISH HOTELS) and across the gorge from its famous gdns. Most complete 13th-century castle in Scotland, an HQ for the Jacobite uprising of 1715 and an evocative and v Highland site. Here the invitation in HS advertising to 'bring your imagination' is truly valid. Apr-Sep 9.30am-6.30pm.
                                    HS

1849
MAP 7
A5
✔ **KISIMULL CASTLE, ISLE OF BARRA:** The medieval fortress, home of the MacNeils that sits on a rocky outcrop in the bay 200m offshore. Originally built in the 11th century, it was burnt in the 18th and restored by the 45th chief, an American architect, but was unfinished when he died in 1970. An essential pilgrimage for all MacNeils, it is fascinating and atmospheric for the rest of us, a grim exterior belying an unusual internal layout – a courtyard that seems unchanged and rms betwixt renovation and decay. Open every day in season & has a gift shop. You phone or flip board when you want to visit & they come in the boat (01871 810313). Phone for wint hrs or enq TIC.   HS

1850 **EDZELL CASTLE, EDZELL:** 2km village off main st, signed. Pleasing red sand-
MAP 3 stone ruin in bucolic setting – birds twitter, rabbits run. Notable walled
D1 parterre gdn created by Sir David Lindsay way back in 1604. The wall niches
are nice. Lotsa lobelias! Mary Queen of Scots was here (of course).   HS

1851 **BOTHWELL CASTLE, UDDINGSTON, GLASGOW:** 15km E of city via M74,
MAP 3 Uddingston t/off into main st and follow signs. Hugely impressive 13th-century
A5 ruin, the home of the Black Douglas, o/look Clyde (with fine walks). Remarkable
considering proximity to city that there is hardly any 21st-century intrusion
except yourself. Pay to go inside or just sit and watch the Clyde go by.   HS

1852 **FORT GEORGE, nr INVERNESS:** On promontory of Moray Firth 18km NE via
MAP 4 A96 by village of Ardersier. A vast site and 'one of the most outstanding
A1 artillery fortifications in Europe'. Planned after Culloden as a base for George
II's army and completed 1769, it has remained unaltered ever since and allows
a v complete picture. May provoke palpitations in the Nationalist heart, but
it's heaven for militarists and altogether impressive. It's hardly a ruin of course,
and is still occupied by the army.   HS

1853 **DUNOLLIE CASTLE, OBAN:** Just o/side town via Corran Esplanade towards
MAP 2 Ganavan. Best to walk to or park on Esplanade and then walk 1km. (No park-
D2 ing on main rd below castle.) Bit of a scramble up and a slither down (& the
run itself is note 'safe), but the views are superb. More atmospheric than
Dunstaffnage and not commercialised. You can climb one flight up, but the
ruin is only a remnant of the gr stronghold of the Lorn Kings that it was. The
Macdougals, who took it over in the 12th century, still live in the house below.

1854 **TARBERT CASTLE:** Tarbert, Argyll. Strategically and dramatically o/look the
MAP 2 sheltered harbour of this epitome of a West Highland pt. Unsafe to clamber
D4 over, it's for the timeless view rather than an evocation of tangible history that
it's worth finding the way up. Steps on Harbour Rd next to dental surgery.

1855 **KILCHURN CASTLE, LOCH AWE:** The romantic ruin at the head of L Awe, vis-
MAP 2 ited either by a short walk (1km) from car park off the main A85 5km E of
D2 Lochawe village (betw the Stronmilchan t/off and the Inveraray rd) or by a
fetching wee steamboat from Loch Awe Pierhead (by the station) – call 01838
200440 for details. Pleasant spot for loch reflections. If you go by boat, take tea
in the railway carriage cafe while you're waiting.

1856 **ST ANDREWS CATHEDRAL:** The ruins of the largest church in Scotland
MAP 3 before the Reformation, a place of gr influence and pilgrimage. St Rule's Tower
D3 and the jagged fragment of the huge W Front in their striking position at the
convergence of the main streets and o/look the sea, are remnants of its gr
glory. 7 days 9.30-6.30pm (wint 4pm). Suns 2-4.30pm.

1857 **CRICHTON CASTLE, nr PATHHEAD:** 6km W of A68 at Pathhead (28km S Edin)
MAP 3 or via A7 turning E, 3km S of Gorebridge. Massive Border keep dominating the
D5 Tyne valley. Open Apr-Sept. Nearby is the 15thC collegiate church. Summer
Suns only, 2-5pm. They record Radio 3 religious music here. 500m walk from
Crichton village. Good picnic spots below by the river. See 405/EASY WALKS.
ADMN HS

1858 **TANTALLON CASTLE, NORTH BERWICK:** 5km E of town by coast rd; 500m to
MAP 3 dramatic cliff top setting with views to Bass Rock. Dates from 1350 with mas-
D4 sive 'curtain wall' to see it through stormy weather and stormy history. The
Red Douglases and their friends kept the world at bay. Wonderful beach
nearby (426/BEACHES).   ADMN HS

1859 **RUTHVEN BARRACKS, KINGUSSIE:** 2km along B970 and visible from A9 esp
MAP 5 at night when it's illuminated, these former barracks built by the English
E3 Redcoats as part of the campaign to tame the Highlands after the first
Jacobite rising in 1715, were actually destroyed by the Jacobites in 1746 after
Culloden. It was here that Bonnie Prince Charlie sent his final order, 'Let every
man seek his own safety', signalling the absolute end of the doomed cause.
Life for the soldiers is well described and visualised. Open AYR.   HS

1860 **URQUHART CASTLE, DRUMNADROCHIT, LOCH NESS:** 28km S of Inverness
MAP 5 on A82. The classic Highland fortress on a promontory o/look L Ness visited
D2 every yr by bus loads and boat loads of tourists. Photo opportunities galore
amongst the well-kept lawns and extensive ruins of the once formidable
stronghold of the Picts and their scions, finally abandoned in the 18th
century. New visitor facs to cope with demand.   ADMN HS

1861 **DOUNE CASTLE, DOUNE:** Follow signs from centre of village which is just off
MAP 3 A84 Callander-Dunblane rd. O/look the R Teith, the well-preserved ruin of a
A3 late 14th-century courtyard castle with a Gr Hall and another draughty rm
where Mary Queen of Scots once slept. Nice walk to the meadow begins on
track to left of castle. ADMN HS

1862 **SLAINS CASTLE nr CRUDEN BAY:** 32km N of Aber off the A975 perched on
MAP 4 the cliffs (1.5km vill). Obviously because of its location, but also because there's
E2 no reception centre/postcard shop or proper signposts, this is a ruin that talks.
Your imagination, like Bram Stoker's (who was inspired after staying here, to
write Dracula), can be cast to the winds. The seat of the Earls of Errol, it has been
gradually disintegrating since the roof was removed in 1925. Once, it had the
finest dining-rm in Scotland. The waves crash below, as always. Be careful!

THE BEST PREHISTORIC SITES

1863 ✓ ✓ ✓ **SKARA BRAE, ORKNEY MAINLAND:** 32km Kirkwall by
A965/B9655 via Finstown and Dounby. Can be a windy walk to
this remarkable shoreline site, the subterranean remains of a compact village
5,000 yrs old. It was engulfed by a sandstorm 600yrs later and lay perfectly
preserved until uncovered by another storm in 1850. Now it permits one of
the most evocative glimpses of truly ancient times in the UK. ADMN HS

1864 ✓ ✓ **THE STANDING STONES OF STENNESS, ORKNEY MAINLAND:**
Together with the Ring of Brodgar and the great chambered tomb
of Maes Howe, all within walking distance of the A965, 18km from Kirkwall, this
is as impressive a ceremonial site as you'll find anywhere. From same period as
Skara Brae. The individual stones and the scale of the Ring are v imposing and
deeply mysterious. The burial cairn is the finest megalithic tomb in the UK.
Seen together, they will stimulate even the most jaded sense of wonder. HS

1865 ✓ ✓ **THE CALLANISH STONES, ISLE OF LEWIS:** 24km from Stornoway.
MAP 7 Take Tarbert rd and go rt at Leurbost. The best preserved and most
B1 unusual combination of standing stones in a ring around a tomb, with radiat-
ing arms in cross shape. Predating Stonehenge, they were unearthed from the
peat in the mid-19th century and have become the major historical attraction
of the Hebrides. Other configurations nearby. At dawn there's nobody else
there (except camping New-Agers). VC out of sight is a good one with a nice
caff. Cl Sun. Free. ☕ HS

1866 ✓ **THE CLAVA CAIRNS nr CULLODEN nr INVERNESS:** Here long before the
MAP 4 most infamous battle in Scottish and other histories; well worth finding.
A1 Not so well marked but continue along the B9006 towards Cawdor Castle,
that other gr historical landmark (1827/CASTLES), taking a rt at the Culloden
Moor Inn and follow signs for Clava Lodge (holiday homes), picking up HS
sign to rt. Chambered cairns in grove of trees. Really just piles of stones, but
the death rattle echo from 5,000 yrs ago is perceptible to all esp when no one
else is there. Remoteness inhibits new age attentions and allows more private
meditations in this extraterrestrial spot. HS

1867 ✓ **THE MOUSA BROCH, SHETLAND:** On small island of Mousa, off Shetland
mainland 20km S of Lerwick, visible from main A970; but to see it properly, take boat (01950 431367). Isolated in its island fastness, this is the best
preserved broch in Scotland. Walls are 13m high (originally 15m) and galleries
run up the middle, in one case to the top. Solid as a rock, this example of a
uniquely Scottish phenomenon would once have been a v des res. Also
JARLSHOF in the far S next to Sumburgh airport has remnants and ruins from
Neolithic to Viking times – 18th century, with esp impressive 'wheelhouses'.
ADMN

1868 ✓ **CRANNOG CENTRE, ABERFELDY:** Adj Croft-Na-Caber Water Sports
MAP 3 Centre on L Tay (2151/WATER SPORTS). Superb reconstruction of iron-age
A2 dwelling (there are several under the loch). Credible and worthwhile archeo-
logical project now gr for kids & conveys history well. Displays in progress and
human story told by pleasant humans. Open Apr-Oct 10am-5.30pm, Nov
10am-4pm.

1869   ✓ **KILMARTIN GLEN, nr LOCHGILPHEAD, TEMPLEWOOD:** 2km S of
MAP 2   Kilmartin and 1km (signed) from A816 and across rd from car park, 2 dis-
C3   tinct stone circles from a long period of history betw 3000-1200 BC. Story and
speculations described on boards. Pastoral countryside and wide skies. There
are other sites in the vicinity, and an excl museum/café (2257/MUSEUMS).   HS

1870 **TOMB OF THE EAGLES, ORKNEY MAINLAND:** 33km S of Kirkwall at the foot
of S Ronaldsay; signed from Burwick. A 'recent' discovery, the excavation of
this cliff cave is on private land. You call in at the VC first and they'll tell you the
whole story. Then there's a 2km walk. Allow time; ethereal stuff. Open AYR, Apr-
Oct 9.30am-6pm, Nov-Mar 10am-noon.   ADMN

1871 **CAIRNPAPPLE HILL, nr LINLITHGOW, WEST LOTHIAN:** App from the
MAP 3   'Beecraigs' rd off W end of Linlithgow main st. Go past the Beecraigs t/off and
B4   continue for 3km. Cairnpapple is signed. Astonishing Neolithic henge & later
burial site on windy hill with views from Highlands to Pentlands. Atmos even
more strange by the very 21st-century communications mast next door. Cute
VC!   ADMN HS

1872 **CAIRNHOLY, between NEWTON STEWART/GATEHOUSE:** 1km off main A75.
MAP 1   Signed from rd, a pleasant walk up the glen side. A mini Callanish of standing
B2   stones around a burial cairn on v human scale and in a serene setting with
another site (with chambered tomb) 150m up the farm track. Excellent view –
sit and contemplate what went on 4000-6000 years ago.

1873 **THE BROWN AND WHITE CATERTHUNS, KIRKTON OF MENMUIR, nr**
MAP 3   **BRECHIN:** 5km uphill from war memorial at Menmuir, then signed 1km. Lay-
D2   by with obvious path to both on either side of the rd. White easiest (500m
uphill). These iron-age hill top settlements give tremendous sense of scale
and space and afford an impressive panorama of the Highland line. Colours
refer to the heather-covered turf and stone of one and the massive collapsed
ramparts of the White. Sit here for a while & picture the Pict.

ABERDEENSHIRE PREHISTORIC TRAIL

1874 **EAST AQUHORTHIES STONE CIRCLE, nr INVERURIE, ABERDEENSHIRE:**
MAP 4   Signed from B993 from Inverurie to Monymusk. A circle of pinkish stones with
D3   2 grey sentinels flanking a huge recumbent stone set in the rolling countryside of the Don Valley. Look at Bennachie then wonder what they got up to …
(2008/HILLS).

1875 **LOANHEAD OF DAVIOT STONE CIRCLE, nr INVERURIE, ABERDEENSHIRE:**
MAP 4   Head for the village of Daviot on B9001 from Inverurie; or Loanhead, signed
D2   off A920 rd betw Oldmeldrum and Insch. The site is 500m from top of village.
Impressive and spooky circle of 11 stones and one recumbent from
4000/5000 BC. Unusual second circle adj encloses a cremation cemetery from
1500 BC. Remains of 32 people were found here. Obviously, an important place
for God-knows-what rituals.

1876 **ARCHAEOLINK nr INSCH, ABERDEENSHIRE:** Geographically betw the 2 sites
MAP 4   above and within an area of many prehistoric remnants, a more recent inter-
C2   pretative centre. Impressively modern app to history both from exterior and
within, where interactive and audiovisual displays bring the food hunter-
gatherer past into the culture hunter-gatherer present. Up the hill, 3 adapt-
able staff members alternate as Iron/Bronze/Stone Age natives or visiting
Romans. Easter-Nov 11am-5pm. Wint: Sun-Tues 11am-4pm.   ADMN

1877 **THE GREY CAIRNS OF CANSTER, nr WICK:** 20km S of Wick, a v straight rd
MAP 6   (signed for Cairns) heads W from the A9 for 8km. The cairns are instantly iden-
E2   tifiable nr the rd and impressively complete. The 'horned cairn' is the best in
the UK. In 2500 BC these stone-piled structures were used for the disposal of
the dead. You can crawl inside them if you're agile (or at night, brave). Nearby,
also signed from A9 is:

1878 **HILL O' MANY STANES, nr WICK:** Aptly named place with extraordinary
MAP 6   number of small standing stones; 200 in 22 rows. If fan shape was complete,
E2   there would be 600. Their v purposeful layout is enigmatic and strangely
stirring.

1879 **THE WHITHORN STORY, WHITHORN:** Excavation site, medieval priory, shrine
MAP 1 of St Ninian, VC and café. More than enough to keep the whole family occu-
B3 pied – enthusiastic staff. Christianity in Scotland? This was ground zero (also
1644/COASTAL VILLAGES). Easter-Oct 10.30-5pm daily.

1880 **THE MOTTE OF UR, nr DALBEATTIE:** Off B794 N of Dalbeattie and 6km from
MAP 1 main A75 Castle Douglas to Dumfries rd. Most extensive bailey earthwork cas-
C2 tle in Scotland dating from 12th century. No walls or excavation visible but a
gr sense of scale and place. Go through village of Haugh and on for 2km S.
Looking down to rt at farm buildings the minor rd crosses a ford; park here,
cross footbridge and head to rt – the hillock is above the ford.

1881 **BAR HILL, nr KIRKINTILLOCH:** A fine example of the low ruins of a Roman
MAP 3 fort on the Antonine Wall which ran across Scotland for 200 yrs early ad. Gr
A4 place for an out-of-town walk (758/VIEWS).

1882 **THE BROCHS, GLENELG:** 110km from Ft William. Glenelg is 14km from the
MAP 5 A87 at Shiel Br (1705/SCENIC ROUTES). 5km from Glenelg village in beautiful
B2 Glen Beag. The 2 brochs, Dun Trodden and Dun Telve, are the best preserved
examples on the mainland of these mysterious 1st-century homesteads. Easy
here to distinguish the twin stone walls that kept out the cold and the more
disagreeable neighbours. Free.   HS

1883 **BARPA LANYASS, NORTH UIST:** 8km S Lochmaddy, visible from main A867
MAP 7 rd, like a hat on the hill (200m away). A 'squashed' beehive burial cairn dating
B3 from 1000 BC, the tomb of a chieftain. It's largely intact and you can explore
inside, crawling through the short entrance tunnel and down through the yrs.

1884 **SUENO'S STONE, FORRES:** Signposted from Grant Pk (1631/TOWN PARKS).
MAP 4 More late Dark Age than prehistoric, a 9th or 10th C carved stone, 6m high in
B1 its own glass case. Pictish, magnificent; arguments still over what it shows.

GREAT COUNTRY HOUSES

1885 ✓✓ **HADDO HOUSE:** Tarves, by Ellon. 01651 851440. Designed by
MAP 4 William Adam for the Earl of Aberdeen, the Palladian-style mansion
D2 well known for its musical evenings. Not so much a house, more a leisure land
in the best poss taste, with country park to wander, a pleasant café, estate
shop and gentle education. Austere inside perhaps, but the basements are
the place to ponder. The window by Burne-Jones in the chapel is glorious. Excl
programme of events, both NTS and Haddo House Trust. 🍵   NTS

1886 ✓✓ **MOUNT STUART, BUTE:** 01700 503877. Unique Victorian Gothic
MAP 2 house; echoes 3rd Marquis of Bute's passion for mythology, astron-
D5 omy, astrology and religion. Amazing splendour and scale, but atmos intimate
and romantic. Beautiful Italian antiques, notable paintings and fascinating
attention to detail with surprising humourous touches. Equally grand gdns,
with fabulous walks and sea views. Stylish VC – straight out of *Wallpaper* magazine with restau/coffee shop. May-Aug 11am-4.30pm. Also open Easter
w/end. Cl Tue/Thu. *Spend the best part of a day here!* 🍵

1887 ✓✓ **FASQUE, betw STONEHAVEN and MONTROSE:** W of A92 at
MAP 3 Laurencekirk and through Victorian Fettercairn to Fasque, one of
D1 the most fascinating old houses you'll ever be permitted to wander through.
Home of Gladstone (4 times Prime Minister). Shut down in 1939 till the 1970s,
the world before and betw the wars was preserved and is still there for faded-
grandeur connoisseurs to savour and all of us to sense. Best is below stairs.
Open by appointment only for groups – 01561 340569.

1888 ✓ **MANDERSTON, DUNS:** Off A6105, 2km down Duns-Berwick rd.
MAP 3 Described as the swan-song of the Gr Classical House, one of the finest
E5 examples of Edwardian opulence in UK. *The* Edwardian CH of TV fame. All the
more fascinating because the family still live there. Below stairs as fascinating
as up; sublime gdns (don't miss the woodland gdn on other side of the lake,
or the marble dairy). Open May-end Sept, Thu/Sun 2-5.30pm.

1889
MAP 3
C6
✓ ✓ **TRAQUAIR, INNERLEITHEN:** 01896 830323. 2km from A72 Peebles-Gala rd. Archetypal romantic Border retreat steeped in Jacobite history (ask about the Bear gates). Human proportions, liveability and lots of atmos. An enchanting house, a maze (20th cent) and tranquil duck pond in the gdn. Traquair ale still brewed. 1745 cottage tearoom, pottery and candle-making. Apr-Oct House 12.30-5.30pm (grounds 10.30am-5.30pm June-Aug). Crafty, folky fair in Aug. Woodland walks.

1890
MAP 3
D4
✓ ✓ **NEWHAILES, MUSSELBURGH nr EDINBURGH:** 0131 653 5599. Newhailes Rd, well signed from Portobello end of Musselburgh. NTS flagship project 'stabilising' the microcosm of 18th cent history encapsulated here & uniquely intact. Gr rococo interiors, v liveable, esp library. A rural sanctuary nr the city. Complex opening hrs. Call first.   NTS

1891
MAP 3
D4
GOSFORD HOUSE nr ABERLADY, EAST LOTHIAN: On A198 betw Longniddry and Aberlady, the Gosford estate is behind a high wall and strangely stunted vegetation. Imposing house with centre block by Robert Adam and the wing you visit by William Young who did Glas City Chambers. The Marble Hall houses the remarkable collections of the unbroken line of the Earls of Wemyss. Priceless art, informally displayed. Superb grounds. July afternoons only. Check local TICs.

1892
MAP 3
E6
FLOORS CASTLE, KELSO: 01573 223333. More vast mansion than old castle, the ancestral home of the Duke of Roxburghe, o/look with imposing grandeur the town and the Tweed. 18th-century with later additions. You're led round lofty public rms past family collections of fine furniture, tapestries and porcelain. Priceless; spectacularly impractical. Good gdn centre (2235/GARDEN CENTRES). Annual event prog (phone for details) or floorscastle.com. ☕

1893
MAP 3
D5
MELLERSTAIN, nr GORDON/KELSO: 01573 410225. Home of the Earl of Haddington, signed from A6089 (Kelso-Gordon) or A6105 (Earlston-Greenlaw). One of Scotland's gr Georgian houses, begun by Wm Adam in 1725, completed by Robert. Outstanding decorative interiors esp the library & spectacular exterior 1761. Easter w/end plus May-Sept 12.30-5pm (not Tue). Café/shop 10.30am-5.30pm.

1894
MAP 3
E5
PAXTON, nr BERWICK: 01289 386291. Off B6461 rd to Swinton and Kelso about 6km from A1. Country park & Adam mansion with Chippendales, Trotters and a picture gallery which is an outstation of the National Gallery. They've made a very good job of the wallpapering. 80 acres woodland to walk. Good adventure playground. Restored Victorian boathouse and salmon fishing museum on the R Tweed. Tours (1hr) every 45mins, Apr-Oct 11.15am-4.15pm. Garden 10am-sunset.

1895
MAP 3
D5
THIRLESTANE, LAUDER: 01578 722430. 2km off A68. A castellate/baronial seat of the Earls and Duke of Lauderdale and family home of the Maitlands; it must take some upkeeping. Extraordinary staterooms, esp plaster work; the ceilings must be seen to be believed. In contrast, the nurseries (with toy collection), kitchens and laundry are more approachable. Apr-Oct 10.30am-5pm (last adm 4.15pm). Cl Sat.

1896
MAP 4
D2
FYVIE, ABERDEENSHIRE: 40km NW Aber, an important stop on the 'Castle Trail' which links the gr houses of Aberdeenshire. Before opulence fatigue sets in, see this pleasant baronial pile first. It was lived-in until the 1980s so feels less remote than most. Fantastic roofscape and ceilings. The *best* tearoom. Tree-lined acres; loch side walks. Apr/May, June/Sept Fri-Tues 12-5pm; July/Aug 11am-5pm.   NTS

1897
MAP 4
D3
CRATHES, nr BANCHORY: 25km W of Aber on A93. Amidst superb gdns (1592/GARDENS) a 'fairy-tale castle', a tower house which is actually interesting to visit. Up and down spiral staircases and into small but liveable rms. The notable painted ceilings and the Long Gallery at the top are all worth lingering over. 350yrs of the Burnett family are ingrained in this oak. Apr-Oct 11am-5.30pm. Grounds open AYR 9.30am-dusk. Excl tearm (1033/NE RESTAUS). ☕

ABBOTSFORD, nr MELROSE: Home of Walter Scott (1908/LITERARY PLACES).

These sites are open at all times and free unless otherwise stated.

1898
MAP 2
B5
✓ ✓ **THE AMERICAN MONUMENT, ISLAY:** On the SW peninsula of the island, known as the Oa (pron 'Oh'), 13km from Pt Ellen. A monument to commemorate the shipwrecks in nearby waters, of 2 American ships, the *Tuscania* and the *Ontranto*, both of which sank in 1918 at the end of the war. The obelisk o/look this sea – which is often beset by storms – from a spectacular headland, the sort of disquieting place where you could imagine looking round and finding the person you're with has disappeared. Take rd from Pt Ellen past Maltings marked Mull of Oa 12km, through gate and left at broken sign. Park and walk 1.5km steadily uphill to monument. Bird life good in Oa area.   1-A-2

1899
MAP 3
B4
✓ **WALLACE MONUMENT, STIRLING:** Visible for miles and with gr views, though not as dramatic as Stirling Castle. App from A91 or Br of Allan rd. 150m walk from car park (or minibus) and 246 steps up. Victorian gothic spire marking the place where Scotland's gr patriot swooped down upon the English at the Battle of Stirling Br. Mel Gibson's *Braveheart* increased visitors though his face on the Wallace statue is thanks too far. In the 'Hall of Heroes' the new heroines section requires a feminist leap of the imagination. The famous sword is v big. Cliff top walk through Abbey Craig woods is worth detour. Monument open daily. 01786 472140 for details; hrs vary.   ADM

1900
MAP 5
A1
THE GRAVE OF FLORA MACDONALD, SKYE: Kilmuir on A855, Uig-Staffin rd, 40km N of Portree. A 10ft-high Celtic cross supported against the wind, high on the ridge o/look the Uists from whence she came. Long after the legendary journey, her funeral in 1790 attracted the biggest crowd since Culloden. The present memorial replaced the original, which was chipped away by souvenir hunters. Dubious though the whole business may have been, she still helped to shape the folklore of the Highlands.

1901
MAP 3
A5
CARFIN GROTTO, MOTHERWELL: Between Motherwell and the M8, take the B road into Carfin and it's by Newarthill Rd. Gardens and pathways with shrines, pavilion, chapel and memorials. Latest (June 2001) unveiled by Irish An Taoiseach Bertie Ahern – to those who died, suffered or emigrated during the Great Famine 1845–51. A major Catholic centre and never less than thought-provoking as the rest of us go station to station. Carfin Pilgrimage Centre adj open daily, 10am-5pm AYR. Grotto open at all times.

1902
MAP 3
A5
HAMILTON MAUSOLEUM, STRATHCLYDE PARK: Off (and visible from) M74 at jnct 5/6, 15km from Glas (1616/COUNTRY PARKS). Huge, over-the-top/over-the-tomb (though removed 1921) stone memorial to the 10th Duke of Hamilton. Guided tours Wed/Sat/Sun 3pm in summer, 2pm in wint. Eerie and chilling and with remarkable acoustics – the 'longest echo in Europe'. Give it a shout or take your violin. Info and tickets from Hamilton Museum: 01698 328232.

1903
MAP 3
D6
PENIEL HEUGH, nr ANCRUM/JEDBURGH: (pron 'Pinal-hue'.) An obelisk visible for miles and on a rise which offers some of the most exhilarating views of the Borders. Also known as the Waterloo Monument, it was built on the Marquis of Lothian's estate to commemorate the battle. It's said that the woodland on the surrounding slopes represents the positions of Wellington's troops. From A68 opposite Ancrum t/off, on B6400, go 1km past 'Woodland Centre' up steep, unmarked rd to left for 150m. Park, walk up through woods.

1904
MAP 3
D4
THE HOPETOUN MONUMENT, ATHELSTANEFORD nr HADDINGTON: The needle atop a rare rise in E Lothian and a gr vantage point from which to view the county from the Forth to the Lammermuirs and Edinburgh over there. Off A6737 Haddington to Aberlady rd on B1343 to Athelstaneford. Car park and short climb. Tower usually open and viewfinder boards at top but take a torch; it's a dark climb. Good gentle 'ridge' walk E from here.

1905 **THE PINEAPPLE, AIRTH:** From Airth N of Grangemouth, take A905 to Stirling
MAP 3 and after 1km the B9124 for Cowie. It sits on the edge of a walled gdn at the
B4 end of the drive. 45ft high, it was built in 1761 as a gdn retreat by an unknown
architect and remained 'undiscovered' until 1963. How exotic the fruit must
have seemed in the 18th century, never mind this extraordinary folly. Grounds
open AYR; oddly enough, you can stay here (2 bedrms, 01628 825925).

1906 **THE MONUMENT ON BEN BHRAGGIE, GOLSPIE:** Atop the hill (pron
MAP 6 'Brachee') that dominates the town, the domineering statue and plinth (over
C3 35m) of the dreaded first Duke of Sutherland; there's a campaign group that
would like to see it demolished, but it survives yet. Climb from town fountain
on marked path. The hill race go up in 10mins but allow 2hrs return. His private view along the NE coast is superb (1842/CASTLES; 2251/MUSEUMS).

1907 **McCAIG'S TOWER or FOLLY, OBAN:** Oban's gr landmark built in 1897 by
MAP 2 McCaig, a local banker, to give 'work to the unemployed' and as a memorial to
D2 his family. It's like a temple or coliseum and time has mellowed whatever
incongruous effect it may have had originally. The views of the town and the
bay are magnificent and it's easy to get up from several points in town centre.
(*See* OBAN, p. 312.)

1908 **THE VICTORIA MEMORIAL TO ALBERT, BALMORAL:** Atop the fir-covered
MAP 4 hill behind the house, she raised a monument whose distinctive pyramid
B3 shape can be seen peeping over the crest from all over the estate. Desolated
by his death, the 'broken-hearted' widow had this memorial built in 1862 and
spent so much time here, she became a recluse and the Empire trembled.
Path begins at shop on way to Lochnagar distillery, 45mins up. Forget
Balmoral (1840/CASTLES), all the longing and love for Scotland can be felt here,
the gr estate laid out below.

1909 **THE PROP OF YTHSIE, nr ABERDEEN:** 35km NW city nr Ellon to W of A92, or
MAP 4 pass on the 'Castle Trail' since this monument commemorates one George
D2 Gordon of Haddo House nearby, who was prime minister 1852-55 (the good-
looking guy in the first portrait you come to in the house). Tower visible from
all of rolling Aberdeenshire around and there are reciprocal views should you
take the easy but unclear route up. On B999 Aber-Tarves rd and 2km from
entrance to house. Take rd for the Ythsie (pron 'icy') farms, 100m. Stone circle
nearby.

1910 **THE MONUMENT TO HUGH MacDIARMID, LANGHOLM:** Brilliant piece of
MAP 1 modern sculpture by Jake Harvey rapidly rusting on the hill above Langholm
E22 3km from A7 at beginning of path to the Malcolm obelisk from where there
are gr views (1737/VIEWS). MacDiarmid, our national poet, was born in
Langholm in 1872 and, though they never liked him much after he left, the
monument was commissioned and a cairn beside it raised in 1992. The bare
hills surround you. The motifs of the sculpture were used by Scotland's
favourite Celtic rock band, Runrig, on the cover of their 1993 album, *Amazing
Things*.

1911 **MONUMENT TO AIR CHIEF MARSHALL LORD HUGH DOWDING, MOFFAT:**
MAP 1 In Moffat's charming Station Park, near the Moffat Woollen Mill, this plain
D1 stone memorial comemorates the valour of Lord Hugh Dowding, born in
Moffat in 1882 and Commander-in-Chief of Fighter Command during the
Battle of Britain. He has been compared to Drake and Nelson in his heroic
defence of his country.

1912 **MURRAY MONUMENT, nr NEW GALLOWAY:** Above A712 rd to Newton
MAP 1 Stewart about halfway betw. A fairly austere needle of granite to commemo-
B2 rate a 'shepherd boy', one Alexander Murray, who rose to become a professor
of Oriental Languages at Edinburgh Univ in early 19th century. 10min walk up
for fine views of Galloway Hills; pleasant waterfall nearby. Just as he,
barefoot …

1913 **SMAILHOLM TOWER, nr KELSO and ST BOSWELLS:** The classic Border
MAP 3 tower; plenty of history and romance and a v nice place to stop, picnic what-
D6 ever. Good views. Nr main rd B6404 or off smaller B6937 – well signposted.
Open Apr-Sept 9.30am-6.30pm (Sun from 2pm). But fine to visit at any time
(1713/SCENIC ROUTES).

SCOTT MONUMENT, EDINBURGH: 432/VIEWS.

THE MOST INTERESTING CHURCHES

All 'generally open' unless otherwise stated; those marked (*) have public services.

1914 ✔ ✔ ***ST CONAN'S KIRK, LOCH AWE:** A85 33km E of Oban. Perched
MAP 2 amongst trees on the side of L Awe, this small but spacious church
D3 seems to incorporate every ecclesiastical architectural style. Its building was a labour of love for one Walter Campbell who was perhaps striving for beauty rather than consistency. Though modern (begun by him in 1881 and finished by his sister and a board of trustees in 1930), the result is a place of ethereal light and atmos, enhanced by and befitting the inherent spirituality of the setting. There's a spooky carved effigy of Robert the Bruce, a cosy cloister and the most amazing flying buttresses. A place to wander and reflect.

1915 ✔ ✔ ***ROSSLYN CHAPEL, ROSLIN:** 12km S of Edin city centre. Take A702,
MAP 3 then A703 from ring-route rd, marked Penicuik. Roslin village 1km
C5 from main rd and chapel 500m from village crossroads above Roslin Glen (416/WALKS OUTSIDE THE CITY). Freemason central and New Age fuel station: stories abound of the Holy Grail hidden in the walls. For such a wee chapel, visitors can spend hrs wandering around working the place out with help from copious guidance notes. Founded by a 15th-century Sinclair, Prince of Orkney, who reinterred his illustrious 13th-century ancestor here (the latter just happened to be a Grand Prior of the Knights Templar). All holy meaningful stuff in a *Foucault's Pendulum* sense. But a special place. In restoration till 2010. Episcopalian. Mon-Sat 10-5pm, 12-4.45pm Sun. Coffee shop.

1916 ✔ ✔ **THE ITALIAN CHAPEL, ORKNEY MAINLAND:** 8km S of Kirkwall at
Lamb Holm and the first causeway on the way to St Margaret's Hope. In 1943, Italian PoWs brought to work on the Churchill Barriers transformed a Nissen hut, using the most meagre materials, into this remarkable ornate chapel. The meticulous *trompe l'œil* and wrought-iron work are a touching affirmation of faith. At the other end of the architectural scale, **ST MAGNUS CATHEDRAL** in Kirkwall is a gr edifice, but also filled with spirituality.

1917 ✔ ✔ **QUEEN'S CROSS CHURCH, GLASGOW:** 870 Garscube Rd where it
MAP B becomes Maryhill Rd at Springbank St. C R Mackintosh's only
xC1 church. Fascinating and unpredictable in every part of its design. Some elements reminiscent of The Art School (built in the same year 1897) and others, like the tower, evoke medieval architecture. Bold and innovative, now restored and functioning as the headquarters of The Mackintosh Society. Mon-Fri 10am-5pm, Sun 2pm-5pm. Cl Sat. No services. (815/MACKINTOSH.)   ADM

1918 ✔ ***DURISDEER PARISH CHURCH, nr ABINGTON AND THORNHILL:** Off
MAP 1 A702 Abington-Thornhill rd and nr Drumlanrig (1613/COUNTRY PARKS). If I
D1 lived in this village in the hills, I'd go to church more often. It's exquisite and the history of Scotland is writ on the stones. The Queensberry marbles (1709) are displayed in the N transept and there's a cradle roll and a list of ministers from the 14th century. The plaque to the two brothers who died at Gallipoli is especially touching, while Covenanter tales are writ on the gravestones.

1919 ***CATHEDRAL OF THE ISLES, MILLPORT ON THE ISLAND OF CUMBRAE:**
MAP 2 Frequent ferry service from Largs is met by bus for 6km journey to Millport.
D5 Lane from main st by Newton pub, 250m then through gate. The smallest 'cathedral' in Europe, one of Butterfield's gr works (other is Keble Coll, Oxford). Here, small is outstandingly beautiful. (1327/RETREATS; 1478/CAFÉS.)

1920 **ST CLEMENTS, RODEL, SOUTH HARRIS:** Tarbert 40km. Classic island kirk in
MAP 7 Hebridean landscape. Go by the Golden Road (1709/ROUTES). Simple cruci-
B3 form structure with tower, which the adventurous can climb. Probably influenced by Iona. Now an empty but atmospheric shell, with blackened effigies and important monumental sculpture. Goats in the churchyard graze amongst the headstones of all the young Harris lads lost at sea in the Gr War. There are other fallen angels on the outside of the tower.

1921 ***ST MICHAEL'S CHAPEL, ERISKAY, nr SOUTH UIST/BARRA:** That rare exam-
MAP 7 ple of an ordinary modern church without history or grand architecture,
A5 which has charm and serenity and imbues the sense of well-being that a religious centre should. The focal pt of a relatively devout Catholic community who obviously care about it. Alabaster angels abound. O/look Sound of Barra. A real delight whatever your religion.

1922 ***ST ATHERNASE, LEUCHARS:** The parish church on a corner of what is essen-
MAP 3 tially an Air Force base spans centuries of warfare and architecture. The
D3 Norman bell tower is remarkable.

1923 ***ST FILLAN'S CHURCH, ABERDOUR:** Behind ruined castle in this pleasant
MAP 3 seaside village (1641/COASTAL VILLAGES), a more agreeable old kirk would be
C4 hard to find. Restored from a 12th-century ruin in 1926, the warm stonework
and stained glass create a v soothing atmos (church open at most times, but
if closed the graveyard is v fine).

1924 ***CULROSS ABBEY CHURCH:** Top of Forth-side village full of interesting
MAP 3 buildings and windy streets (1636/COASTAL VILLS). Worth hike up hill (signed
B4 'Abbey', ruins are adj) for views and this well-loved and looked-after church. Gr
stained glass (see Sandy's window), often full of flowers.

1925 ***DUNBLANE CATHEDRAL:** A huge nave of a church built around a Norman
MAP 3 tower (from David I) on the Allan Water and restored 1892. The wondrously
B4 bright stained glass is mostly 20th-century. The poisoned sisters buried under
the altar helped change the course of Scottish history. HS

1926 ***ST MACHAR'S CATHEDRAL, ABERDEEN:** The Chanonry in 'Old Aberdeen'
MAP 4 off St Machar's Dr about 2km from centre. Best seen as part of a walk round
D3 the old 'village within the city' occupied mainly by the university's old and
modern buildings. Cathedral's fine granite nave and twin-spired W Front date
from 15th century, on site of 6th-century Celtic church. Noted for heraldic ceiling and 19/20th-century stained glass. Seaton Park adj has pleasant Don-side
walks and there's the old Brig o' Balgownie. Church open daily 9am-5pm.

1927 ***THE EAST LOTHIAN CHURCHES at ABERLADY, WHITEKIRK, ATHELSTANE-**
MAP 3 **FORD:** 3 charming churches in bucolic settings; quiet corners to explore and
D4 reflect. Easy to find. All have interesting local histories and in the case of
Athelstaneford, a national resonance – a 'vision' in the sky nr here became the
flag of Scotland, the saltire. The spooky Flag Heritage Centre explains.
Aberlady my favourite.

1928 **ABERCORN CHURCH, nr S QUEENSFERRY:** Off A904. 4 km W 11th cent kirk
MAP 3 nestling among ancient yews in a sleepy hamlet, untouched since Covenanter
C4 days. St Ninian said to have preached to the Picts here and Abercorn once on
a par with York and Lindisfarne in religious importance. Church always open.

1929 **CROICK CHURCH, nr BONAR BRIDGE:** 16km W of Ardgay, which is just over
MAP 6 the river from Bonar Br and through the splendid glen of Strathcarron
C3 (1669/GLENS). This humble and charming church is chiefly remembered for its
place in the history of the Highland clearances. In May 1845, 90 folk took shelter in the graveyard around the church after they had been cleared from their
homes in nearby Glencalvie. Not allowed even in the kirk, their plight did not
go unnoticed and was reported in *The Times*. The harrowing account is there
to read, and the messages they scratched on the windows. Sheep graze all
around.

1930 ***THOMAS COATES MEMORIAL CHURCH, PAISLEY:** Built by Coates (of
MAP 3 thread fame), an imposing edifice, one of the grandest Baptist churches in
A5 Europe. A monument to God, prosperity and the Industrial Revolution.
Opening hrs, check TIC – 0141 889 9980. Service on Sun at 11am.

1931 ***THE LAMP OF THE LOTHIANS, ST MARY'S COLLEGIATE, HADDINGTON:**
MAP 3 Follow signs from E main st. At the risk of sounding profane or at least trite,
D4 this is a church that's really got its act together, both now and throughout
ecclesiastical history. It's beautiful and in a fine setting on the R Tyne, with
good stained glass and interesting crypts and corners. But it's obviously v
much at the centre of the community, a lamp as it were, in the Lothians.
Guided tours, brass rubbings (Sat). Monthly summer recitals (Sun afternoon).
Coffee shop and gift shop. Don't miss Lady Kitty's gdn nearby, including the
secret medicinal gdn, a quiet spot to contemplate (if not sort out) your condition. Daily 11am-4pm.

1932 ***DUNKELD CATHEDRAL:** In town centre by lane to the banks of the Tay at its
MAP 3 most silvery. Medieval splendour amongst lofty trees. Notable for 13th-centu-
B2 ry choir and 15th-century nave and tower. Parish church open for edifying ser-
vices and other spiritual purposes.

1933 **RUTHWELL CHURCH, RUTHWELL:** 10 miles SE Dumfries, B724 nr
MAP 1 Clarencefield. Collect keys from Mrs Coulthard, Kirkyett House (bungalow
D2 where you turn off the main rd); she's the fount of all knowledge concerning
this important building. Unique 18ft Runic Cross within Church, dating from
7th century. Carvings depict Biblical scenes with monk's inscription of 'The
Holy Rood' poem. Fascinating history of its creation, preservation during the
religious troubles of 1640, and subsequent restoration in 1823 by the community. Buy the guidebook from Mrs C. And some postcards!

1934 **KEILLS CHAPEL, S of CRINAN:** The chapel at the end of nowhere. From Loch-
MAP 2 gilphead, drive towards Crinan, but before you get there, turn S down the B8025
C4 and follow it for nearly 20km to the end. Park at the farm then walk the last
200m. You are 7km across the Sound from Jura, at the edge of Knapdale. Early
13thC chapel houses some remarkable cross slabs, a 7thC cross & ghosts.   HS

ST GILES CATHEDRAL, EDINBURGH: 407/OTHER ATTRACTIONS.

GLASGOW CATHEDRAL/UNIVERSITY CHAPEL: 759/763/MAIN ATTRACTIONS.

THE MOST INTERESTING GRAVEYARDS

1935 ✓ ✓ **GLASGOW NECROPOLIS:** The vast burial ground at the crest of the
MAP B   ridge, running down to the river, that was the focus of the original set-
xE3 tlement of Glas. Everything began at the foot of this hill and, ultimately, ended
at the top where many of the city's most famous (and infamous) sons and
daughters are interred within the reach of the long shadow of John Knox's
obelisk. Generally open (official times), but best if you can get the full spooky
experience to yourself. Check with TIC 0141 204 4400. (759/MAIN ATTRACTIONS.)

1936 **EDINBURGH: CANONGATE:** On left of Royal Mile going down to Palace.
MAP A Adam Smith and the tragic poet Robert Fergusson revered by Rabbie Burns
E2, (who raised the memorial stone in 1787 over his pauper's grave) are buried
E3, here in the heart of Auld Reekie. Tourists can easily miss this one. **GREY-**
D3, **FRIARS:** A place of ancient mystery, famous for the wee dog who guarded his
C1, master's grave for 14yrs, for the plundering of graves in the early 18th centu-
B2 ry for the Anatomy School and for the graves of Allan Ramsay (prominent
poet and burgher), James Hutton (the father of geology), William McGonagall
(the 'world's worst poet') and sundry serious Highlanders. Annals of a gr city
are written on these stones. **WARRISTON:** Warriston Rd by B&Q or end of cul-
de-sac at Warriston Cres (Canonmills), up bank and along railway line.
Overgrown, peaceful, steeped in atmos. Gothic horrorland (some of those
cruising guys may like that sort of thing). **DEAN** is an Edinburgh secret.

1937 **ISLE OF JURA:** Killchianaig graveyard in the N. Follow rd as far as it goes to
MAP 2 Inverlussa, graveyard is on rt, just before hamlet. Mairi Ribeach apparently
C4 lived until she was 128. In the south at Keils (2km from rd N out of Craighouse,
bearing left past Keils houses and through the deer fence), her father is buried
and he was 180! Both sites are beautiful, isolated and redolent of island history, with much to reflect on, not least the mysterious longevity of the inhabitants & that soon we'll all live this long.

1938 **CAMPBELTOWN CEMETERY:** Campbeltown. Odd, but one of the nicest
MAP 2 things about this end-of-the-line town is the cemetery. It's at the end of a row
C6 of fascinating posh houses, the original merchant and mariner owners of
which will be interred in the leafy plots next door. Still v much in use after centuries of commerce and seafaring disasters, it has crept up the terraces of a
steep and lush overhanging bank. The white cross and row of WW2 headstones are particularly affecting.

1939 **KIRKOSWALD KIRKYARD nr MAYBOLE and GIRVAN:** On main rd through
MAP 1 village betw Ayr and Girvan. The graveyard around the ruined Kirk famous as
B1 the burial place of the characters in Burns' most famous poem and a must for
Burns fans and thrill seekers. Tam O'Shanter, Souter Johnnie and Kirkton Jean
all lie here.

1940 **HUMBIE CHURCHYARD:** Humbie, E Lothian 25km SE of Edin via A68 (t/off at
MAP 3 Fala). This is as reassuring a place to be buried as you could wish for; if you're
D5 set on cremation, come here and think of earth. Deep in the woods with the
burn besides; after-hrs the sprites and the spirits must have a hell of a time.

1941 **ANCRUM GRAVEYARD, nr JEDBURGH:** The quintessential country church-
MAP 3 yard; away from the village (2km along B6400), by a lazy river (the Ale Water)
D6 crossed to a farm by a humpback br and a chapel in ruins. Elegiac and deeply
peaceful (1755/PICNICS).

1942 **BALQUHIDDER CHURCHYARD:** Chiefly notable as the last resting place of
MAP 3 one Rob Roy Macgregor who was buried in 1734 after causing a heap of trou-
A3 ble hereabouts and raised to immortality by Sir Walter Scott and Michael
Caton-Jones. Despite well-trodden path, setting is poignant. For best reflec-
tions head along L Voil to Inverlochlarig. Beautiful Sunday evening concerts in
kirk July/Aug. (check with local TICs). Nice walk from back corner signed
'Waterfall' & gr long walk to Brig O' Turk (2038/GLEN WALKS). Tearoom in OLD
LIBRARY in vill is cosy & couthie, with v good cakes (1501/TEAROOMS).

1943 **LOGIE OLD KIRK, nr STIRLING:** A crumbling chapel and an ancient graveyard
MAP 3 at the foot of the Ochils. The wall is round to keep out the demons, a burn gur-
B4 gles beside and there are some fine and v old stones going back to the 16th
century. Take rd for Wallace Monument off A91, 2km from Stirling, then first rt.
The old kirk is beyond the new.

1944 **CHISHOLM GRAVEYARD, nr BEAULY:** Last resting place of the Chisholms
MAP 5 and 3 of the largest Celtic crosses you'll see anywhere, in a secret and atmos-
D2 pheric woodland setting. 10km S Beauly on A831 to Struy, 1km before Cnoc
Hotel opp Erchless Estate and through a white iron gate on rt. Walk 250m.

1945 **TUTNAGUAIL, DUNBEATH:** An enchanting cemetery 5km from Dunbeath,
MAP 6 Neil Gunn's birthplace, and found by walking up the 'Strath' he describes in his
D2 book *Highland River* (1978/LITERARY PLACES). With a white wall around it, this
graveyard, which before the clearances once served a valley community of
400 souls, can be seen for miles. Despite isolation, it's still used.

THE GREAT ABBEYS

1946 ✓✓ **IONA ABBEY:** This hugely significant place of pilgrimage for new
MAP 2 age and old age pilgrims and tourists alike is reached from
B3 Fionnphort, SW Mull, by frequent Calmac Ferry (5min crossing). Walk 1km.
Here in 563 BC St Columba began his mission for a Celtic Church that changed
the face of Europe. Cloisters, graveyard of Scottish kings and, marked by a
modest stone, the inscription already faded by the weather, the grave of John
Smith, the patron saint of New Labour. Regular services. Good shop
(2189/CRAFT SHOPS). Residential courses and retreats (MacLeod Centre adj,
01681 700404) include a 'Christmas house party' (2296/MAGICAL ISLANDS). HS

1947 ✓✓ **PLUSCARDEN ABBEY, betw FORRES and ELGIN:** A fully working
MAP 4 monastic community (1324/RETREATS) in one of the most spiritual of
B1 places. Founded by Alexander II in 1230 and being restored since 1948.
Benedictine services (starting with Vigil & Lauds at 4.45am through Prime-
Terce-Sext-None-Vespers at 5.30pm and Compline at 8pm) open to public.
The ancient honey-coloured walls, the brilliant stained glass, the monks'
Gregorian chant: the whole effect is a truly uplifting experience. The bell rings
down the valley. Services aside, open to visitors 9am-5pm.

1948 ✓✓ **PAISLEY ABBEY:** Town centre. An abbey founded in 1163, razed (by
MAP 3 the English) in 1307 and with successive deteriorations and renova-
A5 tions ever since. Major restoration in the 1920s brought it to present-day
cathedral-like magnificence. Exceptional stained glass (the recent window
complementing the formidable Strachan E Window), an impressive choir and
an edifying sense of space. Sunday Services (11am, 12.15pm, 6.30pm) are
superb, esp full-dress communion and there are open days; phone 0141 889
7654 for dates. Otherwise Abbey open AYR Mon-Sat 10am-3.30pm. Café/shop.

1949 ✓✓ **JEDBURGH ABBEY:** The classic abbey ruin; conveys the most com-
MAP 3 plete impression of the Border abbeys built under the patronage of
D6 David I in the 12th century. Its tower and remarkable Catherine window are
still intact. Excavations have unearthed example of a 12th-century comb. It's
now displayed in the excellent VC which brilliantly illustrates the full story of
the abbey's amazing history. Best view from across the Jed in the 'Glebe'. May-
Sep 9.30am-6.30pm, Oct-Mar until 4.30pm. Sun 2-4.30pm. HS

1950   ✓ **DRYBURGH ABBEY, nr ST BOSWELLS:** One of the most evocative of
MAP 3   ruins, an aesthetic attraction since the late 18th century. Sustained innu-
D6   merable attacks from the English since its inauguration by Premonstratensian
Canons in 1150. Celebrated by Sir Walter Scott, buried here in 1832 (with his
biographer Lockhart at his feet), its setting, amongst huge cedar trees on the
banks of the Tweed is one of pure historical romance. 4km A68. (1731/VIEWS.)
Apr-Sept 9.30-6.30, Oct-Mar till 4.30, Sun 2-4.30.   HS

1951 **CROSSRAGUEL ABBEY, MAYBOLE:** 24km S of Ayr on A77. Built 1244, one of
MAP 2 first Cluniac settlements in Scotland, an influential and rich order, stripped in
E6 the Reformation. Now an extensive ruin of architectural distinction, the
ground plan v well preserved and obvious. Open daily if you're passing.   HS

1952 **SWEETHEART, NEW ABBEY nr DUMFRIES:** 12km S by A710. The endearing
MAP 1 and enduring warm red sandstone abbey in the shadow of Criffel, so named
D2 because Devorguilla de Balliol, devoted to her husband (he of the Oxford
College), founded the abbey for Cistercian monks and kept his heart in a cas-
ket which is buried with her here. No roof, but the tower is intact. (895/SW
HOTELS.) Nice tearoom adj if you can sit out and gaze at the ruins while eating
yr fruit pie.   HS

1953 **MELROSE ABBEY:** Another romantic setting, the abbey seems to give an
MAP 3 atmos to the whole town. Built by David I (what a guy!) for Cistercian monks
D6 from Rievaulx from 1136, there wasn't much left, spiritually or architecturally,
by the Reformation. Once, however, it sustained a huge community, as
evinced by the widespread excavations. There's a museum of abbey, church
and Roman relics; soon to include Robert the Bruce's heart, recently excavated in the gdns. Nice Tweed walks can start here. Same hrs as Jed.   HS

1954 **ARBROATH ABBEY:** 25km N of Dundee. Founded in 1178 and endowed on an
MAP 3 unparalleled scale, this is an important place in Scots history. It's where the
D2 Declaration was signed in 1320 to appeal to the Pope to release the Scots
from the yoke of the English (you can buy facsimiles of the yellow parchment;
the original is in the Scottish Records Office in Edin). It was to Arbroath that
the Stone of Destiny (on which Scottish kings were traditionally crowned) was
returned after being 'stolen' from Westminster Abbey in the 1950s and is now
at Edinburgh Castle.   HS

THE GREAT BATTLEGROUNDS

Chosen for accessibility and sense of history as well as historical significance.

1955 CULLODEN, INVERNESS: Signed from A9 and A96 into Inverness and about
MAP 5 8km from town. Extensive battlefield on either side of the rd before you even
E2 get to the (v full-on) VC. Positions of the clans and the troops marked out
across the moor; flags enable you to get a real sense of scale. If you go in
spring you see how wet and miserable the Moor can be (the battle took place
on 16 April 1746). No matter how many other folk are there wandering down
the lines, a visit to this most infamous of battlefields can still leave a pain in
the heart. Centre 9am-6pm (winter 11am-4pm) Cl 2 weeks in Jan. Ground
open at all times for more personal Cullodens.   NTS

1956 BATTLE OF THE BRAES, SKYE: 10km Portree. Take main A850 rd S for 3km
MAP 5 then left, marked 'Braes' for 7km. Monument is on a rise on rt. The last battle
A2 fought on British soil and a significant place in Scots history. When the clearances, uninterrupted by any organised opposition, were virtually complete
and vast tracts of Scotland had been depopulated for sheep, the Skye crofters
finally stood up in 1882 to the Government troops and said enough is
enough. A cairn has been erected nr the spot where they fought on behalf of
'all the crofters of Gaeldom', a battle which led eventually to the Crofters Act
which has guaranteed their rights ever since. At the end of this rd at
Peinchorran, there are fine views of Raasay (which was devastated by clearances) and Glamaig, the conical Cuillin, across L Sligachan.

1957 GLENCOE: Not much of a battle, of course, but one of the most infamous mas-
MAP 2 sacres in British history. Much has been written (John Prebble's *Glencoe* and
D2 others) and the new VC provides audiovisual scenario. There's the Macdonald
monument nr Glencoe village and the walk to the more evocative Signal Rock
where the bonfire was lit, now a happy wood-land trail in this doom-laden
landscape. Many gr walks. (1982/SPOOKY PLACES, 1378/PUBS)

1958 SCAPA FLOW, ORKNEY MAINLAND and HOY: Scapa Flow, surrounded by
various of the southern Orkney islands, is one of the most sheltered anchor-
ages in Europe. Hence the huge presence in Orkney of ships and personnel
during both wars. The Germans scuttled 54 of their warships here in 1919 and
many still lie in the bay. The *Royal Oak* was torpedoed in 1939 with the loss of
833 men. Much still remains of the war yrs (especially if you're a diver,
2024/DIVING): the rusting hulks, the shore fortifications, the Churchill Barriers
and the ghosts of a long-gone army at Scapa and Lyness on Hoy. Excl 'tour' on
MV Guide with remote controlled camera exploring 3 wrecks. 01856 811360.

1959 LILLIARD'S EDGE, nr ST BOSWELLS: On main A68, look for Lilliard's Edge
MAP 3 Caravan Park 5km S of St Boswells; park and walk back towards St Boswells to
D6 the brim of the hill (about 500m), then cross rough ground on rt along ridge,
following tree-line hedge. Marvellous view attests to strategic location. 200m
along, a cairn marks the grave of Lilliard who, in 1545, joined the Battle of
Ancrum Moor against the English 'loons' under the Earl of Angus. 'And when
her legs were cuttit off, she fought upon her stumps'. An ancient poem etched
on the stone records her legendary … feet.

1960 KILLIECRANKIE, nr PITLOCHRY: The first battle of the Jacobite Risings where,
MAP 3 in July 1689, the Highlanders lost their leader Viscount (aka Bonnie) Dundee,
B2 but won the battle, using the narrow Pass of Killiecrankie. One escaping soldier
made a famous leap. Well-depicted scenario in VC; short walk to 'The Leap'.
Battle viewpoint and cairn is further along rd to Blair Atholl, turning rt and
doubling back nr the Garry GH and on, almost to A9 underpass (3km from VC).
You get the lie of the land from here. Many good walks.

1961 BANNOCKBURN, nr STIRLING: 4km town centre via Glas rd (it's well sign-
MAP 3 posted) or jnct 9 of M9 (3km), behind a sad hotel & car-rental centre. Some vis-
B4 itors might be perplexed as to why 24 June 1314 was such a big deal for the
Scots and, apart from the 50m walk to the flag-pole and the huge statue,
there's not a lot doing. But the 'Heritage Centre' does bring the scale of it to
life, the horror and the glory. The battlefield itself is thought to lie around the
orange building of the High School some distance away, and the best place to
see the famous wee burn is from below the magnificent Telford Br. Ask at
centre (5km by road).

MARY, QUEEN OF SCOTS 1542–87

LINLITHGOW PALACE: Where she was born (1843/RUINS).

HOLYROOD PALACE, EDINBURGH: And lived (392/MAIN ATTRACTIONS).

1962
MAP 3
A4
INCHMAHOME PRIORY, PORT OF MENTEITH: The ruins of the Priory on the island in Scotland's only lake, where the infant Queen spent her early years in the safe keeping of the Augustinian monks. Short journey by boat from quay nr lake hotel. Signal the ferryman by turning the board to the island, much as she did. Apr-Oct. 7 days. Last trip 5.15pm (3.15 Oct). Delights of the Trossachs surround you. Good pub fd on way home (1402/PUB FD).   HS

1963
MAP 3
D6
MARY QUEEN OF SCOTS' HOUSE, JEDBURGH: In gdns via Smiths Wynd off main st. Historians quibble but this long-standing museum claims to be 'the' house where she became ill in 1566, but somehow made it over to visit the injured Bothwell at Hermitage Castle 50km away. Tower house in good condition; displays and well-told saga. Mar-Nov 10am-4.30pm (4.30 June-Aug), Sun 1-4.30pm. Wint hrs vary slightly.

1964
MAP 3
C4
LOCH LEVEN CASTLE, nr KINROSS: The ultimate in romantic penitentiaries; on the island in the middle of the loch and clearly visible from the M90. Not much left of the ruin to fill out the fantasy, but this is where Mary spent 10 months in 1568 before her famous escape and her final attempt to get back the throne. Sailings Apr-Sept, 9.30am-6.30pm (last outward 5.15pm) from pier at National Game Angling Academy (Pier Bar serves while you wait) in small launch from Kirkgate Park. 7min trip, return as you like.

1965
MAP 1
C3
DUNDRENNAN ABBEY, nr AUCHENCAIRN and KIRKCUDBRIGHT: Mary Queen of Scots got around and there are innumerable places, castles and abbeys where she spent the night. This, however, was where she spent her last one on Scottish soil. She left next day from Pt Mary (nothing much to see there except a beach – it's 2km along the rd that skirts the sinister MoD range – the pier's long gone and … well, there's no plaque). The Cistercian abbey of Whitemonks (established 1142), which harboured her on her last night, is now a tranquil ruin.   HS

'In my end is my beginning,' she said, facing her execution which came 19 yrs later.

1966
MAP 3
D4
Her 'death mask' is displayed at **LENNOXLOVE HOUSE**, nr **HADDINGTON**; it does seem on the small side for someone who was supposedly 6 feet tall!

1967
MAP 4
D3
BLAIR MUSEUM nr PETERCULTER, ABERDEEN: Scotland's 'Catholic treasury' in college at Blairs on the S Deeside Rd. Massive & austere former pile cl 1986, with adj chapel a repository for religious artefacts, history of the seminary & the 'official' memorial portrait of the recently dead queen – the start of the legend. Apr-Sept, Sat/Sun till 5pm. A lock of Bonnie Prince Charlie's hair is also here (but no T-shirts).

BONNIE PRINCE CHARLIE 1720–88

1968
MAP 7
A5
PRINCE CHARLIE'S BAY, ERISKAY: The uncelebrated, unmarked and beautiful beach where Charlie first landed in Scotland to begin the Jacobite Rebellion. Nothing much has changed and this crescent of sand with soft machair and a turquoise sea is still a secret place. 1km from township heading S. (2301/MAGICAL ISLANDS.)

1969
MAP 5
B3
LOCH NAN UAMH, nr ARISAIG, THE PRINCE'S CAIRN: 7km from Lochailort on A830 (1718/SCENIC ROUTES), 48km Ft William. Signed from the rd, a path leads down to the left. This is the 'traditional' spot (pron 'Loch Na Nuan') where Charlie embarked for France in Sept 1746, having lost the battle and the cause. The rocky headland also o/look the bay and skerries where he'd landed in July the year before to begin the campaign. This place was the beginning and the end and it has all the romance necessary to be utterly convincing. Is that a French ship out there in the mist?

1970 **GLENFINNAN:** The place where he 'raised his standard' to rally the clans to
MAP 5 the Jacobite cause. For a while on that August day in 1745 it had looked as if
C2 only a handful were coming. Then they heard the pipes and 600 Camerons
came marching from the valley (where the viaduct now spans). That must
have been one helluva moment. Though it's thought that he actually stood on
the higher ground, there is a powerful sense of place and history here. The VC
has an excellent map of Charlie's path/flight through Scotland – somehow he
touched all the most alluring places! Tower can be climbed (NTS). Consider also
the monument from L Shiel itself (1718/JOURNEYS).

CULLODEN, nr INVERNESS: 1955/BATTLEGROUNDS.

ROBERT THE BRUCE 1274–1329

1971 **BRUCE'S STONE, GLEN TROOL, nr NEWTON STEWART:** 26km N by A714 via
MAP 1 Bargrennan (8km to head of glen) which is on the S Upland Way (2027/LONG
B2 WALKS). The fair Glen Trool is a celebrated spot in the Galloway Forest Park
(1673/GLENS). The stone is signed and marks the area where Bruce's guerrilla
band rained boulders down on the pursuing English in 1307 after they had
routed the main army at Solway Moss. Good walking, incl Merrick
(2001/HILLS).

1972 **BANNOCKBURN, nr STIRLING:** The climactic battle in June 1314, when Bruce
MAP 3 decisively whipped the English and got himself the kingdom (though
B4 Scotland was not recognised as independent until 1328, just before his
death). The scale of the skirmish can be visualised at the heritage centre, but
not so readily 'in the field' (1961/BATTLEGROUNDS).

1973 **ARBROATH ABBEY:** Not much of the Bruce trail here, but this is where the
MAP 3 famous Declaration was signed that was the attempt of the Scots nobility
D2 united behind him to gain international recognition of the independence
they had won on the battlefield. What it says is stirring stuff; the original is in
Edin (1954/ABBEYS).   HS

1974 **DUNFERMLINE ABBEY CHURCH:** Here, at last, some tangible evidence, his
MAP 3 tomb. Buried in 1329, his remains were discovered wrapped in gold cloth,
C4 when the site was being cleared for the new church in 1818. Many of the
other gr kings, the Alexanders I and III, were not so readily identifiable (Bruce's
ribcage had been cut to remove his heart). With gr national emotion he was
reinterred underneath the pulpit. The church (as opposed to the ruins and
Norman nave adj) is open Apr-Sept 10am-4.30pm. Gr café in Abbot House
thro graveyard (2029/MUSEUMS). Look up & see Robert carved on the skyline.

1975 **MELROSE ABBEY:** On his deathbed Bruce asked that his heart be buried here
MAP 3 after it was taken to the Crusades to aid the Army in their battles. A likely lead
D6 casket thought to contain it was excavated from the chapter house and it did
date from the period. It was reburied here and is marked with a stone. I think
we can believe in this!   HS

1976 **ROBERT BURNS (1759–96), ALLOWAY, AYR AND DUMFRIES:** A well-marked
MAP 1 heritage trail through his life and haunts in Ayrshire and Dumfriesshire. His
D2 howff at Dumfries is v atmospheric. Best is at **ALLOWAY:** The Auld Brig o'
MAP 2 Doon and the Auld Kirk, where Tam o' Shanter saw the witches, dance are
E6 evocative, & the Monument and surrounding gdns are lovely. 1km up the rd,
the cottage, his birthplace, has little atmos, and the Tam o' Shanter Experience
– which has an auditorium and a café – has a shop which is a temple to tat.
AYR: The Auld Kirk off main st by river; graveyard with diagram of where his
friends are buried; open at all times. **DUMFRIES:** House where he spent his
last yrs and mausoleum 250m away at back of a kirkyard stuffed with extravagant masonry. 10km N of Dumfries on A76 at **ELLISLAND FARM** is the most
interesting of all the sites. The farmhouse with genuine memorabilia e.g. his
mirror, fishing-rod, a poem scratched on glass, original manuscripts. There's his
favourite walk by the river where he composed 'Tam o' Shanter' and a strong
atmos about the place. Farmer/curator Les Byers will let you in to see when
he's at home. **BROW WELL, nr RUTHWELL** on the B725 20km S Dumfries and
nr Caerlaverock (1664/BIRDS), is a quiet place, a well with curative properties
where he went in the latter stages of his illness. Not many folk go to this one.

BURNS & A' THAT festival in May is a major new development. I'm the director of it at TGP so I would say it was good, wouldn't I? It's brilliant! Report:
21/EVENTS.

1977 **LEWIS GRASSIC GIBBON (1901–35), ARBUTHNOT, nr STONEHAVEN:**
MAP 3 Although James Leslie Mitchell left the area in 1917, this is where he was born
E1 and spent his formative years. Visitor Centre (01561 361668; Apr-Oct 7 days
10am-4.30pm) at the end of the village (via B967, 16km S of Stonehaven off
main A92) has details of his life and can point you in the direction of the
places he writes about in his trilogy, *A Scots Quair*. The first part, *Sunset Song*,
is generally considered to be one of the gr Scots novels and this area, the
HOWE OF THE MEARNS, is the place he so effectively evokes. Arbuthnot is
reminiscent of 'Kinraddie' and the churchyard 1km away on the other side of
rd still has the atmos of that time of innocence before the war which pervades
the book. New, big film of *Sunset Song* on the way at TGP. His ashes are here in
a grave in a corner. From 1928 to when he died 7yrs later at the age of only 34,
he wrote an incredible 17 books.

1978 **NEIL GUNN (1891–1973), DUNBEATH, nr WICK:** Scotland's foremost writer
MAP 6 on Highland life, only recently receiving the recognition he deserves, was
D2 brought up in this NE fishing village and based 3 of his greatest yarns here,
particularly *Highland River*, which must stand in any literature as a brilliant
evocation of place. The **STRATH** in which it is set is below the house (a nondescript terraced house next to the Stores) and makes for a gr walk
(2044/GLEN AND RIVER WALKS). There's a commemorative statue by the harbour,
not quite the harbour you imagine from the books. Gunn also lived for many
yrs nr **DINGWALL** and there is a memorial on the back rd to Strathpeffer and
a wonderful view in a place he often walked (on A834, 4km from Dingwall).

1979 **JAMES HOGG (1770–1835), ST MARY'S LOCH, ETTRICK:** 'The Ettrick
MAP 3 Shepherd' who wrote one of the great works of Scottish literature,
C6 *Confessions of a Justified Sinner*, was born, lived and died in the valleys of the
YARROW and the **ETTRICK**, some of the most starkly beautiful landscapes in
Scotland. **ST MARY'S LOCH** on the A708, 28km W of Selkirk: there's a com-
memorative statue looking over the loch and the adj and supernatural seem-
ing L of the Lowes. On the strip of land betw is **TIBBIE SHIELS** pub (and hotel),
once a gathering place for the writer and his friends (e.g. Sir Walter Scott) and
still a notable hostelry. Across the valley divide (11km on foot, part of the S
Upland Way (2027/LONG WALKS), or 25km by rd past the Gordon Arms Hotel is
the remote village of **ETTRICK**, another monument and his grave (and Tibbie
Shiels') in the churchyard. His countryside is stark and beautiful. The James
Hogg exhib is at Bowhill House Visitor Centre. Tel 01750 22204.

1980 **SIR WALTER SCOTT (1771–1832), ABBOTSFORD, MELROSE:** No other place in
MAP 3 Scotland (and few anywhere) contains so much of a writer's life and work. This
D6 was the house he rebuilt from the farmhouse he moved to in 1812 in the coun-

tryside he did so much to popularise. The house is still lived in by his descendants and the library and study are pretty much as he left them, including 9,000 rare books, antiquarian even in his day. Pleasant grounds and topiary and a walk by the Tweed which the house o/look. His grave is at **DRYBURGH ABBEY** (1950/ABBEYS). House open Apr-Oct 10am-5pm; Sun 2-5pm (in summer 10am).

1981 **ROBERT LOUIS STEVENSON (1850–94), EDINBURGH:** Though Stevenson
MAP A travelled widely – lived in France, emigrated to America and died and was buried in Samoa – he spent the first 30 yrs of his short life in Edin. He was born and brought up in the New Town, living at **17 HERIOT ROW** from 1857-80 in a fashionable town house which is still lived in (not open to the public). Most of his youth was spent in this newly built and expanding part of the city in an area bounded then by parkland and farms. Both the **BOTANICS** (388/OTHER ATTRACTIONS) and **WARRISTON CEMETERY** (1936/GRAVEYARDS) are part of the landscape of his childhood. However, his fondest recollections were of the **PENTLAND HILLS** and, virtually unchanged as they are, it's here that one is following most poignantly in his footsteps. The 'cottage' at **SWANSTON** (a delightful village with some remarkable thatched cottages reached via the city bypass/Colinton t/off or from Oxgangs Rd and a br over the bypass; the village nestles in a grove of trees below the hills and is a good place to walk from), the ruins of **GLENCORSE CHURCH** (ruins even then and where he later asked that a prayer be said for him) and **COLINTON MANSE** can all be seen, but not visited. The fact is, Edinburgh has no Stevenson Museum (though his lifetime was relatively recent and his acclaim international). Pity that the **HAWES INN** in South Queensferry where he wrote *Kidnapped* has recently had its history obliterated by a brewery makeover.

J.K. ROWLING (we don't give a lady's birthdate): Scotland's most successful writer & ever as the creator of Harry Potter, rich beyond her wildest dreams, was once (& famously) an impecunious single mother scribbling away in Edinburgh coffee-shops. The most-mentioned is opp the Festival Theatre & is now a Chinese restau (upstairs), but not listed. The **ELEPHANT HOUSE** (283/COFFEESHOPS) was another & gives you the idea. Harry Potter country as interepreted by Hollywood can be found at **GLENFINNAN** (1970/MARY, CHARLIE AND BOB) and **GLENCOE** esp around the **CLACHAIG INN** (1273/INNS). JKR lives nr Aberfeldy – you might see her in another coffee-shop, the one at **HOUSE OF MENZIES** (2202/WHERE TO BUY ART), tho she no longer scribbles publicly.

IRVINE WELSH (c1958–): Literary immortality awaits confirmation. Tours (*that* toilet etc) likely any day. **ROBBIE'S BAR:** might suffice (348/'UNSPOILT' PUBS); you will hear the voices.

THE REALLY SPOOKY PLACES

1982 **HIDDEN VALLEY, GLENCOE:** The secret glen where the ill-fated Macdonalds
MAP 2 hid the cattle they'd stolen from the Lowlands and which became (with poli-
D2 tics and power struggles) their undoing. A narrow wooded cleft takes you betw the imposing and gnarled '3 Sisters' Hills and over the threshold (God knows how the cattle got there) and into the huge bowl of Coire Gabhail. The place envelops you in its tragic history, more redolent perhaps than any of the massacre sites. Park on the A82 5km from the VC 300m W of 2 white buildings on either side of the rd (always cars parked here). Follow clear path down to and across the R Coe. Ascend keeping burn to left; 1.5km further up, it's best to ford it. Allow 3hrs. (1957/BATTLEGROUNDS.)   2-B-2

1983 **UNDER EDINBURGH OLD TOWN:** Mary King's Close, a medieval st under the
MAP A Royal Mile closed in 1753 (The Real Mary King's Close 08702 430160); and the
D3 Vaults under South Br – built in the 18th century and sealed up around the time of the Napoleonic Wars (Mercat Tours 0131 557 6464). History underfoot for unsuspecting tourists and locals alike. Glimpses of a rather smelly subterranean life way back then. It's dark during the day, and you wouldn't want to get locked in.

1984 **THE YESNABY STACKS, ORKNEY MAINLAND:** A cliff top viewpoint that's so wild, so dramatic and, if you walk near the edge, so precarious that its supernaturalism verges on the uneasy. Shells of lookout posts from the war echo the melancholy spirit of the place. ('The bloody town's a bloody cuss/No bloody trains, no bloody bus/And no one cares for bloody us/In bloody Orkney' – first lines of a poem written then, a soldier's lament.) Nr Skara Brae, it's about 30km from Kirkwall and way out west.

1985 THE FAIRY GLEN, SKYE: A place so strange, it's hard to believe that it's mere-
MAP 5 ly a geological phenomenon. Entering Uig on the A855 (becomes A87) from
A1 Portree, there's a turret on the left (Macrae's Folly). Take rd on rt marked Balnaknock for 2km and you enter an area of extraordinary conical hills which, in certain conditions of light and weather, seems to entirely justify its legendary provenance. Your mood may determine whether you believe they were good or bad fairies, but there's supposed to be an incredible 365 of these grassy hillocks, some 35m high – how else could they be there?

1986 CLAVA CAIRNS, nr CULLODEN, INVERNESS: Nr Culloden (1955/BATTLE-
MAP 5 GROUNDS) these curious chambered cairns in a grove of trees nr a river in the
E2 middle of 21st-century nowhere can be seriously Blair Witch (1866/PREHIS-TORIC SITES for details).

1987 THE CLOOTIE WELL on the road betw TORE on the A9 and AVOCH: Spooky
MAP 5 spooky place on the rd towards Avoch and Cromarty 4km from the r/bout at
D1 Tore N of Inverness. Easily missed, but it's on the rt side of the rd going E. What you see is hundreds of rags (actually pieces of clothing) hanging on the branches of trees around the spout of an ancient well. They go way back up the hill behind and have probably been here for decades. Don't wish you were here. This has what you'd call strong (but strange) vibrations.

1988 BURN O'VAT, nr BALLATER: This impressive and rather spooky glacial curios-
MAP 4 ity on Royal Deeside is a popular spot and well worth the short walk. 8km
C3 from Ballater towards Aberd on main A93, take A97 for Huntly for 2km to the car park at the Muir of Dinnet nature reserve. Some scrambling to reach the huge 'pot' from which the burn flows to L Kinord. Forest walks, busy on fine weekends, but v odd when you catch it quiet.

1989 CRICHOPE LINN, nr THORNHILL: A supernatural sliver of glen inhabited by
MAP 1 water spirits of various temperaments (and Spanish schoolkids on the wrong
D1 day – go figure). Take rd for Cample on A76 Dumfries to Kilmarnock rd just S of Thornhill; at village (2km) take left for 2km. Discreet sign and gate in bank on rt is easy to miss, but quarry for parking 100m further on, on left, is more obvious. Take care – can be very wet and very slippy. Gorge is a 10-min schlep from the gate. More than dignity has been lost.

1990 SALLOCHY WOOD, LOCH LOMOND: B837, N of Balmaha, look for Sallochy
MAP 2 Wood car park on the left. Cross back over the rd, away from L Lomond, and
E4 follow the trail signs, up the hill. After the large cedar tree, the path takes you into the woods. Slippery going (on the exposed tree roots) then an unexpected clearing in middle of dense undergrowth. This is the ruined hamlet of Wester Sallochy. Surrounded by gloomy conifers, the roofless buildings still stand, awaiting the return of their long-dead tenants. Not a place to visit at night, but some do, and they leave their mark …

THE NECROPOLIS, GLASGOW: 1935/GRAVEYARDS.

HAMILTON MAUSOLEUM, STRATHCLYDE PARK: 1902/MONUMENTS.

LOANHEAD OF DAVIOT, nr OLDMELDRUM, ABERDEENSHIRE:
1875/PREHISTORIC SITES.

SECTION 9

Strolls, Walks and Hikes

Popular and notable hills in the various regions of Scotland but not including Munros or difficult climbs. Always best to remember that the weather can change v quickly. Take an OS map on higher tops. See p. 12 for walk codes.

1991
MAP 6
B2

✔ ✔ **SUILVEN, LOCHINVER:** From close or far away, this is one of Scotland's most awe-inspiring mountains. The 'sugar loaf' can seem almost insurmountable, but in good weather it's not so difficult. Route from Inverkirkaig 5km S of Lochinver on rd to Achiltibuie, turns up track by Achin's Bookshop (2188/CRAFT SHOPS) on the path for the Kirkaig Falls; once at the loch, you head for the Bealach, the central waistline through an unexpected dyke and follow track to the top. The slightly quicker route from the N (Glencanisp) following a stalkers' track that eventually leads to Elphin, also heads for the central breach in the mt's defences. Either way it's a long walk in; 8km before the climb. Allow 8hrs return. At the top, the most enjoyable 100m in the land and below – amazing Assynt. 731m. Take OS map.   2-C-3

1992
MAP 6
B3

✔ ✔ **STAC POLLAIDH/POLLY, nr ULLAPOOL:** This hill described various-ly as 'perfect', 'preposterous' and 'gr fun', certainly has character and, rising out of the Sutherland moors on the rd to Achiltibuie off the A835 N from Ullapool, demands to be climbed. Route everyone takes is from the car park by L Lurgainn 8km from main rd. Head for the central ridge which for many folk is enough; the path to the pinnacles is exposed and can be off-putting. Best half day hill climb in the N. 613m. Allow 3-4hrs return.   2-B-3

1993
MAP 2
D5

✔ **GOAT FELL, ARRAN:** Starting from the car park at Cladach before Brodick Castle grounds 3km from town, or from Corrie further up the coast (12km). Worn path, a steady climb, rarely much of a scramble but a rewarding afternoon's exertion. Some scree and some view! 874m. Allow 5hrs.   2-B-2

1994
MAP 2
E3

✔ **THE COBBLER (BEN ARTHUR), ARROCHAR:** Perennial favourite of the Glas hill walker and, for sheer exhilaration, the most popular of 'the Arrochar Alps'. A motorway path ascends from the A83 on the other side of L Long from Arrochar (park in lay-bys nr Succoth rd end; there are always loads of cars) and takes 2.5-3hrs to traverse the up'n'down route to the top. Just short of a Munro at 881m, it has 3 tops of which the N peak is the simplest scramble (central and S peaks for climbers). Way not marked; consult.   2-B-3

FIVE MAGNIFICENT HILLS IN THE TROSSACHS

1995
MAP 3
A3

✔ **BEN VENUE and BEN AN:** 2 celebrated tops in the Highland microcosm of the Trossachs around L Achray, 15km W of Callander; strenuous but not difficult and with superb views. Ben Venue (727m) is the more serious; allow 4-5 hrs return. Start from Kinlochard side at Ledard or more usually from behind L Achray Hotel: 100m along 'Forest Path' go left and then it's way-marked. Ben An (415m) starts with a steep climb from the main A821 along from the time-share mansions. Scramble at top. Allow 2 to 3hrs.   2-B-3

1996
MAP 3
A3

BENN SHIAN, STRATHYRE: Another Trossachs favourite and not taxing. From village main rd (the A74 to Lochearnhead), cross bridge opp Monro Hotel, turn left after 200m then path to rt at 50m a steep start through woods. O/look village and views to Crianlarich and Ben Vorlich (*see below*). 600m. 1.5hrs.   2-B-3

1997
MAP 3
A4

DOON HILL, THE FAERIE KNOWE, ABERFOYLE: Legendary hillock in Aberfoyle, only 1hr up and back, so a gentle elevation into faerie land. The tree at the top is the home of the 'People of Quietness' and there was once a local minister who had the temerity to tell their secrets (in 1692). Go round it 7 times and your wish will be granted, go round it backwards at your peril (well, you wouldn't would you?). Go from end of main st and opp jnct of Trossachs/Callander rd take small rd turning left at the Covenanter.   1-B-1

1998
MAP 3
A3

BEN VORLICH: The big hill itself is also approached from the S Lochearn rd; from Ardvorlich House 5km from A84. Enter 'East Gate' and follow signs for open hillside of Glen Vorlich. Track splits after 1.5km, take right then SE side of come to N ridge of mountain. Allow 5hrs ret.   2-B-3

1999 ✓ **DUNADD, KILMARTIN, N of LOCHGILPHEAD:** 8km N on A816. Less of a
MAP 2　hill, more of a lump, but it's where they crowned the kings of Dalriada for
C3　half a millennium. Stand on top when the Atlantic rain is sheeting in and …
you get wet like the kings did. Kilmartin House Museum nearby for info & gr
food (2257/MUSEUMS).　　　　2-B-2

2000 **CRIFFEL, NEW ABBEY, nr DUMFRIES:** 12km S by A710 to New Abbey, which
MAP 1　Criffel dominates. It's only 569m, but seems higher. Exceptional views from
D2　top as far as English lakes and across to Borders. Granite lump with brilliant
outcrops of quartzite. The annual race gets up and back to the Abbey Arms in
under an hr; you can take it easier. Start 3km S of village, t/off A710 by one of
the curious painted bus shelters signed for Ardwell Mains Farm. Park before
the farm buildings and get on up.　　　　2-A-2

2001 **MERRICK, nr NEWTON STEWART:** Go from bonnie Glen Trool via Bargrennan
MAP 1　14km N on the A714. Bruce's Stone is there at the start (1971/MARY, CHARLIE
B2　AND BOB). The highest peak in S Scotland (843m), it's a strenuous though
straightforward climb in glorious scenery. 4hrs.　　　　2-B-3

2002 **NORTH BERWICK LAW:** The conical volcanic hill, a beacon in the E Lothian
MAP 3　landscape. **TRAPRAIN LAW** nearby, is higher, tends to be frequented by rock
D4　climbers, but has major prehistoric significance as a hillfort citadel of the
Goddodin and a definite aura. NBL is easy and rewarding – leave town by Law
Rd, path marked beyond houses. Car park and picnic site. Views 'to the
Cairngorms' (!) and along the Forth.　　　　BOTH 1-A-1

2003 **RUBERSLAW, DENHOLM, nr HAWICK:** This smooth hummock above the
MAP 3　Teviot valley affords views of 7 counties, incl Northumberland. Millennium
D6　plaque on top. At 424m, it's a gentle climb taking about 1hr from the usual
start at Denholm Hill Farm (private land, be aware of livestock). Leave
Denholm at corner of Green by shop and go past post office. Take left after
2km to farm.　　　　2-A-2

2004 **TINTO HILL, nr BIGGAR and LANARK:** A favourite climb in S/Central
MAP 3　Scotland with easy access to start from A73 nr Symington, 10km S of Lanark.
B6　Park 100m behind Tinto Hills farm shop, after stocking up with rolls and juice.
Good track, though it has its ups and downs before you get there. Braw views.
707m. Allow 3hrs.　　　　2-A-2

2005 **DUMGOYNE nr BLANEFIELD:** Close to Glasgow & almost a mountain, so a
MAP 3　popular non-strenuous hike. Huge presence, sits above A81 & Glengoyne
A4　Distillery (open to public). App from Strathblane War Memorial via Campsie
Dene rd. 7km track, allow 3–4 hrs (or take the steep way up from the distillery).
Refresh/replenish in Killearn (917/CENTRAL HOTELS, 1415/PUB FOOD). Take care
on outcrops.　　　　2-A-2

2006 **CONIC HILL, BALMAHA, LOCH LOMOND:** An easier climb than the Ben up
MAP 2　the rd and a good place to view it from, Conic, on the Highland fault line, is
E4　one of the first Highland hills you reach from Glas. Stunning views also of L
Lomond from its 358m peak. Ascend thro woodland from the corner of
Balmaha car park. Watch for buzzards and your footing on the final crumbly
bits. May be closed for lambing season Apr-May. 1.5hrs up.　　　　2-A-2

2007 **KINNOULL HILL, PERTH:** Various starts from town (the path from beyond
MAP 3　Branklyn Gdn on the Dundee Rd is less frequented) to the wooded ridge
C3　above the Tay with its tower and incredible views to S from the precipitous
cliffs. Surprisingly extensive area of hill side common and it's not difficult to
get lost. The leaflet/map from Perth TIC helps. Local lurv spot after dark. 1-A-1

2008 **BENNACHIE, nr ABERDEEN:** The pilgrimage hill, an easy 528m often busy at
MAP 4　w/ends but never a let-down. Various trails take in 'the Taps'. Trad route from
C3　Rowan Tree nr Chapel of Garioch (pron 'Geery') signed Pittodrie off A96 nr
Pitcaple. Also from Essons car park on rd from Chapel-Monymusk, which is
steeper. Or from other side the Lord's Throat rd, a longer, more forested app
from banks of the Don. All car parks have trail-finders. From the fortified top
you see what Aberdeenshire is about. 2hrs. Bennachie's soulmate, **TAP O'**
NOTH, is 20km W. Easy app via Rhynie on A97 (then 3km).　　　　2-B-2

The following ranges of hills offer walks in various directions and more than one summit. They are all accessible and fairly easy. See p. 12 for walk codes.

2009 **WALKS ON SKYE:** Obviously many serious walks in and around the Cuillins
MAP 5 (2022/MUNROS, 2031/SERIOUS WALKS), but almost infinite variety of others. Can do no better than read a gr book, *50 Best Routes on Skye and Raasay* by Ralph Storer (avail locally), which describes and grades many of the must-dos.

2010 **LOMOND HILLS, FIFE, nr FALKLAND:** The conservation village lies below a
MAP 3 prominent ridge easily reached from the main st esp via Back Wynd (off which
C3 there's a car park). More usual app to both E and W Lomond, the main tops, is from Craigmead car park 3km from village towards Leslie trail-finder board. The celebrated Lomonds (aka the Paps of Fife), aren't that high (West is 522m), but they can see and be seen for miles. Also start from radio masts 3km up rd from A912 E of Falkland.   3-10KM CIRC XBIKES 2-A-2

An easy rewarding single climb is **BISHOP'S HILL**. Start opp the church in Scotlandwell. A steep path veers left and then there are several ways up. Allow 2hrs. Gr view of L Leven, Fife and a good swathe of Central Scotland. Gliders glide over from the old airstrip below.

2011 **THE EILDONS, MELROSE:** The 3 much-loved hills or paps visible from most of
MAP 3 the Central Borders and easily climbed from the town of Melrose which nes-
D6 tles at their foot. Leave main sq by rd to stn (the Dingleton rd), after 100m a path begins betw 2 pebble-dash houses on the left. You climb the smaller first, then the highest central one (422m). You can make a circular route of it by returning to the golf course. Allow 1.5hrs.   3KM CIRC XBIKES I-A-2

2012 **THE OCHILS:** Usual app from the 'hillfoot towns' at the foot of the glens that cut
MAP 3 into their S-facing slopes, along the A91 Stirling-St Andrews rd. Alva, Tillicoultry
B4 and Dollar all have impressive glen walks easily found from the main streets where tracks are marked (2039/GLEN AND RIVER WALKS). Good start nr Stirling from the Sheriffmuir rd uphill from Br of Allan about 3km, look for pylons and a lay-by on the rt (a reservoir just visible on the left). There are usually other cars here. A stile leads to the hills which stretch away to the E for 40km and afford gr views for little effort. Highest point is Ben Cleugh, 721m. Swimming place near-by is Paradise (1756/PICNICS).   2-40KM SOME CIRC XBIKES 1/2-B-2

2013 **THE LAMMERMUIRS:** The hills SE of Edin that divide the rich farmlands of E
MAP 3 Lothian and the valley of the Tweed in the Borders. Mostly a high wide moor
D5 land but there's wooded gentle hill country in the watersheds of the southern rivers and spectacular coastal scenery betw Cockburnspath and St Abbs Head. (1812/WILDLIFE; 2072/COASTAL WALKS.) The eastern part of the S Upland Way follows the Lammermuirs to the coast (2027/LONG WALKS). Many moorland walks begin at the car park at the head of Whiteadder Reservoir (A1 to Haddington, B6369 towards Humbie, then E on B6355 through Gifford), a mysterious loch in the bowl of the hills. Excellent walks also centre on Abbey St Bathans to the S – head off A1 at Cockburnspath. Through village to Toot Corner (signed 1km) and off to left, follow path above valley of Whiteadder to Edinshall Broch (2km). Further on, along river (1km), is a swing bridge and a fine place to swim. Circular walks possible; ask in village.
5-15KM SOME CIRC MTBIKES 1/2-B-2

2014 **THE CHEVIOTS:** Not strictly in Scotland, but they straddle the border and
MAP 3 Border history. There are many fine walks starting from Kirk Yetholm (incl the
E6 Pennine Way which stretches 400km S to the Peak district and St Cuthbert's Way; 1897/LONG WALKS) incl an 8km circular route of typical Cheviot foothill terrain. See 'Walking in the Scottish Borders' avail from all Border TICs (an excl guide). Most forays start at Wooler 20km from Coldstream and the border. Cheviot itself (2,676ft) a boggy plateau, Hedgehope via the Harthope Burn more fun.

THE CAMPSIE FELLS, nr GLASGOW: 780/WALKS OUTSIDE THE CITY.

THE PENTLAND HILLS, nr EDINBURGH: 414/WALKS OUTSIDE THE CITY.

✓ ✓ *There are almost 300 hills in Scotland over 3000ft as tabled by Sir Hugh Munro in 1891. Those selected here have been chosen for their relative ease of access both to the bottom and thence to the top. All offer rewarding climbs. None should be attempted without proper clothing (esp boots) and sustenance. You may also need an OS map. The weather can change quickly in the Scottish mts.*

2015
MAP 3
B3
BEN CHONZIE nr COMRIE: An easy & gr starter Munro (931m) in accessible & splendid scenery. Ascent not steep. Detail: 2046/GLENWALKS.

2016
MAP 2
E3
BEN LOMOND, ROWARDENNAN, LOCH LOMOND: Many folk's first Munro, given proximity to Glas (soul and city). It's not too taxing a climb and has rewarding views (in good weather). 2 main ascents: 'tourist route' is easier, from toilet block at Rowardennan car park (end of rd from Drymen), well-trodden all the way; or 500m up past Youth Hostel, a path follows burn – the 'Ptarmigan Route'. Circular walk poss. 974m. 3hrs up.

2017
MAP 6
B3
AN TEALLACH, TORRIDON: Sea-level start from Dundonnell on the A832 S of Ullapool, so easy to find. This, one of the most awesome peaks in Scotland is not the ordeal it looks. Path well trod and once up there are gr scrambling opportunities for the nimble. Peering over the pinnacle of Lord Berkeley's Seat 2000' into the void is a jaw-drop. Take a day (a good day). 1,062m.

2018
MAP 5
C1
BEINN ALLIGIN, TORRIDON: The other gr Torridon trek – you may as well go for it! Car park by br on rd to Inveralligin and Diabeg, walk thro woods over moor by tumbling river. Left at fork then a steepish pull up onto the Horns of Alligin. You can cover 2 Munros in a circular route that takes you across the top of the world, up there with mighty Liathach and Beinn Eighe. 985m.

2019
MAP 2
B2
BEN MORE, MULL: The 'cool, high ben' sits in isolated splendour, the only Munro, bar the Cuillins, not on the mainland. Sea-level start from lay-by on the coast rd B8073 that skirts the southern coast of L Na Keal at Dhiseig House, then a fairly clear path through the bleak landscape. Tricky nr the top but there are fabulous views across the islands. 966m.

2020
MAP 5
D1
BEN WYVIS, nr GARVE: Standing apart from its northern neighbours, you can feel the presence of this mt from a long way off. Just to N of main A835 rd from Inverness-Ullapool and v accessible from it, park 6km N of Garve (48km from Inverness) and follow marked path by stream and through the forest. Vast plantations all around but you leave them behind and the app to the summit is by a soft and mossy ridge. Magnificent 1,046m.

2021
MAP 3
C1
LOCHNAGAR, nr BALLATER: Described as a fine, complex mt, its nobility and mystique apparent from afar, not least Balmoral Castle. App via Glen Muick (pron 'Mick') rd from Ballater to car park at L Muick (1698/LOCHS). Path to mt well signed and well trodden. 18km return, allow 6-8hrs. Steep at top. Apparently on a clear day you can see the Forth Br. 1,155m.

2022
MAP 5
B2
BLA BHEINN, SKYE: The magnificent massif, isolated from the other Cuillins, has a sea-level start and seems higher than it is. The *Munro Guide* describes it as 'exceptionally accessible'. It has an eerie jagged beauty and – though some scrambling is involved and it helps to have a head for exposed situations – there are no serious dangers. Take B8083 from Broadford to Elgol thro Torrin, park 1km S of the head of L Slapin, walking W at Allt na Dunaiche along N bank of stream. Bla Bheinn (pron 'Blahven') is an enormously rewarding climb. Rapid descent for scree runners, but allow 8hrs. 928m.

2023
MAP 3
A2
BEN LAWERS, between KILLIN and ABERFELDY, PERTHSHIRE: The massif of 7 summits includes 6 Munros that dominate the N side of L Tay. They are linked by a twisting ridge 12km long that only once falls below 800m and, if you're v fit, it's poss to do the lot in a single day starting from the N or Glen Lyon side. The Munro or non-bagger can have an easier day of it knocking off Beinn Ghlas then Ben Lawers from the VC 5km off the A827. 4/5 hrs.

2024
MAP 3
A2
MEALL NAN TARMACHAN: The part of the ridge to the W of Lawers (above), which takes in a Munro and several tops, is not arduous and is immensely impressive. In 3hrs you can get up, along some of it and back, and feel gr for the rest of the week. Start 1km further on from NTS VC down 100m track and through gate. Head up into saddle, paths indistinct, but just climb.

✔ ✔ *Once again, these walks require preparation, route maps, v good boots etc. But don't carry too much. Sections are always poss. See p. 12 for walk codes.*

2026 **THE WEST HIGHLAND WAY:** The 150km walk which starts at Milngavie 12km
MAP 2 o/side Glas and goes via some of Scotland's most celebrated scenery to emerge in Glen Nevis before the Ben. The route goes: Mugdock Moor-Drymen-L Lomond-Rowardennan-Inversnaid-Inverarnan-Crianlarich-Tyndrum-Br of Orchy-Rannoch Moor-Kingshouse Hotel-Glencoe-The Devil's Staircase-Kinlochleven. The latter part from Br of Orchy is the most dramatic. The Br of Orchy Hotel (01838 400208) (1266/ROADSIDE INNS – not cheap!) and Kingshouse (01855 851259) are both historic staging posts, as is the Drover's Inn, Inverarnan (913/CENTRAL HOTELS). It's a good idea to book accom (allowing time for muscle fatigue) and don't take too much stuff. Info leaflet/pack from shops or Ranger Service (01389 722600).

START: Officially at Milngavie (pron 'Mull-guy') Railway Stn (reg service from Glas Central, also buses from Buchanan St Bus Stn), but actually from Milngavie shopping precinct (Douglas St) 500m away. However, the country-side is close. Start from other end on Glen Nevis rd from r/bout on A82 N from Ft William. Way is well marked, but you must have a route map.   2-B-3

2027 **THE SOUTHERN UPLAND WAY:** 350km walk from Portpatrick S of Stranraer
MAP 1 across the Rhinns of Galloway, much moorland, the Galloway Forest Park, the
A3 wild heartland of Southern Scotland, then through James Hogg country (1979/LITERARY PLACES) to the gentler E Borders and the sea at Pease Bay (official end, Cockburnspath). Route is Portpatrick-Stranraer-New Luce-Dalry-Sanquhar-Wanlockhead-Beattock-St Mary's L-Melrose-Lauder-Abbey St Bathans. The first and latter sections are the most picturesque but highlights include L Trool, the Lowther Hills, St Mary's L, R Tweed. Usually walked W to E, the SU Way is a formidable undertaking … (Info from Ranger Service: 01835 830281).

START: Portpatrick by the harbour and up along the cliffs past the lighthouse. or Cockburnspath. Map is on side of shop at Cross.   2-B-3

2028 **THE SPEYSIDE WAY:** A long distance route which generally follows the valley
MAP 4 of the R Spey from Buckie on the Moray Firth coast to Aviemore in the
C1 foothills of the Cairngorms (there are plans to complete the route to Newtonmore in the next couple of years), with side spurs to Dufftown up Glen Fiddich (7km) and to Tomintoul over the hill between the R Avon (pron 'A'rn') and the R Livet (24km). The main stem of the route largely follows they valley bottom, criss-crossing the Spey several times – a distance of around 100km, and is less strenuous than SU or WH Ways. The Tomintoul spur has more hill-walking character and rises to a gr viewpoint at 600m. Throughout walk you are in whisky country with opportunities to visit Cardhu, Glenlivet and other distilleries nearby (1587/WHISKY). Info from Ranger Service: 01340 881266.

START: Usual start is from coast end. Spey Bay is 8km N of Fochabers; the first marker is by the banks of shingle at the river mouth.   1-A-3

2029 **GLEN AFFRIC:** In enchanting Glen Affric and L Affric beyond (2037/GLEN AND
MAP 5 RIVER WALKS; 1665/GLENS; 1750/PICNICS), some serious walking begins on the
C2 32km Kintail trail. Done either W-E starting at the Morvich Outdoor Centre 2km from A87 nr Shiel Br, or E-W starting at the Affric Lodge 15km W of Cannich. Route can include one of the approaches to the Falls of Glomach (1676/WATERFALLS).   2-C-3

2030 **ST CUTHBERT'S WAY:** From Melrose in Scottish Borders (where St Cuthbert
MAP 3 started his ministry) to Lindisfarne on Holy Island off Northumberland (where
D6 he died). 100km but many sections easy. Bowden–Maxton a stroll by the Tweed esp fine. Check local TICs.   2-A-3

✓ ✓ ✓ *None of these should be attempted without OS maps, proper equipment and preparation. Hill or ridge walking experience may be essential.*

2031 **THE CUILLINS, SKYE:** Much scrambling and, if you want it, serious climbing
MAP 5 over these famously unforgiving peaks. The Red ones are easier and many walks
A2 start at the Sligachan Hotel on the main Portree-Broadford rd. Every July there's
a hill race up Glamaig; the conical one which o/look the hotel. Most of the Black
Cuillins incl the highest, Sgurr Alasdair (993m), and Sgurr Dearg, 'the
Inaccessible Pinnacle' (978m), can be attacked from the campsite or the youth
hostel in Glen Brittle. Good guides are *Introductory Scrambles from Glen Brittle* by
Charles Rhodes, or *50 Best Routes in Skye and Raasay* by Ralph Storer both available locally, but you will need something. Take extreme care! (2/BIG ATTRACTIONS;
1248/1249/HOSTELS; 1681/WATERFALLS; 2002/MUNROS; 1742/PICNICS.)   3-C-3

2032 **AONACH EAGACH, GLENCOE:** One of several poss major expeditions in the
MAP 2 Glencoe area and one of the world's classic ridge walks. Not for the faint-
D2 hearted or the ill-prepared. It's the ridge on your rt for almost the whole
length of the glen from Altnafeadh to the rd to the Clachaig Inn (rewarding
refreshment). Start from the main rd. Car park opp the one for the Hidden
Valley (1982/SPOOKY PLACES). Stiff pull up then the switchback path across.
There is no turning back. Scary pinnacles two-thirds over, then one more
Munro & the knee-trembling, scree-running descent. On your way, you'll have
come close to heaven, seen Lochaber in its immense glory and reconnoitred
some fairly exposed edges and pinnacles. Go with somebody good as I did.
(1704/SCENIC ROUTES; 1378/BLOODY GOOD PUBS; 1245/ HOSTELS; 1957/BATTLE-
GROUNDS.)   3-C-3

2033 **BEN NEVIS:** Start on Glen Nevis rd, 5km Ft William town centre by br opp
MAP 2 youth hostel or from VC (4km town) over br and past Achintee Farm (gentler
D1 start). These paths lead to the same main route which continues to the top
(many consider the tourist route to be v dull, but it is the safest). Allow the
best part of a day (and I do mean the best – the weather can turn quickly
here). For the more interesting arête route, consult locally. Many people are
killed every yr, even experienced climbers. It is the biggest, though not the
best; you can see 100 Munros on a clear day (i.e. about once a yr.) You climb it
because ... well, because you have to. Ben Nevis Inn for that post-walk pint
(2349/FT WILLIAM).   2-B-3

2034 **THE FIVE SISTERS OF KINTAIL and THE CLUANIE RIDGE:** Both generally
MAP 5 started from A87 along from Cluanie Inn (1382/BLOODY GOOD PUBS) and they
C2 will keep you rt; usually walked E to W. Sisters is an uncomplicated but inspiring ridge walk, taking in 2 Munros and 2 tops. It's a hard pull up and you
descend to a point 8km further up the rd (so arrange transport). Many side
spurs to vantage-points and wild views. The Cluanie or S ridge is a classic
which covers 7 Munros. Starts at inn; 2 ways off back onto A876. Both can be
walked in a single day (Cluanie allow 9hrs). (1246/HOSTELS.)   3-C-3

From the Kintail Centre at Morvich off A87 nr Shiel Br another long distance
walk starts to Glen Affric (2029/LONG WALKS).

2035 **GLEN MORE FOREST PARK:** from Coylumbridge and L Morlich; 32km. (2)
MAP 5 joins (3) beyond L Morlich and both go through the Rothiemurchus Forest
E3 (2059/WOODLAND WALKS) and the famous **LAIRIG GHRU,** the ancient Rt of Way
through the Cairngorms which passes betw Ben Macdui and Braeriach.
Ascent is over 700m and going can be rough. This is one of the gr Scottish
trails. At end of June, the Lairig Ghru Race completes this course E-W in 3.5hrs,
but generally this is a full-day trip. The famous shelter, Corrour Bothy betw
'Devil's Point' and Carn A Mhaim, can be a halfway house. Nr Linn of Dee,
routes (1) and (2/3) converge and pass through the ancient Caledonian Forest
of Mar. Going E-W is less gruelling and there's Aviemore to look forward to!

GLEN AFFRIC: Or rather beyond Glen Affric and L Affric (2037/GLEN WALKS;
1665/GLENS), the serious walking begins (2029/LONG WALKS).

See also GREAT GLENS, *p. 204. Walk codes are on p. 12.*

2036
MAP 3
B1
✓ **GLEN TILT, BLAIR ATHOLL:** A walk of variable length in this classic High-land glen, easily accessible from the old Blair Rd off main Blair Atholl rd nr Bridge of Tilt Hotel, car park by the (v) old bridge. Trail leaflet from park office and local TICs. Fine walking and unspoiled scenery begins only a short distance into the deeply wooded gorge of the R Tilt, but to cover the circular route you have to walk to 'Gilbert's Br' (9km return) or the longer trail to Gow's Br (17km return). Begin here also the gr route into the Cairngorms leading to the Linn of Dee and Braemar, joining the track from Speyside which starts at Feshiebridge or Glenmore Forest (2035/SERIOUS WALKS). **UP TO 17KM CIRC XBIKE 1-B-2**

2037
MAP 5
C2
✓ **GLEN AFFRIC, CANNICH, nr DRUMNADROCHIT:** Easy short walks are marked and hugely rewarding in this magnificent glen well known as the first stretch in the gr E-W route to Kintail (2034/SERIOUS WALKS) and the Falls of Glomach (1676/WATERFALLS). Starting pt of this track into the wilds is at the end of the rd at L Affric; there are many short and circular trails indicated here. Car park is beyond metal rd 2km along forest track towards Affric Lodge (cars not allowed to lodge itself). Track cl in stalking season. Easier walks in famous Affric forest from car park at Dog Falls. 7km from Cannich (1750/PICNICS). Waterfalls and spooky tame birds. Good idea to hire bikes at Drumnadrochit or Cannich (01456 415251). Don't miss Glen Affric (1665/GLENS). **5/8KM CIRC BIKE 1-B-2**

2038
MAP 3
A3
✓ **BALQUHIDDER TO BRIG O' TURK:** Easy amble thro' the heart of Scotland via Glenfinglas (1697/LOCHS) with handy pubs (1405/PUBFOOD) & tearms (1501/ TEAROOMS) at either end. Not circ so best to arrange transport. Usually walked this way round (start at Rob Roy graveyard – 1942/GRAVEYARDS), then Ballimore & past Ben Vane to the reservoir & Brig o' Turk. **18KM XCIRC XBIKE 2-B-2**

2039
MAP 3
B4
✓ **DOLLAR GLEN, DOLLAR, nr STIRLING:** The classic fairy glen in Central Scotland, positively hoaching with water spirits, reeking of ozone and euphoric after rain, the erosion has taken its toll & path no longer goes into the gorge. 20km from Stirling by A91, or 18km from M90 at Kinross jnct 6. Start from top of tree-lined ave on either side of burn or from further up rd signed Castle Campbell where there's a car park and a path down into glen. The Castle at head of glen is open 7 days till 6pm (Oct-Mar till 4pm), and has boggling views. There's a circular walk back or take off for the Ochil Tops, the hills that surround the glen. There are also first-class walks (the hill trail is more rewarding than the 'Mill Trail') up the glens of the other hillfoot towns, Alva and Tillicoultry; they also lead to the hills (1881/HILL WALKS). **3KM + TOPS CIRC XBIKE 1-A-2**

2040
MAP 3
B4
✓ **RUMBLING BRIDGE, nr DOLLAR:** Formed by another burn running off the same hills, an easier short walk in an Ochil Glen with something of the chasmic experience and the added delight of the unique double br (built 1713). There's a pt here at the end of one of the walkways under the br where you are looking into a Scottish jungle landscape as the Romantics imagined. Nr Powmill on A977 from Kinross (jnct 6, M90) then 2km. Up the road is **THE POWMILL MILKBAR** serving excellent home-made food for 40 yrs. It's 5km W on the A977. Open 7 days till 5pm (6pm weekends) (1488/TEAROOMS). Go after your walk! **3KM CIRC XBIKE 1-A-1**

2041
MAP 3
C1
✓ **GLEN CLOVA:** Most dramatic of the Angus glens. Most walks from end at Acharn esp W to Glen Doll & the Loops of (Loch) Brandy walk. Enq at Glen Clova Hotel (1289/GET-AWAY-FROM-IT-ALL) & repair there afterwards. Easy, rewarding walks! Check hotel for details.

2042
MAP 3
C3
FALKLAND, FIFE: If you're in Falkland for the Palace (1826/CASTLES) or the tea-room (1502/TEAROOMS), this short amble up an enchanting glen should be added to your afternoon. Head thro vill for 'Falkland Estate' and School (an activity centre for visiting groups) – you can take a car into the estate – and gdns are behind it. Glen and refurb path are obvious. Gushing burn, waterfalls – you can even walk behind one of them! Good café/restau in vill (979/FIFE RESTAUS). **3KM CIRC XBIKE 1-A-2**

2043
MAP 6
C3
THE BIG BURN WALK, GOLSPIE: A non-taxing, perfect little glen walk through lush diverse woodland. Variations poss, but start just beyond Sutherland Arms (1075/HIGHLAND INEXP HOTELS) in the garage yard which is just off the A9 before

Dunrobin Castle. Go past derelict mill and under aqueduct following river. A real supernatural trail unfolds with ancient tangled trees, meadows, waterfalls, cliffs and much wildlife. 3km to falls, return via route to castle woods for best all-round intoxication.   6KM CIRC XBIKE 1-B-1

2044 **THE STRATH at DUNBEATH:** The glen or strath so eloquently evoked in Neil
MAP 6 Gunn's *Highland River* (1978/LITERARY PLACES), a book which is as much about
D2 the geography as the history of his childhood. A path follows the river for many miles. A leaflet from the Dunbeath Heritage Centre points out places on the way. It's a spate river and in summer becomes a trickle; hard to imagine Gunn's salmon odyssey. It's only 500m to the broch, but it's worth going into the hinterland where it becomes quite mystical (1945/GRAVEYARDS).   1-A-1

2045 **TWEEDSIDE, PEEBLES:** The river side trail that follows the R Tweed from town
MAP 3 (Hay Lodge Park) past Neidpath Castle (1748/PICNICS) and on through classic
C5 Border wooded countryside crossing river either 2.5km out (5km round trip), at Manor Br 6km out (Lyne Footbr, 12km). Pick up 'Walking in the Scottish Borders' at local TIC.   5/12KM CIRC XBIKE 1-A-1
Other good Tweedside walk between Dryburgh Abbey & Bemersyde House grounds and at Newton St Boswells by golf course.

2046 **GLEN LEDNOCK, nr COMRIE:** Can walk from Comrie or take car further up to
MAP 3 monument or drive further into glen to reservoir (9km) for more open walks.
B3 From town take rt off main A85 (to Lochearnhead) at Deil's Cauldron restau. Walk and Deil's Cauldron (waterfall and gorge) are signed after 250m. Walk takes less than 1hr and emerges on rd nr Lord Melville's monument (climb for gr views back towards Crieff, about 25 mins). Other walks up slopes to left after you emerge from the tree-lined gorge rd. There's also the start of the hike up **BEN CHONZIE**, 6km up glen at Coishavachan. BC (931m) is one of the easiest Munros, with good path & gr views esp to NW. 3/5KM CIRC XBIKE 1-A-1

2047 **BRIDGE OF ALVAH, BANFF:** Details: 2063/WOODLAND WALKS, mentioned here
MAP 4 because the best bit is by the river and the br itself. The single span crossing
D1 was built in 1772 and stands high above the river in a sheer-sided gorge. The river below is deep and slow. In the rt light it's almost Amazonian.

2048 **THE GANNOCHY BRIDGE AND THE ROCKS OF SOLITUDE, nr EDZELL:** 2km
MAP 3 N of village on B966 to Fettercairn. There's a lay-by after br and a wooden door
D1 on left (you're in the grounds of the Burn House). Through it is another green world and a path above the rocky gorge of the R North Esk (1km). Huge sandstone ledges over dark peaty pools. You don't have to be alone (well maybe you do).   2KM XCIRC XBIKE 1-A-1

2049 **Nr TAYNUILT:** A walk (recommended by readers) which takes in education
MAP 2 with recreation. It goes via Bonawe Ironworks (2265/MUSEUMS) and L Etive
D2 along the river side to a swing br and thence to Inverawe Smokehouse (open to the public; café). Walk back less interesting but all v nice. Ask in Taynuilt for start.   10 KM CIRC BIKE 1-A-1

WOODLAND WALKS

2050 ✔ ✔ **ARDNAMURCHAN:** For anyone who loves trees (or hills, gr coastal
MAP 2 scenery & raw nature), this far-flung peninsula is a revelation. App
C1 from S via Corran ferry on A82 S of Ft William or N from Lochailort on A830 Mallaig–Ft William rd (1718/SCENIC ROUTES) or from Mull. Many marked & unmarked trails (see Ariundle below) but consult TIC & local literature. To visit Ardnamurchan is to fall in love with Scotland again. Woods esp around L Sunart.

2051 ✔ **RANDOLPH'S LEAP nr FORRES:** Tricky to explain how to find this spec-
MAP 4 tacular gorge of the plucky little Findhorn lined with beautiful beech-
A2 woods and a gr place to swim or picnic (1749/PICNICS), so listen up. Go either: 10km S of Forres on the A940 for Grantown, then the B9007 for Ferness and Carrbridge. 1km from the sign for Logie Steading (2178/SHOPPING) and 500m from the narrow stone br, there's a pull-over place on the bend. The woods are on the other side of the rd. Or: take the A939 S from Nairn or N from Grantown and at Ferness take the B9007 for Forres. Approaching from this direction, it's about 6km along the rd; the pull-over is on your rt. If you come to Logie Steading you've missed it; don't – you will miss one of the sylvan secrets of the N. Trailboard at Logie Steading for orientation.

2052   ✓ **LOCHAWESIDE:** Unclassified rd on N side of loch betw Kilchrenan and
MAP 2   ✓ Ford, centred on Dalavich. Illustrated brochure available from local hotels
D3   around Kilchrenan and Dalavich post office, describes 6 walks in the mixed,
mature forest all starting from car parking places on the rd. 3 starting from the
Barnaline car park are trail-marked and could be followed without brochure.
Avich Falls route crosses R Avich after 2km with falls on return route. Inverinan
Glen is always nice. The track from the car park N of Kilchrenan on the B845
back to Taynuilt isn't on the brochure, may be less travelled and also fine. The
pub at Kilchrenan is a cracker (1379/PUBS).   2-8KM CIRC XBIKE 2-A-2

2053   ✓ **PUCK'S GLEN nr DUNOON:** Close to the gates of the Younger Botanic
MAP 2   ✓ Garden at Benmore (1590/GARDENS) on the other side of the A815 to
D4   Stracher 12km N of Dunoon. A short, exhilarating woodland walk from a convenient car park. Ascend thro' trees then down into a faery glen, foll the burn
back to the rd. Some swimming pools.   3KM CIRC XBIKE 1-A-1

2054   ✓ **ROTHIEMURCHUS FOREST, nr AVIEMORE:** The place to experience the
MAP 5   ✓ magic and the majesty of the gr Caledonian Forest and the beauty of
E3   Scots pine. App from B970, the rd that parallels the A9 from Coylumbridge to
Kincraig/Kingussie. 2km from Inverdruie nr Coylumbridge follow sign for L an
Eilean; one of the most perfect lochans in these or any woods. Loch circuit
5km (1693/LOCHS). Good free brochure for all forest activities from TICs.

2055   ✓ **ARIUNDLE OAKWOODS:** Strontian. 35km Ft William via Corran Ferry.
MAP 2   ✓ Walk guide brochure at Strontian TIC. Many walks around L Sunart and
C1   Ariundle: rare oak and other native species. You see how v different Scotland's
landscape was before the Industrial Revolution used up the wood. Start over
town br, turning rt for Polloch. Go on past Cosy Knits, with good home-baking
café and park. 2 walks; well marked.   5KM CIRC MTBIKE 1-A-2

2056   **BALMACARRA, LOCHALSH WOODLAND GARDEN:** 5km S Kyle of Lochalsh on
MAP 5   A87. A woodland walk around the shore of L Alsh, centred on Lochalsh House.
B2   Mixed woodland in fairly formal gdn setting where you are confined to paths.
Views to Skye. A fragrant & verdant amble. Ranger service.   CIRC XBIKE 1-A-1

2057   **THE BIRKS O' ABERFELDY:** Circular walk through oak, beech and the birch (or
MAP 3   birk) woods of the title, easily reached and signed from town main st (1km).
B2   Steep-sided wooded glen of the Moness Burn with attractive falls esp the higher one spanned by br where the 2 marked walks converge. This is where Burns
'spread the lightsome days' in his eponymous poem.   3KM CIRC XBIKE 1-A-2

2058   **THE HERMITAGE, DUNKELD:** On A9 2km N of Dunkeld. Popular, easy, accessi-
MAP 3   ble walks along the glen and gorge of R Braan with pavilion o/look the Falls
B2   and, further on, 'Ossian's Cave'. Also uphill Craig Vean walks starts here to good
view pt (2km). Several woody walks around Dunkeld/Birnam – good leaflet
from TIC. 2km along river is **RUMBLING BRIDGE**, a deep gorge, & beyond it gr
spots for swimming (1745/SWIMMING HOLES).   2KM CIRC XBIKE 1-A-1

2059   **GLENMORE FOREST PARK, nr AVIEMORE:** Along from Coylumbridge (and
MAP 5   adj Rothiemurchus) on rd to ski resort, the forest trail area centred on L
E3   Morlich (sandy beaches, good swimming, water sports). Visitor centre has
maps of walk and bike trails and an activity programme.

2060   **ABOVE THE PASS OF LENY, CALLANDER:** A walk through mixed forest (beech,
MAP 3   oak, birch, pine) with gr Trossachs views. Start from main car park on A84 4km N
A3   of Callander (the Falls of Leny are on opp side of rd, 100m away) on path at back,
to the left – path parallels rd at first (don't head straight up). Way-marked and
boarded where marshy, the path divides after 1km to head further up to crest
(4km return) or back down (2km). Another glorious walk is to the **BRACKLINN
FALLS** – signed off E end of Callander Main St; start by the golf course (1km).
Also loop to the Craggs (adding another 2km).   2 OR 4KM CIRC XBIKE 1-A-1

2061   **LOCH TUMMEL WALKS, nr PITLOCHRY:** The mixed woodland N of L Tummel
MAP 3   reached by the B8019 from Pitlochry to Rannoch. Visitor centre at Queen's
B2   View (1734/VIEWS) and walks in the Allean Forest which take in some historical sites (a restored farmstead, standing stones) start nearby (2-4km). There
are many other walks in area and the Forest Enterprise brochure is worth following (available from VC and local TICs). (1702/LOCHS.)

2062   **THE NEW GALLOWAY FOREST:** Huge area of forest and hill country with
MAP 1   every type and length of trail incl section of S Upland Way from Bargrennan
B2   to Dalry (2027/LONG WALKS). Visitor centres at Kirroughtree (5km Newton

Stewart) and Clatteringshaws L on the 'Queen's Way' (9km New Galloway) with easy routes around them. Glen and L Trool are v fine (1549/GLENS); the 'Retreat Oakwood' nr Laurieston has 5km trails. Kitty's in New Galloway has great cakes and tea (1494/TEAROOMS). There's a river pool on the Raiders' Rd (1754/PICNICS). One could ramble on …

2063 **DUFF HOUSE, BANFF:** Duff House itself is the major attraction around here
MAP 4 (2278/PUBLIC GALLERIES), but if you've time it would be a pity to miss the wood-
D1 ed policies and the meadows and riverscape of the Deveron. An illustrated map on the back of the free brochure for the house (available from local TICs) shows the route. To the Br of Alvah where you should be bound is about 7km return. See also 1912/GLEN AND RIVER WALKS.

2064 **TORRACHILTY FOREST and ROGIE FALLS nr CONTIN and STRATHPEFFER:**
MAP 5 Enter by old br just o/side Contin on main A835 W to Ullapool or further along
D1 (4km) at Rogie Falls car park. Shame to miss the falls (1698/WATERFALLS), but the woods and gorge are pleasant enough if it's merely a stroll you need. Ben Wyvis further up the rd is the big challenge (2020/MUNROS).

2065 **ABERNETHY FOREST nr BOAT OF GARTEN:** 3km from village off B970, but
MAP 5 hard to miss because the famous ospreys are signposted from all over
E2 (1799/BIRDS). Nevertheless this woodland reserve is a tranquil place among native pinewoods around the loch with dells and trails. Many other birdies twittering around your picnic. They don't dispose of the midges.

2066 **FOCHABERS** on main A98 about 3km E of town are some excellent woody
MAP 4 and winding walks around the glen and Whiteash Hill (2-5km). Further W on
C1 the **MORAY COAST: CULBIN FOREST** – head for Cloddymoss or Kentessack off A96 at Brodie Castle 12km E of Nairn. Acres of Sitka in sandy coastal forest.

WHERE TO FIND SCOTS PINE

Scots pine, with oak and birch etc, formed the gr Caledonian Forest which once covered most of Scotland. Native Scots pine is v different from the regimented rows of pine trees we associate with forestry plantations and which now drape much of the countryside. It is more like a deciduous tree with reddish bark and irregular foliage; no two ever look the same. The remnants of the gr stands of pine are beautiful to see, mystical and majestic, a joy to walk among and no less worthy of conservation perhaps than a castle or a bird of prey. Here are some places you will find them:

ROTHIEMURCHUS FOREST: 2054/WOODLAND WALKS.

GLENTANAR, ROYAL DEESIDE: Nr Ballater, 10-15km SW of Aboyne.

Around **BRAEMAR** and **GRANTOWN-ON-SPEY**.

STRATHYRE, nr CALLANDER: S of village on rt of main rd after L Lubnaig.

ACHRAY FOREST, nr ABERFOYLE: Some pine nr the Duke's Pass rd, the A821 to L Katrine, and amongst the mixed woodland in the 'forest drive' to L Achray.

BLACKWOOD OF RANNOCH: S of L Rannoch, 30km W of Pitlochry via Kinloch Rannoch. Start from Carie, fair walk in. 250-year-old pines; an important site.

ROWARDENNAN, L LOMOND: End of the rd along E side of loch nr Ben Lomond. Easily accessible pines nr the loch side, picnic sites etc.

Shores of **LOCH MAREE, L TORRIDON** and around **L CLAIR, GLEN TORRIDON:** Both nr the **BEINN EIGHE NATIONAL NATURE RESERVE** (1814/GREAT WILDLIFE RESERVES). Visitor Centre on A832 N of Kinlochewe.

GLEN AFFRIC, nr DRUMNADROCHIT: 1541/GLENS. Biggest remnant of the Caledonian Forest in classic glen. Many strolls and hikes poss. Try Dog Falls (on main rd) for Affric introduction.

Native pinewoods aren't found S of Perthshire, but there are fine plantation examples in southern Scotland at:

GLENTRESS, nr PEEBLES: 7km on A72 to Innerleithen. Mature forest up the burn side, though surrounded by commercial forest.

SHAMBELLIE ESTATE, nr DUMFRIES: 1km from New Abbey beside A710 at the Shambellie House, 100yds sign. Ancient stands of pine over the wall amongst other glorious trees; this is like virgin woodland. Planted 1775–80. Magnificent.

2067
MAP 2
B5
KINTRA, ISLAY: On Bowmore-Pt Ellen rd take Oa t/off: then Kintra signed 7km. Park in old farmyard by campsite (1298/HIGHLAND CAMPING). A fabulous beach (1650/BEACHES) runs in opp direction and a notable golf course behind it (2098/GOLF IN GREAT PLACES). This walk leads along N coast of the Mull of Oa, an area of diverse beauty, sometimes pastoral, sometimes wild, with a wonderful shoreline. Many gr picnic spots.

ANY KM XCIRC XBIKE 2-B-2

2068
MAP 4
E2
THE BULLERS OF BUCHAN, nr PETERHEAD: 8km S of Peterhead on A975 rd to/from Cruden Bay. Park and walk 100m to cottages. To the N is the walk to Longhaven Nature Reserve, a continuation of the dramatic cliffs and more sea bird city. The Bullers is at start of walk, a sheer-sided 'hole' 75m deep with an outlet to the sea thro a natural arch. Walk round the edge of it, looking down on layers of birds (who might try to dive-bomb you away from their nests); it's a wonder of nature on an awesome coast. Take gr care (& a head for heights).

2069
MAP 6
B1
CAPE WRATH and the CLIFFS OF CLO MOR: Britain's most NW point reached by ferry from 1km off the A838 4km S of Durness by Cape Wrath Hotel; a 10min crossing then 40min minibus ride to Cape. Ferry holds 12 and runs May-Sept (check TIC at Durness for times: 01971 511259). At 280m Clo Mor are the highest cliffs in UK; 4km round trip from Cape. MoD range – access may be restricted. In other direction, the 28km to Kinlochbervie is one of Britain's most wild and wonderful coastal walks. Beaches incl Sandwood (1648/BEACHES). While in this NW area: **SMOO CAVE** 2km E of Durness.

2070
MAP 6
B2
OLD MAN OF STORR, nr LOCHINVER: The easy, exhilarating walk to the dramatic sea stack, 3km from lighthouse off unclassified rd 14km N Lochinver. Park and follow sheep tracks; cliffs are high and steep.

1-B-2

2071
MAP 1
D3
ROCKCLIFFE TO KIPPFORD: An easy stroll along the 'Scottish Riviera' through woodland nr the shore (2km) past the 'Mote of Mark' a Dark Age hill ft with views to Rough Island. The better cliff top walk is in the other direction to Castlepoint.

2072
MAP 3
E5
ST ABBS HEAD: The most dramatic coastal scenery in S Scotland, scary in a wind, rhapsodic on a blue summer's day. Extensive wildlife reserve and trails through coastal hills and vales to cliffs. Cars can go as far as lighthouse, but best to park at VC nr farm on St Abbs village rd 3km from A1107 to Eyemouth and follow route (1812/WILDLIFE).

5-10KM CIRC XBIKE 1-B-2

2073
MAP 2
C1
SINGING SANDS, ARDNAMURCHAN: Park at Arivegaig 3km Acharacle and cross wooden br, following track round side of Kentra Bay. Follow signs for Gorteneorn, and walk through forest track and woodland to beach. As you pound the sands they should 'sing' to you whilst you bathe in the the beautiful views of Rum, Eigg, Muck and Skye (and just possibly the sea). Check at TIC for directions and other walks booklet.

10KM RET XCIRC BIKE 1-B-1

2074
MAP 4
C1
EAST FROM CULLEN on the MORAY COAST: This is the same walk mentioned with reference to Sunnyside (1535/BEACHES), a golden beach with a fabulous ruined castle (Findlater) that might be your destination. There's a track E along from harbour. 2hrs return. Superb coastline.

8KM XCIRC XBIKE 1-A-1

2075
MAP 5
E1
CROMARTY, THE SOUTH SUTOR: The walk, known locally as 'The 100 Steps' tho' there are a few more than that, from Cromarty village (1653/COASTAL VILLAGES; 1516/TEAROOMS) round the tip of the S promontory at the narrow entrance to the Cromarty Firth. E of vill; coastal path hugs shoreline then ascends thro' woodland to headland. Good bench! Go further to top car park and viewpt panel. Return by rd. There may be dolphins out there!

5KM CIRC XBIKE 1-A-1

2076
MAP 3
D4
THE CHAIN WALK, ELIE: Unique and adventurous headland scramble at the W end of Elie (and Earlsferry), by golf course. Hand- and footholds carved into rock with chains to haul yourself up. Watch tide; don't go alone.

2-B-2

2077
MAP 2
D5
COCK OF ARRAN, LOCHRANZA: This round trip starts in the moors but descends to brerathtaking coastal trail past some interesting spots (see 2332/FANTASTIC WALKS IN THE ISLANDS). Gr for twitchers, ramblers & fossils (strong boots needed)! Approx 6 hrs from village. Take a picnic.

2-B-2

SECTION 10

Sports

Those listed open to non-members and available to visitors (incl women) at most times, unless otherwise stated. Handicap certificates may be required.

AYRSHIRE (MAP 2)

2078
E6
✓ ✓ ✓ **TURNBERRY:** 01655 331000. Ailsa (championship) and Arran. Sometimes poss by application. Otherwise you must stay at hotel. (868/AYRSHIRE HOTELS.) Superb. Golf academy a gr place to learn.

2079
E6
✓ ✓ **ROYAL OLD COURSE, TROON:** V difficult to get on. No wimmen. Staying at Marine Highland Hotel (01292 314444) helps. Easier is **THE PORTLAND COURSE:** Across rd from Royal. Both 01292 311555. And 874/AYRSHIRE HOTELS for the adj Piersland House Hotel.

2080
E5
✓ **GLASGOW GAILES/WESTERN GAILES:** 01294 311347/311649. Superb links courses next to one another, 5km S of Irvine off A78.

2081
E6
OLD PRESTWICK: 01292 477404. Original home of the Open and 'every challenge you'd wish to meet'. Hotels opp cost less than a round. Unlikely to get on w/ends (Sat members only).

EAST LOTHIAN (MAP 3)

Note: There is a gr booklet available at the local TIC, entitled 'Golf in East Lothian'.

2082
D4
✓ ✓ **GULLANE NO.1:** 01620 842255. One of 3 varied courses surrounding charming village on links and within driving distance (35km) of Edin. Muirfield is nearby, but you need intro. Gullane is okay most days except Sat/Sun. (Handicap required for no.1 only – under 24 men, 30 ladies.) No.3 best for beginners. Visitor centre acts as clubhouse for non-members on nos. 2/3. Clubhouse for members/no.1 players only.

2083
D4
✓ ✓ **NORTH BERWICK EAST AND WEST:** E (officially the Glen Golf Club) has stunning views. A superb cliff-top course and is not too long, 01620 892726/892135. W more taxing (esp the classic 'Redan') used for Open qualifying; a v fine links. Also has 9-hole kids' course, 01620 892666.

2084
C4
MUSSELBURGH LINKS: The original home of golf (really: golf recorded here in 1672), but this local authority-run 9-hole links is not exactly top turf and is enclosed by Musselburgh Racecourse. Nostalgia still appeals though. 0131 665 5438. ROYAL MUSSELBURGH nearby compensates. It dates to 1774, fifth-oldest in Scotland. Busy early mornings and Fri-Sun, 01875 810139.

NORTH EAST

2085
MAP 3
D2
✓ ✓ **CARNOUSTIE:** 01241 853789. 3 good links courses; even poss (with handicap cert) to get on the championship course (though w/ends difficult). Every hole has character. Buddon Links is cheaper and often quiet. Combination tickets available. A well-managed and accessible course, increasingly a golfing must.

2086
MAP 4
E3
✓ **MURCAR, ABERDEEN:** 01224 704354. Getting on Royal Aber Course is difficult for most people, but Murcar is a testing alternative, a seaside course 6km N of centre off Peterhead rd signed at r/bout after Exhibition Centre. Handicap cert needed. Other municipal courses incl charming 9-hole at Hazlehead.

2087
MAP 4
E2
✓ **CRUDEN BAY, nr PETERHEAD:** 01779 812285. On A975 40km N of Aber. Designed by Tom Simpson and ranked in UK top 50, a spectacular links course with the intangible aura of bygone days. Quirky holes epitomise old-fashioned style. W/ends difficult to get on.

2088
MAP 4
A1
✓ **NAIRN:** 01667 452787. Traditional seaside links course and one of the easiest championship courses to get on. Good clubhouse, friendly folk. Nairn Dunbar on other side of town also has good links. Hand cert reqd.

2089
MAP 6
C3
✓ **ROYAL DORNOCH:** 01862 810219. Sutherland championship course laid out by Tom Morris in 1877. Amongst top 10 courses in UK, but not busy or incessantly pounded. No poor holes. Stimulating sequences. Probably the most northerly gr golf course in the world – and not impossible to get on.

FIFE (MAP 3)

2090
D3
✓ ✓ ✓ **ST ANDREWS:** 01334 466666. The home and Mecca of golf, v much part of the town (2357/HOLIDAY CENTRES) and probably the largest golf complex in Europe. Old Course most central, celebrated. Application by ballot the day before (handicap cert needed). For Jubilee (1897, upgraded 1989) and Eden (1914, laid out by Harry S. Holt paying homage to the Old with large, sloping greens), apply the day before. New Course (1895, some rate the best) easiest access. Less demanding are the new Strathtyrum and Balgove (upgraded 9-hole for beginners) courses. All 6 courses contiguous and 'in town'; the newish Dukes Course (part of Old Course Hotel) is 3km away. Reservations (and ballot) 01334 466666. A whole lot of golf to be had – get your money out!

2091
C3
✓ **LADYBANK:** 01337 830814. Best inland course in Fife; Tom Morris-designed again. V well kept and organised. Good facs. Tree-lined and picturesque.

2092
D4
ELIE: Book 01333 330301. Splendid open links maintained in top condition; can be windswept. The starter has his famous periscope and may be watching you. Adj 9-hole course, often busy with kids, is fun. (01333 330955)

2093
D3
CRAIL: 01333 450686. Balcomie Links originally designed by the legendary Tom Morris, or Craighead Links new sweeping course. All holes in sight of sea. Not exp; easy to get on.

2094
D3
LUNDIN LINKS: 01333 320202/ladies 320832. Challenging seaside course used as Open qualifier. Some devious contourings. There is a separate course for women. (01333 320022)

ELSEWHERE

2095
MAP 3
B3
✓ ✓ ✓ **GLENEAGLES:** 0800 704705. Legendary golf the mainstay of resort complex in perfect Perthshire (hotel 01764 662231 report 1211/CO-HOUSE HOTELS). 3 courses incl PGA centenary which will host Ryder Cup in 2014. No handicap certs reqd.

2096
MAP 2
E4
✓ ✓ **LOCH LOMOND GOLF CLUB, LUSS:** 01436 655555. On A82 1km from conservation village of Luss. Exclusive American-owned club; membership expensive & the list's closed. We can buy a cheaper season ticket to see the annual Scottish Open (July; info: 01436 655559); but no access to plebs to clubhouse. 18 holes of scenic golf by the Loch. This is golfing for gold.

2097
MAP 3
E6
✓ ✓ **ROXBURGHE HOTEL GOLF COURSE nr KELSO:** 01573 450331. Only championship course in the Borders. Designed by Dave Thomas along banks of R Teviot. Part of the Floors Castle estate. Open non-res. Fairways bar/brasserie clubhouse. Details (925/BORDER HOTELS).

GOOD GOLF COURSES IN GREAT PLACES

All open to women, non-members and inexpert players.

2098
MAP 2
B5
✓ **MACHRIE:** 01496 302310. Isle of Islay. 7km Pt Ellen. Worth going to Islay (BA's airstrip adj course or Calmac ferry from Kennacraig nr Tarbert) just for the golf. The Machrie (Golf) Hotel is sparse but convenient. Old-fashioned course to be played by feel and instinct. Splendid, sometimes windy isolation with a warm bar and restau at the end of it. The notorious 17th, 'Iffrin' (it means Hell), vortex shaped from the dune system of marram and close-cropped grass, is one of many gr holes. 18.

2099
MAP 2
C6
✓ **MACHRIHANISH:** 01586 810213. By Campbeltown (10km). Amongst the dunes and links of the glorious 8km stretch of the Machrihanish Beach (1647/BEACHES). The Atlantic provides thunderous applause for your triumphs over a challenging course. 9/18.

2100
MAP 1
D3
✓ **SOUTHERNESS, SOLWAY FIRTH:** 01387 880677. 25km S of Dumfries by A710. A championship course on links on the silt flats of the Firth. Despite its prestige, visitors do get on. 10-12pm and 2-4pm. Under the wide Solway sky, it's pure – southerness. 18.

2101 ✓ **ROSEMOUNT, BLAIRGOWRIE:** 01250 872622. Off A93, S of Blairgowrie.
MAP 3   An excellent, pampered and well-managed course in the middle of green
C2   Perthshire, an alternative perhaps to Gleneagles, being much easier to get on
(most days) and rather cheaper (though not at w/ends). 18.

2102 ✓ **BOAT OF GARTEN:** 01479 831282. Challenging, picturesque course in
MAP 4   town where ospreys have been known to wheel overhead. Has been called
A3   the 'Gleneagles of the North'; certainly best around, tho not for novices. 18.

2103 **GLENCRUITTEN, OBAN:** 01631 562868. Picturesque course on the edge of
MAP 2 town. Head S (A816) from Argyll Sq, bearing left at church. Course is signed.
D2   Quite tricky with many blind holes. Can get busy, so phone first. 18.

2104 **GAIRLOCH:** 01445 712407. Just as you come into town from the S on A832, it
MAP 6 looks over the bay and down to a perfect, pink, sandy beach. Small clubhouse
A3   with honesty box. Not the world's most agonising course; in fact, on a clear
day with views to Skye, you can forget agonising over anything. 9.

2105 **HARRIS GOLF CLUB, SCARISTA, ISLE OF HARRIS:** 01859 502331 (the cap-
MAP 7 tain, but no need to phone). Just turn up on the rd betw Tarbert and Rodel
B3   and leave £7 in the box. First tee commands one of the gr views in golf and
throughout this basic, but testing course, you are looking out to sea over
Scarista beach (1653/BEACHES) and bay. Sunset may put you off your swing.

2106 **NEW GALLOWAY:** Local course on S edge of this fine wee toon. Almost all on
MAP 1 a slope but affording gr views of L Ken and the Galloway Forest behind. No
C2   bunkers and only 9 short holes, but exhilarating play. Easy on, except Sun. Just
turn up.

2107 **MINTO, DENHOLM:** 01450 870220. 9km E Hawick. Spacious parkland in
MAP 3 Teviot valley. Best holes 3rd, 12th & 16th. **VERTISH HILL, HAWICK:** 01450
D6   372293. A more challenging hill course. Both among the best in Borders. 18.
Best holes 2nd & 18th. An excl guide to all the courses in the Borders in avail
from TICs – 'Freedom of the Fairways'.

2108 **TAYMOUTH CASTLE, KENMORE:** 01887 830228. Spacious green acres
MAP 3 around the enigmatic empty hulk of the castle. Well-tended and organised
B2   course betw A827 to Aberfeldy and the river. Inexp, and guests at the
Kenmore Hotel (994/PERTHSHIRE HOTELS) get special rate. 18.

2109 **GIFFORD:** 01620 810267. Dinky inland course on the edge of a dinky village,
MAP 3 bypassed by the queue for the big E Lothian courses and a guarded secret
D5   among the regulars. Generally ok, but phone starter (above) for avail. 9.

2110 **STRATHPEFFER:** 01997 421011. V hilly (and we do mean hilly) course full of
MAP 5 character and with exhilarating Highland views. Small-town friendliness. You
D1   are playing up there with the gods and some other old codgers. 18.

2111 **ELGIN:** 01343 542338. 1km from town on A941 Perth rd. Many memorable
MAP 4 holes on moorland/parkland course in an area where links may lure you to
B1   the coast (Nairn, Lossiemouth). 18.

2112 **DURNESS:** 01971 511364. The most N golf course on mainland UK, on the
MAP 6 wild headland by Balnakeil Bay, looking over to Faraid Head. The last hole is
B1   'over the sea'. Only open since 1988, it's already got cult status. 2km W Durness.

2113 **ROTHESAY:** 01700 503554. Sloping course with breathtaking views of Clyde.
MAP 2 Visitors welcome. What could be finer than taking the train from Glas to
D5   Wemyss Bay for the ferry over (5/FAVOURITE JOURNEYS) and 18 holes. Finish up
with fish 'n' chips at the W End (1468/FISH AND CHIPS) on the way home.

2114 **TRAIGH, ARISAIG:** 01687 450337. A830 Ft William-Mallaig rd, 2km N Arisaig.
MAP 5 Pronounced 'try'- and you may want to. The islands are set out like stones in
B3   the sea around you and there are 9 hilly holes of fun.

*In a good yr the Scottish ski season can extend from Dec (or even Nov) till the 'lambing snow' of late April. And on a good day it can be as exhilarating as anywhere in Europe. Here's a summary (**distances in kilometres**):*

	GLENSHEE	CAIRNGORM	NEVIS RANGE	GLENCOE	THE LECHT
DIST/EDIN	130	215	215	165	200
DIST/GLASGOW	170	235	200	150	160
NR CENTRE	Perth 65	Inverness 45	Ft Will 10	FT Will 40	Aberdeen 95
NR TOWN	Braemar 20	Aviemore 15	Ft Will 10	Ballachulish 20	Tomintoul 11
NO OF RUNS	38	19	35	19	21
EASY	10	3	7	4	7
INTERMED	13	6	12	6	7
DIFFICULT	13	9	11	7	6
ADVANCED	2	1	5	2	1
NO OF TOWS	23	16	12	7	15
CAFÉS	3	3	2 + units	2	1 + 1 unit
GOOD FOR	*Size*	*Size*	*Uplift*	*Fewer crowds*	*Fewer crowds*
	Access from rd	*Non-skiing*	*Access*	*Nr road*	*Nr road*
	Views Glas Maol	*Views*	*Views/Sunsets*	*Views*	*Families*
	2 distinct areas	*Intermediate*	*Ski School*	*Most alpine*	*Beginners*
	Snowboarding	*Snowboarding*	*Café*		

2115 GLENSHEE

MAP 3
C1

BASE STATION: 013397 41320. **SCHOOL:** 01250 885 216 or 0870 443 0253 or 013397 41320.

WHERE TO STAY

DALMUNZIE HOUSE HOTEL: 01250 885 224. 9km S. Country house. Golf. Family-run. MED.EX

BRIDGE OF CALLY HOTEL: 01250 886231. 36km S (1272/INNS). **GLENISLA, KIRKTON OF GLENISLA:** 01575 582223. 32km SE. INX

SPITTAL OF GLENSHEE: 01250 885215. 8km S. Cheap 'n' cheerful. MED.INX

WHERE TO EAT

CARGILL'S BISTRO, BLAIRGOWRIE: 01250 876735 (1006/PERTHSHIRE EATS).

DALMUNZIE/BRIDGE OF CALLY HOTEL/GLENISLA: *as above.*

APRÈS-SKI

BLACKWATER INN: 17km S on main rd. A good all-round pub. Occasional live music.

SKI HIRE

BASE STATION: 01339 741320. **CAIRNWELL SKI SCHOOL:** 08704 430253 at Spittal of Glenshee.

2116 CAIRNGORM

MAP 5
E3

BASE STATION: 01479 861261. **SCHOOL:** 01479 810296 or 01479 810656 or 01479 861261 or 01540 651272.

WHERE TO STAY

CORROUR HOUSE: 01479 810220. 11km W (1219/COUNTRY-HOUSE HOTELS). INX

AVIEMORE BUNKHOUSE: 01479 811181 (1233/HOSTELS).

HILTON COYLUMBRIDGE HOTEL: 01479 810661. 10km W. Nearest and best of modern Aviemore hotels. 2 pools/sauna. Ski hire. Okay restau. Comfort when you need it. MED.EX

CAIRNGORM, AVIEMORE: 01479 810630. Main st of main town. Busy bar. Rms not unreasonably priced and lots of them. INX

THE CROSS, KINGUSSIE: 01540 661166. (1044/HIGHLANDS HOTELS) . MED.INX

WHERE TO EAT

THE CROSS, KINGUSSIE: 01540 661166. See above.

HAMBLETTS & CAFÉ MAMBO, AVIEMORE: 01479 810300 (1088/HIGHLANDS RESTAUS).

THE BOATHOUSE, KINCRAIG: 01540 651394 (1089/INEXP HIGHLANDS RESTAUS).

THE OLD BRIDGE INN, AVIEMORE: Welcoming, good atmos (1407/BEST FOOD).

APRÈS-SKI

THE WINKING OWL, AVIEMORE: At end of main st. Owl's Nest.

CAFÉ MAMBO: See above.

SKI HIRE

HILTON COYLUMBRIDGE HOTEL: 01479 810661. Behind hotel, run by Mountain Ski school and nearest to slopes. And base station. Open mornings and 4–6.30pm.

2117 THE NEVIS RANGE/AONACH MOR
MAP 2
D1
BASE STATION: 01397 705825. **SCHOOL:** 01397 705825.

WHERE TO EAT and STAY

See FORT WILLIAM, *p. 309.*

APRÈS-SKI

No pub in immediate vicinity. Nearest all-in ski centre is **NEVIS SPORT, FORT WILLIAM:** 01397 704921. Bar (side entrance) till midnight. Self-serve café all day till 5pm (4.30pm Sun). Bookshop and extensive ski/outdoor shop on ground floor. Also ski hire.

SKI HIRE

As above (01397 704921), also **ELLIS BRIGHAM** (01397 706220), and base stn.

2118 GLENCOE
MAP 2
D2
BASE STATION: 01855 851226. **SCHOOL:** 01855 851226 or 01855 851200.

WHERE TO EAT and STAY

See FORT WILLIAM, *p. 309*, and also:

ISLES OF GLENCOE HOTEL, BALLACHULISH: 01855 811602. Modern development leisure centre incl pool. Good touring base (1226/KIDS).

CLACHAIG INN, GLENCOE: 01855 811 252. Famous 'outdoor inn' for walkers, climbers etc with pub (1378/BLOODY GOOD PUBS), pub food and inexp accom.

KINGSHOUSE HOTEL: 01855 851259. The classic travellers' inn 1km from A82 through Glen and nr slopes (8km). Pub with food/whisky. Inexp rms but v basic, esp bunks.

APRÈS-SKI

As above, especially Clachaig Inn and Kingshouse.

SKI HIRE

At base stn.

THE LECHT

BASE STATION: 019756 51440. **SCHOOL:** 019756 51412. In redevelopment; rolling completion over 2004.

WHERE TO STAY

Nearest town (28km S) with big choice of hotels is Ballater. But also:

GLENAVON HOTEL, TOMINTOUL: 01807 580218. On sq in Tomintoul, the nearest town. The most ski- and hiking-friendly place in the zone.   INX

RICHMOND ARMS HOTEL, TOMINTOUL: 01807 580777. On sq. Trad hotel, log fires, local beers. A v good prospect. 24 rms.   MED.INX

WHERE TO EAT

GREEN INN, BALLATER: 01339 755701 Picking up again after new owner-ship, also has rms.   MED.EXP

STATION RESTAURANT, BALLATER: 01339 755050 (1034/BEST REST NE).

GORDON HOTEL, TOMINTOUL: 01807 580206. The local hotel with the most aspirational menu.   INX

APRÈS-SKI

GLENAVON HOTEL, TOMINTOUL: 01807 580218. Good large bar for skiers, walkers (S end of Speyside Way is here) and locals.

ALLARGUE HOTEL, COCKBRIDGE: 019756 51410. On rd S to Ballater 5km from slopes and o/look Corgarff Castle and the trickle of the R Don. Rms also.

SKI HIRE

At base stn.

WEATHER AND ROAD REPORTS

Dial 09001 654 then:

655 **CAIRNGORM**; 656 **GLENSHEE**; 658 **GLENCOE**; 660 **NEVIS RANGE**; 657 **THE LECHT**; 659 **CROSS-COUNTRY SKI REPORT**

ALL CENTRES REPORT: 09001 654654.

THE BEST SLEDGING PLACES

Locals will know where the best slopes are. Here's my suggestions for EDIN/GLAS:

EDINBURGH

THE BRAID HILLS: The connoisseur's choice, you sledge down friendly and not-too-challenging slopes in a crowded L S Lowry landscape that you will remember long after the thaw. Off Braid Hills Drive at the golf course. Can walk in via Blackford Glen Rd. **CORSTORPHINE HILL:** Gentle broad slope with woodland at top and trails (413/CITY WALKS) and a busy rd at the bottom. App via Clermiston Rd off Queensferry Rd. **QUEEN'S PARK:** The lesser slopes that skirt Arthur's Seat, and further in around Hunter's Bog for the more adventurous or less sociable sledger.

GLASGOW

KELVINGROVE PARK: At Park Terr side. No long runs but a winter wonderland when the rime's in the trees. **GARTNAVEL HOSPITAL GROUNDS:** In W end (Hyndland) off Gr Western Rd. You can play safe sledging into the playing field, or more adventurously through the woodlands. **QUEEN'S VIEW:** On A809 N of Bearsden 20km from centre. A v popular walk (787/BEST VIEWS) is also a gr place to sledge. Variable slopes off the main path. The Highlands can be seen on a clear day. **RUCHILL PARK:** In N of city (788/BEST VIEWS) and **QUEEN'S PARK** in S.

2122
MAP 3
C3
✓ **PERTH LEISURE POOL:** 01738 492410. A perfect example of the mega successful water-based leisure-land. Large, shaped pool with o/side section (open also in winter, when it's even more of a novelty); 2 flumes, 'wild water channel', whirlpools etc. 25m 'training' pool for lengths (sessions). Outdoor kids' area. Excellent facility. Daily 10am-10pm.

2123
MAP 5
D2
✓ **AQUADOME, INVERNESS:** 01463 667500. Inverness's all-weather attraction. Leisure waters; incl 3 flumes, wave machine and toddler area. Huge competition pool for serious swimming and luxurious health suites; massages, hydrotherapy and (ladies) that essential bikini line wax. All in all, a bigger splash. Mon-Fri 7.30am-10pm, Sat-Sun until 5pm.

2124
MAP 3
D4
✓ **DUNBAR POOL:** 01368 865456. Model of its kind, o/look old harbour (where folks used to swim on a summer's day) and castle ruins. Cool, modern design amidst the warm red sandstone. Flumes and wave machine that mimics the sea o/side; lengths just possible in betw (though it's often v crowded). Phone for opening hours.

2125
MAP 2
E5
MAGNUM CENTRE, IRVINE: 01294 278381. From Irvine's throughway system, follow signs for Harbourside, then Magnum. Big shed still unalluring and looking rather tatty – well… established! This phenomenally successful pleasuredrome provides every conceivable diversion from the monotony of my namesake o/side. From soothing bowls to frenetic skating, pools, cinema, cafés, courses, you name it. Secrete endorphins and other hormones.

2126
MAP 2
E5
VIKINGAR!, LARGS: 01475 689777. Suddenly fulfilled all the needs and gaps in this busy visitor area of the Clyde coast – a pool and sports centre, a theatre, an indoor attraction and a dab of heritage. There's something irresistible about Norse history being told in a sing-song Ayrshire accent. 'Your Viking will be with you shortly, no.' Longhouse interior, the gods and a big AV about the Battle of Largs. Phone for times (or pray to Njord and get the ferry to Cumbrae instead).

2127
MAP 3
A5
THE TIME CAPSULE, MONKLANDS: 01236 449572. They say Monklands, but where you are going is downtown Coatbridge about 15km from Glas via M8. Known rather meanly as the 'Tim Capture' (local joke – you don't want to know!). A leisure (rather than swimming) pool and ice-rink lavishly fitted out on prehistoric monster theme. Even if you haven't been swimming for yrs, this is the sort of place you force the flab into the swimsuit. Cafés and view areas. Facs of the clean-up-your-act variety (e.g. squash, health suite). 10am-9pm.

2128
MAP 3
A5
DOLLAN AQUA CENTRE, TOWN CENTRE PARK, EAST KILBRIDE: 01355 260000. An excl family leisure centre. 50m pool, fitness facs, soft play area and Scotland's first interactive flume, (aquatic pin ball machine with you as the ball!) – there had to be a twist. Mon, Wed, Fri 7.30am-9.30pm; Tue, Thur 8am-9.30pm; Sat & Sun 8am-5pm.

2129
MAP B
xA3
SCOTSTOUN LEISURE CENTRE: 0141 959 4000. Clydeside expressway then A814, rt at Victoria Park lights, first left after r/about. Danes Drive. If 'modernity is suburban' this is state of the art. 10 lane pool, sports halls, health suite, dance studio and gym. Outdoor footie and tennis – it's enormous. Mon, Wed, Fri 7.30am-10pm, Tue & Sun 9am, Thu 10am, Sat 9am-6pm.

2130
MAP 3
D3
EAST SANDS LEISURE CENTRE, ST ANDREWS: 01334 476506. From S St take rd for Crail then follow signs. About 2km from centre. Bright and colourful centre o/look the E Sands, the less celebrated beach of St Andrews. Mainly a fairly conventional pool with 25m lane area as well as 50m water slide, toddlers' pool etc. Also 2 squash courts, gym with Pulsestar machines, 'remedial suite', bar and café. 7 days 9am-10pm.

2131
MAP 3
C4
BEACON LEISURE CENTRE, BURNTISLAND: 01592 872211. On the front of this quietly-getting-on-with-it Fife town nr Kirkcaldy. Family fun pool centre with 'landmark' beacon thing and external flume tubes. It does work. Loadsa kids and 'waves' do come. Latest swimming in area (9.30pm, but check). 7 days.

2132
MAP 4
D3
BEACH LEISURE CENTRE, ABERDEEN: 01224 655401. Beach Esplanade across rd from beach itself. Multisports facility with bars and cafés. 'Leisure' Pool isn't much use for swimming (Aber has many others, 2004/SWIMMING POOLS) but it's fun for kids with flumes etc. Lynx Ice Arena is adj for skating, curling, ice hockey. O/side is the long long beach and the N Sea. Call for times.

THE BEST SWIMMING POOLS AND SPORTS CENTRES

For EDINBURGH, *see p. 68; for* GLASGOW, *see p. 108. And see* LEISURE CENTRES *p 266.*

2133
MAP 3
E1

✓ **STONEHAVEN OUTDOOR POOL, STONEHAVEN:** The 'Friends of Stonehaven Outdoor Pool' won the day (eat your hearts out N Berwick) and they've saved a gr pool that goes from length to strength. Fabulous 1930s Olympic-sized heated salt-water pool. There are midnight swims in midsummer most Wednesdays (is that cool, or what?). June-Aug only: 10am-7.30pm (10-6pm w/ends). Heated saltwater heaven.

2134
MAP 2
E4

✓ **GOUROCK BATHING POOL:** 01475 631561. The only other open-air (proper) pool in Scotland that's still open! On coast rd S of town centre 45km from central Glas. 1950s-style leisure. Heated, so it doesn't need to be a scorcher (brilliant, but choc-a-block when it is). Open May-Sep weekdays until 8.30pm, weekends until 4.30pm.

2135
MAP 2
E4

✓ **THE WATERFRONT, GREENOCK:** 01475 797979. Easily spotted at the waterfront at Customhouse Way – vast building resembling a modernist whale carcass; a rather groovy one at that. Big leisure pool, proper swim pool, 65m flume, ice rink, gym and more. Undeniably fun, by the way. Daily AYR until 9pm Mon-Fri, 4.30pm Sat-Sun.

2136
MAP 3
C4

✓ **CARNEGIE CENTRE, DUNFERMLINE:** 01383 314200. Pilmuir St. Excellent all-round sports centre with many courses and classes. 2 pools (ozone-treated), 25m, and kids' pool. Lane swimming lunch time and evenings. Authentic Turkish and Aeretone Suite with men's, women's and mixed sessions. Large gym with Powersport stations etc. Badminton, squash, aerobic classes. Usually open till 9pm (including pool), but check. Keeping Dunfermline fitter then most of us.

2137
MAP B
xE1

✓ **THE LEISUREDROME, BISHOPBRIGGS:** 0141 772 6391. 147 Balmuildy Rd. At the N edge of Glas, best reached by car or 1km walk from stn; adj Forth and Clyde Canal walkway (776/CITY WALKS). Large, modern, efficient with 25m pool, multi gym, sauna, games hall, café etc. Mon & Fri 9am-10.30pm, Tue 7.30am, Wed & Thu 8am, Sat & Sun 9am-10pm.

2138
MAP 3
B4

✓ **LINLITHGOW POOL:** 01506 846358. On edge of pleasant town off rd to Lanark. Modern light and airy sports centre with sauna and steam room at the pool side and W Lothian outside the windows. Excellent community facility, well designed and laid out. All towns should enjoy this quality of life. Daily till 9pm, gym 10pm.

2139
MAP 6
B3

✓ **LOCHBROOM LEISURE CENTRE, ULLAPOOL:** 01854 612884. 2 streets back from waterfront, but central. Games hall & v nice pool, easy to get in & out, tiny sauna. Small-town friendly atmos. 7 days till 8pm (Sat/Sun 6pm).

2140
MAP 3
D6

GALASHIELS POOL: 01896 752154. An award-winning pool in the Central Borders on the edge of parkland with picture windows bringing the outside in. No leisurama nonsense, just a good deck-level pool (25m) (Teviotdale Leisure Centre). Modern pool in Hawick also good. Phone for opening hrs.

2141
MAP 4
D3

ABERDEEN BATHS: 01224 587920. City well served with swimming pools. 3 in suburbs are not esp easy to find, though Hazlehead (01224 310062) is signed from inner ring road to W of centre. Only open to public from 6pm weekdays, all day w/ends. Bon Accord Baths are a fine example of a municipal pool; recently refurbished, they're centrally situated behind the W end of Union St. Annie Lennox learned to swim here. The newer Beach Leisure Centre has just about thought of everything (2132/LEISURE CENTRES). Hrs vary.

2142
MAP 6
C3

GOLSPIE SWIMMING POOL: 01408 633437. A neat little pool (20m) next to the High School. Nothing too high tech, but a friendly atmos and a friendly mural at one end. Hrs vary.

2143
MAP 2
B5

MACTAGGART CENTRE, BOWMORE, ISLAY: 01496 810767. Eco-friendly pool (heated by adj distillery) o/look bay. Interesting whisky cask shaped ceiling and good fitness suite. Laundry facs. Cl Mon.

2144
MAP 3
D4
✓ **ELIE WATERSPORTS, ELIE:** 01333 330962/077966 84532 (day) 330942 (night). Gr beach location in totally charming wee town where there's enough going on to occupy non-watersporters. Easy lagoon for first timers and open season for non-experienced users. Wind-surfers, kayaks, water-ski. Also mt bikes and inflatable 'biscuits'. (969/971/FIFE HOTELS, 1410/PUB FOOD, 1955/GOLF).

2145
MAP 2
D2
✓ **LINNHE MARINE:** 01631 730401 or 07721 503981. Lettershuna, Port Appin. 32km N of Oban on A828 nr Portnacroish. Established, personally run business in a fine sheltered spot for learning and ploutering. They almost guarantee to get you windsurfing over to the island in 2hrs. Individual or group instruction. Wayfarers, Luggers and fishing-boats. Moorings. Castle Stalker and Lismore are just round the corner, seals & porpoises abound; the joy of sailing. May-Sept.

2146
MAP 2
D5
✓ **SCOTTISH NATIONAL WATERSPORTS CENTRE, CUMBRAE:** 01475 530757. Ferry from Largs then learn all about how to pilot things that float. You need to book – call them, then bob about 'doon the watter'.

2147
MAP 3
C4
✓ **PORT EDGAR, SOUTH QUEENSFERRY:** 0131 331 3330. At end of village, under and beyond the Forth Road Br. Major marina and water sports centre. Berth your boat, hire anything from a Wayfarer to a canoe or just use the jetty to kick off some windsurfing or jet-skiing. Big tuition programme for kids. Home to Port Edgar yacht club.

2148
MAP 3
A5
✓ **STRATHCLYDE PARK:** 01698 266155. Major water sports centre 15km SE of Glas and easily reached from most of Central Scotland via M8 or M74 (jnct 5 or 6). 200-acre loch and centre with instruction on sailing, canoeing, windsurfing, rowing, water-skiing and hire facs for canoes, Mirrors and Wayfarers, windsurfers and trimarans. Call booking office for sessions and times.

2149
MAP 5
E3
✓ **LOCH INSH WATERSPORTS, KINCRAIG:** 01540 651272. On B970, 2km from Kincraig towards Kingussie and the A9. Marvellous loch side site launching from gently sloping dinky beach into shallow forgiving waters of L Inch. Hire of canoes, dinghies (Mirrors, Toppers, Lasers, Wayfarers) and windsurfers as well as rowing boats; river trips. An idyllic place to learn. Watch the others and the sunset from the balcony restau above (1089/INEXP HIGHLAND RESTAUS). Sports 9am-5pm, Apr-Oct.

2150
MAP 5
E3
✓ **LOCH MORLICH WATERSPORTS nr AVIEMORE:** 01479 861221. By Glenmore Forest Park, part of the plethora of outdoor activities hereabouts (skiing, walking etc). This is the loch you see from Cairngorm and just as picturesque from the woody shore. Canoes/kayaks/rowing boats and dinghies (Wayfarers, Toppers, Optimists) with instruction in everything. Evening hire poss. Good campsite adj (1306/CAMPING WITH KIDS).

2151
MAP 3
A2
✓ **CROFT-NA-CABER, nr KENMORE, LOCH TAY:** 01887 830588. S side of loch, 2km from village. Purpose-built water sports centre with instruction and hire of windsurfers, canoes, kayaks, dinghies, motor boats as well as waterskiing, river rafting (down the Tay from Aberfeldy to white water at Grandtully: pure exhilaration), archery, clay shooting, quad biking. A v good all-round activities centre in a gr setting. Timeshare chalet accom avail (for short stays 01887 830236).

2152
MAP 5
D3
GREAT GLEN WATER PARK: 01809 501381. 3km S Invergarry on A82. On shores of tiny L Oich and L Lochy in the Gr Glen. Wonderful spot, with many other lochs nearby. Day visitors welcome with windsurfers, Wayfarers, kayaks, canoes and also mountain bikes and fishing rods for hire. Mainly, however, a chalet park with all the usual condo/timeshare facs (you can rent by the week).

2153
MAP 2
E5
CLYDE MUIRSHIEL REGIONAL PARK, CASTLE SEMPLE CENTRE, LOCHWINNOCH: 01505 842882. 30km SW Glas M8 jnct 28A, A737 past Johnstone then A760. Also 20km from Largs via A760. Loch (nr village) is 3km x 1km and at the Rangers Centre you can hire dinghies and canoes etc (also mountain bikes). Bird reserve on opp bank (1816/WILDLIFE). Peaceful place to learn. Nov-Mar 10am-4pm, Apr-Oct 10am-8pm.

2154 **KIP MARINA, INVERKIP:** 01475 521485. Major sailing centre on Clyde coast
MAP 2 50km W of Glas via M8, A8 and A78 from Greenock heading S for Wemyss Bay.
E4 A yacht heaven as well as haven of Grand Prix status. Sails, charters, pub/restau, chandlers and myriad boats. Diving equipment and dinghies for hire.

2155 **LOCHORE MEADOWS, nr LOCHGELLY:** 01592 414300. From Dunfermline-
MAP 3 Kirkcaldy motorway take Lochgelly t/off into town and follow signs for
C4 Lochore Country Park. Small, safe loch for learning and perfecting. Canoes and dinghies for hire. Equipped for disabled. Park contains 2 good adventure playgrounds for wide age range.

2156 **LOCHEARNHEAD WATERSPORTS:** 01567 830330. On A85 nr jnct with A84 is
MAP 3 a water sports centre where they suggest you'll never be out of your depth.
A3 Certainly the loch is wide open and (usually) gently lapping. Kayaks, Canadian canoes and water-skiing. Café.

2157 **GALLOWAY SAILING CENTRE, LOCH KEN, nr CASTLE DOUGLAS:** 01644
MAP 1 420626. 15km N on A713 to Ayr. Dinghies, windsurfers, canoes, kayaks, tuition.
C2 Also the Climbing Tower so you can zip-wire & take the leap of faith! All this by a serene loch nr Galloway Forest. Phone for times & courses. Open Mar-Nov.

2158 **RAASAY OUTDOOR CENTRE, nr SKYE:** 01478 660266. Excl activity place! Day
MAP 5 visits or holidays.
B2

THE BEST DIVING SITES

Scotland's seas are primal soup, full of life and world-class sites as hard core divers already know. The E coast can be tricky if the wind is blowing from the N or E, therefore the W coast is preferable (the further N the better). Thanks to the Gulf Stream it's not cold, even without a dry suit, and once you're down it's like flying thro the Botanics (says my friend Tim Maguire). So when you see all those crazies walking into the sea, remember, they may know something that you don't know. Some day I will go down!

2159 WEST COAST

MAP 6
MAP 7 **THE OUTER HEBRIDES:** excellent with fantastic visibility esp off the W coast of **HARRIS** where you can plop in virtually anywhere.

ST KILDA: offers the best diving in the UK, but it's the hardest to get to. On the edge of the Continental Shelf and the whale migration route, it has huge drop-offs and upwellings of life. Book boat and board well in advance.

THE SUMMER ISLES: from Ullapool harbour. Wrecks, lee shores and unpolluted waters.

MAP 2 **OBAN:** Scuba central with lots of sites in the neighbourhood and easy access
D2 to the isles. Charter a boat and search for scallops in **THE GARVELLACH** or dive the wrecks in the **SOUND OF MULL**. Somewhere off **TOBERMORY** there is reputedly, one of Scotland's most enigmatic wrecks, a Spanish galleon. Easier to find are dolphins off the coasts of **ISLAY & TIREE** and see 1681/DOL-PHINS for other likely spots.

All W Coast sea lochs are good for general wildlife diving.

2160 EAST COAST

MAP 3
D4 ✓ **ST ABBS HEAD:** Accessible from the shore (1936/COASTAL WALKS) or by boat from **EYEMOUTH**, a marine reserve, so leave the lobsters alone. The spectacular Cathedral Rock is encrusted with green and yellow dead men's fingers and in August /Sept is a sanctuary for breeding fish (this cathedral is as beautiful as St Giles and is distinctly non-denominational). Nearby shore-based diving at **DUNBAR** is shallow, safe and simple.

MAP 3 **THE ISLE OF MAY:** across the Forth is more advanced. Take a boat from
E5 Anstruther (1795/BIRDS). Main site is Piccadilly Circus, a central atrium fed by gullies, full of friendly seals.

✓ ✓ **SCAPA FLOW:** The world-famous underwater burial site where the Germans scuttled their fleet in 1918. Think Gaudalcanal, but colder. Although the scrappies have been in, there are still dozens and cruisers down there. Most lie in 35-40m deep, so plan carefully. Majorly eerie!

DIVE OPERATORS (Don't leave home without one).

EDINBURGH: Edinburgh Diving Centre 0131 229 4838.

COLDINGHAM, BORDERS: Scoutscroft Dive Centre 01890 771669.

OBAN: Puffin Dive Centre 01631 566088. Oban Divers 01631 562755.

SKYE: Dive & Sea the Hebrides 01470 592219.

MULL: Seafare Chandlery & Diving 01688 302277.

ULLAPOOL: Atlantic Diving Services (Achiltibuie) 01854 622261.

ORKNEY: Diving Cellar 01856 850055. European Technical Dive Centre 01856 731269. Scapa Scuba 01856 851218. Scapa Flow Charters 01856 850879.

Wide network of v helpful local diving clubs around the country. Contact Scottish Sub Aqua Club 0141 425 1021.

THE BEST WINDSURFING

FOR BEGINNERS AND INSTRUCTION (see also WATER SPORTS).

CROFT-NA-CABER, KENMORE, LOCH TAY: 01887 830588.

LINNHE MARINE, nr OBAN: 01631 730401.

LOCHORE MEADOWS, LOCHGELLY, FIFE: 01592 414300. (No instruction.)

TIGHNABRUAICH SAILING SCHOOL, TIGHNABRUAICH: 01700 811717.

SCOTTISH NATIONAL WATERSPORTS CENTRE, CUMBRAE: 01475 530757.

STRATHCLYDE PARK, nr MOTHERWELL and GLASGOW: 01698 266155. Lots to do in this recreational zone of the conurbation. Water may not be so turquoise. 1493/COUNTRY PARKS.

ELIE, EAST NEUK OF FIFE: 01333 330962. Small, friendly windsurfing and water sports operation on the beach (beyond the Ship Inn).

WINDSURFING SPOTS

2162 WEST COAST

MAP 2 **MACHRIHANISH:** Wave-sailing, fabulous long beach (1647/BEACHES). Mainly
C6 at Air Force base end. Big waves, for the more advanced.

E6 **PRESTWICK/TROON:** Town beaches.

E5 **ISLAND OF CUMBRAE:** Millport beach.

E4 **MILARROCHY BAY, LOCH LOMOND:** 8km from Drymen (45km N of Glas). W/end centre run by 7th Wave. Second beach up from Balmaha. Picturesque.

2163 EAST COAST

MAP 4 **FRASERBURGH:** Town beach. Also surfing.

MAP 3 **LUNAN BAY:** 12km N of Arbroath. Also surfing.

MAP 3 **CARNOUSTIE:** Town beach.

MAP 3 **ST ANDREWS:** W Sands. Also surfing.

MAP 3 **LONGNIDDRY/GULLANE:** 25/35km E of Edin via A1 and A198.

2164 NORTH COAST

MAP 6 **THURSO:** Many beaches nr town and further W. (1660/BEACHES)

FOR ENTHUSIASTS

2165
MAP 2
A2

✓ **ISLAND OF TIREE:** The windsurfing capital of Scotland. 40km W of Mull. Countless clean, gently sloping beaches all round island (and small inland loch) allowing surfing in all wind directions. Accom basic: Tiree Lodge Hotel (01879 220368), Kirkapol Guest House (01879 220729) or self-catering (Oban TIC 01631 563122). Loganair fly every day except Sunday (0845 7733377) and Calmac run ferries from Oban every day (01475 650100).

INFORMATION/BOARD HIRE:

BOARDWISE, GLASGOW: 1146 Argyle St 0141 334 5559.

BOARDWISE, EDINBURGH: Lady Lawson St 0131 229 5887.

THE BEST SURFING BEACHES

A surprise for the sceptical: Scotland has some of the best surfing beaches in Europe. Forget the bronzed beachboys and lemon bleached hair, surfing in Scotland is titanium-lined, rubber and balaclavas, and you get an ice-cream head even encased in the latest technology. The main season is Sept-Dec.

2166 WEST COAST

MAP 7
C1

✓✓ **ISLE OF LEWIS:** Probably the best of the lot. Go N of Stornoway, N of Barvas, N of just about anywhere. Leave the A857 and your day job behind. Not the most scenic of sites, but the waves have come a long way, further than you have. Derek at Hebridean Surf Holidays (01851 705862) will tell you when and where to go.

MAP 2
C6

✓ **MACHRIHANISH:** Nr Campbeltown at the foot of the Mull of Kintyre. Long strand to choose from (1647/BEACHES). Clan Skates in Glasgow (0141 339 6523) usually has an up-to-date satellite map and a idea of both the W and (nearest to central belt) Pease Bay (*see below*).

2167 NORTH COAST

MAP 6
D1

✓ **STRATHY BAY:** Nr Bettyhill on the N coast halfway betw Tongue and Thurso on the A836. Go past the village, park at the graveyard. Once in the foam, paddle to the rt. From here to Cape Wrath the power and quality of the waves detonating on the shore justify comparisons with Hawaii.

MAP 6
D1

✓ **THURSO:** Surf City, well not quite, but it's a good base to find your own waves. Esp to the E of town at Dunnet Bay – a 5km long beach with excellent reefs at the N end. They say it has to be the best right-hand breaking wave on the planet!

MAP 6
E2

WICK: On the Thurso rd at Ackergill to the S of Sinclair's Bay (1337/HOUSE PARTIES). Find the ruined castle and taking care, clamber down the gully to the beach. A monumental reef break, you are working against the backdrop of the decaying ruin drenched in history, spume and romance.

2168 EAST COAST

MAP 4
E3

NIGG BAY: Just S of Aberdeen (not to be confused with Nigg across from Cromarty) and off the vast beach at Lunan Bay (1654/BEACHES) betw Arbroath and Montrose.

MAP 3
E4

✓ **PEASE BAY:** S of Dunbar nr Cockburnspath on the A1. The nearest surfie heaven to the capital. The caravan site has parking and toilets. V consistent surf here and therefore v popular.

INFORMATION/BOARD HIRE:

GLASGOW: **BOARDWISE:** 1146 Argyle St 0141 334 5559.

                 CLAN SKATES: 45 Hyndland St 0141 339 6523.

EDINBURGH: **BOARDWISE:** Lady Lawson St 0131 229 5887.

                 MOMENTUM: Bruntsfield Pl 0131 229 6665.

SECTION 11

Shopping

signifies notable *café*.

2170
MAP 3
B1
HOUSE OF BRUAR, PITLOCHRY: Courtyard emporia and shopaholic honey pot on the A9 N of Blair Atholl esp for those who just missed Pitlochry. Self-s restau v good (big on Aberdeen Angus beef), retail food side well selected (good range of Scottish cheeses, Mackie's ice cream, MacSween's haggis, etc). Outdoor wear with big labels (Musto, Patagonia), golf shop & gdn centre. Falls nearby for more spiritual sustenance (1678/WATERFALLS). 7 days, till 6pm (5pm in winter).

2171
MAP 3
D3
CRAIL POTTERY, CRAIL, FIFE: At the foot of Rose Wynd, signposted from main st (best to walk). In a tree-shaded Mediterranean courtyard and upstairs attic is a cornucopia of brilliant, useful, irresistible things. Open 10am-5pm. Don't miss the harbour nearby, one of the most romantic neuks in the Neuk. Pity there's nowhere decent in Crail for tea.

2172
MAP 4
A1
ANTA FACTORY SHOP, FEARN, nr TAIN: Off B9175 from Tain to the Nigg ferry, 8km through Hill of Fearn, on corner of disused airfield. Shop with adj pottery. Much tartan curtain fabric; many rugs, throws and pots. You can commission furniture to be covered in their material. Pottery tour by arr. Shop. AYR daily 9.30am-5.30pm (Sun 11-5pm, summer only), pottery Mon-Fri only.

2173
MAP 6
C3
TAIN POTTERY: Off the A9 just S of Tain (opp side of A9 to rd signed for Anta at Fearn; see above). Big working pottery featuring crafts by Pippa Lee and NTS tartan ceramics among others. Daily in summer, 10am-5pm. Cl Sun in wint.

2174
MAP 6
B2, B3
HIGHLAND STONEWARE, LOCHINVER and ULLAPOOL: On rd to Baddidarach as you enter Lochinver on A837; and in Mill St, Ullapool, on way N beyond centre. A modern large-scale pottery business incl a shop/warehouse and studios that you can walk round (Lochinver is more *engagé*). Similar to the 'ceramica' places you find in the Med, but not too terracotta – rather, painted and heavy-glazed stoneware in set styles. Gr selection, pricey, but you may have luck rummaging in the Lochinver discount section. Mail-order service. Open AYR.

2175
MAP 3
B2
MACNAUGHTON'S, PITLOCHRY: Station Rd on corner of main st, this the best of many. A vast old-fashioned outfitter with acres of tartan attire – incl obligatory tartan pyjamas & dressing gowns! Make their own cloth, and 9m kilts prepared in 10 wks. This really is the real McCoy. 7 days till 5.30pm (4pm Sun).

2176
MAP A
xE1
KINLOCH ANDERSON, EDINBURGH: Commercial St, Leith. A bit of a trek from uptown, but firmly on the tourist trail and rightly so. Experts in Highland dress and all things tartan; they've supplied *everybody*. They design their own tartans, have a good range of men's tweed jackets; even rugs. Mon-Sat 9am-5.30pm (5pm winter).

2177
MAP 5
D2
MADE IN SCOTLAND, BEAULY: Station Rd on way out of town to Inverness. Large emporium & restau of things made in Scotland. Well... some are better than others. AYR 9.30am-5.30pm, Sun 10-5pm.

2178
MAP 4
A2
LOGIE STEADING nr FORRES: Estate courtyard in beautiful countryside 10km S of Forres signed from A940 Forres-Grantown rd. Nr pleasant woodland walk and picnic spot. For directions, see 2051/WOODLAND WALKS. Art and ceramics from Highland artists and workshops. Second-hand books. Tearoom. Mar-Dec, 7 days 10.30am-5pm.

2179
MAP 4
A1
BRODIE COUNTRY FARE: By main A96 betw Nairn and Forres, nr Brodie Castle (1824/CASTLES). Not a souvenir shoppie in the trad sense, more a drive-in one-stop shopping experience on the taste by-pass. Deli food, a fairly up-market boutique designer womenswear and every crafty tartanalia of note. The self-serve restau gets as busy as a motorway café. 7 days till 5.30/7pm Thurs.

2180
MAP 5
D1
FALLS OF SHIN VISITOR CENTRE, nr LAIRG: Self-serve café/restau in the VC and shop across the rd from the Falls of Shin on the Achany Glen rd 8km S of Lairg (1691/WATERFALLS). Good basic food in an unlikely emporium of all things Harrods (Mohammed al Fayed's estate is here). They come from miles around at Xmas for hampers etc. 9.30am-6pm AYR.

2181 **MORTIMER'S & RITCHIE'S, GRANTOWN ON SPEY:** 3 & 41-45 High St (the main
MAP 4 st) respectively of this respectable Speyside holiday town where fishing gear is
B2 somewhat in demand (though odd to find 2 similar high-quality shops adj).
Mortimer's more exclusively angling for your custom, but both have a big range
of flies. Outdoor clothing with all the big names betw them and every shade of
olive. Ritchie's also have guns if you want to kill something. Both cl Sun.

2182 **EDINBANE POTTERY, EDINBANE, SKYE:** 500m off A850 Portree (22km) –
MAP 5 Dunvegan rd. Long-established and reputable working pottery where all the
A2 various processes are often in progress. Earthy pots of every shape and size;
unusual 'lantern' plant holders. Open AYR 9am-6pm. 7 days (not w/ends wint).

2183 **SKYE SILVER, COLBOST, SKYE:** 10km Dunvegan on B884 to Glendale. Long
MAP 5 established and reputable jewellery made and sold in an old schoolhouse by
A2 the rd in distant corner of Skye, but 3 Chimneys restau nearby (2322/ISLANDS
RESTAUS). Well-made, Celtic designs, good gifts. Mar-Oct 7 days, 10am-6pm.

2184 **KILN ROOM POTTERY AND COFFEE SHOP, LAGGAN:** On main A889 route
MAP 5 to Ft William and Skye from Dalwhinnie. Simple, usable pottery (tho pottery
D3 itself no longer in use) with distinctive warm colouring. Selected knitwear and
useful things. Home-made cakes and scones; 1491/COFFEE SHOPS. 9am-6pm, 7
days. Now with hostel out back v inx incl comfy lounge with gr vista and
unique seven-person hot-tub spa (01528 544231). ☕

2185 **GLENELG CANDLES, GLENELG:** Signed from glen rd which comes over the
MAP 5 hill from Shiel Bridge (1705/SCENIC ROUTES) and hard to miss. Wooden
B2 cabin/coffee shop with multifarious candles and local art. Excl home-made
food (1497/COFFEE SHOPS). Easter-Oct 9.30pm-5.30pm daily. ☕

2186 **BALNAKEIL, DURNESS, SUTHERLAND:** From Durness & the main A836 rd, take
MAP 6 Balnakeil & Faraid Head rd for 2km W. Founded in the 1960s in what one imag-
B1 ines was a haze of hash, this craft village is still home to those seeking to 'down-
shift'. Varied paintings, pottery, weaving & a bookshop in the different prefab
huts where community members live & work (the site used to be an early warn-
ing station). Lotte Glob *is* (01971 511354) v good. Bistro & a restau. Some businesses seasonal, some not. All open in summer, daily 10am-6 pm (mostly).

2187 **SKYE BATIKS, PORTREE, SKYE:** In centre near TIC. V original Sri Lanka 'batiks'-
MAP 5 cotton fabrics of ancient Celtic designs in every shape and size. Mainly hand-
A2 made, majorly colourful; a unique souvenir of Skye. Island Outdoors adj has
outdoor 'fashion' & all-important midge helmets.

2188 **ACHIN'S BOOKSHOP, LOCHINVER:** At Inverkirkaig 5km from Lochinver on
MAP 6 the 'wee mad rd' to Achiltibuie (1712/SCENIC ROUTES). Unexpected selection of
B2 books in the back of beyond providing something to read when you've
climbed everything. Outdoor wear too and gr hats. The path to Kirkaig Falls
and Suilven begins at the gate. Easter-Oct 7 days; 9.30am-6pm (wint Mon-Sat
10am-5pm). Adj café 10am-5pm, summer only.

2189 **IONA ABBEY SHOP:** Iona via Calmac ferry from Fionnphort on Mull. Crafts
MAP 2 and souvenirs across the way in separate building. Proceeds support a wor-
B3 thy, committed organisation. Christian literature, tapes etc, but mostly artefacts from nearby and around Scotland. Celtic crosses much in evidence, but
then this is where they came from! Mar-Oct 9.30am-5pm.

2190 **OCTOPUS CRAFTS, nr FAIRLIE, nr LARGS:** On main A78 Largs to Ardrossan
MAP 2 rd, just S of Fairlie. Smaller setup than above, but, crafts, wines and cookshop
E5 an excellent restau (1447/SEAFOOD RESTAUS) and a seafood deli. An all-round
road side experience – the sign says Fencebay Fisheries. Everything here is
hand-made and/or hand-picked. Even the wines are well chosen. Good pots.
Glass and wood. They also run courses. Cl Mon.

2191 **BALBIRNIE CRAFT CENTRE, MARKINCH:** Follow signs for Balbirnie Park from
MAP 3 Glenrothes road system, but off the A92. Farmyard courtyard of craft work-
C3 shops and retail in country park nr Balbirnie House Hotel (965/FIFE HOTELS).
Jewellery, glasswork, ceramics, leather and embroidery – bit of everything
really. Nice that something's made in Glenrothes that isn't made in millions. 7
days (Sun afternoons only).

2192 **BORGH POTTERY, BORVE, ISLE OF LEWIS:** On NW coast of island a wee way
MAP 7 from Stornoway, but not much of a detour from the rd to Callanish where you
C1 are probably going. Alex and Sue Blair's pleasant gallery of handthrown pots
with diff glazes; domestic and gdn wear. Some knits. Open AYR 9-6pm. Cl Sun.

274   S H O P P I N G

2193 **ROSEHALL CRAFT SHOP nr LAIRG:** If all else fails, follow signs for Raven's
MAP 6 Rock trail then ask someone. Otherwise, off the A837 E of the Achness Hotel.
C3 Lady Jean Gilmour's place. Pop in for home baking and a chat at least! Easter-
Oct daily until 5pm.

2194 **HOUSE OF MENZIES nr ABERFELDY:** Adj to Menzies Castle (1835/CASTLES)
MAP 3 on rd to Glen Lyon. Mainly art & wine on sale here & coffee shop. Report:
B2 2202/ART. The glen awaits. ☕

2195 **GALLOWAY LODGE PRESERVES, GATEHOUSE OF FLEET:** On main st of com-
MAP 1 pact town. Packed with local jams, marmalades, chutneys and pickles. Scottish
C2 pottery by Scotia Ceramics, Highland Stoneware and Dunoon. Good presents
and jam for yourself. 10am-5pm Mon-Sat, and Sun afternoons in summer.

2196 **CRAFTS AND THINGS, nr GLENCOE VILLAGE:** On A82 betw Glencoe village
MAP 2 and Ballachulish. Eclectic mix of so many baubles that some are literally hang-
D2 ing from the rafters. Mind, body & spirit books (like this one) and reasonably
priced knit/outerwear. Good coffee shop, with local artist's work on walls. All-
round nice place. Summer season, daily until 5.30pm, wint Fri-Sun only. ☕

2197 **THOMAS CHIPPENDALE SCHOOL OF FURNITURE:** 01620 810680. B6369
MAP 3 Haddington to Gifford Rd. Anselm Fraser runs cabinet-making courses here
D5 and welcomes visitors weekdays 9-4.30pm. Check out the work and commis-
sion something.

2198 **DRUMLANRIG CASTLE, nr THORNHILL, nr DUMFRIES:** A whole day out of
MAP 1 things to do (1613/COUNTRY PARKS) including the craft centre in the old sta-
D1 ble/courtyard to the side of the house. Studio-type shops with tartan, jew-
ellery and 'bodging'! Hire a bike and ride while you decide.

2199 **KIRKCUDBRIGHT HIGH ST:** A run of craft shops by the Tolbooth Arts Centre.
MAP 1 Inc Jo Gallant textiles, Cranberries (general), Gill's jewellery and the High St
C3 Gallery. Browse on, then walk round to the Corner Gallery (2222/WOOLLIES).

WHERE TO BUY ART

*These galleries, all outside the dealer & public-gallery concentrations in Edin &
Glas, cater also for tourists… but they're all a cut above the rest. See also* SMALL
GALLERIES, EDINBURGH *p. 71,* GLASGOW *p. 109.*

2200 **McEWAN GALLERY nr BALLATER, DEESIDE:** A surprising place but for many
MAP 4 years this cottage gallery has been dealing in 19th/20th century, mainly
C3 Scottish art. They wrote the book! Summer exhibs, but open AYR 11am-5pm
(Sun 2-6pm). Wint hrs 01339 755429. 300m up A939 Tomintoul rd.

2201 **THE LOST GALLERY, MIDDLE OF NOWHERE, ABERDEENSHIRE:** Signed for
MAP 4 Bellabeg on A944 nr Strathon vill. 3km up farm rd, then another 3km on rough
C3 track to a fab studio/gallery with varied work by contemp Scots & the owners.
AYR 11am-5pm. Cl Tues. 01975 651287 if you get… lost.

2202 **HOUSE OF MENZIES nr ABERFELDY:** On Weem rd across the river from
MAP 3 Aberfeldy then B846, signposted 'Dull' (yes, dull!). This beautifully converted
B2 farm steading is far from it! Selected art from Edinburgh's Wasp art co-operative & a surprising range of New World wines. Café open AYR 10am-5pm (Sun
from 11am). Cl Mon Oct-Jan, Mon/Tues Jan-Mar. ☕

2203 **STRATHEARN GALLERY, CRIEFF:** 32 W St (on Main St). Accessible & afford-
MAP 3 able. The Maguires do know what you like. Fine and applied arts. 7 days till
B33 5pm (Thu-Sat in wint).

2204 **TOLQUHON GALLERY, nr ABERDEEN:** 01651 842343. Betw Ellon and
MAP 4 Oldmeldrum and nr Haddo House (1754/COUNTRY HOUSES) and Pitmedden
D2 (1605/GARDENS) – follow signs for castle, an interesting ruin for kids to clam-
ber. Real art at realistic prices. (Pron 'T'hon'.) 11am-5pm, Sun 2-5pm. Cl Thu.

2205 **JUST ART, FOCHABERS:** 64 High St, the A96 through Fochabers E of Elgin.
MAP 4 Changing exhibs of serious and selected mainly Scottish artists. Good ceram-
C1 ics. An interesting stop on this rd along the coast. See 2237/GARDEN CENTRES.

2206 **McINTOSH GALLERY, KINGUSSIE:** Main St. Crowded with pictures & also
MAP 5 rugs. Across st, **SOMETHING DIFFERENT** is a real treasure-trove of cool
E3 things. Good on you, Ruby!

2207 **ST ANDREWS FINE ART:** Crowded walls of Scottish art from 1800-present.
MAP 3 Includes some good work from kent contemporaries. Peploe-Redpath and
D3 their chums. Cl Sun.

2208 **KRANENBURG & FOWLER FINE ARTS, OBAN:** Star Brae & Stevenson St.
MAP 2 01631 562303. Geoff & Jan source work from artists that ranges from the
D2 polite to the interesting. Small group of regular exhibitors and others. Mon-
Sat 9.30am-5.30pm. Suns when exhib 12-4pm.

2209 **MORVEN GALLERY, BARVAS, ISLE OF LEWIS:** Coast rd just N of Barabhas
MAP 7 30km from Callanish and those stones. Janice Scott's excl farm steading kind
C1 of gallery with well-selected work, mainly local. Painting, tapestry, ceramics
and fab original knits. Baking. AYR Apr-Sept 10am-5pm. Cl Sun. ☕

2210 **SCOTTISH SCULPTURE WORKSHOPS, LUMSDEN nr ALFORD and HUNTLY:**
MAP 4 01464 861372. Main st of ribbon town on A97. Not a place to see work for sale
C2 (mainly commissions), but work being made. They also look after the sculpture
gdn at end of st towards Alford by the school. Workshops open AYR. Mon-Fri
9am-5pm.

2211 **THE GLASGOW ART FAIR:** The Scottish market place for contemporary art.
MAP B Mainly home-grown but London galleries with Scottish connections. Held in
D3 mid April in pavilions in George Square. 0141 552 6027 for details. (829/ESS.
CULTURE/FESTIVALS) ☕

**THE DEGREE SHOWS, EDINBURGH/GLASGOW & DUNCAN OF
JORDANSTONE, DUNDEE, ART SCHOOLS:** Work from final-year students.
Discover the Bellanys, Howsons, Douglas Gordons & Simon Starlings of the
future. 2-week exhibition after manic first night (mid June).

Prints by many contemp Scottish artists available from:

GLASGOW PRINT STUDIOS: 22 King St, Merchant City/Tron area.

EDINBURGH PRINTMAKERS WORKSHOP: 23 Union St off Leith Walk

PEACOCK VISUAL ARTS, ABERDEEN: 21 Castle St.

THE BEST JUNKYARDS

2212 ✓**AULDEARN ANTIQUES, AULDEARN, nr NAIRN:** Doris and Roger Milton's
MAP 4 cornucopia of junk, quality antiques and architectural salvage in an old
A1 manse 2km from main st (via Lethen Rd) which is 3km from main A96 Nairn-
Forres rd. Serene spot for browsing through courtyard of shops and a church-
ful of furniture. Kids welcome. 7 days until 5.30pm.

2213 **SAM BURNS' YARD, PRESTONPANS, nr EDINBURGH:** 01875 810600. On the
MAP 3 coast rd out of Musselburgh; if you get to Prestonpans you've missed it. By a
C4 gate in the wall you'll see cars on the kerb of a long straight stretch. The yard
has piles of old bikes, assorted 'stuff' and is full of domestic and office furniture stored both outdoors and in sheds. Popular with Sunday browsers picking thro' mountains of junk. 7 days 9.30am-5pm, Sun from 11am.

2214 **EASY (EDINBURGH ARCHITECTURAL SALVAGE YARD):** 554 7077. Couper St
MAP A off Coburg St (at N end of Gr Jnct St nr mini roundabout). Warehouseful of
xD1 original house fittings and the place to go for baths, sinks, radiators, fireplaces,
doors (there are rows of them) & all the other bits of Old Edin that used to be
thrown out but which are now worth lots. Open Mon-Fri 9am-5pm, Sat 12-5pm.

2215 **TAYMOUTH ARCHITECTURAL ANTIQUES, DUNDEE:** 01382 666833.
MAP 3 Magdalen Yard Rd off Riverside (the airport) rd, t/off by the railway br. Mainly
D3 big architectural stuff like fireplaces & church pews, but worth a browse, esp
if you're doing up a house. Open Tues-Sat.

2216 ✓**THE SCOTTISH ANTIQUE CENTRES:** 2 locations: 1) 2km W of Doune on
MAP 3 A84, Stirling–Callendar rd. 01786 841203; 2) Outside Abernyte betw Perth
A3 & Dundee on A 90. Not junkyards, more high flautin'. 40,000 sq ft of antiques,
repro & gifts. 7 days, 10am-5pm.

2217 ✓ ✓ **LYNDA USHER, BEAULY:** 01463 783017. Fabulous ladies' knitwear
MAP 5 and linen from a fabulous lady. V selective and based on the owner's
D2 personal choice; Lynda is a big name in Scottish knitting circles. Open AYR;
Mon-Sat 9.30am-5.30pm (till 5pm in winter).

2218 ✓ ✓ **BELINDA ROBERTSON, EDINBURGH:** 0131 225 1057. 22 Palmerston
MAP A Pl, Edin. Queen of the commissioned cashmere creations; you can
B3 only choose from the *prêt-à-porter* collection in her showroom here (or in
London). Her team of 7 girls design and process the stock which is made up
in Hawick. HILARY ROHDE's the other cashmere designer par excellence. She's
too big-time even to give out a phone-number (and I promised I wouldn't).

2219 ✓ **JUDITH GLUE, KIRKWALL, ORKNEY:** Opp the cathedral. Distinctive hand-
made jumpers, the runic designs are a real winner. Also the widespread but
individual Highland and Joker stoneware (jewellery and animal clocks v popular), condiments and preserves. The landscape prints of Orkney are by twin sister, Jane. Open AYR 7 days 9.30am-5.30pm (Suns only in summer, 10am-6pm).

2220 ✓ **FLORAIDH-TWEED & WOOL COLLECTION, SKYE:** 01471 833421. In S on
MAP 5 Sleat adj Eilean Iarmain Hotel (2311/ISLAND HOTELS). Small, packed &
B3 tasteful selection of woolly things for women, with some local crafts.
Somebody here has the 'good eye'. Mon-Fri.

2221 **RAGAMUFFIN, SKYE:** On Armadale Pier, so one of the first or last things you
MAP 5 can do on Skye is rummage through the Ragamuffin store and get a nice knit.
B3 Every kind of jumper and some crafts in this Aladdin's cave within a new build;
incl tweedy things and hats.

2222 **CORNER GALLERY, KIRKCUDBRIGHT:** 75 St Mary's Street (01557 332020).
MAP 1 Anne Chaudhry's resplendent knitwear shop with some very nice gear indeed.
C3 Woollens not just for middle-aged blokes on the golf course: remember – it
can be designer-standard too! Easter–Dec 10am-5pm daily. (Cl Thurs afternoon
in winter, and completely Jan-Mar.)

2223 **JOHNSTON'S CASHMERE CENTRE, ELGIN:** Large Mill Shop kind of operation
MAP 4 and full-blown visitor attraction nr the Cathedral (1847/RUINS). 'The only
B1 British mill to transform fibre to garment' (yarns spun at their factory in Elgin
and made into garments in the Borders) and though this is more British High
St than Bloomingdale's, New York, these jumpers will keep you just as warm.
Mon-Sat 9am-5.30pm, Sun 11am-5pm. Slight variations in winter.

2224 **LOCHCARRON VISITOR CENTRE, GALASHIELS:** If you're in Galashiels (or
MAP 3 Hawick), which grew up around woollen mills, you might expect to find a
D6 good selection of woollens you can't get everywhere else; and bargains. Well,
tough! There's no stand-out place, but L Carron (incl Vivienne Westwood!) is a
big tourist attraction with mill tours (Open AYR 4 times a day), exhibits and an
okay mill shop. Hawick did invent the Y-front.

2225 **HAWICK CASHMERE:** Factory in Hawick since 1874, with VC beside the river
MAP 3 on Duke St. Also shops in Kelso & Edinburgh. 'State-of-the-art colours and
D6 designs'. Not only, but mostly cashmere. 10am-5.30pm Mon-Sat.

HARRIS TWEED

2226 **TWEEDS & KNITWEAR, 4 PLOCKROPOOL, DRINISHADDER:** Organised
MAP 7 operators (they even cater for coach parties) with weaving demonstrations &
B3 wool & knitwear for sale as well as tweed. Cl Sun.

JOAN McCLENNAN: NO 1A, DRINISHADDER: Further down the Golden Rd
(1709/SCENIC ROUTES). I don't know, but I've been told, this is where you find
the real golden fleece. Go look for it.

LUSKENTYRE HARRIS TWEED: NO 6, LUSKENTYRE: 2km off W coast on
main rd S to Scarista and Rodel. Donald and Maureen Mackay's place is
notable for their bright tartan tweed. 9.30am-6pm Cl Sun.

BREANISH TWEED, 1A MELBOST, by STORNOWAY: 01851 701524 (ring for
directions & opening, usually Mon-Fri). Lightweight, handwoven tweed incl cashmere & made-to-measure tailoring. This is the one you want you fashionistas!

2227 ✓ **KINLOCHLAICH HOUSE, APPIN:** On main A28 Oban-Ft William rd just N
MAP 2 of Pt Appin t/off, the West Highlands' largest nursery/gdn centre. Set in a
D2 large walled gdn filled with plants and veg soaking up the climes of the warm
Gulf stream. Donald Hutchison and daughter nurture these acres enabling
you to reap what they sow; with a huge array of plants on offer it's like visiting a friend's gdn and being able to take home your fave bits. Charming cottages for let 01631 730342. 7 days: 9.30am-5.30pm (10.30am Sun). Cl Sun in
winter.

2228 ✓ **DOUGAL PHILIP'S NEW HOPETOUN GARDENS, nr S QUEENSFERRY:**
MAP 3 01506 834433. The mother of all (Scottish) garden centres with 16 demon-
C4 stration gardens (incl Oriental & Scottish). Orangery tea-room has commanding
views and tasty home-made stuff. AYR 10am-5.30pm. Tearm closes 4.30pm. ☕

2229 ✓ **INSHRIACH, nr KINCRAIG, nr AVIEMORE:** On B970 betw Kincraig and
MAP 5 Inverdruie (which is on the Coylumbridge ski rd out of Aviemore), a gdn
E3 centre, nay a nursery, that puts most others in the shade. Specialising in
alpines and bog plants, but with neat beds of all sorts in the grounds (and a
wild gdn) of the house by the Spey and frames full of perfect specimens, this
is a potterer's paradise. Mar-Oct Mon-Fri 9am-5pm, Sat/Sun 10am-5pm.

2230 ✓ **DOBBIES, MILNGAVIE, GLASGOW:** Formerly Findlay Clark's, the original
MAP B home of the gdn centre chain in Campsie countryside N of city, 20km
xB1 from centre via A81 or A807 (Milngavie or Kirkintilloch rds) or heading for
Milngavie (pron 'Mullguy'), turn rt on Boclair Rd. Vast gdn complex and all-
round visitor experience; an institution. 'Famous' coffee shop (the famous
waitresses are local babes and what they turn into), saddlery with everything
except horses; labels from Crabtree & Evelyn to Fisons, plus books, clothes and
piles of plants; and live pets. 9am-9pm (till 7pm in winter). ☕

2231 ✓ **GLENDOICK, GLENCARSE, nr PERTH:** On A85, 10km from Perth, in the
MAP 3 fertile Carse of the Tay. A large family-owned gdn centre notable esp for
C3 rhododendrons and azaleas, a riot of which can be viewed in the nursery
behind (May only). Pagoda Garden (they practice what they preach). V popular coffee shop with superior home-baking. 7 days till 6pm, 5pm wint. ☕

2232 **BRIN HERB NURSERY, FLICHITY, nr INVERNESS:** Off A9 S of Daviot, 12km S
MAP 5 of Inverness, then 10km SW to Farr. An old school and playground dedicated
D2 to herbs, plants and all the potions and lotions that come from them. Tearoom
in the school room. Mar-Oct 9.30am-6pm, Sun 12.30-5pm (summer only). ☕

2233 **THE TREE SHOP, CAIRNDOW, LOCH FYNE:** A gdn centre specialising in trees
MAP 2 & shrubs. Part of the Ardkinglas Estate nr (1km) the Woodland Garden
E3 (1607/GARDENS) with UK's tallest tree. The shop on the main A83 L Lomond-
Inveraray rd also does houseplants & all the usual greeneries. Café. 7 days
9.30am-5pm (6pm in summer).

2234 **TEVIOT SMOKERY, WATER GARDENS AND COFFEE SHOP:** 01835 850253.
MAP 3 On A698 between Jedburgh & Kelso. Nicer when small but still lovely gardens
E6 and good food. ☕

2235 **FLOORS CASTLE, KELSO:** 3km outside town off B6397 St Boswells rd (gdn
MAP 3 centre has separate entrance to main visitors' gate in town). Set amongst love-
E6 ly old greenhouses within walled gdns some distance from house, it has a
showpiece herbaceous border all round. Nice coffee shop and patio. 'V good
roses'. Centre is open AYR. 10am-5pm. (1892/COUNTRY HOUSES.) ☕

2236 **CHRISTIE'S NURSERY, KIRRIEMUIR:** 01575 572977. On long straight stretch
MAP 3 of A926 to Blairgowrie in the village of Westmuir, 3km from Kirriemuir.
D2 Looking towards the Sidlaw Hills, this is a family-run nursery specialising in
hardy plants (orchids, alpines etc) with unique stocks of rare plants. This is
where those in the know go for gentians, (they are world specialists), primu-
las and advice about the rock gdn. Mar-Oct 10am-5pm; cl Sun, Tues. Outwith
these times, phone first esp Jan when you might want your bulbs!

2237 **CHRISTIE'S, FOCHABERS:** On A98 going into town from Buckie side. Huge
MAP 4 gdn centre and forest nursery, with tearm/restaurant. Good for shrubs, indoor
C1 plants etc and a gr place for keen and not-so-keen gardeners to browse

around. Famous floral clock and aviary – an all-round shopping/recreational experience. 9am-5pm, 7 days (from 10am Sun).

2238 RAEMOIR GARDEN CENTRE, BANCHORY: On A980 off main st 3km n of
MAP 4   town. A friendly family-run gdn centre & excl coffee-shop that keeps the fas-
D3   tidious gardeners hereabouts happy. And this is Deeside. If it's good enough for them… 7 days 9am-5.30pm. Tearm till 5pm. ☕

2239 KESKE NURSERIES, CLACHAN, NORTH UIST: In the remote heart of wild and
MAP 7   watery N Uist on main rd to Benbecula S of Lochmaddy and just after Clachan
B3   Stores and the t/off for Bayhead a cottage nursery and a … bus full of plants. Idiosyncratic app, but certainly the Hebridean choice for trees, shrubs, veg and bedding plants. Go on, make a statement – plant a tree in this treeless tract. Open AYR 1pm-5.30pm. Cl Sun.

2240 SMEATON NURSERY AND GARDENS, EAST LINTON: 01620 860501. 2km
MAP 3   from village on N Berwick rd (signed Smeaton). Up a drive in an old estate is
D4   this walled gdn going back to early 19th century. Wide range; good for fruit (and other) trees, herbaceous etc. Nice to wander round, an additional plea-sure is the 'Lake Walk' halfway down drive through small gate in woods. 1km stroll round a secret finger lake in magnificent mature woodland. You're only supposed to go during gdn hrs Mon-Sat 9.30am-4.30pm; Sun 10.30am-4.30pm. Phone for wint hrs.

2241 THE CLYDE VALLEY: The lush valley of the mighty Clyde is gdn centre central.
MAP 3   Best reached say from Glas by M74, jnct 7, then A72 for Lanark. Betw Larkhall
B5   and Lanark there's a profusion to choose from and many have sprouted cof-fee/craft shops. Pick your own fruit in summer and your own picnic spot to eat it. Sandyholm at Crossford is rec.

2242 BINNY PLANTS, ECCLESMACHAN: 01506 858155. Through village and up
MAP 3   driveway past the big house (now a hospice). Down in dell this is run by a
B4   respected nurseryman, Billy Carruthers. Grasses, ferns and perennials flourish-ing here may also flourish for you. Thurs-Mon 10am-5pm, or call for apptmt.

2243 DOBBIES, MONIFIETH: 01382 530333. Big! We wouldn't call it beautiful. Daily
MAP 3   9am-6pm (until 8pm Wed & Thurs). There are other Dobbies plant supermar-
D3   kets. The one outside Edinburgh has the attraction of the Butterfly Farm adj (1761/KIDS).

SECTION 12

Museums, Galleries, Theatres and Music

For EDINBURGH GALLERIES, *see p. 71;* GLASGOW, *see p. 109.*

2244
MAP 3
D4
✔ ✔ **MUSEUM OF FLIGHT, nr HADDINGTON, E LOTHIAN:** 01620 880308. 3km from A1 S of town. In the old complex of hangars and nissen huts at the side of E Fortune, an airfield dating to World War I (there's a tacky open-air market on Sundays), a large collection of planes from gliders to jets and esp wartime memorabilia has been respectfully restored and preserved. Inspired and inspiring displays; not just boys' stuff. Marvel at the bravery back then and sense the unremitting passage of time. From E Fortune the airship R34 made its historic Atlantic crossings. AYR 7 days; 10.30am-5pm (till 6pm Jul-Aug, 4pm wint). ☕

2245
MAP 3
D3
✔ ✔ **THE SECRET BUNKER, nr CRAIL/ANSTRUTHER:** 01333 310301. The nuclear bunker and regional seat of government in the event of nuclear war – a twilight labyrinth beneath a hill in rural Fife so vast, well documented and complete, it's utterly fascinating and quite chilling. Few 'museums' are as authentic or as resonant as this, even down to the 1950s records in the jukebox in the claustrophobic canteen. Makes you wonder what 300 people would have felt like incarcerated down there, what the Cold War was all about and what secrets They are cooking up these days for the wars yet to come. Apr-Oct 10am-5pm.

2246
MAP 3
D3
✔ ✔ **VERDANT WORKS, DUNDEE:** 01382 225282. West Henderson's Wynd nr Westport. Award-winning heritage museum that for once justifies the accolades. The story of jute and the city it made. Immensely effective high-tech and designer presentation of industrial & social history. Excl for kids. Almost continuous guided tour. Café. 7 days 10am-6pm; wint Wed-Sun till 4.30pm. ☕

2247
MAP 7
B1
✔ ✔ **THE BLACKHOUSE VILLAGE, GEARRANNAN, nr CARLOWAY, LEWIS:** 01851 643416. At the end of the rd (3km) from A858 the W coast of Lewis, an extraordinary reconstruction of several blackhouses, the trad thatched dwelling of the Hebrides. One is working Black House Museum (set 1955) with café. Another is a hostel & 4 of them are self-cat accom. Gr walk starts here with viewpts. Apr-Sept 11-5.30pm. Cl Sun. ☕ Also:

2248
MAP 7
C1
✔ **THE BLACKHOUSE AT ARNOL, LEWIS:** 01851 710395. The A857 Barvas rd from Stornoway, left at jnct for 7km, then rt through township for 2km. A single blackhouse with earth floor, bed boxes and central peat fire (no chimney hole), occupied both by the family and their animals. Remarkably, this house was lived in until the 1960s. Smokists may reflect on that peaty fug. Open AYR 9.30am-6.30pm (4.30pm in wint). Cl Sun.   HS

2249
MAP 3
C4
✔ **THE ABBOT HOUSE, DUNFERMLINE:** Maygate in town centre 'historic area'. V fine conversion of ancient house demonstrating the importance of this town as a religious and trading centre from the beginning of this millennium to medieval times. Encapsulates history from Margaret and Bruce to the Beatles. One of the few tourist attractions where 'award-winning' is a reliable indicator of worth. Café and tranquil gdn; gate to the graveyard and Abbey. 7 days 10am-5pm. ☕

2250
MAP 2
C3
✔ **EASDALE ISLAND FOLK MUSEUM:** On Easdale, an island/township reached by a 5min (continuous) boat service from Seil 'island' at the end of the B844 (off the A816, 18km S of Oban). Something special about this grassy hamlet of white-washed houses on a rocky outcrop which has a pub, a tearoom and a craft shop, and this museum across the green. The history of the place (a thriving slate industry erased one stormy night in 1881, when the sea drowned the quarry) is brought to life in displays from local contributions. Easter-Sept 11am-5pm.

2251
MAP 6
C1
✔ **STRATHNAVER MUSEUM, BETTYHILL:** 01641 521418. On N coast 60km W of Thurso in a converted church which is v much part of the whole appalling saga: a graphic account of the Highland clearances told through the history of this fishing village and the Strath that lies behind it from whence its dispossessed population came; 2,500 folk were driven from their homes – it's worth going up the valley (from 2km W along the main A836) to see (esp at Achenlochy) the beautiful land they had to leave in 1812 to make way for

sheep. If interested in general Strathnaver developments, ask the fabulous Angela at Bettyhill TIC. Museum: Apr-Oct Mon-Sat 10am-5pm (cl at lunchtime).

2252 ✓ **APPLECROSS HERITAGE CENTRE:** Along the strand from the Applecross
MAP 5 Inn (1286/GET-AWAY-FROM-IT-ALL) adj lovely church built on ancient
B2 monastery, a well-designed building & lay-out of the story of this remarkable, end-of-the-world community. May-Oct 12-5pm.

2253 ✓ **THE MUSEUM OF SCOTTISH LIGHTHOUSES, FRASERBURGH:** At
MAP 4 Kinnaird Head nr Harbour. A top attraction, so signed from all over.
E1 Purpose-built and v well done. Something which may appear to be of marginal interest made vital. In praise of the prism and the engineering innovation and skill that allowed Britain once to rule the seas (and the world). A gr ambition (to light the coastline) spectacularly realised. *At Scotland's Edge* by Allardyce and Hood (or its follow-up) is well worth taking home. Gt patter from the 4 guides. Apr-Oct 10am-5pm, till 6pm July/Aug; wint closes at 4pm.

2254 ✓ **BRIGHT WATER VISITOR CENTRE and GAVIN MAXWELL HOUSE,**
MAP 5 **EILEAN BAN off KYLEAKIN, SKYE:** 01599 530040. You don't have to be a
B2 Maxwell fan, *Ring of Bright Water* reader or even an otter watcher to appreciate this remarkable restoration of this fascinating man's last house on the island now under the Skye Bridge. Island itself is a natural haven & the Stevenson Lighthouse superb. Limited access only due to funding probs. Contact centre. One guided tour per day Apr-Sept; accessed from Skye Bridge.

2255 ✓ **SURGEONS' HALL MUSEUM, ROYAL COLLEGE OF SURGEONS, EDIN-**
MAP A **BURGH:** 0131 527 1649. 18 Nicolson St. 2 separate small museums left
D3 out of the Edin section's 'attractions', but too good to miss. Displays of 'pathological anatomy' in the classic Playfair Hall in the main st (opp Festival Theatre; pre-booked tours only) & the History of Surgery round corner at 9 Hill Square. Extraordinary & somewhat macabre exhibits in 'the home of medicine'. Mon-Fri 12-4pm. Free.

2256 **WEST HIGHLAND MUSEUM, FORT WILLIAM:** Cameron Sq off main st, listed
MAP 2 building next to TIC. Good refurb yet retains mood; the setting doesn't over-
D1 shadow the contents. 7 rms of Jacobite memorabilia, archeology, wildlife, clans, tartans, arms etc all effectively evoke the local history. Gr oil paintings line the walls, incl a drawn battle plan of Culloden. The anamorphic painting of Charlie isn't so bonny, but a fascinating snapshot all the same. Cl Sun except July/Aug (2-5pm).

2257 **KILMARTIN HOUSE:** N of Lochgilphead on the A816. 01546 510278. Centre for
MAP 2 landscape and archeology interpretation – so much to know of the early peo-
C3 ples and Kilmartin Glen is littered with historic sites. Intelligent, interesting, run by a small independent trust. Excellent organic café (1422/VEGN RESTAUS) & bookshop without usual tat. Some nice Celtic carvings. AYR 10am-5.30pm daily. ☕

2258 **PICTAVIA, BRECHIN:** 01356 626241. S of Brechin on the Forfar rd at Brechin
MAP 3 Castle. Centre opened summer '99 to give a multimedia interpretation of our
D2 Dark Age ancestors. Sparse on detail, high on interactivity. Listen to some music, pluck a harp and argue about the Battle of Dunnichen – was it that important? AYR Mon-Sat 9-6pm, Sun 10am-6pm (5pm winter).

2259 **CROMARTY COURTHOUSE MUSEUM, CROMARTY:** 01381 600418. Church
MAP 5 St. Housed in the 18th cent courthouse, this award-winning museum uses
E1 moving & talking models to bring to life a courtroom scene & famous Cromarty figures to paint the varied history of this important Highland town. Entrance includes multilingual taped tours of the town 7 days. 10am-5pm (winter 12-4pm). Jan & Feb – by appoint.

2260 **SUMMERLEE HERITAGE PARK, COATBRIDGE:** 01236 431261 West Canal St.
MAP 3 Follow signs. Here in the Iron Town is this tribute to the industry, ingenuity
A5 and graft that powered the Industrial Revolution and made Glas gr. Anyone with a mechanical bent or an interest in the social history of the working class will like it here; totty kids and bored teens may not. Tearoom. 7 days, 10am-5pm (Winter (10am-3.30pm)).

2261 **SKYE MUSEUM OF ISLAND LIFE:** Kilmuir on Uig-Staffin rd, the A855, 32km N of
MAP 5 Portree. The most authentic of several converted cottages on Skye where the
A1 poor crofter's life is recreated for the enrichment of ours. The small thatched

township includes agricultural implements as well as domestic artefacts, many of which illustrate an improbable fascination with the royal family. Flora Macdonald's grave is nearby (Apr-Oct; 1900/MONUMENTS). Cl Sun.

2262 **AUCHENDRAIN, INVERARAY:** 8km W of town on A83. A whole township
MAP 2 reconstructed to give a v fair impression of both the historical and spatial
D3 relationship betw the cottages and their various occupants. Longhouses and byre dwellings; their furniture and their ghosts. 7 days. Apr-Sept 10am-5pm.

2263 **INVERARAY JAIL:** 'The story of Scottish crime and punishment' (sic) told in
MAP 2 'award-winning' reconstruction of courtroom with cells below, where the
D3 waxwork miscreants and their taped voices bring local history to life. Guided tours of Peterhead can't be far off. Open AYR, 9.30am-6pm (wint 10am-5pm).

2264 **ARCTIC PENGUIN aka MARITIME HERITAGE CENTRE, INVERARAY:** 'One of
MAP 2 the world's last iron sailing ships' moored so you can't miss it at the loch side
D3 in Inveraray. More to it than would seem from the outside; displays on the history of Clydeside (the *Queens M* and *E* memorabilia etc), Highland Clearances, the Vital Spark. Lots for kids to get a handle (or hands) on. And a 'puffer' for nostalgic trips. 7 days 10am till 6pm; 5pm winter.

2265 **BONAWE IRONWORKS MUSEUM, TAYNUILT:** At its zenith, (late 17th – early
MAP 2 18th century), this ironworks was a brutal, fire-breathing monster, as 'black as
D2 the Earl of Hell's waistcoat'. But now, all is calm as the gently sloping grassy sward carries you around from warehouse to foundry and down onto the shores of L Etive to the pier, where the finished product was loaded on to ships to be taken away for the purpose of empire-building (with cannonballs). Apr-Sept daily until 6.30pm; Oct-Nov daily until 4.30pm; cl Dec-Mar.

2266 **SCOTTISH FISHERIES MUSEUM, ANSTRUTHER:** 01333 310628. In and
MAP 3 around a cobbled courtyard o/look the old fishing harbour in this busy East
D3 Neuk town. Excellent evocation of trad industry still alive (if not kicking). Impressive collection of models and actual vessels incl those moored at adj quay. Crail and Pittenweem harbours nearby for the full picture (and fresh crab/lobster). Open AYR 10am-5.30pm, Sun 11am-5pm (cl 4.30pm in winter).

2267 **ROBERT SMAIL'S PRINTING WORKS, INNERLEITHEN:** 01896 830206. Main
MAP 3 St. A trad printing works till 1986 and still in use. Fascinating vignettes/instant
C6 history. Have a go at hand setting, then have a go at a Caldwell's ice-cream (1536/ICE CREAM). Apr-Oct, Thur-Mon 10am-6pm, Sun 1-5pm. W/ends in Oct. (Cl 1-2pm).

2268 **MYRETON MOTOR MUSEUM, ABERLADY:** 01875 870288. On Drem rd, past
MAP 3 Luffness Mains. Ideal 'little' museum in old barn w restored vehicles dating from
D4 1896. Even for the Luddite, engineering seems an aesthetic here. Dr Finlay's Casebook fans prepare yourselves. 7 days till 4pm; wint Suns only 1-3pm.

2269 **SHAMBELLIE HOUSE MUSEUM OF COSTUME, NEW ABBEY, nr DUMFRIES:**
MAP 1 Another obsession that became a museum. On 2 floors of this country house
D2 set among spectacular woodlands. Fab frocks etc from every 'period'. Apr-Oct 11am-5pm. Accommodating tearoom staff.

2270 **WICK HERITAGE CENTRE, WICK:** 01955 605393. On Bank Row. Amazing civic
MAP 6 museum run by volunteers. Jam-packed with items about the sea, town and
E1 that hard land. Somebody should ensure these people get MBEs or something. Easter-Oct 10am-5pm. Cl Sun.

2271 **ABERDEEN MARITIME MUSEUM:** 01224 337700. Shiprow. Aberdeen faces
MAP 4 the sea – and this place tells you the stories. Films, exhibits, photos and paint-
D3 ings, from sail to oil. Decent cafe. Mon-Sat 10am-5pm, Sun 12-3pm.   ADM

2272 **THE SCOTTISH MARITIME MUSEUM:** Spread out over 3 sites, Irvine (01294
MAP 3 278283), Braehead (0141 886 1013) and Dumbarton (01389 763444).
A5 Dumbarton has the ship model experiment tank, Braehead (off J25A of the
MAP 2 M8) has hands-on engines, while Irvine boasts a massive shed (Victorian
E4, E5 engine shop) full of the bits that non-engineers never usually see, as well as the hulk of an old clipper at Irvine harbour. Completely fascinating. More resonant than The Big Idea (1772/KID-FRIENDLY) along the road? You judge! Irvine and Braehead open daily. AYR, Dumbarton Mon-Sat.

For EDINBURGH, *see p. 62–64;* GLASGOW, *p. 103–104.*

2273 ✓✓ **DUNDEE CONTEMPORARY ARTS:** Nethergate (01382 432000). State
MAP 4 of contemporary art gallery (by award-winning architect Richard
D3 Murphy) with great café (1162/DUNDEE RESTAUS), cinema facilities, etc. which
has transformed the cultural face of Dundee. People actually come from
Edin/Glas for the openings. More evidence of the city's changing status. ☕

2274 ✓ **ABERDEEN ART GALLERY:** Schoolhill. Major gallery with temp exhibits
MAP 3 and eclectic permanent collection from Impressionists to Bellany. Large
D3 bequest from local granite merchant Alex Macdonald in 1900 contributes fas-
cinating collection of his contemporaries: Bloomsburys, Scottish, Pre-
Raphaelites. Excellent watercolour rm. An easy and rewarding gallery to visit.
10am-5pm (Sun 2-5pm).

2275 ✓ **THE FERGUSSON GALLERY, PERTH:** Marshall Pl on corner of Tay St in
MAP 3 distinctive round tower (former waterworks). The assembled works on
C3 two floors of J D Fergusson 1874-1961. Though he spent much of his life in
France, he had an influence on Scottish art and was pre-eminent amongst
those now called the Colourists. It's a long way from Perth to Antibes 1913 but
these pictures are a draught of the warm S. Mon-Sat 10-5pm.

2276 ✓ **KIRKCALDY MUSEUM AND ART GALLERY:** Nr railway stn, but ask for
MAP 3 directions (it's easy to get lost). One of the best galleries in central Scot-
C4 land. Splendid introduction to the history of 19th/20th-cent Scottish art. Lots of
Colourists/McTaggart/Glasgow Boys. And Sickert to Redpath. Museum ain't bad.
Kirkcaldy doesn't get a lot of good press, but this and the parks (1626/PARKS)
are worth the journey (plus Valente's – 1457/FISH AND CHIPS). 7 days till 5pm.

2277 ✓ **HORNEL GALLERY, KIRKCUDBRIGHT:** Broughton House where he lived,
MAP 1 now a fabulous evocation with collection of his work and atelier as was.
C3 'Even the Queen was amazed'. The beautiful gdn stretching to the river is a
real eye opener. House closed in 2003 and 2004 for renovation. Garden open
11am-4pm. NTS

2278 ✓ **DUFF HOUSE, BANFF:** Nice walk and easy to find from town centre.
MAP 4 Important outstation of the National Gallery in meticulously restored
D1 Adam house with interesting history and spacious grounds. Ramsays,
Raeburn, portraiture of mixed appeal and an El Greco. Maybe OTT for some,
but major attraction in the area (go further up the Deveron, 2063/WOODLAND
WALKS). Nice tearm. ☕

2279 ✓ **SCULPTURE AT GLENKILN RESERVOIR, nr DUMFRIES:** Take A75 to
MAP 1 Castle Douglas and rt to Shawshead; into village, rt at T-jnct, left to
C2 Dunscore, immediate left, signed for reservoir. Follow rd along loch side and
park. Not a gallery at all but sculpture scattered amongst the hills, woods and
meadows around this reservoir in the Galloway Hills 16km SE of Dumfries.
One or two are obvious, the others you just have to find: Epstein, Moore, Rodin
in the gr outdoors!

2280 **THE PIER ART CENTRE, STROMNESS, ORKNEY MAINLAND:** 01856 850209.
On main st (1634/COASTAL VILLAGES), a gallery on a small pier which could have
come lock, stock and canvases from Cornwall. Permanent St Ives-style collection of Barbara Hepworth, Ben Nicholson, Paolozzi and others shown in a *sim-
patico* environment with the sea o/side. Also temporary exhibs. Open Tues-Sat
10am-5pm. Cl Sun/Mon.

2281 **PAISLEY ART GALLERY AND MUSEUM:** 0141 889 3151. High St. Permanent
MAP 3 collection of the world famous Paisley shawls and history of weaving tech-
A5 niques. Other exhibs usually have a local connection and an interactive ele-
ment. Notable Greek Ionic-style building. Mon-Sat 10am-5pm, Sun 2-5pm.

2282 **ROZELLE HOUSE, AYR:** In Rozelle Park and the only art in these parts.
MAP 2 Temporary exhibs change every month (incl local artists' work). 4 galleries,
E6 and additional 5 rms featuring the Gaudi collection in Rozelle Hse; craft shop.
AYR Mon-Sat 10am-5pm, Apr-Oct also Sun 2-5pm.

For EDINBURGH, *see pp. 71-72; and* GLASGOW, *see pp. 110-111.*

2283 ✓ **DUNDEE REP:** 01382 223530. Tay Sq. Cornerstone of Dundee's cultural
MAP 3 quarter (with DCA – 2273/GALLERIES). Houses Scotland's only rep co.
D3 Ambitious prog. Anyone into contem Scottish drama comes here. Good
café/restau.

2284 ✓ **MULL LITTLE THEATRE, DERVAIG, MULL:** 01688 302828. 'The smallest
MAP 2 theatre in Britain' is still there after more than 25 years. On edge of dinky
B2 Dervaig, 10km from Tobermory. Bar & acceptable restau adj at the Druimard
Country-House Hotel. Tiny auditorium, so you're almost on top of the actors.
Never predictable. Its incongruity is part of its appeal. Easter-Sept. Curtain up
8.30pm. Cosy seats; cosy intervals. Box office also in Tobermory main st.

2285 ✓ **EDEN COURT THEATRE, INVERNESS:** 01463 234234. An important the-
MAP 5 atre complex making a vital contribution to the cultural life of the
D2 Highlands. Diverse programme of theatre, dance, variety, all kinds of music,
opera, trad – the occasional coup. Easy to book by credit card; lots do sell out.
Theatre bar and the Ness over there. Cinema programme of selected art-
house/first-run movies. And restau getting back on track!

2286 ✓ **BOWHILL LITTLE THEATRE, BOWHILL HOUSE, nr SELKIRK:** 01750
MAP 3 22204. Tiny theatre off the courtyard below Bowhill House with intermit-
D6 tent mixed programme (must phone), but always delightful, esp with supper
afterwards in Courtyard Restau (also phone to book).

2287 ✓ **PITLOCHRY THEATRE:** 01796 484626. Modern rep theatre across river
MAP 3 from main st performing usually 6 plays on different nights of the week.
B2 Well-chosen programme of classics and popular works, the 500-seat theatre is
often full. V mixed Sunday concerts and foyer fringe events. Coffee bar and
recently extended restau menu. Also: Port-Na-Craig adj, by river & The Old
Armoury (1010/1007 PERTHSHIRE EATS).

2288 ✓ **BYRE THEATRE, ST ANDREWS:** 01334 476288. Abbey St or South St.
MAP 3 Recent lottery-funded major reconstruction. Gr auditorium & café-bar.
D3 Major social hub for town & gown. Wills sightings poss till summer 2004.

2289 **CUMBERNAULD THEATRE:** 01236 732887. Nr old part of this new town on a
MAP 3 rise o/look the ubiquitous dual carriageway (to Stirling). Follow signs for
A4 Cumbernauld House. Bar/café-restau and 258-seat theatre (in the round) with
a mixed programme of one-nighters and short runs of mainly Scottish touring companies. Also concerts, drama workshops and kids' programmes.

2290 **THE WYND, MELROSE:** 01896 823854. 100-seater arts venue which regularly
MAP 3 entertains locals and even Edin folk. From classic Ibsen and musicals to folk,
D6 jazz, dance and film. Intimate atmos in an intimate town.

2291 **CAMPBELTOWN PICTURE HOUSE:** 01586 553899. Campbeltown, Argyll.
MAP 2 Cinema Paradiso on the Kintyre peninsula. Lovingly preserved art deco gem;
C6 a shrine to the movies. Opened 1913, closed 1983, but such was the tide of
nostalgic affection that it was refurbished and reopened resplendent in 1989.
Shows mainly first-run films. To see a film here and emerge onto the
esplanade of Campbeltown L is to experience the lost magic of a night at the
pictures. Prog: weepictures.co.uk

2292 **THE NEW PICTURE HOUSE, ST ANDREWS:** 01334 473509. On North St. 'New'
MAP 3 means 1931 and, apart from adding another screen (the small Cinema 2), it
D3 hasn't changed much, as generations of students will remember with fond-
ness. Mainly first-run flicks; Oct-May, a prog of late-night cult/art movies.

2293 **THE ROXY, KELSO:** 01573 224609. Horsemarket. A cinema from my youth, still
MAP 3 remarkably here and unchanged; still the smell of hot celluloid. Few better
E6 places to watch a first-run movie or an art flick and enjoy 'real Scottish pop-
corn'. Sun, Tues, Wed, Sat (early) and bingo on Mon, Thur & Fri/Sat.

✓ **TOLBOOTH, STIRLING:** 01786 274000. See p. 316.

✓ **LEMON TREE, ABERDEEN:** 01224 642230. 1132/ABERDEEN RESTAUS.

SECTION 13

The Islands

2294
MAP 5
B2
RAASAY: A small car ferry (car useful, but bikes best) from Sconser betw Portree and Broadford on Skye takes you to this, the best of places. The distinctive flat top of Dun Caan presides over an island whose history and natural history is Highland Scotland in microcosm. The village with rows of mining-type cottages is 3km from jetty. The Outdoor Centre (01478 660226) in the big hoose (once the home of the notorious Dr No who, like others before him, allowed Raasay to go to rack and ruin) has courses galore. They'll put you up if they've got rm (mostly bunkrooms). The views from the lawn, or the viewpoint above the house, or better still from Dun Caan with the Cuillins on one side and Torridon on the other, are quite brilliant (2329/ISLAND WALKS). Dolphin Café at the House is licensed. Big refurb on the way for the Outdoor Centre at TGP. The island hotel (15 rms, MED.EX) has bar but could do with some TLC. There's a ruined castle, a secret rhododendron-lined loch for swimming, seals, otters and eagles. Much to explore. Go quietly here. *Regular Calmac ferry from Sconser, but not Sun.*

2295
MAP 2
C4
JURA: Small regular car ferry from Pt Askaig on Islay takes you into a different world. Jura is remote, scarcely populated and has an ineffable grandeur indifferent to the demands of tourism. Ideal for wild camping, alternatively the serviceable hotel and pub (2319/ISLAND HOTELS) in the only village (Craighouse) 15km from ferry at Feolin. Walking guides available at hotel and essential esp for the Paps, the hills that maintain such a powerful hold over the island. Easiest climb is from Three Arch Br; allow 6hrs. In May they run up all of them and back to the distillery in 3hrs. Jura House's walled gdn is a hidden jewel set above the S coastline; myriad wildflowers and Australasian trees with scenic walks to the shore (1680/GARDENS). The Corryvreckan whirlpool (2338/ISLAND WALKS) is another lure, but you may need a 4-wheel drive to get close enough, and its impressiveness depends upon tides. Orwell's house (Barnhill; where he wrote 1984) is not open, but there are many fascinating side tracks: the wild west coast; around L Tarbert; and the long littoral betw Craighouse and Lagg. (Also 1655/BEACHES; 1937/GRAVEYARDS.) With one rd, no st lamps and over 5,000 deer the sound of silence is everything. *Western Ferries (01496 840681) regular 7 days, 5min service from Pt Askaig.*

2296
MAP 2
B3
IONA: Strewn with daytrippers – not so much a pilgrimage, more an invasion – but Iona still enchants (as it did the Colourists), esp if you can get away to the Bay at the Back of the Ocean (1622/BEACHES) or watch the cavalcade from the hill above the Abbey. Or stay: **ARGYLL HOTEL** best (01681 700334; 1282/GET-AWAY HOTELS) or B&B. Abbey shop isn't bad (2189/CRAFT SHOPS). Pilgrimage walks on Wed (10am from St John's Cross). Bike hire from Finlay Ross shop 01681 700357. Everything about Iona is benign; even the sun shines here when it's raining on Mull. *Reg 15min Calmac service from Fionnphort till 6pm (earlier in winter).*

2297
MAP 5
A3
EIGG: After changing hands, much to-do and cause célèbre, the islanders seized the time and Eigg is (in-fighting apart) theirs; and of course, ours. A wildlife haven for birds and sealife; otters, eagles and seal colonies. Scot Wildlife Trust warden does weekly walks around the island. July is the 'Month of Music' with lots of ceilidhs. Refurb tearoom at pier. Licenced and evening meals. Bicycle hire 01687 482469. 2 croft houses at Cleadale near Laig bay and the Singing Sands beach; contact Sue Kirk 01687 482405. She also offers full board accom and caters for vegn and other diets. 2,000 sheep on island. Gr walk to Sgurr an Eigg – an awesome perch on a summer's day. *CalMac (from Mallaig) 01687 462403 or (better, from Arisaig) Arisaig Marine 01687 450224 every day except Thurs in summer. No car ferry; but motorbikes poss. Day trips to Rum and Muck.*

2298
MAP 5
A3
RUM: The large island in the group S of Skye, off the coast at Mallaig. The Calmac ferry plies betw Canna, Eigg, Muck and Rum but not too conveniently and it's not easy to island-hop and make a decent visit (but *see below*). Rum the most wild and dramatic has an extraordinary time-warp mansion in Kinloch Castle which is mainly a museum (guided tours tie in with boat trips). Below stairs a hostel contrasts to the antique opulence above. Also a bistro run in conjunction with hostel (no lunch). Rum is run by Scottish

Natural Heritage and there are fine trails, climbs, bird-watching spots. Coffee-shop at the Community Hall (open for day-trippers). 2 simple walks are marked for the 3hr visitors, but the island reveals its mysteries more slowly. The Doric temple mausoleum to George Bullough, the industrialist whose Highland fantasy the castle was, is a 9km (3hr) walk across the island to Harris Bay. Sighting the sea eagles may be one of the best things that ever happens to you. *Calmac ferry from Mallaig via Eigg (2hrs 15mins) or Canna at an ungodly hr. Better from Arisaig (Murdo Grant 01687 450224) Tues/Thur/Sat/Sun in summer (3hrs ashore).*

2299
MAP 2
C5
✓ **GIGHA:** Romantic small island off Kintyre coast; with classic views of its island neighbours. Easy access to mainland (20min ferry trip) contributes to an island atmos that lacks any feeling of isolation. Like Eigg, Gigha was bought by the islanders so its fragile economy is even more dependent on your visit. The island currently remains a whole estate; with gdns open at the main house (1601/GARDENS), a tearm nr ferry and a hotel (2316/ISLAND HOTELS) providing comfortable surroundings. The locals are relaxed and friendly; with bike hire (07766 112619), B&B (CHP) and good home-cooking available at the post office on the ferry rd (01583 505251). Best Walk: Left after golf course (9 hole), through gate and follow track (signed Ardaily) past Mill L to Mill and shore; gr views to Jura (1-B-2). See: Double Beach, where the Queen once swam off the Royal Yacht; two crescents of sand on either side of the N end of the isthmus of Eilean Garbh (seen from rd but path poorly marked). *Calmac ferry from Tayinloan on A83, 27km S of Tarbert (Glas 165km). One an hour in summer, fewer in winter. Cars exp and unnecessary.*

2300
MAP 2
B2
✓ **ULVA:** Off W coast of Mull. A boat leaves Ulva Ferry on the B8073 26km S of Dervaig. Idyllic wee island with 5 well-marked walks incl to the curious basalt columns similar to Staffa, or by causeway to the smaller island of Gometra; plan routes at boathouse 'interpretive centre' and tearoom (with Ulva oysters). Meet shaggy dog Bertie, who is more than happy to be your guide to the island should you desire some 4-legged company. No accom. A charming Telford church has services 4 times a yr. Ulva is a perfect day away from the rat race of downtown Tobermory! *All-day 5min service in summer (not Sats) till 5pm. Ferryman: 01688 500226.*

2301
MAP 7
A5
✓ **ERISKAY:** Made famous by the sinking nearby of the SS *Politician* in 1941 and the salvaging of its cargo of whisky, immortalised by Compton Mackenzie in *Whisky Galore*, this Hebridean gem has all the 'idyllic island' ingredients: perfect beaches (1968/MARY, CHARLIE AND BOB), a hill to climb, a pub (called the Politician and telling the story round its walls; it sells decent pub food all day in summer), and a small, frequent ferry. There's only limited B & B and no hotel, but camping is ok if you're discreet. Eriskay and Barra together – the pure island experience. (Also 1921/CHURCHES *and see* THE WESTERN ISLES *p. 297*). *Car ferry from Ludaig, S Uist has been replaced by a causeway. Ferry from Barra (Airdmhor) rn by Calmac (40 mins): 5 a day in summer, wint hrs vary.*

2302
MAP 7
A5
✓ **MINGULAY:** Deserted mystical island nr the southern tip of the Outer Hebrides, the subject of one of the definitive island books, *The Road to Mingulay*. Now easily reached in summer by daily trip from Castlebay, Barra with 1.5hr journey and 3hrs ashore (enquire at TIC or Castlebay Hotel). Last inhabitants left 1912. Ruined village has the poignant air of St Kilda; similar spectacular cliffs on W side with fantastic rock formations, stacks and a huge natural arch – best viewed from boat. Mingulay was bought by NTS in '99. Only birds & sheep live here now.

2303
MAP 2
B4
✓ **COLONSAY:** Accessible to daytrippers in summer (with the ferry round trip); this island haven of wildlife, flowers and beaches (1646/BEACHES) deserves more than a few hrs exploration. Congenial hotel and pub; self-catering units nearby. Some holiday cottages, but camping discouraged. Coffee/craft/shop adj to hotel and pantry at the pier. A wild 18-hole golf course and bookshop (sic) adj. Semi-botanical gdns adj to Colonsay House and fine walks, esp to Oronsay (2333/ISLAND WALKS). Don't miss the house at Shell Beach which sells oysters and honey. *Calmac from Oban (or Islay). Crossing takes just over 2hrs. Times vary.*

2304
MAP 7
B3
THE SHIANTS: 3 magical, uninhabited tiny islands off E coast of Harris. Read about them in one of the most detailed accounts (a 'love letter') to any small island ever written: 'Sea Room' by the guy who owns them, Adam Nicolson.

There's a bothy & it is poss to visit by visiting first his website, but you'll have to find that for yourself.

2305 **LISMORE:** Sail from Oban (car ferry) or better from Pt Appin 5km off main A828,
MAP 2 the Oban-Ft William rd, 32km N Oban and where there's a seafood
C2 bar/restau/hotel (1454/SEAFOOD RESTAUS), to sit and wait. A rd goes down the
centre of the island, but there are many hill and coastal walks and even the nr
end round Pt Ramsay feels away from it all. History, natural history and air. Bike
hire on island from Mary McDougal 01631 760213 who will deliver to ferry or
Port Appin Bikes 01631 730391. Tearoom (not always open) 3km S of ferry, a
pleasant stroll. *Calmac service from Oban, 4 or 5 times a day (not Sun). From Pt
Appin (32km N of Oban) several per day. 5mins. Last back 8.15pm 9.30 Fri & Sat, but
check (6.15pm winter).*

CALMAC: 08705 650000

THE BEST ISLAND HOTELS

2306 ✓ ✓ **THE HOUSE OVER-BY at THE THREE CHIMNEYS, SKYE:** 01470
MAP 5 511258. At Colbost 7km W of Dunvegan by the B884 to Glendale.
A2 Eddie & Shirley Spear's quietly luxurious and tastefully decorated rms, adj or
just over-by from their accolade-laden restau (in world's top 50 – *Restaurant*
magazine) (2322/ISLAND RESTAUS). Separate dining rm for healthy buffet b/fast.
Outside the sheep, the sea and the sky. Setting new standards in the
Highlands, this is where to come for the pamper-yourself w/end.
6RMS JAN-DEC T/T PETS CC KIDS INX

2307 ✓ **CASTLEBAY HOTEL, BARRA:** 01871 810223. Prominent position o/look
MAP 7 bay and ferry dock. You see where you're staying long before you arrive.
A5 Exceptionally good value hotel at the centre of Barra life with nice owners who
are always there. Good restau and bar meals (2342/WESTERN ISLES). Adj bar one
of the best bars for craic and car culture in Scotland and with more than a dash
of the Irish (1380/BLOODY GOOD PUBS). 12RMS JAN-DEC T/T PETS CC KIDS INX

2308 ✓ **KINLOCH LODGE, SKYE:** 01471 833333. S of Broadford in Sleat Peninsula,
MAP 5 18km Ryliakin, 55km Portree. The ancestral, but not overly imposing
B2 home of Lord and Lady Macdonald with new build house adj – adding 5 v
well appointed rms and spacious, country drawing rm. Lady Mac is Claire
Macdonald of cookery fame, so her many books for sale in 'the shop', cookery
courses thro' yr and her hand in all the wonderful things you eat (all meals in
the Lodge itself). Some Lodge rms small and less exp. See 2321/RESTAUS.
9+5RMS JAN-DEC X/T XPETS KIDS LOTS

2309 ✓ **PORT CHARLOTTE HOTEL, ISLAY:** 01496 850360. New owners of com-
MAP 2 fortable, classy island hotel. Modern, discreet approach in this fine white-
B5 washed village (1638/COASTAL VILLAGES), good whisky choice, and good,
bistro-style food from chef Billy Broderick. Tourists in summer, hardcore twitchers in winter… and us anytime. 10RMS JAN-DEC T/T PETS CC MED.EX

2310 ✓ **HARBOUR INN, BOWMORE, ISLAY:** 01496 810330. 2 doors up from the
MAP 2 harbour in centre of main town on lovely, quite lively Islay. Rms contem-
B5 porary & comfy, nice lounge with views & notable restau. Bar with malts & bar
meals (LO 8.45pm). 2 rms are adj. 7RMS JAN-DEC T/T PETS KIDS MED.EX

2311 ✓ **EILEAN IARMAIN, SKYE:** 01471 833332. Isleornsay, Sleat. 60km S of
MAP 5 Portree. Tucked into the bay this Gaelic inn with its gr pub and good food
B3 provides famously comfortable base in S of the island. 6 rms in main hotel
best value (6 are in house over-by). Also 4 suites over-by – nice but exp.
12RMS + 4SUITES JAN-DEC T/T PETS CC KIDS EXP

2312 ✓ **SCARISTA HOUSE, SOUTH HARRIS:** 01859 550238. 21km Tarbert, 78km
MAP 7 Stornoway. On the W coast famous for its beaches and o/look one of the
B3 best (1653/BEACHES). Tim & Patricia Martin's civilised retreat & home from
home. Fixed menu meals in dining rooms o/look sea. No phones, but many
books. The golf course over the rd is exquisite. Refurb in progress at TGP. Check
wint opening! 5RMS JAN-DEC X/X PETS CC KIDS EXP

2313 ✓ **CALGARY FARMHOUSE, MULL:** 01688 400256. 7kms S of Dervany (30
MAP 2 mins Tobermory) nr beautiful Calgary Beach. Roadside bistro/restau
B2 (2327/ISLAND RESTAUS) with rms and gallery/coffee shop. Excl island hospi-

tality – Matthew's furniture in public rms & 'Art in Nature' sculpture walking woods at back down to the beach. Bohemia in the bay. Get up early to see the otters (tho' we didn't). 2 self-cat suites above gallery. Good mod-Brit cooking.

9RMS APR-OCT X/X PETS CC KIDS MED.INX

2314
MAP 2
B2

✓ **HIGHLAND COTTAGE, TOBERMORY:** 01688 302030. Breadalbane St opp fire stn. Trad Tobermory st above harbour (from r/bout on rd in from Craignure). 6 comfy rms named after islands (all themed, one called Nantucket). Their reputation grows and it's harder to get in but foodies should try hard. Everything here is small but perfectly formed – relaxed atmos with fine dining.

6RMS FEB T/T XPETS CC KIDS MED.EXP

2315
MAP 2
D5

✓ **KILMICHAEL, BRODICK, ARRAN:** 01770 302219. On main rd to castle/ Corrie, take left at bend by golf course and you're in the country. 3km down track is this haven from Brodick & beyond. Country-house refined, so not gt for kids. Rms in house or garden courtyard – painstaking detail in food and environs.

6RMS JAN-DEC T/T PETS CC KIDS EXP

2316
MAP 2
C5

THE GIGHA HOTEL, ISLE OF GIGHA: 01583 505254. A short walk from the ferry on an island perfectly proportioned for a short visit; easy walking and cycling. Residents' lounge peaceful with dreamy views to Kintyre. Menu with local produce, eg Gigha prawns & scallops (in bar or dining rm) but ask what's fresh (not frozen)! Island life without the remoteness. Also self-cat cottages. 2299/ISLANDS.

13RMS FEB-NOV T/T PETS CC KIDS MED.EX

2317
MAP 5
A2

VIEWFIELD HOUSE, PORTREE, SKYE: 01478 612217. One of the first hotels you come to in Portree on the rd from S (driveway opp gas stn); you need look no further. Individual, grand but comfortable, full of antiques and memorabilia, though not at all stuffy; this is also one of the best-value hotels on the island. Log fires, 4-course dinner. The Macdonalds like you to eat in & in Portree there is nowhere better.

12RMS APR-OCT T/X PETS CC KIDS MED.EX

2318
MAP 5
B1

FLODIGARRY, SKYE: 01470 552203. Staffin, 32km N of Portree. A romantic country house o/look the sea, with Flora Mac's cottage in the grounds. Good food, gr craic in the bar. Report: 1150/COUNTRY-HOUSE HOTELS.

12RMS + 7COTT JAN-DEC T/X PETS CC KIDS EXP

2319
MAP 2
B4

JURA HOTEL: 01496 820243. Craighouse, 15km from Islay ferry at Feolin. Serviceable, basic hotel o/look Small Isles Bay; will oblige with all walking/exploring requirements. Pub is social hub of island. Rms at front may be small, but have the views.

17RMS JAN-DEC X/X PETS CC KIDS INX

2320
MAP 7
A5

ISLE OF BARRA HOTEL, BARRA: 01871 810383. The other hotel in Barra (see Castlebay, above) exterior, but comfortable inside with gr setting and rms o/look fab Tangasdale Beach. Nr Seal Bay (1657/BEACHES) and other quiet places. Bar the locals like. 3km from town (and bike hire, 2342/WESTERN ISLES).

42RMS APR-OCT X/T PETS CC KIDS MED.INX

✓ **ARGYLL HOTEL, IONA:** 01681 700334 (1282/SEASIDE INNS). MED

2321
MAP 5
B2

✔ ✔ **KINLOCH LODGE, SKYE:** 01471 833333. In S on Sleat Peninsula, 55km S of Portree signed off the 'main' Sleat rd, along a long characterful track. Lord and Lady MacDonald's family home/hotel offers a taste of the high life without hauteur; a setting and setup especially appreciated by Americans and other visitors. Lady Claire's stints at the stoves are renowned, as are the cookery books that result. Dinner almost a theatrical event, (the dining-rm: lined with oils, furnished with antiques, glinting with silver). Fixed menu. Perfect cheeses but you simply must leave rm for the puds.　　EXP

2322
MAP 5
A2

✔ ✔ **THE THREE CHIMNEYS, SKYE:** 01470 511258. Colbost. 7km W Dunvegan on B884 to Glendale. Shirley and Eddie Spear's classic restau in a converted cottage on the edge of the best kind of nowhere. They shop local for everything so best ingredients. AYR. Lunch (except Sun & wint months). Dinner LO 9.30pm. It's a long rd to Colbost, but you find out why Shirley's cooking has won just about every Scottish award. Best to stay, the wine-list is just too tempting.　　EXP

2323
MAP 2
B5

✔ **PORT CHARLOTTE HOTEL and HARBOUR INN, BOWMORE, ISLAY:** 01496 850360 and 01496 810330. Both excl island inns, with dining rms & bar meals using local produce that are as good as anything comparable on the mainland. Both look over the western sea. Reports: 2309/2310 ISLAND HOTELS.

2324
MAP 7
B2

✔ **BONAVENTURE, LEWIS:** 01851 672474. Aird Uig N of Timsgarry on B8011, about 30kms W of Stornoway via A858. This is about as far-flung as you can get and many will be the most wee westerly restau in the UK. Often fully booked for dinner. Chef/prop Richard Leparoux prepares French-Scottish food from mainly local ingreds (obviously). Nautical theme in unusual ex-RAF base and poss a short hike (or car) up Forsnabhal for a spectacular panorama or sunset. Phone to book & for opening. Dinner only.　　MED

2325
MAP 2
D5

✔ **KILMICHAEL HOTEL, ARRAN:** 01770 302219. 3km from seafront rd in Brodick, this is the place to go for dinner. Report: 2315/ISLAND HOTELS.　　MED

2326
MAP 7
A5

CASTLEBAY HOTEL, CASTLEBAY: 01871 810223. V decent plain cooking in informal dining-rm or bar o/look castle and bay. Scores mainly when fresh from the bay (lobster) or off the beach (cockles in garlic butter), but their sticky toffee pudding is exactly as it ought to be. Inexpensive wines.　　MED

2327
MAP 2
B2

CALGARY FARMHOUSE AND DOVECOTE RESTAU, MULL: 01688 400256. 7km from Dervaig on B8073 nr Mull's famous beach. Roadside farm setting with inexp light, piney bedrms and a bistro/wine bar restau using local produce. For Mod-Brit cuisine. Gallery/coffee shop in summer. A quiet spot for most cosmo meal on Mull.　　INX

2328
MAP 5
A2

AN TUIREANN, SKYE: 01478 613306. On Struan Rd, edge of Portree (direction Uig from main rd into Portree from Sligachan). Not so much a restau, more a café-bar in an arts centre. This is where to go in Skye for interesting local and national touring exhibs and for contemp mainly vegn snacks and meals. Nice soups. Good coffee. 10am-4.30pm, cl Sun.　　INX

LOCHBAY SEAFOOD, SKYE: 12km N Dunvegan (2341/SKYE).　　INX

CREELERS, ARRAN: 01770 302810. Edge of Brodick (2339/ARRAN).　　MED

BUSTA HOUSE, SHETLAND: 01806 522506. 35km N of Lerwick (2345/SHETLAND).　　MED

✔ **ARGYLL HOTEL, IONA:** 01681 700334 (1256/SEASIDE INNS).　　MED

For walk codes, see p. 12.

2329
MAP 5
B2

DUN CAAN, RAASAY: Still one of my favourite island walks – to the flat top of a magic hill (1725/VIEWS). Take ferry (2294/MAGICAL ISLANDS), ask for route from Inverarish. Go via old iron mine; looks steep when you get over the ridge, but it's a dawdle. And amazing.　　10KM XCIRC XBIKE 2-B-2

2330 **THE LOST GLEN, HARRIS:** Take B887 W from Tarbert almost to the end
MAP 7 (where at Hushinish there's a good beach, maybe a sunset), but go rt before
B2 the Big House (signed Chliostair Power Stn). Park here or further in and walk
up to dam (3km from rd). Take rt track round reservoir and the left around the
upper loch. Over the brim you arrive in a wide, wild glen; an overhang 2km
ahead is said to have the steepest angle in Europe. Go quietly; if you don't see
deer and eagles here, you're making too much noise on the grass.
12KM RET XCIRC XBIKE 2-B-2

2331 **CARSAIG, MULL:** In S of island, 7km from A849 Fionnphort-Craignure rd nr
MAP 2 Pennyghael. 2 walks start at pier: going left towards Lochbuie for a spectacu-
C3 lar coastal/woodland walk past Adnunan Stack (7km); or rt towards the
imposing headland where, under the cliffs, the Nuns' Cave was a shelter for
nuns evicted from Iona during the Reformation. Nearby is a quarry whose
stone was used to build Iona Abbey and much further on (9km Carsaig), at
Malcolm's Pt, the extraordinary Carsaig Arches carved by wind and sea.
15/20KM XCIRC XBIKE 2-B-2

2332 **COCK OF ARRAN, LOCHRANZA:** Turn right at church & follow signs. 11km cir-
MAP 2 cular walk into Glen Chalmadale and high into moorland (260m), then drops
D5 down to magnificent shoreline. Here eagles catch the updraft and peregrines
lose it. Divers and ducks share the shore with seals. About 1km from where
you meet the shore, look for Giant Centipede fossil trail. Futher on at opening
of wall pace 350 steps and turn left up to Ossian's Cave. Path crosses Fairy Dell
Burn and eventually comes out at Lochranza Bay. Allow 6hrs & stout boots
(good walk desc from y hostel). 11KM CIRC XBIKE

2333 **COLONSAY:** (2303/MAGICAL ISLANDS). From hotel or the quay, walk to Colonsay
MAP 2 House and its lush, overgrown intermingling of native plants and exotics
B4 (8km round trip); or to the priory on Oronsay, the smaller island. 6km to 'the
Strand' (you might get a lift with the postman) then cross at low tide, with
enough time (at least 2hrs) to walk to the ruins. Allow longer if you want to
climb the easy peak of Ben Oronsay. Tide tables at hotel. Nice walk also from
Kiloran Beach (1646/BEACHES) to Balnahard Beach – farm track 12km ret.
12+6KM XCIRC BIKE 1-A-2

2334 **THE OLD MAN OF STORR, SKYE:** The enigmatic basalt finger visible from the
MAP 5 Portree-Staffin rd (A855). Start from car park on left, 12km from Portree.
A2 There's a well-defined path through woodland & then towards the cliffs and a
steep climb up the grassy slope to the pinnacle which towers 165ft tall. Gr
views over Raasay to the mainland. Lots of space and rabbits and birds who
make the most of it. To be the location of major environmental animation
piece by notable nva organisation in summer 2004. 5KM XCIRC XBIKE 2-B-2

2335 **THE QUIRANG, SKYE:** See 1723/VIEWS for directions to start pt. The strange
MAP 5 formations have names (e.g. the Table, the Needle, the Prison) and it's possible
A1 to walk round all of them. Start of the path from the car park is easy. At the first
saddle, take the second scree slope to the Table, rather than the first. When
you get to the Needle, the path to the rt betw two giant pinnacles is the easiest of the 3 options. From the top you can see the Hebrides. This place is
supernatural; anything could happen. So be careful. 6KM XCIRC XBIKE 2-B-2

2336 **HOY, ORKNEY:** There are innumerable walks on the scattered Orkney Islands
and on Hoy itself; on a good day you can get round the north part of the
island and see some of the most dramatic coastal scenery anywhere. A passenger ferry leaves Stromness 2 or 3 times a day and takes 30mins. Make
tracks N or S from jnct nr pier and use free Hoy brochure from TIC so as not to
miss the landmarks, the bird sanctuaries and the Old Man himself.
20/25KM CIRC MTBIKE 2-B-2

2337 **CORRYVRECKAN, JURA:** The whirlpool in the Gulf of Corryvreckan is notori-
MAP 2 ous. Betw Jura and Scarba; to see it go to far N of Jura. From end of the rd at
C3 Ardlussa (25km Craighouse, the village), there's a rough track to Lealt then a
walk (a local may drive you) of 12km to Kinuachdrach, then a further walk of
3km. Phenomenon best seen at certain states of tide. There are now boat trips
from Crinan and Oban – consult TICs. Consult hotel (2319/ISLAND HOTELS) and
get the walk guide. (2295/MAGICAL ISLANDS) 6/24KM XCIRC XBIKE 2-C-2

2338 **SGURR AN EIGG:** Unmissable treat if you're on Eigg. Take to the big ridge. Not
MAP 5 a hard pull, and extraordinary views & island perspective from the top.
A3 (2297/MAGICAL ISLANDS)

2339
MAP 2 **FERRY:** Ardrossan-Brodick, 55mins. 6 per day Mon-Sat, 4 on Sun. Ardrossan-Glas, train or rd via A77/A71 1.5hr. Claonaig-Lochranza, 30mins. 9 per day (summer only). *The best way to see Arran is on a bike. See foot of page. Winter sailings – call TIC.*

WHERE TO STAY

KILMICHAEL HOUSE, BRODICK: 01770 302219. Period mansion 3km from the main rd and into the glens. Elegant interior & furnishings in house and courtyard rooms. V discreet hence no groups or kids. Still *the* place to eat on Arran, but book (2315/ISLAND HOTELS). Now also has a self-cat cottage.

6RMS JAN-DEC T/T XPETS CC XKIDS MED.EX

AUCHRANNIE HOUSE, BRODICK: 01770 302234. Old house enlarged and recently refurbed. Pool, gym – predictable country-house manner & grub. Somewhat overshadowed by spa facs in grds. Travelodge meets Schrader (they wish!) in stylish mod rooms, restau fits all sizes. Gr poolside facs. Conservatory restau (two AA rosettes) and busy with bar meals. Burgeoning time-share in grounds, and new leisure club.

28RMS JAN-DEC T/T XPETS CC KIDS MED.EX

ARGENTINE HOUSE, WHITING BAY: 01770 700662. Seaside home on the front at Whiting Bay, a GH run by Swiss couple, the Baumgärtners. Look no further for dinner & vegns catered for. Stargazers welcome!

5RMS MAR-JAN X/T PETS CC XKIDS MED.INX

LOCHRANZA HOTEL: 01770 830223. Small hotel with tranquil views across bay and 13thC castle. In village. Basic accom but home-spun hosp, soups, pâtés, scones & more (scones). Beer garden & Dillon the lab. Food all day in season. 7RMS EASTER-DEC T/T PETS CC KIDS INX

S.Y. HOSTELS: at Lochranza (01770 830631) and Whiting Bay (01770 700339). Both busy Grade 2s in picturesque areas (Mar-Oct), 25 and 15km from Brodick.

CAMPING AND CARAVAN PARKS: at Glen Rosa (01770 302380) 4km Brodick; Lamlash (01770 600251), Lochranza (01770 830273). And Glen Rosa has idyllic river side camping.

WHERE TO EAT

✓ **THE LIGHTHOUSE:** 01770 850240. Restau & 12-bed bunkhouse at Pirnmill looking over to Kintyre. Newly established funky vibe. Maritime blue & pine – wholesome menu. 9am-8pm – grt home-made food in unusual West End chic (1500/BEST TEAROOMS & CAFES). Best place on island for sundowners & cappucinos; then just bunk-up. BYOB. 7 days. Jan-Dec 9am-8pm. 12 bunks. INX

CREELERS, BRODICK: 01770 302810. Art, seafood & atmos (when you find the place open). Phone ahead – hrs can be a tad unpredictable. (1448/SEAFOOD RESTAUS). MED

BURLINGTON HOTEL, WHITING BAY: 01770 700255. Kitchen under the direction of Robin Gray who also runs an organic produce business. The sous-chefs work abroad in the winter and the food is top-notch. Nice music in the background. Easter-Oct, dinner daily. INX

THE DISTILLERY RESTAURANT: 01770 830264. At the Distillery Visitor Centre, Lochranza. Good light menu in light even clinical rm with running water accompaniment. Daily 10am-6pm in season. Phone out of season. INX

BRODICK BAR: Best pub food in Brodick? Yes. Bar snacks, then turns into more of a bistro in the eve. Food until 10pm. Off N end of main st by Royal Mail. Bar open till midnight. CHP

WINEPORT, CLADACH: 01770 302977. Simple bistro in developing 'centre' at start of Goat Fell walk. No frills, but you'll want that pasta and beer once you're off the hill. While you're there, have a look at the adj microbrewery and its pleasant Arran ales.

WHAT TO SEE

BRODICK CASTLE: 5km walk or cycle from Brodick. Impressive museum and gdns. Tearoom. Flagship NTS property. (1860/CASTLES.)   NT

GOAT FELL: 6km/5hr gr hill walk starting from the car park at Cladach nr castle and Brodick or sea start at Corrie. Free route leaflet at TIC. (1993/HILLS.)   2-A-2

GLENASHDALE FALLS: 4km, but 2hr forest walk from Glenashdale Br at Whiting Bay. Steady, easy climb, silvan setting. (1679/WATERFALLS.)   1-B-1

CORRIE: The best village 9km N Brodick. Go by bike. Good pub. (1645/COASTAL VILLAGES.)

MACHRIE MOOR STANDING STONES: Off main coast rd 7km N of Blackwater Foot. Various assemblies of Stones, all part of an ancient landscape. We lay down there.

GLEN ROSA, GLEN SANNOX: Fine glens: Rosa nr Brodick, Sannox 11km N.   1-B-2

WHAT TO DO

GOLF: Lots of it. Brodick (01770 302513); Lochranza (01770 830273); Lamlash (01770 600296); Whiting Bay (01770 700487). Corrie and Machrie (9 holes). **TENNIS/SWIMMING:** Enquiries TIC. **CYCLE HIRE:** Brodick 3 places along front, but esp Brodick Cycles (302460); also Whiting Bay (700382). 3-speed or mountain bikes. **PONY TREKKING:** Lots of opportunities – try Cairhouse Centre (860466), Brodick Trekking (302800) or North Sannox (810222).

TOURIST INFO: 01770 302140. **CALMAC:** 08705 650000.

THE BEST OF ISLAY AND JURA

2340
MAP 2
FERRY: Kennacraig-Pt Askaig: 2hrs, Kennacraig-Pt Ellen: 2hrs 10 mins. Pt Askaig-Feolin, Jura: 5mins, frequent daily (01496 840681).

BY AIR: from Glas to Pt Ellen Airport in S of island. BA 08457 733377.

WHERE TO STAY

PORT CHARLOTTE HOTEL, PORT CHARLOTTE: 01496 850360. Restored Victorian inn and gdns on seafront of conservation village. Restful place, restful views. Good bistro-style menu, the best around. New owners taking it onwards & upwards. Report: 2309/ISLAND HOTELS. 10RMS JAN-DEC T/T PETS CC KIDS MED.EX

HARBOUR INN, BOWMORE: 01496 810330. Nice conservatory with bay views, contemp furnishings and well crafted food by Scott Chance, def best bet in town. Report: 2310/ISLAND HOTELS.   7RMS JAN-DEC T/T PETS CC KIDS MED.INX

KILMENY FARM, nr BALLYGRANT: 01496 840668. Margaret and Blair Rozga's top-class GH just off the rd S of Pt Askaig (the ferry). Huge attention to detail, great home-made food, house party atmos and a shared table. Tho small.
3RMS JAN-DEC X/X XPETS XCC KIDS MED.INX

GLENMACHRIE, nr PORT ELLEN: 01496 302560. On A846 betw Bowmore & Pt Ellen adj airport. Sister GH of Kilmeny Farm (above). Here it's Rachel's award-winning farmhouse with enormous care taken over food and gt meals. Farmers with a green sensibility.   5RMS JAN-DEC X/T PETS XCC XKIDS MED.INX

THE MACHRIE, PORT ELLEN: 01496 302310. 7km N on A846. Restau and bar meals in clubhouse atmos. Restau in old byre and 15 lodges in the grounds. You'll likely be here for the golf – so you might overlook its rather bleak setting. The gr beach (1650/BEACHES) *is* over there.
16RMS JAN-DEC T/T XPETS CC KIDS MED.INX

LOCHSIDE HOTEL, BOWMORE: 01496 810244. Probably best selection of Islay malts in the world; so gr bar & bar meals in lochside, actually seaside setting. Rms 50-50.   MED.INX

BRIDGEND INN, BRIDGEND: 01496 810212. Middle of island on rd from Pt Askaig, 4km Bowmore. Roadside inn with good pub meals & surprising no of rms. A fine stopover.   10RMS JAN-DEC T/T PETS CC KIDS MED.EX

JURA HOTEL, CRAIGHOUSE: 01496 820243. The hotel for the island. Situated in front of the distillery by the bay. Front rms best. You'll have fun in the bar. Report: 2319/ISLAND HOTELS.   18RMS JAN-DEC X/X PETS CC KIDS INX

CAMPING, CARAVAN SITE, HOSTEL at Kintra Farm. 01496 302051. Off main rd to Pt Ellen; take Oa rd, follow Kintra signs 7km. July-August B&B in farmhouse. Grassy strand, coastal walks. **ISLAY YOUTH HOSTEL** Pt Charlotte 01496 850385.

WHERE TO EAT

HARBOUR INN, BOWMORE and **PORT CHARLOTTE HOTEL:** *see above.*

CROFT KITCHEN: Pt Charlotte. 01496 850230. Joy and Douglas Law have combined this coffee (latte, macchiato) and gift shop by day, with restau by night (Lagavulin Scallops!). Easter-October 10am-8.30pm (not Wed even). Book in season.   INX

BALLYGRANT INN: 01496 840277. S of Pt Askaig. Small, cared-for, basic pub with (3) rms. Nice family will welcome yours.   INX

ARDBEG DISTILLERY CAFÉ: 5km E of Pt Ellen on the whisky rd. Gr local rep for food. Cl 5pm.   INX

WHAT TO SEE

ISLAY: THE DISTILLERIES esp Laphroaig and Lagavulin (classic settings) by Pt Ellen; tours by appointment. Bowmore has regular glossy tour; Ardbeg, open daily, good cafe (1578/WHISKY); **MUSEUM OF ISLAY, WILDLIFE INFO AND FIELD CENTRE** (18200/WILDLIFE): all at Pt Charlotte; **AMERICAN MONUMENT** (1766/MONUMENTS); **OA and LOCH GRUINART** (1800/BIRDS); **PORT CHARLOTTE** (1638/COASTAL VILLAGES); **KINTRA** (2067/COASTAL WALKS); **FINLAGGAN:** The romantic, sparse ruin on 'island' in L Finlaggan: last home of the Lords of the Isles. Off A846 5km S of Pt Askaig, check TIC for opening. **ISLAY MARINE CHARTERS:** 01496 850436. Wildlife cruises incl whales in summer.

JURA: (2295/MAGICAL ISLANDS); **THE PAPS OF JURA; CORRYVRECKAN, BARN-HILL** (2337/ISLAND WALKS); **KILLCHIANAIG, KEILS** (1937/GRAVEYARDS); **LOWLANDMAN'S BAY** (1655/BEACHES); **JURA HOUSE WALLED GARDEN;** utterly magical in the right light (1608/GARDENS).

WHAT TO DO

GOLF at Machrie (2098/GOLF IN GREAT PLACES); **PONY-TREKKING** at Rockside Farm (01496 850231), Ballyvicar (01496 302251); **SWIMMING** at Bowmore (01496 810767); **BIKE HIRE:** Bowmore (01496 810336), Pt Ellen (01496 302349); **MARINE CHARTERS:** 01496 850436.

TOURIST INFO: 01496 810254. **CALMAC:** 08705 650000.

THE BEST OF SKYE

2341
MAP 5 **THE BRIDGE:** the hump (which is all it has given to a lot of the locals); unromantic but convenient; from Kyle. **THE FERRIES:** Mallaig-Armadale, 30mins. Tarbert (Harris)-Uig, 1hr 35mins (Calmac, as Mallaig). **THE BEST WAY TO SKYE** is Glenelg-Kylerhea, 5mins. Continuous Apr-Oct 01599 511302. Wint sailings: check TIC.

WHERE TO STAY

HOUSE OVER-BY: 01470 571258. Reports: 2306/ISLAND HOTELS

EILEAN IARMAIN: 01471 833332. 15km S of Broadford on A851. V Gaelic inn on bay with dreamy views, good food and gr pub. Main hotel best value (with cottage annexe); suites over rd more inex (2311/ISLAND HOTELS).
            12RMS JAN-DEC T/X PETS CC KIDS EXP

FLODIGARRY: 01470 552203. 30km N Portree on A855. Far-flung N of the island; the views exceptional. Relaxed country-house ambience; local liveliness in the bar. (1218/COUNTRY-HOUSE HOTELS)
            11RMS + 7COTT JAN-DEC T/X PETS CC KIDS EXP

VIEWFIELD HOUSE, PORTREE: 01478 612217. One of the oldest island houses; it's been in the MacDonald family over 200 yrs. Unique and antique atmos. Gr dinner. (2317/ISLAND HOTELS.) 12RMS APR-OCT T/X PETS CC KIDS MED.EX

SABHAL MÒR OSTAIG: 01471 888000. Part of the Gaelic College in Sleat off A851 N of Armadale. Pron *Sawal More Ostag*. Excl inx rms in modern build o/looking Sound of Sleat. Penthouse spectac. B/fast in bright café. Best deal on the island & you could enrol to learn Gaelic.

80RMS JAN-DEC X/X XPETS CC XKIDS CHP

CUILLIN HILLS HOTEL, PORTREE: 01478 612003. On the edge of Portree (off rd N to Staffin) nr water's edge. Secluded mansion house hotel with nice conservatory. Decor slightly iffy (you may like leather-studded furniture and draped 4-posters) but gr views from most rms. 28RMS JAN-DEC T/T PETS CC KIDS MED.EX

SKEABOST: 01470 532202. 11km W of Portree on A850. Old-style country house in grounds with 9-hole golf and salmon fishing on R Snizort. New owners imminent at TGP. TLC reqd. 26RMS MAR-DEC T/T PETS CC KIDS MED.EX

THE STEIN INN, WATERNISH: 01470 592362. Off B886, the Waternish rd which is 5km Dunvegan on the rd to Portree. Distant but v Skye location in vill row on the water & nr Lochbay (see below). Ancient inn with atmos pub (1260/SEASIDE INNS) & 5 nice rms above. An excl retreat. 5RMS JAN-DEC X/X PETS CC KIDS CHP

GRESHORNISH HOUSE HOTEL: 01470 582266. 5km from Dunvegan-Portree rd (A850) about 30km Portree & on its own peninsula along L Greshornish ... so quite far away. Comfy small co house hotel with inimitable madame in charge. Nice to take over with family or mates (not exp; 1336/HOUSE PARTIES). 2 Billiard rms. Home-made food. 6RMS JAN-DEC X/T PETS CC KIDS MED.INX

S.Y. HOSTELS: At Kyleakin (biggest, nearest mainland), Armadale (interesting area in S), Broadford, Glen Brittle (v Cuillin), Uig (for N Skye, ferry to Hebrides). **INDEPENDENT HOSTELS** at Kyleakin & Staffin (1249/1248/HOSTELS) & many others.

WHERE TO EAT

THREE CHIMNEYS: 01470 511258. 7km W of Dunvegan on B884. Superb home cooking, best in the islands. Report: 2322/ISLAND RESTAUS. MED

KINLOCH LODGE: 01471 833333. 13km S Broadford off A851. Classy food in almost theatrical atmos at Lady Claire's table(s). Report: 2321/ISLAND RESTAUS.

EXP

LOCHBAY SEAFOOD: 01470 592235. 12km N Dunvegan off A850. Small; simple fresh seafood in loch-side setting, Apr-Oct. Cl Sun & Sat (dinner in July/Aug only). Report: 1442/SEAFOOD RESTAUS. INX

AN TUIREANN CAFE: 01478 613306. Nr Portree. Coffee shop/gallery. Good food and chat in a cultural caff. Cl Sun. Report: 2328/ISLAND RESTAU; 1426/VEGN RESTAUS.

HARBOUR VIEW, PORTREE: 01478 612069. Bosville Terr on rd to Staffin and N Skye with harbour view at least from the door. Local seafood in intimate bistro dining rm. 7 days Easter-Oct lunch and dinner (not Sun lunch). LO 9.30pm. Also next door:

THE CHANDLERY: 01478 612846. The more upmarket end of the Bosville Hotel restau has had recent uplift. Seafd taken seriously here & building local rep. Open Apr-Oct for lunch & LO 10pm. MED

CREELERS, BROADFORD: 01471 822281. Just off A87 rd from Kyleakin and bridge to Portree as you come into Broadford. Small cabin seafood restau and t/away round back, but excl local rep. 12-9pm (& t/away till 10pm). Cl Wed.

THE OLD SCHOOL, DUNVEGAN: 01470 521421. On main rd/st in Dunvegan. Long established, serviceable bistro. Good vegn. 7 days, lunch and dinner in season. LO 9pm. Cl Jan/Feb.

PASTA SHED, ARMADALE: no number. On the quayside at Armadale where the Mallaig ferry comes in. A real pizza hut, but best to get Alistair MacPhail to knock you up some super-fresh seafood. Amazone teas & herbs from garden adj. 7 days in season 9am-5.30pm (7.30 high season).

SLIGACHAN HOTEL: Surprisingly decent seafood in hotel dining-rm situation (The Cairidh). 7-9pm. 7 days. Best book.

THE STABLES: Coffee shop/restau of the Clan Donald Centre/Museum of the Isles on A851 1km N of Armadale. Decent self-serv comfort food & cakes. Apr-Oct till 5.30pm.

WHAT TO SEE

THE CUILLINS (2/BIG ATTRACTIONS); **RAASAY** (2294/MAGICAL ISLANDS), (2339/ISLAND WALKS); **THE QUIRANG** (1723/VIEWS), (2335/ISLAND WALKS); **OLD MAN OF STORR** (2334/ISLAND WALKS); **DUNVEGAN** (1833/CASTLES); **EAS MOR** (1681/WATERFALLS); **ELGOL** (1727/VIEWS); **SKYE BATIKS** (2187/CRAFT SHOPS); **SKYE MUSEUM OF ISLAND LIFE** (2261/MUSEUMS); **FLORA MACDONALD'S GRAVE** (1900/MONUMENTS); **SKYE SILVER, EDINBANE POTTERY** and **CARBOST CRAFT** (2183/2182/CRAFT SHOPS); **FAIRY POOLS** (1742/PICNICS); **SLIGACHAN HOTEL** (above).

WHAT TO DO

GOLF at Skeabost (*previous page*) and Sconser (01478 650351); **FISHING:** ask at hotels; Skeabost, Eilean Iarmain (*previous page*) and Greshhornish House; **SWIMMING** at Portree Pool (01478 612655); **BIKE HIRE:** Island Cycles (01478 613121); Fair Winds Bicycle Hire (01471 822270); **RIDING:** (01470 582419 or 01478 612945).

CEILIDHS: In this most Highland of islands 2 hoolies are worth mentioning, all welcoming to visitors; **SKYE SCENE CEILIDH, TIGH NA SCIRE, PORTREE** (enquire TIC). Mon and Wed in season and Tues (July-Sept). Touristy, but charming. **FLODIGARRY COUNTRY HOUSE HOTEL:** 32km N Portree. V north, v Staffin and the stuff of a damned good shindig. Every Sat, plus other nights. Backpackers from adj hostel (1248/HOSTELS), locals and hotel guests happily get down. Till 11.30pm-ish. **AROS CENTRE** on main rd just S of Portree also has full programme of trad & contemp Scottish music thro'out yr. Check TIC.

TOURIST INFO: 01478 612137. **CALMAC:** 08705 650000.

THE BEST OF THE WESTERN ISLES

2342
MAP 7
FERRIES: Ullapool-Stornoway, 2hrs 40mins, (not Sun). Oban/Mallaig-Lochboisdale, S Uist and Castlebay, Barra; up to 6.5hrs. Uig on Skye-Tarbert, Harris (not Sun) or Lochmaddy, N Uist 1hr 40mins. Also Leverburgh, Harris-Otternish, N Uist (not Sun) 1hr 10mins. Local passenger ferry: Ludag, S Uist-Eoligarry, Barra (01851 701702). Winter sailings – call TIC.

BY AIR: BA 3 times daily (2 Sat; not Sun). Inverness/Glas/Edin. Local 01851 703240. BA Otter to Barra/Benbecula from Glas (1 a day). Linkline 08457 733377.

WHERE TO STAY

SCARISTA HOUSE, S HARRIS: 01859 550238. 20km S of Tarbert. Nr famous but often deserted beach; celebrated retreat. Also self-catering accom. Report: (2321/ISLAND HOTELS).

RODEL HOTEL, S HARRIS: 01859 520210. Hotel at the end of the rd, the A859, S of Tarbert, S of everywhere. Superb setting, you are truly away from it all. Recent makeover, so comfy & contemp (2 self-cat). Gastropub menu (open non-res), all home-made with local produce.

4(+2)RMS APR-DEC X/T PETS CC KIDS MED.EX

CASTLEBAY HOTEL, CASTLEBAY, BARRA: 01871 810223. O/looks ferry terminal in main town. Excellent value. Good food. Brilliant bar (2307/ISLAND HOTELS; 1380/BLOODY GOOD PUBS).

ISLE OF BARRA HOTEL, BARRA: 01871 810383. Modern purpose-built hotel on gr beach 3km W of Castlebay. Seaviews are why we're here (2320/ISLAND HOTELS).

ROYAL HOTEL, STORNOWAY, LEWIS: 01851 702109. The best value and most central of the 3 main hotels in town. Barnacle bistro and Boatshed (probably 'best' hotel dining). All owned by same company. Some rms OK-ish, some not, so see first (bedrms in the **CABARFEIDH** are better; 01851 702604).

26RMS JAN-DEC T/T PETS CC KIDS MED.INX

PARK GUEST HOUSE, STORNOWAY: 01851 702485. James St. Refurbished town house with surprisingly good menu and comfy rms tho guest-housey. A place to eat even if not staying. More accom on way at TGP.

7+2GDN RMS JAN-DEC X/T XPETS XCC XKIDS TOS CHP

LEACHIN HOUSE, TARBERT, N HARRIS: 01859 502157. 2km N on A859. Small, Victorian family house. Personal touch in furnishings, food and your excursions. Shared dinner. A Wolsey Lodge. 2RMS JAN-DEC X/T XPETS XCC KIDS INX

LOCHBOISDALE HOTEL, LOCHBOISDALE, S UIST: 01471 822270. In last town nr tip of Uists at ferry terminal o/look bay. Mainly fishing hotel with all rods catered for. Gr local bar. But rms vary & some ain't so great.

18RMS JAN-DEC X/T PETS CC KIDS MED.EX

POLLACHAR INN, S UIST: 01878 700215. S of Lochboisdale nr small ferry for Eriskay/Barra (2199/ISLANDS) an inn at the end of the known world. Excl value, good craic and the view/sunset across the sea to Barra. Refurb has improved.

11RMS JAN-DEC T/T PETS CC KIDS MED.INX

HOSTELS: Simple hostels within hiking distance. 2 in Lewis, 3 in Harris, 1 each in N and S Uist (Barra pending). Excellent hostelling holiday prospect (1240 & 1241/ HOSTELS).

WHERE TO EAT

BONAVENTURE, AIRD UIG: 01851 672474. 30km W of Stornaway to the end of the rd (A858 then B8011). A corner of France far from home. Report 2324/ISLAND RESTAUS.

THE THAI CAFE, STORNOWAY: 01851 701811. 27 Church St opp police stn. An unlikely find but prob the best place to eat in this town – Mrs Panida Macdonald's restau an institution here & you may have to book. Gr atmos, excl real Thai cuisine, though you couldn't be further in every respect from Bangkok. Lunch & LO 11pm. Cl Sun.

PARK GUEST HOUSE and **THE BOATSHED**, at the **ROYAL HOTEL, STORNOWAY:** (*see above*). The top two dining-rms in town. Park is a restau so don't be put off by guesthouse tag. V TOS (Tues-Sat). Latter slightly up-market with seafood emphasis. High teas then LO 9pm.

TIGH MEALROS, GARYNAHINE, LEWIS: 01851 621333. On A858 22km SW Stornoway. 2km S of Callanish. Unpretentious surf 'n' turf. Scallops (dived) a special. BYOB. Open AYR. LO 9pm.

COPPER KETTLE, DALBEG, LEWIS: 01851 710592. 6km N of Carloway W of Stornoway. Signed off main rd down track to lily-filled lochan. Tables on terrace in summer for tea and tiny restau with excellent plain cooking. Must book dinner.

COFFEE SHOPS at **AN LANNTAIR GALLERY, STORNOWAY,** and **CALLANISH VISITOR CENTRE, LEWIS.** The latter esp good. Daytime hrs (1865/PREHISTORIC SITES).

SCARISTA HOUSE, HARRIS: (*see above*). Dinner possible for non-residents. A nice drive from Stornoway. Fixed menu. Book.

FIRST FRUITS TEAROOM, TARBERT, HARRIS: Nr TIC and ferry to Uig. Home-cooking that hits the spot. Good atmos. 10.30am-4.30pm Apr-Sept.

TOURIST INFO: (Stornoway) 01851 701818. **CALMAC:** 08705 650000.

2343
MAP 2 **FERRY:** Oban-Craignure, 45mins. Main route; 6 a day. Lochaline-Fishnish, 15mins. 9-15 a day. Kilchoan-Tobermory, 35mins. 7 a day (Sun – summer only). Winter sailings – call TIC.

WHERE TO STAY

HIGHLAND COTTAGE, TOBERMORY: 01688 302030. Breadalbane St opp fire stn a street above the harbour. Report: 2314/HOTELS.
6RMS FEB-DEC T/T XPETS CC KIDS TOS MED.EX

GLENGORM CASTLE nr TOBERMORY: 01688 302321. Minor rd on right going N outside town. Glen Gormenghast! Fab views over to Ardnamurchan from this baronial pile. Luxurious bedrms in family home – use the library & grand public spaces. B&B only. Self-cat.   6RMS JAN-DEC X/X PETS CC KIDS MED.INX

TIRORAN HOUSE: 01681 705232: In S of Mull, a treat and a retreat way down the SW of Mull nr Iona. Light, comfy house in glorious gdns with excl food & flowers. Report: 1281/GET AWAY HOTELS.
6RMS + 2COTT MAR-NOV X/X XPETS CC KIDS MED.EXP

ARGYLL HOTEL, IONA: 01681 700334. Nr ferry and on seashore o/looking Mull on rd to abbey. Laid-back, cosy accom, cottage rms, home cooking, good vegn. (1256/SEASIDE INNS)   16RM FEB-OCT X/X PETS CC KIDS MED.INX

CALGARY FARMHOUSE, CALGARY: 01688 400256. Nr Dervaig on B8073 nr Mull's famous beach. Gallery/coffee shop and good bistro/restau. Report: 2313/HOTELS.   9RMS APR-OCT X/X PETS CC KIDS MED.INX

TOBERMORY HOTEL: 01688 302091. On waterfront. Creature comforts, gt view & restau. Competes well with other Mull seafd lunches. Middle of the quays.   16RMS JAN-DEC X/T PETS CC KIDS MED.INX

WESTERN ISLES, TOBERMORY: 01688 302012. Presiding high above town, classic views over bay; but new owners so not much to say so far.
26RMS JAN-DEC T/T PETS CC KIDS MED.EX

DRUIMARD COUNTRY HOUSE, DERVAIG: 01688 400345. Small, country place beside Mull Little Theatre does get listed in guides. Takes pride in their food, but for sale at TGP.   5RMS JAN-DEC T/T PETS CC KIDS MED.EX

S.Y. HOSTEL: In Tobermory main st on bay (1171/HOSTELS).

CARAVAN PARKS: At Fishnish (all facs, nr Ferry) Craignure and Fionnphort.

CAMPING: Calgary Beach, Fishnish and at Loch Na Keal shore.

WHERE TO EAT

HIGHLAND COTTAGE: 01688 302030. As above and 2314/ISLAND HOTS. Also the local night out. Small so must book.   MED

THE GLASS BARN: 2km Tobermory centre. Highly recommended (1498/TEA-ROOMS).   INX

ISLAND BAKERY, TOBERMORY: 01688 302225. Main St. Bakery-deli with excl take-away pizza by Joe Reade, the son of the cheese people (and the Glass Barn above). Home-made pâtés, quiches, salads. Buy your picnic here. 7 days LO 7.30pm (w/end only in wint).   CHP

THE ANCHORAGE, TOBERMORY: 01688 302313. Main St opp pier. Family-owned by fishing folk, so mainly seafood. Homely and friendly & not bad at all. For sale at TGP. 7 days, lunch and LO 7pm. Winter hrs will vary.   INX

CALGARY FARMHOUSE: 01688 400256. Dovecote Restaurant. Local produce in atmospheric wine-bar setting, run by mellow people (2327/ISLAND RESTAUS). Coolest dining rm on the island.   INX

ARGYLL HOUSE, SALEN: 01680 300555. On main A849 half-way betw Craignure & Tobermory. Caff by day, decent pizza & pasta joint in evening but LO 8pm.   INX

MULL POTTERY, TOBERMORY: 01688 302592. Fun mezzanine café above working pottery just outside Tobermory on rd S to Craignure. Evening meals and usual daytime offerings. Locals do recommend. AYR. 7 days.

WHAT TO SEE

TOROSAY CASTLE: Walk or train (!) from Craignure. Fabulous gdns and fascinating insight into an endearing family's life. Teashop. (1832/CASTLES.) **DUART CASTLE:** 5km Craignure. Seat of Clan Maclean. Impressive from a distance, good view of clan history and from battlements. Teashop. (1831/CASTLES.) **EAS FORS:** Waterfall on Dervaig to Fionnphort rd. V accessible series of cataracts tumbling into the sea (1650/WATERFALLS). **THE MISHNISH:** No mission to Mull complete without a night at the Mish (1375/BLOODY GOOD PUBS), MacGochann's over the bay no contest.

WHAT TO DO

Excursions to **IONA** (from Fionnphort) and **ULVA** (from Ulva Ferry) (2296/2300/MAGICAL ISLANDS); **STAFFA** (from Fionnphort or Iona) and **THE TRESHNISH ISLES** (Ulva Ferry or Fionnphort). Marvellous trips in summer (1794/BIRDS); walks from **CARSAIG PIER** (2331/ISLAND WALKS); or up **BEN MORE** (2019/MUNROS); **CROIG** and **QUINISH** in N, nr Dervaig and **LOCHBUIE** off the A849 at Strathcoil 9km S of Craignure: these are all serene shorelines to explore. **AROS PARK** forest walk, from Tobermory, about 7km round trip. **GOLF:** Tobermory (01688 302020). Craignure (01688 302372). Both 9 holes. **FISHING:** Info: 'Tackle and Books' (01688 302336).

TOURIST INFO: 01688 302182. **CALMAC:** 08705 650000.

THE BEST OF ORKNEY

2344 **FERRY:** Northlink (0845 6000449) Stromness: from Aber – Tue, Thu, Sat, Sun, takes 6hrs; from Scrabster – 2/3 per day, takes 1.5hrs. John O'Groats to Burwick (01955 611353), 40mins, up to 4 a day (May-Sept only). Pentland Ferries from Gill (nr J o'Groats) to St Margaret's Hope (01856 831226) – 3 a day, takes 1hr.

BY AIR: BA (08457 733377) to Kirkwall: from Aber – 3 daily; from Edin – 2 daily; from Glas – 1 daily; from Inverness – 2 daily; from Wick – 1 daily (not w/ends).

WHERE TO STAY

FOVERAN HOTEL, ST OLA: 01856 872389. A964 Orphir rd; 4km from Kirkwall. Scandinavian style hotel is a friendly informal place serves trad food using best local ingredients; separate vegn menu. offering gr value. Comfortable light rms recently refurbished; gdn o/look Scapa Flow. Good restau.

8RMS JAN-DEC T/T XPETS CC KIDS MED.INX

AYRE HOTEL, KIRKWALL: 01856 873001. Roy and Moira Dennison have spent several years refurb their family hotel in line with TIC standards; which has resulted in them having the highest grading on the mainland. Situated on the harbour front, the whole place is well tidy and well established. It's where to stay in Kirkwall.

33RMS JAN-DEC T/T PETS CC KIDS MED.EX

CLEATON HOUSE HOTEL, WESTRAY: 01857 677508. Beautifully refurbished former Victorian manse. Panoramic seascapes, relaxed atmos & wonderful food.

6RMS JAN-DEC T/T PETS CC KIDS MED.EX

BARONY HOTEL, BIRSAY: 01856 721327. 40km from Kirkwall. Basic accom in wild corner by loch. Brown trout fishing, walks, sea air. Cabin style 'HMS Hampshire' bar.

10RMS MAY-OCT T/T PETS CC KIDS MED.INX

MERKISTER HOTEL, HARRAY: 01856 771366. A fave with fishers and twitchers; handy for archaeological sites and just poss the Orkney hotel of choice. À la carte or table d'hôte in the conservatory o/look the loch.

13RMS JAN-DEC T/T PETS CC KIDS MED.INX

STROMNESS HOTEL: 01856 850298. Orkney's biggest hotel, recent refurb. Central and picturesque. We haven't stayed.

42RMS JAN-DEC T/T PETS CC KIDS MED.INX

WOODWICK HOUSE, EVIE: 01856 751330. Comfy country house and gdn, nr shore with views of islets. It's a gr retreat. Home cooking, local produce. Good value.

7RMS JAN-DEC X/X PETS CC KIDS TOS MED.INX

S.Y. HOSTELS: At Stromness (excellent location, 01856 850589), Kirkwall (the largest, 01856 872243). Other hostels at: Hoy, N & S Ronaldsay, Birsay, Sanday.
PEEDIE HOSTEL, KIRKWALL: 01856 875477. Ayre Rd; by the sea. Private bedrm, own keys.
BIS GEOS HOSTEL, WESTRAY: 01857 677420. Hostel with 2 self-catering cottages. Traditional features & luxuries.
THE BARN, WESTRAY: 01857 677214. Four-star self-catering hostel in renovated stone barn. Gr views.

CAMPING/CARAVAN: At Kirkwall (01856 879900) and Stromness (01856 873535).

WHERE TO EAT

THE CREEL INN & RESTAURANT, ST MARGARET'S HOPE: 01856 831311. On S Ronaldsay, 20km S of Kirkwall. In the wild area where seals vie with the fishermen. Excl table (2 AA rosette) though fairly exp. Many sauces over meat or fish. Clootie for pud or Orkney cheeses. Popular with the islanders. Dinner only. Seal Rescue Centre nearby. Also well-appointed 3 rms, a good choice B+B. 3RMS TOS MED

FOVERAN HOTEL, ST OLA: 01856 872389. 4km Kirkwall. *As above.* MED

WOODWICK HOUSE, EVIE: 01856 751330. *As above.* TOS MED

THE HAMNAVOE RESTAURANT, STROMNESS: 01856 850606. 35 Graham Pl off main st. Seafood is their speciality, but they do haggis, neeps and tatties. Apr-Oct; Tue-Sun 6.30pm-late. Nov-Mar open w/ends only. INX

JULIA'S CAFÉ & BISTRO, STROMNESS: 01856 850904. Gr home baking, blackboard & vegn specials. Internet access. A favourite with the locals. Gets busy – fill yourself up before the ferry journey! Open AYR, 7 days 7.30am-10pm (cl 5-6.30pm). Phone for winter opening hrs. CHP

WHAT TO SEE

SKARA BRAE: 25km W Kirkwall. Amazingly well-preserved underground labyrinth, a 5,000-year-old village (1863/PREHISTORIC SITES).

THE OLD MAN OF HOY: on Hoy; 30min ferry 2 or 3 times a day from Stromness. 3hr walk along spectacular coast (2336/ISLAND WALKS).

STANDING STONES OF STENNESS, THE RING OF BRODGAR, MAES HOWE: Around 18km W of Kirkwall on A965. Strong vibrations (1864/PREHISTORIC SITES).

YESNABY SEA STACKS: 24km W of Kirkwall. A precarious cliff top at the end of the world (1984/SPOOKY – or spiritual – PLACES).

ITALIAN CHAPEL: 8km S of Kirkwall at first causeway. A special act of faith. (1916/CHURCHES).

SKAILL HOUSE: 01856 841501. At Skara Brae. 17th-century 'mansion' built on Pictish cemetery. Set up as it was in the 1950s; with Captain Cook's crockery in the dining-rm looking remarkably unused. Apr-Sep; 7 days 9.30am-6pm (or by appointment). Tearoom and VC and HS link with Skara.

ST MAGNUS CATHEDRAL (1916/CHURCHES); **STROMNESS** (1634/COASTAL VILLAGES); **THE PIER ARTS CENTRE** (2280/INTERESTING GALLERIES); **TOMB OF THE EAGLES** (1870/PREHISTORIC SITES); **MARWICK HEAD** and many of the smaller islands (1801/BIRDS); **SCAPA FLOW** (1858/BATTLEGROUNDS; 2161/DIVING); **HIGHLAND PARK DISTILLERY** (1583/WHISKY); **PUFFINS:** (1803/BIRDS)

CRAFT TRAIL and ARTISTS' STUDIO TRAIL: Take in some of the trad arts & crafts in the isles. Lots of souvenir potential. Ask at TIC for details & maps.

WHAT TO DO

GOLF: Golf courses open to public at Kirkwall and Stromness. **SWIMMING:** Pools at Kirkwall, Stromness, Hoy and Sanday. **FISHING:** Permits not required, though permission needed to fish at L of Skile. **SCUBA DIVE:** PADI training, trips, hire, shop at Burray (01856 731269) and Stromness (01856 850055 or 01856 851218). **BIKE HIRE:** Kirkwall (01856 875777), Stromness (01856 850255).

TOURIST INFO: 01856 872856 or 01856 850716.

2345 **FERRY:** Northlink (0845 6000 449), Aber-Lerwick: Mon, Wed, Fri – dep 7pm, 12 hrs. Tue, Thurs, Sat, Sun – dep 5pm (via Orkney, arr 11.45pm), 14hrs.

BY AIR: BA (linkline 08457 733377, Shetland 01950 460345) sto Sumburgh: from Aber (4 a day, 2 Sat, 2 Sun). From Inverness (1 a day). From Glas (2 a day, 1 Sat). From Edin (1 a day).

WHERE TO STAY

BURRASTOW HOUSE, WALLS: 01595 809307. 40 mins from Lerwick. Most guides & locals agree this is the place to stay on Shetland. Peaceful Georgian house with views to Island of Vaila. Wonderful home-made/produced food. Full of character with food (set menu), service & rooms the best on the island.
5RMS MAR-DEC X/T PETS CC KIDS MED.EX

HERRISLEA HOUSE HOTEL, TINGWALL: 01595 840208. 7km NW of Lerwick. Refurbished country house in beautiful setting. Incorporating Starboard Tack café-bar, open daily till 11pm. Basic, good home cooking and useful children's play area.
13RMS JAN-DEC T/T PETS CC KIDS MED.INX

BUSTA HOUSE HOTEL: 01806 522506. Historic country house at Brae just over 30 mins from Lerwick. Elegant & tranquil. High standards, gr malt selection.
20RMS JAN-DEC T/T PETS CC KIDS TOS MED.EX

SUMBURGH HOTEL, SUMBURGH: 01950 460201. Refurbished manor house in v S of mainland 42 km from Lerwick. Next to airport and Jarlshof excavations. Sea views as far as Fair Isle (50km S). Beaches and birds! Wide and relatively cheap menu.
32RMS JAN-DEC T/T PETS CC KIDS MED.INX

KVELDSRO HOTEL, LERWICK: 01595 692195. Pron 'Kel-ro'. Probably best proposition in Lerwick; o/look harbour. Reasonable standard at a price. Locals do eat here.
16RMS JAN-DEC T/T X/PETS CC KIDS MED.EX

WESTINGS, THE INN ON THE HILL, WHITENESS: 01595 840242. 12 km from Lerwick. Breathtaking views down Whiteness Voe. Excellent base for exploring. Large selection of real ales and three different menus. Campsite alongside.
6RMS JAN-DEC T/T PETS CC KIDS MED.INX

ALMARA B&B, HILLSWICK: 01806 503261. We don't usually venture into the world of the B&B in this book but, although we haven't stayed ourselves, couldn't ignore numerous good reports of Mrs Williamson's four-star establishment. Friendly family home with good food & nice vibes.

S.Y. HOSTEL in Lerwick, Isleburgh House: 01595 692114. Beautifully refurbished and v central. Also home of excl Isleburgh House Café. Open Apr-Sept.

CAMPING BODS (fisherman's barns). Cheap sleep in wonderful sea-shore settings. **THE SAIL LOFT** at Voe; **GRIEVE HOUSE** at Whalsay; **WIND HOUSE LODGE** at Mid Yell; **VOE HOUSE** at Walls; **BETTY MOUAT'S COTTAGE** at Dunrossness; **JOHNNIE NOTIONS** at Eashaness. Remember to take sleeping mats. Check TIC for details.

CAMPING/CARAVAN: CLICKIMIN, LERWICK 01595 741000. **LEVENWICK** 01950 422207. **THE GARTHS, FETLA** 01957 733227. **WESTINGS, WHITENESS** 01595 840242.

WHERE TO EAT

BURRASTON HOUSE, WALLS and BUSTA HOUSE HOTEL, BRAE: (see above). The best meal in the islands.
MED

SUMBURGH HOTEL, SUMBURGH: (see above). The organically farmed smoked salmon 'possibly the best in the world' according to one local.
MED.INX

MONTY'S BISTRO, LERWICK: 01595 696555. Mounthooley St nr TIC. Renovated building in light Med décor. Best bet in town. Good service and quality menu using Shetland's finest ingredients. Bistro: Cl Sun/Mon. Lunch and LO 9pm.
TOS MED

Pub food also recommended at the following:

THE MID BRAE INN, BRAE: 32km N of Lerwick, 01806 522634. Lunch and supper till 8.45pm (9.30pm w/ends), 7 days. Big portions of the filling pub-grub variety. **THE MERRYFIELD HOTEL, BRESSAY:** 01595 820207. 5 mins ferry ride from Lerwick to Bressay. Better known for its seafood rather than accommodation, both bar and dining rm menus worth a look. LO are for those off the 8pm ferry. Don't miss the return ferry at 10.30pm Sun-Thurs and 12.45am, Fri & Sat. INX.MED

HAVLY, LERWICK: 01595 692100. 9 Charlotte St. Norwegian-style café with family-friendly atmos. Gr homemade soup, baking, waffles. Open Mon-Fri 10am-3pm, Sat 10am-4.45pm.

DA HAAF RESTAURANT, SCALLOWAY: 01595 880747. Part of the North Atlantic Fisheries College, Port Arthur. Basically a canteen but fresh Shetland seafood overlooking the harbour at reasonable prices more than makes up for the plastic trays and fluorescent lights. Lunch & LO 8pm. INX

SCALLOWAY FISH AND CHIP SHOP: New Rd, by the castle. Quite the freshest and best fish and chips in Shetland (if not Scotland, some say); can also sit in.

OSLA'S CAFE, LERWICK: 01595 696005. Mounthooly St, just up from Monty's. Best café. Incredibly good value. Cosy & very child-friendly. Art exhibitions on walls. Upstairs La Piazza is a good bet for supper. LO 9.30pm.

THE PEERIE SHOP CAFE, LERWICK: 01595 692817. A local delicacy!

WHAT TO SEE

MOUSA BROCH and **JARLSHOF** (1867/PREHISTORIC SITES), also **CLICKIMIN** broch. **OLD SCATNESS:** 01595 694688. A fascinating, award-winning excavation – site of one of the world's best-preserved Iron Age villages. Ongoing and accessible; climb the tower and witness the unearthing first-hand. Tours, demonstrations & exhibitions. 5 mins from airport. Open July-Aug only.

ST NINIAN'S ISLE, BIGTON: 8km N of Sumburgh on W Coast. An island linked by exquisite shell-sand. Hoard of Pictish silver found in 1958 (now in Edin). Beautiful, serene spot.

SCALLOWAY: 7km W of Lerwick, a township once the ancient capital of Shetland, dominated by the atmospheric ruins of Scalloway Castle.

SHETLAND WOOLLEN COMPANY is worth a rummage.

NOUP OF NOSS, ISLE OF NOSS, off BRESSAY: 8km W of Lerwick by frequent ferry and then boat (also direct from Lerwick 01595 692577 or via TIC), May-Sept only. National Nature Reserve with spectacular array of wildlife.

UP HELLY AA: Festival in Lerwick on the last Tuesday in Jan. Ritual with hundreds of torchbearers and much fire and firewater. Norse, northern and pagan. A wild time. Permanent exhibition at St Sunniva Street, Lerwick.

SEA RACES: The Boat Race every summer from Norway. Part of the largest North Sea international annual yacht race.

BONHOGA GALLERY & WEISDALE MILL: 01595 830400. Former grain mill housing Shetland's first purpose-built gallery. Café.

ISLAND TRAILS: Historic tours of Lerwick and the islands. Book through TIC or 01950 422408. Day trips, evening runs or short tours.

SWIMMING: at Clickimin Leisure Complex, Lerwick 01595 741000, Scalloway 01595 880745. Also at Unst, Yell, Brae, Whalsay, Aith and Sandwick. **GOLF RANGE:** at Moor Park, Gulberwick 01595 694959.

TOURIST INFO: 01595 693434.

SECTION 14

Local Centres

2346 ## WHERE TO STAY

MAP 2
E6

✓ **THE IVY HOUSE:** 01292 442336. 3km from centre on rd to Alloway. Small but v well-appointed establishment, more a superior restau with rms. Esp good bathrms. Serious chef (872/AYRSHIRE HOTELS).

5RMS JAN-DEC T/T PETS CC KIDS EXP

✓ **LOCHGREEN HOUSE:** 01292 313343. Monktonhall Rd, Troon 12km N on way in from Ayr. White seaside mansion nr famous golf courses of Troon (2079/GREAT GOLF). Elegant setting and décor; civilised wining and dining (875/AYRSHIRE HOTELS). 40RMS (7 IN COURTYARD) JAN-DEC T/T PETS CC KIDS EXP

✓ **SAVOY PARK:** 01292 266112. 16 Racecourse Rd. Period mansion run by the Hendersons for 40 yrs. V Scottish, v Ayrshire. Lovely grdn for summer b/fast (1322/SCOTTISH HOTELS). 15RMS JAN-DEC T/T PETS CC KIDS MED.INX

FAIRFIELD HOUSE: 01292 267461. Fairfield Rd. 1km centre on the front. Ostensibly the 'best' hotel in town. 'De luxe' facs incl pool/sauna/steam, conservatory brasserie and breakfast and notable (tho' only 1 AA rosette) Fleur de Lys restau. Only 3 rms have seaview. 44RMS JAN-DEC T/T PETS CC KIDS EXP

THE ELLISLAND: 01292 260111. 19 Racecourse Rd. On rd towards Alloway of many hotels (see Savoy Park, above). A recent makeover by the Costley group who have Lochgreen & Brig o' Doon (above). Reopening at TGP but expected to be excl. Reports please.

RAMADA JARVIS: 01292 269331. Dablair Rd. Centrally situated, best bedbox in town with facs incl pool. Café Le-to opposite (see below) for more charming meals. 118RMS JAN-DEC T/T PETS CC KIDS MED.INX

THE RICHMOND: 01292 265153. 38 Park Circus. Best of bunch in sedate terrace nr centre. John and Anne are nice folk.

6RMS JAN-DEC X/T XPETS XCC KIDS CHP

PIERSLAND, TROON: 01292 314747. 12km N of Ayr (874/AYRSHIRE HOTELS).

BRIG O'DOON, ALLOWAY: 01292 442466. 5km S of Ayr. Romantic, many weddings, few rms.

ENTERKINE HOUSE, ANNBANK: 01292 521608. 10km town centre across ring rd. Country house comforts (873/AYRSHIRE HOTELS).

WHERE TO EAT

Ayr is well served by the 5 places below which cover the range from seriously good food to trad Scottish caff cuisine. Look no further than:

✓ **FOUTERS:** 01292 261391. 2 Academy St (879/AYRSHIRE RESTAUS). The best in town.

✓ **IVY HOUSE:** 01292 442336. Restau of hotel above 845/AYRSHIRE RESTAUS. The best just outside town. Also **CAFÉ IVY** for lighter meals.

✓ **THE HUNNY POT:** 37 Beresford Terr. 01292 263239. Wholemeal-slanted, kid-friendly, GM-free café – good home baking and light meals. Mon-Sat 9am-10pm, Sun 10.30am-9pm.

THE STABLES: 41 Sandgate, downtown location in courtyard of shops. Coffee shop/bistro with wine bar ambience and enlightened attitude. Imaginative Scottish menu. Good teas, good beers. No smk rm. Till 5pm. Cl Sun. INX

✓ **THE TUDOR RESTAURANT:** 8 Beresford St. Superb caff. They don't make 'em like this any more! Till 8pm. Report: 1487/TEAROOMS.

THE REST ...

CECCHINI'S: 01292 317171. 72 Fort St (also in Troon at 72 Fort St). Excl Italian & Med restau run by the estimable Cecchini family. Mon-Sat, lunch & LO 10pm.

PIERRINO'S: 01292 269087. Alloway Pl. The other credible Italian. LO 10pm.

INX

CAFÉ LE-TO: 01292 288598. Dablair Rd opp Ramada Jarvis hotel. Good contemp café/restau with Italian emphasis & local rep. 7 days, LO 9pm/10pm. INX

ELLIOTS, PRESTWICK: 01292 677677. 132 Main Rd (the main rd). All-purpose bar/restau/diner with sports TV, ladies who lunch, nights of white satin. Part of local chain but not bad at all. 7 days till late.

MANCINI'S, AYR: Ice-cream & a' that. 1533/ICE CREAM.

WHAT TO SEE

CULZEAN (1825/CASTLES); **HEADS OF AYR** (1722/SCENIC ROUTES) and **THE ELECTRIC BRAE** nr (3km S Dunure on the A719); **BURNS HERITAGE TRAIL** (1976/LITERARY PLACES); **GAILES/TROON/PRESTWICK/TURNBERRY/BELLE-ISLE** (see GREAT GOLF, p. 260); **MAGNUM, IRVINE** (2125/LEISURE CENTRES); **KIDZ PLAY** (1773/KIDS); **BURNS 'N' A' THAT** (21/EVENTS).

WHAT TO DO

SWIMMING: V good pool complex at Beach Harbour Rd (01292 269793), and at Prestwick, off the road in from Ayr (01292 474015). **RIDING:** Ayrshire Equitation Centre, all standards, country setting. Book! 01292 266267. **TENNIS:** Good all-weather courts at Citadel Pl and Craigie Av near Craigie Park. Just turn up.

TOURIST OFFICE: 22 Sandgate. 01292 678100. Jan-Dec.

THE BEST OF DUMFRIES

2347 **WHERE TO STAY**

MAP 1
D2

CAIRNDALE: 01387 254111. Surprising spa concealed within this corporate friendly old faithful; conference centre now being added. Visiting somebodies stay here. Café is popular lunch venue for all sorts.
91RMS JAN-DEC T/T PETS CC KIDS EXP

STATION HOTEL: 01387 254316. 49 Lovers' Walk. The best all-round business/tourist hotel in town with decent upgrading of the trad stn-hotel elegance and ambience (from 1896); central and often full. 'Bistro' as well as dining-rm.
32RMS JAN-DEC T/T PETS CC KIDS MED.EX

ABBEY ARMS 01387 850489 (862/SW HOTELS). **CRIFFEL INN** 01387 850305 both in **NEW ABBEY** 12 km S of Dumfries A710. 2 gr pubs on either side of the green in this lovely wee vill where Sweetheart Abbey is the main attraction (1952/ABBEYS). 4/5RMS JAN-DEC X/T PETS CC KIDS INX

EDENBANK: 01387 252759. Reasonably priced place on Laurieknowe (main rd to Dalbeattie going SW) nr centre. Also handy for the football for those having nightmares on Terregles St. 10RMS JAN-DEC T/T PETS CC KIDS INX

No SYH, Dumfries College accom: ask at TIC.

WHERE TO EAT

PIZZERIA IL FIUME: 01387 265154. In Dock Park nr St Michael's Br, underneath Riverside pub. Usual Italian menu but gr pizzas and cosy tratt atmos. 5.30-10pm daily. INX

BENVENUTO: 01387 259890. 42 Eastfield Rd, off Brooms Rd – follow signs for Cresswell Maternity Hospital. Sort of surreal wooden hut setting next to owner's chippy. 5pm-late. Tues-Sun. INX

BRUNO'S: 01387 255757. 3 Balmoral Rd, off Annan Rd. Well-established Italian eaterie beside **BALMORAL** chippy (1470/FISH AND CHIPS). 6-10pm, Cl Tue. INX

MA-DONNA'S: 01387 253876. Lane beside Theatre Royal. Informal atmos, food, drink & poss a bit of a knees-up. Owners Mark & Donna (geddit?) used to be at the estimable Anchor at Kippford. INX

HULLABALOO: 01387 259679. At Robert Burns Centre which also houses local art-house cinema. Contemporary pasta/wrap/burger kind of place –

good though. Opens from 11am for coffee, then lunch, then dinner. Daily in summer, Tues-Sat winter. LO depend on movie times. INX

THE OLD BANK: 01387 253499. Snacks in converted bank. Very old-school, but lovely cakes. INX

WHAT TO SEE

ROCKCLIFFE (1639/COASTAL VILLAGES); **ROCKCLIFFE TO KIPPFORD** (2071/COASTAL WALKS); **SOUTHERNESS** (2100/GOLF IN GREAT PLACES); **SWEETHEART ABBEY** (1952/ABBEYS); **CRIFFEL** (2000/HILLS); **CAERLAVEROCK** (1793/BIRDS); **CAERLAVE-ROCK CASTLE** (1844/RUINS); **ELLISLAND FARM** (1976/LITERARY PLACES). **GARDENS** (all off A75): **CASTLE KENNEDY GARDENS** 75 acres laid out around 2 acre lily pond, 2 lochs; rare species. Apr-Sep 10am-5pm. **GLENWHAN GARDENS, DUNRAGIT** enchanting 12 acre hill side, tamed and lovingly hewn into lush overflowing haven. Gr views and walks. Apr-Oct 10am-5pm. **THREAVE GARDEN, nr CASTLE DOUGLAS** for all seasons. AYR 9.30am-sunset.

WHAT TO DO

SWIMMING: Modern pool on river side nr Buccleuch St Br (01387 252908); **GOLF:** Southerness 25km S on A710 or Powfoot, 20km SW on B724 (01461 700276); **RIDING:** Barend at Sandyhills on 34km S on A710 (01387 780533).

TOURIST OFFICE: Whitesands. 01387 253862. Jan-Dec.

THE BEST OF DUNFERMLINE AND KIRKCALDY

2348 ## WHERE TO STAY

MAP 3
C4 **KEAVIL HOUSE HOTEL, CROSSFORD, DUNFERMLINE:** 01383 736258. 3km W of Dunfermline on A994 towards Culross (1636/COASTAL VILLAGES) and Kincardine. Rambling mansion house in grounds within a suburban area of town, converted into modern business-type hotel with all facs incl separate leisure club (not bad pool). Best Western.

47RMS JAN-DEC T/T PETS CC KIDS MED.EX

DUNNIKIER HOUSE, KIRKCALDY: 01592 268393. 3 km centre in parkland area. Prob the only half-decent hotel hereabouts but not exp. We can say no more. 15RMS JAN-DEC T/T PETS CC KIDS TOS MED.INX

STRATHEARN HOTEL, KIRKCALDY: 01592 652210. Forget the 2 'business' hotels, the Dean Park and the Parkway. This hotel on Wishart Pl opp Ravenscraig Park on coast rd and main rd E from town, about 3km from centre may suffice. Ravenscraig is a beautiful coastal park for respite.

18RMS JAN-DEC T/T PETS CC KIDS MED.EX

THE BELVEDERE, W WEMYSS, nr KIRKCALDY: 01592 654167. However, this is worth the 8km trek E of town via A955 coast rd. At beginning of neat village, a curious mixture of dereliction and conservation. Views of bay and Kirkcaldy from comfortable rms in cottages and on the seafront, all white and with red-tiled roofs. Harmless pictures, decent menu.

21RMS JAN-DEC T/T PETS CC KIDS MED.INX

No hostels (Burgh Lodge, Falkland, is miles away, but good; 1250/HOSTELS).

WHERE TO EAT IN AND AROUND DUNFERMLINE

TOWNHOUSE: 01383 432382. 48 East Port in centre. This is the credible restau in Dunfermline by the youngest of the Brown family who run the Bouzy Rouges (565/GLAS) & the Roman Camp (907/CENTRAL HOTS), so they know what they're doing. Light, modern feel to room & menu. Open all day 12-LO9.30pm. Lunch, dinner or just grazing. Best in town no doubt. MED

IL PESCATORE, LIMEKILNS: 01383 872999. 7km from town via B9156 or to Rosyth, then Charlestown. Local favourite and the best pasta etc around. Now has 6 inexp rms above. Good for birthdays or a stroll after dinner. 7 days, LO 11pm. INX

LUIGI'S: 01383 726666. Entrance of Kingsgate mall on Douglas St. The local choice for standard Italian fare. Cl Mon. Fri-Sun lunch, Tues-Sun dinner LO 11pm. INX

NOODLE BAR: 01383 624222. 41 Carnegie Drive. Recently opened at TGP so looks fresh. Noodles & other Chinese staples. 7 days LO 10.30-11pm. INX

WHERE TO EAT IN AND AROUND KIRKCALDY

THE OLD RECTORY, DYSART: 01592 651211. 5km E (980/FIFE RESTAUS).

LA GONDOLA: 640085. N Harbour. The best Italian with live Enzo on Suns. INX

FEUARS ARMS: 205025. 66 Commercial St. V good pub food west of town nr high flats. Best in town for informal meal and atmos. Lunch and dinner w/ends. INX

BAR ITZD: 01592 204257. Main St E end. Café-bar with Tex–Mex menu & accoutrements. May date rapidly (may not). 7 days. LO 9.30pm. INX

MAXIN: 01592 263406. 5 High St at the W end. The best Chinese. 7days. INX

VALENTE'S: 01592 205774. Not sit-in, but *absolutely the best* fish and chips. Take them to Ravenscraig Park nearby, walk along the coves. 2 branches. Report: 1457/FISH 'N' CHIPS.

WHAT TO SEE

ABBOT HOUSE, DUNFERMLINE (2249/MUSEUMS); **PITTENCRIEFF & RAVEN-SCRAIG PARKS, DUNFERMLINE** (1625/TOWN PARKS) and **BEVERIDGE PARK, KIRKCALDY** (1626/TOWN PARKS); **CARNEGIE CENTRE, DUNFERMLINE** (2136/SWIMMING POOLS); **DUNFERMLINE ABBEY** (1974/MARY, CHARLIE AND BOB); **KIRKCALDY ART GALLERY** (2276/PUBLIC GALLERIES); **PILLANS, KIRK-CALDY** (1529/BAKERS); **BETTY NICOL'S** (1398/REAL ALES).

WHAT TO DO

SWIMMING/INDOOR SPORTS: *As above.* **GOLF:** Kirkcaldy is nr some of the best (see Golf, p. 260). **TENNIS:** Both towns have municipal and private courts. Check TIC.

TOURIST OFFICES

DUNFERMLINE: 1 High Street. 01383 720999. Jan-Dec.

KIRKCALDY: 19 White's Causeway. 01592 267775. Jan-Dec.

THE BEST OF FORT WILLIAM

WHERE TO STAY

MAP 2
D1

✓ ✓ **INVERLOCHY CASTLE:** 01397 702177. 5km out on A82 Inverness rd. One of Scotland's gr hotels. Victorian elegance recently refurb & impeccable service. 1040/HIGHLANDS HOTELS. 17RMS JAN-DEC T/T XPETS CC KIDS LOTS

✓ **LIME TREE STUDIOS:** 01397 701806. Achintore rd as you come in along the loch from S, last 'hotel' of many almost at end of main st. Unassuming, but at TGP all about to change – major refurb into regional art-gallery space, but still rms above. These are prob the best inx rms in town.
5(+5NEW)RMS JAN-DEC X/X XPETS CC XKIDS INX

GLENLOY LODGE, NORTH OF BANAVIE: 01397 712700. The Haynes' rather splendid hideaway up the Caledonian Canal at Glen Loy. 1920s lodge house with cared-for grounds, occ pine martens, and sense of peace. Non-res can dine, and they do – but you'll want to stay. Pat cooks, Gordon does the cheese and excl value wine (Dinner MED). 7RMS DEC-OCT X/X XPETS CC KIDS TOS MED.EX

THE MOORINGS: 01397 772797. Banavie (follow signs), 5km out on A830 Corpach/Mallaig rd. O/look the Caledonian canal by 'Neptune's Staircase'. Good location, ok dining-rm (1 AA rosette).
29RMS JAN-DEC T/T PETS CC KIDS TOS MED.INX

HIGHLAND HOTEL: 01397 702291. Union Rd. High above town (best place to be), with gr views esp when you walk out the front door to the terraced lawns. Rms basic but foyer has character. Conveyor belt to the Highlands, but you may find untrendy tackiness charming. Very old school.
110RMS MAR-DEC X/T PETS CC KIDS MED.INX

ONICH HOTEL: 01855 821214. At Onich 16km S on A82. Loch side; good value (1056/HIGHLANDS HOTELS).

LODGE ON THE LOCH: 01855 821237. In Onich, quite stylish peace and quiet (1055/HIGHLAND HOTELS).

S.Y. HOSTEL at GLEN NEVIS: 01397 702336. 5km from town by picturesque but busy Glen Nevis rd. The Ben is above. Grade 1. Fax poss. Many other hostels in area (ask at TIC for list) but esp **FW BACKPACKERS:** 01397 700711, Alma Rd.

ACHINTEE FARM: 01397 702240. On app to Ben Nevis main route & adj Ben Nevis Inn (see below). GH/self/c & bunkhouse. A walkers' haven.

CAMPING/CARAVAN SITE, GLEN NEVIS: 01397 702191. Nr hostel. Well-run site, mainly caravans (also for rent). Many facs incl restaus and much going on.

WHERE TO EAT

✓ ✓ **INVERLOCHY** (as above): 3 AA rosettes. Best for miles.

✓ **CRANNOG:** 01397 705589. On loch front. Seafood (1451/SEAFOOD RESTAUS).

THE MOORINGS: 01397 772797. 5km by A830. (*See above.*)

FACTOR HOUSE: 01397 701420. At entrance to Inverlochy on A82, 5km centre. New bar/restau under same management at TGP augurs well for Fort W.

No 4: 01397 704222. Cameron Sq behind the TIC. Best bet in main st area. Mixed reviews followed high initial expectations. Reports please! À la carte and daily specials. Lunch and LO 9.30pm. Daily in season, cl Sun in winter. MED

AN CRANN, BANAVIE: 01397 772077. 7km centre via Mallaig rd & signed at Banavie. A local favourite, this stone barn nestling in countryside offers eclectic mix. V Scottish, v friendly. Gr atmos. Easter-Oct: 5-9pm Mon-Sat; phone first. INX

CAFÉ BEAG, GLEN NEVIS: 01397 703601. 5km along Glen Nevis rd; past VC. Alpine-looking cabin, cosy atmos; open fires, books, games. Restau, bar & coffee-stop. May-Oct till 6pm (9pm Jun-Aug). INX

CAFÉ CHARDON: Coffee shop upstairs at Peter Maclennan's well-kent emporium in the main st (or access via side lane). The auld alliance continues here with pastry thingies and snacks in unsurprising rm. Mon-Sat 9-4.30pm. CHP

BEN NEVIS INN at ACHINTEE: On main app to the Ben iself. Reach across river by footbridge from VC or by rd on rt after Inverlochy/Glen Nevis r/bout on A82 (3km). Excl atmos inn in converted farm building. Good grub/ale & walking chat. LO 9pm. Cl wint.

WHAT TO SEE

Most of the good things about Ft William are outside the town, but these incl some v big items esp the Ben and the Glens (Glens Nevis as well as Coe):

GLENCOE: 30km S (1704/SCENIC ROUTES; 2032/SERIOUS WALKS; 1957/BATTLE-GROUNDS); **GLEN NEVIS** (1667/GLENS); **BEN NEVIS:** 6km E on Glen Nevis rd (2033/SERIOUS WALKS); **WEST HIGHLAND WAY** (2026/LONG WALKS); **STEALL FALLS**, Glen Nevis (1683/WATERFALLS); **GLENCOE SKIING** (2118/SKIING); **AONACH MOR SKIING** (2117/SKIING) **MUSEUM** (2256/MUSEUMS). **NEVIS RANGE GONDOLA:** Aonach Mor (*see below*), open AYR, is a big attraction. Go up for the incredible view and the air and the Ben over there. **MOUNTAIN BIKE WORLD CUP/BEN NEVIS RACE** (23/EVENTS).

WHAT TO DO

GOLF: Ft William Golf Club (01397 704464). 5km towards Inverness on A82; **SWIMMING/SPORTS:** Lochaber Centre (01397 704 359). Beyond main st and Alexandra Hotel. Squash, sauna, 2 gyms, climbing wall, swimming (with flume). **TENNIS:** One court at Lochaber Centre, free of charge. **SKIING:** Aonach Mor (01397 705825). 12km via A82. Scotland's most modern ski resort (2117/SKIING). Gondola goes up in summer for the view. **BIKE HIRE:** Off-Beat Bikes (01397 704008). Main St and ski base stn.

> **TOURIST OFFICE:** Cameron Square. 01397 703781. Jan-Dec.

THE BEST OF THE BORDER TOWNS

2350
MAP 3
WHERE TO STAY

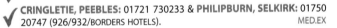 **ROXBURGHE HOTEL, KELSO:** 01573 450331 (925/BORDERS HOTELS).
LOTS

✓ **BURTS, MELROSE:** 01896 822285 (927/BORDERS HOTELS). MED.EX

✓ **CRINGLETIE, PEEBLES:** 01721 730233 & **PHILIPBURN, SELKIRK:** 01750 20747 (926/932/BORDERS HOTELS). MED.EX

✓ **EDENWATER, EDNAM, nr KELSO:** 01573 224070 (928/BORDERS HOTELS).
MED.EX

✓ **CLINT LODGE nr ST BOSWELLS:** 01835 822027 (935/BORDERS HOTELS). INX

✓ **FAUHOPE, GATTONSIDE:** 01896 823184 (938/BORDERS HOTELS). INX

✓ **CADDON VIEW, INNERLEITHEN:** 01896 830208 (937/BORDERS HOTELS).
MED.INX

CHURCHES, EYEMOUTH: 01890 750401 (929/BORDERS HOTELS). MED.EX

WOODLANDS, GALA: 01896 754722. Windyknowe Rd off A7 in Edin direction, A72 to Peebles. Substantial mansion above town centre with elegant hall, spacious public rms and local reputation for food and service.
10RMS JAN-DEC T/T PETS CC KID MED.EX

JEDFOREST COUNTRY HOTEL, JEDBURGH: 01835 840222 (933/BORDERS HOTELS).

EDNAM HOUSE HOTEL, KELSO: 01573 224168 (934/BORDERS HOTELS).

DRYBURGH ABBEY HOTEL nr ST BOSWELLS: 01835 822261 (931/BORDERS HOTELS).

HUNDALEE HOUSE, JEDBURGH: 01835 863011. 1km S. Jedburgh off A68. Lovely 1700 manor house in 10 acre gdn. Brilliant value, gr base, views of

Cheviot hills. Nr the famously old Capon Tree.

5RMS MAR-OCT X/T XPETS XCC KIDS CHP

GLEN HOTEL and HEATHERLIE HOTEL, SELKIRK: 01750 20259/21200. Both family-run hotels in manor houses with views over town. Well-run, dependable. Selkirk makes a good touring centre.

8/7RMS JAN-DEC T/T X/T PETS/XPETS CC KIDS INX

S.Y. HOSTELS: V good in this area (1237/HOSTELS).

WHERE TO EAT

✓ **MARMIONS, MELROSE:** 01896 822245 (939/BORDERS HOTELS).

✓ **CRINGLETIE, PEEBLES:** 01721 730233 (926/BORDERS HOTELS); **PHILIP-BURN, SELKIRK:** 01750 20747 (932/BORDERS HOTELS); **EDENWATER, EDNAM, nr KELSO:** 01573 224070 (928/BORDERS HOTELS).

✓ **ROXBURGHE HOTEL and FAIRWAYS:** Adj brasserie in the clubhouse o/look the course (Fri/Sat only, dinner: 01573 450331). 925/BORDERS HOTELS

✓ **BURT'S HOTEL, MELROSE and KING'S ARMS:** (927/BORDER HOTELS) Local faves (940/BORDERS HOTELS).

✓ **AULD CROSS KEYS, DENHOLM:** 01450 870305; **HORSESHOE INN, nr PEEBLES:** 01721 730225; **WHEATSHEAF, SWINTON:** 01890 860257 (1421/1420/1401 PUB FOOD). **CRAW INN, AUCHENCROW:** 01890 761253 (1269/ROADSIDE INNS).

✓ **CHAPTERS, nr MELROSE:** 01896 823217 (941/BORDERS RESTAUS).

LAZELS, PEEBLES: 01721 720602 (1224/HOTELS THAT WELCOME KIDS).

SUD ITALIA, GALASHIELS: 01896 750007. Reasonable Med option in downtown Gala. Nice people. Lunch and LO 9.30/10pm. Cl Tues & Sun lunch.

BRYDONS, HAWICK: 01450 372672. 16 High St. Once Brydons were bakers, now they have this oddly funky family caff-cum-restau. Home cooking, good folk – this is a totally Hawick experience. All day and dinner Fri/Sat.

LE BISTRO, DENHOLM: 01450 870530. Corner of the green on rd from Hawick. Pop local choice (tho Hawick is bereft), antiques & art adj. Lunch & dinner Fri/Sat.

HERGÉ'S BAR BISTRO, GALASHIELS: 01896 750400. 58 Island St on rd to Peebles. Wine-bar ambience, locals rate it. Sat night-pub only. Lunch and 6-9pm. Cl Mon.

OBLO'S, EYEMOUTH: 01890 752527. Italian plus good vegn. Glossy & fun. All day till late (1469/FISH AND CHIPS).

WHAT TO SEE

THIRLESTANE CASTLE, LAUDER (1895/COUNTRY HOUSES); **TWEED FISHING** (see below); **PENIEL HEUGH** (1903/MONUMENTS); **MARY QUEEN OF SCOTS' HOUSE** (1963/MARY, CHARLIE AND BOB); **ANCRUM** (1941/GRAVEYARDS; 1755/PICNICS); **ABBEYS** (1949/JEDBURGH; 1950/DRYBURGH; 1953/MELROSE); **PRIORWOOD** (1603/GARDENS); **ABBOTSFORD** (1980/LITERARY PLACES); **EILDON HILLS** (2011/HILL WALKS); **RUBERSLAW** (2003/HILLS); **SCOTT'S VIEW/IRVINE'S VIEW** (1731/1732/VIEWS); **LILLIARD'S EDGE** (1959/BATTLEGROUNDS); **LOCHCARRON** and **CHAS WHILLANS** (2224/2225/WOOLLIES).

WHAT TO DO

SWIMMING: V good leisure facs both in and around Hawick and Galashiels. Galashiels Pool (01896 752154) at Livingston Pl up the hill from the one-way main st is excellent (2003/SWIMMING POOLS). Hawick's Teviotdale Leisure Centre (01450 374440) has squash courts, a gym (Universal) and a pool with fun stuff as well as lane swimming. Jedburgh and Selkirk also have pools. **GOLF:** Good courses at Minto, nr Denholm (01450 870220) (18); Selkirk (01750 20621) (9); Melrose (01896 822855) (9); Hawick (01450 372293) (18); Jedburgh (01835 863587) (9). All picturesque, in fair condition, available to visitors.

RIDING: Cowdenknowes, Earlston (01896 848020). Kailzie Stables nr Peebles. **TENNIS:** Galshiels, Abbotsford Terr; Hawick, Wilton Lodge Park; also Melrose. **CYCLE HIRE:** Galashiels, 58 High St (01896 757587); Hawick, 45 N Br St (01450 373352); Peebles, 3 High St (01721 720844). **FISHING:** There can be last-minute vacancies even on the famous Tweed. Tweed Foundation (01896 848271); J Leeming's independent agency (01573 470280). Tackle: Angler's Choice, Melrose (01896 823070); Tweedside Tackle, Kelso (01573 225306).

TOURIST INFORMATION:

JEDBURGH: Murray's Green. 01835 863435. Jan-Dec. **GALASHIELS:** 01896 755551. Apr-Oct; **HAWICK:** Common Ground. 01450 372547. Apr-Oct; **MELROSE:** Adj Abbey. 01896 822555.

THE BEST OF OBAN

2351
MAP 2
D2
WHERE TO STAY

✓ **CALEDONIAN HOTEL:** 0871 222 3415. Lashings of money & style spent on this refurbed seafront hotel. Can't beat the captain's rooms – comfort & urban facs. Restau & café.   59RMS JAN-DEC T/T PETS CC KIDS EXP

✓ **MANOR HOUSE:** 01631 562087. Gallanach Rd. On S coast rd out of town towards Kerrera ferry, o/look bay. Quiet elegance in contemp style, and a restau that serves (in an intimate dining-rm) prob the most 'fine-dining' dinner in town. Bedrms also prob the cosiest, but the competition ain't great. More delightful than de-luxe. Nice bar.   11RMS JAN-DEC T/T PETS CC KIDS EXP

✓ **DUN NA MARA, BENDERLOCH:** 01631 720233. Off main A828 Oban-Ft William rd at Benderloch 12km n of Oban. Gorgeous setting with beach adj for fab contemp conversion of seaside mansion. This place prob deserves a tick or two but we haven't stayed at TGP.   7RMS JAN-DEC X/T XPETS CC KIDS MED.INX

✓ **BARRIEMORE HOTEL:** 01631 566356. Corran Esplanade. The last in a long sweep of hotels to N of centre and streets above the rest. Nice people in residence, gr view of the sea. New restau so now do dinner (864/ARGYLL HOTELS).   13RMS MAR-OCT X/T PETS CC KIDS INX

GLENBURNIE HOTEL: 01631 562089. Corran Esplanade. And this one is also good. Run by the inimitable Strachan family, tea & shortbread on arrival.   14 RMS MAR-OCT X/T PETS CC KIDS MED.EX

CLACHNAHARRY INN: Rd in from W (2km centre). Report: 1395/REAL ALE.

S.Y. HOSTEL: 01631 562025. On Esplanade (i.e. on the front).

WHERE TO EAT

✓ **EE-USK, FISH CAFÉ:** 01631 565666. North Pier. Brand new seafd wine bar & restau – steel, glass, stripped wood. Sophisticated surroudings for yachties, trippers & locals in new pierfront development. The Macleods have moved this excl fish place from previous space. This *is* glam & fish to die for. The name is the phonetic pron of the gaelic for 'fish'. 7 days, LO 10pm.   MED

✓ **THE WATERFRONT AT THE PIER:** 01631 563110. In the port, by the station, an old favourite that's serious about seafood. 'From pier to pan' is about right. Blackboard menu & monkfish à la carte. 2 AA rosettes are well-deserved served in clean, airy upstairs rm. Open L and LO 9pm ish, Mar-Dec.   MED

THE MANOR HOUSE: (*see above*). The best hotel dining-rm in town. Creative sauces on fresh seafood and other good things. Booking essential.   EXP

SIRLOIN: 01631 569900. 1004 George St, the main st E of the bay. Was Ee-Usk (see above) but now a char-grill steakhouse. Owned by ubiquitous local entrepreneurs the Macleods. All locally sources meats & established rep to maintain. Stylish, laid-back & gr staff. 7 days LO 10pm.   INX

JULIE'S COFFEE HOUSE: 01631 565952. 33 Stafford St opp Oban Whisky Visitor Centre. Only 6 tables, so fills up. Nice approach to food (snacky, but hot dishes) & customers. Ice-cream from Luca's (the best, so some discernment here). 7 days 10.30am-5pm, Sun 12-4.30pm.   INX

THE STUDIO: 01631 562030. Craigard Rd off main st at Balmoral Hotel. Up the hill to find this here forever, candle-lit restau. Way beyond time for a makeover but who needs it? Surprising menu. Often have to book. Apr-Oct, 5-10pm.INX

THE KITCHEN GARDEN: 01631 566332. 14 George St. Deli-café that's often busy & you may have to queue to go upstairs to the small gallery caff. Not a bad cup of coffee & ciabatta sandwich. Aimed at local gastros & visiting yachties – everything Ratty reckoned was necessary for a picnic or just messing about in boats. Gt rare whiskies, fresh-squeezed OJ. Deli heaven. 7 days 9am-5.30pm (Suns 11-4pm).

CAFÉ NA LUSAN: 01631 567268. 9 Craigard Rd nr The Studio (*above*). Well it says it's 'simple, relaxed, friendly' & all this is true. Organic & internet kind of caff we like. Excl salads. (Cherry Records for rare grooves downstairs). 7 days 11.30am-9.30pm (till 3.30 Sun/Mon). INX

WHAT TO SEE

DUNOLLIE CASTLE: On rd to Ganavan (1853/RUINS); **GLEN LONAN:** Gr wee glen starting 8km out of town (1672/GLENS); **SEALIFE CENTRE:** 16km N on A28 (1788/KIDS); **RARE BREEDS FARM:** 4km S from Argyll Sq (1789/KIDS); **OBAN INN:** (*see* WHISKY, *p. 193*); **McCAIG'S TOWER or FOLLY:** You can't miss it, dominating the skyline. A circular granite coliseum. Superb views of the bay. Many ways up, but a good place to start is via Stevenson St, opp Cally Hotel. Free, Open AYR (1907/MONUMENTS). **KERRERA:** The island in the Sound reached by regular ferry from coast rd to Gallanach (4km town). Ferries at set times, but several per day – check TIC. A fine wee island for walking, pack your lunch but look for the tea gdn. **LISMORE:** The other, larger island (2305/MAGICAL ISLANDS). Ferry from Oban (Calmac) or Pt Appin (passengers only). **DUNSTAFFNAGE CASTLE:** Signed and visible off A85 betw Oban and Connel (7km). 13th-century. V early type of castle, more of a ft, really. Unoccupied, except for the odd Clan McDougall spectre rattling around in the dungeons. Pity about the post-industrial approach rd, but there is a chapel in the woods. **ARDCHATTAN:** 20km N via Connel. Along N shore of L Etive, a place to wander amongst ruins and gdns. Tearoom. If you're along that way, go to the end of the rd at Bonawe where the famous granite that cobbled the world was (and still is) quarried. Ironworks open as a museum is a tranquil place (2265/MUSEUMS).

WHAT TO DO

GOLF: Glencruitten (01631 562868) (2103/GOLF IN GREAT PLACES); **SWIMMING:** Atlantis Leisure Centre at Dalriach Rd (01631 566800); **PONY-TREKKING:** Achnalarig Farm, Glencruitten (01631 562745); **WINDSURFING:** Linnhe Marine (01631 730227), 32km N via A828. (2008/WATER SPORTS); **FISHING:** Plenty on lochs and R Awe and Avich – check TIC; **BIKE HIRE:** Hazelbank Cycles (01631 566476).

TOURIST INFO: Argyll Sq. 01631 563122. Jan-Dec.

THE BEST OF PERTH

WHERE TO STAY

✓ **BALLATHIE HOUSE, KINCLAVEN:** 01250 883268. 20km N of Perth via Blairgowrie rd A93/left follow signs after 16km just before the famous beech hedge; or A9 and 4km N, take B9000 through Stanley. Former baronial hunting lodge beside the R Tay. Relaxed and informal atmos in definitive country house. New riverside rms. Kevin MacGillivray's award-winning food. Fishing by arrangement with Estate office.

42RMS JAN-DEC T/T PETS CC KIDS TOS LOTS

✓ **KINFAUNS CASTLE:** 01738 620777. A90 main Dundee Rd, 10 mins Perth centre in lofty country setting. Magnificent building, well refurb and decent dining.

16RMS FEB-DEC T/T PETS CC LOTS

HUNTINGTOWER HOTEL: 01738 583771. Crieff rd (1km off A85, 3km W of ring route A9 signed). Elegant, modernised mansion house o/side town. Good gdns with spectacular copper beech. Subdued, panelled restau with decent menu (esp lunch) and wine list. Business-like service.

34RMS JAN-DEC T/T PETS CC KIDS TOS MED.EX

ROYAL GEORGE: 01738 624455. Tay St by the Perth Br over the Tay to the A93 rd to Blairgowrie and relatively close to Dundee rd and motorway system. Br is illuminated at night. Georgian proportions and some faded elegance – last visit, we saw real Chelsea Pensioners. Mums and farmers and visiting clergy seem happy here.

39RMS JAN-DEC T/T PETS CC KIDS MED.EX

WHERE TO EAT

✓ **LET'S EAT:** 01738 643377. 77 Kinnoull St. The place to eat (1002/PERTHSHIRE RESTAUS).

✓ **63 TAY STREET:** 01738 441451. 63 Tay St on riverside. Seriously good bistro. Report: (1003/PERTHSHIRE EATS).

KERACHER'S: 01738 449777. Corner of South St and Scott St. Seafood corner restau run by notable local supplier. Downstairs lounge and upstairs bistro style dining. Excl ingredients and service. Cl Mon. Lunch and LO 9.30/10pm.

INX(BAR)/MED

METZO: 01738 626016. 33 George St. Very plush bistro-style newcomer & très cosmopolitan. Bit of a local favourite. Lunch & dinner daily, LO 9.30pm (10pm Fri).

INX

EXCEED: 01738 626000. 65 Main St in Bridgend, on the N side of the Tay. Very suave, very classic Franco-Scottish eats in unlikely location. Long may they thrive. Mon-Sat, lunch and LO 10pm

INX

KRUNGTHAI: 01738 633090. 161 South St. Authentic fare offered by Thai owner/chef has earned good local rep but many curries (and was that a paratha?). Open late daily, lunch Tues-Sat only.

INX

PACO'S: 01738 622290. Now a bit mega. Still the happy burger 'n' pasta 'n' Mex restau in Mill St (behind M&S) but also a newer café on St John's Place by the city hall & church (daily until 7pm, 5pm Sun). Young atmos in both, LO in restau 11pm.

INX

THAT BAR (THE LOFT): 01738 634523. 147 South St. Perthshire trendy, designery bar (with pool table & big TV). Predictable food upstairs. Somewhere to watch more TV.

INX

MARCELLO'S: 143 South St. Pizza pasta pitstop. Takeaway only. Noon-11pm (midnight Fri/Sat). Good looking guys knead the dough.

INX

DELI-CIOUS: 46 Methven St. Small, cheery take-away and sit-in coffee shop. Some hot dishes. Excl sandwiches. 7.30am – evening, Suns 11am-7pm.

INX

HOLDGATE'S FISH TEAS: South St. A classic!

INX

CONCERTO'S: 8-10 North Port. 01738 443000. Formerly '1774', this is now a smart bistro whose name anticipates the opening of the new concert hall in late '04. Very 'Perth'. Lunch & dinner daily.

CAFFÈ CANTO: 62-64 George St. Handy for a quick focaccia & a glass of wine. Daily until 5pm (5.30pm Sat).

OLD SHIP INN: Skinnergate (off High St). Here for the beer. A traditional-style wee howf with some real ales – a good escape from retail Perth.

WHAT TO SEE

KINNOULL HILL (2007/HILLS); **FERGUSSON GALLERY** (2275/PUBLIC GALLERIES); **GLENDOICK** (2231/GARDEN CENTRES).

BELL'S CHERRYBANK CENTRE/BRANKLYN GARDENS: Cherrybank is off Glasgow Rd, 18 acres of formal gdns around the offices of the whisky company, notable esp for heathers. Open May-Sept 10am-5pm (Sun 12-5pm). Branklyn is signed off Dundee Rd beyond Queen's Br; park and walk 100m. A tightly packed cornucopia of typical gdn flowers & shrubs. Open Mar-Oct 7 days 9.30am-6pm.

PERTH THEATRE: 01738 621031. Established 1935 and Scotland's most successful repertory theatre (Ewan MacGregor got his first break here). Bar/coffee bar and restau. Essential all-round centre even for non-theatregoers.

WHAT TO DO

SWIMMING: Excellent large leisure centre with flumes pool and 'training' pool for lengths. Part of it is outdoors. Best app via Glasgow Rd (01738 492410) (2122/LEISURE CENTRES). **SPORTS CENTRE:** The Gannochy or 'Bells' Complex for multigym (Universal), squash (5 courts), badminton etc. Hay St off Barrack St (01738 622301). **GOLF:** Interesting course on Moncreiffe Island in the middle of the Tay (01738 625170). Officially known as the King James VI Golf Club. Excellent course at Blairgowrie (01250 872622) (2101/GOLF IN GREAT PLACES).

TOURIST INFO: Lower City Mills. 01738 450600. Jan-Dec.

THE BEST OF STIRLING

2353
MAP 3
B4

WHERE TO STAY

✓ **STIRLING HIGHLAND:** 01786 475444 (909/CENTRAL HOTELS).

✓ **QUEENS HOTEL, BRIDGE OF ALLAN:** 01786 833268. 7km Stirling Centre (910/CENTRAL HOTELS).

✓ **BOUZY ROUGE at the SHERIFFMUIR INN:** 01786 823285. 15km Bridge of Allan. Only 4 rms but stylish stopover in empty countryside (908/CENTRAL HOTELS).

PARK LODGE: 01786 474862. 32 Park Terrace off main King's Park Rd, 500m from centre. Posh-ish hotel in Georgian town (they say 'country') house nr the park and golf course. Objets and lawns. French chef/prop.
10RMS JAN-DEC T/T PETS CC KIDS MED.EX

PORTCULLIS HOTEL: 01786 472290. Castle Wynd, no more than a cannonball's throw from the castle & one of the best locations in town. Pub & pub food (hearty, v popular, may be noisy); upstairs only 4 rms, but 3 have brilliant views of Castle/graveyard/town & plain.
4RMS JAN-DEC T/T PETS CC KIDS MED.INX

STIRLING MANAGEMENT CENTRE: 01786 451666. Not strictly speaking a hotel, but is as good as. Fully serviced rms on the univ campus (7km from centre in Br of Allan – & v good restau choice). Excl leisure facs nearby. No atmos but a business-like option.
76RMS JAN-DEC T/T XPETS CC KIDS MED.INX

THE GOLDEN LION: 01786 475351. 8 King St. V central, large, functional with very interior and not that 'great' Great Food Stop. Handy for shops/stn/Stirling stuff.
67RMS JAN-DEC T/T PETS CC KIDS MED.EX

THE GEAN HOUSE, ALLOA: 01259 219275. 12km E (916/CENTRAL HOTELS).

S.Y. HOSTEL: 01786 473442. On rd up to castle in recently renovated jail is this new-style hostel, tho still very SYH (1231/HOSTELS). The **WILLY WALLACE HOSTEL** 01786 446773 at 77 Murray Pl (corner with Friars St) is more funky. Upstairs in busy centre with many caffs & pubs nearby. Unimposing entrance but bunkrms for 56 backpackey folk.

WHERE TO EAT

✓ **THE TOLBOOTH:** 01786 274000. Jail Wynd betw 2 streets leading to castle (250m). Stirling's bright new arts centre & audiorium has gr café-bar (11am-late) & restau (6-9.30pm). Contemp British cuisine in stylish rms. CHP/MED

HERMANN'S: 01786 450632. Mar Place House on rd up to (& v close to) Castle. Hermann Aschaber's (with Scottish wife, Kay) corner of Austria where schnitzels and strudels figure along with trad Scottish fare. 2 floor, ambient well run rms with cheery staff. LO 9.30pm. MED

SCHOLARS at the **STIRLING HIGHLAND HOTEL:** 01786 473052. The up-market, up-by-the-Castle eaterie in town, the Stirling Highland a good conversion of an old school hence the name (909/CENTRAL HOTELS). MED

PIZZA EXPRESS: 01786 474950. 26 King St in middle of main shopping area The chain (but still one of the best chains) with reliably good pizza & good designery ambience. Also open later than most. 7 days 11.30/midnight. INX

THE COTTAGE: 01786 446124. 52 Spittal St on rd up to castle. Tearm/caff with home-made aft tea-type fare but hot mains with Scottish no-nonsense approach. Upstairs and down. Lunch & (Fri/Sat only) dinner. CHP

PAPA JOE'S: 01786 446414. Nr TIC in town centre. Popular, big Tex-mex/Italian/everything kind of menu. Woody ambience. LO 10/11pm. INX

CAMBIO: 01786 461041. 1 Corn Exchange on Main St corner & rd going to castle. Contemp bar/restau with OK food till 7.45pm (Mon-Wed till 5pm). INX

THE EAST INDIA COMPANY: 01786 471330. 7 Viewfield Pl. Still proclaim to be the best Indian in town tho a bit shabby now. Good atmos in woody base-ment rm. Open 7 days till 11pm. INX

CORRIERI'S: 01786 472089. On rd to Br of Allan at Causewayhead. For 70 yrs this excl café/restau nr busy corner below the Wallace Monument. Pasta/pizza & ice-cream as it should be. 7 days, LO 9.30pm. Cl Tues. CHP

ITALIA NOSTRA: 01786 473208. 25 Baker St. Gr name. The tratt to try. Busy atmos. Decent wine list. Usual pastas. 7 days. 10.30 (12 w/ends). CHP

THE BARNTON BAR AND BISTRO: 01786 461698. Barnton St nr stn. Perenially popular. Jukebox. All-day breakfast, baked potatoes, hefty sandwiches. Newspapers. 7 days. Food till 7.30pm (8pm summer), then bar takes over. CHP

BIRDS & BEES: 01786 473663. Betw Stirling & Br of Allan at Causewayhead, Easter Cornton rd. Gr pub & pub grub worth finding. A roadhouse which is the Scottish *pétanque* (French *boules*) centre. Good for kids. 7 days. LO 9.15/10pm. INX

ALLAN WATER CAFE, BRIDGE OF ALLAN: 8km up the rd in Br of Allan main st nr br itself. Great café, the best fish 'n' chips 'n' ice cream (1477/CAFÉS). CHP

CLIVE RAMSAYS: Gt deli & café/restau in Bridge of Allan main st. V cool caff with snack & graze menu. INX

WHAT TO SEE

STIRLING CASTLE (1822/CASTLES); **WALLACE MONUMENT/THE PINEAPPLE** (1899/1905/MONUMENTS); **BANNOCKBURN/SHERIFFMUIR** (1961/BATTLE-GROUNDS); **THE OCHILS** (2012/HILL WALKS; 2038/GLEN AND RIVER WALKS); **LOGIE OLD KIRK** (1943/GRAVEYARDS); **PARADISE** (1756/PICNICS); **DUNBLANE CATHE-DRAL** (1925/CHURCHES).

STIRLING OLD TOWN JAIL: St John's St on rd up to Castle. Guided tour and put-up job, but rather well done. Live actors. Kids will be quiet or simply tortured. Open AYR 5.30pm (3.30pm winter).

THE GHOST WALK: A stroll through old part of the town nr the castle: 'a world of restless spirits and lost souls' (sound familiar?). Info: TIC or 01592 872788.

RAINBOW SLIDES: Nr Railway Stn. A leisure centre with good 25m pool and gym (Pulsestar) and for kids 3 water slides of varying thrill factors. Open 7 days (Sat and Sun till 4pm). Check times: 01786 462521.

WHAT TO DO

SWIMMING/SPORTS: (*see above*). There's also a pool at the University Sports Centre and at the Stirling Highland Hotel (with squash). **GOLF:** Stirling Golf Course v central at Queen's Rd. Quite testing and one of best in area (01786 464098). **BIKE HIRE:** Stewart Wilson Cycles, 49 Barnton St (01786 465292).

TOURIST INFO: Dumbarton Rd. 01786 475019. Jan-Dec.

THE BEST OF WICK AND THURSO

2354

MAP 6
D1, E1

WHERE TO STAY

✓ **FORSS HOUSE HOTEL, nr THURSO:** 01847 861201. 8km W on A836. The MacGregor's family home set in 20 woodland acres by the sea is the best quality hotel for miles. Popular restau (you should book), over 210 malts in the bar comfortable spacious rms and 3 chalets in the grounds too. Breakfast in the conservatory then birds, walks, old mill and waterfall. Fishing.

13RMS JAN-DEC T/T PETS CC KIDS MED.EX

✓ **PORTLAND ARMS, LYBSTER:** 01593 721208. On main A9 20km S of Wick and 45km S of Thurso by A895. A coaching inn since 1851; still hospitable. Small rms are a bit, well, small but this is a homely hotel with decent food in a choice of settings. Log fires. Feels part of the community. While in Lybster, pop down and see Waterlines (WHAT TO SEE, below).

22RMS JAN-DEC T/T PETS CC KIDS MED.INX

✓ **BORGIE LODGE HOTEL, nr BETTYHILL:** 01641 521332. A836 12km E of Tongue. Secluded trad huntin', shootin', fishin' sort of a place: 20 hill lochs and 2 rivers with salmon and trout. Shooting on the adj 12,000 acre estate and Jacqui's acclaimed cooking to come home to. Getaway people like it too though. Another MacGregor establishment – Peter's brother has Forss House (above).

8RMS JAN-OCT X/T PETS CC KIDS MED.INX

ROYAL HOTEL, THURSO: 01847 893191. Trail St in town centre. Sprawling stone inn upgraded to comfortable commercialism. All mod cons but still no sign of the pool/leisure complex. Some say it can be cold here in Thurso – so take your vest. A hotel for visitors. 102RMS JAN-DEC T/T XPETS CC KIDS MED.INX

MACKAY'S HOTEL, WICK: Union Street. 01955 602323. Basic but welcoming. Business travellers during week, family-run (the Lamonts).

27RMS JAN-DEC T/T XPETS CC XKIDS MED.INX

QUAYSIDE B&B, WICK: 25 Harbour Quay. 01955 603229. Brenda Turner's great little establishment, keeping the punters happy since '96. Basic, economical and friendly – with parking (she told us to say).

6RMS (2SELF-CAT) JAN-DEC X/X XPETS CC KIDS CHP

ACKERGILL TOWER, nr WICK: 01955 603556. A rare treat (1259/HOUSEPARTIES)

S.Y. HOSTEL: 01955 611424. At Canisbay, John O'Groats (7km). Wick 25km. Regular bus service. The furthest-flung youth hostel on the mainland. Thurso now has a backpacker hostel – **SANDRA'S** at 24-26 Princes St. Cheap 'n' cheerful with snack bar adjacent. 01847 894575.

NAVIDALE HOUSE, by HELMSDALE: 01431 821258. Not stayed but we hear it's v good.

WHERE TO EAT

✓ **CAPTAIN'S GALLEY, SCRABSTER:** 01847 894999. Seafood with simplicity & integrity. Report: 1443/SEAFOOD RESTAUS. INX

✓ **FORSS HOUSE HOTEL, PORTLAND ARMS, BORGIE LODGE HOTEL:** (*all as above*)

✓ **LA MIRAGE, HELMSDALE:** 60km S so a fair drive, but Viva Las Vegas! (1086/INEXP HIGHLAND RESTAUS). INX

THE FERRY INN, SCRABSTER: 01847 892814. 3km W of Thurso in busy pt area o/look BP and ferry terminal for Orkney. 'Turf' (meat) on upper deck and 'surf' (fish) on top deck. Adj bar. Lunch and 6-9.30pm, 7 days. INX

OLD SMIDDY INN, THRUMSTER: 01955 651256. 7km S of Wick on A9. Bar/restau/café full of smiddyish stuff. Snacks, meals and blackboard specials. 7 days; Sun-Thur 12-2pm, 5.30-8.30pm; Fri and Sat all day. LO 9pm.   CHP

WHAT TO SEE

DUNBEATH: 32km S of Wick (1978/LITERARY PLACES; 2044/GLEN AND RIVER WALKS); **CAIRNS OF CAMSTER:** 15km S of Wick (1877/PREHISTORIC SITES); **BETTYHILL MUSEUM:** 50km W of Thurso (2251/MUSEUMS); **NORTH COAST BEACHES** (1660/BEACHES); **CASTLE of MEY** (1841/CASTLES).

WICK HERITAGE CENTRE: 01955 605393. In town centre; June-Sept. Mon-Sat 10am-5pm. (2270/INTERESTING MUSEUMS). **CAITHNESS GLASS CENTRE, WICK:** 01955 602286. Home of popular gift ware; factory and VC; by the airport.

WATERLINES: Lybster harbour. 01593 721520. All-new visitor centre telling Lybster's tale at its harbour. Good history – the big contrast between then and now. Plus tearoom! May-Sep, daily, 11am-5pm.

THE TRINKIE: A walk along the rocky coast E of Wick or drive through housing schemes until cliff rd appears (ask locals). Flat rocks, an open-air pool; a good spot. 2km further for the 'Brig O'Trams'.

WHALIGOE STEPS: On A9 N of Lybster; down track nr cottages and septic tank, by Cairn O' Get sign. Infamy regained after Billy Connolly's visit; 318 (Keith counted) stone cliff steps to sea where herrings used to be landed and cured. Unsignposted so ask locally for directions if lost, and go carefully.

WILDLIFE CRUISE, JOHN O' GROATS: 01955 611353. June-Aug; 90min trips to sea stacks, birds and **JOHN O' GROATS – ORKNEY:** May-Sept day trips. White water adventures and 'nature shows', try **NORTH COAST MARINE ADVENTURES,** Easter-Oct. 07867 666273.

WHAT TO DO

SWIMMING: Wick (01955 603711), Thurso (01847 893260). Both central. **GOLF:** Wick (01955 602726), Thurso (01847 893807), Reay (01847 811288). **SURFING AND WINDSURFING:** Esp round Thurso. TIC have leaflet about beaches. **ALLSTAR FACTORY:** bowling, cinema, the whole entertainment centre idea (01847 895050).

TOURIST INFO:

WICK: Whitechapel Rd. 01955 602596. Jan-Dec.

THURSO: Riverside. 01847 892371. Apr-Oct.

HOLIDAY CENTRES

2355
MAP 3
B2

PITLOCHRY

WHERE TO STAY

KILLIECRANKIE HOUSE: 01796 473220 (993/PERTHSHIRE HOTELS).   MED.EX

PINE TREES: 01796 472121. Off Main St (992/PERTHSHIRE HOTELS).   MED.EX

DUNFALLANDY HOUSE: 01796 472648. Just out of town (2km), but away from all that. Good-value Georgian mansion; not one for the kids, though.
8RMS JAN-OCT MED/INX

WHERE TO EAT

THE OLD ARMOURY: 01796 474821. (1007/PERTHSHIRE EATS).   INX

KILLIECRANKIE HOUSE: Go those miles (5) to dinner; or bar meals! (*above*).
INX

PORTNACRAIG: 01796 472777. By theatre, on river. An insider choice.   INX

OLD SMITHY: 01796 472356. Main St. Coffees/restau. 7 days. LO 9pm.   INX

PRINCE OF INDIA: 01796 472275. Off main st by McNaughton's. Unusually good Indian and good late bet. MED

MOULIN INN: 01796 472196. Notable for pub food and atmos (1279/REAL ALE). 6km uphill. LO 9.30pm. CHP

WHAT TO SEE

THE SALMON LADDER: From Main St and across dam to see 34-pool fish ladder (salmon leaping May-Oct, if you're lucky) and Hydro Board displays (sic); **BEN VRACKIE:** Local fave with fab Trossachs views climbed from Moulin (2km from town). Rd behind Moulin Inn. Car park. 734m. Scree at top; and goats; **FASKALLY WOODS/LINN OF TUMMEL WALKS:** Well-marked woodland walks around L Faskally and Garry R. Can incl the Linn (rapids) and Pass of Killiecrankie (1829/BATTLEGROUNDS). Start: town/Garry bridge/visitor centre; **WOOLLEN SHOPS:** Many major chains and local shops in one small area/the main st. **PITLOCHRY THEATRE** (2287/THEATRES); **QUEEN'S VIEW** (1734/VIEWS); **EDRADOUR DISTILLERY** (1582/WHISKY); **MACNAUGHTON'S** (2175/OUTDOOR SHOPS); **MOULIN INN** (1388/REAL ALE).

2356
MAP 2
D3 # INVERARAY

WHERE TO STAY

GEORGE HOTEL: 01499 302111. On main st and in the Clark family for centuries (no, really – 1790). A gr value hotel – ales, good pub food, real fires. 855/ARGYLL HOTELS CHP

LOCH FYNE HOTEL: 01499 302148. On A83 rd out of town towards W, o/look loch. Big hotel, but personally run. Good bar meals. 859/ARGYLL HOTELS. MED.INX

WHERE TO EAT

THE GEORGE/LOCH FYNE HOTELS: Bar meals esp. (*See above.*) CHP

LOCH FYNE OYSTER BAR: 01499 600236. 14km E on A83. INX

CREGGANS INN: 01369 860279. 32km E and S via A83/A815. On opp bank of L Fyne, but 35mins by rd. Bar meals/restau. MED

WHAT TO SEE

INVERARAY CASTLE: Home of the Duke of Argyll and clan seat of the Campbells. Spectacular entrance hall; chronicle of Highland shenanigans unfurls in the gilded apartments. Fine walks in grounds esp to the prominent hill and folly (45mins up). Apr-Oct. **ARDKINGLAS WOODLAND:** 17km E on A83 (1607/GARDENS). **AUCHINDRAIN:** 8km S on A83; **INVERARAY JAIL** (2263/MUSEUMS); **ARGYLL WILDLIFE PARK:** 4km S on A83 (1709/KIDS)

2357
MAP 3
D3 # ST ANDREWS

WHERE TO STAY

OLD COURSE HOTEL: 01334 474371 (964/FIFE HOTELS). LOTS

RUFFLETS: 01334 472594 (966/FIFE HOTELS). MED.EX

RUSACKS: 01334 474321. Long-standing golfy hotel nr all courses and overlooking the 18th of the Old. Nice sun-lounge and b/fast o/looking the greens. Reliable & quite classy for a Macdonald Hotel, the recent new owners. 78RMS JAN-DEC T/T PETS CC KIDS MED.EX

ST ANDREWS BAY: 01334 837000 (967/FIFE HOTELS). MED.EX

OLD STATION: 01334 880505 (968/FIFE HOTELS).

INN ON NORTH STREET: 01334 474664. 127 North St. Corner of Murray park where there are numerous GH options. This a hipper, younger alternative to the stalwart, elegant but exp offerings above. Lizard bar in basement is happening place, the Oakrooms on street level is quite civilised café-bar, so all corners are covered. Comfy, contemporary rms. 13RMS JAN-DEC T/T PETS CC KIDS MED.EX

WHERE TO EAT

THE PEAT INN: 01334 840 206. 15km SW (974/RESTAU).　　　　EXP

THE VINE LEAF: 01334 477497. 131 South St. Inauspicious entrance belies civilised St Andrews fav restau with menu that covers all bases, good vegn, good wines. Morag & Ian Hamilton know how to look after you and what you like esp for pud. Tues-Sat dinner only.　　　　MED

THE DOLL'S HOUSE: 01334 477422. Church Sq. V central café/restau that caters well for kids (and teenagers). Eclectic range, smiley people and tables outside in summer.　　　　INX

GRANGE INN: 01334 472670. 4km E off Anstruther rd A917. V popular country pub in several rms with good local rep. Always busy. Report: 1409/PUB FOOD.
　　　　INX

BROONS: 01334 478479. 117 North St. Adj to New Picture House. Locally fashionable upstairs bistro with simple contemporary menu & nice people. 7 days lunch & dinner. LO 9pm.　　　　INX

PIZZA EXPRESS: 01334 477109. Logies Lane on Church Sq off North St. Usual menu in bright, modern space. Handily open late (12pm 7 days).　　　　INX

BALAKA BANGLADESHI RESTAURANT: 01334 474825. 'Best Curry in Scotland' winner. Certainly as good as many in Edin or Glas. Celebrated herb & spice gdn out back which supplies other restaus in St Andrews.　　　　MED

BRAMBLES: Long-standing definitive St A coffee-shop. Cramped & cosy & usually a queue. (1517/TEAROOMS).　　　　CHP

NORTH POINT: 24 North St (1517/TEAROOMS).

JANETTA'S: 31 South St. Known for ice-cream (1535/ICE-CREAM), but pop caff. Open 7 days till 5/5.30pm.

OLD COURSE & RUFFLETS: Top end, top dining rms (*see above*).

INN ON NORTH ST: 01334 474664 (*see above*).

WHAT TO SEE

THE TOWN ITSELF: The lanes, cloisters, gdns and the University halls and colleges; the harbour and the botanic gdns. Perfect lawns; **THE CASTLE RUINS:** Founded in 13th cent on promontory; good for clambering over. 'Escape tunnel' to explore (if not tall). Spooky by night along this shore; **BRITISH GOLF MUSEUM:** Sophisticated audio-visual exhibition illustrating history and allure of the game. Even non-players will enjoy. **THE HIMALAYAS:** the most brilliant putting green; piles of fun, near the beach. Apr-Oct till 8pm, 7 days. Many **GOLF COURSES** (2090/GREAT GOLF); **WEST SANDS/KINSHALDY BEACH** (1658/BEACHES); **LEUCHARS CHURCH:** 9km by A91 N (1922/CHURCHES); **TENTSMUIR:** 20km by A91/A919 N (1818/WILDLIFE); **NEW PICTURE HOUSE** (2292/THEATRES); **JANETTA'S** (1535/ICE CREAM); **ST ANDREWS FINE ART**; **CATHEDRAL** (1856/RUINS); **EAST SANDS** (2130/LEISURE CENTRES).

2358
MAP 4
C3, D3

ROYAL DEESIDE: BALLATER AND BANCHORY

WHERE TO STAY

RAEMOIR, BANCHORY: 01330 824884. Large mansion in secluded grounds 3km town by Raemoir Rd off A93. Relaxed and discreet. 9-hole golf and tennis. Growing rep for food.　　　　LOTS

DARROCH LEARG, BALLATER: 01339 755443. Town mansion above/off (at tight bend) A93 on way in from Braemar. Excellent nosh. (1013/NE HOTELS.)
　　　　MED

BANCHORY LODGE, BANCHORY: 01330 822625 (1022/NE HOTELS).　　　　EXP

TOR-NA-COILLE, BANCHORY: 01330 822242. Town mansion above/just off main A93 on way in from Ballater. Nr golf. Antiques in tasteful/individual rms.
　　　　EXP

WHERE TO EAT

DARROCH LEARG, BALLATER: 01339 755443. The other Deeside hoteliers aspire to. (*see above*).

THE OAK ROOM, BALLATER: 01339 755858.   EXP

THE BLACK-FACED SHEEP, ABOYNE: 01339 887311. Near main rd. Coffee shop/gift shop with excellent home-baking. Daytime hrs (1490/TEAROOMS).

MILTON RESTAURANT: 01330 844566 (1033/NE RESTAUS).   MED

WHAT TO SEE

CRAIGIEVAR/DRUM (1838/1839 CASTLES); **FASQUE** (1887/COUNTRY HOUSES); **CRATHES** (1592/1897 GARDENS/COUNTRY HOUSES); **BALMORAL** (1840/CASTLES); **LOCHNAGAR** (2021/MUNROS); **ALBERT MEMORIAL** (1908/MONUMENTS); **GLEN MUICK** (1698/LOCHS); **CAMBUS O'MAY** (1757/PICNICS); **GOLF:** Well-managed/picturesque courses, open to visitors at both Ballater (013397 55567), and Banchory (01330 822447). Both 18 holes; **FISHING:** Difficult, not impossible, on Dee or on R Feugh (N bank only) – permits from Feughside Inn (01330 850225); **WALKS:** Walks down both sides of the Dee, esp Ballater to Cambus O'May, 7km; **VIEWPOINTS:** Up Craigendarroch, the Hill of the Oaks, Ballater, from Braemar Rd (45mins). Scolty Hill and Monument, Banchory. Ask for directions; **RAEMOIR GARDEN CENTRE** (2238/GARDEN CENTRES); **BURN O' VAT** (1988/SPOOKY PLACES); **MACEWAN GALLERY** (2200/WHERE TO BUY ART); **BRAEMAR–LINN OF DEE, BALLATER–TOMINTOUL** (1714/1715/SCENIC ROUTES).

LIST OF MAPS

NOTE: The maps give general guidance on attractions in an area –
they are not exact. For more precise details, refer to the text.

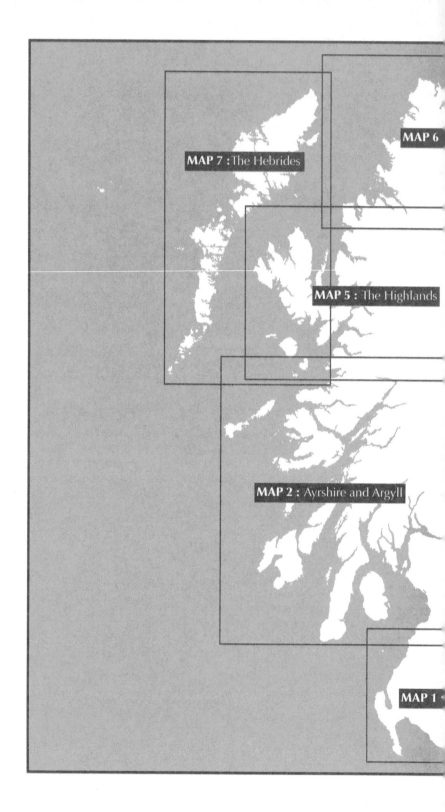

MAP 6

MAP 7 : The Hebrides

MAP 5 : The Highlands

MAP 2 : Ayrshire and Argyll

MAP 1

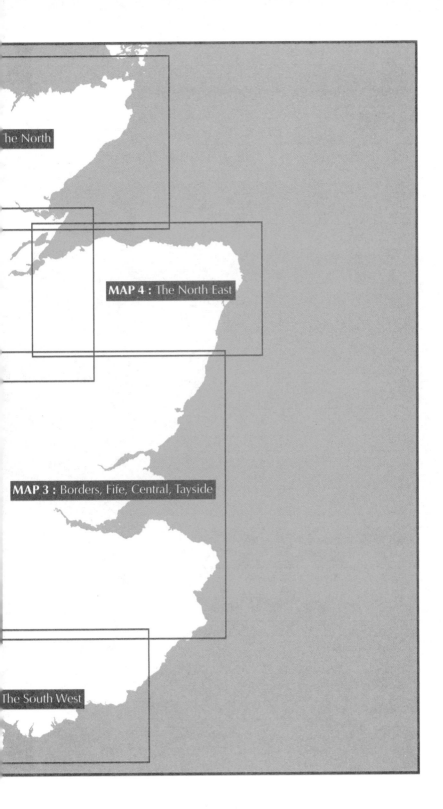

The North

MAP 4 : The North East

MAP 3 : Borders, Fife, Central, Tayside

The South West

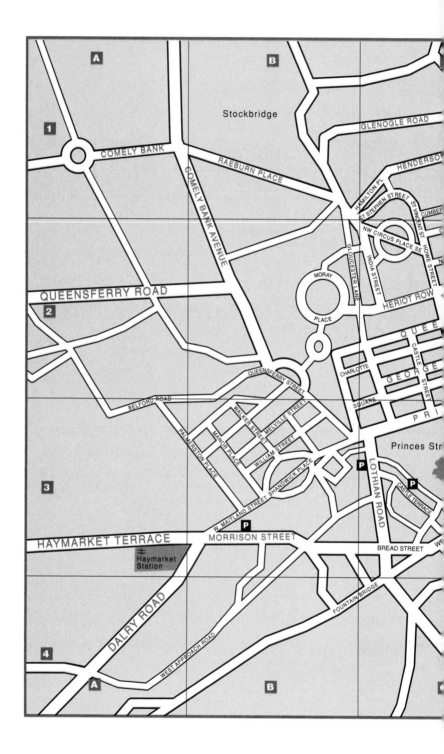

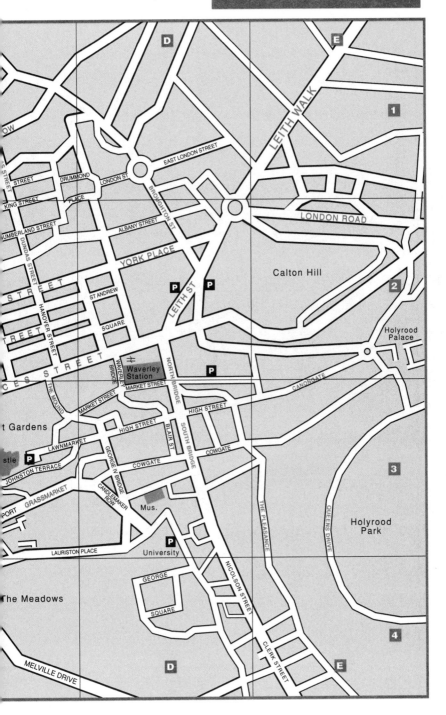

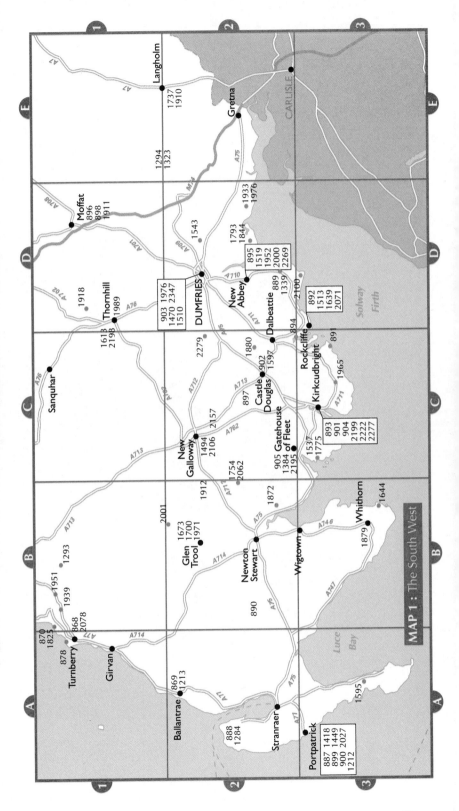

MAP 1 : The South West

MAPS

331

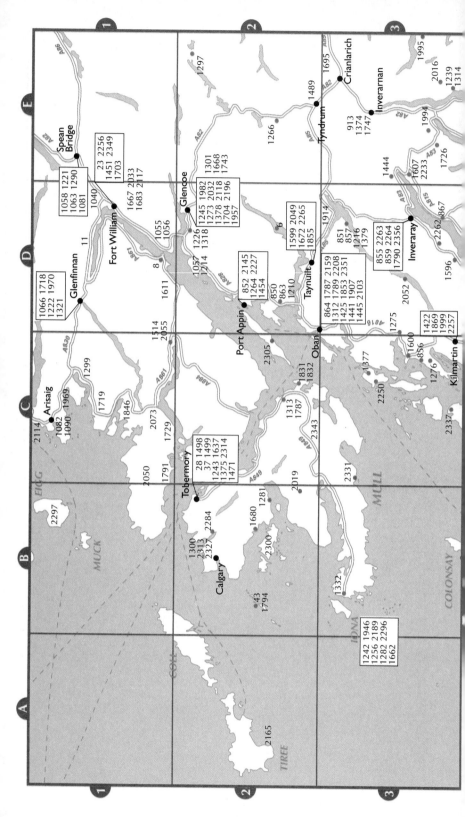

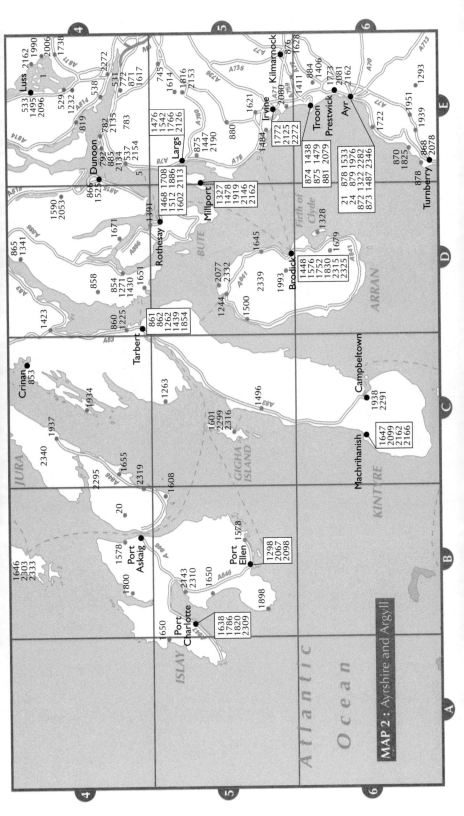

MAP 2 : Ayrshire and Argyll

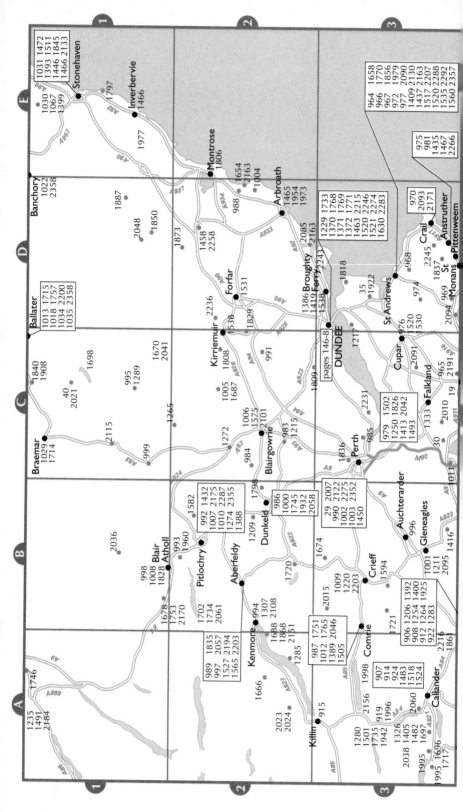

MAPS

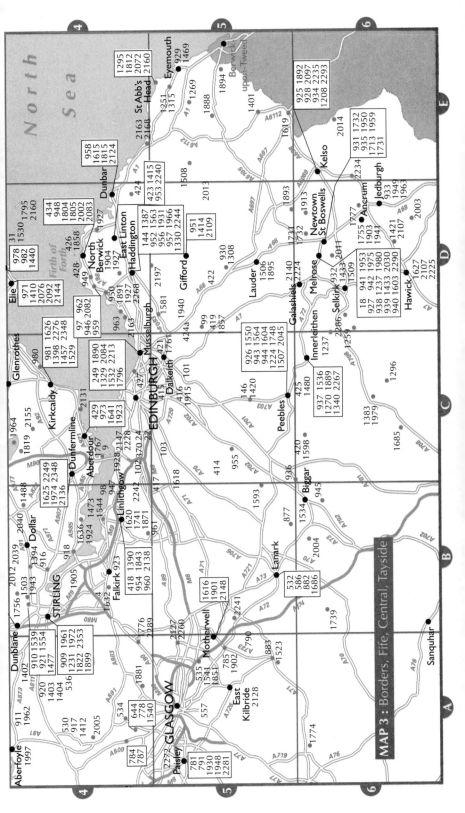

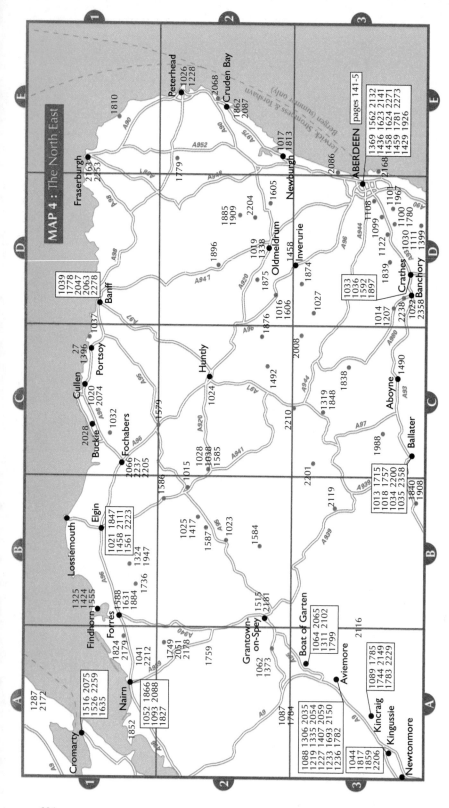

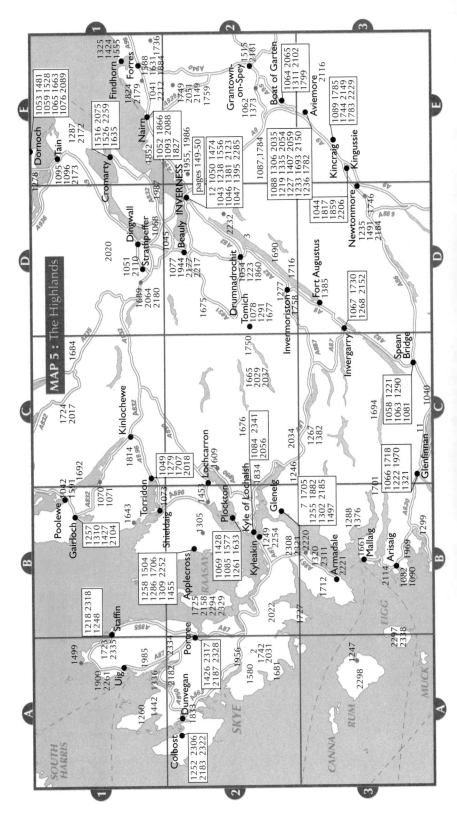

MAP 5 : The Highlands

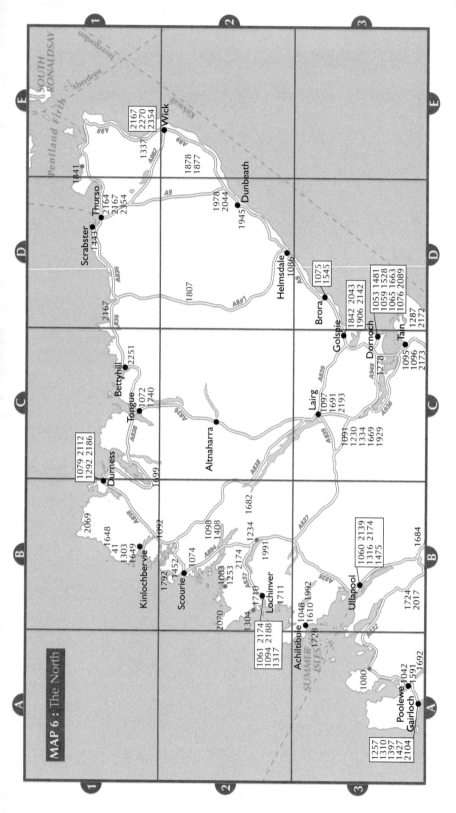

MAP 6 : The North

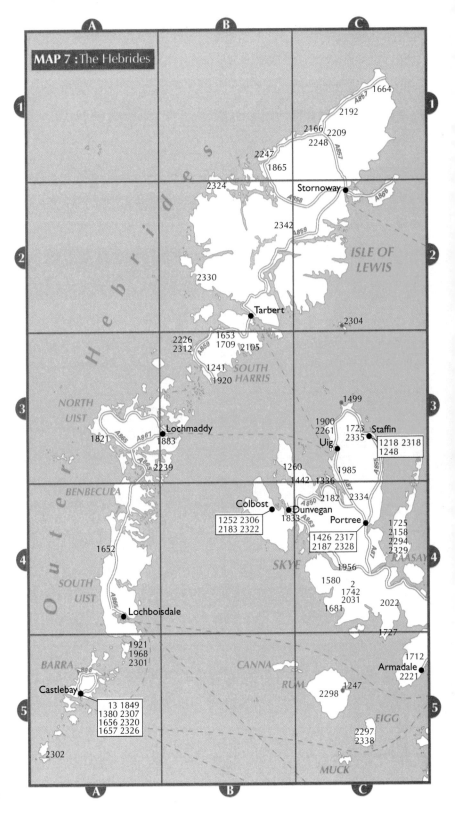

MAP 7 : The Hebrides

A B C

1 1

ISLE OF LEWIS

1664
2192
2166 2209
2248
2247
1865
2324
Stornoway
2342

2 2

2330
Tarbert
2304

NORTH UIST
2226 1653
2312 1709 2105
1241
1920 SOUTH HARRIS
1821
Lochmaddy
1883
2239

1499
1900
2261 1723
2335 Staffin
Uig 1218 2318
1248
1985
1260
1442 1336

3 3

BENBECULA
Colbost
2182 2334
1252 2306 Dunvegan
2183 2322 1833 Portree
1426 2317
2187 2328
1725
2158
2294
2329
RAASAY
1652
1956
SKYE
1580 2
1742
2031
1681 2022

4 4

SOUTH UIST
Lochboisdale
1727

1921 1712
1968 Armadale
BARRA 2301 CANNA 2221
Castlebay RUM 2298 1247
13 1849
1380 2307 EIGG
1656 2320
1657 2326 2297
2302 2338
MUCK

5 5

A B C

MAPS   339

INDEX

Note: the numbers listed against index entries refer to the page number on which the entry appears and not the entry's item number.

356   INDEX

QUICK-REFERENCE GUIDE TO THE CODES

In many entries, special codes are used. These are described below for quick reference. Full explanations can be found in the section on 'Using This Book' (p.11).

1. The Item Code

Each entry has its own item number, e.g. **1269**.

MAP 2	see Map 2 in the map section
B2	the entry's map co-ordinate using the map grid
xC1	the entry can be reached by leaving the map at grid reference C1

2. The Hotel Code

Below each hotel recommended is a band of codes as follows:

20RMS   JAN-DEC   T/T   PETS   CC   KIDS   TOS   LOTS

20RMS	the total number of rooms
JAN-DEC	the hotel is open all year round
APR-OCT	the hotel is open April – October
T/T	T/: direct-dial phones in the bedrooms /T: TVs in the bedrooms
PETS	the hotel accepts dogs and other pets, probably under certain conditions
XPETS	the hotel does not generally accept pets.
CC	major credit cards (e.g. Access and Visa)
XCC	credit cards not accepted
KIDS	children are welcome and special provisions/rates may be available.
XKIDS	special provisions/rates are not usually made. Check by phone.
TOS	the hotel is part of the Taste of Scotland scheme

The following indicate the approximate cost per night per person:

LOTS	over £75
EXP	Expensive: £55-75
MED.EX	Medium (expensive): £40-55
MED.INX	Medium (inexpensive): £32-40
INX	Inexpensive: £25-32
CHP	Cheap: less than £25

3. The Restaurant Code

The cost of an average dinner per person with a starter, a main course and dessert (excluding wine, coffee or extras):

EXP	Expensive: more than £30
MED	Medium: £20-30
INX	Inexpensive: £12-20
CHP	Cheap: under £12